ENGENDERING PSYCHOLOGY
BRINGING WOMEN INTO FOCUS

FLORENCE DENMARK

Pace University

VITA RABINOWITZ

Hunter College

JERI SECHZER

Pace University

ALLYN AND BACON

Boston • London • Toronto • Sydney • Tokyo • Singapore

To those who paved the way and to those who will follow the path

Senior Series Editor: Carolyn Merrill
Vice President, Director of Marketing: Joyce Nilsen
Series Editorial Assistant: Lara Zeises
Production Editor: Christopher H. Rawlings
Editorial-Production Service: Omegatype Typography, Inc.
Composition and Prepress Buyer: Linda Cox
Manufacturing Buyer: Megan Cochran
Cover Administrator: Jennifer Hart
Electronic Composition: Omegatype Typography, Inc.

Copyright © 2000 by Allyn & Bacon
A Pearson Education Company
160 Gould Street
Needham Heights, MA 02494

Internet: www.abacon.com

Library of Congress Cataloging-in-Publication Data

Denmark, Florence.
    Engendering psychology / Florence L. Denmark, Vita Carulli
Rabinowitz, Jeri A. Sechzer.
        p.   cm.
    Includes bibliographical references and index.
    ISBN 0-205-14685-6 (alk. paper)
    1. Women—Psychology.   2. Sex role—Psychological aspects.   3. Sex
discrimination against women.   4. Feminist theory.   I. Rabinowitz,
Vita Carulli.   II. Sechzer, Jeri A.   III. Title.
HQ1150.D45   2000
155.6'33—DC21   99-19908
                                                          CIP

Printed in the United States of America
10   9   8   7   6   5   4   3   2   1   04   03   02   01   00   99

CONTENTS

PREFACE

Over the last few decades, the psychology of women and women's studies have grown from courses given occasionally in colleges and universities to major fields with scholarly recognition. There has also been an explosion in the number of research articles on women and gender. Why then, when there are now so many books on the psychology of women, and more each year on the psychology of men, do we offer yet another text in this area? We three authors have come together to write what we believe is a different kind of book, both in the information it presents and the approach to its subject matter.

We have set out to create a text that captures the richness and variety of the new scholarship on women and conveys that excitement to the student in a useful and meaningful way. We write at a time when the traditional boundaries among the academic disciplines are breaking down. Research relevant to understanding women is emerging from fields as broad as the natural and biological sciences, the social sciences, and the humanities. Although unabashedly feminist in perspective, our text attempts to present a balanced view of the ongoing debates relevant to the lives of women. We see gender as a social construction mediated by parents, teachers, the media, religion, culture, and other forces, and consider gender as a status variable; that is, female and male are seen not merely as different but as unequal, with male being dominant or superior. We also recognize the biological foundations that may play a role in gender development and the expression of gender throughout the life span.

We have written this book primarily for undergraduate classes in the psychology of women. However, it can also be used for courses on gender or women's studies. It is a text that can stand alone or be used in conjunction with a book of readings or other material that an instructor would assign. In addition, sections of this text could be used as a supplement to such courses that include units on gender roles, gender issues in developmental psychology, and human sexuality. With its wealth of references, this book encompasses recent as well as classic studies and thus can serve as a valuable resource for advanced students and faculty conducting research on women.

We have filled gaps in the existing literature with material not ordinarily included in textbooks on women. The text includes topics that needed to be addressed in more depth (e.g., the origins of stereotypes) and explores new issues that have recently arisen (e.g., the sexuality of disabled women). For example, we have provided current information about the physical and mental health of women and the inherent gender bias in research, human sexuality, and older adulthood.

Although this text aims to provide a thorough discussion of a wide range of topics germane to the psychology of women, it is by no means exhaustive. The subject of each chapter alone yields enough information to fill an entire book. Our attempt to capture a comprehensive view of the numerous issues that pervade women's lives has forced us to limit our attention to any one topic in particular. Readers interested in pursuing topics in greater depth can utilize the references and suggested readings to locate additional information.

In addition, we have made a concerted effort to use appropriate or correct terminology when referring to women and men from various ethnic and racial groups. However, this has proved to be an extremely difficult task because language is a complex area in which consensus does not currently exist. For example, women and men from Spanish-speaking countries may be referred to as Hispanic or Latina and Latino, or women and men from an individual country may be called Chicana and Chicano. In addition, some individuals speak of themselves as black and others use African American. It is unclear which designation is preferable to these individuals, and different people have different preferences. When citing the work of different researchers and scholars, we felt uncomfortable imposing a particular ethnic and racial terminology and have decided to present the categories with the terminology used by the authors themselves. We hope that our readers will understand and accept our rationale.

The organization of this book combines a developmental and topical approach. All chapters are self-contained and can be readily rearranged according to a given instructor's preference. The text consists of thirteen chapters and an epilogue. The first chapter sets the tone for the book, beginning with an exploration of the meanings of sex and gender, discusses sex discrimination in science and in society, and provides for the conduct of gender-fair research. The origins of gender stereotypes are revealed in an extensive review of religion and mythology that reaches back to roots in the middle ages and to the ancient Greeks. The biology of sex and gender incorporates basic as well as current scientific findings that illuminate the interaction of biological and psychological factors that affect gender.

Engendering Psychology seeks to incorporate the new scholarship on the intersection of women and race, ethnicity, class, age, and sexual orientation. To address specific concerns about race, ethnicity, and class, the text includes a comprehensive chapter by Dr. June Chisholm (Chapter 4), who is an expert in this area. However, our interest in the psychological aspects of race, ethnicity, and class, as well as age and sexual orientation, is not confined to any chapter but is reflected throughout the text. Similarly, international and cross-cultural experiences of women and girls are included in relevant portions of the text. Other chapters examine the psychological development of girls and women; topics incorporate how females grow up, aspects of their abilities and achievements, and their careers. Also included are extensive chapters on human sexuality and intimate relationships. The remaining chapters are devoted to topics of vital importance to the lives of girls and women: violence and exploitation, psychological health, and physical health. These chapters examine these issues from a historical perspective, as well as from psychosocial and cultural perspectives, and bring in new scholarship and fresh views on topics such as elder abuse, female infanticide, gay bashing, changing patterns of eating disorders, gender issues in stress and pain, and the intersection of ethnicity and race with physical and mental health. Power and power relations inextricably intertwined with gender are woven throughout the book. The epilogue raises questions about the future realities and potentialities of women's and girls' experiences and forecasts trends in the study of women and gender.

Special features in the text include detailed outlines prior to each chapter, suggestions for additional readings, a series of questions designed to stimulate critical thinking and discussion, and a glossary of relevant terms.

We have many varied goals for this edition. In the general sense, it is hoped that readers of *Engendering Psychology* will internalize a valuing of women, their own lives, and experiences. Beyond that, readers should come to understand the concept of gender as a social construct, as well as recognize the importance of equality of power and the subsequent need for activism and change.

In a more structured sense, readers should grow in some of the following ways:

1. Deeper understanding of women: A woman may find validation and a sense of empowerment in being a woman and in being part of a larger group of women with common concerns and experiences; men may be better able to connect with the experiences of their female family members, friends, and other significant women in their lives.
2. The knowledge that "woman" is a diverse and multifaceted category: Women must be looked at with regard to all aspects of their lives other than their gender.
3. Critical thinking skills: Through learning about the psychology of women, readers will be able to perceive human behavior more accurately and equitably and critically evaluate psychological research.
4. An appreciation that women have been and continue to be an oppressed group globally: By understanding the plight of women, we gain insight about other oppressed groups and how gender intersects with other systems of discrimination.
5. Future concerns: An interest in and commitment to working toward social, legal, political, and health changes that advance women and other nondominant groups.

If this book guides and enlightens without being overwhelming and encourages a cooperative dialogue between student and instructor, it will have accomplished our intent. We want to encourage the development of an informed and challenged student in psychology, as gender issues become more salient in the twenty-first century.

ACKNOWLEDGMENTS

We wish to acknowledge the valuable contributions made by the following individuals. First, we are grateful to June Chisholm, who not only contributed Chapter 4 on race, ethnicity, and culture, but also expanded our outlook on diversity throughout this book. The manuscript has been greatly enhanced by careful readings and comments of many colleagues, especially Ruth Abrams, Leonore Loeb Adler, Kathleen Barker, Rabbi Steven Bayar, Matthew Erdelyi, Elizabeth Haines, Barry Keating, Daniela Martin, David Riccio, Bonnie R. Seegmiller, and Deborah Tolman.

A special word of thanks to our editor, Carolyn Merrill, senior editor at Allyn and Bacon, for shaping the perspective of the text, encouraging and guiding us throughout our writing, and staying on top of this project. We also wish to thank Carolyn's former assistant, Amy Goldmacher, for handling the many questions that arose during the preparation of this book.

We also thank the many students at Pace University, Hunter College, and the Graduate Center of CUNY who have discussed topics germane to this text in a variety of contexts in and out of the classroom. We also wish to acknowledge the contributions of the many reviewers of this volume: Marlene K. Adelman, Norwalk Community College; Thomas Boone, Brandeis University; Grace Calliano, Kennesaw State University; Claire Etaugh, Bradley University; Mary Gotch, Solano Community College; William Gragoin, Georgia Southwestern State University; Norine L. Jalbert, Western Connecticut State University; Melinda Jones, University of Pittsburgh-Bradford; Korrel Kanoy, Peace

College; Pat Lefler, Lexington Community College; Toby Silverman, William Patterson College; Michael Stevenson, Ball State University; and Yvonne Wells, Suffolk University.

We were especially fortunate to have several doctoral students at Pace University who provided invaluable assistance: Kelly Adams, Khaya Eisenberg, Scott Gallagher, Erica Heitner, Nicola Holder, Milagras Sanchez, and Sara Schulman.

Last but not least, we thank our husbands and children for their patience and understanding throughout the writing of this text.

FLORENCE L. DENMARK

Florence L. Denmark is an internationally recognized scholar and researcher. She received her Ph.D. from the University of Pennsylvania in social psychology. Denmark's current position is that of Robert Scott Pace Distinguished Professor of Psychology at Pace University in New York. She was previously the Thomas Hunter Professor of Psychology at Hunter College and the Graduate Center, CUNY. She also has received four honorary doctoral degrees.

Denmark holds fellowship status in the American Psychological Association (APA) and the American Psychological Society. She is also a member of the Society for Experimental Social Psychology (SESP) and a Fellow of the New York Academy of Sciences. She received several APA awards for Distinguished Education and Training, Public Interest Senior Career, and Distinguished International Contributions to Psychology, and is a recipient of the Carolyn W. Sherif Award from APA's Psychology of Women Division. Denmark's most significant research has emphasized women's leadership and leadership styles, the interaction of status and gender, women in cross-cultural perspective, and the contributions of women to psychology.

VITA CARULLI RABINOWITZ

Vita C. Rabinowitz is Associate Professor of Psychology at Hunter College and the Graduate School and University Center of the City University of New York. She received her doctorate in social psychology at Northwestern University, where she developed a life-long love of research methodology from Donald T. Campbell and Thomas D. Cook. Her current research and writings are in the area of sex and gender bias in behavioral and biomedical research, feminist perspectives on research methods, models of helping and coping, and implicit memory. In 1992, she received the Kurt Lewin Award for Outstanding Contributions to Social Psychology from the New York State Psychological Association.

JERI ALTNEU SECHZER

Jeri A. Sechzer is Visiting Professor of Psychology at Pace University. She received her doctorate in behavioral neuroscience at the University of Pennsylvania. Sechzer's main research interests concern sex and gender bias in behavioral and biomedical science, behavioral toxicology and early development, bioethics, and values in science. She is a Fellow of the American Psychological Association (Divisions 35—Psychology of Women, and 6—Behavioral Neuroscience and Comparative Psychology), the American Association for the Advancement of Science (AAAS), the New York Academy of Medicine, and the New York Academy of Sciences. Sechzer has been the recipient of many honors and awards. Some of these include a Leadership Award of the Exxon Education Foundation, the Outstanding Women in Science Award of the Association for Women in Science (AWIS, New York Chapter), and, most recently, the Wilhelm Wundt Award of the New York State Psychological Association for her scientific contributions to psychology.

JUNE F. CHISHOLM

June F. Chisholm is Associate Professor of Psychology at Pace University and Adjunct Professor at New York University Medical Center. She is a clinical psychologist who worked for many years as a Senior Psychologist in the outpatient psychiatric department at Harlem Hospital Center, providing psychological services to an ethnically diverse, primarily poor, urban population. She is in private practice in Manhattan. Her clinical and research interests include issues in the psychological treatment of women of color, psychological assessment of children and adults, parenting, community psychology, violence, and prejudice in the theory and practice of psychology.

CHAPTER 1

EXPLORING SEX AND GENDER

Ignorance about women pervades academic disciplines in higher education, where the requirements for the degree seldom include thoughtful inquiry into the status of women, as part of the total human condition.
—Carolyn Sherif

Psychology has nothing to say about what women are really like, what they need and what they want, essentially, because psychology does not know.
—Naomi Weisstein

It may be a pleasure to be "we," and it may be strategically imperative to struggle as "we," but who, they ask, are "we"?
  Ann Snitow

We exist at moments, at the margins and among ourselves. Whether or not we have transformed the discipline of psychology, and whether or not we would like to, remain empirical and political questions. . . . At the level of theory, methods, politics, and activism, it is safe to say that feminist psychology has interrupted the discipline.
—Michelle Fine

It feels glorious to "reclaim an identity they taught [us] to despise."
—Michelle Cliff

DISTINCTION BETWEEN SEX
AND GENDER
  The Limits of Biology
  Why Gender?
  Beliefs about Gender
  Gender Stereotypes

SEX DISCRIMINATION IN SOCIETY AND
SCIENCE: BLATANT, SUBTLE, AND COVERT
  Sex Discrimination in Society
  Sex Discrimination in Science
FEMINIST PERSPECTIVES AND IDEOLOGY
  Feminism: Not a "Brand Label"

1

It has been more than 20 years since Sherif and Weisstein penned the preceding sentiments that reverberated throughout psychology. More recently, the field of the psychology of women has begun to correct its androcentric (male-centered) bias and the literature on the psychology of women continues to expand. One of the authors of this textbook, Florence Denmark, commented in 1980 that women in psychology had gone from "rocking the cradle to rocking the boat." In fact, there are now several journals (e.g., *Feminism and Psychology, Sex Roles,* and *Psychology of Women Quarterly*) exclusively concerned with women and gender. The psychology of women is also interdisciplinary because it is informed by research conducted across a wide number of disciplines, such as biology, sociology, anthropology, history, media studies, economics, education, and linguistics.

As Fine suggests in the preceding quote, however, "interrupting" the discipline of psychology means that psychology has been made to pause and reconsider its theoretical assumptions and where they have led us. This is distinct from transforming the discipline and the social structures that have impeded the progress of women in society. Today, women and the issues that they care about receive greater attention from scientists, researchers, and laypersons. Few would dispute that women have made great strides in North America over the last quarter-century. Yet, clearly not all women have thrived. Subtle, and sometimes not-so-subtle, forces continue to support belief systems and traditions that are sources of inequity for girls and women.

In this chapter, we discuss the distinctions between sex and gender. The chapter also explores and critically examines traditional approaches to psychological research and the biases therein. Psychological research, like any research enterprise, is subject to the perils of researchers' own stereotypes and attitudes. These stereotypes affect the way that women and female psychologists are perceived. Sexism in both society and science is explored and gender-fair solutions for sexism in research will be considered. Feminist research, due to its critique of scientific procedures and findings, is particularly suited to uncovering biases that are related to race, ethnicity, disability, and sexual orientation, as well as gender. Feminists in psychology have begun to focus on the societal forces that afford privilege for some at the expense of others. Therefore, feminist psychologists are positioned at the forefront of social change as they uncover bias in science and society and advance the study and understanding of girls and women.

To make psychology a stronger science and profession that better serve the public interest, certain changes are necessary. Specifically, sensitivity to issues concerning women, gender, and diversity must be emphasized. Psychology should include a gendered perspective in its domains of science, practice, education, and public interest. Psychology must make visible women's viewpoints and experiences. **Engendering**

psychology refers to cultivating such a psychology in which gender considerations are mainstreamed or integrated throughout the discipline (Denmark, 1994).

In addition to distinguishing between sex and gender, this chapter discusses the obstacles faced and the advances made in research as sensitivity to gender issues becomes more and more salient in psychology.

DISTINCTION BETWEEN SEX AND GENDER

The girl pictured in Figure 1.1 is mystified by the distinction between sex and gender. Let us investi-

gate the meanings of these terms to clear up her confusion.

The Limits of Biology

The terms **sex** and **gender** are often misunderstood and misused. All animals, including humans, are differentiated by sex, but only humans are differentiated by gender. Sex, very simply, refers to the biological differences in the genetic composition and reproductive structures and functions of men and women. Two biological sexes exist in mammals and in many

FIGURE 1.1 The Sex–Gender Distinction

nonmammalian species, although recent controversies question the actual number of biological sexes that exist (see Chapter 3).

Biological differences between females and males exist on many levels: chromosomal, genetic, hormonal, and neurological. There is widespread misinformation and lack of understanding of these processes and interrelationships. For example, people's unfounded beliefs concerning hormones make the distinction of sex even more confusing. Many individuals believe that estrogen and progesterone are uniquely female hormones, while androgens are hormones that belong exclusively to males. However, all these hormones are found in both men and women, but in varying concentrations.

Why Gender?

Biological differences between men and women become social distinctions in most societies. Though gender is based on sex, it is actually comprised of traits, interests, and behaviors that societies place on or ascribe to each sex. In an age of technological advancement in much of the Western industrial economies, the different life experiences of males and females are not mainly due to hormones or reproductive capacities, but primarily to the *social context* that determines gender, that is, what is considered "feminine" and what is "masculine." By social context, we mean the total social sphere in which people find themselves: their personal history, immediate situation, their society and culture. The social context influences and determines the beliefs and behaviors that many people mistakenly believe are directly linked to being female or male. Gender is also more than just a category. Gender is a set of reciprocal activities that comprise being female and male, and all females and males are involved in the ongoing, day-to-day activities that make up "doing" gender (West & Zimmerman, 1987) or living up to society's prescriptions for gender based on their sex.

Gender is a socially constructed concept that refers to how differences between girls and boys and women and men are created and explained by society. It refutes notions that most differences between women and men are due to biology and are normal and immutable. It refutes notions of biological essentialism and what we consider to be either female or male. The concept of gender illuminates the *social construction* of difference between the sexes and underscores the fact that, while we may observe many different behaviors and attitudes between women and men, there is not necessarily a biological basis for these differences. For example, gender is quickly constructed, even for the newborn. A visit to a greeting card shop will demonstrate that foremost on the mind of those who congratulate new parents is the sex of the newborn. Girls' cards are dominated by themes of daintiness and physical attractiveness. Boys' cards are dominated by themes of strength and sports. The difference between the types of cards for female and male infants reveals how early gender is constructed and how the ideals for each sex are based on images that maximize the differences between females and males. For example, within 24 hours of birth, mothers and fathers were more likely to describe female infants as softer, finer featured, smaller, and more inattentive than male infants, even though male and female infants were not significantly different from each other in terms of birth weight or birth length (Rubin, Provenzano, & Luria, 1974). Nothing much has changed since 1974.

Although classified ads no longer specify the sex of the applicants that they are seeking, consider the following listing for a fictitious position. As you read the description, think about your own match with this position.

> *We are looking to hire the ideal member of the female sex. Applicants should be compassionate, patient, and kind. A nurturing woman is preferred.*

In actuality, the traits listed refer to aspects of the female *gender* and not the female *sex*. Many women, perhaps yourself included, possess these attributes; however, many women do not conform to this stereotypical characterization. In fact, several *men* are more suited to this description than some women!

Now consider the following position:

> *We are looking to hire the ideal member of the female gender. Essential requirements: must have breasts and have given birth for this position as a baby's wet nurse.*

The second ad demonstrates the incorrect usage of the term female *gender.* Possession of breasts, having given birth, and the capacity to nurse a baby are traits limited only to biological females, and the correct term is female *sex.*

This leads us to a very important question. If some critical behaviors or traits are not due to real differences, what is the purpose of creating such difference? Psychologists sometimes disagree about this, and we address this issue later. But first we need to consider some of the psychological processes that are involved in how beliefs about gender and gender-related activities are adopted and maintained by individuals.

Beliefs about Gender

Many theoreticians assert that children are *socialized* to act in accordance with their cultural dictates, presumably through the societal rewards and punishments that accompany adoption of society's values and norms. This acceptance of culture and its continuation into adulthood lead to the reinforcement and perpetuation of gender stereotyping. This view is known as the **cultural approach** to explaining the origin of gender stereotypes from a sociocultural perspective (Deaux & Kite, 1993).

A second framework, the **structural approach,** emphasizes the common positions that certain groups occupy within the social structure. Rather than stressing early socialization experiences, adherents of this approach focus on the ongoing structural and social role requirements that channel our experience, from the family to the societal level. For example, occupational roles were found to be a strong determinant of the traits ascribed to women and men, outweighing gender information (Deaux & Kite, 1993).

Beliefs about gender might also be explained from a cognitive perspective. **Stereotyping** is one example of a more general categorization process that is necessary in order for people to deal with the complexities of human existence. To cope with a potentially unmanageable amount of information, people learn to streamline information processing by grouping people into manageable categories based on some similarity among members. Unfortunately, perceived similarities among females (or males) may be inaccurate and perpetuate the formation of faulty gender stereotypes (Deaux & Kite, 1993). Interest in exploring racial and ethnic stereotypes, as well as gender stereotypes, arose in psychology at least in part due to the rise of feminism (Deaux, 1995).

Many real-life examples of stereotyping can be found in discrimination cases that have been brought before the courts. Imagine that you had worked for a number of years at a Fortune 500 firm in the United States. You had established a strong track record by being praised for your work by clients, winning new clients for the firm, and working extremely hard and to high standards. Each year, a few individuals make partner. Based on your stellar performance, which exceeds the performance of many other women as well as men, you expect to be made a partner of the firm, even though there are only a few partners, about 1 percent, who are women. Instead of receiving a partnership, however, you are told that you have interpersonal problems, you are too "macho," and that you even need a "course at charm school." A colleague even advises you to wear makeup if you want to be seriously considered for partner (*Hopkins* v. *Price Waterhouse,* 1985, p. 117). What would you do? Ann Hopkins lived through these experiences and decided to take the firm of Price Waterhouse to court (see Box 1.1).

According to cognitive social psychologists, at root in the Hopkins case is the notion of **stereotypes.** In general, stereotypes are generalized and oversimplified beliefs about groups of people (Harré & Lamb, 1986). Whereas prejudice refers to an attitude toward a group, which is usually negative, such as hostility or dislike, stereotypes are widely shared and socially validated beliefs or cognitions about whole groups of people that are then applied to individual members of that group (Lott, 1995). Stereotypes, the outcome of normal human cognitive processes called categorization, are highly efficient and organize much of what we perceive in the social world (Fiske & Taylor, 1991). For example, we quickly perceive a person's sex, race, occupation, or ethnicity, and we then form impressions based on this limited information. These impressions are not necessarily accurate ("Tim's sister is a president of a major university. I bet she doesn't have children"). The content of

Box 1.1

Psychology, Stereotyping, and the Law:
The Case of *Hopkins* v. *Price Waterhouse*

Susan Fiske and her colleagues, Donald Bersoff, Eugene Borgida, Kay Deaux, and Madeline Heilman, took psychological findings about the character and operation of stereotyping into sex discrimination litigation. The case, well-known in legal circles, involved the employment of Ann Hopkins at Price Waterhouse (a leading accounting firm). Hopkins was, by virtually all accounts, a competent, committed, hard-working, and effective professional. Although successful in her job, Hopkins was denied partnership, and she promptly filed a complaint in federal court. Social psychologist Susan Fiske testifed on her behalf, primarily citing research findings on stereotyping, conditions that encourage it, indicators that reveal it, consequences of it,

and remedies to prevent it. The judge ruled in Hopkins's favor, and Price Waterhouse, not surprisingly, appealed. After Hopkins's appellate victory, the case eventually was reviewed by the U.S. Supreme Court. Although research on sex stereotyping had been introduced in other legal proceedings (e.g., Goodman & Croyle, 1989), review by the Supreme Court made this case unique. It was the first such case to examine psychological research on sex stereotyping. The American Psychological Association entered with an *amicus curiae* (friend of the court) brief, expanding psychology's involvement. The result, possibly attributable in part to psychology's role, was victory for Hopkins.

Source: From "Resolving Legal Questions with Psychological Data," by E. F. Loftus, 1991, *American Psychologist, 46,* pp. 1046–1047. Copyright 1991 by the American Psychological Association. Reprinted by permission.

stereotypes will vary based on how they are cognitively organized, for example, around age, status, or gender, and who holds the stereotypes. Many young people believe that the elderly tend to be lonely, for example, but in actuality at least one study showed that adolescents were just as likely to report feeling lonely when alone as were the aged (Larson, Csikszentmihalyi, & Graef, 1982).

We next look more closely at **gender stereotypes,** that is, how males and females are represented. How are gender stereotypes expressed? How do gender stereotypes develop? What is the relationship of sexism to stereotypes? What are the implications of both racism and sexism for women of color? (See Chapter 2 for a full discussion of the origin of gender stereotypes.)

Gender Stereotypes

Gender is often classified into feminine and masculine qualities or behaviors and is prone to stereotyping as a result. Research conducted in the 1970s and 1980s (e.g., Broverman, Vogel, Broverman, Clarkson, & Rosenkrantz, 1972; Deaux & Emswiller, 1974;

Spence, Helmreich, & Stapp, 1974) found that women were evaluated as more communal and expressive than men and that men were believed to be more competent, agentic, and instrumental than women. Moreover, these differences extended beyond evaluations to beliefs about occupations and appropriate roles. People who are not labeled feminine or masculine are termed *androgynous* individuals, since they have a mixture of the traits traditionally assigned to one sex or the other (e.g., Bem, 1974).

In considering how stereotypes are organized, we first need to consider the basis for their organization. Because an individual's sex is typically highly visible and salient to observers (race, ethnicity, and age are other examples), sex is a foundation for cognitive categorization. The result is a number of gender stereotypes that are based on whether a person is perceived to be male or female. Furthermore, when researching the stereotypes that people hold, many gender stereotypes may actually be a mixture of sex, race, and/or class (see Box 1.2). Not only are the characteristics that are ascribed to men and women different, but these same characteristics also have different amounts of desirability.

Box 1.2 _____

Stereotypes of Women
by Race and Class

BLACK WOMEN	WHITE WOMEN
Hostile	Warm
Dirty	Vain
Emotional	Dependent
Superstitious	Intelligent

MIDDLE-CLASS WOMEN	LOWER-CLASS WOMEN
Intelligent	Talkative
Ambitious	Irresponsible
Competent	Dirty
Happy	Dependent

Source: Adapted from "Race X Class Stereotypes of Women," by H. Landrine, 1985, *Sex Roles, 13,* pp. 65–75. Copyright 1985 by Plenum Publishing. Adapted with permission.

The extent to which gender stereotypes reflect actual differences between men and women is debatable. Whatever truth does exist within the roles ascribed to men and women may originate in biology or environment or be a function of the interaction of the two. However, it is dangerous to take a gender stereotype and apply it to every individual, no matter how truthful it might seem to be at a group level (Deaux & Kite, 1993). Yet, gender-associated processes are often so deeply ingrained and subtle that most of us do not even realize how strongly they affect our behavior, thoughts, feelings, language, interactions with others, and the structures of social institutions.

Returning to the example of Ann Hopkins, the testimony of a cognitive psychologist at the trial pointed out that a number of conditions encouraged the use of gender stereotypes for *outgroups,* or individuals who are not perceived as members of one's own group. These conditions included Hopkins's near-solo status in the firm; her job, which was traditionally held by men; and her personal attributes, which made her fit for her job as a manager but which were not typical for women and could "create dissatisfaction among their subordinates." Furthermore, female stereotypes are elicited when judgments are made of ambiguous traits,

such as an individual's "warmth," "collegiality," or "interpersonal skills." It was Hopkins's gender, not her track record, that was narrowly evaluated and became the primary category within which she was judged. Future research needs to consider the institutionalization of discrimination by examining the environment or "playing field" in which women are evaluated.

In sports, for example, athletes, coaches, and referees expect that the playing field will be level; that is, players from all teams must subscribe to the same rules in order for fairness and equality to prevail. In social life, however, playing fields are not necessarily level and pose considerable influence in facilitating or negating the stereotyping process. One playing field that concerns us is that of science, including psychology. As we will see, science is not isolated and immune from antifemale prejudices, stereotypes, and discrimination.

SEX DISCRIMINATION IN SOCIETY AND SCIENCE: BLATANT, SUBTLE, AND COVERT

Sex Discrimination in Society

Sex discrimination, the harmful and unequal treatment of individuals due to their sex, is a function of both internal processes, such as the cognitive categorization that underlies much stereotyping, and the power that men have to invoke antifemale prejudices through everyday practices that deny women the same privileges that men enjoy. Before reading on, answer the questions in Box 1.3.

According to Benokraitis and Feagin (1995), **sexism** produces greater disadvantages for women than men because it is women who are targeted more frequently. Although men may experience discrimination due to other social variables (religion, age, race, or sexual preference), their gender neutralizes these other sources of discrimination. Being female, on the other hand, predicts discrimination more than other variables. In addition, being female is braided with additional social variables, such as age, race or ethnicity, and social class, to produce greater disadvantage (Benokraitis & Feagin, 1995).

Blatant Sexism. After answering the questions in Box 1.3, you may notice that the behaviors that you

BOX 1.3

A Self-Study

Using the scale below, indicate how often the event has happened to you over the course of your life.

1	2	3	4	5	6
the event never happened					the event happens almost all the time

Answer 1: If the event has NEVER happened to you.
Answer 2: If the event happened ONCE IN A WHILE.
Answer 3: If the event happened SOMETIMES.
Answer 4: If the event happened A LOT.
Answer 5: If the event happened MOST OF THE TIME.
Answer 6: If the event happened ALMOST ALL THE TIME.

1. How many times have people made inappropriate or unwanted sexual advances to you because you are a woman?
2. How many times have you been treated unfairly by your co-workers, fellow students, or colleagues because you are a woman?
3. How many times have you wanted to tell someone off for being sexist?
4. How many times have you been denied a promotion or a raise because you are a woman?
5. How many times have you been picked on, hit, pushed, shoved, or threatened with harm because you are a woman?
6. How many times were you forced to listen to sexist jokes or degrading sexual jokes?
7. How many times have you gotten into an argument or fight about something sexist that was done or said to you or to somebody else?
8. How many times have people failed to show you the respect that you deserve because you are a woman?
9. How many times have you been treated unfairly by teachers or professors because you are a woman?
10. How many times have you been treated unfairly by your boyfriend, husband, or other important man because you are a woman?

Source: Adapted from "The Schedule of Sexist Events: A Measure of Lifetime and Recent Sexist Discrimination in Women's Lives," by E. A. Klonoff and H. Landrine, 1995, *Psychology of Women Quarterly, 19*, pp. 439–472. Reprinted with the permission of Cambridge University Press and the authors.

experienced varied along a number of dimensions. According to Benokraitis and Feagin, sexism varies as a function of its visibility, intentionality, and ease of documentation. **Blatant sexism** occurs when women are treated in a transparently harmful and unequal way. Physical violence, sexist jokes, degrading language, sexual harassment, and unequal treatment under the law or in employment fall into this category. The effects of this treatment, such as inequality in employment, are documented in statistics.

Subtle Sexism.   **Subtle sexism** is less apparent than blatant sexism because it is less visible to others as well as to ourselves. Benokraitis and Feagin make the point that we have internalized negative cultural messages regarding the inferiority of women, despite all our outward attempts to say that we believe in the equality of women. For example, when three or four male faculty members congregate in a parking lot to chat, other faculty merely think that they are sharing information or passing the time of day together and wave when passing by the group. When three or four female faculty members form a group, however, other faculty members may feel that they can joke to the threesome or foursome that they are forming a "cabal." When men form a group, onlookers do not experience any message except a wave or inattention. For a cluster of women, however, the message is different. When they form a group, it is inferred to be for the sinister purposes of plotting, intrigue, or conspiracy. According to Benokraitis and Feagin, subtle sexism is not necessarily manipulative, intentional, or malicious; however, it can be. Furthermore, it can be documented, though it is difficult to do so because many people do not perceive it as a threat.

Covert Sexism. In distinction to blatant and subtle forms of sexism, **covert sexism** is intentional, hidden, and frequently hostile. This form of sexism refers to behavior that is deliberate in attempting to thwart women and assure their failure. Applications for jobs or promotion are "lost" but then found after the job is filled or the promotion occurs. Covert sexism can be very difficult to prove or document, and strategies, such as sabotage of a woman on the job, are easy to deny (Benokraitis & Feagin, 1995).

Sex Discrimination in Science

According to most traditional definitions, **science** is a knowledge-based activity that depends on facts accumulated through systematic and objective questioning, hypothesis testing, methodological study, analysis, and presentation. In most college classrooms, science is presented as a dispassionate activity (Rabinowitz & Sechzer, 1993). As conventionally presented, a scientist is not sentimental, irrational, emotional, or imprecise (Fausto-Sterling, 1992; Rabinowitz & Sechzer, 1993). Historians of science, however, have pointed to a number of errors that scientists generally have committed (e.g., Jacklin, 1981). Vita Rabinowitz and Susan Weseen (1997) have noted that "As in other scientific fields, the history of psychology is replete with examples of failures to replicate results, peculiar omissions and preoccupations, and misrepresentations of findings" (p. 626). Commonly, different scholars interpret the "same findings" quite

differently at different times. To take just one example, American social psychologists (with the important exception of Solomon Asch) have tended to interpret Asch's famous research on the effects of group pressure as supporting the notion that people are conforming, and this interpretation has gained force over time. European psychologists (and Asch himself) saw the same work as suggesting that people are remarkably independent of group pressure (Asch, 1951; Friend, Rafferty, & Bramel, 1990). Gender comparisons in science are particularly fraught with difficulty and subject to misinterpretation.

Men's prominence in the history of the field of psychology parallels sex-role stereotypes pervading our society. Psychology might have more accurately been called the psychology of men (see Box 1.4). Most research in the first half of the twentieth century was carried out by men with a predominance of male subjects. In the rare event that a study did include some female subjects, sex differences were not reported. In fact, close to 95 percent of all early research never looked at sex comparisons (Denmark, 1976; Sechzer, Rabinowitz, & Denmark, 1994).

The few studies carried out in the early years of the twentieth century that did look at sex differences (and were carried out by male investigators) overwhelmingly concluded that females were inferior based on an idea called the *variability hypothesis.* This hypothesis, which was prominent in the early 1900s, posited that males were more variable than females on many dimensions, and this greater variability indicated their higher status. Only Leta Hollingworth, a female psychologist conducting research during this time, found no female–male differences in variability (Denmark & Fernandez, 1993). In 1914, Hollingworth found that when birth weight and length of neonates were examined, the female sex (if any) was favored in terms of variability (Montague & Hollingworth, 1914). Hollingworth also concluded that women's physical and mental performance did not fluctuate according to the phases of the menstrual cycle, as had been previously surmised (Hollingworth, 1914). Lowie and Hollingworth (1916) reported that the objective evidence of cross-cultural, biological, and psychological studies did not support the notion of innate female inferiority. Thus, not only did Hollingworth

Box 1.4 _____

A Psychologist Remembers

In 1991, the annual conference of the American Psychological Association was held in San Francisco. A friend of the authors of this text attended the meetings and has told this story widely:

I was standing at a publisher's book stall and was admiring their new textbook on the psychology of women. It was very enjoyable to consider the scope and depth of recent scholarship on women, as many of the topics were long neglected. I made a few comments to the publisher's representative. Within a few moments, I noticed that another psychology professor joined me and the bookseller in the book stall. A couple of minutes later, I heard the professor ask, "Where are your psychology of men textbooks?"

I have to say, in all honesty, that without missing a beat I wheeled around, quickly scanning his badge for his name and university affiliation, and advised him, in as nonchalant a voice as I could gather, "Why don't you examine any introductory psychology textbook published before 1978. Most of the human subjects, and even the rats, were white and male."

The psychologist looked taken aback at first and then his facial expression changed and he looked down. After about 10 seconds, he nodded his head up and down slowly and looked back up and said, "I need to think about this, don't I." I nodded back. He smiled and walked away.

I went back to paging through the new textbook. At that moment, I knew that psychology, and some psychologists, were being challenged during a wholesale change in the production of psychological knowledge. It was a great moment.

and her colleagues refute the variability hypothesis based on scientific research, but they also elucidated the gender bias underlying the hypothesis. Yet, during this period, the history of the field of psychology tended to neglect women's roles and contributions to the field—a serious omission, as the reader will see (Russo & Denmark, 1987).

In the late nineteenth and early twentieth centuries, myths about women's inferiority pervaded society. The popularity of Social Darwinism reinforced the belief that men were superior to women as a result of natural selection based on sex. Early female psychologists had their hands full attempting to disprove notions such as the debilitating effect of the menstrual cycle on women and women's emotional fragility (see Box 1.5). As psychoanalytic theory became more popular, female psychologists were forced to contend with concepts such as penis envy and inferior superego development in women. As these beliefs grew more widespread, the disadvantaged position of women in psychology became more salient (Denmark & Fernandez, 1993).

As social psychology and human learning blossomed in psychology, so too did the idea that environmental factors in gender-based behavior were of importance in understanding gender differences (Denmark & Fernandez, 1993). Viola Klein (1950) aptly summarized our cognitive heuristics or shortcuts in describing male versus female behavior. She pointed out our cultural tendency to note a wide variation in male abilities and dispositions while women were summarized in homogeneous terms. Klein keenly noted a fact regarding stereotyping in research that was carried out well into the 1960s: Male researchers tended to note the wide individual differences of men ("us"), but tended to view women as a distinct psychological type ("them") (Denmark & Fernandez, 1993). "Whether she is strong-willed or meek, single-minded or hesitant, gentle or quarrelsome—she is supposed to possess a particular version of whatever trait she manifests and her stubbornness or submissiveness, her capriciousness or lack of humor will be found 'typically feminine'" (Klein, 1950, p. 4)

In writing about the psychological processes involved in the construction of differences among social groups, Erika Apfelbaum (1979) commented that

Box 1.5

G. Stanley Hall

G. Stanley Hall is considered to be one of the founders of modern psychology. Most accounts of Hall focus on his early concerns with functionalism, that is, the study of mental functions and adaptive processes. Many functionalists were influenced by Darwin's evolutionary theory, which was used by Hall to support his theory of sex differences. Leslie Diehl (1988) maintains that, excepting scholarship by feminists (Rosenberg, 1982; Shields, 1975), most historians have ignored Hall's interest in women's nature and sex differences. Hall, in fact, was a leader of the movement against coeducation in the early part of the twentieth century. Although males and females were represented in most grade schools and high schools by the turn of the century, the fledgling presence of women in colleges and universities renewed the controversy. His views on evolution influenced his theory of human development (G. S. Hall, 1904, in Diehl, 1988). Adolescence was a period of biological differentiation, which necessitated different roles for men and women in life as well as in education. It was especially during the period of adolescence that Hall thought that women should be separated from men due to the danger of damage to the female reproductive system. Coeducation could potentially feminize men in Hall's views. Furthermore, coeducation was both an attack on the role of women as mothers and therefore on the future of humanity. Furthermore, in Hall's view, "the truest measures of the effects of education on the development of the re-

productive organs were the reduced number of marriages among female college graduates and the smaller number of children produced" (Diehl, 1988, p. 300). Hall's views were hardly unanimously accepted by the public or psychologists, but he singled out feminists for special attack, charging them with wanting to deny the monthly pain of menstruation of young girls (1908, p. 10, 240) and with trying to "escape the monthly function" (1904, p. 609) in their research and theorizing.

Hall's writings on the topic have enjoyed near obscurity, but his role in the lives of women undergraduates was potentially more potent. Hall was a chief administrator at Clark University from 1888 through 1920. In 1889, he prevailed with the board of trustees at Clark to deny women admission to the university and later, under public and state pressure, took a stance that would void women's chance to be fully admitted to undergraduate and master's programs. Yet, he did enroll women in graduate programs. According to Diehl, the paradox of the psychological theoretician and administrator was due to the fact that to Hall women students were unusual and not typical of women in general. Alternatively, perhaps the women at Clark University appealed to Hall's own proclivities as a theoretician. For example, just as Hollingworth enrolled at Columbia where there were instructors who shared her perspective on sex differences, Hall himself could have attracted female students who ascribed to his own views on sex differences (Rosenberg, 1982).

marking, excluding, and grouping make up the first sequence of processes necessary to establish domination. . . . The segregated, subordinated group, its autonomy removed, now exists only by reference to the norms, rules and regulations set by the dominant group; that is, it exists within an imposed dependency relation that benefits the latter. (pp. 197–198)

Research that focuses on sex differences due to either biology or person-based differences contributes, in some instances, to the notion that women are deficient. It "is seen in the explanations for women's lack of achievement motivation, their excessive fear of success, their lack of self-confidence, or their desire for children" (Kahn & Yoder, 1989, p. 424). Such re-

search contributes to the status quo because it reflects the belief that differences between men and women, attributed to either biology or early socialization, are permanent and intractable (Kahn & Yoder, 1989; Prilleltensky, 1989). Furthermore, such research can sound as if it is blaming the victim, as the context in which these differences emerge is left unexamined and unchallenged (Kahn & Yoder, 1989; Ryan, 1971).

Attention to social and contextual variables yields correctives to many long-standing truisms in sex difference research. For example, for many years scientists concluded that boys were naturally better at math than girls (Benbow & Stanley, 1980). However, many factors other than biology could account for this finding. In a study of mathematically gifted girls and boys (Fox, 1987), girls were significantly less confident in their abilities than were their male counterparts. In fact, girls take fewer math courses in high school than boys do (Peterson & Crockett, 1987). Moreover, the perceived usefulness of mathematics plays a role in the discrepancy between males and females. As females tended to perceive less utility for mathematics in the future, so too did their test scores diminish (Hilton, 1987).

Motivation could also help explain the differences. Denmark and Francois (1987) have noted that, because studies have shown that enjoying math may be considered unfeminine, performing well "on the SAT mathematics test may not be very important to girls. They might not consider themselves 'high achievers' even if they did receive high scores" (p. 65). As noted earlier by Fennema and Sherman (1977), math *ability* has also been confounded with math *training,* as well as with parents' attitudes, teachers' attitudes, and informal math experiences.

More recently, a meta-analysis of gender differences (Hyde, Fennema, & Lamon, 1990) comprising the testing of 3 million people found no gender differences in math ability with the one exception of the area of problem solving. Here males scored noticeably higher beginning in high school, with the differences increasing during college. For further information on gender differences in mathematical aptitude, see Chapter 6.

FEMINIST PERSPECTIVES AND IDEOLOGY

The women's and feminist movements have raised the consciousness of both women and men revealing how our everyday lives and social norms reinforce male dominance. Although there have been individual women who acted to change male dominance or patriarchy in their own particular sphere, feminist movements arose to develop and implement broad-based social actions to challenge a whole range of social and cultural traditions regarding sex and gender (Stockard & Johnson, 1992). The beginnings of **feminism** date back to 1903 with the founding of the Women's Social and Political Union (WSPU) in Britain by Emmeline Pankhurst and her daughters, which initiated the **"first wave of feminism"** (Humm, 1992). In the United States, the first formally organized convention for women's rights was held in 1848 in Seneca Falls, New York. The conference, attended by 300 people and organized by Elizabeth Cady Stanton and Lucretia Mott, produced a document endorsing women's rights, The Declaration of Sentiments, which paralleled the Declaration of Independence.

Feminism: Not a "Brand Label"

The term *feminism* was not used until the twentieth century and refers to the belief that women and men are equal and should be equally valued as well as have equal rights (Offen, 1988). Feminism has a broad-based perspective and encompasses several different ideologies, each with a unique frame of reference. Yet, many of these theories and viewpoints intersect and are not strictly exclusive. All, however, criticize the ways in which women have been "oppressed, repressed, and suppressed" and "celebrate the ways in which so many women have 'beaten the system,' taken charge of their own destinies, and encouraged each other" (Tong, 1989, pp. 1–2).

There is not one type of feminist, just as there is not one type of sexist. Feminism is a broad movement that enables researchers to adopt different perspectives of feminism as they conduct research and generate theory. The term *feminist* does not accurately portray the various views that inform the scholarship that is considered feminist. The term *feminist,* however, is many times used by nonfeminists as a caricature of individuals who are characterized by negative traits as discussed later.

One viewpoint, **socialist feminism,** does not focus on individuals as does liberal feminism, but on social relations and how social institutions preserve and promote male dominance. Socialist feminism emphasizes the need to change our economic system as a precondition to gender equality. Economic and sexist oppression are seen as fundamental aspects of society that reinforce each other. For example, most social feminists believe that a few wealthy white people exploit the working class and all men exploit women.

Social feminists often study the relationship of inequalities stemming from social class, race, and ethnicity, as well as from gender. Social feminism stresses unity and integration, both in the sense of integrating all aspects of women's lives and of producing a unified feminist theory (Tong, 1989). These groups call for a fundamental restructuring of social institutions and social relationships.

Radical feminism, a second feminist perspective, focuses on the control of women by men. While social feminists emphasize both economic and sexist oppression, the position of radical feminists is that men's oppression of women is primary and serves as a model for all other oppression (e.g., economic and racial). The goal of radical feminism is the abolition of class and gender inequality and the creation of a new culture and society based on a more balanced integration of female and male power. Radical feminists also believe that in order to end the oppression of women it is necessary to establish women-centered systems and beliefs. Therefore, change is needed on all levels.

The theory of radical feminism is still evolving and therefore is not as well developed as those of the other feminist groups. One reason is that, unlike the other feminist groups, radical feminists reject feminisms rooted in theories developed by men. The theory of radical feminism must be developed by women and must be based on women's experiences. Because of oppression, women have had few chances to come together to understand their experiences and to develop theories (Rosser, 1992). Research in this domain often looks at sexuality and violence against women in order to understand the origin of males' greater power in our society.

A third feminist perspective, **cultural feminism,** seeks to emphasize the characteristics and qualities of women who have been devalued and ignored in our society—qualities such as female tendencies toward being nurturing, caring, and concerned for the needs of others. Cultural feminism supports the idea that our society should acknowledge and honor unpaid work contributed by women in our culture.

A fourth feminist perspective, **liberal feminism,** focuses on equality. This perspective defines a feminist as one who believes that females are entitled to total social and legal equality with males and who supports revisions in values, mores, and laws in order to achieve this equality. This feminist perspective also believes that males and females are more alike than different and that, if given similar, equal opportunities and situations, women and men will behave similarly.

Liberal feminism is sometimes referred to as "equal opportunity feminism" (Stockard & Johnson, 1992). Liberal feminists do not seek special privileges, but simply demand that everyone receive consideration without discrimination on the basis of gender. Over the last 25 years, liberal feminists have championed changes in our language, changes in how the media represent women, and even changes in religious practices. According to Stockard & Johnson (1992), "These attempts have met with such success that some authors have suggested that we are in a postfeminist era" (p. 18).

The label *feminist* is considered somewhat stigmatizing by some, and many people therefore tend to avoid classifying themselves as such. Yet the same people will express views consistent with those of liberal feminism. For example, in a recent teaching experience, one of the authors asked the class how many of them would call themselves feminists and she got a minimal reaction. However, when she asked them how many believed in justice and equality for all races, classes, and sexes, the students responded unanimously in the affirmative.

THE FEMINIST CRITIQUE IN PSYCHOLOGY: MULTIPLE ISSUES

Feminists are not antiscience. Indeed many prominent feminist researchers within psychology have dedicated their careers to demonstrating how rigorous scientific research can dispel myths and stereotypes harmful to women. Feminist researchers, like feminists in other domains, vary in the problems that they tackle and the specific research methods that they use to approach problems.

Research and theorizing on gender differences continue and are popular among some feminists. Some feminist psychologists focus almost exclusively on differences between women and men in their writing and research (e.g., Belenky, Clinchy, Goldberger, & Tarule, 1986; Gilligan, 1982). According to these authors, gender differences do emerge and show that women are more caring, are more interpersonally effective in leadership skills, and have other special characteristics. These characteristics are consistent with many gender stereotypes of women, as distinct from men and men's stereotypical cluster of traits.

Other feminist research psychologists, using the scientific method, have tended to find fewer gender differences than researchers such as Gilligan and others who depend on case histories and alternative research approaches (Eagly, 1995a). While noting that some large gender differences have been found in psychology, such as women smiling much more than men (Hall, 1984), these feminist psychologists have argued that most differences are zero to moderate in size (Hyde & Plant, 1995). Furthermore, they say that by focusing on differences, the similarities, which are equally important, become obscured. As we shall see throughout this book, women and men are more alike than they are different.

The above example of a gender difference, women smiling more than men, is explained by Hyde and Plant as due to the social dominance of men in interpersonal situations. These researchers argue that research that focuses on gender differences does not help promote the causes of women and the social change that is needed. Furthermore, problems in gender comparison research revolve around difficulties in defining and measuring differences and in removing values in the interpretation of results. Continuing to focus on differences between males and females may serve to keep women in inferior social positions. Researchers with this perspective advocate integrating feminist research into each area of psychology, which would obviate any need for a separate study of the psychology of women. Focusing instead on similarities, which are more common, may help women more easily gain legal and social parity with men. Conversely, others have argued that a focus on similarity has obscured important gender differences and that a focus on such differences could "enhance women's ability to understand the antecedents of inequality and to improve their status in society" (Eagly, 1995b, p. 155).

We now know that although sex differences have been studied in psychology since its inception it is often not clear precisely what is being studied. Terms like sex, gender, male, female, masculine, and feminine have been used too loosely or inclusively to de-scribe everything from the biological sex of participants to the social or situational factors considered appropriate to males and females. Whenever males and females are compared and differences assessed, so many uncontrollable variables are correlated with biological sex that we can never know which variable played a causal role in a gender difference. For instance, male and female groups in any one study may be different in height, body fat composition, educational background, social skills, athletic experience, eating habits, and other variables too numerous to measure. Feminist researchers have pointed to the dangerous and unscientific tendency to interpret gender differences as originating in innate biological differences—sex differences—without evidence supporting those claims (Rabinowitz & Sechzer, 1993).

It is by now well known that many long-established "sex differences," on reexamination, are bound by historical, social, and contextual factors and do not endure over time, populations, or situational context. For example, as we will see in Chapter 6, the difference in mathematical ability between males and females is shrinking over time in the United States. Many gender differences have been reinterpreted as power or status differences. Moreover, the conventional focus on sex differences in the psychological literature obscures the many ways in which males and females are similar.

Problems and Biases in Research

Almost thirty years ago, coinciding with the women's movement in the 1970s, a few feminist psychologists began raising questions about how we did research in psychology and related fields, including **bias in research methods.** They noted, for example, that the research questions posed reflected men's interests and concerns more than women's and that gender-role stereotypes affected all aspects of the research. They pointed out that male research participants were much more commonly used than female participants and that findings based on males were indiscriminately generalized to females. Increasingly, feminists noticed that the bias in the choice of research participants, with its attendant biases in many other aspects of the research, was rampant in animal research as well as human research and in health and biomedical research as well as behavioral and social research (Sechzer, Rabinowitz, & Denmark, 1993; Sechzer, Zmitrovich, & Denmark, 1985). In some cases, findings based solely on male animals have been generalized to human females (Sechzer et al., 1994)! Over the past three decades, clear progress has been made in psychology toward the conduct of gender-fair research. There is recent evidence that related fields like biomedicine are following suit, due largely to a federal mandate established by the U.S. government in the mid-1990s to include women and ethnic minorities in research that is relevant to both males and females. But progress in the conduct of nonsexist research in biomedicine, health, and some areas of research practice in psychology has been slow and, in certain quarters, grudging. Let us briefly review how feminist psychologists, along with psychologists of color, gay male and lesbian psychologists, and other scholars who represent disenfranchised groups in psychology and society, are changing the practice of psychological research.

> [A]s historians and sociologists have begun to identify the ways in which the development of scientific knowledge has been shaped by its particular social and political context, our understanding of science as a social process has grown. (Keller, 1982, p. 312)

Traditional, Nonsexist, and Feminist Approaches to Research

Among many but by no means all researchers, there is increased understanding and acceptance of the fact that science is not, and cannot be, value free. Our values arise from our experience of our gender, race and ethnic background, social class, and other influences, and they enrich at the same time that they constrain our work. Values affect all phases of a research project, from the choice of what to study to the conclusions drawn from the results. Pervasive beliefs about the objectivity of science prevent us from seeing the nature and limits of scientific knowledge and have worked to preserve the status quo in society (Rabinowitz & Sechzer, 1993).

Rabinowitz and Sechzer (1993) and Denmark, Russo, Frieze, and Sechzer (1988) have reviewed many of the issues that arise in the nuts and bolts of conducting more gender-fair research, such as the formulation of research questions, the conduct of the literature review, the choice of research participants and research designs, the operationalization of variables, and the analyzing and interpretation of results. These issues are discussed next.

Question Formulation.   Traditional psychology has begun its analysis from men's experience, particularly white middle-class men's experiences. Questions have been asked about the conditions under which females are cognitively impaired, but not about when males are so impaired, just as they have been asked about male sexual arousal far more often than female sexual arousal. In psychological research in general, the concentration has been on topics such as aggression, conflict, dominance, work achievement, and cognitive processes and has downplayed topics such as affiliation, cooperation, family issues, and emotional processes. As an essential corrective to male bias in psychology, the experiences, concerns, and perspectives of girls and women need to be better integrated into mainstream psychology.

Reviewing the Psychological Literature.   Most researchers get their ideas from reading other people's work. Many bodies of literature are rife with sexist assumptions and research practices and are unreliable guides for feminist research. While analyzing scholarly literature, we need to identify likely sources of bias and consider how different research participants, treatments, designs, and measures might affect the results of the study.

Sample Selection.   Descriptions of respondents in the research report typically include the sex of respondents. This is largely due to scientific convention, but also reflects assumptions that sex is a variable that affects results. There is a serious problem with conceptualizing sex (along with other respondent variables) as an independent variable. It is a descriptive rather than a conceptual variable, and it has obvious biological (genetic, hormonal, physiological), psychological (developmental, experiential), and sociocultural (socialization, economic, educational, political) components. Males and females are therefore not randomly assigned to gender, and gender comparisons are fraught with problems in interpretation, as we have already noted.

Research Design. There are few topics in psychology for which it is safe to assume that gender is completely irrelevant. Feminist psychologists remind the scientific community that gender matters and that we need to reflect this in our research. For instance, they caution that gender is a complex problematic independent variable; if it is used as a subject (respondent) variable, it needs to be taken apart and analyzed so that we can better understand which of the many facets of gender may be important in a given area. Beyond our respondents, we need to take into account the sex of experimenters, confederates, and other people involved in our research.

It is by now a truism in research methodology that the choice of research design depends on the research question. Causal questions call for true experimental and quasi-experimental designs when they are ethical and feasible to implement. But despite their unique advantages in permitting causal inferences, experiments frequently do not illuminate the processes underlying the relationships among variables and, as we have noted, they are poor vehicles for understanding respondent variables like gender, race, and class. Given what many feminist researchers have found to be the inherent sexism of traditional scientific psychology, more and more feminists are exploring the use of alternative research methods, particularly qualitative methods, in their work. Diverse methods are needed to capture the rich array of personal, situational, and structural factors that shape, and are shaped by, women and girls (Riger, 1992).

Operationalizations. Females and males throughout the life-span differ in the ideas, objects, and events to which they are exposed, the behaviors that they are able to practice, and the outcomes that they receive in the real world. For these reasons, we expect them to enter any experimental situation with different orientations, attitudes, perceptions, expectations, and skills.

Females and males respond to the same stimuli quite differently, and we need to determine the meaning to respondents of experimental stimuli, tasks, and tests before assuming that all respondents share the researchers' perceptions and assumptions.

Data Analysis and Interpretation. We have discussed some of the most serious problems in testing for and interpreting gender differences. We need to be sure not to exaggerate or minimize such differences. Oversimplified conclusions regarding gender differences can provide seemingly scientific justifications for sexist stereotyping and discriminatory practices.

Guidelines for avoiding sexism in psychological research have been developed to aid in conducting gender-fair research (Denmark et al., 1988). As both experienced research psychologists and psychology students conduct research, they need to confront the potential for sexism at various stages of the research process. Box 1.6 provides you with a series of sexism-related research problems and gender-fair research solutions.

Mapping Solutions for Gender-Fair Research

It is important when reporting gender differences to avoid value judgments about the direction of the differences, as these kinds of judgments have been used against women in the past. Thus, male rationality has been contrasted with female emotionality, male dominance with female submission, male independence with female dependence, and so on. The unspoken assumption underlying such evaluations is that if a response is more associated with females than males, there must be something wrong with it.

These critiques and correctives of traditional scientific practice, born in the 1970s, have woven their way into mainstream psychology. Increasingly, the insights and perceptions of 1990s feminist theory are changing our conceptions of the socially and culturally structured differences among people and are promising to change the practice of psychology still further (Sechzer, Griffin, & Pfafflin, 1994; Stewart, 1998). According to the leading feminist theorist and

BOX 1.6

Sexism-Related Research Problems and Gender-Fair Research Solutions

Science produces knowledge, but it is also a *human* and *social process*. Therefore, the production of knowledge can be affected by human values and assumptions that are relevant at one or more stages of the research process. The result, which many reviews of the literature support, is that science can produce highly biased knowledge, especially when conducting human research related to gender, race, ethnicity, disability, sexual preference, or socioeconomic status.

The following guidelines, although focused on gender, are based on principles that can be applied to other forms of bias as well.

QUESTION FORMULATION

Problem: Gender stereotypes that are associated with the topic being studied can bias question formulation and research outcomes.
Example: Some studies have defined leadership only in terms of dominance, aggression, and other styles that emphasize characteristics congruent with a male stereotype.
Correction: Recognize the existence of a range of leadership styles, including those that emphasize egalitarian relationships, negotiation, conflict resolution, and consideration of others. The limits of any definition that is used should be specified.

RESEARCH METHODS

Problem: The selection of research participants is based on stereotypic assumptions and does not allow for generalizations to other groups.
Example: On the basis of stereotypes about who should be responsible for contraception, only females are looked at in studies of contraception.
Correction: Both sexes should be studied before conclusions are drawn about the factors that determine the use of contraception.

Problem: The sex and race of research participants, experimenters' confederates, and persons in direct contact with the participants are not specified. Potential interactions of sex and race or other variables may create unexplained variance.

Example: More helping behavior by males rather than females is found in studies that use a young female confederate who needs help. Such results may be a function of the sex of the confederate or an interaction of participant and confederate, rather than a difference due to the gender of the research participants.
Correction: Control for or vary the sex and race of persons involved in the research. Try to include experimenters and participants who are members of racial minorities. At a minimum, specify the sex and race of everyone involved in the research.

DATA ANALYSIS AND INTERPRETATION

Problem: Serendipitous gender differences are reported, but no report is made when differences are not found. Care must be taken to avoid giving a skewed image of the actual data.
Example: "In analyzing data, we found that males and females differed significantly on. . . ."
Correction: Any nonhypothesized sex or gender differences should be reported and the need for replication indicated to assure that the difference is not artifactual. When gender differences are not found and where such an observation is relevant, this too should be reported so that future research can confirm or disconfirm the lack of any nonhypothesized gender differences.

Problem: Misleading implications of findings of gender differences are not addressed. Statistical significance is not clearly distinguished from the substantive significance.
Example: "The spatial ability scores of women in our sample are significantly lower than those of the men, at the .01 level." The reader is left to assume that perhaps women should not become architects or engineers.
Correction: "The spatial ability scores of the women are significantly lower than those of the men, at the .01 level. Successful architects score above 32 on our spatial ability test . . . ; engineers score above 31. . . . Twelve percent of the women and 16% of the men in our sample score above 31; 11% of the women and 15% of the men score above 32."

(continued)

BOX 1.6 Continued

CONCLUSIONS

Problem: Results based on one sex are generalized to both.

Example: Threshold measurements in shock sensitivity for rats have been standardized for males, but are often generalized to both sexes.

Correction: There should be empirically determined norms for male and female study participants that reflect differences in weight, body fat, and so on.

Problem: Evaluative labeling is used for results.

Example: Male aggressiveness is used as the standard of acceptability. Females are described as unaggressive or submissive.

Correction: Use neutral, objective descriptions, such as "the mean score for the aggression measure was higher for males than females."

Source: From "Guidelines for Avoiding Sexism in Psychological Research: A Report of the Ad Hoc Committee on Nonsexist Research," by F. L. Denmark, N. F. Russo, I. H. Frieze, and J. A. Sechzer, 1988, *American Psychologist, 43,* pp. 582–584. Copyright 1988 by the American Psychological Association. Reprinted by permission of the publisher.

methodologist Abigail Stewart, contemporary feminist theories have even more to offer psychology. Stewart wrote specifically of improving and enriching research in personality, but her analysis has broader implications for all of psychology. She points to six areas where feminist theories can help us to get behind invalid and limiting assumptions that render research less exciting and revealing than it might be, and she holds forth the promise of enriching psychological research generally.

Specifically, the practices that Stewart calls for are these:

1. Look for what has been left out of traditional research in an area, because features of women's experience have been left out of the discipline. For instance, the assumption that everyone has an equal chance of succeeding or failing to get what they want is not likely to be valid.

2. Analyze your own position as it affects your understanding and the research process. Our positions as educated middle-class professionals bias how we view all aspects of the research, even how we see the routine process of obtaining informed consent. Our respondents' understanding of events, stimuli, and tests needs to become central to our analyses.

3. Use gender as an analytic tool, a category of analysis, a socially constructed concept that has different and layered meanings in different cultural and historical contexts.

4. Consistent with the notion of gender as an analytic tool, gender is not (only) about difference, but is also about dominance or power relations. As Stewart notes, power is a critical aspect of gender requiring analysis in our research.

5. Explore other aspects of social position. Given the power dimension of gender and moved by the evidence of the importance of power relations within groups of women who differ by race and class, for example, Stewart argues that we must consider how all axes of structural power in a culture shape and define gender and the research topic under investigation.

6. Give up the search for a unified self: individual personalities derive from multiple and conflicting positions. One is not, for example, entirely dominant or subordinate, but dominant and subordinate along particular dimensions and in particular contexts.

We conclude, along with Stewart, that contemporary theoretical and epistemological advances in feminist analyses can be mined for insights into how to improve theory and research in psychology, especially if they devote far greater attention to cultural diversity.

Feminist psychologist Hope Landrine challenges feminist psychology in a multicultural world to develop explicit theoretical frameworks through which sociocultural variables and differences will become coherent. Specifically, Landrine calls for models for understanding cultural variables and a theory of relationships between culture and behavior that neither romanticizes cultures nor renders difference deviant. She writes (Landrine, 1985):

> *Culture is not just an additional variable that demarcates the local limits of otherwise universal gender-related principles and gender differences, nor is it simply an additional, moderating variable whose inclusion will allow researchers to account for a larger percentage of the variance in human behavior. Rather, culture is us, it is each of us, and thus only it can be known, revealed, and discovered in social science. Researchers need to understand that European American culture is the structure and content of feminist psychology and is the only thing that is discovered and revealed in feminist data, constructs, therapies, and theories on gender. (pp. 65–75)*

Landrine concludes that culture will be regarded with dignity, and the sociology of knowledge in feminist scholarship advanced, when European American cultures are treated like all others.

FORMAL RECOGNITION OF THE PSYCHOLOGY OF WOMEN

The field of the psychology of women emerged in an effort to help rectify the problems discussed previously. Feminism became an issue during the 1960s, as the women's liberation movement increased its activity. During that time, women's centers, women's studies programs, and college courses about women and their contribution to psychology were developed.

The psychology of women itself basically encompasses all psychological issues pertaining to women and their experience. This includes male gender-role behavior mediated by the interactions with females. Official acceptance of the field within psychology came in 1973 when the American Psychological Association (APA) established **Division 35,** the Division of the Psychology of Women (Denmark & Fernandez, 1993).

The impact of the growth of the psychology of women, both in the United States and internationally, is shown by the following events. APA's nonsexist research guidelines (discussed earlier in this chapter), promoted through the efforts of Division 35 activities, have opened the way for the adoption of nonsexist guidelines in many disciplines besides psychology, including sociology and anthropology. The adoption of a form of these guidelines has occurred in many other countries as well. The preparation of nonracist, nonageist, and nonheterosexist guidelines was the direct result of the landmark APA guidelines. As Division 35 grew, it functioned to provide a forum for the development of an in-depth focus on understanding both the psychological and the social realities of women. Courses in the psychology of women are now taught in many countries, including Israel, Ireland, the Netherlands, and Argentina, as well as the United States.

Overall, the psychology of women affects all of psychology by highlighting methodological biases and emphasizing the need to use representative samples to yield generalizable data. In addition, the psychology of women or gender has also blossomed into an interdisciplinary field—women's studies. The cross-fertilization of women's studies and psychology has resulted in an increased awareness of class and racial issues, as well as gender issues. The psychology of women continues to give rise to feminist pedagogy, which fosters the development of feminist identity, shared leadership during the learning process, and integration of emotional and factual learning, resulting in greater overall congruence and enhanced self-esteem.

Ethnic Minorities

Just as there is no universal male experience, no female experience is universal. Women, like men, vary greatly in their ethnicities, classes, ages, and life experiences. Psychologists are increasingly acknowledging and studying diverse groups of women. Unfortunately, the vast majority of classical research focuses on white, middle-class women, and perspectives of women of color and particularly poor women are virtually absent from psychology (Reid, 1993).

Pamela Trotman Reid has urged psychologists to analyze women in multiple contexts, to expand our focus to include multiple races and classes in our studies, and to consider gender alongside other major status characteristics. She has challenged psychology, particularly the psychology of women, to deal honestly and fully with female ethnicity and class (Reid, 1993).

Racial, ethnic, and class stereotypes interact with gender to promote subordination. Women may be in triple jeopardy, suffering oppression on the basis of gender, race or ethnicity, and class. As a result of being discriminated against and excluded because of both race and class, a woman may readily come to accept society's attribution of inferiority because of her gender. These factors have interesting ramifications for research with minority women, whose experience is unique (Hunter College Women's Studies Collective, 1995).

Today, some researchers are meticulous in providing demographic information about the populations that they have studied. However, this effort is not sufficient. Although the race and social class of participants are included as descriptors, they are typically not evaluated as factors that affect the experience and shape the responsiveness of participants. For example, in research on college students, we see little or no recognition of the privilege associated with being White, middle class, and well educated. Questions about the impact of race remain reserved for people of color, and queries on social class are saved for working class and poor people (Reid, 1993).

Ethnic minority women in the field of psychology have unfortunately been few and far between, and the history of ethnic minority female psychologists is minimal. Until 1940, only four Black universities offered psychology as a major, and few Blacks attended predominantly White universities. Sadly, the involvement of Asian, Native American, and Hispanic women in psychology is even less monitored.

EMERGENCE OF THE PSYCHOLOGY OF MEN AS A DISTINCT FIELD

The psychology of men has been documented and studied over the centuries. The **men's movement** has encompassed military, political, religious, and economic events that have benefited many men. Recently, men have begun to come together in an attempt to better understand themselves within the context of social institutions that give rise to and nurture sexist values and the context of their prescribed and strictly masculine gender role. The American Psychological Association recently established Division 51, the Society for the Psychological Study of Men and Masculinity.

Men, like women, have been affected by emotional and psychological boundaries. Herbert Goldberg was a prominent figure of this movement in the 1970s. His book, *The New Male,* stresses a man's need to become more sensitive to the emotional and physical aspects of the self. In fact, some researchers have found that adherence to certain aspects of the male gender role can be detrimental to men's mental health and self-image (Goldberg, 1980).

In response to this, small groups of men were formed all over the nation in an effort to educate and raise consciousness regarding this issue. The first Men and Masculinity conference was held in 1974 (Lamm, 1977) and has continued to meet regularly to this day. The primary function of these conferences is to provide an arena for the concern that males in the United States (and elsewhere) are prevented from actualizing their full potential as human beings and for discussion about the harm that assigning female and male gender-role can cause.

Many spin-offs have resulted from these male consciousness-raising experiences, and political repercussions were felt in the form of efforts to change laws that discriminate against men in their roles as fathers and as husbands, that is, divorce legislation, child custody, and visitation. Currently, the men's movement has diversified to include various groups across the country (Gross, Smith, & Wallston, 1983), such as antisexist groups and groups that are all-male and believe that males have suffered because of the actions of feminist women. This particular aspect of the 1990s men's movement is epitomized by individuals like Robert Bly, who rails against men's "softness" and emphasizes their need to reestablish their "truly" masculine identity.

SOCIOBIOLOGY AND SOCIAL CONSTRUCTION THEORY

In psychology as in all sciences, research findings are put into a theoretical framework to give meaning and coherence to facts and to generate future research. Two major theories with sharply contrasting perspectives currently vying for influence in the social sciences, including psychology, are sociobiology and social construction theory.

Sociobiology or evolutionary theory was developed by Harvard biologist E. O. Wilson in 1975, who argued that psychological traits, like physical ones, are selected through an evolutionary process because they are adaptive; that is, they serve to maintain the species. Proponents of this view believe, for instance, that women stay home to nurture children, whereas men are the breadwinners, because these distinct, sexually differentiated roles maximize the chances that women's and men's genetic legacy, in the form of their children, will survive and thrive (Wilson, 1975). In Wilson's own words:

> It pays males to be aggressive, hasty, fickle, and undiscriminating. In theory it is more profitable for females to be coy, to hold back until they can identify the male with the best genes . . . human beings obey this biological principle faithfully. (1978, p. 156)

The second theory, **social constructionism,** is often traced to French philosopher Michael Foucault (1978). Social constructionists believe that human behavior is not solely biologically determined, but rather arises in response to historical, cultural, and social conditions. This view further suggests that human behavior does not have essential elements that have universal meanings across times, places, and circumstances. Behavior can be best understood by examining its historical, cultural, and social milieu. For instance, as we will see in Chapter 8, the meaning of a sexual act depends on the particular context in which it occurs. Thus, men who have sex with other men while they are in prison rarely consider themselves, or are considered by others, gay. Throughout this text we will see the impact of social construction on gender.

PSYCHOLOGICAL RESEARCH AND SOCIAL CHANGE

Behavior is viewed by social constructionists as more amenable to change, provided that the negative social environment is altered. In fact, historically, psychology is a field that has focused on changing people. Techniques for changing behavior, increasing knowledge about oneself, and decreasing unhealthy or unproductive thoughts and actions are used in numerous educational and treatment environments. Yet research has shown that the strength of these techniques alone is often not enough to effect individual change. Problems that are ingrained in society's structural fabric require more than individual modifications in behaviors and attitudes to solve them. Social institutions and environments that allow women to be victimized and treated unequally must be changed.

According to Kahn and Yoder (1989), the psychology of women can serve to foster rather than inhibit social change. For psychology to facilitate this process, psychologists and their students need to understand how behavior is shaped by external forces and to also imagine a society in which the roles, health, and issues pertinent to women are addressed so that solutions enhance women's well-being. Psychological research that concentrates on changing establishments such as the workplace, academic settings, business institutions, and the family looks at real people within complex social environments. The subsequent chapters of this text assemble the research and findings that will help to shape, we hope, a psychology of social change in the future.

SUMMARY

The terms *sex* and *gender* are distinct. Sex refers to biological and genetic differences. Gender refers to the different clusters of traits, interests, and behaviors that societies ascribe to each sex. While some traits and abilities are statistically different between the sexes, due to either socialization or biology, many "differences" in behavior are nonexistent, small, or moderate. The *social constructionist* perspective in psychology examines how differences are created and then used to justify nonneutral differences between men and women, which ultimately prove to be disadvantageous to women.

Theoreticians and researchers have developed different explanations for beliefs about gender. Some psychologists believe that gender is an outcome of socialization (*cultural approach*). Others believe gender is an outcome of the varying positions that women and men occupy in society (*structural approach*). Yet other psychologists have focused on the *stereotypes,* that is, cognitive rules of thumb that are widely held, oversimplified beliefs. Individuals use stereotypes when they cope with information (*information processing approach).* These *gender stereotypes,* or beliefs about what is appropriately feminine or masculine behavior, are influenced by sex, race, and class. The stereotypes associated with gender affect an individual's access to resources and power, but so too does the environment or social context in which women care for others and engage in paid employment.

Sex discrimination underlies both everyday life and the practice of science. *Sexism* constantly reproduces the power inequities between genders on a daily basis and varies along a number of dimensions. There are different types of sexism: *blatant, subtle,* and *covert.* Historically, myths about women's inferiority pervaded psychological science as well as society, as witnessed in the difficulties women had in achieving parity with men in higher education. Paradoxically, some researchers insist on sex differences between men and women, but note the superiority of women to men along a number of psychological dimensions. Psychologists themselves are divided regarding the implications of sex difference research. *Feminists* in psychology, just as "women" themselves, are not a homogeneous group. The term feminist when used by itself does not accurately portray the various views that inform scholarship that is considered feminist. Some of the types of feminists identified were *social feminists, radical feminists,* and *liberal feminists.*

In science, values influence the questions asked, the methods pursued, and the interpretation of data. A variety of problems and *biases* occurs in research. Some of these are exclusion of women as research participants, publication bias, gender differences in self-report, and an overreliance on college-age participants. Further problems in research concern the difficulty in discerning confounds. Are observed differences due to gender or are they due to *status* and *power?* Feminists have critiqued traditional research strategies and provided a number of solutions for *gender-fair research.* Such solutions hinge on accepting that science can never be completely *value neutral.* In this context, *social change* brought about by psychological research promises to challenge the status quo. The psychology of women and gender has received recognition by the American Psychological Association. The importance of ethnicity, race, and class to the conduct of research can only enhance the production of knowledge that aims to maximize women's well-being.

Now that we have initiated the process of bringing women into focus, the next chapter will review the origins of the stereotypes and images of women that remain with us today.

KEY TERMS

Bias in research methods (p. 14)
Blatant sexism (p. 8)
Covert sexism (p. 9)
Cultural approach (p. 5)
Cultural feminism (p. 13)
Division 35 (p. 19)
Engendering psychology (pp. 2–3)
Feminism (p. 12)
First wave of feminism (p. 12)

Gender (p. 3)
Gender stereotypes (p. 6)
Liberal feminism (p. 13)
Men's movement (p. 20)
Radical feminism (p. 13)
Science (p. 9)
Sex (p. 3)
Sex discrimination (p. 7)
Sexism (p. 7)

Social constructionism (p. 21)
Socialist feminism (p. 12)
Sociobiology (p. 21)
Stereotypes (p. 5)
Stereotyping (p. 5)
Structural approach (p. 5)
Subtle sexism (p. 8)

DISCUSSION QUESTIONS_____

1. What is the difference between sex and gender?

2. What are the processes that underlie the development of beliefs regarding gender?

3. What are the problems with research that focuses on gender differences?

4. Develop a list of the ways that sexism interacts with ageism or classism or racism. For example, what are the traits that might be ascribed to women who are young, Hispanic, and poor versus the traits of women who are old, Black, and middle class? Describe why this may occur.

5. What is feminism? How has feminism positively affected research in psychology?

SUGGESTED READINGS_____

Benokraitis, N. V., & Feagin, J. R. (1995). *Modern sexism: Blatant, subtle, and covert discrimination* (2nd ed.). Englewood Cliffs, NJ: Prentice Hall.

Bohan, J. S. (1992). *Seldom seen, rarely heard: Women's place in psychology.* Boulder, CO: Westview.

Denmark, F. L., & Paludi, M. A. (1993). *The psychology of women: A handbook of issues and theories.* Westport, CT: Greenwood Press.

Faludi, S. (1991). *Backlash: The undeclared war against American women.* New York: Crown.

Fine, M., Weis, L., Powell, C., & Wong, L. M. (1997). *Off white: Readings on race, power, and society.* New York: Routledge.

Tavris, C. (1992). *The mismeasure of woman: Why women are not the better sex, the inferior sex, or the opposite sex.* New York: Touchstone.

CHAPTER 2

THE ORIGIN OF GENDER STEREOTYPES IN MYTHOLOGY AND RELIGION

You may go over the world and you will find that every form of religion which has breathed upon this earth has degraded women. There is not one which has not made her subject to man.
—Elizabeth Cady Stanton

It is always difficult to describe a myth; it cannot be grasped or encompassed; it haunts the human consciousness without ever appearing before it in fixed form. The myth is so various, so contradictory, that . . . at first its unity is not discerned . . . [and] woman is at once Eve and the Virgin Mary. She is an idol, a servant, the source of life, a power of darkness; she is the elemental of darkness; she is the elemental silence of truth, she is artifice, gossip, and falsehood; she is healing presence and sorceress; she is man's prey, his downfall, she is everything that he is not and that he longs for, his negation and his raison d'etre.
—Simone de Beauvoir

From 3000 B.C.E. to C.E. 1100, man's view of himself as superior in all ways to women soon became enshrined in the law and custom of the world's earliest civilizations, those of the Near East. [A] Woman became a chattel first of her father, then of her husband, then of her son.
—Reay Tannahill

GENDER SCHEMAS AND STEREOTYPES: AN OVERVIEW

For most people, the words *male* and *female* conjure up very different images. Beyond anatomical and physical characteristics, these words bring to mind generalized notions of two different types of behaviors, personality traits, and other attributes. The stereotypes depict men as stronger, more rational, objective, aggressive, and outgoing and women as weaker, more emotional and submissive, but warm and caring. Specific characteristics considered socially desirable for males differ from those considered socially desirable for females: males should be aggressive, assertive, independent, unemotional, dominant, not easily influenced, better in math and science, unexcitable, decisive; females should be tactful, gentle, aware of others' feelings, dependent, insecure, indecisive, emotional, but not aggressive.

These and other stereotypes of male and female are evident not only in the United States, but also in most if not all major societies in both western and eastern cultures, as well as in developing countries. At a time when women have expanding opportunities for advancement and empowerment, portrayals of women that exemplify these stereotypes continue to oppress them and limit their many prospects for change.

What are stereotypes and how are they defined? Stereotypes have been extensively studied by social psychologists who regard them as cognitive categorizations or schemas of specific social groups. They are defined as generalized beliefs about the characteristics and qualities of members of identifiable social groups. Stereotypes influence how information from the environment is perceived, stored, remembered, and transmitted.

Do we know what factors are crucial to the formation of stereotypes, especially gender stereotypes? Current research has explored some of the factors that may be involved in the formation of gender stereotypes. Eagly (1987) suggests that the typical social roles performed by men and women in society call for the characteristics that people have come to associate with each sex. Men have tended to occupy positions that require attributes like agency, independence, instrumentality, and task orientation whereas women have tended to occupy positions that require communality, emotional expressiveness, and nurturance. According to Eagly, men and women develop the personality characteristics needed to fill certain roles. Thus, she feels that men and women are born with the same personality potential, but differing social roles select and develop some personality characteristics at the expense of others that may not be needed. In another social role analysis, Hoffman and Hurst (1990) found that objective sex differences in personality are not necessary for the formation of gender stereotypes; the fact of the division of labor based on sex is sufficient. In this more cognitive explanation, gender stereotypes arise to justify or rationalize gender roles.

In her review of the literature, Valian (1998) takes a cognitive approach by emphasizing that the most salient and distinctive social role occupied by women is motherhood, and the most obvious characteristic of motherhood is physical nurturance. Throughout human history, women have borne, nursed, and cared for infants. This has constrained women's mobility, and thus it made sense for them to remain at home and assume child-care and homemaking responsibilities. This act of physical nurturance is extrapolated to the personality realm, so that women are seen—whether they are or not—as more psychologically nurturing as well. According to Valian, the perception of this single salient difference creates and amplifies other gender differences.

Recent cross-cultural research has suggested that some aspects of gender stereotypes are remarkably similar across cultures. For example, in one major study of "typical characteristics" of men and women, Williams and Best (1990) asked college students in twenty-five countries to rate the extent to which each of three hundred adjectives were associated with males and females in their own culture. In at least nineteen of the countries, males were associated with the following adjectives: adventurous, aggressive, autocratic, daring, dominant, enterprising, forceful, independent, masculine, stern, and strong; women were associated with the following adjectives: affectionate, feminine, sensitive, sentimental, submissive, and superstitious. In some countries (such as Japan and Nigeria), male-associated items were rated more favorably than female-associated items, and in other countries (such as Italy and Brazil), female-associated items were perceived as more positive. Interestingly, the only major societal variable that differed between the countries with the positive and negative stereotypes for men and women was religion. Countries with religious traditions in which females were visible in religious ceremonies and were portrayed as virtuous and powerful, for instance as deities or saints, had much more positive views of women than countries whose religious traditions did not feature women prominently.

As we will see, since earliest history, myths and religions have embodied images of women as inferior—socially, culturally, and biologically—which have since become entrenched in other cultural representations. In more recent times, we see these depictions in the economy, with underpaid and undervalued female employees at virtually all career levels (Blier, 1984). As social movements arise to threaten the social order vis à vis the status of women, "it has been a recurrent phenomenon that corresponding 'scientific' theories emerge that implicitly defend the *status quo*" (Blier, 1984, p. vii).

How did these gender stereotypes and images come about? When and why did they arise and how were they maintained? What is the place of women in our society and how did that place develop? What are some of the ways in which women in various times and places have attempted to effect change?

This chapter addresses these questions. To answer them we need a historical context, "for every human event is the product of the interplay of the forces of the past and the responses of the forces of the present" (Swidler, 1976, p. 4). A historical context is especially relevant in pursuing and understanding societal attitudes and the status of women. Thus it is essential to explore how attitudes toward women developed in past societies and how they are prevalent in today's society. We will also see whether attempts to change attitudes about the status of women in the past were successful. Finally, we will discuss how these images of women enshrined in mythology and religion are affecting women's lives in contemporary society.

MYTHOLOGY AND RELIGION

Women as a Source of Evil

There exist many stories in early myths and religions about the creation of man and woman and about the evil, destructiveness, and mysteries of women. Many of us are familiar with the story of Pandora in classical Greek mythology. Pandora was the first mortal woman in Greek mythology; out of curiosity, she opened the cover of a forbidden jar containing Hope together with all the evils of mortals. Hope alone remained in the jar, but the evils within flew out and were scattered throughout the world and "for mortals devised sorrowful troubles." Pandora is seen as the origin of all the world's evils (Morford & Lenardon, 1995).

In the history of India, both female and male deities were worshipped. Traces of these beliefs and practices are found in the mythology that apparently predated the beginning of religion in India, as well as in the rural cultural traditions as far back as the third millennium **B.C.E.** The ancient goddess who was held to have high power came to be named **Shakti.** She was held to be able to create as well as destroy, and the term *to have shakti* meant to have the energy of creation and destruction. In primitive times, this power was thought of as *femininity*. So the goddess, or "mother" as she was called, who can bring forth life is also the purveyor of death. The critical association that India has made throughout 4,000 years of worship and religious development is that this "primordial femininity" needs the control of a "primordial masculinity" (Carmody, 1989, p. 42), that is considered consistent, cerebral, and without fervor. It was thought that if this ancient goddess was not controlled she would create turmoil and upheaval through the excess use of her energy. According to Carmody, the social constraints on women still found in Hindu society have found sanction in this primitive concept of the nature of the female.

Perhaps the most famous story portraying the evil of women is found in the story of Genesis in the Old Testament of the Hebrews. Adam and Eve, the first man and woman, were placed in the Garden of Eden by the Lord. They were forbidden by the Lord to eat fruit from the tree of knowledge. Eve could not resist temptation. She ate the fruit of the tree and gave the fruit to Adam. And, as the serpent told them, they both "knew both good and evil" (Genesis III.5). For succumbing to temptation, Adam and Eve were punished by the Lord by being forced to leave the Garden of Eden. For Eve's punishment for what she had done she was told by the Lord, "I will greatly multiply thy sorrow and thy conception; in sorrow shalt thou bring forth children; and thy desire shall be to thy husband, and he shall rule over thee" (Genesis III.16). Eve then, as the first woman, is seen as the source of original sin and as responsible for the fall of humanity. She is also seen as subordinate to her husband and subject to his rule. And, although "Genesis symbolically depicts the change of status for *both* woman and man, sadly it has been the woman's loss rather than the man's that has been emphasized" (Carroll, 1983, p. 16). In most western religions, Eve is considered the source of original sin, on which many theological principles are based.

Historian Leonard Swidler has written in great detail about the story of Eve in Genesis, and it is worthwhile to consider his work. He tells that there are two traditions about Eve. The first, before her Fall (before she is beguiled by the serpent and eats fruit from the forbidden tree), depicts her as the equal of man. But then, after the Fall, she is depicted as subject to man. These two traditions are to be found in the older scriptural tradition in the Yahwist story of creation (Swidler, 1976). The writer of the older script did not judge woman as lesser or inferior even though she was created after Adam. Swidler quotes from the older script, "Yahweh God said, 'It is not good that the man should be alone. I will make him a helpmate'" (Swidler, 1976, pp. 25–26). God then created all the animals and birds, and man gave names to each of them. No helpmate suitable for Adam was found.

> *So Yahweh God made the man fall into a deep sleep. And while he slept, he took one of his ribs and enclosed it in flesh. Yahweh God built the rib he had taken from the man into a woman, and brought her to the man. The man exclaimed: "This at last is bone from my bones, and flesh from my flesh! This is to be called woman, for this was taken from man." This is why a man leaves his father and mother and joins himself to his wife, and they become one body. Now both of them were naked, the man and his wife, but they felt no shame in front of each other. (Genesis 2:18–25, quoted by Swidler, p. 25–26)*

Swidler finds it significant that the creation of woman came after that of all the animals. In Genesis, before woman was created, God gave man dominion over the animals of the land, sea, and earth. This speaks to man's relationship to woman—her creation was related to man's solitude. Swidler does not believe that the creation of woman was an afterthought and a portrayal of women as closer to animals than men, but a creation that evolved from Adam "with the intermediate creations serving to establish the stage for the higher creation that was attained with the modeling of woman" (Swidler, 1976, pp. 25–26). In this view woman is not simply an addition to humankind in the person of Adam, but Adam himself, symbolized by his rib, is modeled into woman. She was created as the perfecting ingredient of humankind. In the coming together of man and woman, it is woman who brings perfection (Tavard, 1973).

Here we have a biblical account of woman before and after her fall (the pre- and postlapse period). We know that the prelapse state of Eve, that is, woman as the equal of man, is not how women are perceived now in contemporary society, nor was it the state in the development of most formal religions. Some aspects of these two views of women do emerge early in the formation of traditional religions, but the prelapse view fades with time, with a focus on the postlapse events that reversed the ideal universe attained in the Garden of Eden. Swidler summarizes this in a quote by Tavard:

> There were two traditions [developed] about woman. The one corresponded to the order of society, in which woman, though protected by many laws, was inferior to man. The other echoed the legends of the origins as recorded in the Yahwist text: originally woman was the higher and better part of mankind. (Swidler, 1976, pp. 27–28)

The prelapse tradition or state of woman seems not only to have faded but also to have been lost. In the focus on the postlapse tradition, women are clearly depicted as different from and secondary to males—incomplete, an aberration, and in other derogatory terms. This is found in special concern about women's reproductive functioning. For example, menstruating women in Judaism are depicted as unclean, particularly in orthodox Judaism. (In other religions and cultures, menstrual blood is also considered a pollution.) In the New Testament, there is the image of woman as Madonna (Virgin Mary) or as whore (Mary Magdalene). This sends double messages about female sexuality (these dichotomies will be discussed further in Chapter 8).

There are parallels to these legends throughout the myths and religions across various cultures, which have been interwoven into the religions of the East and West. Even when goddesses and women were accorded power in these sagas, these powers were still associated with some form of evil, destructiveness, or mystery.

Primitive Cultures.   Both men and women in nonliterate societies have handed down culture and myths that were unique to their "sex-specific roles and needs" (Carmody, 1989, p. 36). Many of the attitudes

and practices of these cultures, as well as those from obsolete religions, have left their mark on the major world religions. Primitive cultures were polytheistic, believing in special gods and goddesses with none as the supreme being. The males were gods of wisdom, water, thunder, and war; females were goddesses of the moon, fertility, summer, birth, and fruits of the earth. The myths and the gods and goddesses that participated in them became "woven tightly into the fabric of early religion" (Tannahill, 1982, p. 53). The time period we speak of for primitive societies throughout the world ranged from the various parts of the **Stone Age** through the **Bronze Age.** The **Paleolithic Age** (Old Stone Age) ranged from more than 25,000 B.C.E. to 10,000 B.C.E., the **Mesolithic Age** from 10,000 to about 7000 B.C.E., and the **Neolithic Age** from 7000 to about 3500 B.C.E. The Bronze Age ranged from about 3500 to 1000 B.C.E.* Table 2.1 describes these primitive ages.

The various pantheons (gods and goddesses) in these primitive cultures featured females in prominent roles. In Stone Age cultures, goddesses abounded, and there were many matriarchal cultures in which women alone were thought to be responsible for offspring. Here a child's legitimacy depended on knowing who the mother was. In this era, people believed in

TABLE 2.1   Ages for Primitive Societies: 25,000 to 1000 B.C.E.

The Paleolithic Age ranged from more than 25,000 to 10,000 B.C.E.

The Mesolithic Age ranged from 10,000 to about 7000 B.C.E.

The Neolithic Age ranged from 7000 to about 3500 B.C.E.

The Bronze Age ranged from 3500 to about 1000 B.C.E.

---

*Recently, the designations B.C.E. (before the common era) and **C.E.** (common era), used originally in some circles to avoid the Christian references in the designation B.C. (before Christ) and A.D. (*anno domini,* in the year of the Lord), have gained wider use and are most likely to be used even more broadly in the future. We use B.C.E. and C.E. in this book.

parthenogenesis because the process of sexual reproduction was not yet discovered. In contrast, in patriarchal cultures, which developed later, the paternity of the child had to be proved, because inheritance, bloodline, and legitimacy were established through the father. In many primitive tribes in Europe, Asia, and North America, matrilinear social organization granted women important rights over their children and principal roles in tribal decisions and rules (Carmody, 1989).

In these nonliterate societies, women played an important part as gatherers of food and probably provided more food on a continual basis than did the men, who were hunters. Women and their goddesses were tied to fertility of the earth and human fertility. The female divinities were not just associated with fertility and life, but also death. According to Gimbutas (1982), among Old European statues only 2 to 3 percent of the total number are of males; the rest are of females. She states that

> *Judging by the stereotypes that recur in figures over the millennia, the religions of Old-Europe (7000 to 2000 B.C.E.) were polytheistic and dominated by female deities. The primary goddess inherited from the Paleolithic age was the Great Goddess, whose functions included the gift of life and increase of material goods, death wielding . . . and regeneration. (p. 16)*

These assertions have been questioned by others who maintain that, although the roles of goddesses were important, few goddesses were a supreme power; they were often subordinate to husbands or brothers (this differs from later Greek and Roman mythology and religions in which goddesses were more abundant and attributed with much more power).

Despite these powerful images in which women were portrayed as fertility goddesses and earth mothers, they were, at the same time, perceived as threatening and a source of fear. In Sumerian literature (the Sumerian kingdom existed from about 2800 to 2360 B.C.E.), the fertility goddess, Inanna, was very powerful. This belief goes back to early Neolithic times when women were believed to be the sole childmakers, as well as cultivators of the soil. In somewhat later

Babylonian times (2067 to 2025 B.C.E.), the fertility goddess and earth mother Ishtar (a variation of Inanna) was not always thought of as kind and gentle. There was something uncontrollable about her, and when roused she became warlike and destructive, revealing that sex has its deadly as well as life-giving side. Other goddesses, like Anath of ancient Canaan, were seen as shrewish and bloodthirsty (Noss, 1949; Ringgren & Strom, 1967; Tannahill, 1982).

In Egypt, also during the second millennium B.C.E. (2000 to 1000 B.C.E.), gods first appeared as animals, but then gradually assumed human forms, though often with some animal parts. The ankh, originally the Egyptian symbol of the generative principles of both women and men, has come to represent the female. It is shown in Figure 2.1. Goddesses also became known and worshipped, although they too were less powerful than and subordinate to the male gods. One exception was Isis. As the goddess of fertility, Isis was also versed in magic. Isis is usually represented with a cow's horns and a lunar or solar disk. By about 1500 B.C.E., she had become one of the most renowned of goddesses. She was so popular that Isis cults of worship extended and survived as far as Spain, North Africa, and Germany for centuries and were

FIGURE 2.1   The Ankh

Source: From *The Egyptian Gods and Goddesses: The Mythology and Beliefs of Ancient Egypt,* by C. Barrett, 1996, London: Diamond Books. Reproduced by permission of the author.

known as late as the second century B.C.E. Although worshipped as a fertility goddess, Isis, with her magic powers over life and death, was adored yet feared (Anderson & Zinsser, 1988; Ringgren & Strom, 1967). Thus, although women in mythology have been worshipped for their power to give life, they have also been feared and resented for their power to take it away (Lederer, 1968; Tannahill, 1982). Isis is represented in Figure 2.2.

FIGURE 2.2 Isis

Source: From *The Egyptian Gods and Goddesses: The Mythology and Beliefs of Ancient Egypt,* by C. Barrett, 1996, London: Diamond Books. Illustration reproduced by permission of the author.

Women and the Moon. Many goddesses were known as moon goddesses: Ishtar of Babylonia and Isis of Egypt, as discussed above; Aphrodite and Artemis of Greece; Astarte, worshipped by the Canaanites, early Hebrews, and Phoenicians; and Cybele and Hecate, worshipped by the Greeks. In these times, the moon was still closely associated with women and fertility, and the moon goddesses were worshipped for their power to create life and growth. The words *menses* and *menstruation* also relate to the moon. Menstruation means "moon change" (*mens* refers to both the moon and the month) (Lederer, 1968, p. 35). This association of the moon and women can be traced back to nonliterate cultures that believed that the light of the moon was crucial for growth. Rather than the sun, the moon was thought to germinate seeds and stimulate plant growth. People in these cultures also believed that without the power of the moon women could not bear children nor animals their young. Thus, the moon became the symbol of fertility for tribes that had not yet discovered the sexual basis of reproduction. It was believed that the moon was able to impregnate women. This belief was so potent that women would sleep on their abdomens in order to prevent the light of the moon from falling there and would also rub spittle on their abdomens to prevent pregnancy (Harding, 1971).

These nonliterate people believed that women "must be of the same nature of the moon, because of their monthly cycle which is of the same duration as the moon" (Harding, 1971, p. 21). Later, as these early societies became agricultural and tribes settled down, it was necessary to have a system of planting and searching for edible roots and fruits to feed the people. Women then had the responsibility for all planting and harvesting; because of their moon nature, it was thought that they and only they had the power to make things grow.

In later mythology, these beliefs came to focus on the concept of moon goddesses who had the power of fertility and were the givers of life, but also had the negative side of the destructiveness of nature and death. This duality of the moon goddess means that, although she produces light and thus understanding and intelligence, under certain conditions her light "may also produce darkness, her intelligence may result in confusion . . . and may pass over into madness" (Harding, 1971, p. 24). Although in many religions the bright and dark aspects of the moon were represented by one goddess, in some religions they are represented by two. The early Greeks recognized Selene as the goddess of both phases of the moon, but sometime later each phase of the moon came to be represented separately by different goddesses; Aphrodite came to represent the light moon while Hecate represented the dark side. The waxing phase of the moon represented the power of growth; the waning phase of the moon represented the power of destruction and death. During the moon's dark phase, storms and floods, destruction by pests, as well as ghosts were feared but expected. These two phases of the moon, good and evil, have also been compared with women's nature. The waxing and waning of the moon have been associated with women's instability. With some ambivalence, women are venerated as both the givers of life and the consumers of the dead, with the power of life and death. The moon also came to be considered a source of inner emotional storms and conflict and in this way could influence the onset of lunacy, that is, intermittent insanity, supposed to change in intensity with the phases of the moon (Harding, 1971). Current notions of women's instability can be traced all the way back to these "mythical" lunar associations. As late as 1971, many superstitions related to the moon were still found in isolated areas of Europe, Great Britain, and the southern part of the United States (Harding, 1971).

Another important concept among primitive tribes was that of *mana*. Mana is a Melanesian term for the widespread belief in an occult force or some supernatural power that is different from persons or spirits. Mana is either good or bad, and refers to one's experience of a powerful and silent force in things or other persons. This force is believed to be able to go from objects in nature to humans, between persons, and back to nature. Mana is thought to permeate everything, but especially the alien and unusual (Hays, 1964; Noss & Noss, 1984). Although both men and women are subject to the experience of mana in others, it is women, with their powers of the moon, men-

struation, and fertility, that makes them alien or unusual and mysterious. Thus it was believed that women were filled with mana, which could be positive, but more important, negative. This concept of mana is another way of perceiving women as ambivalent; their negative or bad mana can lead to sickness, mutilation, terror, and even death in men. This belief would in time result in attempts to protect men from the bad mana of women and would later be entwined into developing religious and social forms to protect men from the "dangerous sex" (Hays, 1964, pp. 34–38).

Magic and fear were also associated with women because of their monthly period and menstrual blood. Blood was seen as a positive, intrinsic power, a vitalizing and revitalizing agent, and was used in many magical rituals and in dealing with the gods and spirits. There was no understanding of the cause and meaning of menstrual blood and so it was considered magical. Box 2.1 describes the taboo of blood and menstruation.

The specialness of menstruation may have caused envy among men, who were "denied" this power, and no cultural rite, no matter how intensely practiced, could endow males with the power to menstruate and to bear children. Whether menstruation was recognized as a puberty rite among primitive tribes is uncertain, but among some of these early tribes there were attempts by men to imitate the menarche. According to Tannahill (1982), the practice of *subincision* evolved as a puberty rite in primitive tribes and was continued in some tribes into the twentieth century in central Australia and New Guinea. This puberty rite was actually a type of mutilation where the "underside of the penis was split from the point nearest the scrotum, sometimes for as little as an inch, sometimes for almost its whole length" (Tannahill, 1982, p. 44). The blood that ensued was referred to as "men's menstruation" (Tannahill, 1982, p. 44). This association of magic power with menstrual blood and hence with women was to be used by magicians and sorcerers even as late as the seventeenth century.

However, as formal religions began to develop and incorporate myths, women were granted less and

BOX 2.1

The Second Taboo:
Blood and Menstruation

While the first taboo among primitive tribes was incest, the second taboo was blood. In the prehistoric period, blood was considered as life. Early writings concluded that blood was not only crucial for life but that it was "the essence of life itself" (Tannahill, 1982, p. 43). Blood held a mystical meaning especially with regard to menstruation with significance regarding the position of men and women. It is most likely that the taboo regarding menstruation came about through ignorance, not through deliberate sexism.

The real meaning of menstruation was unknown not only to primitive tribes and the Hebrews whose treatment of women during menstruation is discussed later, but it was not until recent times that scientists elucidated the biological function of menstruation. To prehistoric society, menstrual blood was magical. To these people it was magical because losing this blood did not cause pain, illness or even death. There was little understanding, but mystical wonder that this blood flowed for several days and then stopped. It was only seen in women, young women and brought about a certain element of fear. With this, menstrual blood was associated with power of women who menstruated and this concept of awesome power persisted even as late as the seventeenth century and perhaps still does in some parts of the world (Harding, 1971; Tannahill, 1982).

Source: From "The Second Taboo" in *Sex in History* (p. 43), by R. Tannahill, 1982, New York: Stein and Day. Copyright 1980, 1982 by Reay Tannahill. Reproduced by permission of the publisher.

---

less power. Menstruation came to be considered taboo, and restrictions including isolation were placed on women during their menstrual period. Even in some primitive societies today, women are physically isolated in huts during their menstrual period (Small, 1999). Tannahill (1982) suggests that perhaps in the beginning women may not have protested these restrictions if their menstrual periods pained and distressed them. The recurring theme was that women were unclean, unstable, and primitive. We shall discuss these taboos again under the various religions in

which they were adopted and still exist in one form or another. But regardless of how these restrictions or taboos developed, they did not favor women, but oppressed them. As formal religions coevolved with patriarchy, men were considered increasingly important—the representatives of the species—and women were considered variants of men. This perception has its roots in the biblical story of Creation, described earlier. In other creation myths, like that of Pandora, who was created by Zeus, man is always created first, the more important of the species and the "normative." Woman is created second, a variant or different version of man. These beliefs or attitudes have been maintained with "the division of responsibility, opportunity, and privilege that still prevails between male and female humans, and the patterns of psychological interdependence that are implicit in this division" (Dinnerstein, 1976, p. 4).

China before Confucius

Perceptions of Female and Male. In China, perhaps as early as 1000 B.C.E., unknown philosophers (several centuries before Confucius) distinguished between energy modes that acted together in every natural object, the *yin* and the *yang*. The yang is described as masculine: active, warm, dry, bright, procreative, positive. According to Noss (1949), "it [the yang] is seen in the sun, in anything that is brilliant, the south side of a hill, the north side of a river, fire" (p. 295). The yin is described as a mode of energy in a lower and slower key. Yin is "fertile and breeding, dark and cold, wet, mysterious, secret; the female or negative principle in nature. It is seen in the shadows, quiescent things, the north side of a hill, the shadowed south bank of a river" (Noss, pp. 295–296). Men and women are the products of the interrelationship of these two energy sources in varying degrees. They show differing proportions of each, men being celestial or predominantly *yang* and of great worth; women are earthly, predominantly *yin* and of little account.

Here too, early in the East, we can find the dominance and superiority of males over females. If we explore further and trace the development of many of the world's major religions, we will see that they progressed in lockstep with the development of patriarchy, "a form of social organization in which descent and succession are traced through the male line" (Young, 1987, p. 21).

RELIGIONS ORIGINATING IN INDIA

The world's great religions were born in what we call the Middle East and South Asia (formerly, India was considered part of the Far East) (Noss & Noss, 1984, p. i). Buddhism, Hinduism, and Jainism, the chief religions of India, have remained largely in India and Asia, while Judaism and Christianity have spread to Europe and the Americas. Islam, although largely represented in the Middle East, is also spreading to the Western world in increasing numbers.

The religions of India represent the transition of a people from **polytheism** to **pantheism,** that is, from the belief and worship of many gods to the precept that god is not a personality, but that God, the universe, and the human soul are all one and the same; there is no distinction anywhere (Zaehner, 1958).

The major religions of India are interrelated and based on the classical Indian creed, the **Vedic** literature. Early Hinduism built further on this literature, whereas Jainism and Buddhism began as a rejection of these doctrines. All these religions offer a path to salvation as a way to meet peoples' need to adjust to life and the world. The motive of Hindu, Jainist, and Buddhist thought has been to "*escape* from the degrading . . . experiences and misleading appearances of the physical world into mental and spiritual realms that have an unshakable reality and guarantee eternal satisfaction" (Noss, 1949, p. 97). Hinduism is based on the belief that man's error is in his "*thinking:* his miseries due to fallacies in his conception of things" (Noss, 1949, p. 97); Jainism, however, primarily emphasizes "*behavior,* how one acts; one must behave so as to avoid contamination by matter, defiling as pitch and destructive of all spirituality of being" (Noss, 1949, p. 98). Early Buddhism identifies the chief errors of man in the area of "*feeling;* it is our desires that must be reigned in and prevented from flooding us with misery" (Noss, 1949, p. 98). Although all three religions are in basic agreement with each other on the

necessity of seeking salvation, each has a different approach to the path of salvation. We shall see that these basic doctrines, especially those of early Hinduism, had a serious negative impact on women and continue to do so. To understand the development of restrictions on the people of India, especially on women, it is necessary to pursue the history of the development of these religions.

Brahmanism and Early Hinduism: From Polytheism to Pantheism

The Aryan Immigration.   Sometime around 1500 B.C.E. (the second millennium), organized tribes of people, known as Aryans, traveled in hordes into northwest India and began their centuries-long conquest of this enormous country. The Aryans were tall and light-skinned Indo-Europeans who proceeded to conquer the Dasas (Dasyus), the darker-skinned tribes of India. The Dasas were a people of mixed origin and diverse ethnic composition. History shows them to have had well-developed systems of art and architecture, which combined to produce the Bronze Age. They had a religion of which many ideas and beliefs would help to germinate *Hindu* doctrines of reincarnation and the law of Karma. The Dasas primarily worshipped mother-goddesses, the bull, and a special fertility god (Noss & Noss, 1984; Ringgren & Strom, 1967). Several centuries passed before the Indo-Europeans completely conquered this vast land. In doing so, the Indo-Europeans "were eventually to remake, and be remade by India" (Noss & Noss, 1984, p. 73). Figure 2.3 shows the invasion of the Indo-Europeans (Indo-Aryans) and their spread throughout India.

After defeating and subjugating the Dasas, the Aryans, who up to this time had been nomads, began to settle into tribes in different village groups. Gradually, they became a pastoral and agricultural people. The family life of the existing non-Aryan (Dasa) tribes was matriarchal with matrilineal descent and inheritance. Goddesses figured very importantly in their religious ceremonies. There was a sense of mutuality between non-Aryan men and women in which each one's role was recognized, appreciated, and supported (Carroll, 1983). The Aryans changed all this and enforced *their* patriarchal system on the Dasas,

FIGURE 2.3   Historical Buddhist Sites

Source: From *Man's Religions* (pp. 99–128), by J. B. Noss, 1949, New York: Macmillan. Copyright
© 1949. Reprinted by permission of Prentice-Hall, Inc., Upper Saddle River, NJ.

which restricted the power and roles of women. Yet even in this early period women certainly fared better than they would later on as India continued to develop. In contrast to the matrilinear system, each Aryan tribe had a chieftain called a *rajah* who made the rules of the tribe and also protected its members. The father (*pitar*) was the head of the family, the master of the household, and the owner of its property.

He was also the family priest. The wife and mother (*matar*) during this early period was relatively free and much less isolated than her female descendants would be. Although she had authority in her home over her children and black servants, the mother was still subject to restriction by her husband, but not rigidly so. This would not be true of Brahmanism or later Hinduism.

Like the Dasas, the Aryans worshipped various deities, male, female, and animal. As they became more settled in India, the Aryans developed religious texts now known as classic Vedic literature in which the gods, goddesses, and their powers were glorified. By the end of the seventh century B.C.E., the Aryans had a well-established social stratification system that eventually became the *caste* or *Varna system* (Noss, 1949; Carroll, 1983; Noss & Noss, 1984). This social system was based on color (*varna*) and appears to have developed from the Aryan's firm rules of **endogamy** and **exogamy**, which forbade marriage outside one's racial group and also with near kin. The austere enforcement "undoubtedly was influenced more by their [Aryans] being outnumbered by a subject, black-skinned, allegedly inferior people" (Carroll, 1983, p. 23). Although the first division of society was based on "unadulterated race or color discrimination . . . *varna (caste)* became a method of separation and discrimination by virtue of *jati*, or birth, and then by color" (Carroll, 1983, p. 23). There is still some controversy about the meaning of *caste* (Noss, 1949; Noss & Noss, 1984; Carroll, 1983). The four original castes were the *Brahmans, Kshatriyas, Vaisyas,* and the *Sudras.* They are described in Table 2.2.

As the caste system became more rigid, its impact on women soon proved to be severe. "Not only did Hindu thought and scriptures relegate females to a lowly status, but they were assigned the low caste standing of Sudras, irrespective of the caste into which they were actually born. They were doubly damned as women and as Sudras and were therefore banned by decree . . . from contact with the scriptures, deities and Brahmins" (Carroll, 1983, p. 15). This is an excellent example of how, in places with racial and ethnic discrimination, we also find discrimination and oppression of women.

TABLE 2.2   The Caste System

The different castes originally were:

1. The **Brahmans,** the priests who would become the highest caste with the color white as its distinction.
2. The **Kshatriyas,** the warrior and official caste with red for its color.
3. The **Vaisyas,** which consisted of peasants and craftsmen with yellow as its color of distinction.
4. The **Sudras,** the servant and slave caste.

There was also the untouchable caste (the pariahs or outcasts) who were not permitted to have anything to do with the other castes.

The Brahmans or priests eventually became the highest caste, with the Kshatriyas next. Brahmans were rapidly increasing in number and made religion and the search for knowledge their life work. The Brahmans were raised to great prestige because of the superstitious regard of the people for sacrificial prayer. However, it took a long time for the caste stratification to change India proper. The people of pre-Aryan and early Aryan India were not too affected by the caste system, and even as late as the fourth century B.C.E. there was a fairly flexible structure between the two upper castes (Carroll, 1983; Noss, 1949; Noss & Noss, 1984; Ringgren & Strom, 1967).

Source: From *A History of the World's Religions* (9th ed.) by Noss/Noss, © 1994. Adapted by permission of Prentice-Hall, Inc., Upper Saddle River, NJ.

The Brahmans, who evolved as the highest and most powerful caste, wrote voluminous texts showing a growing sense of the principle of unity in the universe. This became a pantheistic doctrine in which **Brahma** (sometimes referred to as Brahman) was declared the creator of the universe and the *ultimate reality.* The Brahma was all that was objective and all that was subjective. Thus, according to the Brahmans, man and the universe are all one, the Brahma. While the concept of Brahma as the one god or the ultimate reality developed, two doctrines were adopted that would succeed in permanently altering the outlook of India well into the present time. These were the doctrine of *transmigration of souls* (**reincarnation** or Samsara) and the *law of* **Karma.** Transmigration of souls or Samsara states that

> the soul of man who dies does not, except in the case of one who turns into indistinguishable oneness with Brahma, pass into a permanent state of being in heaven or hell or elsewhere; the soul, rather, is reborn into another existence which will terminate in due time and necessitate yet another birth. The nature of the next birth will be determined by The Law of Karma, the notion that one's status in the present life is the result of one's thoughts and deeds in the past life. Karma had an ethical consequence fixing one's lot in future existences. (Noss, 1949, pp. 122–123)

These two doctrines had strong social consequences. The lower castes were looked at as having sinned in their previous existence, whereas the upper castes, especially the Brahmans, were considered, according to the doctrine, to have led exemplary previous lives. These doctrines acted to reinforce the social discrimination of the caste system. This negative aspect of life, the constant reincarnation or rebirths and the fear of one's next existence, brought about a great pessimism in the Indian people. Hindus called the process of rebirth *The Wheel* and studied and worked on how to escape it and become one with Brahma, thus achieving eternal salvation (Moksha, or freedom from Karma and reincarnation). We shall see in the section on Later Hinduism that the adoption of these two doctrines had even greater impact on women.

Toward the close of this early period, the Brahmans were growing in number and power and gradually became the elite of the caste system. Religion and its doctrines were still being formed. The priests or Brahmans now occupied the central power in India. They performed sacrifices as part of the path to achieving freedom from rebirth and reincarnation; the deities, however, held less significance. It was the sacrifice that would achieve the desired result.

The caste system was still not in its final form, but hard and fast rules were being drawn. On the one hand, a member of the Brahman caste had every right to enjoy his exalted position because of the good deeds he had performed in his previous lives, which entitled him to his high position. Along with this

standing, he had every right to expect that after death he would indeed achieve salvation with Brahma. On the other hand, especially for lower castes and for outcasts, escape from the Wheel of Karma appeared to be a hopeless situation, and people who understood these concepts became extremely pessimistic. They faced the seemingly eternal continuation of the cruel round of rebirth and the hopelessness of escaping the law of Karma. Gradually, a great depression spread throughout the entire country. The people of the second caste, the Kshatriyas, were now becoming discontented with their position, but to question the Law of Karma would be seen as the worst of heresies. However, two heresies did arise that, while rejecting Brahmanism, still sought a way to salvation and release from reincarnation and the Law of Karma.

Jainism and Buddhism

During the sixth century B.C.E., there was a religious awakening in India that was the result of the spreading pessimism described previously. This awakening was apparent first in a rejection of Brahmanism and in the rise of two new religions, Jainism and Buddhism, which the Brahmans considered heresies. There was an urgency about this movement or rebellion. People saw these new religions as an answer and as a means of escaping from their growing misery and the doctrine of birth, rebirth, and Karma. The usual philosophical speculation or priestly sacrifices did not help. It was the caste system under which the individual suffered most. These two religions and the later development within Hinduism emerged as the three major eastern religions, each of which involved concepts of reincarnation and salvation. In each, we find many examples of the domination of the male over the female (Noss, 1949).

Jainism.   In its rejection of early Hinduism or Brahmanism, Jainism was essentially atheistic and extremely ascetic. According to Webster's dictionary, *ascetic* is the practice or way of life characterized by contemplation and rigorous self-denial for religious purposes. Critical minds objected to the idealism of Brahmanism that resolved the substantial world of everyday into a single unknowable entity—Brahma. Yet they believed in the doctrine of reincarnation (Samsara) and Karma. Although they believed in the reality of the physical world, they also believed that it was possible to achieve Moksha and transcend one's physical state to become one with the universe, but not with any supreme being.

The founder of Jainism was Mahavira (Great Man or Hero). He was born in India and lived from 599 to 527 B.C.E. He was said to have come from the second highest caste, Kshatriya. His father was said to have been a wealthy rajah and Mahavira and his family lived in great luxury. Mahavira married and had a daughter, but he was never content with his princely life. It is believed that at 30 years of age he gave up his wealth, family, and belongings to practice asceticism and complete withdrawal from all worldly things. He eventually joined a group of monks and took their pledge to neglect his body and forsake all care of it and to suffer all calamities arising from divine powers or man or animals.

Mahavira wandered naked for years searching for a way of release from the cycle of birth, death, and rebirth. He became convinced that "(1) saving one's soul from evil (purging contamination from the soul) is impossible without practicing the severest asceticism, and (2) maintaining the purity and integrity of one's own soul involved practicing *ahisma* or noninjury to any and all living beings" (Noss, 1974, p. 108). In his wanderings, he refused raw food of any kind and accepted in his begging bowl only the food that had been left over by the person for whom it was originally prepared.

After 13 years of wandering, Mahavira finally came to a town called Grimbibhikagama not far from a sal tree. There, in a deep meditation, he is said to have had the experience of a complete and full **Nirvana.** He had finally achieved a complete victory over his body as well as the needs and desires that keep one attached to the physical world. After this, Mahavira began to journey all over India, teaching people his way or path to salvation and making converts. At the age of 72 he cut all worldly ties and engaged in the practice of self-starvation (*sallakhana*). Upon his death it was said with certainty that he was finally liberated from rebirth and reincarnation.

Mahavira's path to salvation necessitated taking of the Five Worldly Vows that he developed for his system of asceticism. These vows include

(1) Not to kill, (2) Not to speak untruth, (3) Not to steal, (4) Renunciation of all sexual pleasure. I shall not give way to sensuality, nor cause others to do so, nor consent to it in others, (5) Renunciation of all attachments, whether to little or much, small or great, living or lifeless things; neither shall I myself form such attachments, nor cause others to do so, nor consent to their doing it. (Noss, 1949, pp. 99–100)

Mahavira had specific comments about women with regard to the fourth vow: "The greatest temptation in the world [is] women. . . . Men forsooth say, 'These are the vessels of happiness.' But this leads them to pain, to delusion, to death, to hell, to birth as hell-beings or brute beasts" (Noss, 1974, p. 113).

For some time after the death of Mahavira, women were excluded from pursuing the higher forms of perfection and release and were not permitted to enter the temples. For the Jain text says,

Infatuation, aversion, fear, disgust and various kinds of deceit are ineradicable from the minds of women; for women, therefore, there is no Nirvana. Nor is their body a proper covering: therefore they have to wear a covering. In the womb, between the breasts, in their navel and loins, a subtle emanation of life is continually taking place. How can they be fit for self-control? A woman may be pure in faith and even occupied with a study of the sutras or the practice of a terrific asceticism: in her case there will still be no falling away of karmic matter. (Campbell, 1962, p. 237)

The Jains subsequently became divided into two groups, the more liberal Shvetambras and the conservative Digimbaras. The first group admitted women to their monastic orders and assumed that they had a chance to enter Nirvana (to achieve salvation) without being reborn as men; the Digimbaras, however, persisted in their conservative ways and adhered to the original "vows," accepting their founder's verdict about women, that they are the cause of "all sinful acts" (Noss, 1974, p. 116). Women in this group were excluded from higher forms of perfection and release and were not admitted to their temples. The Digimbaras felt that women could not achieve salvation until they were reborn as men. This was the only hope that women had.

The Five Great Vows could apply only to Jainist ascetics. For the layperson these vows were relaxed, especially the fourth vow regarding renunciation of sexual pleasures. This vow now stated that one should always be faithful to husband or wife and be pure in thought and word. Jainist ideology did have some effect on Indian thought, and some of the doctrines were to be subsequently adopted in later Hinduism. Jainism today numbers about 5 million adherents, mainly in the Bombay area of India. This religion never spread beyond India, as did Buddhism.

Buddhism. Although Buddhism came about nearly a generation after Jainism, it still shares some of the same motives and principles, most notably a world-denying movement of escape as a means of achieving salvation, but in a different way. Although it was based on worldly renunciation, Buddhism was moderate in comparison with Jainism. Siddhartha Gautama, the founder of Buddhism, lived about 2,500 years ago (536–476 B.C.E.) in India, and the religion he founded spread beyond India to Nepal and then came to embrace most of Asia. It is now popular in the United States. See Figure 2.3 for historical Buddhist sites.

Similar to the life of Mahavira, Gautama was born to a wealthy family in northern India. According to the many legends about his life, Gautama is said to have been protected from all hardships. His father was a chieftain of the Sakya clan, a warrior group, and was determined that his son should not have to learn about or experience the hardships of life or know about old age, disease, suffering, and death. While still young, Gautama married his cousin and soon after their son was born. Yet with all the riches he and his family were accustomed to he became dissatisfied and unhappy. Legend has it that a god appeared to him in the form of a very feeble and fragile old man, and for the first time Gautama began to learn about suffering and old age. When a second apparition appeared, that of a diseased man, Gautama learned for the first time about physical illness and misery. Finally, Gautama saw yet

another specter. It was the body of a dead man on a funeral pyre. Thus he came to learn about the awful fact of death. These sights continued to distress him and he was unable to find peace. Sometime later Gautama was confronted with a fourth specter, an ascetic monk in a yellow robe. This monk had apparently gained true peace within his soul, and it is said that Gautauma learned how "freedom from the miseries of old age, disease and death could be won" (Noss & Noss, 1984, p. 108). For some time after these apparitions, Gautama had thoughts about leaving his family and going out into the world in a homeless state as a religious mendicant. He did this shortly after his son was born.

He too wandered for six years throughout India, testing Brahman and Jainist philosophy with different teachers in different places to see if he could realize the "realm of nothingness" through various practices. He also tested the extreme asceticism of Jainist philosophy. But he was disappointed with both. Gautama pursued all kinds of meditation with no effect. He did not give up, and over time his thinking became much more meaningful as a result of all his religious experiences. Gautama did not follow the extreme ascetic practice of the Jains nor did he return to his former state of pleasure and lust. Instead, he sought a middle path toward renunciation and salvation. Gautama finally came to a place called Bodhi-gaya and, similar to Mahavira's sal tree, he is said to have sat under a fig tree, which afterward came to be called the Knowledge or Bodhi-tree. There he entered into deep meditation, which totally freed him from all desire for worldly things, and he was able to attain enlightenment or Nirvana, the experience he had sought for so long, "a state of fulfillment and release from the bondage of worldly existence (Samsara)" (Carmody, 1989, p. 237). Gautama realized that when one reached enlightenment, one was free of desire and the suffering it caused, and that he had been able to escape into a higher form of consciousness. The Buddhist scriptures say that Gautama passed into a state of awareness and knew neither satisfaction or dissatisfaction.

From then on Gautama became the Buddha, the enlightened one. After this enlightened state had passed, he knew that he had to teach this way of salvation to all who would listen. The Buddhist order was then established. At that time in India, the caste system was not fully in place, and members of any caste were welcome to join the new order. Many Kshatriyas and those of lower castes as well as some Brahmans joined his order, now known as the Sangha.

Basic rules were written and customs adopted: the wearing of a yellow robe, the requirement for a shaven head, carrying a begging bowl, and daily meditation. Members of the order also had to follow the ten precepts of Buddha listed in Table 2.3.

One became a Buddhist by "taking refuge in the 'three jewels' that Buddhists treasure—the Buddha himself, the *Dharma* (teaching), and the Sangha (the Buddhist order)" (Carmody, 1989, p. 68).

In its beginning, Buddhism was more egalitarian than other Indian religions and than it would later become. Buddha gave the same teachings to female as well as male disciples, and they were all taught that the same spiritual path to salvation was open to all, regardless of gender. Sometime around the beginning of the common era and after the death of Buddha, a theological controversy emerged among Buddhists, some of whom engaged in efforts to prove that women were inferior to men and therefore incapable of the highest order of attainment. Orders of monks and nuns were established with the creation of rules for both. But there were special rules that applied only to the nuns. Among these rules, known as The Eight Chief Rules, supposedly formulated by Buddha himself, "were the most notable and the most stifling" (Barnes, 1987, p. 118). These rules included a requirement that each nun treat every monk as her senior and superior. Nuns were forbidden ever to revile or admonish any monk. All formal ceremonies had to be carried out under the guidance or in the presence of monks, as was the settlement of penances for any erring nuns.

Early concepts of Buddhism charged its followers to love all humans with a mother's love. Interestingly, this charge involved only sons and said nothing about daughters: "As a mother, even at the risk of her own life, protects her son, her only son, so let him [the follower] cultivate love without measure toward all beings." Although Buddhism eventually adopted the general bias toward women and clearly went along with the Indian tendency to subject women to men's control, Buddhism did give women another option not available in Brahmanism or Jainism. There were many female Buddhist teachers who lectured on the responsibilities of wives and husbands and on household management. Moreover, laywomen also could become Buddhists by following a less rigorous path and still gain merit. It was these laywomen who financially supported most of the Buddhist orders regardless of caste or gender. These groups of women were also a major force in the survival and spread of Buddhism.

TABLE 2.3 The Ten Precepts of Buddha

All Buddhists undertook to obey the precepts. They included:

1. Refrain from destroying life (*ahisma*).
2. Do not take what is not given.
3. Abstain from unchastity.
4. Do not lie or deceive.
5. Abstain from intoxicants.
6. Eat moderately and not after noon.
7. Do not look on at dancing, singing, or dramatic spectacles.
8. Do not affect the use of garlands, scents, or unguents, or ornaments.
9. Do not use high or broad beds.
10. Do not accept gold or silver.

As you can see, the first 4 vows of Buddha are the same as those in the Jainist order. The remaining 6 vows of Buddha detail aspects of the Jain's 5th vow, but in a moderate way to show the middle path between the two. As described earlier, the 5th vow of the Jains was to renounce all attachments. Buddhist philosophy, like the Jain's philosophy, was essentially atheistic or agnostic.

Source: From *A History of the World's Religions* 9/e by Noss/Noss, © 1994. Adapted by permission of Prentice-Hall, Inc., Upper Saddle River, NJ.

However, Buddhism eventually lost ground to Hinduism in India. It is still very prominent in many Asian countries and has spread to the United States and other Western countries. The total number of Buddhists in the world is 325 million. Most of the schools of Buddhism that exist today have become fully egalitarian, offering greater opportunities within the teachings to women. Many of the problems that women in Buddhist countries (China, Japan, and Tibet) face today have more to do with entrenched social values than with Buddhist theories and practices. Figure 2.4 illustrates the spread of Buddhism through Asia and the Middle East.

Later Hinduism

As Brahmanism (early Hinduism) failed to hold its people through priestly sacrifices and its philosophy, a compelling need developed to escape from increasing pessimism. This motivated people to attempt to find a practical means to achieve relief from their growing misery. The Kshatriyas formed the major group that

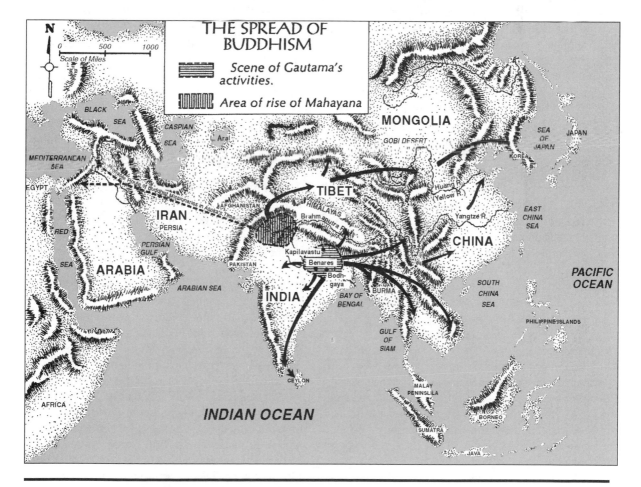

FIGURE 2.4 Spread of Buddhism

Source: From *Man's Religions* (pp. 99–128), by J. B. Noss, 1949, New York: Macmillan. Copyright © 1949. Reprinted by permission of Prentice-Hall, Inc., Upper Saddle River, NJ.

did not like either the social or religious implications of Brahmanism. Its idealistic model struck many as absurd. As discussed earlier, Jainism and then Buddhism expressed their revolt and offered a different path to salvation, rejecting the sacrificial system of Brahmanism as useless and misleading. These new religions also refused to give the Brahmans "first place or prescriptive rights in discovering the way from misery to freedom" (Noss, 1984, pp. 177–178).

In the turmoil that ensued during the rise of Jainism and Buddhism, Brahmanism began, of necessity, to change. Instead of using tactics against Jainism and Buddhism or outlawing these religions, Brahmans declared that many of the principles of these two "heretical" religions were valid and proceeded to adopt them. For example, from Jainism they absorbed the principle of noninjury to living beings or *Ahisma,* which resulted in the renunciation by many of eating meat and the gradual development of vegetarianism. This doctrine, together with the concept of reincarnation, brought about the veneration of the cow, a widespread feature of the Hindu religion. All parts of the cow, including its excreta, were hallowed and the killing of a cow could be punishable by death. In many areas of India today, particularly in the villages, the cow is still a sacred animal. Another adaptation came from Buddhism: the Brahmanists included in their principles the moral desirability of quenching desire and in this way prepared for the final entrance to Nirvana. Hinduism was now on its way to being redefined. Three ways to achieve release from misery and pessimism and three paths to salvation were worked out and clearly specified. The first of these, and of relevance to the status of women, was the *Way of Works* or the *Karma Marga.*

Indian society had by now become patriarchal, particularly in marriage. Marriage by mutual consent between bride and bridegroom was discouraged and **polygamy** was actively encouraged, especially for the upper castes, for the purpose of transmitting esteemed male traits and improving bloodlines. Of great importance was the Way of Works, which governed how to carry out rites, ceremonies, and duties that would add to one's merit for achieving salvation. The *Code of Manu,* which was a list of rules of life, was well established by 200 B.C.E. There was a list of "man's

debts" that he owed in order to achieve good works. There was of course a separate Way of Works for women. Women's duty was to meekly serve their men: "In childhood, a female must be subject to her father, in youth to her husband, and when her lord is dead to her sons; a woman must never be independent" (Noss, 1984, p. 188). There were also restrictions regarding meals; wives had to eat separately from their husbands and were also to be the last in the family to be fed. "The most excellent of all good works that she can do is to seek to please him by manifesting perfect obedience to him." Included in the Way of Works is the custom of **suttee,** one of the oldest customs for women. The Code of Manu states, "She must on the death of her husband allow herself to be burnt alive on the same funeral pyre; then everybody will praise her virtue" (Noss & Noss, 1984, p. 181). This custom, once widely practiced in India, is now forbidden by law. It is, however, apparently still practiced in the religious circles of some regions of India (Ward, 1999). Isolated instances of self-immolation by widows are still taking place, despite strict precautions taken by the police.

From the thirteenth to the eighteenth century in India, female infanticide was practiced. In the extreme, Brahmanic religion sanctioned this, along with the practice of suttee and a ban on widow remarriage. All these practices were part of the devaluation of women (Robinson, 1985).

Female infanticide is discussed in Chapters 3, 4, and 11 as an ongoing practice in several Asian countries. With particular concern about this practice in India, Robinson (1985) wrote that female infanticide has been outlawed and was virtually eradicated in that country. However, female infanticide is still carried out and may even be increasing in parts of India. Some families apparently feel that it is too costly to raise daughters given the costs of dowries and weddings. Indian sons are better able than daughters to hold prestigious jobs and bring money into the family. In other circumstances, women have so little emotional and financial support from partners, family, or other sources that, in desperation, they neglect their infants until they die (Ward, 1999). Scrimshaw (1984) has depicted infanticide as follows:

Perhaps the greatest tragedy in today's world is that modern contraceptives and even induced abortion have not sufficiently replaced infanticide as a means of fertility control. Further, infanticide has been superceded in many societies by abandonment, neglect, and differential care rather than methods of fertility control less costly in terms of lives and resources. (p. 462)

Throughout the centuries Hinduism became more flexible and liberal. Six different systems or approaches to reach salvation gradually developed. One of these included the Yoga system, a practice of mental discipline based on meditation and concentration as a way to release and salvation. Childhood marriage was outlawed along with infanticide and suttee. Modern legislation in India now permits divorce and legislates that women have the same political rights as men. Western religion and science have had an impact on Hinduism in its approach to education, social welfare, and women. A wider variety of opinion and disagreement about religion is now tolerated. Intellectual freedom has unfolded so that adherents of Hinduism can deny aspects of the teachings as long as they do not break completely with the code of social regulations (e.g., dietary restriction, marriage laws, and cow veneration). In the nineteenth century, Christian missionaries and educators also had an impact on Hinduism. Polytheism was denounced, and religious services took on more of the western Christian character. In the twentieth century, accepting the advances of science and technology, secular groups formed. These groups raise more radical issues including the rejection of all religion. They condemn the pessimistic tone of Hinduism and its world-denying perspective.

The concept of the exclusiveness of castes is finally crumbling under the weight of globalization and modernization. For example, in today's world, castes must travel together on modern transportation and work in the same environment. In 1948, when India became independent from Great Britain, India abolished "untouchability" and forbade its practice, but it has taken a long time for this integration to take place. Additional changes took place. Mahatma Gandhi, who was a champion of women's rights, set changes in motion so that women would be considered capable of attaining salvation. The Constitution of 1947

banned discrimination of women in all social, political, and economic matters.

In the late 1970s, birth control promoted by the government of Prime Minister Indira Gandhi was opposed. However, in 1980, during her second administration, family planning began to be practiced. The reasons for this were twofold: the population in India in 1981 was in excess of projections, and birth control was crucial to the effort to improve the health and welfare of Indian women.

Because women in India were considered to be among the most neglected, many Hindu reformers began to focus on the needs of women and to champion education for them. Their efforts improved the status of women, and education became available to all females. Tradition, however, hampered the efforts of reformers and still continues to subvert their successors' endeavors (Carroll, 1983).

Although these changes have been positive for women, the force of tradition still impedes progress. Even in current times, tradition keeps wives subservient to their husbands. In the late 1970s, there were reports of suicide among women, most of whom had been highly educated and who had been married only a short time. At first, it was thought that they had been murdered by their husbands who had tired of them and sought the dowry that a new wife would bring. Analysts later speculated that many were overwhelmed by the changes brought about by marriage and found that they could not cope with the move to a new household and the restrictions of marriage and, in some cases, motherhood. After their education, they had envisioned broader and more liberal horizons and, failing that, had become extremely depressed (Carmody, 1989).

In rural areas the pressures on women were comparable. The patterns of life were traditional, essentially untouched by the events occurring after India gained its independence in 1947. These patterns have continued, even with the positive changes. Hindu festivals include god and goddess worship. According to Carmody (1989), "the majority of Hindus, men as well as women, have sought to improve their Karma, make a living, prosper with healthy children all by worshipping gods and goddesses" (pp. 59–60). In small villages and outlying areas, contemporary reforms have had little impact. These people still rely on ancient traditions and worship of gods and goddesses, along with their understanding of the concepts of reincarnation and rebirth.

Education appears to be one of the most important changes necessary for the improvement of conditions for women. "[R]eligion has historically been and continues to be one of the main inhibitors of the education of females" (Carroll, 1983, p. 55). Religion could be a positive influence if certain aspects of Hinduism were modified or eliminated. Carroll (1983) has speculated on whether such reform could be accomplished and the conditions under which reform could progress. She feels that without a centralized authority or a charismatic leader emerging in India, the potential for the advancement of women is poor.

There are more than 795 million Hindus in the world; 700 million of these religious adherents live in India, representing 80 percent of the country's population.

Summary of Religions Arising in India

In this review of the religions of India we have looked at the ways in which women were perceived and treated from ancient times. These gender stereotypes, formulated thousands of years ago, have continued to be maintained in one form or another to the present. We have also considered the changes in the status of women, both positive and negative, throughout these thousands of years. In the early development of Hinduism (Brahmanism), we saw negative changes for women that, as Hinduism developed further, became even worse, starting with the change from a matrilineal to a patriarchal society. In early Jainism, there were few if any improvements for women, except for one branch of Jainists who accepted women as capable of reaching enlightenment and salvation. Buddhism showed the most improvement for women overall as the religion matured. Although experiencing many changes for women in the religious, social, and economic areas, later Hinduism is still burdened by a tradition that offers a poor outlook for change. Today, although modified regarding their attitudes toward

women, these religions are still plagued with the images developed in their formative periods.

We will continue to explore these considerations as we move on to the other major religions from their inception to more modern times.

MONOTHEISTIC RELIGIONS*

The prevailing ideas of the religions of India differ profoundly from those that developed in the Middle East. Noss (1974) has provided a concise description of these differences. **Monotheism,** the belief in one God who reveals himself to his people, had replaced polytheism and pantheism. In monotheistic religions, God is the creator and sustainer of the universe and is anthropomorphized as a person with a proclaimed interest in good moral behavior. Monotheistic religion is a way of comprehending and mastering life rather than negating it as in the religions of pantheism. Asceticism or self-denial is not considered crucial whereas nature is a created reality—"a stage on which the drama of divine–human relationship is enacted" (Noss, 1974, p. 334). This relationship is brought about by God, not man.

Monotheism is a revealed religion belonging to Judaism, Christianity, and Islam; in contrast, the religions of India are those in which people, by discipline and reflection, obtain their own enlightenment and achieve salvation. In monotheistic religions, people turn to a single source of revelation from a great God, whereas in the Indian religions people seek many sources of help to achieve salvation. Thus, monotheistic religions, with few exceptions, give great importance to the human community and consider the relationship between God and humans as a "person-to-person encounter in which the moral element is prominent" (Noss, 1974, p. 355).

Judaism was the first monotheistic religion to develop in the Middle East and marked this transition from pantheism and polytheism. Centuries later Judaism gave rise to Christianity and although the two religions may have influenced each other historically,

*Although we are not endorsing any particular gender for God, we are going to follow the traditional and historical use of God as *he.*

each has its own internal dynamism and distinct characteristics. Islam was the last monotheistic religion to develop and did so in the midst of Judaism and Christianity. It was surely influenced by some of their beliefs and practices. Although monotheism is almost exclusively associated with these three religions, it may also be seen now in some specific Hindu groups and perhaps even elsewhere (Parrinder, 1983). The development toward a monotheistic theology began almost four millenia ago, and even though monotheism was a latecomer on the stage of history, it nevertheless has had profound effects on the development of Western civilization.

Although we are cognizant of the contributions of monotheistic religions, we are also concerned with the attitudes and beliefs about males and females that these religions encompassed. We will see that the attitudes and beliefs about men and women that we find today were profoundly shaped by these religions from their inception thousands of years ago that carried over to Western culture. The late Juanita Williams (1987) wrote about the perception of women as a necessary evil throughout history. Some of her thoughts are summarized in Box 2.2.

The basic source of traditional attitudes toward women and men in Judaism and Christianity derives from the story of Genesis in the Old Testament. As we showed earlier, virtually all major religions have a strong emphasis on the two sexes acting in ways consistent with a patriarchal society. This is especially evident in Judaism and Christianity. The Adam and Eve story shows that because of Eve's gullibility and treachery she brings about the downfall of Adam and of succeeding generations. Consequently, she is condemned to suffer childbirth, to work hard, and to be a faithful and submissive wife. The Adam and Eve story can be perceived as a rationale for patriarchy.

Judaism: From Polytheism to Monotheism

With a history going back 4,000 years, Judaism is the oldest of the revealed religions. The belief in one God is the basis of the Jewish religion, and it is believed that this God is the creator and ruler of the universe and is eternal, transcendent, and the only god to be

---

BOX 2.2 _____

Women as Property

During most of the history of Western civilization, women have always been regarded basically as property and with no rights of their own. A creed of early Puritan belief was the requirement that women be kept in a subordinate position. John Milton, a Puritan poet, insisted strongly on the inferiority of women and the need for men to guard their authority over women to deter them from foolish action. He expressed a theme of woman as an intrusive nuisance in a man's world in his *Paradise Lost,* when he has Adam mournfully ask, after the Transgression, why God created "this novelty on earth, this fair defect," instead of filling the world with men, or finding some other way to generate mankind (Rogers, 1966).

This mythic perception of woman as a necessary evil has successfully survived the evolution of ideas and intellectual changes. The basic ideas of woman's inferiority and unfitness to be man's equal continue to be thematically important in determinants of attitudes toward her (Williams, 1987, p. 5).

Source: From *Psychology of Women: Behavior in a Biosocial Context,* Third Edition, by Juanita H. Williams. Copyright © 1987, 1983, 1977, 1974 by Juanita H. Williams. Reprinted by permission of W. W. Norton & Company, Inc.

---

worshipped. God communicates to his people through the prophets, and Moses is considered to be the most illustrious of all the prophets throughout the history of Judaism. In a covenant made 4,000 years ago, God promised Abraham a land for all his generations. On Mount Sinai, God revealed the Ten Commandments and the Torah to Moses (Flower, 1997). The Torah contains the five Books of Moses (Genesis, Exodus, Leviticus, Numbers, and Deuteronomy). The Torah is the "ultimate, unchanging word of the Divine Law" (p. 6). To Jews, God is all-knowing and all-seeing and he and he alone can reward or punish. It is believed that one day God will send a messiah who will be a descendent of David. Then the age of the redemption will begin and the dead will be resurrected.

The oldest of the revealed religions, Judaism has survived for over 4,000 years in spite of conquests, exile, antisemitism, and slaughter. In the 1930s anti-semitism, which had been prevalent throughout Europe, increased dramatically with the rise of Hitler. It culminated in the Nazi Holocaust in which over six million Jews were put to death in gas chambers during World War II. When these horrendous facts became known after the war, it shocked and devastated the international community. It was decided that a separate state was needed for the protection and safety of those Jews who survived. On May 14, 1948, the United Nations voted to establish the state of Israel. The creation of a separate state in Palestine for Jews was seen by the Jewish people as the fulfillment of the promise made by God to Abraham and then Moses millennia earlier. Jews still believe that they were "chosen by God to be an example of light and love to all mankind" (Flower, 1997, p. 6) through the teachings as revealed to Moses.

Denominations of Judaism.   In the mid-1800s, egalitarian movements in Europe and advances in science brought changes in Judaism. Many no longer wanted to accept that the Torah was revealed as was believed in Orthodox Judaism. Changes in ritual and dietary law were also desired. Under the guidance of Rabbi Isaac Wise (1819–1900), the Reform movement began. It is the most liberal branch of Judaism and is still evolving. Basically, Reform Judaism emphasizes the ethics of Judaism rather than the rituals and dietary laws. Women and men sit together rather than separated as in Orthodox Judaism. In the Orthodox religion, when a boy reaches age thirteen, he enters adulthood with the rite of Bar Mitzvah. In Reform Judaism, both boys and girls partake in this rite—but with girls the rite is called Bat Mitzvah. Commentaries and interpretations on the law became part of Reform practice. These were radical and very progressive changes and not everyone was happy with them. Instead, a middle ground soon developed in Europe—Conservative Judaism.

Two concepts or ideologies dominate Conservative Judaism. The first stresses the centrality of religion in Jewish life; the second is a strong sense of tradition, history, and the continuity of Jewish life. Professor Solomon Schechter, a leader in the Conser-

vative movement, spoke of the "organic unity" of Jewry (Noss, 1974, p. 415). Tradition is stressed, both in ritual and dietary law, but there are commentaries and interpretations of the laws. As in Reform Judaism, women and men sit together and both boys and girls partake in the rite of adulthood at age thirteen. The Conservative movement has not been very successful in Europe or in Israel but is in the United States where it contains the largest membership in all branches of Judaism. The Conservative movement also gave rise to the Reconstructionist branch of Judaism, somewhat to the left of Conservatism. Rabbi Mordecai Kaplan, a former Conservative rabbi, was the founder of Reconstructionism. This branch of Judaism allows a wide spectrum of clergy, from traditional practice to left-wing ideology. Reconstructionism also believes that religion evolves with social change. These are just some of the basic differences in these branches of Judaism. There are many other differences, especially with regard to the interpretation of the Bible and ritual and dietary law.

Holidays.   All branches of Judaism observe five major holidays. These include Rosh Hashanah, which occurs in September or October and ushers in the Jewish New Year, and eight days later, Yom Kippur, the Day of Atonement. Yom Kippur is a 24-hour period of fasting and is spent mainly in the synagogue atoning for sins committed against God and praying for forgiveness for the year. It is the most sacred day of the year. Hanukkah, the Festival of Lights, begins in December, often very close to Christmas. This is a commemoration of the victory of Judas Maccabaeus in the second century C.E. and the rededication of the temple in Jerusalem. Passover (*Pesach*), observed in March or April, celebrates the liberation of the Jews from bondage in Egypt by the intervention of God through the Prophet Moses. Passover occurs very close to Easter. Seven weeks after Passover, Jews celebrate Pentecost (*Shavuot*). This commemorates the giving of the law to Moses on Mt. Sinai.

Population of Jews.   There are at least 14 million Jews worldwide. Approximately 6 million live in North America, 5 million in Israel, 2.4 million in Europe,

1.1 million in Latin America, 165,000 in Africa, and 85,000 in Oceania.* Almost 84 percent are Ashkenazis of eastern and northern European ancestry; 10 percent are considered Oriental; and 4 percent are Sephardic, people of Iberian ancestry (*Encyclopedia Britannica,* 1999).

The Religion of the Early Hebrews. Judaism, like Hinduism, started as an ethnic religion. As in the other religions, stereotypes of women in Judaism developed along with the early development of the Hebrew religion and continued with the Judaic order that followed. These stereotypes are still evident today. To appreciate how these stereotypes took shape, we need to look back at the history and foundation of Judaism through the Common Era.

The story of the founding of Judaism is the story of Abraham and his wife, Sarah. It is recorded in detail in the books of Genesis and Exodus from the Hebrew Bible or Old Testament. Although the Bible provides the most complete history of the development of the religion of the Jews, the story of Abraham and several other writings have been considered oral traditions, passed down through generations. There was no reliable record of written Hebrew before the tenth century B.C.E. which, as we will see, was after the Hebrews escaped from Egypt under the leadership of Moses and settled in the land of Canaan (Cahill, 1998; Parrinder, 1983). The Hebrews were members of an ancient northern Semitic tribe and were the ancestors of the Jews and descendants of the patriarchs of the Hebrew Bible or Old Testament (*Encyclopedia Britannica,* 1999).

It is speculated that Abraham was born about 1900 B.C.E. near a place called Ur in Babylonia, along the border of Mesopotamia. This area of the Near East was known as the Fertile Crescent, the most ancient cradle of civilization. After he reached maturity, Abraham married Sarah. Abraham, his father Terah, and family decided to leave the area of Ur and proceeded to a place called Harran on the border of the Arabian desert. Although the family of Abraham increased their wealth, the region was a hostile area of fighting

*Oceania includes Australia, Melanesia, Micronesia, and Polynesia.

and invasion by various tribes including the Indo-Aryans who, some centuries later, would invade and conquer India. It was here that a voice came to Abraham and said:

> Get thee out of thy country, and from thy kindred, from thy father's house, unto the land that I will show thee.
> And I will make of thee a great nation, and I will bless thee,
> and make thy name great; and be thou a blessing.
> (Genesis 12:1,2)

Abraham gave his allegiance to this God who had spoken to him and took his family to Canaan (Palestine) where he built an altar to worship his God, whom he called El Shaddai. Soon, a famine came to Canaan and Abraham and Sarah went to Egypt, where they prospered greatly. God revealed himself again to Abraham and made a covenant with him. He would be Abraham's God and God to all his generations. He promised to give Abraham and his descendants the land of Canaan (Genesis 17:1–9). But Abraham was unhappy because he and Sarah did not have any children. God promised that she would soon have a child and said that Abraham's child and all the children of his descendants should be circumcised at eight days "and my covenant shall be in your flesh for an everlasting covenant" (Genesis 17:10–14). By this covenant between God and man, the children of Abraham would not be able to forget God and God would never forget them. Sarah conceived and bore a son whom she named Isaac and who was circumcised at eight days as God instructed.

As recorded in Genesis, God tested Abraham, telling him to take his son Isaac and "offer him up" on the mountain for a sacrifice to his God. Abraham obeyed and was prepared to slay his son, but at the critical moment, God's messenger stopped him, saying that now God knew Abraham was in awe of him and provided a ram for the sacrifice instead of Isaac (Genesis 22:1–18). Noss (1974) has suggested that the story of Isaac lays the foundation for the substitution of animals for sacrifice instead of humans. This was the first crucial episode in the formation of Judaism.

Abraham and his descendants prospered in Canaan but once again it is told that a famine came and decimated the land. So, Abraham and Sarah's descendants left Canaan and made their way to Egypt. For generations they flourished in Egypt until about 1580 B.C.E., when the Egyptians began to expel many groups. The descendants of Abraham were not expelled and continued to live peacefully. Sometime during the thirteenth century B.C.E., a "mad pharaoh, Ramses II, came to power" (Noss, 1984, p. 359). He decided to build great works—cities and temples—and, because he needed large numbers of unpaid laborers, made slaves of the Hebrews.

The story of the Exodus and of Moses, the greatest prophet in the Hebrew Bible, begins to unfold during the time the Hebrews were slaves in Egypt. Moses saw an Egyptian beating a Hebrew and killed him. Fearful for his life, Moses fled to the land of Midian. Years later, with the Hebrews still in bondage to the Egyptians, God was revealed to Moses in a flame of fire coming from a bush (the "burning bush"). God gave Moses instructions about the liberation of the Hebrews from their slavery and Moses returned to Egypt (Exodus 3:1–22). Among God's miracles that forced the Pharaoh to free the enslaved Hebrews was the slaughter of the first born in every house of the Egyptians. God passed over the houses of the Hebrews so that no harm came to their children. After the Pharaoh agreed to let the Hebrews go, Moses led them to the Red Sea which, through another of God's miracles, parted, so all the Hebrews could cross out of Egypt to the land on the other side. Once they were safely across, the sea closed, destroying the Egyptians who had tried to follow (Exodus 14:15–31). It is this event, known as Passover, that Jews all over the world celebrate in the spring (Cahill, 1998; Noss, 1984).

The leadership of Moses makes its greatest contribution to Judaism after the crossing of the Red Sea. During the wandering of the Hebrews in the desert, Moses acted as an intermediary between his people and God. He went up on Mount Sinai where God was again revealed to him. God wanted to make another covenant with the Hebrew people. The terms of the covenant were inscribed on two tablets; the first was the Ten Commandments and the second was the **Torah** (Exodus 20:1–22). The Hebrews, carrying the sacred

tablets in the Ark of the Covenant (Noss, 1974, p. 365), wandered in the desert for forty years until they reached the border of Canaan and prepared to invade it. Moses was not to enter Canaan and died before the invasion. His young general, Joshua, replaced him. The invasion was a long process and took years of fighting but finally the Hebrews succeeded. The Hebrews captured and entered Canaan (Palestine) and captured Jerusalem. This was the promised land to which God led them.

It is not known just when Moses and the Hebrews left Egypt or actually how long they wandered in the desert (although according to the traditional account, it was forty years), but it is estimated that the Hebrews entered Canaan or Palestine about 1200 B.C.E. From the time they entered Canaan they were known as Israelites.* This name would not change until late in the fifth century B.C.E. when they would become known as Jews (*Encyclopedia Britannica,* 1999).

The kingdom of Judah was established in the southern part of Canaan, and Solomon was made their king. He erected a temple for the worship of God about 930 B.C.E. According to custom, the temple was the only site where Jewish prayer and sacrifice could be carried out and was under the supervision of the priestly order. A pilgrimage to the temple was mandatory. However, in 597 B.C.E. Nebuchadnezzar, the king of Babylon, sacked Jerusalem and reduced the entire area to rubble. The temple in Jerusalem was destroyed. Nebuchadnezzar took captive and carried away the king, all the nobles, and many other renowned groups to Babylon, (Kings 24:14–16). Others who were able fled to Egypt and surrounding coun-

*Originally there were 12 tribes of Hebrews who left Egypt with Moses, each named for the son or grandson of the great Patriarch Jacob, whose name God changed to Israel (Genesis 32:22–30). When they entered Canaan they called themselves the 12 tribes of Israel, hence the name Israelites. Ten of the tribes formed the Kingdom of Israel in the north; the other two tribes—Benjamin and Judah—formed the southern kingdom of Judah. Following the conquest of the northern kingdom in 721 B.C.E. by the Assyrians, the ten tribes were gradually assimilated by other groups and disappeared from history. Only the people of the tribes of Benjamin and Judah remained. Thus, this section on Judaism and Christianity relates to events concerning the descendants of those two tribes of Israel who had settled the southern kingdom of Judah.

tries in the Mediterranean. The rest of the Israelites continued to stay on in Judah. The change in the status of the Israelites who survived the fall of Jerusalem was so profound that the name *Hebrew* was dropped and history has spoken of them since as Judeans or Jews, of which the latter has continued to the present time (Noss, 1974). In Babylonia, the Jews were permitted comparative freedom to live their old way of life. Although no longer able to worship and offer sacrifice to the God at the temple in Jerusalem, the only place they knew, the Jews maintained their faith. They established places to meet, teach, pray, and hold religious discussions. Meetings were held on the Sabbath and the discussions became the origin of the sermon and were standard. These practices foreshadowed what would become the synagogue and the official writing down of the oral tradition of the Torah, which would include the place of women.

About fifty years later (539 B.C.E.), Babylon was captured by Cyrus the Great, the founder of the Persian empire. He allowed the Jews to return to Jerusalem and Judah. Many Jews remained in Babylon but thousands returned. Cyrus the Great helped the Jews rebuild the temple in Jerusalem and the priests again became dominant. Distinct from the temple, synagogues began to develop in Jerusalem and throughout Judah. When the Jews returned to Jerusalem they found not only the Jews who remained after it was destroyed, but also an increase in the number of many different groups: the Edomites, Sodomites, and Samaritans, as well as other religious Jewish sects who held specific thoughts about women. The hopes of the Jews to rebuild the kingdom of Judah was not to be realized even a century later.

By the fifth century B.C.E., the Jews had become dependent on their own religious authorities even though they were under Persian rule. The supreme authority was the high priest in the temple in Jerusalem. Authority was also vested in the learned profession of the scribes who were devout and who began writing down the oral tradition of the Torah (the Hebrew Bible) and other sacred writings that would become Hebrew law. Those who had special talents for preaching in the synagogues would later be known as rabbis or teachers and would become part of the Pharisees.

This was the beginning of the period of formative Judaism that began around 450 B.C.E. in Palestine. It was during this time that Judaism began to take root and of which we have written records (Noss & Noss, 1984). Attitudes toward women began to be clearly defined and included in the religious scriptures. There were many social and cultural forces during the several hundred years that the scriptures were being written down that would help shape the perspectives of women and the restrictions on them that would evolve.

During the Babylonian exile, the Jews were exposed to a different culture. After the return to Judah, the Jews were under the rule of the Persians and continued to experience their practices. In 332 B.C.E., Alexander the Great of Greece drove the Persian armies out of Asia Minor and seized Palestine. Exposure to Greek society and culture had a strong influence on the Jews. The Greeks governed Palestine until 63 B.C.E., when the Romans took control. By 70 C.E., the Jews, discontented with the treatment of the Romans, rebelled. This resulted in indescribable slaughter— the complete devastation of Jerusalem and the temple by the Romans. More than the city was destroyed; the priests, their sacrifices, and religious groups "passed from the scene of history never to have importance or even reality again" (Noss, 1974, p. 547). Only the Pharisees (Rabbis) and the then-heretic group called Christians would survive. The Jews underwent a great dispersion; some fled to Babylon, others to Syria, Egypt, North Africa, and Spain. This dispersion made it all the more important for the definitive form of the Hebrew Bible to finally, after several centuries, take shape so as to ensure its applicability to the Jews now living in different countries. The Jews had come to see Judaism less as a faith than as a way for life to be lived (Harris, 1923).

The writing of the scriptures and the final shape of the Hebrew Bible would take until the first century C.E. to be completed. It was put into its present canon and fixed about 90 C.E.—that is, no longer subject to change. Some years later, the leading rabbis of the first and second centuries C.E. codified the interpretations and commentary on the oral law and compiled them in the form of the Mishna, which was the first part of the **Talmud.** The second part of the Talmud, the Gemara, included the commentaries and discussions on the Mishna and completed the Talmud. The Talmud functioned as a guide for the operative conduct of Jewish life and also contained an important section describing the place of women in Jewish life. Carmody (1989) has commented that "[T]he Hebrew bible is our best source about the *religious experience* of women before the Common Era" (p. 135) and that the Talmud is the most "important document about the *official status* of women in Judaism of the Common Era" (p. 135).

Swidler (1976) describes the sociocultural forces in which formative Judaism developed. For most of this time, Jewish women lived in a patriarchal society. It was assumed that men were in charge of all affairs, from leadership to teaching to legislation. Women were considered lesser than men and they were to follow them. This was essentially the general pattern, although there were famous biblical exceptions in which women were heroines and leaders. This inferior status of women was the general model in the ancient world of the Middle East (Palestine, Egypt, Babylonia, etc.), also known as the Fertile Crescent. Most of these civilizations were male dominated. Men were in charge of the government, ran businesses, administered the law and education, and often controlled theology and religious practices. Women were second-class citizens without any power or prestige. *The Social World of Ancient Israel* (Matthews & Benjamin, 1995) provides additional information on women in the Israelite patriarchy.

However, by the fifth and fourth centuries B.C.E. in many parts of classical Greek society, Hellenism (Box 2.3) flourished. Here, as well as in Egypt and Rome, Hellenistic society was essentially individualistic and the status of women was considerable. Women had greater freedom, they took part in sports, and they owned and ran businesses. In some of these societies, women in rural areas had greater freedom than those in the cities. In the Hellenistic period the status of women in marriage was also elevated. Marriage continued to be monogamous for both partners, and there was an equal right for either partner to seek divorce for infidelity. Inheritance laws favored women. In the Hellenistic world, there was also an increase in sensitivity toward children and animals.

BOX 2.3 _____

Hellenism

Hellenism relates to the cultural model generated by Alexander the Great of Greece. Hellenism came to dominate the Near East and eastern Europe in the late centuries before the Common Era through the early centuries of the Common Era and spread through the Middle East, affecting the Jews during the period of formative Judaism. Hellenism combined unprecedented religious and racial tolerance. Many Jews, particularly women, welcomed Hellenism, but the plain people were slow to respond to its precepts. The Jewish scribes and rabbis for obvious reasons strongly opposed this new culture (Noss & Noss, 1984).

Source: From *A History of the World's Religions* (9th ed.) by Noss/Noss, © 1994. Adapted by permission of Prentice-Hall, Inc., Upper Saddle River, NJ.

This change was also seen in attitudes toward slaves, who were treated more as equals than inferiors. This was in contrast to earlier Greek society and other societies where women were frequently classed as inferior *along* with children and slaves. In Greece, these changes were especially noted in and around Sparta where society was more individualistic, but not as much for society in Athens and Macedonia, where societal structures tended to be more patriarchal.

In contrast, the status of Jewish women during this same period seems to have reached a nadir in Western history (Bullough, 1974). Swidler has suggested that because the Hellenistic culture was so attractive and pervasive, many Jews saw it as a threat to Jewish identity. In protecting the Jewish character, they proceeded to insulate the Jewish community from these influences. They expanded restrictions on one-half of their community, the female half, in order to remove them from the pervading influence of Hellenism. This action prevented the higher status of Hellenistic women from reaching and influencing women in the Jewish community. This helped to ensure the procreation and survival of Judaism as a part of carrying out the Covenant with God.

Attitudes of Major Jewish Groups. As noted, this period was the time of the writing of the Hebrew scriptures, and by 90 C.E. this canon or doctrine was fixed and no longer subject to change. These writings also "fixed" the images and perceptions of women and the laws and restrictions to be placed on them. Three major groups of men came to have important influence on the religious customs and rituals of the Jews in Palestine: the *Pharisees,* the *Essenes,* and the *Sadducees.*

The Pharisees. The Pharisees were devoted to the written Torah or Bible. They paid much attention to the oral traditions (interpretations and commentaries about the Bible) that accompanied the Bible. They concerned themselves with moral obedience, ceremonial purity, and spiritual growth. They came to control the synagogue with regard to doctrine and politics. The Pharisees perceived

> woman as "in all things inferior to the man" as "evil" as "overcome by the spirit of fornication more than men," as ones who "in their heart plot against men," and that every man should "guard his senses from every woman." Such an attitude could hardly be without wide social effects in the areas which came under the influence of the Pharisees. (Swidler, 1976, p. 56)

Other writings by the Pharisees are equally derogatory to women. The Scribes and Rabbis were part of the Pharisees. As described earlier, the Rabbis and the Christians were the only groups that would survive to current times.

The Essenes. The Essenes lived in different parts of Palestine during the second century B.C.E. at about the same time as the Pharisees. Their beliefs were similar to the Pharisees. They believed in the Messiah and in preparation for his coming and withdrew from society into virtually monastic seclusion. They were very religious, practiced nonviolence, and rejected all politics. These extremely pious men had no women and renounced all sexual desire. According to Josephus, an historian of the first century C.E., the Essenes thought of women as a distraction, and therefore did not bring wives into their community, nor did they have slaves. They were very concerned with sexual

morality. However, some Essenes who were not as zealous did take wives, but they lived apart from their extremely devout brethren. The Essenes are thought to have been involved in the writing of the *Dead Sea Scrolls* found in Israel in 1947. The texts of some of these scrolls relate clearly to the Essenes' perception of women, describing them as prostitutes with seductive ways. Their writings express misogynism (hatred of women) and a fear that women will lead mankind astray.

The Sadducees. The third group were the Sadducees. They represented the ruling hierarchy or class of the time and separated themselves from the general public. The Sadducees believed in the written law and the views of the ancient fathers as they appeared in the Bible or Torah. They rejected the traditional and oral law and opposed the Pharisees. They rejected the belief in angels as well as the concept of resurrection in the afterlife. They were very liberal for their time and were often accused of favoring the Greek (Hellenistic) style of life. They were patriotic but also wished to protect the Jewish institutions in Palestine. To do this, they compromised with the Romans and for some time were successful. This group, like the Essenes, would not survive.

The Rabbis. The Rabbis evolved from the Pharisees and came to prominence after the dispersion in 70 C.E. By the beginning of the Common Era the Rabbis were highly respected. They believed that to be a Jew meant that one had to live according to the Holy Scriptures. But the Rabbis declared themselves to be the only ones who could explain what the Scriptures meant. The Rabbis along with the Scribes were responsible for copying, interpreting, explaining, and protecting the holy Scriptures. Rabbinic Judaism developed in an already highly structured patriarchal system. Although they did write positive evaluations of women, overall they gave women a disadvantaged status. Women were subordinate to men in every facet of life, whether religious, social or legal; they were of inferior mind and function. Within their subordinate position, women were depicted favorably by the Rabbis. Some examples of positive images of women include "He who has no wife dwells without good, without help, without joy, without blessing, without atonement" (Genesis Rabbah 18:2). Rabbis praised women for being supportive, resourceful, and self-sacrificing. They wrote of the sadness and darkness that descends upon the death of one's wife. Nonetheless, the Rabbis produced a concept of Judaism in this well-established patriarchal society that presented a world with men at the center. The laws that the Rabbis wrote were perceived as "divinely ordained" (Baskin, 1984) and only considered a woman in relationship to a man; her duty was to be completely under his control and to contribute to his comfort. If women realize their obligations, they are revered and honored and their praises loudly sung. If they do not fulfill their responsibilities, their husbands can divorce them, punish them, and treat them harshly, from which there is no protection. On the other hand, a woman could not divorce her husband or seek refuge from him. In the case of adultery by either the wife or husband, the punishment was death by stoning. But for the man there was little castigation if he had sex with an unmarried woman. (Niditch [1991], however, has speculated about how strictly these laws were implemented for both men and women.) There were exceptions to these denigrating perceptions of women. In the history of the development of Judaism many women were heroines; Esther, who saved her people, and Ruth, who accepted the God of her mother-in-law, are examples. The only woman described in the book of Jewish laws (the Talmud) as learned in Jewish law is Beruriah, the wife of a Rabbi. But she is later transformed into an adulteress who commits suicide (Baskin, 1984).

The Synagogue.   Women were not permitted to take an active role in the development of rabbinic Judaism nor were they permitted to have the religious education that men could have. Study of the Torah and other Scriptures were closed to women by several but not all groups. They could not assume an equal part in religious practices. They were separated from men in the synagogue, but it is not clear just when this practice started. It apparently did not exist in earlier temple worship. Archeological studies of first-century synagogues do not show separation of men and women. However, it was believed that separation would prevent distraction of the men from their prayers by

avoiding sexual arousal by the women. Women had to enter their section of the synagogue by certain gates, but were forbidden entrance if they were menstruating or were within seven days of their cycle. Women were placed in a court either behind the men or in a gallery above the men. The separation was seen as just one part of the distinctions between men and women and became a principle for temple worship for centuries to come (now only for Orthodox practice) (Swidler, 1976).

Menstruation.   The responsibility of the husband was to produce children, but it also became a responsibility of the wife. The writers of biblical law had contemptuous feelings about the way women's reproductive systems functioned. Menstrual blood was now seen as totally incompatible with any ritual worship or sacrifices made to God. A woman was declared unclean from the beginning of her menstrual period until seven days had passed. After her child was born, she was considered unclean for 40 days after the birth of a boy, but for 80 days after the birth of a girl (Carmody, 1989). As discussed earlier, menstrual blood and other bodily secretions were deemed a pollution in other cultures as well (Douglas, 1969; Swidler, 1976), and, as we have seen and will continue to see, this was not unique to Judaism. Additional laws state that whatever a menstruating woman touches or sits on is impure. If a man has intercourse with a menstruating woman, he shall be unclean for seven days, and every bed on which he lies shall be unclean (Leviticus 15:23–34). A more severe punishment for this practice is possible, in which the man and woman are cut off from their people (Leviticus 20:18).

The life of women during the time of formative Judaism was negative. Women remained uneducated and were considered the property of their husbands. They were castigated for their reproductive function and considered unclean. Polygamy was permissible for men, but **polyandry** was not permitted for women. On the other hand, while women were separated from men and from their religious practice, men did appreciate women's many skills and contributions. These were mainly involved in household activities, procreation (especially if a boy was born), child rearing, and other domestic talents. Husbands were not always harsh and abusive, but often loving and caring. However, in their early morning prayers, men thanked God for not creating them as women. Across the centuries, these concepts of Jewish women were undoubtedly internalized so that women not only accepted their inferior status and treatment, but also considered themselves to be inferior and to deserve such treatment.

In his review of the condition of women in the period of formative Judaism, Swidler concludes that the markedly inferior status of women and the potent misogynism during this phase were not mitigated by the sincere affection that men showed their wives and children (Swidler, 1976). The religious and patriarchal structures that were written into the Bible and other scriptures surely had an overwhelming influence on the history of Jewish life and Judaism, which continues to the present time.

In more recent times, feminist ideas have begun to enter Jewish discourse and there have been increasing efforts at reform. Conservative, Reform, and Reconstructionist Judaism, although still embroiled in controversies concerning the status of women, have undergone many changes. Feminists are involved in all branches of Judaism, working to make transformations that are acceptable to today's women. Women and men, too, have expended considerable effort in Orthodox Judaism to modify the laws that have kept women on the fringes of religious practice and under the restrictions on marriage and divorce. Women have been ordained as Rabbis and Cantors in Reconstructionist, Reform, and Conservative Judaism. However, many Jewish women feel that until actual changes are made in laws of rabbinic Judaism, women will still be dealing with a patriarchal structure in which women are not equal to men in their capacity for religious participation. Although rabbinic laws at present are unlikely to change, many continuing advances will surely influence and affect Judaism.

Christianity

Christianity is the most widespread of the great religions and has the largest number of adherents. It is a monotheistic religion that began as a movement within Judaism. Christianity centers on the life and work of Jesus of Nazareth who lived as a human being for about 30 years in Palestine and was crucified by the Romans sometime between 29 and 33 C.E. Jesus was a Jew as were his chief followers, the Apostles, who accepted him as the "Christ," the anointed or chosen one (Encyclopedia Britannica, 1999; Noss, 1974). Jesus Christ is considered "God, Man, Icon" (Flower, 1997, p. 19). Christians believe that Jesus is divine, the son of God, but was made a man and came down to Earth to carry out God's will and that he died on the cross for their sins. They believe that Jesus was resurrected from the dead after three days and for the next 40 days, based on testimony of contemporary witnesses, was seen by his disciples on many occasions and then ascended to heaven. The meaning of Christ's death is salvation. Salvation depends on "the grace, the divine favor of God, shown in the atonement for man's sins by the death of Jesus Christ on the cross" (Flower, p. 25). Jesus, although he is divine, walks among his followers on earth. He "is present in them and they in Him, in their belief and trust" (p. 25). In this way, "Christians do not worship a dead hero, but the living Christ (Parrinder, 1983, p. 420).

Christians believe Jesus to be the Messiah or Christ as was prophesied in the Hebrew Bible and "in unique relation to God whose son He was declared to be" (Flower, p. 19). Christ is from the Greek—Khristos—which is a translation from the Hebrew word *mashiah* (anointed one). This is the name Jesus was called when the budding faith was being communicated to the people outside of Palestine. Christians consider Jesus to be the "human face of God" (p. 19). He is the way to reach God. "I am the way, and the truth and the life. No one comes to the father except through me" (John 14:6). Christians are able to draw close to God by following Jesus' life and teachings.

Although monotheistic, the belief in one God is complicated by the doctrine of the Trinity—the Father, the Son, and the Holy Spirit. The Nicene Creed explains this in that "the one God is revealed in three persons: the Father, the Son and Holy Spirit. They are three persons in the same substance and as such are united—but yet separate" (Flower, p. 24). This concept of the Trinity is not accepted by all branches of Christianity.

Next in importance to Jesus Christ is the Bible. The Bible for Christians is comprised of the Old Testament (the Hebrew Bible) and the New Testament. The New Testament is considered by Christians to be the realization of the Old Testament, because the figure of Jesus and his life and teachings as told in the Gospels by His **Apostles,** fulfill the prophesies of the coming of the Messiah as written in the Old Testament.

Through Jesus' disciples (Apostles), the Christian faith spread through the Greek and Roman world. By the year 315 C.E., the Emperor Constantine declared that Christianity was the official religion of the Roman Empire. This became the basis of civilization for the Middle Ages in Europe. As Christianity continued to spread, major separations developed as a result of differences in doctrine and practice. These separations include the Roman Catholic Church, which acknowledges the Bishop of Rome, the Pope; the Eastern or Orthodox Church; and the Protestant church which was organized during the sixteenth century C.E. Reformation. However, all branches of Christianity recognize the authenticity of the Bible.

There are sacraments carried out in all branches of Christianity. A sacrament is defined as "an outward and visible sign of an inward spiritual grace. It is through the sacraments that God, through the Holy Spirit, is present in mankind" (Flower, 1997, p. 26–27). The Roman Catholic and Eastern churches recognize seven sacraments: baptism, confirmation, marriage, ordination, penance, anointing of the sick, and mass (communion). The Protestant churches observe only the 2 main sacraments—baptism and communion.

Holidays.   Christians observe several major holidays. Lent commemorates the forty days that Jesus spent in the wilderness before beginning his ministry and also commemorates the forty years that the Jews spent wandering in the desert. Good Friday, falling sometime during March or April, is the day of the crucifixion of Jesus Christ and is a day of sadness followed by the joy of the resurrection on Easter, which is a major festival. Forty days after Easter is Ascension day, which commemorates the ascension of Jesus

into heaven. Ten days after the ascension of Jesus is the Pentecost, the day that God sent the Holy Spirit to all of Jesus' Apostles. The largest festival is that of Christmas, held on December 25th, celebrating the nativity of Jesus. It is a time for gifts, family gatherings, singing carols, and feasting.

Population.   There are at least 1.9 billion Christians worldwide—about 30 percent of the world's population. Approximately 1 billion are Roman Catholic, 400 million are Protestant, and 220 million are Eastern Orthodox. About 70 million are Anglican Christians and 175 million are from other Churches outside the main category of Christianity but are in some way related to Protestantism. In East Asia, Christians are not highly visible and total approximately 75 million. There are factions of Christians in other areas of the world (*Encyclopedia Britannica,* 1999).

Jesus and the Development of Christianity

The story of Christianity is the story of Jesus of Nazareth but it is also the story of a religion that developed from the faith "that in its founder God was made manifest in the flesh and dwelt among them" (Noss, 1974, p. 417). From the time of the resurrection when the disciples came to believe that Jesus was the character of God on earth, the key elements of the Christian doctrine were in place. Jesus did not write down his teachings and relied on his disciples to carry out his work and preach what he taught. The major sources of his teachings come from the Gospels and **Epistles** in the New Testament, composed after Jesus' death.

Jesus was born about 4 B.C.E. (Smith, 1993).* Prior to his birth, as told in the gospels, the angel Gabriel was sent by God to the virgin girl Mary in Nazareth. He told her that she would conceive and give birth to a son called Jesus. When she told him that it could not be because she was not having inter-

---

*It was not until the middle of the sixth century C.E. that the Church started to figure time as before and after the *birth* of Christ. The monks whose calculations were followed miscalculated when they computed the year of Jesus' birth (Noss, 1974).

course with any man, the angel replied that the "Holy Spirit will come upon you, and power of the Most High will overshadow you. For that reason also what is born will be called holy. God's Son" (Luke 1:26–38). Mary became pregnant. Some months later Mary and her husband Joseph began their travel to Bethlehem. We are all familiar with the story of how Joseph and Mary could not find proper lodgings and so Jesus was born in a manger. The Gospel of Luke tells that when the shepherds heard an angel say "There was born to you today a Savior, who is Christ the Lord," in David's city, the shepherds traveled to Bethlehem and found Mary with her infant (Luke 2:8–20). When Jesus was eight days old, he was circumcised, according to Jewish law, and Mary and Joseph went to the temple in Jerusalem to offer a sacrifice in honor of Jesus' birth. Figure 2.5 portrays Palestine at the time of Jesus.

The world in which Jesus grew up and started his ministry was a complex one. The Jews had been under foreign influence and were oppressed under Roman rule. The concept of monotheism as well as the problem of keeping the people from straying from their religion and from being influenced by other groups created a great deal of tension. The issue of how to resolve the situation differed among the different Jewish groups (e.g., the Essenes, Pharisees, Sadducees, and Zealots) and ranged from outward rebellion (the Zealots), to accommodation (the Sadducees), to remaining within society and revitalizing Judaism by adhering strictly to the law (the Pharisees), or to the Essenes who continued to withdraw into their community to continue with their celibate lives, praying, fasting, and keeping the Sabbath while awaiting the Messiah as prophesied in the Hebrew Bible. To this problem Jesus would later offer another option. In contrast to the Sadducees, Jesus wanted change. Instead of holiness and strictly adhering to ritual law, Jesus stressed God's compassion and questioned whether the social system that the code of holiness structured was a compassionate one. That difference would be important in the splitting off from Judaism and the development of Christianity.

There is little known or written about Jesus' early life. It has been assumed (but is undocumented) that his earthly parents, Mary and Joseph, were common people who led quiet religious lives, making the yearly trip to pray in the temple in Jerusalem on Passover as was the custom. It was also thought that Jesus worked as a carpenter with his father and other family members (Noss, 1974).

When Jesus was about 30 years old, he had a profound experience. This came about when he was baptized by John. John came out of the desert where he had lived the life of an ascetic. He appeared quite suddenly on the shore of the Jordan River with an important message: "Repent! for the Kingdom of Heaven is coming" (Matthew 3:2). John was certain the end of the present age was at hand and that the Messiah would judge the people. Only those who repented could face the day of wrath that would take place. He said that the Messiah was already beginning his task. John went on to preach throughout Palestine. He took those convinced of the need to repent down to the Jordan River, immersed them into the water to signify their repentance and the washing away of their sins against the Lord. He became known as John the Baptist. John preached social and individual righteousness. He attracted much attention but denied being the Messiah; instead he professed to prepare the way for the people to accept the Messiah. Jesus came to him asking to be baptized. John immersed Jesus in the water of the Jordan River. As Jesus came out of the water "He saw the heavens being parted and, like a dove, the spirit coming down upon Him; and a voice came out of the heavens: You are my Son, the beloved; I have approved you." (Mark 1:10–11).

Immediately after his baptism, Jesus went into the Judean wilderness for 40 days and nights. He did not eat; he was tempted by the Devil but refused to yield. It is this 40-day period that Christians observe as Lent. Soon after Jesus returned from the wilderness, John the Baptist was arrested for his preaching. Jesus then crossed the Jordan and began to make his way to Galilee. He accepted the first of his disciples— Simon Peter and his brother Andrew, and James and his brother John. Jesus' message was urgent, proclaiming the good news from God "that the time has come and the reign of God is near; repent, and believe

FIGURE 2.5   Palestine in the Time of Christ

Source: From *Man's Religions* (pp. 99–128), by J. B. Noss, 1949, New York: Macmillan. Copyright
© 1949. Reprinted by permission of Prentice-Hall, Inc., Upper Saddle River, NJ.

this good news" (Mark 1:15). This was the beginning of his ministry.

Jesus started his ministry by speaking in the synagogues, and as the crowds grew larger, he preached to the people in marketplaces and open fields. The Gospels tell of the miracles that Jesus performed—at the wedding feast at Cana, where he changed water into wine; of his healing of a child in Capernum; the multiplication of loaves of bread and fishes; raising Lazarus from the dead; and calming the terrible storm on the Sea of Galilee.

Jesus' message was clear. "The appointed time has been fulfilled, and the kingdom of God has drawn near, Be repentant YOU people, and have faith in the good news" (Mark 1:15). Jesus attracted enormous crowds. His preaching was lucid and understandable to the ordinary Jew. He told the people that the new age was dawning and that when it came, the reign of God would be supreme. He taught that God's will was ultimate and that everyone should have faith in his powers. He impressed on the people that faith and obedience to God's will were vital and would lead to the love and understanding of God and enable the people to walk in the ways of God. He assured them that by accepting the will of God, all of them might enter into the kingdom—but only if they repented and returned to the true loyalty of God (Flower, 1997; Noss, 1974).

Jesus' teachings can be summed up by his Sermon on the Mount, preached to an enormous crowd. In his sermon, Jesus spoke of overturning the status quo that was adhered to by the Pharisees and Sadducees. It is an extensive work and can be found in its entirety in Matthew (Matthew 5:3–12). Jesus also gave a simple prayer, "The Lord's Prayer" (Matthew 6:9–13). This prayer, said with reverence and humility, became a fundamental prayer for Christian services and is recited throughout the world.

Although Jesus' teachings attracted large numbers of Jews wherever he went in Palestine, it soon became evident that not enough people were heeding his message. Until this time Jesus had been preaching to his fellow Jews, but then he carried his ministry to non-Jews. Jesus claimed that purity of the heart was absolutely more important than the ritual cleansing required by Judaic law. Jesus declared that it was the

thoughts people had that propelled them to evil deeds, not the forsaking of the law. His popularity aroused the concern and anger of some religious groups, especially the Pharisees who held to the legality of Judaism and Judaic law, as well as that of the Sadducees who were the priestly rulers and whose power depended on the good will of the Romans. Concern arose about whether Jesus was indeed the promised King of the Jews or the Messiah. His increasing popularity seemed to say so. However, Jesus did not see himself as the Messiah but as God's son who came to teach them the ways of God and the way to reach God. On the Passover before his crucifixion, Jesus rode into Jerusalem on a donkey. It was perceived that he did so in the style of a ruler. The people expected Jesus to declare that he was the King and rise up against Rome. But Jesus had denied this saying that the Kingdom of God was not literal. Many of his followers were disillusioned, including Judas, one of his own disciples. Jesus had come to be considered dangerous in the eyes of the leaders who, with the disillusioned Judas, arranged for his arrest. The Passover supper Jesus shared with his Apostles before his arrest is known as The Last Supper. Jesus was charged with blasphemy—that he claimed to be the Messiah and the Son of God. The Roman rulers sanctioned the arrest of Jesus and passed the death sentence with insurrection as the reason. His death was by crucifixion on a Friday. John, Jesus' most beloved Apostle, as well as Jesus' mother Mary, Salome, Mary Magdalene, and Mary, the mother of the Apostle James, stayed there through the darkness until Jesus died. Crucifixion was not a Jewish but a Roman method of capital punishment. Many Jews as well as others were said to have been crucified as rebels on meager evidence (Flower, 1997; Parrinder, 1993; Smith, 1994).

Jesus foretold that he would be put to death and at The Last Supper on Passover tried to prepare the Apostles for his departure. Jesus told them that through his death the disciples would understand the need for his sacrifice and would understand the significance of his death for the salvation of all humanity.

Jesus' body was taken off the cross and buried. Two days later, on Sunday, the tomb was found empty by Mary Magdalene; Mary, the mother of James; and other women. This was the day of the resurrection of

Jesus, to be known as Easter Sunday. Jesus then began to reappear to his Apostles in corporeal form. Now the Apostles began to understand what Jesus was. He told them the meanings of his life and death—he came to "minister, and to give His life, a ransom in exchange for many" (Mark 10:45). "His death was to free the people from sin and reconcile them with God, with whom they would then live in harmony. He was the ultimate, perfect sacrifice" (Flower, 1997, p. 21–22). Thus, after Jesus, no additional sacrifice would be necessary. His work would be carried out by his Apostles who would proclaim him the Messiah.

Forty days after his resurrection, Jesus ascended to heaven. Ten days later, at the Jewish festival of the Pentecost, the Apostles gathered in a room in Jerusalem. Suddenly, they heard a noise like a stiff breeze which proceeded to fill the entire room. Tongues of fire appeared and descended on each of the Apostles who then began to speak in different languages. This was the Holy Spirit of which Jesus had spoken (Acts 1:9–11; 2:1–4). Thus, the Holy Spirit of God was deemed to have "endowed His followers with its power" (Flower, 1997, p. 22). Now Jesus' Apostles were enabled to continue with his ministry, invested with the Holy Spirit, and act as Jesus' representatives on earth. The resurrection and ascension of Jesus became the focus of Christianity. To Christians, it seemed that in his willingness to suffer death for the redemption of humanity, Jesus gave to them the clearest understanding of the quality of "the redemptive love of God himself" (Noss, 1974, p. 437).

Through the continuing efforts of Jesus' Apostles, especially **Paul** (St. Paul), the new faith spread through Persia, Asia, and Africa, reaching across the sea to Rome. At the same time, Christianity began to adapt to the different beliefs and cultures of these countries.

Jesus and Women in the Pre-Christian Palestine

Quite early in Jesus' ministry, women formed an important part of the crowds that followed him. The Gospels tell of his egalitarian attitude toward women. Jesus had sensitive and sympathetic relations with many women such as Martha and Mary, the sisters of Lazarus whom Jesus brought back from the dead. As related earlier, women stayed by him during and after his crucifixion, and after the resurrection, his first appearance was to the women who found his tomb empty. Carmody (1989) has written about Jesus' stance toward women. She describes how the Gospels tell of Jesus' teachings about divorce. In rejecting divorce, Jesus spoke of the unity of the man and woman as being "one flesh" and which bound both to the marriage (Mark 10:17–31). The prevailing law at the time gave men exclusive control over the right to divorce. The denial of divorce would be a positive benefit to women, protecting them from abandonment and poverty, and keeping them from being set adrift in a male-centered society. Jesus rejected the custom that it was one's duty to marry and procreate. He felt that if a man or woman wanted to have a life of religious service, then an unmarried state was permissible. In this way, Jesus made it possible for men as well as women to lead a monastic life. Jesus also spoke against a double standard for morality and marital fidelity. Yet, he did not absolutely reject the patriarchal culture that was part of Judaism and that of other cultures. He felt that men should be the ones to set moral examples in the community. As evidence of this, twelve men, but no women, became his Apostles, although he did accept women as his students, something the Rabbis of the time would never permit (Carmody, 1989).

The Gospels also relate that Jesus prevailed against Jewish customs, especially the prohibition against activity on the Sabbath, for which he was severely criticized. He healed many, including women, on this holy day of rest. He dealt compassionately with all kinds of women, among them prostitutes and women who were "unclean" (menstruating) according to the law and who were to be shunned (Thurston, 1998). In his positive attitude toward women, Jesus not only took from Judaism what would be important for his own teachings, but went against the laws of Judaism as well. His new movement, not yet called Christianity, seemed to accept and welcome women. Carmody (1989) quotes Ben Witherington who, in explaining why Christianity differed from Judaism, said "Thus, the community of Jesus, both before and after

Easter, granted women *together* with men (not segregated from men . . .) an equal right to participate fully in the family of faith. This was a right that women did not have in contemporary Judaism or in many pagan cults" (Witherington, 1984, p. 127).

As we turn to the development of Christianity and the role of women in this new religion, we will explore whether these attitudes toward women were maintained.

Catholicism

Christianity began after the death of Jesus. In the development and spread of Christianity, the concept of the Church as a teaching authority became prominent. It began with the postulate that "God came to earth in the person of Jesus Christ to teach people how to live in this world so as to inherit eternal life" (Smith, 1994, p. 22). As Christianity spread throughout Rome, it was initially subject to official persecution, but by 380 C.E., it became the official religion of the Roman Empire. It essentially continued until 1054 C.E. when it divided into the Eastern Orthodox Church and the Roman Catholic Church. Then, in the sixteenth century, another great division occurred with the Protestant Reformation.

Roman Catholics see their church as beginning with Jesus and Peter and continuing through an unbroken succession of 20 centuries of popes to the present time. They see the Protestants as beginning in 1517 and the Eastern Orthodox church as beginning with the earlier splits from the Catholic church.

Protestants see their churches in the direct historical line of succession from the early churches of the first and second centuries. Protestants disagree on various issues, but all denominations try to make their congregations more or less like the congregations of the first century of Christianity.

Throughout the 20 centuries of Christianity, particularly in Roman Catholicism, there has been conflict between two motifs in the theological understanding of male–female relations: equivalence and subordination. This conflict between the two views, one that affirmed the equivalence of man and woman as human persons and the other that defined woman as subordinate to men socially and even ontologically, can be traced through the whole of Christian history (Carroll, 1983).

The traditional biblical reference for both of these basic positions have come from Paul's letters. Paul, an Apostle of Jesus, has been considered the "second founder of Christianity" (Noss, 1974, p. 441). He was very important in the spread of Christianity throughout the Roman Empire. Before 65 C.E., Paul wrote to the Galatians the *equivalence* position: "There is no such thing as Jew and Greek, slave and free, male and female; for you are all one person in Christ Jesus" (Paul's letter to the Galatians 3:68).

There is evidence that early Christianity regarded redemption by Jesus as overturning systems of social discrimination, bringing all persons to a new status before God. But beginning with the post-Pauline period, the social order, according to the concept of subordination, demanded that men as husbands have authority over women, both as wives and children. Women must act as obedient followers and carry out his commands, as must children and servants. This theology of subordination has been maintained by insinuating that women are, in fact, morally, ontogenically, logically, and intellectually inferior to the man and therefore less capable of an independent life. A woman's inferior status can lead to sin when she acts independently. The *subordinate* position implies that:

> As in all congregations of God's people, woman should not address the meeting. They have no license to speak, but should keep their place as the law directs. If there is something they want to know, they can ask their husbands at home. It is a shocking thing that a woman should address the congregation. (Paul's first letter to the Corinthians, 14:34–35)

Paul's letter of equivalence suggests that early **Pauline** Christianity accepted the radical egalitarianism of Jesus and his movement. But according to Carmody (1989), the Church did not accept Paul's vision and intent to define the Christian community on an egalitarian basis. The patriarchalism of the Judaic culture and the contemporary Hellenistic culture (which was different then from that in early Judaism) began to penetrate the Church's vision for family life and the community. Whether this was the reason for Paul's subordinate position has not been clarified. The theme of subordination has never been the sole view of women in Christianity, although for much of its history it has been the dominant and official one. The concept of equivalence has been present, but only recently has it come to be the dominant view and then only by liberal churches. Equivalence takes the creation story of Genesis, where both male and female are created in the image of God, as *normative.*

After the split from the Eastern Orthodox Church, the Roman Catholic Church continued to evolve. If it was true that Jesus Christ came to earth to teach people how to live in order to merit eternal life, it was crucial for his teachings to continue. The Gospels may not be sufficient because they contained ambiguities. If the Bible is studied individually, it may be given different interpretations. From these problems arose the concept of a "supreme court to adjudicate between truth and error" (Smith, 1994, p. 223). The formation of such a teaching authority resulted in the doctrine of "papal infallibility." The earthly head of the Church is the Pope, successor to St. Peter in the Bishopric of Rome. The Doctrine of papal infallibility asserts that "when the Pope speaks officially on matters of faith and morals, God protects him from error" (Smith, 1994, p. 223).

A second concept that developed in Catholicism was the Church as the Sacramental Agent—to know what sacraments should be done and to be able to carry them out. As indicated earlier, the Roman Catholic Church observes seven sacraments, paralleling the important moments and needs during one's lifetime. Two need to be repeated often: reconciliation (confession) and the Church's central sacrament, the Mass, also known as the Holy Eucharist or Communion.

These two concepts of the Church as a *teaching authority* and *sacramental agent* are two of the most important central perspectives in Roman Catholicism. There are other important aspects of the Catholic Church but they are beyond the scope of this section.

The Virgin Mary.   Christian tradition has it that Mary, the only mortal born without original sin, al-

though a virgin, conceived and gave birth to Jesus Christ, the Son of God. She is the principal saint, also known as the Blessed Virgin Mary, Our Lady, and the Mother of God (from the Greek theotokos). Her name in Hebrew is Miriam.

The events of Mary's life and the birth of Jesus as told in the New Testament have already been reviewed. Although few other details of her life are mentioned or implied, tradition has it that she was the daughter of St. Anne and St. Joachim and that she was presented and dedicated at the temple in Jerusalem as a virgin at a young age. According to a doctrine issued in the fifth century C.E., Mary was "assumed" directly into heaven. However, it was not until 1950 that Pope Pius XII's bulla *Munificentissimus Deus* made Mary's assumption into heaven an article of faith. In 1854, the Roman Catholic Church proclaimed the dogma of the Immaculate Conception—declared in the bulla *Ineffabilis Deus* of Pope Pius IX, according to which Mary was conceived without original sin. The Roman Catholic Church also teaches that Mary was freed from actual sin by a special grace of God (*Encyclopedia Britannica,* 1999).

While Catholics but not all Protestant denominations have accepted the Pope's 1950 bulla, Mary's virginity has served as an important symbol of Christianity's ascetic ideal, almost since the Church was organized. From the earliest times in the Catholic Church, it was believed that Mary's intercession was especially effective on behalf of humanity, and since the Middle Ages, the most prevalent expressions of Marian devotion has been the recitation of the rosary. According to the Church, Mary is the mediatrix of all graces. The study of doctrine about Mary is called Mariology and the veneration and devotion to Mary is called Mariolatry (*Columbia Encyclopedia,* 1993).

Devotion to Mary has increased in many parts of the world and in some cases has been carried to an idolatrous extreme. Mary is the most famous and venerated of mother figures and she has grown to be an immense personality throughout the world. It is claimed that two billion Hail Marys are said daily. Why is this happening? Why did five million people, many non-Christian, visit Lourdes this year to drink the healing waters and ten million travel to Guadeloupe to pray to Mary? Why the need to talk with her?

Apparitions of Mary have been reported for centuries but have always been infrequent events. Each apparition was said to have been accompanied by miraculous healings, messages from heaven, and other signs of supernatural intervention. Sightings were reported in New York City in 1970, and in 1981, sightings began in Medjugorje in Bosnia. There Mary is said to have appeared to six young peasants and has continued to deliver messages to them. No fewer than 11 million believers have flocked to the site. A more recently reported occurrence began in January, 1993, with a retired truck driver, Ray Doiron in Renault, Illinois. Mary appeared to him and told him to pray for peace, reject evil, and welcome God. For the past 20 years, Mr. Doiron had been visiting the Our Lady of the Snows shrine in Belleville, Illinois. After the appearance of Mary in his home, he began to be visited by her at the shrine. When people learned of this, they too began to visit the shrine from early in the morning to late in the evening. The crowds soon became too great and a nearby amphitheater is in use with almost 6,000 visitors a day (*Life Magazine,* 1996).

Theologians and clergy are uneasy about these sightings, which seem to have multiplied out of proportion. The Church as yet has not made a definitive statement about the sightings but are asking serious questions concerning the sudden rise in appearances of Mary.

One explanation for the increase in the frequency of appearances of Mary is that the emotional need for her is so irresistible to a profoundly troubled world that people, even those without an obvious link to Mary, are being drawn to her. It is known that in the Muslim world, Mary is revered as a pure and holy saint, but it is remarkable to many that large numbers of Muslims are making pilgrimages to Christian shrines (*Life Magazine,* 1996).

It also seems that more feminists are rediscovering the feminine symbol that Mary presents. As the Bible's most famous and revered woman, Mary may now have become a symbolic player in the fight for the ordination of women. These women point out

that Pope John Paul II loves Mary and visits Mary shrines—yet he stands by the long-term rationale for a males-only priesthood. This dichotomy is also seen in the fact that Mary adorns the banners of the liberals seeking a more prominent role for women in all the churches, but, at the same time, Mary glorifies the banners of the many conservatives who want to preserve the ministries as all-male. Despite intransigence, the fight is having an effect. The church is beginning to redefine women's roles and, according to many clergy, the all-male celibate priesthood may be endangered, a sign that culture may be stronger than theology.

With the elevation of Mary today, whether as a symbol for feminists or as solace for a sorely troubled world, her cultural importance now seems to far transcend any dogmatic or institutional boundaries that could never have been anticipated.

Eastern Orthodoxy

The Eastern Orthodox Church has far more similarities than differences with the Catholic Church. Both observe the same Sacraments but while they believe in a teaching authority, two differences are evident. The Catholic Church regards as doctrine the Immaculate Conception, Assumption of Virgin Mary, the idea of purgatory, and so on. The Eastern Orthodox Church considers these as "additions" that Orthodox Christians may or may not need to endorse (Smith, 1994).

In the Roman Catholic Church, dogmas are, in the final analysis, delivered by the Pope. In contrast, Eastern Orthodoxy believes that God's truth is revealed through the "conscience of the Church" or Christian consensus. Thus the Eastern Church does not have a Pope but the titular head of the Church is the Patriarch of Constantinople. Church dogmas reflect the consciences of the Orthodox Christians (Noss, 1974; Smith, 1994).

While Eastern Orthodoxy may seem more egalitarian, it, too, like Catholicism, maintains that an all-male clergy was part of God's plan for the Church. So it, too, is imbued with the patriarchal system that only recently shows signs of changing (Carmody, 1989).

Protestantism. On October 31, 1517, Martin Luther began his theological and ecclesiastical opposition to Catholicism by nailing 95 theses to the church door in Wittenberg, Germany. The causes that led to the break from Roman Catholicism are complex and still being debated. However, the basic cause was the development of a new concept or philosophy of Christianity. Luther's interest was to restore to all Christians the liberty of the Gospel. And, because men and women were images of God, they shared the fundamental abilities and the rights to this liberty.

Although Luther disagreed with Roman Catholic positions on some major issues, his arguments and references were generally conservative doctrinal positions very much in the mainstream of ancient and medieval Christian theology.

Luther rejected the concept of Papal Infallibility and considered it idolatrous because it prevented the type of critical deliberation that would avoid limitations and errors. Protestants believe that God speaks to his people through the Bible and insist that every word and letter in it was dictated by God. Thus, the Bible contains no historical, scientific, or other errors. This is known as bibliolatry.

Another concept in Protestantism is the deification of private religious experience in which what is experienced must be the work of the Holy Spirit. For Protestants, the Bible presents the clearest picture of God's goodness and the way the people can relate to it. In this way "the Bible is, for Protestants, ultimate"(Smith, 1994, p. 229).

There is some recognition that with each individual's encounter with God's word in the Bible as a centering force in their religion, there can be uncertainty and risks. If you misread the Bible, different truths may emerge. The formation of different groups within Protestantism may be evidence of these different interpretations of the Bible. In addition, other differences among the Protestant denominations are in their church government. Nevertheless, Protestants, regardless of their denomination, prefer these problems rather than the security of doctrines or institutions which they consider to be fallible.

Although the mainstream Protestant reform groups abolished celibacy among priests and Christian monasteries, they did not substitute a new inclusion of women in the Protestant married clergy. Therefore, Reformation on the whole did not have a liberating effect on women.

In beginning this section on Protestantism, we noted that one reason for the break from Catholicism was that Luther, on the other hand, wanted to restore to all Christians the liberty of the Gospel. And, because men and women were images of God, they shared the basic capacities and rights related to this liberty (Carmody, 1989, p. 174). On the other hand, the reformers kept with the patriarchal tradition which advocated silence and submission of women based on the order of creation (man was created first in the image of God and woman created second) and based on the punishment for the sin of Eve. However, in time, cultural changes with regard to women were made.

One of the most critical distinctions among the major divisions of the Protestant Reformation was church government. It was these difference that ultimately most influenced the places of women in Protestant churches.

There are four basic divisions of Protestantism, all dating from the sixteenth-century Reformation: the Lutherans, the Reformed, the Anglicans, and the Anabaptists.

The Lutherans. Luther and the northern princes set up churches in Germany. The important ecclesiastical appointments were made from the top down—from the princes of each German state (e.g., Saxony, Prussia). There was no democracy. When the Lutheran church came to the United States, it was not until 1918 that somewhat democratic reforms were made (Evans, 1976).

The other half of the Lutherans were the Scandinavians. These nations all had powerful and somewhat democratic parliaments as well as kings. Sweden, Denmark, and Norway all became Lutheran states and were later joined by Finland. All these churches were generally ruled by their somewhat democratic parliaments. Scandinavian Lutheranism followed Scandinavians to the United States. They spoke well for women. But it was not until 1938 that the Norwegian parliament began to ordain women. By 1958, European Lutheran churches and many of those in the United States began to ordain women as clergy.

The Reformed Tradition. Sometimes called the Calvinist tradition, the Reformed tradition has historically fought over Calvin's doctrines of predestination. This tradition began in the Swiss city-state Canton of Zurich by Zwingili in 1518. Zwingili advocated free-will in opposition to Calvin's position. Zwingili's position has been accepted by almost all Reformed churches today.

The original Reformed churches were historically somewhat democratic because the church government was modeled after their elected city–state governments. Middle-class males, but not poor males, could vote. With few exceptions, women could not. Reformed churches spread to cities in Switzerland, Germany, and Holland, to some French cities (The Huguenots), a few Hungarian towns, the Church of Scotland (Presbyterian), to the Scotch-Irish in Northern Ireland, and to many English cities (the Congregationalists or "Puritans"). When the churches emigrated to North America, many split off (e.g., the Church of Scotland became the "Christian church" or "disciples of Christ."

The Reformed churches all had democratic governments that encouraged education for all their members, including women. Their clergy was highly educated (in the United States, the Reformed churches founded Harvard, Yale, Princeton, and many other colleges).

The Anglican Tradition. This tradition began in 1532 when King Henry VIII of England decided to divorce in order to marry Anne Boleyn. The King broke with the Pope, seized control of all churches in England, as well as church land and property for himself and his allies. He eliminated all who opposed his "religious" reforms, replacing them with his friends and associates.

In the beginning the Anglican church differed little from the Catholic church except that church authorities were appointed directly by the King and, of course, divorce was permissible. The Bible was translated and published in English. By 1551, married clergy were permitted. The Anglican church remained completely hierarchical in government; Anabaptist (Brownists) and Reformed (Puritans, Congregationalists, Presbyterians) churches were now organized illegally in urban and working class areas (Langer, 1948).

There were many conflicts between the English kings and parliament that existed well into the next century. Since 1660, the governing power of the Anglican church in England has remained partly democratic. The Protestant Episcopal church in the United States was organized as an American denomination separate from the English state church after the Revolutionary War (Ahlstrom, 1972).

The Anabaptist Churches. These were originally working class and peasant churches of the Reformation and were opposed by Lutheran state authorities, Roman Catholic state authorities, Reformed church authorities, and Anglican English state authorities. The movement started in Switzerland by Felix Mantz about 1525. Women were part of this local congregation and may have already started to vote in its decision-making process. The congregation was expelled in 1526 for opposing infant baptism (Williams, 1962). The Anabaptist movement rapidly spread across northern and central Europe, organizing house-churches of the poor, often led by ex-Roman Catholic clergy. They were opposed by local authorities almost everywhere. Women played a major role in town events and even in a military battle in Munster, Germany.

Regarding the role of women in the Anabaptist movement, Williams (1962), in summarizing sixteenth century Anabaptist policies, stated that "Nowhere else in the Reformation Era were women so nearly the peers and companions in the faith and martyrdom in missionary enterprise. . . . The Anabaptist insistence on the conventional principle of freedom of conscience for all adult believers and thereby the extension of the priesthood of the Christophorous laity to women constituted a major breach in the patriarchalism and a momentous step in the Western emancipation of women (Williams, 1962, pp. 506–507).

Thus far, our discussion has provided some concept of the principles of Protestantism and the major divisions within it in which women have played some part, depending on their particular group membership. We can also see that in the Reformation, the patriarchal system was still functioning. Rather than discussing in more detail the role and progress of women in each of the groups within these divisions, we will describe events in the **Quakers** and in the **Puritan** groups. Beginning in the seventeenth century in England and then in the United States, the Quakers became very important in pioneering leadership in the emancipation of women; in the Puritan groups, women suffered severely and many were killed.

Puritanism.   Puritanism did not develop in England until the late sixteenth century and was brought to America soon after. English Puritans elaborated on the relations between male and female in marriage. The Puritan husband was to be the benevolent ruler; the wife, although a subordinate partner, was to be a docile helpmate to her husband in all things. This view of family harmony had another side, a constant suspicion that women (and servants) were secretly rebellious against authority but was frequently thought to be more prevalent among women than men, since women were the "weaker vessel." This was thought to be the fact because "the Devil [could] more easily prevail in her and . . . continues to resort to women as the easier victim of temptation" (Perkins, 1596). Perkins specified that one of the reasons women easily succumb to the devil is that they are by nature insubordinate and wish to repudiate their divinely appointed inferiority to men. This makes women an easy target for the devil.

Whether this was one of the concepts that led to the association of women and witchcraft is uncertain. However, there were witchcraft trials and burning of witches long before Puritanism developed in England. In 1431, the French heroine Jeanne d' Arc was burned at the stake as a witch by the English. After that, the French were decidedly unenthusiastic about witchcraft trials. However, thousands of "witches," mostly peasant women with local enemies, were convicted and burned during that century in Germany, Scotland, and Spain. Almost all the victims were women, although some men were also convicted as witches.

The Puritans who came to America brought the same ideology along with them. Puritanism flourished in Massachusetts, which was a bastion of Puritan orthodoxy. The elaboration on relations between husband and wife continued with the idea of women's subordination. The suspicions of witchcraft were augmented by a now famous Puritan tract on witches— Cotton Mather's 1689 *Memorable Providences, Relating to Witchcrafts and Possession.* This book was probably one of the causes of the 1692 Salem witch trials. Cotton Mather was one of the clergy in Salem that year (Ahlstrom, 1972).

In the summer of 1692, hysteria concerning witches, provoked in part by the Puritan clergymen, gripped Salem village. The governor of Massachusetts created a special court to try suspected witches, and by that autumn, twenty people were hanged. Most were local women, but two Puritan clergymen had also been victims of witchcraft associations and were convicted. All died protesting their innocence. The verdict was not based on "tortured" confessions but on "eyewitness" testimony, including neighbors who were certain that they saw the victims carry out impossible things like floating through the air and changing themselves into non-human animals. Although twelve local clergymen actively opposed the trials, warning about the dangers of such testimony, three clergymen actively supported the trials. Interestingly, Cotton Mather's father, Increase Mather, wrote about these cases, attacking the Salem witchcraft court decisions. Finally, Massachusetts Governor Phipps was convinced by Increase Mather's manuscript that innocent people had been falsely convicted and hanged. He disbanded the court and ended the trials in late 1692 (Ahlstrom, 1972).

Although many people in Massachusetts probably believed witches did exist, this was in part provoked by the sermons and writing of the clergy. The Massachusetts clergy became more interested in fair trials than witchhunts. The people in Massachusetts gradually became disgusted with these trials after the Salem events, and they were never again repeated in America. One of the trial judges, Samuel Sewall, later made a very sad public confession in church, that he had been wrong at the witchcraft trials (Ahlstrom, 1972; Smith, Handy, & Loetscher, 1960).

Quakerism.   Quakerism continued these Puritan attitudes but was more charismatic and egalitarian. This was especially due to Margaret Fell and George Fox's beliefs about Eve. They believed in women's subordination to men because of Eve's part in the fall; they also proclaimed that this condition of subordination *ended* when a woman accepted Jesus Christ as Savior, because her original equal position to men before the fall was then automatically restored by God. Therefore, Christian women should now actively proclaim God's word in public; just as women like the Samaritan woman at the well, Mary Magdalene and Lydia, did in the New Testament. The parallelisms of Adam's fall and Christ's new salvation and reconciliation for humans has been a traditional theme in Christian theologies (Ahlstrom, 1972).

George Fox (1624–1691) searched for the Holy Spirit during the English Civil War, and actively began to travel and preach a mystical or spiritual version of Christianity about 1648. The traditional date for the founding of the Society of Friends or Quakers is 1652, when Fox held a crucial organizational meeting at Swarthmore Hall in England, the home of some of his most loyal associates, as well as patrons Thomas Fell (1595–1658) and his wife, Margaret Fell (1614–1702).

The Quakers treated all members, men and women, as "saved in Christ" and therefore equal in church roles and responsibilities. They abandoned separate clergy, believing that all their adult members, both men and women, were "priests" or clergy. Fox, Margaret Fell, and other Quakers, both men and women, became aggressive missionaries, which often landed their members in jail (and sometimes hanged) in both England and America. Fox himself visited America where some Quakers had already settled.

Another Quaker, William Penn, obtained a charter from the English king to create a place of settlement and refuge for Quakers in America in the new colony of Pennsylvania in 1681. The Quakers in America had formerly helped Roger Williams and Anne Hutchinson create the colony of Rhode Island (1636) and were the first English settlers of New Jersey (1674) (Ahlstrom, 1972; Smith, Handy, & Loetscher, 1960).

Some important examples of Quaker women taking active roles were Mary Fisher, Ann Austin, Mary Clark, and Mary Dyer, who attempted to preach Quaker Christianity in the closed Puritan state of Massachusetts between 1651 and 1655. Mary Fisher and Ann Austin were jailed naked for five weeks and inspected for bodily tokens of witchcraft, and their library of over 100 books was confiscated. They were expelled to Barbados from where they had come from England. Mary Clark was severely whipped, held in prison for ten weeks and then expelled to Rhode Island. Mary Dyer was hanged (Ahlstrom, 1972; Irwin, 1979).

Religion differed in different areas of the colonies. While Massachusetts was the stronghold of Puritanism, Rhode Island became home for dissidents, with the Middle Colonies having many Quakers. The southern colonies were loyal to the Church of England, although Maryland was settled by Roman Catholics. Nevertheless, the major influence was that of the Puritans made up of British believers who themselves had emigrated to America to find "religious liberty."

Eventually, the concepts of the patriarchal order began to be overcome, but only in the Christian movements in the nineteenth century as a result of the Enlightenment. This allowed modern Christians to identify with redemption and reform in the direction of egalitarian rights and opportunities, a way to justify the equivalence of all persons and to provide access to opportunities for self-expression. This shift was basic for all modern theologies of liberation, including the feminism that arose in the nineteenth- and twentieth-century drives for women's suffrage in the United States. This feminist movement was the biggest single change in public concepts of women in the last two centuries. These concepts are highly evident today in women's continuing struggle for equality with men.

Thus, the early "narrow thought in Christianity, as much as in any other religion, has restricted the acceptance of women as full human beings" (Carroll, 1983) and is still with us today. The classic in Western literature that has most systematically argued for the general biological inferiority of women is Plato's *Republic*. Included in this theme is the mythical belief that women have weaker brains and weaker educational needs than men, which was previously supported by "scientific" data. The resultant attitudes are still encountered daily by young women embarking on education in science, mathematics, law, medicine, and other allegedly masculine fields.

In religious hierarchy, power and prestige have been reserved exclusively for males. Until very recently in most denominations, only men could be priests, ministers, or rabbis. Although the first female Protestant cleric was ordained in 1853, it was not until 1972 that the first female Reform rabbi was ordained, and in 1976 the first female Episcopal priest was ordained. At first, their positions were highly controversial, but as time passed, though still the subject of some dispute, their numbers have increased. At present, the Catholic church does not have female clergy, although Roman Catholic women can now participate in mass as lectors and in the distribution of the Eucharist. Nuns have become more independent and involved in the community, and there is a strong movement toward equality in the church.

There is some evidence that religious beliefs and training may affect gender-related attitudes, although religion is not the most important shaper of gender roles (Wilson, 1978). In a nationwide sampling of college students in 1973, students who identified themselves as Seventh Day Adventists, Mormons, or Baptists, particularly if they were white, showed the greatest differences between sexes in occupational choices and disapproval of careers for married women. Students who identified themselves as Quakers, Unitarians, or of no religious preference showed the fewest differences between sexes in these two areas (Rhodes, 1983).

Islam

There are millions of Muslim women in the many Muslim countries throughout the world. Complex elements comprise the picture of the Islamic woman; that is, the basic Islamic rites and aspects of its interpreta-tion in each of the Muslim countries, as well as the politics of each of these countries, make it difficult to write about the place of women in Islamic society, especially at this critical moment in history.

A *Muslim* is "one who submits" or "one who commits *himself* to Islam." The word *Islam* means "submission" or "surrender." "One who thoughtfully declares 'I am a Muslim' has done more than affirm *his* membership in a community. . . . [He is saying] 'I am one who commits himself to God'" (Adams, 1965, p. 496). In the beginning, Islam was a challenge to other religions, primarily Judaism and Christianity. The force and clarity of Islamic thought have great appeal for those who have accepted it. It has been estimated that at least 1 billion people now consider themselves adherents to Islam, and the number is increasing. Since its inception, Islam has held to its one basic scripture, which has been preserved in its initial textural purity. The Qur'an (or Koran), the bible of the Muslims, was revealed to Muhammad, the Muslim prophet, about 531 C.E. (Noss & Noss, 1984; Ringgren & Strom, 1967; 1997 Britannica Book of the Year).

Pre-Islamic Arabia.   At the time of Muhammad's birth, the Arabian peninsula was populated by seminomadic tribes. They were neither politically or spiritually united; their main loyalty was to the tribe. It was an inhospitable land, and tribes were forced to move from one area to another along this peninsula, seeking a more favorable climate in which they could find food and water. The Arabian people had a polytheistic religion and worshipped many gods and goddesses, animals, demons, wells, and stones, similar to the tribes of Abraham.

Muhammad was born about 571 C.E. in Mecca, a small town in western Arabia. It is said that Muhammad's father, a Quraysh Cherish of the Hashemite clan, died before Muhammad was born. His mother died when Muhammad was six years old, and he was brought up first by his paternal grandfather and then by his uncle. Growing up in impoverished circumstances surely shaped Muhammad's feelings about poor people. He was angered by the social inequities and the mistreatment of women and children, and he condemned female infanticide (Carroll, 1983; Ringgren & Strom, 1967).

Muhammad entered the service of Khadija, the widow of a wealthy merchant. Khadija was attracted to Muhammad and admired his ability to assist her in the management of her trading business. Muhammad married Khadija when he was 25 and she was 40. It was said that she had considerable influence on his thoughts, especially about the social problems in Arabia. She also had sufficient wealth so that he was free to pursue his meditations. Khadija and Muhammad had six children, but only his daughter Fatima survived him and lived to see her father's Islam grow and prosper. Khadija died in 621 C.E. Until then, she was Muhammad's only wife. After Khadija's death, Muhammad took four wives, which was then permitted by the Koran (Carmody, 1989; Carroll, 1983; Ringgren & Strom, 1967).

When he was 40 years old, Muhammad began to receive revelations from the God, Allah. Khadija supported his belief that Allah had chosen him to be a prophet. Khadija became known as the First Mother of the Faithful and was his first convert. Her uncle Waraqah also believed in Muhammad's visions and decided that he was the successor of Moses and was destined to be the prophet of his Arab people for his God, Allah. At first Muhammed spoke about his revelations only to his family circle, but soon Allah commanded him to preach to his tribe, where he obtained his first disciples. But many members of Muhammad's own tribe were hostile to his ideas. His main supporters were liberated slaves and poor people. Muhammad began to preach a consistent monotheism. See Box 2.4 for this verse.

Eventually, more and more tribes followed Muhammad, converting to Islam. When about 60 of his converts moved to Yathrib, he went there himself in 622 C.E. and this town would eventually be named after him, The Prophet's City, *madinal an-nabi* or Medina. This event marked the beginning of the Muhammadan era. After his followers abandoned their old tribal groups in Mecca, strong enmity developed between the new religionists and the Meccans. This triggered a holy war in the cause of the God, Allah. Muhammad and his new Islamites became strong

---

BOX 2.4

Koran Verse

Say Allah is One
The Eternal God
He begot none,
Nor was he begotten
None is equal to him.

Koran 81.I–14 [cp. Rev.6.12–14]. Pelican trs., p. 17, II.3–11

---

enough to attack Mecca, and in 630 C.E. it was conquered. Muhammad began the ritual of the pilgrimage to the holy city of Mecca, which became a precedent for all rituals and which still survives. Muhammad died in Medina on June 8, 632 C.E. at about the age of 59. He was buried in Mecca. By then he and the new Islam held sway over nearly the entire Arabian peninsula.

Muhammad's revelations are preserved as originally written in the Qur'an (meaning reading or recitation) or Koran. The Qur'an was not completed until after Muhammad's death, partly through writings and by relying on oral tradition. In volume it is comparable to the New Testament. To faithful Muslims, the Qur'an is the very word of Allah brought down and revealed to Muhammad, just as the Ten Commandments had been revealed to Moses on Mt. Sinai (Ringgren & Strom, 1967). Let us look at what is in the Qur'an and what it means for the status of women both during the formative period of Islam and in current times.

The Qur'an. In the doctrine of the Qur'an, the "absolute oneness of God" is its principal tenet. "There is no God but Allah, and Muhammad is his prophet." This is the Islamic creed. Allah is omnipotent and omniscient (all-powerful and all-knowing). Polytheism and the Christian belief in the Trinity are denied. All is dependent on the will of Allah. There will be judgment and retribution; the good will enter Paradise and the wicked are damned to Hell. The patriarchs of the Jews as well as Jesus are all considered prophets and the recipients of revelations by Allah, but the absolute and perfect revelation came through Muhammad, who is the last in the long succession of prophets.

The basic plan of worship in the Qur'an involves the Five Pillars of Islam, which are the demands made of all adherents of Islam. These are described in Table 2.4.

Male circumcision is not mandated by law in the Qur'an but is generally observed in all Muslim countries. Pork is regarded as unclean and the eating of it is prohibited, as is the drinking of alcohol (Ringgren & Strom, 1967).

Impact of Islam on Women.   Many pre-Islamic traditions were carried over to Islam, but others were not. There were both patriarchal and matriarchal systems at the time of Muhammed, but Islam abolished all matriarchy. Women were no longer controlled by their families but by their husbands and their husbands' relatives. Despite the patriarchal system of most pre-Islamic marriages, the woman retained blood kinship with her tribe and could seek protection with her own tribe if maltreated by her husband. Polyandry gave way to polygamy (Ringgren & Strom, 1967).

TABLE 2.4   The Five Pillars of Islam

The five basic demands are:

1. **The Creed:** There is no God but Allah.

2. **The Ritual Prayer:** It is now said five times a day at fixed hours.

3. **Almsgiving:** A kind of tithe for the poor and sick and for other purposes.

4. **Fasting:** Total abstinence from food and drink and sexual intercourse from sunrise to sunset during the month of Ramadan.

5. **Pilgrimage to Mecca:** This is obligatory for any believer once during *his* lifetime if *he* can possibly undertake it.

Source: From *World Religions* (pp. 503–504), edited by Geoffrey Parrinder. Copyright © 1983 by the Hamlyn Publishing Group Ltd. Reprinted by permission of Facts On File, Inc.

Muhammad was familiar with the doctrines of Christianity and Judaism. He disapproved of the celibacy of Christianity. He did not equate women with evil and uncleanliness. Muhammad was sympathetic to women and concerned with their treatment, especially of widows. He did not consider women's menstruation as unclean or menstrual blood as pollution, although he did order women not to pray during this time and precluded their presence at the **Mosque.** The question of whether women should attend the Mosque engaged the attention of Muslim doctors. Many, if not most, preferred that they not pray in the Mosque, but they were constrained by tradition, which said that women could not be prevented from attendance but may not be perfumed.

The Qur'an is clear about full religious responsibility for women. Women are directed to participate in the stated obligations equally with men. In practice, however, this was not carried out. It is said that Muhammad allowed women to pray in the mosque with him, while other stories say that this was possible only with the permission and presence of the husband. Muhammad replaced the practice of polyandry with polygamy but restricted the practice to only four wives. There was a proviso that all wives were to be treated equally. He did this out of concern for the large numbers of women whose husbands were killed in battle and who needed to be taken care of. Divorce was not to be undertaken rashly by husbands. Although under Islam divorce benefited men, stipulations allowed divorced women to keep their dowries, and they were to be sent away with kindness and no loss of reputation. Previously, women were punished if they committed adultery by being beaten or even stoned to death. This punishment was not in the Qur'an but originated from the Torah of the Jews. Muhammad modified this law and urged leaders to let the accused go on the premise that it is better to make an error in forgiveness than in punishment (Noss, 1974).

However, a few years after Muhammad's death, conditions for women worsened under the rule of Umar, who succeeded him. Umar attempted to limit women to praying at home. After much opposition even from his wife and son, he virtually succeeded in this by appointing separate imams (teachers) for men and women. He also prevented Muhammad's wives from making pilgrimages but later changed his decision. Umar supported the trend toward excluding women from taking part in religious life and in all communal aspects of that life. This practice of exclusion was one of two significant factors in early Islam that contributed to the rapid decline of the status of women. The other factor was the seclusion of women. Smith (1985) describes seclusion as a custom beginning specifically with the Prophet's relegation of his wives to a separate place apart from normal social interaction with men. Women stayed at home and were not permitted to speak directly with men. Any conversation had to be carried out with a curtain between them. This led to the direct withdrawal of women from normal society, which came to be essentially a male society. Seclusion in this new religion resulted in a diminished role for women. Smith argues that the practice of seclusion would not have come about if the men of the time had not encouraged it. The institution of *hijah* or seclusion behind a curtain was said to be a divine revelation by Allah. The freedoms that women had enjoyed became virtually nonexistent.

The custom of veiling also diminished the role of women in this early period of Islam. Women had to keep their faces covered if they went out. Many women also covered one of their eyes. This practice, which emphasized both the obedience of women and their chastity, pervaded all Muslim lands.

It seems apparent that at no time during or immediately after the time of the prophet did women hold strong positions of leadership in the religious sphere. Only a few women in the very early days of Islam served as collectors and transmitters of traditions or in public affairs. The practice of exclusion and seclusion kept women from making any progress. There appears to be no convincing evidence that the establishment of Islam and the social revolution that ensued expanded opportunities for women that were previously not available to them. The establishment of Islam as a religiocultural system reduced the chances for women to participate in public life. Smith (1985) argues that codification of the laws in the Qur'an taken as divine revelation and the imposition of seclusion alleged to be based on divine revelation were crucial factors that increased the exclusion of women. The rapid implementation of exclusion and seclusion that followed Muhammad's death should be seen as the predominant attitude of men about the unsuitability of women to take part in public life and leadership. Women were willing to submit to these restrictions and accept that they were a part of divine revelation. Smith suggests strongly that considerable investigation needs to be done to obtain a clearer picture of the status of women at the time of the Prophet.

SUMMARY

In this chapter we described many of the origins of sex and gender stereotypes in mythology and religion. We recounted the early development of specific religions and how the attitudes toward and treatment of women evolved along with the evolution of the religions. We examined the representations of women in the different religions and societies in which they lived, the status of these women, the restrictions placed upon them, and the impact of these attitudes and restrictions. Attempts were made by women as well as some men to change conditions for women but, at least until recently, few changes endured. Some changes were reversed by the ensuing leader or ruler of that particular society. In some societies, restrictions were intensified for ideological, political, or economic reasons.

These stereotypes and biases are so deeply intertwined in our religious practices and education that many have not even questioned their validity until recent times. Naomi Goldenberg (1985) has written about the religious forces that are now beginning to replace the traditional male gods. She believes that the emergence of feminist theology has begun to shake the very roots of Western religions and may yet overthrow existing forms of Judaism, Christianity, and Islam. Other critiques of religion question and dispute the traditional patriarchal concept, its texts, and practices. The "development of the multicontextualization of feminist theology across ethnic, cultural and religious lines" (Ruether, 1993, p. xvi) has created an important literature. These women have "found their own distinctive voice" (Ruether, 1993, p. xvi). The continued development of women's rights movements throughout most of the world appears to be forcing crucial changes in the way religions treat women and the way women experience their religion. These changes may be the only hope for the various religions to endure into the next century.

The impact of these changes would indeed have substantial implications for society in general but especially for women. Societal change has often come about through manipulation and transformation of the religious institutions and beliefs that have always served to maintain the status quo. We have seen that in the many periods throughout civilization, the fortunes of women changed along with religious transformations as well as through political changes and developments in science and technology. These transformations will profoundly affect both Western and Eastern cultures and those in the developing world in ways that we cannot possibly anticipate.

KEY TERMS

Apostle (p. 54)	Mosque (p. 68)	Puritan (p. 64)
B.C.E. (p. 27)	Neolithic Age (p. 29)	Quaker (p. 64)
Brahma (p. 36)	Nirvana (p. 38)	Reincarnation (p. 37)
Bronze Age (p. 29)	Paleolithic Age (p. 29)	Shakti (p. 27)
C.E. (p. 29)	Pantheism (p. 34)	Stone Age (p. 29)
Endogamy (p. 36)	Parthenogenesis (p. 30)	Suttee (p. 42)
Epistle (p. 54)	Paul (p. 58)	Talmud (p. 49)
Exogamy (p. 36)	Pauline (p. 59)	Torah (p. 48)
Karma (p. 37)	Polyandry (p. 52)	Vedic (p. 34)
Mesolithic Age (p. 29)	Polygamy (p. 42)	
Monotheism (p. 44)	Polytheism (p. 34)	

DISCUSSION QUESTIONS

1. Are you a participating member of your religious group? What are the restrictions, if any, toward women?

2. Are the attitudes toward girls and women in your religious or cultural group restrictive or liberal? Do they still reflect the stereotypes described in this chapter?

3. What changes have been made concerning women's roles in your religious group or in your particular house of worship?

4. What changes do you feel are still needed in religious or cultural groups to make it possible for women to participate equally with men?

5. Do you approve of women becoming priests, ministers, rabbis, or other religious leaders? What changes could these women bring about in the major religions?

6. How would you describe the daily home life and workday of ordained women religious leaders?

7. Should lesbians be permitted to become active religious leaders? Why or why not?

SUGGESTED READINGS

Carroll, T. F. (1983). *Women, religion and development in the third world.* New York: Praeger.

Goldenberg, N. R. (1985). *Changing of the gods: Feminism and the end of traditional religions.* Boston: Beacon Press.

Haddad, Y. Y., & Findley, E. B. (Eds.). (1984). *Women, religion and social change.* Albany, NY: State University of New York Press.

Morford, M. P. O., & Lenardon, R. J. (1995). *Classical mythology* (5th ed.). White Plains, NY: Longman Publishers.

Sharma, A. (Ed.). (1987). *Women in world religions.* Albany, NY: State University of New York Press.

CHAPTER 3

BIOLOGY OF SEX AND GENDER

Anatomy is destiny.
—Sigmund Freud

*Although the girl is not yet a woman, her record to date offers convincing
evidence that the gender identity gate is open at birth . . . and that it
stays open at least for something over a year after birth.*
—John Money

*As Darwin demonstrated . . . we males have been born the fittest for
three billion years. From that constantly on-the-make little tree mouse
(the lemur . . .) to Mailer the magnificent, the DNA of the male Y
chromosome has programmed us to lead our sisters.*
—Edgar Berman, *The Complete Chauvinist*

*The origin of homosexuality has also been the subject of extensive debate
over the years. Much of that discussion has revolved around the
question: Do homosexual men and women develop a permanent sexual
orientation prenatally or early in life, as the essentialists maintain, or do
they choose their sexual orientation within a social context?*
—Mary Roth-Walsh

IS ANATOMY DESTINY?

Can We Change Sex and Orient Gender?

Can we change sex and orient gender or was Freud correct when he said that "anatomy is destiny" (Freud, 1924)? A recent follow-up of the classic story of "John" and "Joan" addresses these questions. This well-known case, which took place in 1963, involved a set of normal male twins. At seven months of age one of the twins, John, developed phimosis, an abnormal condition where the foreskin around the penis tightens and prevents urination. It is a serious condition and requires circumcision, removal of the foreskin of the penis, to relieve the problem. During the surgical circumcision, which was carried out using a cautery, John's penis was accidentally burned and ablated (amputated). After much discussion and consultation, John was taken to the Johns Hopkins University in Baltimore where he was seen by Dr. John Money, a renowned sex researcher. On Dr. Money's advice, it was decided that it would be best to rear John as a girl. The family was instructed about how to treat the child in a gender-appropriate way. John's name was changed to "Joan." Within the following year, an orchidectomy (removal of the testes) was performed. Sometime later, further surgery was carried out and a vagina was constructed for Joan. The development of Joan was monitored and followed up with yearly visits to the Johns Hopkins Hospital. A psychiatric team, which included female therapists, was located in the family's area, and they arranged a program to foster female identification and role modeling for Joan. The treatment was reported to be progressing successfully, with acceptance of the child as Joan. Money (1975) reported on Joan's progress:

Although the girl is not yet a woman, her record to date offers convincing evidence that the gender identity gate is open at birth for a normal child no less than for one born with unfinished sex organs or one who was prenatally over or underexposed to androgen [male hormone], and that it stays open at least for something over a year after birth. (p. 98)

Money continued to write on the success of this case of sex reassignment, feeling that the outcome reinforced a social-learning theory of sexual identity.

In 1975, when Joan was about 12 years old, she had, according to reports, apparently developed as a normal female, confirming Money's projection that being raised as a female would override the masculinizing effect of male genes and early male hormone output. He strongly believed that sexual identity and sexual behavior were simply a matter of upbringing (Money, 1975; Money & Tucker, 1975). As Joan approached puberty she began to receive female hormones, developing breast tissue, and the perception was that she continued to function as a normal female.

In 1980, however, a British news team interested in reporting on this case came to the United States. They discovered that several psychiatrists had examined Joan when she was 13. The psychiatrists' findings and conclusions seemed to conflict strongly with those reported by Money. They found that Joan was having significant psychological problems concerning her ambivalence with a female role. It became apparent that she was never really content with being a girl and had suspected that she was really a male ever since she was in second grade. Joan had developed a masculine gait that was ridiculed by her classmates.

She also showed interest in what were then commonly considered male occupations. By the time Joan was 14 years old, she started to rebel against her female persona. She sought other medical treatment. Joan stopped taking estrogens, had a mastectomy, and started taking male hormones. Joan then reverted to the male status he had always wanted and began to use his original name, John. Over a period of time, John had a phalloplasty, a surgical procedure to form a penis. When John was 25 years old, he married a woman who already had a family. Scientists report that John, now in his mid-thirties, is happily married, although still suffering from the psychic trauma of his early life (Diamond & Sigmundson, 1997; Holden, 1997; Pinel, 1993).

This case has been closely followed since the 1960s. It received widespread recognition, which in turn influenced many scientific and social disciplines. Numerous texts, including those in psychology, sociology, and women's studies, were rewritten to assert that "conventional patterns of masculine and feminine behavior can be altered. It also cast doubt on the theory that major sex differences, psychological as well as anatomical, are immutably set by the genes at conception" ("Biological Imperatives," 1973). At that time, the newly stated and rapidly accepted view was seen as validation of a theory that the gender identity of the offspring depends on the child's upbringing and environment, a theory that, as of this writing, can still be found in the literature and in some instances continues to be the opinion of some physicians and social scientists. This belief is based on assumptions that (1) individuals are psychosexually neutral at birth and (2) healthy psychosexual development depends on the appearance of the genitals. These assumptions appear to have been influenced strongly by Money and his colleagues (Diamond & Sigmundson, 1997). Because of Money's prominence in the scientific community at the time, such assumptions became entrenched in the academic and medical communities. And, although Joan's reversion to a male occurred several years ago and the longitudinal data have been made available, many textbooks do not reflect these later findings.

Pinel (1993), in his careful and complete review of Joan's case of sex reassignment, regarded it as "sci-

entifically regrettable that so much of a theoretical and philosophical superstructure has been built on the supposed results of a single, uncontrolled and unconfirmed case" (p. 293), adding that it was also regrettable that a British news team rather than scientists uncovered the facts of the case.

In contrast to Money's nurture over nature views, Diamond, a reproductive biologist, has proposed an interactive model of gender identity (Diamond, 1982) that he calls the *biased interaction model*. In this model, sexuality and gender are influenced by environmental forces, but the environmental influence is profoundly affected by the individual's biological make-up (genes and hormones). Gender identity and sexuality are the outcome of the interaction of the two (biology and environment). The fact that the majority of individuals have a gender identity that fits with their biological sex is consistent with Diamond's theory.

Also inconsistent with a strict environmental view of gender identity are studies of a group of children in the Dominican Republic by Imperato-McGinley and her associates (Imperato-McGinley & Peterson, 1976; Imperato-McGinley, Peterson, Gaultieret, & Sturla, 1979), which are described in Box 3.1.

It is not clear how much we can learn about the normal development of gender identity from studies of children with anomalous biological conditions. Clearly, more research with various populations is needed. At the present time, however, gender identity is best viewed as the product of an interaction between biology and the environment.

Nature versus Nurture: Development of Gender Identity

For decades, the relative influence of nature (biology and anatomy) versus nurture (social and cultural learning and the environment) on human development and gender identity has been debated. It is pertinent here to review Freud's psychoanalytic theory, which postulates a model for gender identity for the male and the female that has been one of the most influential theories in the history of psychology and psychiatry. Many of our sex and gender stereotypes are related to

Box 3.1

Nature versus Nurture

In addition to support from human and animal studies for Diamond's theory, evidence has come from the work of Julianne Imperato-McGinley and her associates. For several years they studied a group of male pseudohermaphrodites in the Dominican Republic. These children had normal male sex chromosomes (XY) and male gonads, but they had an inherited enzyme deficit due to a genetic defect that resulted in improperly formed external genitalia at birth. They presented an incompletely formed scrotum which looked like labia and a very small penis that looked like a clitoris with a partially formed vagina. The uneducated parents and probably the physicians who delivered these babies were unaware of any problems. The parents proceeded to rear the children as females.

When the "girls" reached puberty, normal male testosterone production began, causing their penises to fully develop. Puberty was also associated with the onset of other masculine behaviors. The girls indeed became boys. It was most surprising that, despite their rearing as girls, the psychological orientation of the majority of these children also changed and their gender identity "became male," with all the typical male behaviors and attitudes, but with varying degrees of success.

From the results of this study, it was apparent that biology was the ultimate influence on their sexuality and on their final gender identity. This is consistent with the outcome that Diamond's theory predicted. Imperato-McGinley and her colleagues believe that their findings provide evidence that when the sex of rearing, even for a prolonged period, is contrary to the child's biological sex, in the end, the biological sex will prevail if at puberty normal hormone production takes place (Imperato-McGinley & Peterson, 1976; Imperato-McGinley, Peterson, Gaultieret, & Sturla, 1979).

This type of pseudohermaphroditism will be discussed in further detail on p. 90.

Freud's concepts, which stress anatomy, but give little attention to the role of society and learning in shaping behavior, particularly in gender identity. Freud's theory of psychosexual development was based on his belief in the superiority of the male and the phallus. Freud believed that because the female does not have a penis she is biologically inferior to the male, which is an important factor in her personality development. Freud theorized that the adult personality was the result of early experiences, and these experiences of childhood were especially critical. He formulated three stages of early sexual development that we all pass through and that occur in distinctive ontogenetic stages. The later two stages of sexual development, latency and genital, are not relevant here (Freud, 1925, 1931).

Stages of Early Sexual Development. During the first year of life, the child goes through the *oral* stage, with major pleasure derived from sucking and stimulating his or her lips and mouth. By the second year of life, the child enters the *anal* stage with its major focus on elimination and toilet training. Inhibition of bowel movements as well as permitting them to take place is, according to Freud, a means for the child to show his or her independence. Gradually, the child is socialized and conforms to the socially accepted standard of bathroom behavior.

During these early experiences, the mother is the primary love object for both sexes. Both boys and girls pass through these stages with little difference. In the third stage, the development of gender begins to differ. From about 3 years to 5 or 6 years, the child goes through the *phallic* stage. The boy's interest now focuses on his penis, with pleasure obtained by masturbating. According to Freud, the most significant aspect of this stage is the boy's development of the Oedipus complex, which derives from the Greek legend of Oedipus, who unknowingly killed his father, Laius, and married his mother, Jocasta. The boy now desires his mother sexually and hates his father, whom he considers a rival for his mother's love and affection. The boy fears that his father, whom he sees as all-powerful, will punish him by cutting off his penis when he learns of his son's feelings for his mother. As a result, the boy develops *castration anxiety.* When his anxiety becomes too great, the boy attempts to resolve it by suppressing his sexual impulses toward his mother. He then turns toward his father and starts to identify with him. In doing so, the boy comes to acquire his own gender identity and takes on his father's male qualities and characteristics, as well as those normally expected of males by society (Freud, 1925, 1931; Masters, Johnson, & Kolodny, 1995).

For girls, this stage is a different and in some ways a more difficult one as described in Box 3.2.

Questions and criticisms of Freud's theory have been raised because it overemphasizes biological determinants of sexual development, in part setting the stage for the nature versus nurture controversy. The John and Joan case was used to support nurture over nature and as evidence for the malleability of sexual identity and, thus, that anatomy is *not* destiny. ("Anatomy *Is* Destiny," 1997). Many textbooks and instructors have continued to cite this case in support of this theory, even though John's reversion to his male self demonstrates that so many important aspects of sexual differentiation are indeed biologically determined (Diamond & Sigmundson, 1997; Holden, 1997; Reiner, 1997). The consequences of this are major for, as we will see later in this chapter, many babies are born with ambiguous genitalia and internal sexual organs. And, while the policy has been to surgically alter these infants, current reassessment of this practice is occurring. For new data increasingly show that sexual anatomy and its appearance may be less critical than the prenatal hormonally differentiated brain. The psychosexual neutrality or plasticity "gate" that Money (1975) postulated to stay open for at least a year after birth (discussed earlier) may in fact have a much narrower window early in embryonic life when intrauterine hormone exposure virilizes or feminizes the brain and determines sexual dimorphism.

SEX DETERMINATION, DIFFERENTIATION, AND PREGNANCY

How and by what processes do males become males and females become females? And what consequences arise if the process goes awry?

Reproduction and therefore the survival of the species are the evolutionary goal of all organisms.

BOX 3.2 _____

Freud on a Girl's Resolution of Her Electra Complex

According to Freud, for girls, this stage in her development is a different and in some ways a more difficult one. It begins with the girl's recognition that she does not possess a penis. Realizing the superiority of the male because he has a penis and the inferiority of her clitoris, she becomes envious and feels cheated, developing **penis envy.** The girl believes that she originally had a penis but that it was cut off. She blames her mother and begins to reject her and turns to her father.

The girl subsequently forms the opposite version of the Oedipus complex, the **Electra complex** (named after a myth about a Greek princess who helped to kill her mother). As she passes through her Electra complex, the girl develops incestuous feelings for her father. Freud postulates that these feelings derive from her wish to be impregnated by him as a substitute for a penis that she can never have. The girl's resolution of her Electra complex is not as complete as the boy's resolution of the Oedipus complex, and because of this her development is less adequate. According to Freud, for the rest of her life she remains immature compared to men, with feelings of jealousy and inferiority because she does not have a penis (Freud, 1924, 1925, 1931).

Freud's views on the origin of the differences between male and female and on the nature of female personality are primarily biological, relying on anatomical differences. In 1924, Freud wrote that "[T]he feminist demand for equal rights for the sexes does not take us far, for the morphological distinction is bound to find expression in psychical development. 'Anatomy is destiny', to vary a saying of Napoleon's" (Freud, 1924).*

*The paraphrase of Napoleon's epigram can be found in a paper by Freud (1912) on the psychology of love.

Species that do not have effective reproductive mechanisms will not survive very long. There are many factors that affect the process of becoming female or male. As shown in Figure 3.1, the stage is set with chromosomes and genes.

FIGURE 3.1   Chromosomes and Genes

Chromosomes and Genes

Simple organisms such as amoeba and paramecia reproduce by splitting in two to create a pair that is genetically identical to the parent or original organism before division. More complex organisms, including humans, reproduce by combining genetic material of both parents to create an offspring. Each parent donates a reproductive cell known as a gamete or germ cell; the male contributes a **sperm** cell and the female an **ovum** or egg cell. These two cells combine or fuse to create a single cell, which will develop into the offspring. One of the benefits of this reproductive process is that, when genetic material from different cells is combined, genetic diversity is increased and the transmission or inheritance of undesirable traits to the ensuing offspring is lessened or avoided.

Sexual determination and differentiation are an intricate process that is *only initiated* at the time of conception and conception is just the first part of the process to determine the sex and sexual development of the offspring. Every cell in our bodies, other than the sperm and egg (ova), contains two sets of **chromosomes** in its nucleus arranged in pairs (called *diploid*)—23 from the mother and 23 from the father—

making a total of 46 chromosomes. The sperm and ova have only one set of 23 chromosomes. Twenty-two pairs of the chromosomes appear identical and are known as autosomes (independent), which determine the organism's physical development independently of its sex. The twenty-third pair is the sex chromosomes, which will initiate the process toward development of a male or female. The female is represented by the X chromosome and the male by the Y chromosome. The cells of females all contain two chromosomes of one type, XX; the cells of males have one of each, X and Y. The presence of the Y chromosome differentiates the male from the female. The female always contributes an X chromosome. The male can contribute either an X or a Y. If the male contributes an X chromosome, the offspring is destined to be female with a pair of XX chromosomes; if a Y chromosome is contributed, the offspring is destined to be male with an XY chromosome. The functional unit of the chromosome is the gene, and every chromosome consists of several thousands of genes (Carroll & Wolpe, 1996; Hunter, 1995; Masters et al., 1995; Schatten & Schatten, 1983). The genetic information that controls the development of an organism is contained in the DNA that make up these chromosomes, as seen in Figure 3.2.

The production of the gametes, the male and female reproductive cell or sperm and ova (gamete is from the Greek *gamos* meaning *marriage*), differs from that of the somatic cells of the body, each with their 23 pairs of chromosomes. If the gametes too had 23 pairs of chromosomes they would, on merging, produce an organism with 46 pairs or 92 chromosomes. The gametes are produced by the division of special cells in the **ovaries** and **testes** and result in cells that have only one-half the normal number of chromosomes, called haploid cells (in contrast to diploid cells with 23 pairs). In the male, the division of special cells into sperm cells results in one-half of the sperm cells having an X chromosome and the other half a Y chromosome. In the female, division will result in each half of the ova having an X chromosome. Therefore, instead of 23 *pairs* of chromosomes, sperm and ova contain only 23 *single* chromosomes, one member of each pair. An ovum is the largest cell in the human body, approximately the

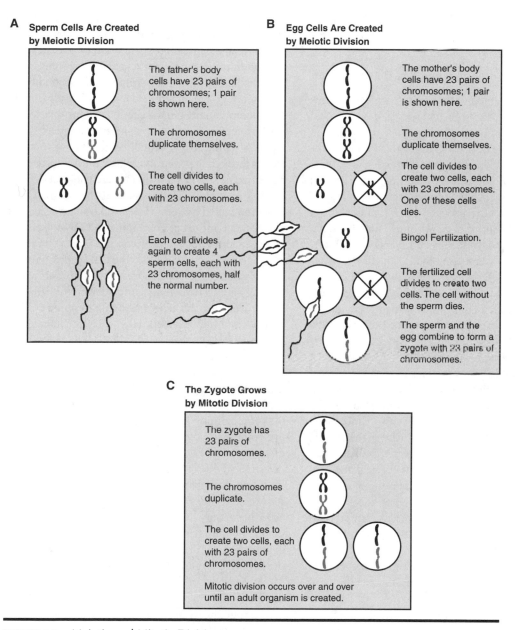

FIGURE 3.2   Meiotic and Mitotic Division

Source: From *Biopsychology* (4th ed.) (p. 36), by John P. J. Pinel, 2000, Boston: Allyn & Bacon. Copyright © 2000 by Allyn & Bacon. Reprinted by permission.

size of the head of a pin. Its yolk contains nutrients to sustain its growth for a few days. On the other hand, sperm are one of the smallest cells in the body and swim by lashing their long tails back and forth to propel them forward (flagellation). The testes produce billions of cells across the life cycle of the male

(Carroll & Wolpe, 1996; Rathus, Nevid, & Fichner-Rathus, 1997).

Fertilization, Conception, and Sex Determination

Fertilization, the union of the sperm and egg, requires the production of ova (eggs) and sperm. It is estimated that at birth about 400,000 unripe ova are present in the female ovary. The process of fertilization, conception, and sexual determination is a complex one. Masters et al. (1995) and Schatten and Schatten (1983) have provided an excellent review and a detailed description of this entire process. Each ova contains a different assortment of chromosomes, thus having a tremendous potential for genetic diversity in the offspring, especially when combined with genetic material of the male. After puberty, on about the fourteenth day of the menstrual cycle, one ovary will produce a ripened ovum each month, which is then gently drawn from the surface of the ovary into the Fallopian tube by the movement of cilia (tiny hairlike structures). If fertilization occurs, it is usually in the upper part of the Fallopian tube, not in the uterus. If the egg is not fertilized, it disintegrates in about 48 hours. After ejaculation into the **vagina,** healthy sperm swim rapidly into the female's reproductive system. Although as many as 200 million or more sperm are in the vagina, only about a few thousand ever reach the Fallopian tubes and only about 200 actually get near the egg. Most sperm spill out of the vagina or clump together and are immobilized, and never reach the female's cervix. Others are damaged or enter the empty Fallopian tube. This appears to be nature's way to assure that only the healthiest sperm get a chance to fertilize the egg. The Y sperm have been shown to move faster than the X sperm, thus increasing their chances of reaching an ovum.

Sperm can stay in the reproductive tract for several hours in a process called **capacitation** that enables the sperm to penetrate the egg. During capacitation, sperm secrete a chemical (acrosin) that dissolves the **zona pellucida,** the jellylike coating around the egg. The egg can enhance this process by embracing the sperm with tiny outgrowths called microvilli on its surface. The egg pulls the sperm inside via these microvilli and moves its nucleus to meet that of the sperm. To prevent penetration by other sperm (polyspermy), an electrical block, temporary but rapid, occurs within thousandths of a second once the sperm attaches itself to the ova's surface. The second block comes about when microscopic vesicles from the ova's membrane begin to secrete proteins that form a hard protective coat that pushes all the other sperm away. After the sperm actually enters the egg, it penetrates through the ova's cytoplasm until it locates the nucleus. The sperm's movements are controlled by the beating of its tail. The nucleus of the ova has been shown to quickly migrate toward the sperm. The two nuclei meet and fuse, combining the DNA from the mother and the father. The intricate process of fertilization may take at least 24 hours. It begins with the first contact that the sperm makes with the surface of the egg, and fertilization is not considered to have taken place until the genetic material from the egg and sperm combine (Masters et al., 1995; Schatten & Schatten, 1983).

Upon fertilization, a single cell is produced—the **zygote.** The zygote contains 23 chromosomes contributed by the sperm and 23 from the egg. These 46 chromosomes with their genetic material will initiate the programming for inherited characteristics such as eye color, hair color, skin color, and blood type. Two of these chromosomes, the sex chromosomes, will determine the sex of the developing embryo. A zygote with two X chromosomes is destined to become a female; a zygote with one X and one Y, a male. Since eggs have only X chromosomes, it is the genetic nature of the sperm penetrating and activating the egg that is the primary determining factor of the sex of the resulting zygote, as shown in Figure 3.2 (Hunter, 1995; Masters et al., 1995; Schatten & Schatten, 1983).

About 30 to 36 hours after fertilization takes place in the Fallopian tube, the single-celled zygote starts to divide, first into two cells, then the two cells into four cells, and so on. Division continues, forming smaller and smaller cells that increase in number. This small mass is called a *morula.* It begins to travel down the Fallopian tube toward the **uterus,** propelled by cilia (hairlike structures) of the Fallopian tube, and will reach it in about 5 to 7 days. Once it enters the uterus, the morula implants itself in the lining of the uterus where it will continue to develop and receive nourishment from the placenta, which is a mass of tissues formed on the wall of the uterus through which the fetus will receive nutrients and oxygen and through which it will eliminate its waste products. Once the zygote is implanted in the uterus, **conception** is complete. This product of conception is known as the *conceptus.* For the first eight weeks of pregnancy or gestation, the conceptus is called an **embryo.** From the ninth week until birth it is called a **fetus** (Carroll & Wolpe, 1996; Masters et al., 1995). "Fertilization is the riskiest of all biological processes. No other basic, necessary physiological mechanism is so chancy, so fragile, and so clearly a matter of life

or death. If successful, the union of sperm and egg bridges the generations and ensures survival of the species" (Schatten & Schatten, 1983, p. 34).

Striking changes take place during pregnancy in both the embryo or fetus and the mother to be. The nine months of gestation are divided into three-month periods called **trimesters.** The process from fertilization to implantation in the uterus is shown in Figure 3.3.

Sexual Differentiation and Pregnancy

When conception is complete, the sex of the embryo is determined. As we said earlier, if an egg is fertilized by a Y-bearing sperm, the fetus is destined to become a male; if by an X chromosome, a female.

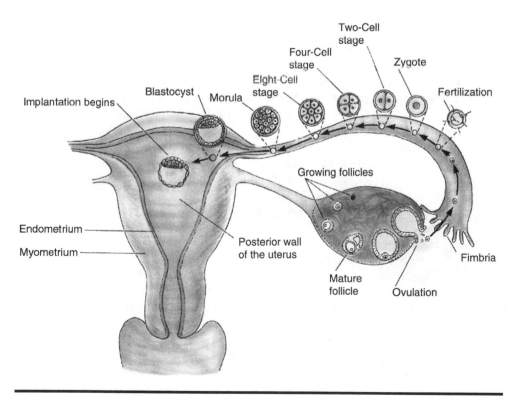

FIGURE 3.3 The Ovarian Cycle, Conception, and the Early Days of the Germinal Stage
Source: From *Human Sexuality in a World of Diversity* (p. 307), by S. A. Rathus, J. S. Nevid, and L. Fichner-Rathus, 1997, Boston: Allyn & Bacon. Copyright © 1997 by Allyn & Bacon. Reprinted by permission.

Sex determination is not enough, however. There is a significant amount of differentiation necessary to complete what we now recognize as the adult male or female. When the genetic material from each parent is combined, sexual differentiation leads to the specific physical differences between males and females. This process is essentially controlled by genetic and hormonal mechanisms. Although genetic coding has predestined the embryo to become a male or female, prior to the differentiation process the fetus is sexually neutral. During the first weeks of development, the male and female embryos are anatomically identical and undifferentiated. By the fifth and sixth weeks of pregnancy, two primitive gonads begin to form. They are bipotential; that is, they can develop into ovaries or testes. Two paired primitive duct systems also develop that will form in both male and female embryos—the Müllerian ducts and the Wolffian ducts. At this point, differentiation appears to depend on the male. For the testes to develop, another step in genetic control must take place. It is currently known that the Y chromosome carries a sex-determining gene, the H-Y gene, which produces an antigen (the H-Y antigen) that stimulates the transformation of the undifferentiated gonads into testes. If the H-Y antigen is not present, the primitive gonads will always develop into ovaries. Other proteins along the Y chromosome have also been hypothesized to initiate the testes-forming process, but these mechanisms are still poorly understood. It has been generally considered that female differentiation is the "default" pathway, because feminization occurs only in the absence of a proper Y chromosome (Hunter, 1995; Ohno, 1979; Rathus, Nevid, & Fichner-Rathus, 1997).

Once the testes begin to develop, other aspects of differentiation occur at three different levels: the internal sex structures, the external genitals, and the brain. These are predominantly controlled by hormones. And even if the sex chromosome pattern is that of the male, XY with 46 chromosomes, without a sufficient amount of the male hormone testosterone at the critical time, anatomic development will be female. Such abnormalities will be discussed later in this chapter.

Internal Sexual Structures.   By the seventh to eighth week in most males, the testes begin to develop. The newly forming testes begin to secrete two different chemicals. One chemical, a Müllerian duct-inhibiting substance, causes substantial shrinking of the ducts, which almost disappear instead of developing into female internal organs. The male hormone **testosterone,** an **androgen,** is the second substance to be secreted and is the principal hormone produced by the testes. Testosterone stimulates the development of the Wolffian ducts into internal male organs: the epididymis, vas deferens, seminal vesicles, and the ejaculatory ducts. In certain tissues, testosterone is then converted to or acts like a prohormone for the formation of dihydrotestosterone, which results in the development of the penis, scrotum, and prostate.* Testosterone and dihydrotestosterone are androgens, hormones that stimulate masculinization (Carroll & Wolpe, 1996).

In contrast, female development does not appear to depend on hormones, but only on the lack of testosterone. Ovaries develop about the twelfth week of gestation, but even if this is delayed the Müllerian duct system will continue its development into a uterus, Fallopian tubes, and part of the vagina. Without sufficient amounts of testosterone, the Wolffian system in the now designated female will shrink with only tiny remnants remaining. By the fourteenth week of gestation, there is a clear difference in the internal structure of the male and female embryo.

At present, it seems that female sexual differentiation does not depend on hormones or even genetic control. Hunter (1995) has speculated about the knowledge of the female differentiation pathway: "maleness tends to be given special prominence in discussions of mammalian sexual differentiation, with femaleness being treated essentially as the permissive, secondary or alternative condition (i.e., the default pathway) in the absence of the prior action of any male-determining sequences" (Hunter, 1995, p. 58).

*Testosterone and other androgens are secreted in varying amounts by the ovaries and the adrenal cortex, as well as by the testes, and serve different functions at different stages of life (Gilman, Rall, Nies, & Taylor, 1990).

He is hopeful that this generalization may be modified and more consideration given to explore the positive steps involved in the formation of the ovary, a specific process deriving from gene-regulated mechanisms, although occurring slightly later than for the male. The course of development of the internal sexual structures is seen in Figure 3.4.

External Genitals and Hormones. The external genitals for both male and female develop from the

FIGURE 3.4 Development of Internal Reproductive Systems

Source: From *Biopsychology* (4th ed.) (p. 51), by John P. J. Pinel, 2000, Boston: Allyn & Bacon. Copyright © 2000 by Allyn & Bacon. Reprinted by permission.

same tissue. Male and female organs that develop from the same tissue are known as *homologous* organs.

In the seventh week of gestation, the external genitals of both male and female still look the same. The undifferentiated tissue from which genitalia will develop exists as a mound of skin or tubercle beneath the umbilical cord. In females, the external genitals develop under the influence of female hormones now beginning to be produced by the placenta and by the mother. The clitoris, vulva, and remaining sections of the vagina can be seen by the eighth week. In the male, stimulation by androgens beginning with the eighth week causes the folds of tissue that would develop into vaginal lips in the female to grow together to form the cylindrical shaft of the penis. The tissue that would develop into the clitoris in the female now develops into the glans of the penis in the male. Other surrounding tissue differentiates into the outer vaginal lips in the female or the scrotum in the male which will eventually contain the testes.

Ovaries and testes develop first in the abdomen during fetal life and remain there through early development. The ovaries begin to descend into the pelvis and testes into the scrotum when the child is about five years of age. The development of external genitalia is seen in Figure 3.5.

Hormones play a crucial role in the development of males and females. Endocrine glands like the gonads begin to secrete hormones directly into the bloodstream, which are then carried to the target organs. For example, the ovaries produce **estrogen** and **progesterone,** the two major female hormones. Estrogen is critical for the development of female sexual characteristics throughout fetal development and in later life, while progesterone acts to regulate the menstrual cycle and, when the female reaches puberty, prepares the uterus for implantation of the embryo and pregnancy. The testes produce androgens (e.g., testosterone), also critical for the male. A male fetus will develop female characteristics if androgens are not secreted at the correct time or if the fetus, due to some defect, is insensitive to androgens.

Brain Differentiation and Dimorphism. Differentiation of the male and female brain begins during prenatal life beginning at about 12 weeks. Hormones in the blood of the fetus have a critical and timely influence. Much of our evidence comes from experiments on animals in which fetal and brain development can be monitored and the influence of hormones can be measured directly. One of the most important structural differences between male and female brains is in the number and location of certain types of nerve connections (synapses) in the hypothalamus. In prenatal sexual differentiation, in the presence of androgen stimulation the brain develops in a male pattern. In the absence of androgen stimulation, the brain develops in a female direction. This hormonal programming starts to take place during prenatal life and determines the type of patterning and function of the hypothalamus and the pituitary gland. Thus, females will have a cyclic sex hormone production and menstrual cycles, while males will have a generally constant level of hormone production. Therefore, female fertility becomes cyclic, whereas male fertility is continuous. Prenatal hormone effects on the developing brain may also influence later behaviors, such as sexual behavior, assertiveness, and aggression. However, the precise nature of these effects and how they come about are unclear (Goldman, 1978; McEwen, 1981; Rubin, Reinisch, & Haskett, 1981).

In the introduction to this chapter, we reviewed the classic case of John and Joan and the final outcome of this case of sex reassignment. The significance of prenatal hormone exposure to the developing brain was one aspect that was not considered at the time that the decision was made to feminize John. Now we know more about the implications of brain development as it is influenced by the intrauterine hormonal milieu. Sexual dimorphism in the brain was first reported by Raisman and Field (1971). More information has emerged since that time, as indicated in this section, and will be discussed further in other sections of the chapter. However, from our review of sexual determination and differentiation, it should be understood that the structure that may be critical for psychosexual development and adaptation is not anatomy—but the brain.

Pregnancy. The length of pregnancy ranges from 36 to 38 weeks and is divided into 3-month (12-week) periods or trimesters.

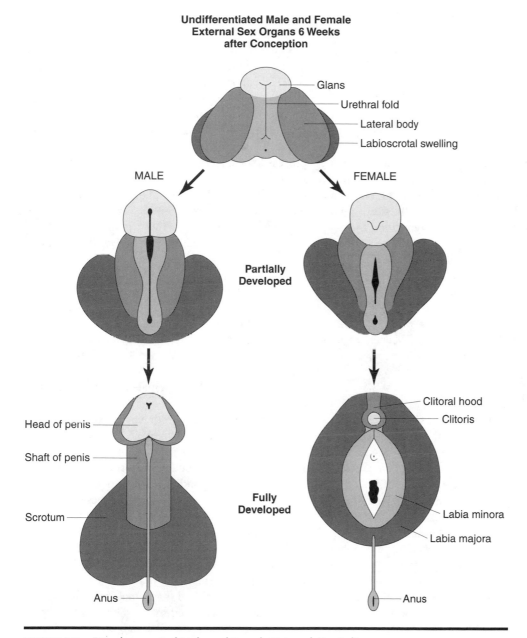

FIGURE 3.5 Development of Male and Female External Genitalia

Source: From *Biopsychology* (4th ed.) (p. 52), by John P. J. Pinel, 2000, Boston: Allyn & Bacon. Copyright © 2000 by Allyn & Bacon. Reprinted by permission.

By the end of the first trimester, the fetus definitely resembles a very small infant. It is about 10 centimeters (4 inches) long and weighs about 19 grams (2/3 ounce). From the end of the twelfth week, fetal development consists of the enlargement and differentiation of the already existing structures.

By the end of the fourteenth week (now the second trimester), movements or "quickening" of the fetus are felt, and by the eighteenth week, the fetal heartbeat can be heard by the physician. During the twentieth week, the fetus begins to open its eyes, and in the twenty-fourth week, it becomes light sensitive and can hear sounds. Movements become more vigorous and the fetus displays sleep and wake periods.

By the third trimester, the fetus develops fat pads and its skin becomes wrinkled and is covered with fine downlike hair, which will disappear before birth. In the seventh month, the fetus turns in the uterus and presents a head-down position in preparation for delivery. If it does not turn, then delivery will be a *breech* presentation (feet first) that will require special skills by the obstetrician during delivery to rotate the infant to a head-down position. By the time of delivery, the average full-term normal infant weighs 3300 grams (7.5 pounds) and is an average of 50 centimeters (20 inches) long (Carroll & Wolpe, 1996; Masters et al., 1995).

Sexual Selection

The possibility of influencing the sex of a fetus has intrigued women and men throughout time. The historical literature abounds with techniques recommended to control the sex of offspring. The ancient Greeks, among them Pythagoras (580–500 B.C.E.), thought in a sexist manner that the noble parts of the fetus derived from male semen, while the base or coarse parts of the fetus derived from female semen. The Greek physician Hippocrates and philosopher Democritus of Abdera, both of whom lived between 460 and 370 B.C.E., had specific assumptions about how sex was determined. Hippocrates believed that the male fetus formed on the right side of the womb and the female on the left. Democratis believed that each testis played an important role in sexual determination; females originated from the left testis and males from the right (Cadden, 1993; Hunter, 1995). According to Mittwoch (1977), this distinction between right and left influenced and indeed led to the general concept of *rightness* being associated with maleness and *leftness* being associated with females, and with the usual sexist attributes. This led to recommendations for special positions during intercourse.

The Hippocratic corpus (a collection of writings by physicians during Hippocrates' time that also claims to include some of those by Hippocrates) held the belief that both parents contribute seed arising from all parts of their bodies to form the fetus, a process known as *pangenesis.* Thus, at the time, this theory explained the resemblance of the offspring to their parents and other members of the family. Another view of the ancient Greeks, which may also have been attributed to Hippocrates, is the belief in two seeds, one contributed by each parent. The philosopher Aristotle (384–322 B.C.E.) also held specific beliefs about reproduction. First, in contrast to the Hippocratic corpus, Aristotle believed that only one seed was necessary for reproduction and that was from the male. Aristotle designated different values based on the poles of temperatures; warm is better than cool; dry is better than wet. In application to sex differences, the male, who is warm, became the superior sex. For Aristotle, the female is cooler, which immediately earned her a lower place in the natural order, and her lack of warmth was responsible for the difference in her reproductive role. Because males are warmer, they have sufficient heat to process their nutrients into semen; females, according to Aristotle, lack sufficient heat and can only produce menstrual blood, which, however, has characteristics that help to form the fetus. Aristotle also held other sexist attitudes. His warm and cold poles of temperature, which defined males as superior and females as inferior, also translate to ability and activity on the part of the male and the opposite, inability and passivity, for the female. Aristotle believed that females were a type of monstrosity or deformed males. Females are representative of either "the weakness of the father's seed or the intractability of the mother's material or some external condition which has, by default, produced a daughter" (Cadden, 1993, p. 24). Aristotle also thought that if the parents had intercourse in a wind coming from the north, a male fetus would form and, in a south wind, a female would result.

Throughout the span of history, many of these concepts persisted. During the late Middle Ages, varieties of these same doctrines, especially those of Aristotle, continued to be espoused in modified forms. Similar beliefs and other legends appeared throughout the Oriental world of Persia, Mesopotamia, and India. Down through the centuries, from ancient Greece until the nineteenth century, there was little progress in the scientific understanding of the reproductive process and sexual determination and so these beliefs were paramount. Hunter (1995) details the very gradual development of knowledge about reproduction by physicians, scientists, and philosophers across the centuries. One interesting concept is the *preformist* or *ovist* theory of reproduction in which the offspring is considered to be already preformed in the egg. The view held by eminent anatomists (e.g., William Harvey and Reguier de Graaf during the seventeenth century) was that all living things derive from eggs. This view held until the invention of the microscope and the discovery of sperm. In the ensuing centuries there continued to be increasing research into the anatomical and physiological bases of the reproductive process. We now have a much more precise understanding of this process, with meticulous details on reproduction.

The fascination with and interest in sexual determination and selection have continued. In many countries, including Western countries, some myths also persist. For example, many men still believe that it is the woman who determines the sex of the fetus, notwithstanding the available knowledge that only the male has the Y chromosome. In these groups, women who give birth to females are blamed for their baby's sex, and in some societies men divorce their wives and marry other women in the hope of siring a male heir (Masters et al., 1995). There is some evidence that creating an acidic or alkaline environment in the vagina will affect the type of sperm (X or Y) to reach the ova in the Fallopian tube. Having intercourse at specific days prior to ovulation is also considered to favor the fertilization of a female or male. Other formulas and diet regimes regularly appear in the literature and will doubtless keep doing so.

However, there are now known scientific and medical reasons for sexual selection. Some inherited diseases may affect one sex more than the other (e.g., hemophilia affects more males than females). With the development of amniocentesis, performed around the sixteenth week of gestation, the sex of the fetus can easily be determined, although such information is not routinely provided. While this procedure is necessary for determining the risk of chromosomal abnormalities in pregnant women over age 30, it also has the advantage of discovering sex-linked abnormalities. The question of abortion in such cases, as well as the aborting of a fetus of an unpreferred sex, has raised moral, ethical, and social issues in many countries. In some countries such as China, where a one-child policy is in effect in an effort to control overpopulation, the incidence of infanticide, primarily of females, is thought to be used to allow for the subsequent birth of a male child. Carroll and Wolpe (1996) report that as of 1992 some 60 million babies, all female, fail to be accounted for in China, India, Pakistan, Bangladesh, Nepal, Egypt, and western Asia. It is believed that female infanticide as well as neglect to the point of death for female babies, who are given less food and medical treatment in these countries, are the reasons for the inability to account for these female babies.

An American volunteer working at an orphanage in Guangzhou, China, was devastated when she observed the bodies of abandoned girls carted away in wheelbarrows to be disposed of by the garbage collectors. Reports are that the government and State Family Planning Commission in China are now trying to stop the situation (Herbert, 1997).

In 1998, a group of physicians at a fertility center in Virginia reported that they are now able to "stack the odds" that a couple can have a baby of the sex that they prefer. This group has developed a DNA detector technique for sorting the X- from the Y-bearing sperm based on the amount of DNA present. The Y-bearing sperm have less DNA than X-bearing sperm. The physicians at the center report a high success rate in sex selection. The couples that they have helped range from those who have a sexual preference in order to avoid transmitting sex-linked genetic diseases to those who already have a child of one sex and would like one of the other sex. This technique has raised questions about the ethics of such selection procedures and the safety in the long term of such techniques (Kolata, 1998).

WHAT HAPPENS IF SOMETHING GOES AWRY?

Incidents of abnormal sexual development have been noted since ancient times, but without any understanding of their origin. These disorders occur not only in humans but also have their counterparts in diverse animal species (Hunter, 1995). Early observations focused on the abnormal appearance of the external genitalia and later included the gonads. As science and technology advanced, we have gained a better comprehension of the basis of many of these sexual abnormalities. Prenatal development and differentiation are the consequence of carefully coordinated developmental processes. Each stage of prenatal development carries the risk of irregularities that can result in abnormal or atypical sexual differentiation. Three major causes of abnormal differentiation have been determined: sex chromosome disorders, hormonal or genetic conditions, and exposure of the fetus to drugs that were given to the mother during her pregnancy or drugs that she ingested by herself. We will review here some of the major disorders that can occur.

Sex Chromosome Disorders

As described earlier, there are normally 46 chromosomes (23 pairs), which include one pair of sex chromosomes, XX or XY. An infant can be born with one or more extra sex chromosomes or with only one sex chromosome. This abnormality takes place after fertilization and during the meiosis (cell division) stage when the fertilized ovum begins to divide. These disorders have a variety of effects on physical appearance, may lead to different physical and psychological clinical syndromes, and can affect sexual behavior.

Klinefelter's Syndrome. This syndrome occurs when a genetic male has an extra X chromosome. This happens when an ovum with an extra X chromosome is fertilized by a Y sperm, resulting in an XXY em-

bryo and giving the offspring a total of 47 instead of 46 chromosomes. The Y chromosome then triggers the development of male genitalia, but because of the extra X chromosome the genitalia are prevented from developing normally. Because testosterone production is reduced, men with Klinefelter's syndrome may have a small penis and small testes. Surface virilization, including pubic and axillary hair, are usually normal. These men are usually tall with a feminized body shape and most often develop gynecomastia (enlarged breasts). They appear to have a low sex drive, may be impotent, and seem to be passive, with low levels of ambition, which is thought to be due to their low testosterone levels. Klinefelter's syndrome is found in about 1 in 700 live births, but is not usually detected until puberty or early adulthood. Testosterone therapy, especially during adolescence, will improve the condition and facilitate the development of secondary sexual characteristics (Hunter, 1995; Masters et al., 1995).

Turner's Syndrome. This disorder has been viewed as the most common chromosome disorder in females. Although the incidence is 1 in 100 at conception, it drops significantly to 1 in 1,000 females at birth. It has been estimated that about 98 percent of embryos or fetuses with an X0 (zero) chromosomal constitution will not survive (Short, 1982). Turner's syndrome comes about when an ovum without any X chromosome is fertilized by an X sperm. This gives the offspring only 45 chromosomes and it is designated as X0. However, if an ovum without an X chromosome is fertilized by a Y chromosome, the ovum will die.

Although external genitalia appear normal in Turner's syndrome, the ovaries never develop properly and are called *streak gonads* (Hunter, 1995). The typical female with Turner's syndrome is short, perhaps due to abnormal bone growth, with skin folds over the neck that appear to be webbed. Birth marks on the skin are also common. Though external genitalia appear normal, menstruation is absent because the ovaries are nonfunctional, and therefore these females are sterile. There may also be abnormalities of the cardiovascular and lymphatic systems. Occasionally, however, menstruation and even pregnancy have been reported (Dewhurst, 1978; Weiss, 1971). Breast development and menstruation may be induced with hormone therapy, but the problems of height and infertility have not been successfully treated.

XYY Syndrome and XXX Syndrome. Chromosomal disorders in which there is an extra X or Y chromosome are rare. They occur at the time of fertilization, when a normal ovum with one X chromosome is fertilized by a sperm that has two Y chromosomes (XYY) or two XX chromosomes (XXX). An XXX condition can also come about when an ovum with two X chromosomes is fertilized by a normal sperm with an X chromosome. Although these individuals may grow up as normal males and females, they may have some genital abnormalities with decreased fertility or infertility. Some of these individuals may shows signs of slight mental retardation. There is at present no known treatment for these syndromes.

Genetic or Hormonal Conditions

Pseudohermaphroditism. A **pseudohermaphrodite** is one who is born with gonads (internal sex organs) that match her or his sex chromosomes, but whose genitals (external sex organs) appear to be that of the other sex. There are two categories of this condition.

Adrenogenital Syndrome (AGS). This type of *female* pseudohermaphrodite has ovaries, Fallopian tubes, a uterus, and a 46 XX chromosome constitution and has normal fertility potential, yet their genitals are masculinized. Masculinization of the genitals can range from mild enlargement of the clitoris to the formation of a penislike structure or even the development of a true penis. The labia may be fused, resembling a scrotum. The genitals appear to be so strongly male that the actual sex of the infant can be wrongly identified.

The most frequent cause of AGS, an inherited disorder, involves an enzyme block of the adrenal glands, resulting in the production of excessive amounts of androgens. When this happens, the female fetus is exposed to large or abnormal amounts of androgens at a crucial period of prenatal development. The genitals are masculinized to varying degrees depending on the amount of male hormone secreted. If

an early diagnosis is not made, the adrenal glands will continue their abnormal production of androgens, and masculinization will persist throughout the girl's development. If a diagnosis of AGS is made at birth or shortly thereafter, treatment can begin in early childhood so that normal androgen output can be attained. Plastic surgery can later modify the appearance of the genitals. Because the internal organs remain normal, fertility may also be normal and pregnancy may even be possible. Today, if a baby is born with questionable male genitals, a chromosome analysis can be easily carried out, thus assuring early treatment of this disorder.

Yet even with early treatment, the behavior of AGS girls may be somewhat different from that of normal girls. AGS girls may show a higher rate of "tomboyism." They may prefer boys to girls as playmates and show little interest in activities associated with girls: playing with dolls, playing house, and imitating the mother's activities. Although there is no problem with their gender identity, AGS females show delayed dating and may have considerable difficulty in establishing close relationships. The question of the incidence of bisexual or lesbian tendencies has been raised regarding AGS females (Carroll & Wolpe, 1996; Hoyenga & Hoyenga, 1993; Hunter, 1995; Masters et al., 1995).

Testicular Feminization Syndrome. This is a type of *male* pseudohermaphrodite and is an inherited condition in which testosterone and other androgens have no effect on the fetus. These androgen-insensitive male pseudohermaphrodites have a 46 XY chromosome pattern and have testes, but are born with female genitals. Even though testosterone secretion at the crucial time in neonatal development is normal, because the fetus is insensitive to it, differentiation occurs as it does in females, with the formation of a clitoris, labia, and vagina. However, in this type of disorder, the fetal testes do produce the Müllerian-inhibiting substance (to which the fetus is sensitive). The Müllerian ducts will shrink and prevent the growth of a uterus and Fallopian tubes, but a vagina ending in a blind pouch can develop.

At birth, the testicular feminized infant resembles a normal female unless the testes have descended into the labia and can be identified on examination of the groin. These children are usually reared as girls with normal development until around puberty. These "girls" have a very feminine appearance; that is, they have physical characteristics highly prized by society. The lack of menstruation brings about medical investigation and a diagnosis is made. There can even be some breast development in these adolescents because the testosterone produced metabolizes into estrogen to which the body is sensitive. When testicular feminization is extreme, some feel it is best that these children be brought up as girls.

A second type of male pseudohermaphroditism is known as the *5-alpha-reductase syndrome* or the *Dominican Republic syndrome,* an endocrine defect referred to earlier in this chapter. In this disorder, an inherited enzyme defect in genetically 46 XY males results in improper formation of male genitalia, even though prenatal testosterone concentration is normal. This is an inherited condition due to a recessive gene. There is a lack of the enzyme that facilitates the conversion of testosterone to dihydrotestosterone, the androgen needed for closure of the scrotum and growth of the penis. Imperato-McGinley and her colleagues (1976) have been involved in studies of these children in the villages of the Dominican Republic. When these babies are born, they appear anatomically to be females, with normal internal sexual structures but a small, clitoris-like penis and incompletely formed scrotum resembling the labia. They are reared as girls. The parents are unaware that anything is wrong with these children. However, when these "girls" reach puberty, they develop male genitalia with all the secondary male sex characteristics and are then considered as true males. Despite being reared as females, in most of the cases their gender identity changes to male. Thus, the forces of socialization have little effect when their hormones come into play at puberty. Imperato-McGinley and her coworkers believe that these studies show that even when a person is reared in a manner counter to her or his biological sex, biological sex will prevail if normal hormones are produced at puberty (Imperato-McGinley et al., 1979). Imperato-McGinley's findings also fail to support Money's earlier theories of nurture and lend support to

Diamond's biased interaction model concepts, both of which were discussed in the beginning of this chapter (Pinel, 1993; Unger & Crawford, 1996).

True Hermaphroditism or Intersexuality.   This disorder is defined as the "possession, at birth, of both male and female characteristics in the gonads and/or in the internal or external genitalia" (Jacobs, 1969, p. 214). The word *hermaphrodite* comes from the Greek god Hermes and Aphrodite, the goddess of sexual love and beauty. According to the Greek legend, Hermaphroditus, the son of Hermes and Aphrodite, became half female and half male when his body fused with that of a nymph with whom he fell in love.

The condition is exceptionally rare. Such individuals are born with both testicular and ovarian tissue, with a variable distribution of each type of tissue. Combinations of these tissues vary; there may be one testis and one ovary or a mixture of both ovarian and testicular tissue (ovotestis). When the gonads are well defined as an ovary or testis, the ovary tends to be found on the left side and the testis on the right. In extreme cases, both testes and ovaries are fully formed.

In the majority of cases, the chromosome constitution of true hermaphrodites is 46 XX compared with 46 XY chromosomes. Since there is testicular tissue, true hermaphrodites usually show signs of masculinization in their external genitalia. Yet, development of breast tissue can appear at puberty. A uterus is frequently present with a Fallopian tube on one side and a vas deferens and epididymis on the other. Both male and female duct systems may also be present on opposite sides of the body. The extent of the development of these structures depends on the amount of ovarian and testicular tissue and the extent of hormone action during fetal life. Although the chromosome constitution of these individuals may be female (46XX) or male (46XY), their sex is considered ambiguous and so too is their gender identity (Hunter, 1995).

It is difficult to estimate the percentage of intersexuals. Fausto-Sterling (1993) quotes Money as suggesting that intersexuals may constitute as much as 4 percent of the population. In her article "The Five Sexes," Fausto-Sterling includes both the true and the pseudohermaphrodites. Her "five sexes" include male; female; true hermaphrodites, whom she calls *herms;* the pseudohermaphrodites described previously: *merms,* males who have testes and some type of female genitalia but no ovaries; and *ferms,* females who have ovaries with some type of male genitalia but no testes. Fausto-Sterling traces the history of hermaphroditism and shows concern about surgical sex assignment or correction when these conditions are diagnosed. She feels that these individuals are compelled by society to choose an established gender role and stay with it. This pattern developed in Europe during the Middle Ages and has lasted until the present time. "For questions of inheritance, legitimacy, paternity, succession to title, and eligibility for certain professions, modern Anglo-Saxon legal conditions require that newborns be registered as male or female" (Fausto-Sterling, 1993, p. 22). Fausto-Sterling raises questions about why this is necessary and points to an apparent cultural need to keep a clear and consistent division between the two sexes. But in her ideal world, intersexuals would be permitted to develop as such with their own interests and abilities. For her, a new ethic of medical treatment would come about where oppositions—"patient and physician, parent and child, male and female, heterosexual and homosexual—would be dissolved" (Fausto-Sterling, 1993, p. 24).

While Fausto-Sterling's ideal world seems far away, a number of intersexuals who have had corrective surgery have found each other primarily through the Internet. They have joined together to protest surgical correction and want to establish a pattern whereby intersexuals will be free to grow and develop with their combination of male and female characteristics and make their own way. It is a group that we shall certainly hear more from in the near future. The social, ethical, and psychological implications are certain to be brought before the public for discussion.

Prenatal Drug Exposure

Drugs taken at any time during pregnancy that can cross the placental barrier can cause damage to the embryo or fetus, which may have many serious consequences, including malformations called *teratogenic.* When pregnant women are given hormones for medical treatment, the hormones enter the circulation and cross the placental barrier. The embryo or fetus exposed to these hormones often suffers detrimental effects. For example, if a pregnant women is given male hormones or drugs mimicking male hormones, the AGS syndrome can result, depending on the amount of drug and the time of pregnancy during which the drugs are administered. Synthetic female hormones can result in malformation of the penis (Masters et al., 1995; Wilson, 1990). The behavior of these children may also be affected. Boys who were exposed to female hormones have been found to be lower in assertiveness and, compared with other males, have less athletic ability. They were perceived as less likely to indulge in physical activity than normal boys. Girls exposed to female hormones during gestation demonstrated heightened femininity (Ehrhardt, Grisanti, & Meyer-Bahlburg, 1977; Masters et al., 1995). More research is needed on available new drugs that may also affect the developing embryo and fetus. Antibiotics that cross the placental barrier may also have adverse effects on the embryo and fetus.

Alcohol. When a pregnant woman consumes alcohol, it circulates throughout her body and also through the fetus. Excessive and repeated amounts of alcohol throughout pregnancy may result in the neonate developing withdrawal symptoms. Alcoholism can also result in vitamin depletion, biochemical imbalance, small-for-dates babies, premature births, or even prenatal death. Physical malformations can occur as part of the **fetal alcohol syndrome,** which include pre- and postnatal growth defects; small brain; joint, limb, or heart malformations; and, most critically, mental retardation (Carroll & Wolpe, 1996; Hyde, 1996b).

Other Addictive Drugs. Heroin, morphine, cocaine, amphetamine, and marijuana may also lead to consequences similar to the fetal alcohol syndrome. Many pregnant women are not single drug abusers but polydrug abusers, which places their babies at a very high risk for teratogenic and other defects. The question of whether cocaine abuse will affect the developing fetus has received positive and negative answers. Recent data suggest that cocaine, too, has adverse effects on the developing fetus. The effect of drugs taken by the father before conception is not as well documented as for the pregnant woman taking drugs, but recent work has suggested that damage to the sperm and their genetic material may occur, with serious effects on the embryo (Lester, Latasse, & Seifer, 1998).

SEXUAL ORIENTATION

Homosexuality and Heterosexuality

Sexual orientation, whether heterosexual, homosexual, or bisexual, is a set of complicated human emotions, cognitions, and behaviors with multiple psychological factors. Although sexual behavior has been speculated on and written about throughout history at least since the time of Aristotle, scientific studies of human sexual behavior only began to be conducted in the late nineteenth century. One of the most noted investigators of human sexual behavior was Alfred Kinsey. In the 1940s, he and his associates carried out a monumental study of human sexual behavior and published their results in two major volumes: *Sexual Behavior in the Human Male* (1948) and *Sexual Behavior in the Human Female* (1953). At the time that these publications appeared, most people considered (and many still consider) homosexual and heterosexual as two distinct categories. During his major study, Kinsey came to perceive heterosexual and homosexual orientation on a seven-point continuum. His *heterosexual–homosexual continuum* varied across seven points from "exclusively heterosexual" to "exclusively homosexual," with the category "equally heterosexual and homosexual" (bisexual) in the center (Kinsey et al., 1948, p. 373).

Defining Sexual Orientation. Sexual orientation refers to one's erotic attraction toward, and interests in developing loving relationships with, members of one's own or the opposite gender. A **heterosexual orientation** refers to an erotic attraction to, and pref-

erence for developing romantic relationships with, members of the opposite gender. A **homosexual orientation** refers to an erotic attraction to, and preference for developing romantic relationships with, members of one's own gender (Nevid et al., 1995, p. 272). A **bisexual** is a woman or man who is sexually oriented to persons of both genders.

Compared with other Western societies in the Netherlands, Germany, France, and the Scandinavian countries, attitudes toward homosexuality in the United States are negative. Many people in the United States hold pejorative attitudes toward homosexuality, although the efforts of groups such as the liberation movement for gay and lesbian civil rights have made inroads in changing public opinion. Such attitudes are considered *homophobic.* A homophobic person is one with an intense and illogical fear of gay men or lesbians and with negative and hostile attitudes and reactions to them. Many hate crimes have occurred against both gays and lesbians and have received nationwide publicity, such as the Matthew Shepard murder in Wyoming in 1998. Whether such media attention has increased or decreased homophobic feelings in this country remains to be studied.

Prevalence of Homosexuality. It is difficult to determine the percentage of gay men and lesbians in the United States not only due to differences in how one defines *homosexual* and *heterosexual,* but also because not all gay men and lesbians willingly report their sexual orientation.

Many surveys have been carried out over the past two decades, each with varying results. Reports on the gay and lesbian population have ranged from 4 to 17 percent (Greene, 1994c). In 1948, when Kinsey carried out his initial studies on white men, he and his colleagues reported that 10 percent of men between 16 and 35 years of age engaged in exclusively homosexual behavior for at least three years and that 4 percent engaged in such behavior throughout their life. About 37 percent of subjects reported at least one homosexual experience during adolescence or adulthood. In surveys of the female population, Kinsey and his colleagues found that about 19 percent of women by age 40 had at least one sexual experience with a member of the same sex and about 2 to 3 percent stated that they were lifelong lesbians (Kinsey et al., 1953). These data became the standard and for years were extensively quoted. At the time that Kinsey's study was published, it generated a storm of public criticism, which led to concerns about whether this type of research should be carried out. Many social scientists raised questions about the accuracy of the study and criticized how the survey samples were collected and analyzed.

A 1991 national representative survey of sexually active U.S. men between 20 and 39 years of age reported that as little as 2 percent had had sexual contact with members of the same sex over the past 10 years, with only about 1 percent stating that they were exclusively homosexual (Billy, Tanfer, Grady, & Klepinger, 1993). These data are remarkably consistent with other recently reported surveys conducted in France, Great Britain, Denmark, and other countries, including the Philippines and Thailand. The results of these surveys, especially in countries where homosexuality is not viewed with negativity or homophobia, seem to indicate that the prevalence of homosexuality and bisexuality may be less than is commonly assumed (see Diamond, 1993, for a review and comments on these studies).

Biological Theories of Homosexuality. In this section we will present theories and research about possible biological foundations of sexual orientation. In Chapter 8 we present a variety of nonbiological theories and additional studies on the determinants of sexual orientaion.

Are people born gay or straight? Why do people become gay or straight? When is sexual orientation determined? For virtually 100 years, homosexuality was considered an illness. Physicians classified homosexuality as a sickness or illness. Until 1973 the American Psychiatric Association listed homosexuality in the DSM-III (Diagnostic and Statistical Manual of Mental Disorders) as a disorder under Section V, Personality Disorders and Certain Other Nonpsychotic Mental Disorders. In 1973, the American Psychiatric Association voted to remove the category of homosexuality from the listing, deciding it was no

longer a psychiatric illness. Following this, in 1975, the American Psychological Association adopted the official policy that "homosexuality *per se* involves no impairment in judgement, stability, reliability, or general social and vocational capabilities and urged all mental health professionals to take the lead in removing the stigma of mental illness that has long been associated with gay and lesbian sexual orientations" (Committee on Lesbian and Gay Concerns [CLGC], 1986; Greene, 1994c, p. 1).

Although much research has been conducted to explain homosexuality, current research is focusing not only on the origins of homosexuality, but also on heterosexuality. As we review some of the theories of sexual orientation, you will see that we still do not know why people become homosexual, bisexual, or heterosexual. In addition, you will also realize that most of the research on homosexuality has been centered on gay men, with little research carried out on lesbian women.*

Genetic Aspects. In 1952, Kallman showed evidence for a genetic component of homosexuality. His study consisted of identical and fraternal male twins for which one of each pair was gay. He reported a surprising 100 percent concordance in the identical twins for homosexuality and only 12 percent for the fraternal twins (Kallman, 1952). This finding of 100 percent concordance is most unusual in the sciences, since studies rarely show such perfect agreement. Studies carried out to duplicate and replicate Kallman's findings were unsuccessful and his work was essentially discarded.

Some recent studies have again raised the question of the genetic aspects of homosexuality. Bailey and Pillard (1991) studied 115 male twin pairs with the adoptive siblings of these twins. These investigators reported that if one identical twin was gay the other twin was three times more likely to be gay in

*We have spoken with many lesbians and gay men and found that the gay community is divided in their opinion on whether homosexuality is innate or an individual choice. Regardless of the factors influencing sexual orientation, it is imperative that everyone be treated fairly regardless of orientation.

comparison with the nonidentical twins. In a subsequent study, Bailey, Pillard, Neale, and Agyei (1993) reported similar data for lesbian women. These findings argue in favor of the genetic aspects of sexual orientation. Yet, caution is urged about depending on such studies alone for closure on a theory. Moreover, the twin studies consisted of only males; not one pair of female twins, for which one of the pair was lesbian, was included.

Recently, studies at the National Cancer Institute have uncovered a region on the X chromosome that may contain one or more genes for homosexuality. Hamer, Hu, Magnusen, Hu, & Pattalucci (1993) studied 76 gay men and set up family trees for each in order to determine whether other family members on either the mother's or father's side had a homosexual orientation. They found 13.5 percent of brothers of homosexuals were also gay, a rate much higher than the 2 percent reported for the general population. The researchers also found that there were more gay relatives on the mother's side, which suggested that a biological disposition for homosexuality would be passed through the mother—an X-linked inheritance pattern. In additional studies of gay brothers, the researchers also found that in 33 of 40 sets of brothers there was a shared stretch of DNA on the long arm of the X chromosome. The researchers were very careful to point out that not all the pairs of subjects tested showed this linkage and that one gene for homosexuality cannot explain the origin of all male homosexuality (Pool, 1993). These findings have been reviewed and the experimental design criticized. Again, further research is needed to replicate these findings.

Neurological and Brain Aspects.   Although many parts of the brain are involved in mammalian sexual behavior, recent attention has come to focus on the hypothalamus. Research in this area has demonstrated that gonadotropin release is under the control of the hypothalamus. The hypothalamus in turn stimulates the anterior pituitary gland to release gonadotropins, which in turn effect the release of gonadal hormones (e.g., estrogen, testosterone). Research on the neural basis of sexual behavior has involved this brain area.

As discussed earlier in this chapter, the female hypothalamus is functionally different from the male hypothalamus in orchestrating the cyclic hormonal pattern in females and the steady hormonal pattern of males. It was thought that hormone release was controlled by the anterior part of the pituitary gland, but, in fact, the hypothalamus controls the cyclic versus steady-state hormone release from the pituitary. Raisman and Field (1971) discovered differences in the male and female hypothalamus, and then Gorski, Gordon, Shryne, and Southam (1978) found that a nucleus in the *medial preoptic area* of the rat hypothalamus was much larger in the male than the female. They called this nucleus the *sexually dimorphic nucleus.*

These nuclei in the rat are the same size at birth; in the male the nucleus grows at a rapid rate, but in the female it does not. It has been found that the size of the sexually dimorphic nucleus in the male rat is highly correlated with sexual activity. These differences have been found in other nonhuman species. In humans, nuclei in both the preoptic and anterior regions of the hypothalamus are considerably larger in males, but the difference is not seen until after about two years of age (Allen, Hines, Shryne, & Gorski, 1989; Hofman & Swaab, 1989; Swaab & Fliers, 1985).

The results of these studies have raised questions about whether differences in hypothalamic size between males and females are related in any way to sexual orientation. To explore these questions, LeVay (1991) analyzed and published the results of a postmortem neuroanatomical study of the brains of gay males and of males and females who were assumed to be heterosexual. LeVay's findings were in agreement with those of Allan, Hines, Shryne and Gorski: the *third interstitial nucleus of the anterior hypothalamus* (INAH3) was more than twice as large in heterosexual men than in heterosexual women and gay men.

These results, published in the journal *Science,* were widely reported in the press and generated positive and negative comments by both the heterosexual and gay communities. First, it will be important to determine whether these results are reliable and can be replicated by other investigators. This was a small group of subjects whose past histories are not known, except that many of the gay men died of AIDS. This is one reason that lesbians were not included in the study. These results should not be taken as proof that homosexuality results from a small INAH3 nucleus. It may be that a gay sexual orientation caused the small nucleus, rather than the opposite, or these findings may be in fact artifactual (Pinel, 1993). Although this is a potentially important scientific finding, its meaning is not clear and awaits further validation with carefully controlled studies.

Prenatal and Postnatal Hormonal Aspects.   Does homosexuality develop as a result of events during the prenatal period? Exposure to different drugs during fetal development, as discussed earlier, can result in a genetic female with male genitals and a genetic male with female genitals. Would such exposure during some stage of prenatal development affect sexual orientation (Hyde, 1996b)?

In view of the previous discussion of sexual dimorphism in the hypothalamus and the findings of LeVay, the earlier work of Ellis and Ames (1987) is relevant. According to their theory, there is a critical period between the middle of the second month to the middle of the fifth month of gestation for hypothalamic development. During this period they theorize that the hypothalamus develops and sexual orientation is determined. Ellis and Ames speculate about whether biological errors affecting hypothalamic development during this critical period could produce homosexuality. This would be a prenatal error affecting development, but would it affect only the hypothalamus or also other central nervous system structures which may or may not be involved in sexual orientation? Would this pertain only to gay men? What of lesbians? This raises the issue of whether the origins of sexual orientation in men are different from the origins of sexual orientation in women.

The effects of prenatal stress (and subsequent changes in hormone levels) have been studied in animals and humans. Some studies show that a substantial percentage of mothers of gay children experienced stress during their pregnancy, compared to mothers of

bisexual and heterosexual children, but other studies failed to replicate these findings.

It has also been speculated by many that homosexuality is associated with current hormone levels. Several studies have demonstrated that the circulating hormone levels of heterosexual women and men and gay women and men do not differ. Although some animal studies have shown an increase in homosexual offspring after prenatal treatment with hormones (Adkins-Regan, 1988; Baum, Erskine, Kornberg, & Weaver, 1990), studies in humans have had conflicting results. However, some support for this view has come from the work of Ehrhardt et al. (1985), who interviewed women whose mothers had been given diethylstilbestrol (synthetic estrogen) during pregnancy. These women reported that they were more sexually attracted to women when compared to control subjects. The investigators concluded that perinatal estrogen exposure seemed to encourage homosexuality in women, but it is not a strong effect because the sexual orientation in all but 1 of 30 subjects was heterosexual.

A review of these studies suggests that biology may play an important role in sexual orientation; however, we have found no *conclusive* body of evidence to support such a biological basis. Consideration of other theories of nonbiological determinants of sexual orientation are described in detail in Chapter 8.

Bisexuality

What is a bisexual individual? How do members of this group differ from gays, lesbians, and heterosexuals?

Defining Bisexuality.   A bisexual is a person whose sexual orientation is to the same and other gender. They are not exclusively homosexual nor are they exclusively heterosexual. On the Kinsey heterosexual–homosexual continuum scale described earlier, they would be included in three of Kinsey's ratings: more than incidentally homosexual, equally heterosexual and homosexual, and more than incidentally heterosexual. These persons are called bisexual or *ambisexual.*

Prevalence.   As with the gay and lesbian population, the incidence of bisexuals is difficult to establish, not only because of sampling methods and sources but because, like gay men and lesbians, bisexuals are identified typically by self-report. Because there are several types of bisexuals, bisexuality may be even more common than is usually thought, and perhaps more common than homosexuality. If we include in the definition of a bisexual a person who has had only incidental sexual contact with someone of the same sex, as well as with someone of the other sex, prevalence would then be even higher. Because of the lack of reliable data, estimates of bisexuality have ranged widely, from less than 5 percent to as much as 11 percent (Hill, 1989). Bisexuals may not be willing to acknowledge their sexual orientations because of the fear of reprisal by the communities in which they are accepted. Heterosexuals and gay men and lesbians are reported to be suspicious or antagonistic toward bisexual women and men. Many bisexuals who are predominantly heterosexual are married and do not want their sexual contacts with gays or lesbians revealed. Therefore, they would be much less willing to openly admit their bisexual orientation. In Latino communities with a strong machismo culture, same-sex contacts by males who are considered heterosexual are hidden and exposure is highly feared. Although it is acceptable for women in these countries to have close relationships with other women, lesbianism is even more restrictive than being gay is for men. Similar conditions almost certainly exist in Asian and other cultural groups in which gender roles are rigidly enforced. In the United States, these groups tend to assimilate into Anglo communities that have more liberal attitudes (Hyde, 1996a, 1996b).

Some bisexuals who have lived as heterosexuals report their first homosexual encounter during adulthood when they begin to have special emotional needs that seem to be best served by their own gender. This is especially prevalent among women (Blumstein & Schwartz, 1976). Heterosexuals, both men and women, may find themselves in situations where they engage in some same-sex sexual behavior, for example, in prison, and then later return to a heterosexual life. Some bisexuals may require special situations to

be responsive to a second gender, for example, becoming high on drugs or alcohol or engaging in a sexual threesome with both genders (Money, 1988).

Theories of Bisexual Orientation.   The cause or origin of bisexuality is still essentially unknown. The research and information available have only raised issues about our theories of sexual orientation. In view of the fact that most of the available information about the development of sexual orientation theorizes that it is fixed or determined before adolescence, the pattern of bisexuality often contradicts these assumptions. Hyde has raised important questions about this apparent contradiction and feels that the time that sexual orientation is actually fixed is unclear. She has also speculated about whether heterosexuality is the norm and why we are all not bisexuals (Hyde, 1996b). More research on bisexuality is needed before its origin can be better understood. Additional discussion on bisexuality with a particular focus on sociocultural factors can be found in Chapter 8.

BIOLOGICAL CHANGES ACROSS THE LIFE-SPAN

From the time of birth (the neonatal period) until the child begins to reach puberty, circulating levels of gonadal hormones are very low, reproductive organs are undeveloped, and males and females differ little in general appearance. Although the sexual organs are immature, the adrenal glands of infant girls begin to produce small amounts of estrogen and the undeveloped testes of males produce small amounts of testosterone.

Puberty and Adolescence

By the time the child reaches 6 or 7 years of age, she or he is well aware of the anatomical differences between boys and girls and most probably between the mother and father. Children soon become aware of intimacy and privacy and usually develop a sense of modesty about exposing their bodies. Subsequently, children are likely to engage in sexual exploration to learn more about these differences.

Puberty represents a period of transition between childhood and adulthood during which an adolescent growth spurt takes place, secondary sex characteristics develop, and fertility is achieved. Puberty is also the time when there is an increase in hormones, often a sudden increase. As puberty approaches, the ovaries begin to function and the testes increase functioning. The adrenal cortex also starts to enlarge and increases its output of steroids, which include the sex hormones. As hormone levels increase, the concentrations in the two sexes begin to differ (Hoyenga & Hoyenga, 1993; Pinel, 1993).

In pubertal females, estrogen levels rise and feminization takes place. Estrogen levels increase to about eight times their level in childhood, along with an increase in progesterone, which helps the breasts to develop and the uterus to reach its adult size. The hips and thighs begin to accumulate fat to produce the typical female shape. The ovaries also produce some androgen (testosterone), which results in the growth of pubic and underarm hair. Acne may also develop. The first indication that puberty has started is the growth spurt and the beginning of breast development, which will continue for several years. Breast growth can begin as early as 8 years of age or as late as 13 years of age. The appearance of pubic hair becomes noticeable shortly after the breasts begin to grow. During this same time, the uterus begins to enlarge and the vagina lengthens. The first menstruation, the *menarche,* occurs as the breasts become fully developed and after the peak growth spurt. Although the menarche is the most obvious indication of sexual maturation, it actually occurs several years after puberty begins. Yet, it presents a dramatic change in the female in contrast to the male, for which there is no single and dramatic sign to indicate when his sperm are viable or that he is now fertile. A girl's awareness of her bodily changes is often accompanied by strong emotional and psychological reactions, especially as she recognizes the fact that she will have a menstrual period on a monthly basis and that she is now fertile. In the United States, the average age of puberty is almost 13 years for white girls and 12½ years for black girls. Earlier in this century, the age at menarche was almost 16 years, but this has gradually decreased.

Nutrition, heredity, socioeconomic conditions, family size, and psychological factors all may influence the age at which the first menstruation occurs. It can vary from as early as 8 years to as old as 16 or later, again with differences in ethnic and minority groups (Basow, 1986; Beal, 1994; Hoyenga & Hoyenga, 1993; Marshall & Tanner, 1969; Masters et al., 1995; Pinel, 1993).

In pubertal males, androgen hormone levels rise to almost 18 times what they were during childhood; however, the adolescent growth spurt and masculinization begin some two years later than feminization for girls. The first change seen in the male is the growth of the testes, then of the penis and the accessory male sex organs: the prostate, seminal vesicles, and epididymis. The increase in androgen levels results in the development of muscle tissue and body hair. Boys' estrogen levels also increase and in some cases lead to breast enlargement. Although usually transient, it is an embarrassing condition for a young boy, and he is usually subjected to much ridicule. This is usually followed by a growth spurt, with the development of pubic and facial hair as well as underarm hair. Boys' sweat glands become active and their voices deepen. One certain indication of puberty is the interest that heterosexual boys begin to show in girls. As puberty proceeds, boys begin to have frequent erections and thoughts about sex, have "wet dreams," and have their first ejaculations. This is the phase when boys may show a renewed interest in masturbating. Boys have different emotional and psychological responses to their first ejaculation and the realization that they too are now fertile. Boys generally begin to show genital development at an average of 11.6 years and reach adult size at about 14.9 years (Beal, 1994; Carroll & Wolpe, 1996; Doyle, 1989; Masters et al., 1995; Pinel, 1993).

A recent report finds that puberty in girls may actually begin as early as age 6. One stimulus for the process comes not from the ovaries or testes but from the adrenal glands, which are usually associated with the production of stress hormones. The adrenal hormones stimulate both physical changes and sexual behaviors. The adrenal hormone associated with these changes is DHEA (dihydroepiandrosterone). Research on DHEA for its activity and effect on other physiological mechanisms has been ongoing but now will undoubtedly focus on its influence on puberty. Data on synthetic chemicals in shampoos, dyes, and detergents are part of this ongoing study (Biondo, 1998; Marano, 1997). The developmental changes that take place during puberty are seen in Figure 3.6. The mature reproductive systems of the male and female are shown in Figures 3.7 on the next page and 3.8 on page 100.

Menstruation and the Menstrual Cycle

The **menstrual cycle** averages about 28 days, but can range from 15 to 45 days. The cycle is usually set with a girl's first menstruation. The human female at birth has about 400,000 primary follicles in her ovaries.

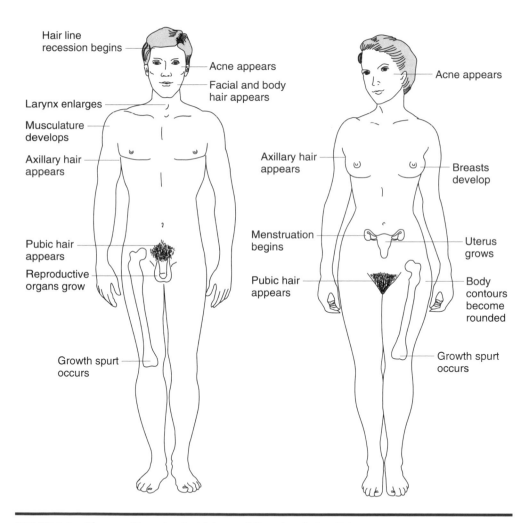

FIGURE 3.6   Changes Occuring in Males and Females during Puberty

Source: From *Biopsychology* (4th ed.), by John P. J. Pinel, 2000, Boston: Allyn & Bacon. Copyright © 2000 by Allyn & Bacon. Reprinted by permission.

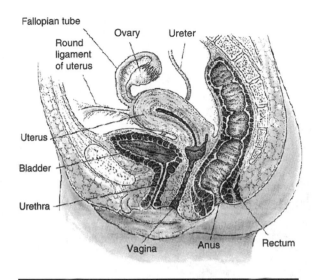

FIGURE 3.7 The Female Reproductive System
This cross-section locates many of the internal sex
organs that compose the female reproductive system.
Note that the uterus is normally tipped forward.
Source: From *Human Sexuality in a World of Diversity* (p. 65),
by S. A. Rathus, J. S. Nevid, and L. Fichner-Rathus, 1997,
Boston: Allyn & Bacon. Copyright © 1997 by Allyn & Bacon.
Reprinted by permission.

Each follicle contains an egg or ovum. With each
menstrual cycle, an ovum is released from the ovary
and begins its trip down the Fallopian tube for possible fertilization and implantation in the uterus.

The menstrual cycle is divided into four phases.
The **follicular phase** is the initial phase, beginning
after the last menstrual period has ended. It lasts from
about 6 to 13 or 14 days. During this phase, estrogen
released from the ovaries stimulates the regrowth of
the *endometrium,* the inner layer of the uterus, which
has diminished after the last menstrual period. At the
same time, the follicles in the ovary begin to ripen
with the next ovum to be released.

In the **ovulation phase,** the second phase, the follicle matures and swells. This phase ends when the
follicle ruptures, releasing the ovum so that it can
travel down the Fallopian tube for possible fertilization and implantation in the uterus. During the third
phase, the **luteal phase,** a group of cells, the *corpus*

luteum, forms in the space that previously held the
now ruptured follicle. For the next 10 to 12 days, the
corpus luteum, a small pouchlike gland, secretes additional estrogen and progesterone via stimulation by
the hypothalamus. These hormones act to increase the
growth of the endometrium in the uterus and to improve the blood supply so that, if the ovum is fertilized, the uterus will be prepared to implant and
nourish a fertilized egg. If within this time the ovum is
not fertilized, the continued high levels of progesterone and estrogen are a signal to the hypothalamus
to decrease production of hormones. When this occurs, the corpus luteum begins to degenerate, and
about 2 days before the end of the normal menstrual
cycle, estrogen and progesterone levels decrease
rapidly and the luteal phase ends.

The fourth and final phase of the cycle is the
menstrual phase. During this phase, the endometrial
cells lining the uterus shrink and slough off. The uterus
contracts in order to expel the dead tissue along with
blood, which passes from the uterine cavity through
the cervix into the vagina. It is these contractions that
cause menstrual cramps, which for some women become extremely painful. Other possible effects of the
menstrual cycle, such as PMS (premenstrual syndrome), are discussed in Chapter 12. The menstrual
flow is known as *menses,* which lasts from about 3 to
7 days. Day 1 after the menstrual cycle ends, the follicular phase begins again and the cycle is repeated
(Carroll & Wolpe, 1996; Hoyenga & Hoyenga, 1993;
Hyde, 1996a, 1996b). The phases of the menstrual
cycle and hormonal changes are shown in Figure 3.9
on page 101.

Earlier in this chapter we described the process
of ovulation, fertilization, conception, and pregnancy.
At this point we have completed a circle in this aspect
of the biology of sex and gender. The next area we explore will be the process of menopause, which marks
the termination of the reproductive life of the female.

Menopause

Just as the age of menarche has decreased, the age of
menopause has increased, making the reproductive
range of women much longer. In the last century,

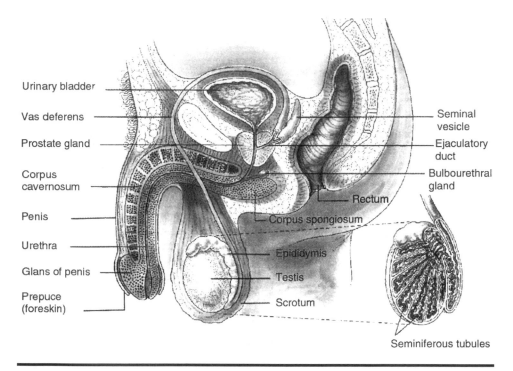

Urinary bladder

Vas deferens

Prostate gland

Corpus
cavernosum

Penis

Urethra

Glans of penis

Prepuce
(foreskin)

Seminal
vesicle

Ejaculatory
duct

Bulbourethral
gland

Rectum

Corpus spongiosum

Epididymis

Testis

Scrotum

Seminiferous tubules

FIGURE 3.8   The Male Reproductive System
The external male sex organs including the penis and the scrotum.
Source: From *Human Sexuality in a World of Diversity* (p. 103), by S. A. Rathus, J. S. Nevid, and
L. Fichner-Rathus, 1997, Boston: Allyn & Bacon. Copyright © 1997 by Allyn & Bacon. Reprinted by
permission.

menopause started in a woman's middle forties, but now the age has increased into the late forties or early fifties (Carroll & Wolpe, 1996).

The term **menopause** refers to the period where menstruation gradually ends, somewhere between 45 and 55 years of age. For the woman, this interval symbolizes a gradual passage from being able to reproduce to becoming infertile. Although menopause is often referred to as the *climacteric,* this term is more appropriately used to describe changes in men as they age, which will be discussed later. During menopause, estrogen production gradually declines, resulting in the cessation of menstruation. As the ovaries age, they cannot respond to stimulation from the anterior pituitary gland to produce estrogen and progesterone. Often, one of the first signs of menopause is irregular cycles. Excessive bleeding during a cycle may also occur. A woman may have amenorrhea (lack of a

cycle) for several months, followed by one or more cycles, but then the menstrual flow gradually ends. Menstruation usually does not stop suddenly, but gradually wanes. Menopause is considered to have occurred when a year has passed without a menstrual cycle.

As estrogen levels decrease, often fluctuating in the early stages of menopause, the primary sex organs are affected. The clitoris and labia become smaller. Due to the lack of estrogen, the vaginal wall is altered, and the vagina often becomes dry and can cause painful intercourse. The ovaries and uterus also begin to undergo changes. Decreased estrogen production also affects the secondary sex characteristics: a decrease in hair on the head and in the pubic area, loss of tone in the breasts, and sometimes the appearance of hair on the upper lip and chin. Wrinkling of the skin may also begin. One of the most important changes is the loss of bone density, which often results in **osteo-**

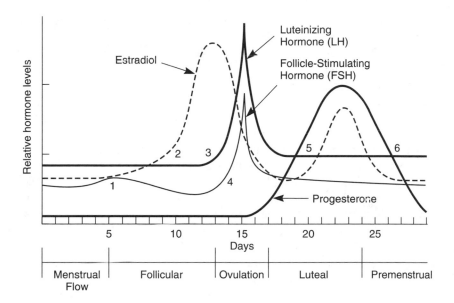

Phases of the human menstrual cycle

1. In response to an increase in FSH, small spheres of cells called ovarian follicles begin to grow around individual egg cells (ova).

2. The follicles begin to release estrogens such as estradiol.

3. The estrogens stimulate the hypothalamus to increase the release of LH and FSH from the anterior pituitary.

4. In response to the LH surge, one of the follicles ruptures and releases its ovum.

5. The ruptured follicle under the influence of LH develops into a corpus luteum (yellow body) and begins to release progesterone, which prepares the lining of the uterus for the implantation of a fertilized ovum.

6. Meanwhile, the ovum is moved into the Fallopian tube by the rowing action of ciliated cells. If the ovum is not fertilized, progesterone and estradiol levels fall, and the walls of the uterus are sloughed off as menstrual flow and the cycle begins once again.

FIGURE 3.9   Hormones during the Menstrual Cycle

Source: From *Biopsychology* (2nd ed.) (p. 63), by John P. J. Pinel, 1993, Boston: Allyn & Bacon. Copyright © 1993 by Allyn & Bacon. Reprinted by permission.

porosis. The aging woman with increasingly brittle bones is at a heightened risk for fracture of the hip and vertebrae. A full discussion of osteoporosis is given in Chapter 13.

The age at which menopause occurs and the symptoms experienced throughout this transition period vary greatly from woman to woman. Even though the ovaries stop producing progesterone and all but a small amount of estrogen, the adrenal glands continue to produce various amounts of these hormones. In many woman, the vacillation of hormone levels causes *hot flashes*. Hot flashes are the most common symptom, affecting about 75 percent of women. The typical hot flash is defined by women as a transient sensation of flushing, sweating, and heat. These sensations are often accompanied by palpitations of the heart and anxiety and can be followed by chills. The terms *hot flash, flush,* and *night sweat* are all used to describe the same symptoms. Symptoms may occur weekly or every few hours. They may last a few seconds to several minutes. Because hot flashes tend to occur more often during the night, women complain of being awakened suddenly and suffer from insomnia. Hot flashes may also be accompanied by headaches. Some women experience mood and other emotional changes that become distressing. Chapter 10 describes some of these changes with a particular focus on psychological and social effects of menopause (Bates, 1981; Carroll & Wolpe, 1996; Kronenberg, 1990).

Treatment of Symptoms.   The treatment of menopausal symptoms and concern about preventing heart disease and osteoporosis are ongoing issues. While the incidence of cardiovascular disease (CVD) in premenopausal women is significantly less than that of men, CVD increases markedly after menopause. This change has been attributed to the loss of estrogen, which protects women against cardiovascular disorders. The use of hormone replacement therapy (HRT) for these purposes has conflicted with the reported increased risk of cancer of the uterus and breast. Nevertheless, scientific studies have shown that not only does HRT alleviate menopausal symptoms, but it can also help to protect women from developing heart disease, from which they were protected before menopause by their circulating levels of estrogen. It has been estimated that estrogen given to postmenopausal women has cut the risk of certain forms of heart disease by 40 to 50 percent. Women who had taken estrogen for more than 15 years had a 40 percent reduction in death rate, as compared with women who did not take estrogen postmenopausally. HRT has also been shown to slow down the loss of bone density, especially when combined with other factors like nutrition and exercise (Galsworthy, 1994; Henderson, Pagnani-Hill, & Ross, 1991; Lindsay & Cosman, 1990; Lobo; 1990; Stampfer et al., 1991).

Even with all the benefits of taking HRT, the risks must be considered and a risk–benefit ratio established. Different women have different risk/benefit ratios depending on genetic and lifestyle factors. The decision to take HRT is a personal one that should be made with a physician. There is an estimated, although disputed, 30 percent increase in breast cancer, as well as an increase in cancer of the uterus with HRT. But adding progestin to estrogen has reduced the risk to the uterus (Curtin, 1994; Martin & Freeman, 1993). There is continuing work by many pharmaceutical companies to develop new drugs and treatments to replace estrogen and reduce the risk of uterine and breast cancer. The drug Evista is one such replacement. It is reported to prevent bone loss and also work as estrogen does to decrease cholesterol. This drug apparently carries no risk for cancer of the uterus and breast and it may be able to be used by women either at risk for breast cancer or who have had breast cancer. The drug Fosomax is now used extensively by postmenopausal women and women with osteoporosis to reduce bone loss and increase bone density. Other drugs, such as salmon calcitonin (Miacalcin) administered nasally, can also reduce bone loss. All these drugs must be taken under a physician's supervision and in the smallest, effective dose for each patient (Prelevic, Balint-Peric, & Petrovic, 1990).

Male Climacteric

In men, the pattern of aging and reproductive change is very different from that of women. There is no definite end to male fertility, no recognizable sign of its termination, as with the cessation of menstrual flow during menopause. Sperm production decreases after 40 years, but men can still be fertile into their 80s. And, although testosterone levels decrease after age 55, there is no rapid and major drop in hormone levels as there is in women.

Only about 5 percent of men experience a condition called the *male climacteric.* It has been referred to as *male menopause.* The male climacteric has been defined as a syndrome experienced by men over age 60, marked by some or all of the following symptoms: "weakness, tiredness, poor appetite, decreased sexual desire, reduction or loss of potency, irritability and impaired ability to concentrate" (Masters, Johnson, & Kolodny, 1994, p. 265). These symptoms occur because of decreased testosterone levels but can be improved or even reversed with testosterone treatment. On experiencing any of these symptoms, men may think that they are suffering from a serious disease, but on seeking a physician's help they can be treated successfully.

However, other problems are more common than the climacteric in aging men. One is the enlargement of the prostate gland, believed to be a consequence of decreasing hormone levels. Approximately 10 percent of men develop this problem at about 40 years, but the incidence increases to almost 50 percent by age 80. The enlarged prostate causes urinary problems ranging from difficulty in initiating urination to nocturnal frequency. Surgery can alleviate these symptoms by removal of the part of the enlarged gland that is pressing against the urethra. To date, nonsurgical treatment has not been very successful. Prostate cancer is also a disease that tends to develop in older men. Various treatments from surgery to female hormone treatment to radiation and implantation of radium seeds have been successful.

Aging and Ageism

In Western cultures, sex has been considered an activity primarily for the young and healthy and not for the older or elderly couple. These myths do not hold up. The need for intimacy and pleasure generally found in sexual activity does not disappear when a woman reaches menopause or when a man's hormonal levels decrease. The biological changes described here do not automatically terminate sexual function, and aging alone does not diminish sexual interest in either males or females. However, in both men and women, aging, with its associated biological changes, does affect the nature of sexual function. The process of aging in both women and men is fraught with psychological consequences that vary across cultures. *Ageism,* prejudice against people because they are old, is a well-known phenomenon in the United States and other industrialized countries. In some other societies, aging is accompanied with high-level recognition and deference. In most Western cultures, ageism is a much more negative experience for women than for men. The psychological consequences of aging and the strategies for coping with these changes are described in Chapter 10.

SUMMARY

This chapter has attempted to take the reader through the biology of sex and gender, beginning from concepts of fertilization and conception through menopause and the climacteric process. In presenting the details of these processes, it should be evident that much scientific and technological advance in reproductive physiology has taken place so that we now have a better understanding of the developmental process and what can go wrong. We have also included a section on nature versus nurture, since new evidence has raised questions about the independence of each of these factors. Whereas, at one time, nurture seemed to be the important factor in developing sex and gender identity, recent work has cast doubt about the validity of this concept.

In the section on homosexuality and bisexuality, we have attempted to provide the most recent infor-

mation about theories of sexual orientation. Although research on the biological aspects of sexual orientation is continuing, no data have yet been shown to be conclusive. Bisexuality is just now becoming of interest to social and biological scientists. Available data have succeeded in raising questions about the nature of heterosexuality itself.

Finally, the section on menopause in women and the climacteric in men closes the circle on the biology of sex and gender and the meaningfulness of such changes to men and women as they age. An understanding of these ontological (developmental) processes early in this volume should assist the reader in relating to the chapters that follow.

KEY TERMS

Androgen (p. 82)
Bisexual (p. 92)
Capacitation (p. 80)
Chromosomes (p. 78)
Conception (p. 81)
Electra complex (p. 77)
Embryo (p. 81)
Estrogen (p. 84)
Fetal alcohol syndrome (p. 91)
Fetus (p. 81)
Heterosexual orientation (p. 92)

Homosexual orientation (p. 92)
Hormone (p. 84)
Menopause (p. 100)
Menstrual cycle (p. 98)
   Follicular phase (p. 99)
   Luteal phase (p. 99)
   Menstrual phase (p. 99)
   Ovulation phase (p. 99)
Osteoporosis (pp. 100–101)
Ovaries (p. 78)
Ovum (p. 78)

Penis envy (p. 77)
Progesterone (p. 84)
Pseudohermaphrodite (p. 89)
Sperm (p. 78)
Testes (p. 78)
Testosterone (p. 82)
Trimester (p. 81)
Uterus (p. 80)
Vagina (p. 80)
Zona pellucida (p. 80)
Zygote (p. 80)

DISCUSSION QUESTIONS

1. How do you feel about John Money's theories of nurture *not* nature in the development of gender identity advanced during the time of the accident that ablated "John's" penis? What perspective do you have on nature *versus* nurture in the development of gender identity? What ethical questions do you think should have been raised at that time? How do you think you would respond if "John" was your child and this terrible accident happened to him?

2. Freud theorized that the Oedipal complex, castration anxiety, and penis envy involve unconscious mechanisms. Does this stage of development as described by Freud seem plausible to you, especially in the 1990s? What criticisms do you have of these views?

3. How does the knowledge of the potential for fetal abnormalities as a result of prenatal drug exposure heighten your awareness of the importance of good prenatal care and health throughout pregnancy? How would you go about assuring that you received proper prenatal care?

4. Do you think that results of self-report sex research studies by Kinsey and more recently by others are valid? Do these reports coincide with your experience or is your experience different? How would you design a sex research study to address today's issues?

5. Have you or anyone you know ever felt that you (he or she) were a male born with a female body or a female born with a male body? What did you do with these feelings? Do you still have these feelings?

6. Have you ever wished that you were a member of the other sex, to be a male with a penis or a female with breasts and a vagina? How did you cope with these feelings?

7. Do you feel that it would be easier to be accepted by society if you were bisexual rather than exclusively homosexual? As a female or male bisexual?

8. If you were either a lesbian or gay, what special problems would you need to overcome to feel at ease with your sexual orientation?

9. How old were you when you realized that society had rigid gender roles? What event triggered this recognition? How did you react to this insight and how did you adapt to these specified gender roles?

SUGGESTED READINGS

Boswell, J. (1980). *Christianity, social tolerance, and homosexuality: Gay people in Western Europe from the beginning of the Christian era to the fourteenth century.* Chicago: University of Chicago Press.

Money, J. (1986). *Lovemaps.* New York: Irvington Press.

Tavris, C. (1992). *The mismeasure of women.* New York: Simon & Schuster.

Boston Women's Health Book Collective. (1984). *The new our bodies ourselves.* New York: Simon & Schuster.

CHAPTER 4

CULTURE, ETHNICITY, RACE, AND CLASS

JUNE F. CHISHOLM, PH.D.

If I didn't define myself for myself, I would be crunched into other people's fantasies for me and eaten alive.
—Audre Lorde

The task of psychologists interested in gender and cultural diversity is to explain the processes through which particular traits and behaviors are produced and maintained. Naming the process as social construction is no longer sufficient. It is especially important that psychologists recognize that social construction is not the same thing as socialization, just as it is certainly not the same thing as biology. Instead, psychologists must look at how interpersonal transactions, sociostructural beliefs, and values, as well as their internalization, cause people to "do ethnicity" in a manner similar to the ways they "do gender."
—Rhoda K. Unger

That which U.S. women have in common must always be viewed in relation to the particularities of a group, for even when we narrow our focus to one particular group of women it is possible for differences within that group to challenge the primacy of what is shared in common. For example, what have we said and what have we failed to say when we speak of "Asian American women"?
—Johnnetta B. Cole

With the changing demographics occurring in the United States, psychology must make substantive revisions in its curriculum, training, research and practice. Without these revisions, psychology will risk professional, ethical and economic problems because psychology will no longer be a viable professional resource to the majority of the U.S. population.
—Christine C. Iijima Hall

The mainstream assumptions of normative behavior will be infused by
that behavior of people of color. Instead of solely valuing independence,
interdependence will be also aspired as a desirable trait. Instead of
viewing separation as a mature developmental response, other cultural
values will be offered as alternatives. For instance, the Japanese concept
of amae positively emphasizes the feeling of filial dependence and
parental indulgence. Along these lines, learned cognitive patterns that
are culturally biased (e.g., locus of control and self-efficacy) will be
reexamined. For instance, instead of solely valuing internal locus of
control and self-reliance as modes of action, the role played by destiny,
fate, and karma will provide alternative acceptable options.
—Lillian Comas-Diaz

In the nineties, I am recognized by those choosing political correctness as an African American woman. Ten years ago I was recognized by those choosing political correctness as a Woman of Color, a designation which is still in use today. Ten years before that, I was recognized by those choosing political correctness as an Afro-American woman and, in solidarity with oppressed women in developing countries, a Third World woman. Ten years before that, I was recognized, with some temerity by the "establishment," as a Black. In my childhood, I was either a Negro (or

Negress for those who also recognized my sex) or Colored. Back then, to be called Colored by some individuals was positive and affirming because, for them, the term connoted a connection and solidarity with people of color around the world. For others, using the term was negative because it referred exclusively to American Blacks and all that is inherent in our status in America. Today, Black has similar connotations. For some, it is an umbrella term recognizing the solidarity with people of the Black Diaspora, that is, people dispersed throughout the world whose ancestors are of African descent (Landrine, 1995). For others, it is a racial designation in which race is either viewed as a biological or genetic fact or a social construction with scientific, sociopolitical, moral, and economic ramifications.

I consider myself fortunate to have been raised within a cohesive, nurturing network of family, friends, and neighbors who enabled me to live through decades of designations and redesignations with an intact sense of self as a confident, intelligent, and capable person who chose to pursue a career in the field of psychology. Some might question the degree of my intactness, considering this career choice and the role the field has had and continues to have in perpetuating stereotypic views about "people like me." Nonetheless, for the past two decades I have been a practicing clinical psychologist and an educator who has worked with men, women, and children from a variety of cultural, ethnic, and socioeconomic backgrounds. The following discussion on culture, ethnicity, race, class, and gender is based in part on a critical review of the literature and my work experience.

As evident in my opening personal statement, any meaningful discussion on this topic, especially as it relates to women of color, requires the use of labels and terms that, for clarity, must be defined. This chapter discusses **gender** with respect to culture, race, ethnicity, and class by focusing on women in five major U.S. ethnic–racial groupings: White (Euro American), African American, Hispanic American, Asian American, and Native American Indian.

It is to be noted that the term **African American** is an **ethnocultural group;** a grouping of people rather than a racial category, even though its use in discussions on race ignores this distinction. The term **Hispanic** refers to all people of Spanish origin and includes a variety of nationalities, ethnicities, and races. **Chicanos** and **Chicanas** are men and women of Mexican origin. **Latinos** and **Latinas** are men and women from Latin America. Some politically conscious women prefer the term *Latina* to Hispanic. For American women of color of Asian descent the preferred term is often **Asian American,** even though the term is overinclusive, referring to people whose ancestors are from China, Japan, Korea, India, Southeast Asia,

and South Asia (Bradshaw, 1994). Likewise the term **Native American Indian** refers to anyone whose ancestors are from one of the 587 American Indian tribes.

The sections on demography and mental and physical health use the U.S. Bureau of Census racial categories: White, Black, Asian/Pacific Islander, American Indian/Eskimo/Aleut, and Hispanic (although this is not a racial group). The terms, *White* and *Black* as used by the Bureau of Census are problematic. A Hispanic can be either White or Black. The term **White** subsumes many ethnocultural groups (e.g., Anglo Americans, Irish Americans, and Polish Americans). The term **Black** is used for African Americans, people from the Caribbean (e.g., West Indians), Black Hispanics, and recent immigrants from Africa.

The following passage from a text entitled *Culture, Ethnicity and Mental Illness* (Griffith & Baker, 1993) illustrates the confusion surrounding ethnic–racial categorization, the consequences of which are problematic for the theory and practice of psychology:

> *The African American population of the United States is a heterogeneous group of individuals who may speak other languages in addition to English. They have different ethnic heritages and skin color. In the early part of this century, they were called Negroes or people of color. As a result of the civil rights activity of the 1960s and the "Black is beautiful" movement, many of these people preferred simply to be called blacks, although some preferred the designation African American. Because the former terminology refers explicitly to skin color and excludes any reference to cultural heritage, some have found it inadequate, preferring to be called African Americans (Baker, 1987; Pinderhughes, 1989). However, "black," "Afro-American," and "African American" continue to be used interchangeably to denote nonwhites born in the United States who are descendants of African slaves, as well as [emphasis mine] recent immigrants from the West Indies, Brazil, and a host of other countries, including those in Africa. (p. 148)*

African American, when so broadly applied, tends to be too inclusive and runs the risk of missing significant differences related to cultural heritage, national origin, and the experience of oppression among people of color of African descent. Moreover, it is unlikely that people of color who are not descendants of African slaves from the United States would refer to themselves as African American, despite any physical resemblance to African Americans. For example, a person of African descent (i.e., parents are African immigrants) who was born in the United States but whose ancestors were not slaves in America would not readily identify with being called an African American, because the term refers to African ancestors who were slaves during the slavery period in American history.

THEORETICAL AND EMPIRICAL RESEARCH ON PEOPLE OF COLOR

Empirical research in which race is a part of the research design is a well-established tradition that has produced a body of knowledge about "minorities" that is widely known and accepted in many scientific circles, albeit with ambivalence, because of the social ramifications of the group investigated. Few studies were designed to highlight racial variations as a major thrust of the research. The practice of grouping individuals into categories such as Black and White that stem from a sociopolitical system structured to protect the **hegemony** (i.e., the domination and power of certain groups) has produced an extensive body of findings based on flawed methodology and lacking rigor, but nonetheless reflecting the bias of the particular researcher, as well as conforming, in a general way, to the socially constructed "truths" about the "races" studied (Graham, 1992).

Campbell (1967) warned psychologists about the danger of perpetuating ethnic stereotyping by the practice of using race as a variable in comparison studies. Azibo (1988) criticizes the scientific basis of a comparative racial paradigm that reinforces the view that a Eurocentric perspective sets the norms by which the African American experience, as well as the experiences of other ethnic groups in the United States, are evaluated and consequently found to be deviant. This approach omits an analysis of within-group variation. Graham (1992) argues, for example, that while

the percentage of studies on African Americans in mainstream psychology has always been low (3.6 percent), there is a growing trend of exclusion of such studies so that in the 1990s the field is in danger of becoming "raceless." Scarr (1988) boldly states:

> There should be no qualms about the forthright study of racial and gender differences; science is in desperate need of good studies that highlight race and gender variables, unabashedly, to inform us of what we need to do to help underrepresented people to succeed in this society. Unlike the ostrich, we cannot afford to hide our heads for fear of socially uncomfortable discoveries. (p. 56)

To better understand the points raised in the preceding section, let us look at a hypothetical research project in which a researcher is interested in the relationship between problem-solving ability and the capacity for logical reasoning. The researcher designs an experiment with a methodology that appears to be objective (i.e., an apparatus is used that contains buttons, panels, and slots). To open the device to obtain a prize, subjects will have to independently combine two different procedures—first pressing the correct button to release a marble and then inserting the marble into the appropriate slot to open a panel. The researcher, interested in developmental issues and cross-cultural differences, conducts this experiment with different populations (e.g., White American children and adults and Liberian children and adults). He finds that White American children under the age of ten were unable to solve the problem, whereas the American adult group was very successful. However, neither the Liberian adult nor Liberian child group was able to solve the problem. One might be tempted to conclude that Liberian adults do not problem solve as well as American adults. Such a conclusion would be false and misleading, but nevertheless would be consistent with previous scientific findings suggesting that Blacks are less intelligent than Whites. However, a finding that shows a difference in performance on some measure between two groups does not automatically mean that the difference reflects *deviancy* or a *deficiency* among the sample that scored lower. In fact, our hypothetical study was actually a real study conducted by Cole and his colleagues (Cole, Gay, Glick, & Sharp, 1971). In a follow-up study, the methodology was changed; that is, the apparatus used to assess problem-solving abilities among a Liberian population was constructed from materials familiar and common in Liberian culture and, not surprisingly, the findings were reversed: the Liberian sample performed better than the American sample!

The traditional theoretical models that have been used at various points in the history of American psychology to understand and explain the nature and experiences of African Americans are instructive in highlighting the complex, complementary relationship between psychological thought and prevailing societal views. For example, the **inferiority model** comprises a vast array of theories that explicitly or implicitly link African Americans' status in society to inherent genetic defects (Jensen, 1985; Shockley, 1971). That is, as a group, African Americans are believed to be genetically inferior to Caucasians, and this inferiority accounts for their marginal status. While this model has been rejected by most social scientists, the controversial book *The Bell Curve* (Herrnstein & Murray, 1994) raises the issues once again.

The **cultural deprivation model** frames the condition of African Americans within the context of **racism,** prejudice, and discrimination. This model explains ethnic identity, self-esteem, school failure, chronic unemployment, family disturbances, and higher rates of more serious psychiatric disorders in terms of oppressive environmental circumstances. Critics of this model point out that it tends to overlook the strengths, competencies, and skills of African Americans and therefore unwittingly perpetuates stereotypic views (Jones, 1991; Landrine, 1995; Moynihan, 1965).

Stereotypic views about other ethnic–racial groups have also been perpetuated through inadequate theoretical formulations and biased research. For example, while the image of the **model minority** may fit some Asian Americans, such as some Japanese, some Chinese, and some Koreans, other Asian groups experience high unemployment (Wong, 1983; Wong & Hayashi, 1989). Moreover, few of these studies examined gender differences (Chow, 1985) and many

misstate the status of Asian American women, who, in general, have not attained the same advantages associated with their male counterparts.

Vazquez-Nuttall, Romero-Garcia, and De Leon (1987) reviewed studies that measured the perceptions of masculinity and femininity of Hispanic American women in North America and questioned the traditional concept that Hispanic culture is one of male dominance and female submissiveness, conceding that the dynamics of the relationships were often more complex than the stereotypes. Indeed, the stereotype of dominant male and submissive female roles in the Mexican-American family is not supported by research that includes an analysis of class, urban–rural, regional, and generational differences (Hurtado, Hayes-Bastista, Burciaga, Valdez, & Hernandez, 1992). This complexity is especially true for women who have come into contact with European American culture by pursuing education and careers.

The research of Hayes-Bastista cited in a report by Winkler (1990) on the impact of poverty found evidence of "cultural vitality." For example, poor Latinos were twice as likely to live in traditional family structures compared to either poor Blacks or Whites; Latinos had the highest rates of working males, higher life expectancy, with a 50 percent lower rate of violent deaths compared to Blacks and 20 percent lower compared to Whites. Additionally, immigrant Latinos exhibited healthier behavior than Latinos born in this country. While there is little doubt that poverty is clearly stressful, is damaging to a sense of well-being, and results in numerous and complex disadvantages, Hayes-Bastista's research provides evidence of more complex dynamics at play that involve strengths as well as weaknesses.

The above research conducted by people of color within psychology supports Greenfield's (1994) ideas about the importance of an **insider's perspective** in the framing of research and interpretation of data. An *insider* social scientist is someone who is from the culture or group being researched. In contrast, an outsider social scientist with an **outsider's perspective** is someone who is not from the culture or group that he or she researches. Greenfield (1994) argues that psychology as a whole, in its attempts to be objective, has overlooked this important phenomenon as a variable influencing the scientific method and the subsequent interpretation of the database generated, while functioning, albeit unconsciously, as "unacknowledged" insiders of Euro-American culture. The outsider's perspective tends to involve the imposition of assumptions about the psychological phenomenon in question, with serious ramifications. It would be a mistake to conclude from Greenfield's analysis that the problem of scientific bias in research on ethnicity, race, gender, and class can be resolved by promoting more research conducted by insiders. Without doubt, more research conducted by insiders is desirable. However, the point to be made here is that a balance between the research generated by insiders and outsiders is necessary. Achieving a balance may reduce if not eliminate the deleterious impact of poorly framed research questions, inadequate methodology, and misleading interpretation of findings on ethnic–racial minorities that misinform the scientific community as well as the community at large.

It is noteworthy that women scholars studying gender raise similar concerns about the psychological understanding of women's experiences that, until recently, was based on theories and research developed by men in a male-dominated profession (Denmark & Paludi, 1993; Miller, 1976; Unger, 1981). Denmark, Russo, Frieze and Sechzer (1988) stress the importance of developing guidelines for conducting nonracist, nonsexist research.

Additionally, there has been a trend to develop supplemental texts to complement traditional texts that at least point out the limitations and misconceptions that persist within the traditional, mainstream approaches, but do little in the way of revising the enterprise that produces them. Information about women presented in the psychological literature on gender has also been flawed by psychologists who fail to seriously consider culture, ethnicity, race, and class as relevant to all aspects of psychological functioning.

FEMINIST PERSPECTIVES

Scholarship within the feminist literature presents an alternative view, but until recently it has also been vic-

tim of the narrow scope that tends to misinform and misconstrue the nature of woman by using a framework that is too inclusive and all encompassing. Women scholars criticized the dominant U.S. institutions and ideologies for being patriarchal and accused mainstream psychology for being "womanless" (Crawford & Marecek, 1989). However, their analyses failed to consider distinctions in class or racial and ethnic inequalities. Espin (1994) acknowledges the narrow-sightedness of some feminists in psychology and agrees with several feminists of color (Anzaldúa, 1990; Combahee River Collective, 1979; hooks, 1984; Lorde, 1984) that "White middle class women do not 'own' feminism, nor is feminism irrelevant to the experiences of Women of Color" (p. 265).

The current epistemology and methodology of psychological thought and practice attempt to revise our understanding of the human condition by examining the psychological significance of cultural, ethnic, racial, and economic influences on individual and group differences. Alternative perspectives for psychological understanding of the human condition are emerging. This understanding reflects contemporary national and international, sociopolitical, and economic realities shaping psychological inquiry and scientific knowledge about human behavior. It appears that the psychological community has become aware of sufficient anomalies in the theoretical models and the tradition of scientific practice and, as Kuhn (1970) has argued in his thesis about the structure of scientific revolutions, has embarked on investigations that will lead the profession to a new set of commitments, as well as new paradigms for the practice of the field.

In 1970, Toni Cade Bambara asked, "How relevant are the truths, the experiences, the finding of white women to black women? Are women after all simply women?" Cole (1986) eloquently expresses the dilemma:

> *[T]o address our commonalities without dealing with our differences is to misunderstand and distort that which separates as well as that which binds us as women. Patriarchal oppression is not limited to women of one race, ethnic group, women in one class, women of one age group or sexual preference, women*

who live in one part of the country, women of any one religion, or women with certain physical abilities or disabilities. While oppression of women knows no such limitations, we cannot, therefore, conclude that the oppression of all women is identical. . . . (pp. 2, 3)

In 1851, at a women's rights convention in Ohio, Sojourner Truth (1795–1883), one of the early feminists of color, articulated these differences when she spoke out against male delegates who warned women that they were going beyond their true natures when they wished to participate in the world of men.

That man over there says that women need to be helped into carriages and lifted over ditches, and to have the best place everywhere. Nobody ever helps me into carriages or over mud puddles, or gives me any best place! And ain't I a woman? Look at me! I could work as much and eat as much as a man—when I could get it—and bear the lash as well! And ain't I a woman? I have borne thirteen children, and seen most all sold off to slavery and when I cried out with my mother's grief, none but Jesus heard me! And ain't I a woman?" (Schneir, 1972, p. 177)

Yamada (1983), an Asian American feminist, asserts that Women of Color experience a double bind in their efforts to be heard by many White majority women, who, she observes, act as though they need to be educated about the plight of Women of Color instead of educating themselves. Simultaneously, they convey the unspoken request that Women of Color talk about what is acceptable and not criticize the values of their dominant White counterparts. She adds, "Asian female interests—which may include focus on family rather than self, fatalism, obedience, inhibition, passivity, self-restraint and adaptiveness—are all positions that are often rejected and criticized as negative role types by White middle-class feminist formulations on sexist oppression" (p. 93).

CULTURE

Discussions on culture and, to a lesser extent, ethnicity, in psychology texts are becoming more prevalent, even though the subject is still deemed by social scientists to be contained within the domain of anthropology. The increasing cultural diversity of the United States challenges the field of psychology (science and practice) into an awareness of the need to develop cultural sensitivity and competencies with respect to theory, practice, and psychological research. Moreover, psychologists need a better understanding of cultural, ethnic, racial, and socioeconomic realities that affect gender. Psychologists need to develop an explicit theoretical model through which sociocultural variables and differences are meaningfully explored. Research citing ethnic differences and speculations about the cultures of others without some theoretical foundation ultimately obscures the relevance of culture, while perpetuating the very conditions that the focus on diversity supposedly challenges (hooks, 1992).

Bullivant (1984), an anthropologist, defines **culture** as a group's program for survival in and adaptation to its environment. The cultural program consists of knowledge, concepts, and values shared by group members through systems of communication. Culture also consists of the shared beliefs, symbols, and interpretations within a human group. Other social scientists view culture as consisting of the symbolic, ideational, and intangible aspects of human societies. For instance, the way you make sense of things depends on your way of making meaning in the world, that is, your world view. Each individual makes unique meanings, but these meanings also have universal human qualities influenced by cultural factors. Culture, therefore, is composed of all those things that people have learned and is reflected in actions, beliefs, values, fears, and the traditions evident throughout their history.

Landrine (1995) suggests that the ways in which psychologists, as social scientists, have traditionally construed meaning from behavior, where behavior is "superficial–mechanical movements irrespective of context," results in comparative studies about women of different ethnic groups who vary in the frequency or prevalence of a specific behavior. The danger in this kind of analysis lies in the mistaken assumption that the *specific behavior,* operationally defined, has identical or similar meanings across ethnic, cultural, and gender boundaries. This researcher proposes a **contextualistic behaviorism** perspective that emphasizes that "behaviors" have no a priori categorical meanings, but must be understood and defined through a careful analysis of the context in which the behavior occurs. What this suggests is that seemingly identical behavior across cultural, ethnic, and gender groups may in fact be categorized in different ways because the "behavior-in-context" changes the meaning depending on the referent group. The example cited in the research findings about the higher incidence of unprotected anal intercourse as a risk factor for HIV infection among young Latinas and the approach to effectively dealing with this risk factor with this group of women illustrates the application of this perspective to research and intervention (see Landrine, 1995, pp. 9–11). It was found that "anal sex" meant something quite different for this young Latina group of women than it did for gay men. Specifically, by engaging in anal sex, these young women could meet the sexual demands of their boyfriends while complying with the larger cultural norm to remain virgins until marriage. According to this culture, virginity means that young women have not engaged in vaginal intercourse, thus keeping the hymen intact. Once the researchers understood the meaning of the behavior-in-context, that is, the significance of anal sex for these young women, the campaign to eliminate this high-risk behavior among this population was different from the one launched to educate gay men about the dangers of this high-risk behavior.

An **ecological model,** derived from field theory, often used within community psychology, is another possible theoretical perspective for the meaningful study of culture, ethnicity, race, and gender. Lewin (1935) posited that human behavior is a function of the interaction of the person and environment: $B = f(P, E)$; that is, "a person's behavior in any situation is jointly determined by the characteristics of that situation, *as he perceives them* [emphasis mine], and by the particular behavioral dispositions of which he is possessed at that time" (Carson, 1969). Barker (1968) and his colleagues at the Midwestern Psychological Field Station of the University of Kansas identified "environments" or what he termed, **"behavior settings."** A behavior setting is a basic environmental unit that entails the naturally occurring spatial and temporal features that surround behavior and the appropriate behavioral match. As an example, Barker uses the analogy of how one comes to understand the behavior of a first baseman in a baseball game. To observe only this player's behavior would not enable one to comprehend the game, which gives meaning to the player's actions. Learning about the aspirations and attitudes of the individual players would also give little understanding of the game. In contrast, by attending more to the game around the player, the ecological environment of the player is made visible (Barker, 1968).

The point to be made here is that theoretical models do exist within psychology that may be more germane to conceptualizing the multiplicative variables of culture, ethnicity, race, and gender as they affect behavior. Spelman (1988) suggests that one way to better understand gender and what it means to be a woman or man is to focus not only on what all women and all men seem to have in common, but also on the meaning of what all women and all men do *not* have in common because of cultural, ethnic, racial, and class differences. Examining both the commonalities and differences is to ask about the extent to which **gender identity** coexists with these other aspects of identity.

Gender Socialized Behavior

According to Miller (1976), the *dominants,* that is, those in power, label their *subordinates* as substandard, defective, and inferior. The preferred roles in the culture are reserved for the dominants, and they define the acceptable roles for the *subordinates,* such as providing services that *dominants* do not want to perform. This is evident when looking at the different status of men and women. Figure 4.1 humorously depicts the polarization of the sexes into two mutually exclusive groups.

One of the earliest and most pervasive tasks of childhood is learning to be a "psychological" male or female, a task that is generally accomplished by the age of three (Bussey & Bandura, 1984; Libby & Aries, 1989). Boys are raised to be independent, self-reliant, aggressive, and achievement-oriented to a greater extent than are girls. Low (1989) found that sexual restraint and industriousness were instilled in girls in about 40 cultures, while boys received such training in fewer than 5 cultures. Chodorow (1979) proposed that the female identity is based on attachment to the mother, whereas the male's is based on detachment. The individual's relationship to the mother in childhood is then posited to give rise to a specific style of thinking and behavior in adulthood. For the female, this style is person-centered or relational; that is, the social context influences thinking and problem solving. For the male, it is object centered or nonrelational. Feminist theorists argue that the relational behavior identified by many to be female is more properly understood as a method of oppression designed by men for women (Hogg & Frank, 1992). It is suggested to be a mechanism of social control for the purpose of excluding one gender from attaining equal access to the social power resources of the other (Hare-Mustin et al., 1989).

Constructs of race, gender, and class help to explain the position of oppressed women nationally and internationally. Gender, ethnicity, and socioeconomic

class are core components of an individual's identity. In studies of 14 countries, Williams and Best (1990) examined how individuals believe themselves to be (the actual self), how they would like to be (the ideal self), and how males and females should be (the ideology of gender). They found small cultural variations in the actual or ideal self, but large cultural variations in the ideology of gender. Specifically, in countries with high socioeconomic development and a high proportion of Protestant Christians, there were highly educated women and large percentages of women were employed outside the home. In those countries the gender ideology was egalitarian. In other cultures, especially those with large proportions of Muslims, such as India, Pakistan, and Nigeria, the gender ideology emphasized the desirability of differences between men and women.

Of special interest is Japan, because it is a modern country that has a gender ideology that is still relatively traditional. But, as Iwao (1993) observes, the gender ideology is very different among those born during the periods 1930–1946, 1946–1955, and 1955–1970.

"Which one of us is the opposite sex?"

FIGURE 4.1   The Polarization of the Sexes
Source: © Leung/Rothco. Reprinted with permission.

Gender-Role Inequality and Abuse

The general pattern around the world is that men have more status and power than women, but this difference is not the same across cultures (Rosaldo & Lamphere, 1974). Cultures differ in the degree of gender inequality. Inequality in this context is meant to convey more than "unequal treatment." It includes the pervasive view that the functions ascribed to women, and hence women themselves, are subordinate in status to men. In some cultures this subordinate status involves a pejorative devaluation of women and women's work that creates a diminished quality of life for them or, in extreme cases, threatens their very lives.

Even in cultures where an ideal of gender equality is stated explicitly, as in Mao's China, the practice is inconsistent with the ideal. In band societies there is often male–female reciprocity and complementarity rather than hierarchy (Triandis, 1994). In stratified societies, socioeconomic and gender inequalities are often correlated. In Africa, for example, in the non-Muslim areas, the status of women was fairly equal to the status of men until the colonial powers took control (Etienne & Leacock, 1980). Under colonization, economic exploitation occurred and gender inequality increased.

One index of gender inequality is the percentage of illiterates who are women. In general, it is desirable to have an equal number of men and women who are literate, as is the case in Scandinavia and Switzerland. In many of the developing countries, however, far more women than men are illiterate. Even in the United States, women did not match the education levels of men until the late 1970s (Triandis, 1994). A second index of gender inequality is the gender-earnings ratio, which indicates how much women earn as a percentage of what men earn. In general, women earn less than men. Table 4.1 shows the gender disparity of earnings between men and women by ethnicity.

Indices of gender abuse include the prevalence of wife abuse, **genital mutilation** of girls and young women, acid throwing, infanticide, and elder abuse (the majority of whom are women). Although husbands can no longer legally beat their wives in the United States, and wives in the United States can legally sue their husbands for damages, the practice remains a reality for far too many women and their families. In India, the phenomenon of bride burning (suttee) has increased in the past 20 years.

TABLE 4.1   Median Weekly Earnings by Race–Ethnicity and Sex

	MEDIAN EARNINGS	PERCENTAGE OF WHITE MEN'S
White men	$595	100.0
White women	444	74.6
Black men	432	72.6
Black women	375	63.0
Hispanic men	371	62.4
Hispanic women	318	53.4

Source: U.S. Department of Labor, Bureau of Labor Statistics, Washington, DC, 1997.

Clitordiction and *infibulation* (technical terms for what is more commonly called female genital mutilation) of girls are practiced in many parts of Africa and the Middle East (see Figure 4.2). According to the World Health Organization, more than 80 million females have been subjected to genital mutilation in Africa, which ranges from the removal of the foreskin of the clitoris to removal of the clitoris and labia, with unsterilized equipment and without anesthesia, and having the two sides of the vulva sewn together. The practice reflects tribal customs and societal values and is considered a significant aspect of a woman's identity. Some men, believing that women's sexual organs are unclean and that clitordiction–infibulation "purifies" women, will not marry women who have not undergone the procedure (Heise, 1994).

What is so inconceivable to those outside the cultures in which these practices are condoned is that they are performed by women and are viewed as a rite of passage. During the late 1990s, the plight of 19-year-old Fauziya Kasinga, who sought asylum in the United States after fleeing Togo when she was 16 to escape having a tribal member "scrape my woman parts off," has drawn international attention and condemnation of this type of gender abuse. The outcry from Westerners has focused on the medical health hazards for these girls and young women, rather than attacking the belief systems that condone the practice. Apropos of this, legislators in several states have responded to reports that the practice of female genital mutilation is occurring in the United States by immigrants from those countries in which the practice is tradition. In 1996, the 104th U.S. Congress passed and enacted Bill HR3247 (introduced by then-Representative Patricia Schroeder), which makes female genital mutilation illegal in the United States.

As Westerners, it is easy to be appalled by the beliefs and practices of some non-Western cultures. However, it is much more difficult to examine the beliefs and practices in one's own culture that, to others outside that culture, are equally appalling and perceived to be abusive to women. An example from American history is illustrative. It is noteworthy that in the nineteenth century doctors in England and the United States performed clitoridectomies on women

Excision (cutting of the clitoris and all or part of the labia minora)

    Infibulation (cutting of the clitoris, labia minora, and part of the labia majora and
    stitching together of most of the vaginal opening)

 ⊘ Over half of all women and girls mutilated

FIGURE 4.2   Countries in Which Genital Mutilation of Women and Girls Is Widely
Practiced, Early 1980s

Source: From *World Watch,* 2(2), (WDC, March–April 1989). Copyright 1989 by the Worldwatch
Institute. Reprinted by permission.

as a viable treatment for masturbation, nymphomania, and psychological problems (Abusharaf, 1998). For more information on clitoridectomy, see Chapters 11 and 13.

In some parts of the world, most notably China, South Korea, India, and Nepal, studies have shown that girls often receive inferior medical care and education and less food than their brothers (Landes, Foster, & Cessna, 1995). In India and China, many women use sonograms and amniocentesis to learn if they are carrying a girl; if they are, the fetus is frequently aborted (Heise, 1994).

Within the past decade, researchers have identified different types of elder abuse, including physical abuse, psychological abuse, material abuse, financial abuse, violation of rights, active neglect, passive neglect, and psychological neglect. In 1984, a California study conducted by the California State Department of Social Services found that the typical abuse victim was female (73 percent) and about 78 years of age; almost two-thirds of the abused were White (65 percent), followed by unknown (17.8 percent), Hispanic (8.8 percent), Black (7.5 percent), and other (2.2 percent) (Landes et al., 1995).

UNITED STATES CULTURE

In the United States, the distinction among groups based on cultural heritage is a hierarchical stratification scheme consisting of a *dominant* culture and a variety of *subcultures.* The **dominant culture** (1) owns and controls the means of production and commerce; (2) has the power to grant and take away livelihoods; (3) owns and controls the channels of communication in the society; (4) decides what, how, and who gets addressed in the media; (5) promotes those aspects of the culture in the media that it considers valuable; and (6) excludes, denigrates, or makes invisible those aspects of culture that it considers inferior or of lesser value. Assumptions of white male supremacy and **white privilege** predominate in American value systems, worldviews, and social institutions (Bullivant, 1984; McLemore, 1991; Triandis, 1994).

A *subculture* is one of those cultures that does not exert the same power and influence on the society at large. These cultures are often portrayed by the dominant culture as being of lesser value (e.g., they are portrayed as marginal, primitive, unsophisticated, exotic, mysterious, etc.). Ironically, aspects of these cultures are frequently "borrowed" by the dominant culture and "valued" when they can be put to profitable commercial use. Examples include Native American Indian jewelry, music stemming from the African American experience (the blues, gospel, jazz), and ethnic cuisines.

Glazer and Moynihan (1970) propose that the melting-pot metaphor describing the cultural composition of the United States in reality does not provide an accurate description. To strengthen their point, they discuss how the Jews, Italians, and Irish of New York City tend to retain their old-world heritages. Similarly, other groups have not relinquished cultural characteristics in order to become totally Americanized.

Within ethnic groups, there are different perspectives on the role of ancestral cultural history. At one extreme are some scholars on the African American experience and some African Americans who question the significance of African roots to contemporary life. This view, that the experience of slavery and subsequent discrimination are mainly responsible for a distinctive African American culture, is challenged by others who point to the fact that Africans who survived slavery and adapted to the customs and traditions of European Americans brought with them a culture that must have affected the nature of their adaptation (Sudarkasa, 1988). At another extreme are Japanese Americans who place so much importance on ancestral history that they label every generation since emigration from Japan with a distinctive name. First-generation Japanese Americans born and raised in Japan are called **Issei;** second-generation Japanese Americans who were born in the United States and experienced the American backlash during World War II, resulting in the internment of many Japanese Americans, are called **Nisei;** third-generation Japanese Americans are called **Sansei** (Greenfield, 1994; Kumekawa, 1993).

African Americans and many individuals from the Asian and Hispanic populations are often reluctant to give up the ethnic customs and traditions learned early in life in favor of Eurocentric middle-class American values and life-styles that may be contrary to their beliefs. African Americans have fought to overcome cultural dominance and discrimination and, through efforts such as the Civil Rights Movement, have sought to understand and maintain their cultural heritage. For some the struggle is more personal and individual. For example, I recently met with a young Korean man for a psychological consultation. He has been in the United States for four years and is the father of two young children, who were born in the United States. He is experiencing emotional conflict about the best ways to raise his children who have never been to Korea and are not acquainted with traditional Korean customs. He is raising his children the "American way" because they are "Americans" and he wants them to be successful here. In contrast to traditional Korean child-rearing practices, his child-rearing methods apparently involve much less discipline and less of an emphasis on honor, self-sacrifice, and the meaning of respect for self and others.

Each group of ethnic minority women has been uniquely influenced by its history prior to its arrival in the United States, as well as its experiences in this country. Consequently, a positive sense of their psychological well-being, if it develops at all, unlike their white counterparts, evolves from a complex, internal conundrum of positive, personal, and collective heritage, plus racism, **sexism,** immigration, acculturation, assimilation, discrimination, and stereotyping.

Ogbu (1994) points out the importance of appreciating the historical power relations between minority and majority groups while studying the culture. Even with an appreciation of diversity, one must still acknowledge the effects of varying sociopolitical relations with the dominant group. That is, the origin and nature of these sociopolitical relations is not merely a function of minority culture. Instead, it varies with each minority–majority group pair.

The designation of *African American woman* presents three aspects of identity—ethnicity, race, and gender—as a totality, an entity. However, I do not think of myself as an *African American* and a *woman;* I am *myself,* which includes but is not limited to both conscious and unconscious conceptions of what an *African American woman* is all about. Yet, I am well aware that in this society my experiences will reflect a blend of racial–ethnic–gender influences that, depending on the referent group of the moment, will determine which of these facets of my identity take precedence over the others. That is, while I share much in common with women of different ethnic and racial backgrounds, I also will have experiences that are more in common with men who share my ethnic and racial heritage.

The need to recognize the differences as well as the common experiences that women share involving race and gender can be seen when one considers the different stereotypes about women and Women of Color that for the latter are based not only on their gender but also on their racial designation. Gender stereotypes affect how women and men think of themselves and how they evaluate their own behavior and the behavior of others. For Women of Color, stress is often the result of significant role strain as we try to accommodate different cultural expectations and values simultaneously.

African American women have been stereotyped as "Aunt Jemina," "Mammy," "sapphire," "whore," and "super woman" (Greene, 1992; Young, 1989), as "matriarchs," and as the prototypical "welfare recipient" (e.g., a lazy, single woman who continues to have children out of wedlock for a larger welfare check). The Native American Indian woman has been stereotyped as the "squaw," a term that became synonymous with "drudge" and "prostitute" (Witt, 1976). The contemporary image of the Native American Indian woman from Hollywood is a Native American Indian Princess, Pocahontas. Hispanic American women have been variously stereotyped as a passive, submissive, male-dominated, all-suffering woman or as a loud, histrionic, hot-tempered "Carmen Miranda" type (Rivers, 1995). The predominant stereotypic image for the Asian American woman is one of reserve, passivity, and sexual attractiveness. They defer to males, elders, and authority figures (Chan, 1987; Fujitomi & Wong, 1976). These different stereotypes of women share a common theme, but their differences reflect conscious and unconscious operations in the collective psyche of Americans about race and ethnicity.

In the following sections on ethnicity and race, gender is secondary to the discussion in an attempt to better elucidate how ethnicity and race become primary, inextricable aspects of identity for people of color, regardless of gender. While gender differences in identity exist in relation to ethnicity and race, the sociopolitical reality of racism in American society, and its pervasive impact on all sectors of society, including the scientific community, calls for separate consideration of race apart from gender, at least initially. To do otherwise seems more likely to obscure rather than illuminate the spectrum of socially transmitted values that are internalized in varying ways by Women of Color.

ETHNICITY

In anthropological terms, an ethnic group is generally understood to designate a population that is largely self-perpetuating; shares fundamental cultural values realized in overt unity in cultural forms; makes up a field of communication and interaction; and has a membership that identifies itself, and is identified by others, as constituting a category distinguishable from other categories of the same order (Narroll, 1964). Barth (1969) stresses that ethnic groups are categories of ascription and identification by the actors themselves and thus have the characteristic of organizing interaction between people. When someone is identified as being a member of an ethnic group, that individual supposedly shares with that group many complex characteristics, such as language, customs, traditions, physical characteristics, religion, and ancestral origin. **Ethnicity** is a key aspect of one's identity. Erikson (1950) began to develop a framework for understanding how the individual is linked to the ethnic group and society. He viewed identity as a process located in the core of the individual, and yet also in the core of his or her communal culture. Ethnic identity may remain hidden and outside awareness. Its effects on feelings, thoughts, perceptions, expectations, and actions of people toward others are not readily understood; nonetheless, it is maintained by a boundary (Barth, 1969). The following self-descriptions offered by these two individuals during a workshop on cultural sensitivity are illustrations.

I'm Syrian and Italian—pure on each side. To belong to both of these ethnic groups where I grew up meant being inferior. I have mixed feelings about my ethnic background because Italians are associated not only with food but with the underground and I have had to be connected with that emotionally. In the Syrian aspect of my life, they have not had a good historical reputation and are considered sort of sleazy—so you might say I come from a kind of underground sleaze. (Pinderhughes, 1989, p. 41)

I now realize my father taught us to hate being Black. We couldn't go out of the house until we straightened our hair—he was ashamed of being Black, and I used to envy kids whose fathers taught them to feel proud. I have to work hard to overcome this—even now. (Pinderhughes, 1989, p. 41)

The cultural indicators of the boundary may change, as well as the cultural characteristics of the members and the organizational form of the group. However, what becomes crucial in understanding the impact of ethnicity on psychological functioning are the mechanisms that permit the continued existence of the ethnic group. Barth (1969) makes the cogent point that ethnic groups persist as significant units despite constant interaction with persons of different cultural–ethnic backgrounds because of shared criteria and signals for identification and the shared codes and values that structure the very nature of such interactions. It is interesting to note that colleagues who have run workshops on racial awareness and identity have shared with me their observations that many White attendees do not think of themselves in terms of "having" an ethnicity or "being" ethnic. Ethnicity is something they associate more with minorities.

According to Goffman (1959), all interethnic relations are maintained by a set of rules that govern interethnic social encounters. Based on Erikson's views on the centrality of ethnicity to one's identity and Goffman's discussion on the systemic rules that shape and maintain interethnic encounters, ethnicity needs to be distinguished from race in psychological research and discourse. Within the psychological literature there are those who propose that the constructs of ethnicity and race be merged into a broader construct (Phinney, 1996). Based on the preceding discussion, combining ethnicity and race for research purposes would seemingly obscure rather than clarify the meaning and usage of both in psychology. I concur wholeheartedly with those who state that race is not ethnicity (Helms & Talleyrand, 1997). Instead, what needs to occur among those studying ethnicity and gender is a shift away from a psychology of groups to a psychology of group processes analyzed on various levels (e.g., intrapsychic, interpersonal, institutional and structural, and sociocultural) (Unger, 1995).

RACE IN AMERICA

Race matters in America. To the non-White person in America, race is the most important defining factor in all aspects of life (West, 1994). Race takes on cultural significance as a result of the social processes that sustain majority–minority status (Pinderhughes, 1989). The subordinate status assigned to persons with given physical traits and the projections made upon them are used to justify exclusion or inclusion within the society. The responses of both those who are dominant, and therefore exclude, and the victims who are subordinate, and therefore excluded, become part of their cultural adaptation. The meaning assigned to class status as well as racial categorization is determined by the dynamics of stratification and stereotyping. Hopps (1982) suggests that true understanding of minority status requires understanding of the various levels of oppression endured by the group. While discrimination and exclusion have existed in this country for a number of groups classified as minorities, oppression has been the most severe, deeply rooted, persistent, and intractable for people of color (Hopps, 1982).

Subordinates can and have coped with the power imbalance between them and the dominants through **horizontal hostility** (Pharr, 1988); that is, members of a subordinate group express hostility in a horizontal direction toward their own group. Consequently, there may be infighting within a subordinate group. According to Pharr (1988), "we may see people destroying their own neighborhoods, displaying violence and crime toward their own kind, while respecting the power of those that make up the norm" (p. 61). Self-hatred is often the result of the internalization of the dominant group's beliefs that those who are subordinates are substandard, defective, and inferior.

The form self-hatred takes varies from subordinate group to subordinate group. For example, among African Americans, both men and women, the preference for light skin and the devaluation of dark skin indicate negative views about the self. One of my patients takes great pride in the fact that she comes from a town in a southern state known for its single, light-skinned African American women. These women are sought out by African American men who are interested in either maintaining or improving their social status by marrying a light-skinned African American woman. Another patient, who is Puerto Rican, recalled with great sadness a conference on Latina women that she attended. According to her, Spanish was the mother tongue for some of the Latina women present, while for others, Spanish was their second language. This distinction created two antagonistic groups in which inclusion–exclusion was seemingly determined by fluency in Spanish and degree of accentedness in English.

An important factor contributing to the **assimilation** or **acculturation** of the minority group is whether the group is a **voluntary minority** or an **involuntary minority.** Ogbu (1994) states that voluntary or immigrant minorities are people (and their descendants) who have voluntarily come to the United States because they believe that the move will ultimately lead to more economic opportunities and greater political freedom. These expectations continue to influence the way that the immigrants perceive and respond to obstacles confronting them in U.S. society (e.g., discrimination). Voluntary minorities do relatively well in education and employment, especially after mastering the language. What is important is that they apparently do not interpret their presence or reception in the United States in terms of having been forced by Euro-Americans. On the other hand, involuntary minorities are people and their descendants who were originally forced against their will by Euro-Americans through slavery, conquest, and colonization to marginally participate in U.S. society. They tend to define themselves and their cultures in opposition to the cultural values of the majority.

Examples of both types include people of color from the Caribbean (e.g., Jamaican Americans) and African Americans, respectively. Although both experience oppressive racism and sexism, West Indian Americans tend to be more successful than their African American counterparts (Brice, 1982).

Featherston (1994) makes the point that Women of Color "live theater of the absurd" daily in their efforts to negate negative assumptions imposed from without and to create internal frames of reference that facilitate authentic self-awareness and expression. She quotes Toni Morrison who, on a segment of Bill Moyer's television series, *World of Ideas,* that I happened to see and that made a lasting impression on me, stated the following about Black–White race relations in the United States:

> To make an American, you had to have all these people from all these different classes, different countries, different languages feel close to one another. So what does an Italian peasant have to say to a German burgher, and what does an Irish peasant have to say to a Latvian? You know, really, they tended to balkanize. But what they could all do is not be Black. So, it is not coincidental that the second thing every immigrant learns when he gets off the boat is the word "nigger." In that way, he's establishing oneness, solidarity, and union with the country. That is the marker. That's the one. Well, these were people who were frightened. I mean, I would be. You go to a strange country, maybe you have some friends there. You need a job. You've cut your bridges. You've said something is terrible back home. You go, and you emigrate, you go someplace else. And if it's under duress, you are facing chaos. And when you are facing chaos, you have to name it, or violate it, or control it in some way. So you want to belong to this large idea, you want to belong. And one learns very quickly what to belong to. And you belong to this non-Black population which is everywhere. But it serves. It serves. It has always served economically a lot of forces in this country. (p. ii–iii)

Racial categorization is arguably questionable, confusing, and tends to have adverse effects on those identified as being members of the ethnic group (Betancourt & Lopez, 1993; Spickard, 1992). The Bureau of Census has divided the U.S. population into four major races: White, Black, Asian/Pacific Islander, and American Indian/Eskimo/Aleut. In the 1970s the Census added Hispanic origin, a group that had previously been labeled "Spanish speaking" or "Spanish surnamed." People who felt that they did not fit into these categories could choose "Other."

Squyres et al. (1996) report that the Bureau of the Census has begun hearings to consider adding new categories to the present census choices. They found that Arab-Americans, for example, are unhappy with their official designation of "White, non-European." Many Native Hawaiians want to be redesignated as American Indians rather than Pacific Islanders, reflecting historical accuracy. Some Hispanics want the Census Bureau to classify them in terms of race, not ethnic origin, and to replace "Hispanic" with "Latino." For those with this view the term *Hispanic* recalls the colonization of Latin America by Spain and Portugal and has become as offensive as the term *Negro* became for African Americans.

Survey results show that people would prefer to be identified as Puerto Rican, Colombian, Cuban, and so on. About one in three Black Americans would like the Census Bureau to adopt the term African American. People from the Caribbean, however, tend to prefer being labeled by their country of origin, such as Jamaican or Haitian American. Africans who are not American also find the term inaccurate. It is imperative that the rich diversity in individual differences that exists within each of these groups not be overlooked.

Scientists in the fields of biology and genetics have been challenging the conventional racial categories of Black, White, and Asian, based mostly on phenotype, that is, observable differences in skin color, hair texture, and the shape of one's eyes and nose, as meaningful ways of organizing information about the variability among people (Begley, 1995). When other variables such as genes or traits are used as criteria to categorize race, surprising combinations occur. Jared, a biologist, for example, groups Asian, Native American Indians, and Swedes together based on the common characteristic of their shovel-shaped incisors (Begley, 1995). Norwegians, Arabians, and the Fulani of northern Nigeria can be considered a racial group because they alone share in common the lactase enzyme that digests milk sugar; other Africans, Japanese, and Native American Indians are lactase deprived and hence could be considered another racial group.

As mentioned earlier, there is extensive literature in psychology on race and the use of race as a variable in comparison studies. Many psychological researchers, along with biologists, acknowledge that race is more a social construction than a genetic or biological reality. Some advocate combining ethnicity and race into a single construct (Phinney, 1996), while others advocate revising the construct race to distinguish it from constructs such as ethnicity and minority (Helms & Talleyrand, 1997; Landrine, 1995).

CLASS

In psychology, **class** is discussed in terms of socioeconomic status of the individual and the group, which signifies, among other things, one's degree of success in achieving a quality of life, standard of living, and life-style idealized in the American Dream. Presumably, the higher the socioeconomic level is, the better the quality of life and the more successful are those who attain it. Conversely, the lower the socioeconomic status, the less successful the individual is in attaining a desirable standard of living, which, according to democratic ideals, is possible for all. Class, defined by income, education, and power and analyzed solely in terms of its relationship with various psychological constructs, such as intelligence, locus of control, achievement motivation, mental health, and the like, obscures the vulnerabilities of designated minorities who are barred from participating as equal players in the capitalistic marketplace of the United States. When gender, race, and ethnicity are included in discussions on class, the politics of deeply institutionalized policies and practices of discrimination and the resilience of racial–ethnic and gender hierarchies becomes apparent.

For example, Sidel's (1993) assessment of poverty in the United States indicates that poverty affects women and ethnic minority families more than others. Single mothers are more likely to be poor than any other demographic group, affecting not only their psychological well-being and physical health, but also exposing their children to the stress associated with poverty. The *feminization of poverty,* a phrase originally coined by sociologist Diana Pearce (Sidel, 1993), refers to social and economic factors resulting in the increased percentage of poor women and children. These include the rapid growth of female-headed families, a labor market that continues to discriminate against female workers, and unpaid domestic responsibilities traditionally reserved for women (e.g., child care).

The manner in which women experience the adverse effects of exclusion based on race, gender, and class can and does differ among and within minority groups. Racial differences between Puerto Rican American and Asian American women can also be observed and foster different responses from the majority group. Distinctions in linguistic and cultural patterns may also, in part, account for differences in responses. For example, degree of accentedness, especially for Spanish-speaking people, tends to correlate negatively with the listener's perception and impression of the speaker's ability and competence (Ryan & Carranza, 1975; Ryan, Carranza, & Moffie, 1977; Steinhart, 1992). Research findings on Asian Americans have led to erroneous notions about their successful adaptation and contributed to the image of Asian Americans as the *model minority.* As noted earlier, while the image may be true for some Asian Americans, it is not true for others (Wong, 1983; Wong & Hayashi, 1989). Moreover, as noted, few of these studies examined gender differences (Chow, 1985). In sum, every woman, regardless of her race–ethnicity and socioeconomic status, is vulnerable to the ill effects of oppression and discrimination.

The ill effects of oppression and discrimination are evident among women and men who report experiencing a sense of marginality and/or invisibility as a function of their race, ethnicity, and/or gender (Chisholm, 1996; Comas-Diaz & Greene, 1994). By marginality, I mean to suggest that many individuals experience a profound schism between their public and private presentations of self, which reflects an awareness of how the dominant "other" perceives (misperceives by "not seeing," stereotyping, etc.) them in those settings away from family, friends, and neighborhood (e.g., work, school, or business) in which there is interaction between designated majority and minority individuals. The "not seeing" results in a sense of invisibility despite the fact that the individual may be highly visible, that is, invisible in terms of influence while being visible in terms of tokenism. The individual experiencing marginality exists uncomfortably in both worlds of the dominant other and the minority group and is perceived and treated differently by both. In the world of work, for example, the marginal person is defined by his or her race and gender, as well as competence. In personal life, he or she often feels set apart from family and friends who experience whatever his or her "successes" may be, as determined by the dominant group, as a moving away from the minority group, physically, as in leaving the old neighborhood, or psychologically, as in emotional distancing from the group.

HISTORICAL OVERVIEW OF THE EXPERIENCES OF WOMEN OF COLOR IN THE UNITED STATES

Ogbu (1994) points out the importance of appreciating the historical power relations between minority and majority groups. Even with an appreciation of diversity, one must still acknowledge the effects of the varying sociopolitical relations that each minority group has with the dominant group. That is, the origin and nature of these sociopolitical relations is not merely a function of minority culture. Instead, it varies with each minority–majority group pair.

The daily lives and activities within the communities of many African, Asian, and Latin American women may not be directly affected by racism and sexism. However, they are linked by racial oppression in both a historical and contemporary sense.

African Americans

Slavery was the lamentable plight for the ancestors of African Americans. Socioeconomic forces and racism originating during that period have been perpetuated through the years. The direct, organized, and secret

methods of groups such as the Ku Klux Klan and economic and legal methods such as Jim Crow laws in the South sustain racist practices. More covert forms of institutionalized racism and discrimination include redlining, a discriminatory practice in which some financial institutions refuse to grant mortgages, loans, or insurance to ethnic minorities living in urban areas heavily populated with ethnic minorities. Subtle but definite strategies for maintaining segregated residential communities, as well as discrimination in hiring, fosters segregation in the workplace and the community.

Traditionally, African American women have had more or less equal status with African American men within the family (Davenport & Yurich, 1991). African American women of necessity have always worked outside the home and have been strong and independent within the family. African American women have traditionally been socialized to be caretakers (Comas-Diaz & Greene, 1994). The traditional feminine role for U.S. women to be homemakers, that is, a wife and mother who remains home with the children, often was not an option for African American women, resulting in a strengthening of feelings of competency and skills of independence born out of the African tradition and survival of slavery (Smith, Burlew, Mosley, & Whitney, 1978).

Native American Indians

Native American Indians were defeated in wars, subjugated through treaties, and forced to relocate and live on reservations as a conquered people. Their historical status approximates that of traditional or classical colonialism. A woman's identity in traditional Indian life is firmly rooted in her spirituality, extended family, and tribe (Green, 1980; Jaimes, 1982; LaFromboise, Berman, & Sohi, 1994; Welch, 1987). While both Indian men and women suffer the consequences of societal dislocation and the denial of basic human rights, women's lives have been particularly affected by the pressing effects of acculturation into the dominant society. Although tribes differed in terms of the specific roles and behavior expected of women, most Native American Indian women experienced greater flexibility and power than did women in European societies. The traditional roles and status of Native American Indian women were undermined by European colonizers, who perceived the women's conduct as subversive to their intended style of socio-political and religious order (LaFromboise, Heyle, & Ozer, 1990). Missionary activity led to the Christian conversion of many Native American Indians. Indian children were forcibly separated from their families and placed in boarding schools to become "civilized," that is, to reject their culture while embracing the culture of the colonizers (Tafoya, 1989; Udall, 1977). Women's roles and power within tribes today vary among Indian communities and according to clan and family structure (LaFromboise, Heyle, & Ozer, 1990).

Hispanic Americans

People of Latin American descent are a heterogeneous group that includes new immigrants and descendants of some of the original Spanish settlers, people with different national origins, and those who do, as well as those who do not, identify closely with their ethnic heritage (Ginorio, Gutierrez, Cauce, & Acosta, 1995).

Chicanos (Mexican Americans), who make up 60 percent of the Latino population (Portes & Truelove, 1987), trace their historical origins to Mexico, which was defeated as a nation in its attempts to maintain and expand its possessions in what is now the United States. Treaties were signed between the two nations. Yet, Mexicans who remained or migrated to the United States were usually not covered by political agreements between the two sovereign nations (Lindsey, 1980). Historically, Chicanas have been ascribed an inferior status to men. Both the economic system and the church sanctioned the continued dominance and sexual abuse by men (Nieto-Gomez, 1976). "Church tradition has directed the women to identify with the emotional suffering of the pure, passive, bystander, the Virgin Mary" (p. 228). From this identification with the Virgin Mary as the ultimate role model, the concept of marianisma (the ideal of womanliness in Latino cultures) grew, along with the expectation that the woman would passively endure the injustices committed against her. The concept of marianisma has been linked with child-rearing attitudes and behaviors in Latino families. Empirical studies report that Latino families are more protective of their children than are White or African American families and that Latino families are more child-centered, placing greater emphasis on the mother–child relationship than on the spousal relationship (Ginorio et al., 1995; Durret, O'Bryant, & Pennebaker, 1975).

A similar situation is found in Puerto Rican society, which accounts for 15 percent of the Latino population, and Puerto Rican women tend to experience similar conflicts as Chicanas (Rivers, 1995). Puerto Rico was acquired by the United States at the end of the Spanish American War. The high rate of unemployment on the island has contributed to the increased migration of Puerto Ricans to the United States during the past 45 years (Ginorio et al., 1995).

The socioeconomic profile of Cuban Americans, who constitute 5 percent of the Latino population, is different from the other groups; the demographic picture of Cuban Americans mirrors the national averages with respect to education and economic status (Portes & Truelove, 1987). Those Cuban immigrants who came to the United States between 1959 and 1965, forming the first wave and settling in Miami, Florida, were successful because (1) they received federal economic benefits due to their status as political refugees, (2) they were educated, professional people, and (3) they formed an ethnic enclave economy that has supported more recent immigrants (Nelson & Tienda, 1985).

The most rapidly expanding Latino subgroup, which comprises 20 percent of the Latino population, is a heterogeneous grouping that includes Central American refugees (e.g., from El Salvador), white-collar and professional workers from South America (e.g., Argentina and Uruguay), and migrants from the Caribbean (Ginorio et al., 1995).

Asian Americans

The number of Asian Americans and Pacific Islanders doubled between 1981 and 1994, from 4.2 million to 8.8 million. Between 1980 and 1991, 46.2 percent of all immigrants admitted to the United States came from Asia. During the 1980s, immigrants from China, Korea, and the Philippines came to the United States and added to the large populations already here from those countries. These immigrants, many highly educated, came basically for family reunification and through employment provisions of the immigration laws. Another group of immigrants and refugees, fleeing from war and unstable economic and political conditions, came from countries of East and Southeast Asia (e.g., Vietnam, Laos, Cambodia, Burma, and China).

The first wave of voluntary immigration occurred among Chinese seeking fortunes in gold around 1848. Subsequent importation of Chinese laborers to the United States was recommended by the U.S. government for the establishment of a transcontinental railroad and to cultivate lands in California. Following this, immigration and naturalization laws functioned to protect the economic interest of the prevailing Eurocentric interests. These various forms of oppression have ramifications for Asian women immigrants, because they faced the problems of sexism within their own cultures and also the racism and sexism of the dominant White culture (Rohrbaugh, 1979). Traditional Asian families have a long history of oppression and exploitation of women. Women are subordinate to men and subject to male authority and control (Song, 1993).

Over 90 percent of the initial Asian immigrants were men (Kim & Otani, 1983) because of legal restrictions and a cultural tendency for women to remain at home. Immigration of women increased slowly and only substantially after 1965, after the new Immigration Act. The combination of exclusion and anti-miscegenation laws (laws prohibiting interracial marriage) acted to suppress the presence of Asian women in the United States to such a degree that the imbalance in the gender ratio was still high as recently as 1970 (Kim & Otani, 1983). Legal restrictions on the immigration of Asian women, laws that revoked citizenship for any U.S. woman who married an "alien ineligible for citizenship" (e.g., the 1922 Cable Act), and the artificial community of single Asian men created by these laws influenced to a great degree both

the status and the role of Asian women when they finally did arrive. The most blatant expression of racism directed against Asian Americans was the internment of Japanese Americans during World War II. Their property was confiscated and they were forcibly moved to detention centers.

Differences between older and younger generations of Asian women are found in (1) employment status: older women are employed in service jobs or factory jobs, especially the garment industry, whereas younger women's employment resembles the distribution for European American women (Glenn, 1986); (2) education (second- and third-generation Asian women are better educated); and (3) the values and life-styles of the younger generation, which are less traditional than those of their parents and grandparents and are often a source of conflict (Almquist, 1989). Asian Americans have been called the model minority due to their *apparent* upward mobility and socioeconomic success in comparison to other American minority groups. But within the Asian community, many, including Asian American women, have not enjoyed such success (Chow, 1985; Wong, 1983).

QUALITY OF LIFE AMONG WOMEN OF COLOR

As indicated earlier, each group of ethnic minority women has been uniquely influenced by its history prior to its arrival in the United States as well as its experiences in this country. Former Secretary of Health and Human Services Margaret M. Heckler acknowledged that large differences between the health status of Whites and ethnic minorities exist; individuals from minority groups are not as healthy and die at a younger age than those of the White majority (Squyres, Jacobs, & Quiram, 1996). Various explanations have been given, including poverty, poor access to health care, high-risk behavior, and inadequate or no health insurance.

Mental Heath

Mirowsky and Ross (1980) discuss two competing hypotheses in studies of the relation between ethnic status and psychological distress. The first, the *minority status perspective,* asserts that the extent to which an ethnic group is both a minority group and disadvantaged and the chronic social stressors associated with the disadvantaged position will produce greater distress; that is, ethnic differences in psychological distress are due primarily to social class effects. The other hypothesis, the *ethnic culture perspective,* states that ethnic psychological well-being varies with different cultural patterns in terms of beliefs, values, and life-styles; that is, there are ethnic effects that are both positive and negative on mental health over and above social class effects.

The Woman of Color who accepts the American standard for femininity, womanhood, and female attractiveness is vulnerable to lowered self-esteem and even self-hatred because of her inability to readily change facial features, hair texture, and skin color, despite the fantastic claims of the lucrative cosmetic industry, which caters to women, ethnic minority women in particular, striving to achieve the impossible (Kaw, 1993; Rivers, 1995; Root, 1995).

Misdiagnoses of mental disorders among people of color has been reported in the literature. African American and Puerto Rican patients are less likely than White patients to be diagnosed as having a psychotic affective disorder and more likely to be diagnosed as having schizophrenia (Garb, 1997; Thomas & Sillen, 1979). Patients from the lower socioeconomic classes are more often assessed to be more seriously disturbed than patients from the higher social economic classes. Moreover, women patients are more often seen to be more disturbed than their male counterparts presenting with identical problems (Garb, 1997). Among immigrants, misdiagnoses of mental disorders by service providers unfamiliar with culture-bound syndromes have been reported (Oquendo, Horwath, & Martinez, 1992). For example, among Latinas, *ataque de nervios* is a condition characterized by a sense of being out of control, in which uncontrollable shouting, attacks of crying, trembling, heat in the chest rising into the head, verbal or physical aggression, dissociative experiences, fainting, and suicidal gestures may occur. This condition may be misconstrued by the Western practitioner as somatization, hysteria, and/or an affective disorder.

Women of Color have been found to experience high levels of depression and anxiety (Kuo, 1984; LaFromboise, Heyle, & Ozer, 1990; Pyant & Yanico, 1991). An American Psychological Association report indicated that among Native American Indians the typical client seeking help from an Indian Health Service-supported, outpatient reservation-based mental health service unit, is depressed, anxious, and/or experiencing situational crises, such as domestic violence, disruption, or victimization, and has been or is currently using drugs or alcohol (Jacobs, Dauphinais, Gross, & Guzman, 1991). Additionally, tragedies occur frequently in Indian communities involving motor vehicle accidents, homicide, and suicide (Indian Health Service, 1989). Consequently, it is widely speculated that primary mental health issues for Native American Indian women are trauma and a cycle of unresolved grief and mourning (LaFromboise, Bennett, James, & Running Wolf, 1995; Root, 1992).

Many studies have found a significant relationship between mental disorders and degree of acculturation of people of color (Escobar, 1993). For example, higher rates of acute depression are sometimes reported for immigrant versus nonimmigrant Latinas (Vega, Warheit, & Meinhardt, 1984), while other studies have shown that the U.S.-born Latinas report more depression than do immigrant Latinas (Ginorio et al., 1995). It is speculated that, for the highly acculturated Latina, conflicts between cultural expectations and achievement in the majority culture in the face of discrimination generate high levels of stress (Amaro & Russo, 1987).

While Women of Color tend to have more positive attitudes toward mental health services and use them more frequently than their male counterparts (Gary, 1987), accurate diagnosis and effective treatment are often impeded by stereotypical attitudes, gender role bias (Chisholm, 1996; Comas-Diaz & Jacobsen, 1991; Sue, 1988; Thomas & Sillen, 1979), and linguistic bias directed towards non-English speaking and/or bilingual clients (Malgady et al., 1987).

Turner and Turner (1992) found in a survey among psychologists listed in the National Register of

Health Service Providers in Psychology that race–ethnicity of the therapist, not gender or age, was a significant factor in therapy outcome for a large percentage of ethnic minority clients. Ethnic minority therapists were more likely to report having ethnic minority clients as well as White clients than were the White therapists in the sample. The Turners surmised:

> White therapists, based on socialization and experience, have certain attitudes—including negative attitudes and stereotypes about various categories of people. A minority client enters the mental health system and needs to be evaluated and treated, but he/she also has attitudes about people who are likely to be the service providers. When therapist and client meet, the therapist's negative attitudes and stereotypes lead him/her to both expect certain behavior from the client and that he/she behaves in certain ways. The African American client or ethnic minority client, [emphasis mine] reacts to these expectations and behaviors, and behaves in such a way as to fulfill the expectations. The therapist notes that the client has behaved in a way consistent with his/her racial attitudes and stereotype and continues to behave in ways consistent with those attitudes and stereotypes. Since no authentic (emphasis mine) encounter takes place, one of the two gives up and leaves the relationship. (p. 8)

Box 4.1 illustrates this factor.

Physical Health

Gender and race affect longevity. The average life expectancy for women in 1994 was approximately 76.8 years. The life expectancy for a White woman was the highest at 79.7 years. For Black women, it was 74.1 years, slightly higher than that of White men (73.2 years), but much higher than that of Black men (64.9 years). For Hispanic women, it was 77.1 years and for American Indian women it was 76.2 years. Data for Asian and Pacific Islander Americans were not available. Women will continue to have longer life expectancies than men, according to the U.S. Census Bureau projections (Leigh, 1994; Squyres et al., 1996), but will be sicker (Sechzer, Griffen, & Pfafflin, 1994).

Cardiovascular Disease, Cancer, and Stroke. Heart disease is the leading cause of death for women, followed by cancer and stroke, with the exception of unintentional injuries as the third cause of death among Native American Indian women. The death rates among women vary depending on race and age. Overall, Black women have higher death rates than White women for most of the major causes of death other than suicide. Black women are more than one and a half times as likely to suffer heart disease, nearly twice as likely to have a stroke, and over two and a half times as likely to die from diabetes (Chideya, 1995; Landes, Foster, & Cessna, 1994; Squyres et al., 1996; Villarosa, 1994; White, 1994). See Table 4.2 on pages 130–131.

Four and a half times as many Black women in New York City are murdered than are White women, and nine times as many die of AIDS (see Figure 4.3 on page 132). Black and White women under age 50 have essentially equal incidence rates of breast cancer. However, after that age, White women have consistently higher rates than their Black counterparts, but survival rates are not similar. According to the 1983–1989 SEER (Surveillance, Epidemiology, and End Results) Program of the National Cancer Institute, the 5-year survival rate was 81 percent for White women and 64 percent for Black women, a difference the institute called "significant" (Landes et al., 1994) (see Figure 4.4 on page 133).

Native Hawaiian women also have higher death rates and lower 5-year survival rates than White women for most types of cancer (Leigh, 1994). Japanese, Shanghai Chinese, Singapore Chinese, and Hawaiian Filipino women have the lowest risk of breast cancer (Petrakis, 1988). The rate of cervical cancer is much higher among Hispanic, Black, Native American Indian, and Chinese American women than for White women (Delgado & Trevino, 1985).

Obesity. Obesity is one of the health-related lifestyle conditions that is a major problem for Black and Hispanic women, who have been found to have

Box 4.1

Cross-Ethnic Counseling

The following clinical vignette illustrates a worst case scenario involving an upper-middle-class White male psychiatrist and a poor, urban young African American woman patient who had been referred by the psychiatrist to see me for a psychological assessment to evaluate for mental retardation and a personality disorder.

L., a 17-year-old African American single female, was being seen once a week in psychotherapy sessions with a White male psychiatrist. A nurse's entry in her chart had suggested the possibility of suicidal behavior, because the patient had indicated during the intake screening that she had taken an overdose of vitamin C. The therapist dismissed the possibility of a suicide attempt because "Everyone knows that vitamin C won't kill you. She's probably slow." I interviewed her and obtained the following information. She was prone to violent outbursts in which she would physically fight against two or more people, males or females, when she felt provoked. She had no psychiatric history or record of misconduct or violence. L. and her boyfriend of 10 months were talking about getting married within the next two years. The emergence of the violent outbursts began several months after the sudden death of her beloved mother and consequent mistreatment by an older sister with whom she was forced to live. Her sister allegedly told L. that, because their mother was dead, she was now the mother, and L. had to obey her and live by her rules or else. Her bereavement was complicated by her intentional refusal to feel grief, sadness, and anger over her loss. Moreover, the lack of emotional support by her family and the dire financial circumstances of staving off homelessness by living with a sister whom she despised contributed to her emotional state. L. had a mercurial quality of becoming hostile and belligerent, while at other times displaying a soft-spoken, sensitive, and compassionate concern for others. She understood her fighting in terms of being easily irritated and as a way of ensuring her safety and of protecting her boyfriend who, since her mother's death, was the only other person in the world that she cared about. What was most significant about her violent behavior was the extent to which she provoked these attacks and her sense of gratification in dealing with them. In relating each incident she became "alive," eager to talk about her moves and countermoves and the harm inflicted on the others. She rarely fought with only one other person; being outnumbered was key to experiencing the "high." She seemed to have little awareness of her provocative behavior or its self-destructiveness. For instance, she described two physical altercations, one in which she deliberately fought back with a gang of girls who attacked her because she had "dissed" (disrespected) one of them, and the other involving her fighting single-handedly with a group of boys who had "dissed" her boyfriend in her presence. The significance of the history and current behavior of this young woman, which at the very least would raise the question of depression and suicidal risk, was apparently misconstrued, overlooked, or, worse, not elicited in the clinical interviews with the treating physician.

---

nearly twice the rate of obesity of White women (Landes et al., 1994; Squyres et al., 1996). Nearly 60 percent of all Native American Indian women on reservations in 1987 and 63 percent of urban American Indian women were found to be obese. Similar findings exist for Pacific Islanders, Native Hawaiian women, and Samoan women (Leigh, 1994). During adolescence and adulthood, body mass index (BMI) and the prevalence of obesity begin to increase with age among Black women and are linked to diets of poverty that are high in fat and low in fruits and vegetables. Of particular concern is the location of the excess fat. Fat that deposits more in the central part of the body has been linked to increased cardiovascular risk factors including hypertension, diabetes mellitus, and plasma lipid abnormalities. The attitudes toward body weight and weight control among Women of Color are seemingly more tolerant to the extent that being overweight or obese is not necessarily equated with being unattractive.

TABLE 4.2 Numbers of Deaths and Rank for Selected Causes of Death, According to Sex and Detailed Race: United States, 1985–1990

SEX, RACE, AND CAUSE OF DEATH	1985	1986	1987	1988	1989	1990	1985	1986	1987	1988	1989	1990
			Num	ber					Ra	nk		
White female												
All causes	666,599	878,529	669,685	911,487	902,989	902,442	—	—	—	—	—	—
Diseases of heart	332,778	333,396	333,669	337,007	323,460	318,002	1	1	1	1	1	1
Cerebrovascular diseases	81,067	79,641	79,810	79,383	76,953	76,502	3	3	3	3	3	3
Malignant neoplasms	190,548	193,971	196,716	200,626	206,856	208,977	2	2	2	2	2	2
Chronic obstructive pulmonary diseases	26,364	27,781	29,578	31,946	33,835	34,945	5	5	5	5	5	5
Pneumonia and influenza	31,480	32,432	32,527	37,308	36,961	38,705	4	4	4	4	4	4
Chronic liver diseases and cirrhosis	7,871	7,817	7,591	7,543	7,797	7,589	10	11	11	11	11	11
Diabetes mellitus	17,547	17,496	17,843	18,684	21,771	21,879	7	7	7	7	7	7
Nephritis, nephrotic syndrome, and nephrosis	8,584	8,602	8,964	9,129	8,514	8,550	9	9	9	10	10	10
Septicemia	7,419	8,194	8,840	9,873	8,829	8,870	11	10	10	9	9	9
Atherosclerosis	13,770	13,091	13,040	12,732	11,139	10,315	8	8	8	8	8	8
Human immuno-deficiency virus infection	—	—	628	788	961	1,149	—	—	24	24	23	23
Unintentional injuries	25,155	25,451	25,874	26,656	26,448	25,586	6	6	6	6	6	6
Suicide	5,831	6,167	6,029	5,810	5,566	5,638	12	12	12	12	12	12
Homicide and legal intervention	3,041	3,123	3,149	3,072	2,971	3,006	17	17	16	18	18	18
Black female												
All causes	110,597	113,112	115,263	119,791	121,249	120,139	—	—	—	—	—	—
Diseases of heart	37,702	38,650	38,813	39,882	39,110	38,073	1	1	1	1	1	1
Cerebrovascular diseases	10,341	10,014	10,055	10,381	10,240	9,754	3	3	3	3	3	3
Malignant neoplasms	21,878	22,616	23,099	23,647	24,112	25,082	2	2	2	2	2	2
Chronic obstructive pulmonary diseases	1,505	1,554	1,733	1,832	2,078	2,027	11	11	11	11	9	10
Pneumonia and influenza	2,674	2,664	2,770	3,144	3,417	3,402	7	6	6	6	6	6
Chronic liver diseases and cirrhosis	1,439	1,341	1,342	1,427	1,334	1,360	12	12	12	12	12	13
Diabetes mellitus	3,874	4,004	4,109	4,332	4,883	5,065	4	4	4	4	4	4
Nephritis, nephrotic syndrome, and nephrosis	2,109	2,057	2,070	2,249	2,119	2,049	8	8	8	8	8	9
Septicemia	1,662	1,720	1,988	2,011	1,912	1,841	10	10	9	10	11	11
Atherosclerosis	1,022	964	942	955	889	817	13	15	15	15	16	16
Human immuno-deficiency virus infection	—	—	739	995	1,320	1,633	—	—	16	14	13	12
Unintentional injuries	3,455	3,550	3,618	3,879	3,901	3,663	5	5	5	5	5	5
Suicide	314	355	328	374	382	374	19	19	19	20	19	20
Homicide and legal intervention	1,666	1,861	1,969	2,089	2,074	2,163	9	9	10	9	10	8

SEX, RACE, AND CAUSE OF DEATH	1985	1986	1987	1988	1989	1990	1985	1986	1987	1988	1989	1990
			Number						*Rank*			
American Indian female												
All causes	2,973	2,936	3,170	3,300	3,548	3,439	—	—	—	—	—	—
Diseases of heart	732	683	755	777	880	807	1	1	1	1	1	1
Cerebrovascular diseases	189	175	185	200	181	201	4	4	4	4	5	4
Malignant neoplasms	456	486	549	557	612	646	2	2	2	2	2	2
Chronic obstructive pulmonary diseases	51	46	71	66	85	91	10	12	8	8	8	8
Pneumonia and influenza	99	85	110	131	142	147	7	7	7	7	7	7
Chronic liver diseases and cirrhosis	147	124	134	162	172	154	6	6	6	6	6	6
Diabetes mellitus	150	137	158	187	211	196	5	5	5	5	4	5
Nephritis, nephrotic syndrome, and nephrosis	56	74	63	53	59	54	8	8	9	10	11	10
Septicemia	39	33	37	50	35	38	12	14	14	12	13	13
Atherosclerosis	26	26	20	26	29	17	15	15	15	15	15	15
Human immunodeficiency virus infection	—	—	3	—	8	3	—	—	25	—	23	29
Unintentional injuries	306	339	305	306	318	299	3	3	3	3	3	3
Suicide	38	37	39	36	35	38	14	13	13	14	13	13
Homicide and legal intervention	39	55	51	50	72	51	12	11	11	12	10	11
Asian or Pacific Islander female												
All causes	6,446	6,719	7,193	7,808	8,354	8,916	—	—	—	—	—	—
Diseases of heart	1,729	1,834	1,875	2,065	2,186	2,360	1	1	2	2	2	1
Cerebrovascular diseases	689	641	719	789	846	924	3	3	3	3	3	3
Malignant neoplasms	1,649	1,752	1,902	2,115	2,236	2,302	2	2	1	1	1	2
Chronic obstructive pulmonary diseases	66	78	82	78	79	85	13	13	12	13	13	13
Pneumonia and influenza	201	226	253	242	328	355	5	5	5	5	5	5
Chronic liver diseases and cirrhosis	66	78	82	78	79	85	13	13	12	13	13	13
Diabetes mellitus	132	175	184	188	231	256	7	6	6	6	6	6
Nephritis, nephrotic syndrome, and nephrosis	68	81	83	80	105	103	12	12	11	12	11	12
Septicemia	44	62	80	59	68	77	15	14	13	14	14	14
Atherosclerosis	46	37	43	46	46	39	14	15	15	15	15	16
Human immunodeficiency virus infection	—	—	10	8	14	16	—	—	24	27	24	22
Unintentional injuries	380	366	407	433	442	487	4	4	4	4	4	4
Suicide	123	118	126	109	143	131	9	9	9	10	8	10
Homicide and legal intervention	79	97	79	109	102	107	11	11	14	10	12	11

Source: From "Mental Health Issues in African-American Women," by J. F. Chisholm, 1996, *Women and Mental Health: Annals of the New York Academy of Sciences, 789,* pp. 167–168. Copyright 1996 by the New York Academy of Sciences. Reprinted with permission.

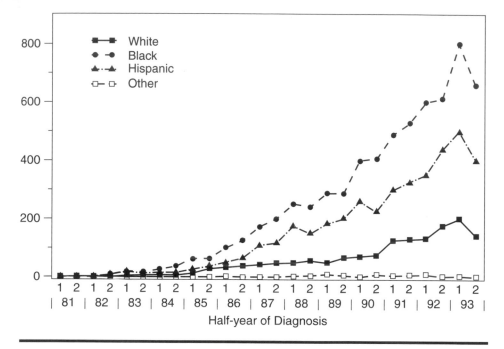

FIGURE 4.3   AIDS Cases in New York City among Women by Race/Ethnicity by Half-Year of Diagnosis

Source: From the New York City Department of Health AIDS Surveillance Unit. From "Mental Health Issues in African-American Women," by J. F. Chisholm, 1996, *Women and Mental Health: Annals of the New York Academy of Sciences, 789,* p. 166. Copyright 1996 by the New York Academy of Sciences. Reprinted with permission.

Cigarette Smoking.   The hazards of cigarette smoking affect not only the smoker, but everyone with whom she comes in contact (e.g., children and the spouse through second-hand smoke and the fetus if the smoker is pregnant). Cigarette smoking has declined among Black and White women since the 1980s but has not changed among Hispanic women (Haynes, Harvey, Montes, Nickens, & Cohen, 1990; Leigh, 1994; Squyres et al., 1996). Surveys show that Asian American women have the lowest rate of smoking; the prevalence rates vary among Native American Indians.

According to a nationwide survey conducted by the Centers for Disease Control and Prevention, the smoking habits of youth suggest a disturbing trend in the 1990s. Among Black youth, smoking rates increased 80 percent since 1991 from 12.6 percent to

22.7 percent; 39.7 percent of white teenagers reported cigarette use, an increase from 30.9 percent in 1991. More than one-third of Hispanic students smoked cigarettes, up from about 25 percent in 1991 (Stolberg, 1998). Chapter 13 provides general information on physical health.

Education

Regardless of education, on average, men still earn more than women at every level of education. The greatest disparity exists for women with professional degrees (60 percent of what men earn) and for those who did not finish high school (65 percent) (Chideya, 1995; Landes et al., 1994; Ortiz, 1994) (see Table 4.3 on page 134).

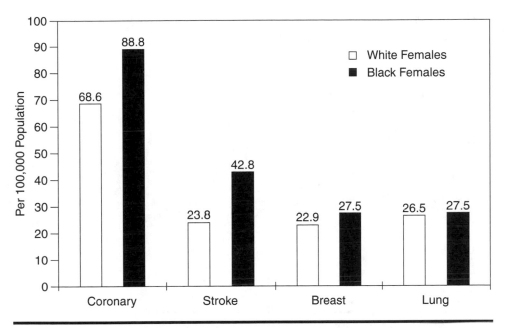

FIGURE 4.4 Age-Adjusted Death Rates for Heart Attack, Stroke, Breast and Lung Cancer for White and Black Females (United States: 1990 Final Mortality)

Source: National Center for Health Statistics and the American Heart Association. From "Mental Health Issues in African-American Women," by J. F. Chisholm, 1996, *Women and Mental Health: Annals of the New York Academy of Sciences, 789,* p. 165. Copyright 1996 by the New York Academy of Sciences. Reprinted with permission.

The proportion of all women attending institutions of higher education rose from 47 percent in 1976 to 55 percent in 1993. By 1993, Asian and Hispanic women made the greatest gains in enrollment over those years (304 percent and 215 percent increase, respectively) (Foster, Squyres, & Jacobs, 1996; Squyres et al., 1996). As of 1994, about 63.2 percent of female high school graduates enrolled in college, compared to 60.6 percent of all high school graduates. In 1992–1993, women obtained a larger percentage (59 percent) of associate degrees (2-year college) than men, and women earned 54 percent of the bachelor's degrees (4-year college); however, they earned fewer degrees at the graduate level (Foster et al., 1996; Squyres et al., 1996). Educational attainment was typically lower among Hispanics of both sexes than among Blacks or Whites. Ginorio and col-

leagues (1995) conclude that Latinas (Hispanic women) receive less familial and institutional support for educational achievement than Latinos (Hispanic men) and are more likely to be encumbered by societal gender-role responsibilities. Those Latinas who do achieve academic success are accordingly less likely to be married and less of a **gender stereotype** than their counterparts who do not attend college or attain college degrees. The proportion of women who have had 12 or more years of schooling increased most dramatically between 1970 and 1991 among Black women. Women of Asian descent, whether born in this country or not, are more likely than other women between the ages of 25 and 54 to have had four or more years of college.

The fields of study in which the most notable gains for women occurred were business and

TABLE 4.3   Median Weekly Earnings of Full-Time Workers, 1997 Annual Average

CHARACTERISTIC	TOTAL	EDUCATIONAL ATTAINMENT		
		Less Than High School	*High School Diploma, No College*	*Bachelor's Degree or Higher*
Total	503	307	534	760
Men	579	335	615	877
Women	431	265	457	654
White	519	310	560	776
Men	595	341	634	899
Women	444	266	469	663
Black	400	291	419	617
Men	432	316	464	651
Women	375	257	393	596
Hispanic	351	285	422	666
Men	371	301	463	745
Women	318	249	382	606

Source: U.S. Department of Labor, Bureau of Labor Statistics, unpublished tabulations from the current population survey, Washington, DC, 1997.

management. Between 1971 and 1990, the proportion of business and management degrees awarded to women rose from 9 percent to 46 percent at the bachelor's level and from 4 percent to 34 percent at the master's level. After declining in the 1970s and 1980s, degrees earned in psychology, social sciences, and education rose in the 1990s. Important inroads were also made by women in the life, physical, and computer sciences (Foster et al., 1996; Squyres et al., 1996).

Employment

In the early 1990s, 59 million women aged 16 years and older were employed or looking for work, or 58 percent of the total female labor force; 74 percent of all women in the workforce were in their child-bearing years (18 to 44 years). The greatest labor force participation was among women between 35 to 44 years of age (77 percent). Over 55 percent of all working women are employed in the following traditionally female occupations: administrative support including clerical, service, and health treatment occupations (e.g., nurses, dieticians, and physician's assistants) and noncollege-level teachers. Many Native American Indian women work primarily in federal and local government jobs. Other women are employed as artists, poets, university instructors, heavy equipment operators, truck drivers, and small farmers (LaFromboise et al., 1994).

While Latinas have the lowest labor force participation, the participation is not equal among the major Hispanic groups in the United States; there are major differences for both men and women in labor force participation, with Chicanos having the highest participation rate among males and Cuban women having the highest participation rate among females. For both genders, Puerto Ricans have the lowest participation rate (Ginorio et al., 1995).

As with Black American women, Asian American women tend to be employed outside the home because they need a second income (Chan, 1991). According to Chu (1988), Filipina women are employed at a higher rate than men because of their high educational levels, whereas Vietnamese women are employed at the lowest rates in part because of lack of skills relevant to the type of employment. Reporting on census data for Los Angeles County from 1980, Chu (1988) states that Korean and Vietnamese women were overrepresented in the lower-paying jobs and underrepresented in managerial and professional jobs. The percent of Filipina and Asian Indian women working in managerial and professional jobs was higher. She also noted that more than half of Japanese women were in white-collar occupations, as were Chinese women.

Recent surveys indicate that 57 percent of all married women over 16 years of age are employed. The percentage of working wives' earnings to family income varied by race: 38 percent for Black working wives, 32 percent for Hispanic wives, and 31 percent for White working wives (Foster et al., 1996). The main reason for the varying percentages was that more Black wives were year-round, full-time workers (64 percent), compared to 53 percent of White wives and 51 percent of Hispanic wives. Additionally, White husbands earned more than Black or Hispanic husbands, although earnings for wives varied little. Consequently, Black wives' salaries were 83 percent of their husbands', Hispanic wives earned 74 percent as much as their husbands, and White women earned 68 percent as much as their husbands.

The number of Caucasian women and ethnic minority women and men attaining professional status is higher than ever before. However, despite their advancement to professional standing, women and ethnic minority men are typically confined to lower-level management positions than Caucasian men, a phenomenon that has been termed the "glass ceiling" effect. The glass ceiling refers to an artificial barrier in the workplace that prohibits qualified employees from advancing beyond certain levels. Biased assumptions inherent in the organizational structure of a company or biases held by key decision makers maintain the glass ceiling phenomenon in the workplace. This results in the exclusion of White women and ethnic minority men and women from the centers of power where important decisions are made. In general, minorities have plateaued at lower levels of the work

force than women (Cyrus, 1993). Stress among professional Women of Color in the corporate world can overwhelm (Campbell, 1993). This stress is more than the typical stress relating to managing homes and families while dealing with office politics and meeting deadlines. The highly competitive atmosphere with its oppressive overtones separates ethnic minority women not only from their White colleagues, but also tends to place them in opposition to their ethnic minority male professional counterparts. Says Audrey Chapman, a therapist and human relations trainer in Washington, D.C., specializing in stress management seminars for women professionals, "The women exhibit a lot of psychosomatic pain in their backs and necks. They have severe menstrual cramps. The pain isn't so much physical as it is mental. Stress leads to the real killers . . . hypertension, diabetes, and strokes" (Campbell, p. 107).

Family Type

Parenting is one of the important functions of family life, regardless of family type. Box 4.2 provides major aspects of parenting.

The Bureau of Labor statistics reported that in 1993 there were 32.7 million families with children under 18 years old; 61 percent of these families had children under 6 years of age, 53 percent of whom had a mother in the labor force. More Black women with children under 6 years old worked outside the home than White women, 73.5 percent compared to 59.1 percent (Landes et al., 1994).

Single-parent families make up 31 percent of all family groups. In 1994, 60 percent of Black families with children under age 18 were female headed, compared with 31 percent among Hispanic families and 21 percent of White families (Rawlings & Saluter, 1995). Forty-five percent of Native American Indian households are headed by women (LaFromboise, Bennett et al., 1995), 42 percent of these women are under the age of 20 when they have their first child, and many never marry (Snipp & Aytac, 1990). Chu (1988) noted that the divorce rate for Asian Americans was much lower than for other women; thus, proportionally fewer Asian women are

Box 4.2

Highlight on Parenting

Effective parenting enables parents to encourage and facilitate the development of healthy, well-adjusted children who are prepared to deal with the vicissitudes of life. By definition, effective parenting presupposes that the quality of the parent–child relationship and parenting skills are sound. In 1990 the U.S. Department of Health and Human Services sponsored a conference that reviewed research on successful families. The following characteristics were found among strong, healthy families: communication, encouragement of individuals, expressing appreciation, commitment to family, religious and spiritual orientation, social connectedness, ability to adapt, clear roles, and time together (Foster et al., 1996). Each of these characteristics may have different definitions and requirements by an ethnic group.

A child, having matured in a family that facilitated the above, has achieved a harmonious balance between her private, inner reality of the self and experience and her public presentation of self in the outer (social) reality. Conversely, ineffective parenting as evidenced in the research on violent youth, for example, indicates disturbances in the parent–child relationship that interfere with a child's development, predisposing the child to later difficulties. Given the ethnic and multicultural diversity, as well as the social class differences within contemporary American society, no one model or ideal child-rearing method exists (Fantini & Cardenas, 1980). There must be a recognition of the community values, the dignity inherent in local cultural customs, and the need for tolerance in relating to cultural diversity. While it is beyond the scope of this chapter to examine the differences in child rearing among and between people of color of different socioeconomic status and ethnocultural backgrounds, it is worthwhile to acknowledge that differences in child rearing relative to our pluralistic society may affect the issues raised in this discussion.

Recent thinking about family systems and our understanding of unconscious motivations help to expand our knowledge about the transmission of family patterns across generations. Not only explicit family rules, but also powerful implicit rules allow the expression of certain feelings and inhibit others. The concept of *quality time* may also serve to illustrate the above ideas. In one sense the term seems euphemistic in that it serves to assuage the guilt and, in some instances, contradict the common sense of some parents who realize that while they are away from their children, parenting responsibilities must be delegated to others or in many cases to the children themselves (e.g., latchkey children). Alternatively, quality time alludes to a psychological space in which ideas, attitudes, fantasies, expectations, intentionality, parent–child schemes, and skills about parenting determine the characteristics of the actual parenting. Achieving quality time on a regular, consistent basis has become close to impossible for all types of families, especially dual-career families, working class families in which both parents have one or more jobs, and single-parent families.

I am reminded of a conversation I had with a colleague whose children are now grown. She said that one advantage of being in academia was the flexible schedule. All through her children's childhood and adolescence she prided herself on "being there for them." She was disturbed by a recent conversation with her adult daughter, whose recollection of her mother during those years was quite different; the daughter felt that her mother had always been preoccupied with work and not "all there." Fabe and Wikler (1978) describe four factors that affect how a working mother will adapt to parenting: (1) the demands of her work, (2) her attitudes about her job, (3) her use of child care, and (4) her personal reaction to motherhood. Even with the involvement of the father in child care, the stress and strain of being responsive to the child's needs and fulfilling other often conflicting responsibilities may affect child rearing vis-à-vis the emotional availability of the parent and the quality of the parent–child interactions; this is especially true for people of color who face discrimination based on cultural or ethnic–racial prejudice.

single heads of households than other groups of women. However, differences exist among Asian groups; the divorce rate was higher among Japanese Americans compared with Vietnamese Americans; the divorce rate for Korean women was relatively high also (Root, 1995).

In 1994, about 38 percent of single parents were divorced, 38 percent had never been married, 20 percent were married but not living with their spouse, and 5 percent were widowed. Parents who were divorced or never married accounted for three of every four single parents (see Box 4.2).

SUMMARY

This chapter reviewed and discussed some traditional psychological theories and the empirical research on people of color (the minorities). The concept of gender and the salience of including, in fruitful ways, an analysis of culture, ethnicity, race, and class into discussions on gender and socialized behavior were explored. A brief historical overview of the experiences of women from four ethnic minority groups (African Americans, Native American Indians, Asian Americans, and Hispanic Americans), as well as a summary of the quality of life issues facing them, were presented.

The scope of psychological inquiry into culture, race, ethnicity, and gender to date has seemingly been limited to identifying and appreciating the diversity among ethnic groups in general and among ethnic women in particular as it pertains to gender. What is also needed and to date has not been done is an analysis into the ethnic boundary that defines the group, that is, the social boundaries structuring social life. As discussed earlier in the chapter, social boundaries involve a complex organization of behavior and social relations such that the nature of interactions among people is in a sense determined by unconscious cueing by fellow members of the ethnic group. It thus entails the assumption that the two are fundamentally "playing the same game," and there is the potential for diversification and expansion of their social relationship to cover eventually all different sectors and domains of activity. On the other hand, a dichotomization of others as strangers, or outsiders, implies a recognition of limitations on shared understandings and interactions. The status of a given group within society helps to determine whether the ethnic meaning for a given group or individual becomes positive, ambivalent, or negative, which bears greatly on how the group and the individual behave.

Theories and research on the complexities in the relationship between self and racial–ethnic identity have shown that when people are secure in their identity they can act with greater openness to others of different cultural backgrounds and with more freedom and flexibility. However, when people internalize negative images of their ethnic background or learn values from the larger society that conflict with those of their family, they can develop a sense of inferiority and self-hate that manifests in different ways (Cobbs, 1972; Klein, 1980; McGoldrick, Pearce, & Giordano, 1982).

For Women of Color in the United States, race, gender, and class are so intertwined that manifestations of their presence constantly permeate our lives. The fictions ascribed to us form a socially constructed reality or pseudoreality of stereotypic images idealized and devalued by society at large and internalized by us in varying degrees. These images capture the shadow rather than the essence of our lives, thereby limiting opportunities and possible experiences and hence curtailing our potential and prohibiting what could be. Similar sentiments are expressed by other women who, while not directly subjected to oppressive forces because of race, nonetheless feel and are oppressed by other forms of discrimination prevalent in our society. Engendering psychology and including in meaningful ways the influences of culture, race, ethnicity, and class will provide psychologists with the tools necessary to shatter the fictive images that destroy us and pave the way for self-definitions that affirm and appreciate our differences as well as our commonalities.

The first four chapters of this volume have provided basic perspectives through which to consider the special topics that follow. It is important to be mindful of basic constructs, gender stereotypes, the biology of sex and gender, and culture, ethnicity, race, and class as they relate to the following chapters.

KEY TERMS

Acculturation (p. 121)
African American (p. 109)
Asian American (p. 109)
Assimilation (p. 121)
Behavior setting (p. 114)
Black (p. 109)
Chicanos and Chicanas (p. 109)
Class (p. 123)
Contextualistic behaviorism (p. 113)
Cultural deprivation model (p. 111)
Culture (p. 113)
Dominant culture (p. 118)
Ecological model (p. 114)

Ethnicity (p. 120)
Ethnocultural group (p. 109)
Gender (p. 109)
Gender identity (p. 114)
Gender stereotype (p. 133)
Genital mutilation (p. 116)
Hegemony (p. 110)
Hispanic (p. 109)
Horizontal hostility (p. 121)
Inferiority model (p. 111)
Insider's perspective (p. 111)
Involuntary minority (p. 121)
Issei (p. 118)

Latinos and Latinas (p. 109)
Model minority (p. 111)
Native American Indian (p. 109)
Nisei (p. 118)
Outsider's perspective (p. 111)
Racism (p. 111)
Sansei (p. 118)
Sexism (p. 119)
Voluntary minority (p. 121)
White (p. 109)
White privilege (p. 118)

DISCUSSION QUESTIONS

1. Are the commonalities among women of different cultures, ethnicities, races, and social classes greater than their differences, such that the "truths" about one group of women are relevant and true for different groups of women? If yes, why? If no, why not?

2. In what ways do culture, ethnicity, race, gender, and class influence your sense of identity?

3. Discuss how a Woman of Color from a voluntary minority might respond differently than a woman from an involuntary minority to discrimination and prejudice experienced in the workplace.

4. Discuss Yamada's assertion that traditional feminist thought about gender causes Women of Color to experience a double bind.

5. In what ways have traditional theories and research methodology within mainstream psychology perpetuated gender and ethnic stereotypes? What steps should psychologists take to reduce and eventually eliminate these types of bias in research?

6. Are Asian American women the model minority? If yes, why? If no, why not?

7. Define marginality. In what ways do oppression and discrimination contribute to men and women experiencing a sense of marginality?

8. Should race and ethnicity be merged into a single construct within psychology? If yes, why? If no, why not?

SUGGESTED READINGS

Anzaldúa, G. (Ed.). (1990). *Making face, making soul—Haciendo caras: Creative and critical perspectives by feminists of color.* San Francisco: Aunt Lute Foundation.

Azibo, D. A. (1988). Understanding the proper and improper usage of the comparative research framework. *Journal of Black Psychology, 15,* 81–91.

Cole, J. (Ed.). (1986). *All American women: Lives that divide, ties that bind.* New York: Macmillan.

Landrine, H. (Ed.). (1995). *Bringing cultural diversity to feminist psychology: Theory, research, and practice.* Washington, DC: American Psychological Association.

Ogbu, J. (1994). From cultural differences to differences in cultural frame of reference. In P. Greenfield & R. Cocking (Eds.), *Cross-cultural roots of minority child development* (pp. 365–391). Hillsdale, NJ: Lawrence Erlbaum.

Pinderhughes, E. (1989). *Understanding race, ethnicity, and power: The key to efficacy in clinical practice.* New York: Free Press.

Song, Y., & Kim, E. (Eds.). (1993). *American mosaic: Selected readings on America's multicultural heritage* (pp. 186–203). Upper Saddle River, NJ: Prentice Hall.

CHAPTER 5

GROWING UP

What are little girls made of, made of?
What are little girls made of?
Sugar and spice and everything nice;
And that's what little girls are made of, made of.
—Mother Goose

Boys were listened to and shown how to do things, which would seem to convey the message that what they have to say is important and that they are mastering new skills. Girls, on the other hand, were treated gently, and at the same time, with a lack of full attention and an imposing of opinions and values. The gentle treatment would seem to convey the message that they are fragile and docile.
—Phyllis Bronstein

In the older times it was seldom said to little girls, as it always has been said to boys, that they ought to have some definite plan, while they were children, what to be and do when they were grown up. There was usually but one path open before them, to become good wives and housekeepers. And the ambition of most girls was to follow their mothers' footsteps in this direction: a natural and laudable ambition. But girls, as well as boys, must often have been conscious of their own peculiar capabilities—must have desired to cultivate and make use of their individual powers.
—Lucy Larcom

The only trouble here is they won't let us study enough. They are so afraid we shall break down and you know the reputation of the College is at stake, for the question is, can girls get a college degree without ruining their health?
—Ellen Henrietta Swallow Richards

. . . all children have creative power.
—Brenda Ueland

This chapter discusses various issues pertaining to the development of gender roles in childhood. According to a recent article in *Newsweek,* the concept of *child* development has become obsolete. Today, girls' development is viewed separately from boys' development because girls face distinct challenges during the course of their childhood.

Gender role development is then described in this chapter in the context of several scientific paradigms, including psychoanalytic, social learning, and cognitive-developmental theories. Distinctions between a feminine and masculine sense of morality are highlighted, and theories proposed by Freud, Kohlberg, and Gilligan are contrasted. Freudian theory links children's moral capacity to their development of a superego at the resolution of the Oedipal conflict. Kohlberg elucidates a developmental series of moral reasoning that is hierarchical in nature and based on research with only male children. Gilligan, on the other hand, describes two different styles of moral reasoning adopted by boys and girls that emerge in the context of their differential upbringing. The chapter also illustrates prevailing images of mas-

culinity and femininity in U.S. society. These gender stereotypes play an influential role in shaping young children's attitudes and emerging gender identity formation. Next, the chapter examines additional forces influencing gender-role development, beginning with parenting and prenatal experiences and continuing with socialization aspects, such as language, play, media, school, and peers. The increase in biological and social distinctions between the sexes that emerges during puberty and adolescence is discussed. Finally, the chapter examines how demographic variables, specifically race and class, influence gender comparisons.

EXPECTATIONS AND GENDER ROLES

When American couples elect to find out the sex of their child during the mother's pregnancy, gender-role expectations and assignments may be set in motion even at this prenatal stage. Often, as the time for delivery nears, preparations are made, such as the selection of the nursery room color and decor and the purchase of gender-appropriate toys and clothing.

Box 5.1_____

The Wonder (and Worry) Years

There may be no such thing as *child* development anymore. Instead, researchers are now studying each gender's development separately and discovering that boys and girls face very different sorts of challenges. Here is a rough guide to the major phases in their development.

	GIRLS	BOYS
0–3 years	Girls are born with a higher proportion of nerve cells to process information. More brain regions are involved in language production and recognition.	At birth, boys have brains that are 5% larger than girls' (size doesn't affect intelligence) and proportionately larger bodies—disparities that increase with age.
4–6 years	Girls are well suited to school. They are calm, get along with others, pick up on social cues, and reading and writing come easily to them.	The start of school is a tough time as boys must curb aggressive impulses. They lag behind girls in reading skills, and hyperactivity may be a problem.
7–10 years	Very good years for girls. On average, they outperform boys at school, excelling in verbal skills while holding their own in math.	While good at gross motor skills, boys trail girls in finer control. Many of the best students but also nearly all of the poorest ones are boys.
11–13 years	The start of puberty and girls' most vulnerable time. Many experience depression; as many as 15% may try to kill themselves.	A mixed bag. Dropout rates begin to climb, but good students start pulling ahead of girls in math skills and catching up some in verbal ones.
14–16 years	Eating disorders are a major concern. Although anorexia can manifest itself as early as 8, it typically afflicts girls starting at 11 or 12; bulimia at 15.	Entering adolescence, boys hit another rough patch. Indulging in drugs, alcohol and aggressive behavior are common forms of rebellion.

Source: From "Boys Will Be Boys," by B. Kantrowitz and B. Kalb, 1998, May 11, *Newsweek,* pp. 54–60. Newsweek–Kantrowitz and Kalb. Copyright © 1998 by Newsweek, Inc. All rights reserved. Reprinted by permission.

Blue is the traditionally appropriate color for newborn boys' clothing, bedding, and room, and pink is the traditional color for girls. Initially, children of either gender may receive soft, cuddly toys to play with that may vary according to gender. For example, it is considered unusual for the growing female child to be given "male" toys such as footballs and trucks. Maccoby and Jacklin (1974) reported that U.S. men prefer to have male children. Similarly, Jaccoma and Denmark (1974) noted that couples in the United States often hope that the firstborn child will be male, based on the assumption that if a female child is born afterward, she will have an older brother to look out for her (Denmark, Nielson, & Scholl, 1993; Jaccoma & Denmark, 1974).

Even before the woman becomes pregnant, there are various strategies that many employ to influence the sex of the embryo. As we learned in Chapter 3, the mother's sex chromosome is consistently an X or female chromosome and the father's sex chromosome may be either a female X or a male Y chromosome. An XX chromosome pairing during fertilization and conception will initiate the process toward the development of a female embryo; an XY chromosome pairing will initiate the process toward male development.

In addition to the early beliefs and practices described in Chapter 3 to influence the sex of the offspring, current beliefs and practices may be based on more reliable scientific data. Women who conceive during times when their vaginal environments are strongly acidic are more likely to have girls, suggesting that a strongly acidic environment may weaken or be detrimental to the male Y chromosome (Rathus, 1988). Timing of fertilization may also be a factor in determining the embryo's sex. Although the Y chromosome is faster, it does not endure as long as the X chromosome. Therefore, if fertilization takes place slightly before ovulation when the ovum (egg) is not completely mature, it is more likely that the embryo will be a female. In this circumstance, the sperm must remain in the female's reproductive tract until the egg is fully mature, which increases the probability that the more enduring X chromosome will outlast the Y chromosome. However, if fertilization occurs right after ovulation when the ovum is fully mature, the greater speed of the Y chromosome may enable it to reach and fertilize the ovum before the X chromosome, making it more probable that the embryo will be a male (Nevid et al., 1995).

SCIENTIFIC THEORIES ON GROWING UP

Three major psychological theories attempt to explain gender-role development: the *psychoanalytic* perspective, *social learning* theory, and the *cognitive-developmental* approach.

Freud's *psychoanalytic theory* posits that children ultimately learn to adopt the male or female role through identification with the same-sex parent, passing through several fixed stages of psychosexual development. Female and male infants begin life in the oral stage of development. The mouth is the original erogenous zone and babies derive nourishment and pleasure entirely from their oral experiences of sucking and feeding. Initially the mother serves as the love object for both boys and girls, and there is minimal psychological differentiation of the sexes. During the anal phase of development, emphasis is shifted away from the infant's feeding experiences involving the mouth, and toilet training assumes a prominent position. Throughout the oral and anal stages of development, boys and girls remain psychologically similar. The onset of the phallic stage during the preschool years ushers in the development of disparate gender roles. At this time, boys and girls discover that they are anatomically different, a revelation that is pivotal in the developing relationship with both parents. Boys discover that they have a penis and take great pride in this organ. Oedipal struggles ensue in which boys harbor sensual feeling for their mothers and resent their fathers as rivals in the competition for the mother's affection. To resolve the guilt inspired by these emotions and to mitigate the intense fear that their fathers will punish them with castration, boys abandon their mothers and identify with their fathers. The process of identification with the father involves internalizing the father's ideals, values, and behaviors and acquiring a masculine gender identity.

The experience of girls during the phallic stage is drastically different. When they discover that they don't have a penis, girls grow angry with their mothers because they perceive themselves to have been castrated and they develop penis envy. An Electra complex ensues in which girls develop sensual feelings for their fathers and resent their mothers. Eventually acknowledging that identification with the father is hopeless, they accept their mother as a role model, but often with lingering ambivalence. Thus, children of both sexes develop images of gender which are largely based on the personalities of their parents. This theory of development, while creative and innovative, is unscientific in nature and denigrates women. By emphasizing the presence or absence of a penis as the pivotal element of gender differentiation, Freud's model of psychosexual development inherently asserts the superiority of the male sex (see also Chapter 3). Therefore, other approaches to gender-role development have been theorized.

Unlike the psychoanalytic approach, *social learning theory* emphasizes the power of the surrounding social environment in influencing children's development of gender images. Although this approach shares Freud's view that children internalize gender images through imitation of their parents, social learning theory proposes that others' reactions serve as the main motivation for internalizing these images. The principle of reinforcement states that reward after the performance of a specific behavior will increase the possibility that this behavior will be performed more frequently in the future. Behaviors followed by punishments will be subsequently abandoned. Relating to gender development, children are consistently rewarded for performing actions that are stereotypically associated with their sex. Hence, they are most likely to adopt gender-typed behaviors into their repertoire. Gender-inappropriate behaviors, which often elicit punishment and criticism from parents, are relinquished.

The concepts of imitation and observational learning are also included in the paradigm of social learning theory. Children have a tendency to copy the behaviors they view others performing. They actively observe what other people are doing and may store up this information to guide them in the future. Therefore, according to this theory, children acquire gender-roles by imitating and observing the behaviors of their same-sex parent. However, children may have their own conceptions about appropriate behavior for boys and girls; neither psychoanalytic nor social learning theory accounts for this possibility.

The *cognitive-developmental perspective* emphasizes the role of the child in her or his own socialization. Based on the model of cognitive development advanced by Piaget and Inhelder, children's shifting cognitive organization underlies their development of gender roles. Children learn their own *gender identity* at an early age and choose to form their own images of behaviors and traits appropriate to their gender. The concept of gender identity forms around two years of age. At this time, girls and boys recognize their sex and identify with their same-sex parent. However, gender remains a fluid construct in their minds and they do not recognize the permanency of being a female or male until *gender constancy* is achieved. Gender identity becomes a crucial aspect of personal

identity once girls and boys realize that their sex is a fixed characteristic. Role models are a springboard for this process; eventually, children use gender as a classification principle and create schemas, or mental categories, organized in terms of gender. They impose structure on their world and actively choose to behave according to these gender-typed rules.

Like social learning theory, the cognitive-developmental view proposes that gender-role learning is a function of a general process in which children use cues from their social environment to form notions of gender-appropriate behavior. The primary weakness of cognitive-developmental theory is that it is incomplete; it does not account for the entire process of gender-role socialization.

In support of cognitive-developmental theory, a recent report states that knowledge about gender begins as early as the first year of infancy (Poulin-Dubois, Serbin, Kenyon, & Derbyshire, 1994). (See Bem's [1981] gender schema theory discussed later in this chapter.) At one year of age, infants can match voices with faces according to gender, at least for female stimuli. Because this knowledge about gender is based on the perceptual characteristics of each gender group, its development is likely to precede the development of knowledge about female- or male-typed activities and traits associated with each gender (Poulin-Dubois et al., 1994). Toddlers, especially boys, are more likely to comply with the demands of the same-sex parent. This may be because of perceived similarities with this parent (Power, McGrath, Hughes, & Manire, 1994).

MORAL DEVELOPMENT

Moral development is another area in which misconceptions about gender exist. Several noted researchers on child development have differentiated between the moral development of females and males. Four such scholars are Freud, Piaget, Kohlberg, and Gilligan.

Freud

According to Freudian theory (as noted earlier in this chapter), children resolve their Oedipal conflicts through identification with the same-sex parent, which results in the acquisition of the superego. The superego fills a self-judgmental function in the child and serves to promote the child's morality. Freud believed that the superego was less developed in girls, because their identification with the same-sex parent was more ambivalent than that of boys. As a result, girls were assumed to have vaguer conceptions of morality than boys did.

Freud concluded that females would not solve moral problems through a rational, impersonal set of rules based on society's values. Rather, they would base their reasoning on their feelings about the people involved and the particular situation. As we mentioned earlier, Freud's theories have been criticized for their unscientific nature and lack of empirical evidence, as well as their obvious gender bias.

Piaget

Piaget's theory, based largely on boys, involves two distinct stages of moral development. The first stage, **morality of constraint** (or heteronomous morality), characterizes children's moral judgments until they are approximately nine or ten years of age. In this stage, children base their moral judgments on what is deemed appropriate by the adults surrounding them. These children tend to base moral judgments on objective consequences. They believe that rules are immutable, and believe in imminent justice or natural retribution for wrongdoing (Piaget, 1932).

The second stage in Piaget's theory is **morality of cooperation** (or autonomous morality). Children in this stage base their moral judgments on intentions rather than consequences, moving from an objective to a subjective orientation. They regard rules as social conventions modifiable by majority wish and realize the foolishness of believing in imminent justice. Piaget believed that interactions with one's peers were crucial for moving from the first stage to the second (Piaget, 1932).

Kohlberg

Drawing on Piaget's theoretical framework, Kohlberg theorized that there were three distinct levels of moral development, each one characterized by two stages as shown in Table 5.1. To develop his theory, Kohlberg gave children moral dilemmas in which several different choices were apparent. He classified the morality of the course of action selected by the children based on the reasons given for their decisions.

In the first level of moral development, **preconventional reasoning,** children base moral decisions on the consequences of their actions. Rewards and punishments signal whether a behavior is good or bad. Stage 1 is called the punishment and obedience orientation because it emphasizes childrens' unswerving

TABLE 5.1   Kohlberg's Stages of Moral Development

STAGE	BASIS OF MORAL REASONING
Preconventional Level	
Stage 1: Punishment and Obedience Orientation	Consequences of actions
Stage 2: Naïve Hedonistic Orientation	Obtaining rewards and personal interests
Conventional Level	
Stage 3: Good Boy–Good Girl Orientation	Gaining others' approval
Stage 4: Social-Order-Maintaining Orientation	Conforming to society's rules
Postconventional Level	
Stage 5: Social Contract/Legalistic Orientation	Balancing the value of community rights and individual rights
Stage 6: Universal Ethical Principle Orientation	Respect for universal human rights

acceptance of the rule of authority. Children adopt the moral prescriptions of authority figures as their own and do not perceive the possibility of other perspectives. In Stage 2, the naïve hedonistic orientation, children have developed the capacity to recognize the existence of alternative points of view and base moral decisions on maximizing their own rewards and self-interest (Kohlberg, 1976).

At the second level of moral development, **conventional reasoning,** individuals abide by internal moral standards that are based entirely on those of parents or society. Stage 3 has been termed the good boy–good girl orientation. In this stage, individuals are apt to uphold societal norms and seek approval from others whom they know personally. In Stage 4, the social-order-maintaining orientation, individuals incorporate the perspective of unknown people when making moral decisions. They believe that the laws and rules of society are wholly applicable to all members of society (Kohlberg, 1976).

Some individuals achieve the highest level of moral development, **postconventional reasoning,** in adolescence or early adulthood, although, according to Kohlberg, not every individual reaches this level. At this level, morality is completely internalized and based on abstract principles and values. Individuals in Stage 5, the social contract/legalistic orientation, believe that the rule system of society represents only one possible system of social order. They perceive inconsistencies between the rights and values of individuals and the rules of law that govern them. Hence, their moral reasoning considers community rights versus individual rights. Kohlberg's highest stage of moral development, Stage 6, is termed the universal ethical principle orientation. In this stage, individuals have developed a moral standard based on universal human rights that sometimes transcend the laws of society. They utilize ethical standards to guide them in making moral decisions (Kohlberg, 1976).

One of the main limitations of Kohlberg's theory is that his studies were conducted largely with boys as subjects. Not surprisingly, he believed that only males achieved the highest level of moral development. Since Kohlberg's results found gender differences favoring men, researchers became curious about the possibility of other gender differences in moral development. Carol Gilligan conducted studies that resulted in a more gender-fair, if problematic, theory of moral development.

Gilligan

Although Kohlberg developed his theory by presenting children of various ages with hypothetical dilemmas, Gilligan felt that this experiment limited the criteria for judgment of children's morality level to their use of abstract, detached justice. She termed Kohlberg's version of morality the *justice perspective* because it focused on contractual obligations and principles of reciprocity. Gilligan (1982) proposed that other moral concerns and values exist, such as care, compassion, and concern for others. The "care perspective" highlights the significance of sustaining interpersonal relationships. Moral decisions are made on the basis of maintaining personal relationships and fostering sensitivity to the needs of others. Gilligan linked the two different conceptions of morality to the distinct patterns of psychological development experienced by females and males. Since she believed female development centers on attachment to the mother, she posited that women would utilize the care perspective when making moral decisions. In contrast, male development emphasizes independence and separation from the mother. Hence, the justice perspective is more aligned with their developmental experience.

In place of presenting children with hypothetical dilemmas, Gilligan and her colleagues asked them (both boys and girls) to describe an actual moral dilemma that they had confronted at some point. They found that girls, more than boys, tended to discuss issues of trust, friendship, and concern for others (Gilligan, 1982).

In sum, Gilligan and her colleagues found that females' moral dilemmas tended to emphasize care, whereas males' moral dilemmas tended to emphasize fairness and justice (Gilligan & Attanucci, 1988). However, subsequent studies suggest that these differences more often reflect the kinds of problems actually experienced by males and females than differences in their own personal value systems.

Cosse (1992) infers from Gilligan's work that the female developmental pathway is based on interpersonal, empathetic relatedness. Female morality in adolescence and beyond is guided by an empathetic understanding of person, context, and situation. Males, on the other hand, follow a pathway that leads to their personal autonomy. They follow an internalized set of rules that is applicable in all situations. In early adulthood, females and males are confronted with the task of integrating these pathways for a complete morality.

Gilligan's perspective on morality is an important critique of Kohlberg's theory because it exposes the bias against women implicit in this theory. Gilligan believes that these two paths to morality are different, but equal, and that there is nothing inherently better or worse in either approach to making moral judgments. Her theory of morality gives a positive view of characteristics that have been continually disparaged by placing value on interpersonal attachment and relationships. All of these attributes—caring, relationships, concern for others' feelings—were previously devalued because they were thought to interfere with the male attributes of logic and reason.

To date, however, empirical support for Gilligan's conceptualization of moral development is inconsistent. Additional research is needed to determine whether males and females reason differently about moral dilemmas.

IMAGES OF FEMININITY AND MASCULINITY

As young children develop socially and cognitively, their images of gender take on a more complex form. It is possible that their gender identification will prove to be dysfunctional, as in the case of **gender identity disorder** (GID). Children who are diagnosed with GID typically display an array of marked cross-gender role behaviors and often express the wish to belong to the other sex. These children may feel an aversion to or actively avoid gender-role behaviors associated with their own sex. Children with GID show both affective and cognitive gender confusion (Zucker et al., 1993).

GID tends to decrease with age. Apparently, children become less inclined to evaluate their own sex

negatively or ambivalently as they mature. This may merely reflect a growing adherence to conventional gender stereotypes. It could also be a manifestation of achievement of concrete operational thought, enabling the children to appreciate the invariant nature of gender (Zucker et al., 1993).

Children's personal gender role orientation may increase or decrease in flexibility in middle childhood and adolescence, depending on several factors. Girls tend to be more flexible than boys in their preferences for engaging in gender-typical or gender-atypical behavior as well as in their standards for the behavior of others. In both boys and girls, flexibility of gender roles for both themselves and others increases from middle childhood to adolescence, perhaps because of the change in perceived flexibility of the child's social environment. Children tend to view their social environment in more rigid terms than adolescents do. In general, the degree of gender-role flexibility exhibited by children and adolescents represents complex developmental and socialization processes (Katz & Ksansnak, 1994).

Children's images of gender play an important role in such areas as popularity in elementary school (Adler, Kless, & Adler, 1992; Powlishta, Serbin, Doyle, & White, 1994), conceptions of personal power (Dyson, 1994), self-esteem (Orr & Ben-Eliahu, 1993), and motivation and personal goals for adolescents (Gibbons et al., 1993). All these areas are salient in terms of personality formation and healthy adjustment. In elementary school, children's peer cultures may be stratified by gender (Adler et al., 1992). In-group/out-group bias may play a role in the development of gender prejudice, as elementary schoolchildren tend to attribute positive traits to members of their own sex and negative traits to the other sex (Powlishta et al., 1994). The tendency to associate exclusively with classmates of their own sex is pervasive. Children are especially attuned to this when there is a danger of being teased about one's secret romantic intentions in having a friend of the other sex (Adler et al., 1992; Dyson, 1994; Powlishta et al., 1994).

This polarization of peer groups into male and female cliques may contribute to the generation and reinforcement of gender-role ideals for "masculine" and "feminine" behavior. An elementary schoolchild's popularity may in fact be determined by her or his adherence to the students' gender-role ideals. However, this is more the case with boys than with girls, and conceptions of gender-typical behavior have actually become more flexible over the years. Whereas boys were once characterized as purely active and girls as passive, boys' and girls' behavior now incorporates elements of both behaviors (Adler et al., 1992).

Dyson (1994) found salient differences between elementary school-aged boys and girls enacting cartoon stories that they authored. Boys wrote stories about the "Ninjas" and the "X-men" that typically excluded females. When females were included, they were not positioned as equal members of the same team. It was also apparent that boys were deeply attracted to the power of male superheroes. Girls, on the other hand, wrote stories in which the characters were predominantly female and expressed feelings about each other. In addition, these superheroines were ambivalent about their physical powers, lamenting the destructiveness of physical violence. When a character proved to be bellicose, its biological sex vacillated as if the female author were struggling with the possibility of being both tough and female.

In a recent study of adolescents and college students, more boys than girls defined conventional masculine attributes as masculine, while more girls than boys viewed these traits as equally connected with masculinity and femininity. Conventional feminine and neutral attributes were judged similarly by both. Male self-esteem was significantly related to the men's conventional masculinity, whereas female self-esteem did not depend on any gender-related attributes. Both male and female self-esteem benefited from having a self-image that was not stereotypically feminine or masculine (Orr & Ben-Eliahu, 1993).

Findings from this study also suggest that gender differences in self-esteem do not emerge until young adulthood, when males tend to perceive themselves as more worthy than females. It appears, then, that masculinity is the stronger predictor of self-esteem, perhaps because society tends to reward masculine traits to a greater extent than feminine traits (Orr & Ben-Eliahu, 1993).

Adolescents' images of women's roles differ cross culturally. In the Philippines, Guatemala, and the United States, teen-agers who were shown images of women working in an office and images of women preparing food described the women in terms of contentment or dissatisfaction. Filipino adolescents also described these women in terms of their apparent organization or disorganization. Guatemalan respondents described both women in terms of hope, hard work, betterment, and family. In the United States, on the other hand, the women were described in terms of their level of contentment and "niceness" (Gibbons et al., 1993).

It is difficult to identify a specific cultural variable resulting in these particular responses, particularly in light of the commonality of many of the responses. In all three samples, the women cooking were described as mothers who were cooking for others. These women were perceived in terms of their relationships with other people. The women engaged in office work were also described similarly in all three samples; traits such as hardworking and wanting something else out of life were attributed to them by respondents from all three countries. However, teen-agers from the United States and the Philippines described these women as yearning or dreaming. Guatemalans connected this yearning to achieving goals or betterment of the self or the family. The adolescents' interpretations of the drawings may reflect not only their views of women and their roles, but their images of their own futures (Gibbons et al., 1993).

In sum, images of gender and its requirements for appropriate behavior begin developing at a very young age and are continually reinforced by the child's surroundings.

CHILDREN'S ATTITUDES TOWARD FEMALES AND MALES

The images and stereotypes employed by children categorizing information by gender are a function of their development, especially cognitive, in addition to environment (Biernat, 1991; Bigler & Liben, 1992; Liben & Signorella, 1993). Bem's **gender schema theory** suggests that children create knowledge structures that organize gender-related information in memory and are used to evaluate new information according to their gender. Gender schemas might include knowledge about the physical appearances of females and males, their typical interests, activities, and personality traits, and expectations about how females and males will react to different situations (Bem, 1981).

Children's gender schemas may be more or less flexible, and this flexibility or rigidity will affect their attitudes toward both females and males. Younger children are more inclined to classify information into very strict gender categories. Stimuli labeled as female or male will have several different traits ascribed to them by these children based on this distinction alone (Biernat, 1991).

As children grow older, gender remains a cue for stereotyping a stimulus, but other cues are acknowledged as well. In addition, older children are cognitively capable of understanding that many characteristics are shared by both sexes and are not in the unique domain of one or the other. Paradoxically, however, a bipolar view of femininity and masculinity seems to develop with age. Although older children are more open to the idea of a woman expressing masculine traits, or vice versa, certain feminine and masculine features (e.g., physical characteristics) are deemed mutually exclusive by these children—more so than by their younger counterparts (Biernat, 1991).

Toy preference is an effective means of gauging children's attitudes toward gender. Bussey and Bandura (1992) found that children chose to play with same-gender toys from as young as 30 months. Boys were more strongly opposed to cross-gender toys than girls were, sometimes attempting to have the stereotypically feminine objects removed, rather than merely ignoring them. Apparently, children adopt traditional patterns of gender-linked conduct from an early age.

Frey and Ruble (1992) found a similar tendency among boys and girls; boys were more likely to restrict themselves to gender-typed toys—at times, even when the cross-gender toy was more attractive. Frey and Ruble suggest that society's attribution of greater power and competence to males may make girls more motivated than boys to adopt cross-gender behavior.

It is also possible that girls' definition of gender-appropriate behavior expands to include gender-neutral as well as stereotypically feminine behavior, whereas boys define gender-appropriate behavior exclusively in terms of stereotypically masculine behavior (Frey & Ruble, 1992).

Although younger children do tend to be more rigid with regard to gender-role consistency, the degree of this rigidity varies with the individual. Children with more flexible norms about gender-role violation may choose a course of action based on factors other than gender, such as attractiveness (Lobel & Menashri, 1993). A preschooler's standards for gender-appropriate or gender-inappropriate behavior are affected by the child's environment, specifically, the parents' values as mediated by their surrounding culture.

Fagot, Leinbach, and O'Boyle (1992) found that toddlers and preschoolers who demonstrated a more pronounced tendency to discriminate nonhuman items (animals and objects) in gender-stereotyped ways generally had mothers who initiated gender-typical play more often, responded more positively to their children's gender-typed play, and initiated less other-gender play with them. In general, these mothers expressed more traditional attitudes concerning appropriate behavior for women and traditional gender roles within the family and rated their own personality as containing fewer other-gender traits. This factor may be partially responsible for determining a child's attitude toward gender and toward members of either gender who engage in cross-gender behavior.

Conversely, increased father participation in child rearing during the preschool and elementary-school years was found to contribute to more nontraditional views regarding employment, as well as less conservative expectations for child rearing. Adolescents tended to express conventional or less conventional attitudes toward the gender roles of their parents in keeping with the atmosphere in which they were raised (Williams, Radin, & Allegro, 1992).

Cross-Cultural Gender Attitudes in Children

In a more global sense, developing gender attitudes in children is a function of the culture in which they are raised. For example, in Jamaica, female-headed households are prevalent, with women serving as both the primary economic provider and the child rearer in the home. Possibly as a result of this, a tendency for a cultural preference for girls in Jamaica has been noted by researchers (Sargent & Harris, 1992).

Jamaican children of both sexes begin performing household chores at a young age, but boys are supervised much less closely than girls are. Parents express higher expectations for their daughters both academically and economically. In fact, parents' differing attitudes favoring female over male children may be reflected in sex differences in terms of health and growth (improved health and growth for female children), patterns of child abandonment (boys being more frequently abandoned than girls), and decisions of foster and adoptive parents (to adopt female rather than male children). Statistics in all these areas parallel the Jamaican cultural preference for girls (Sargent & Harris, 1992).

Portuguese children were found to begin acquiring knowledge of gender stereotypes at age 5, and to continue developing this knowledge beyond age 11. Across all age levels, knowledge of gender stereotypes varied inversely with socioeconomic status, suggesting that Portuguese middle- and upper-class families place a greater emphasis on traditional gender roles. Like Brazilian, Venezuelan, and Chilean children, Portuguese children, especially girls, tended to know more about the female stereotype than the male stereotype. In these countries, the female stereotype is reported to be more favorable than the male stereotype (Neto, Williams, & Widner, 1991). Therefore, knowledge of the preferred stereotype might come more readily.

In Botswana, on the other hand, women are not regarded as highly. Children of both sexes expressed the attitude that women are more suited to domestic careers (e.g., housecleaner), or careers in beauty care (e.g., hairdresser) and care-giving (e.g., nurse). Men, on the other hand, were rated as the best candidates for positions of leadership (e.g., mayor), in technology (e.g., engineer), and in academia (e.g., professor). Apparently, Botswanan children perceive "women's work" as less prestigious than "men's work." Un-

fortunately, the female children also viewed themselves as better suited for "women's work" (Mbawa, 1992).

Finally, in the United States, boys have been traditionally socialized to become future breadwinners for their families, while female socialization has involved preparation for domestic roles as wife and mother. Whereas personality and attractive appearance are seen as essential characteristics for females, males are usually encouraged to be achievement oriented, competitive, and aggressive. Although such priorities eventually have ramifications for career choices (a phenomenon strikingly similar to that of Botswana), change is happening toward more gender-fair attitudes (Denmark, Nielson, & Scholl, 1993). In contrast to Jamaican adults, U.S. men tend to have a preference for male children, while women do not express a preference for either sex. As a rule, parents openly encourage gender-stereotyped behavior in their children; for example, household chores may be assigned according to the child's sex (i.e., boys taking out the garbage and girls doing dishes). However, the majority of U.S. parents make some nontraditional chore assignments (Lackey, 1989).

Overall, attitudes toward gender tend to be differentiated among children worldwide, whether the bias is occasionally in favor of women or, more commonly the case, for men. These attitudes begin developing at a very early age and continue to affect individuals into adulthood, thus creating a culture in which one gender or the other has the upper hand. Such stereotypes are perpetuated most potently at the individual level within the child's own family.

PARENTING

In recent years it has become clear that parents do not bear as much responsibility for socialization of gender roles as was once thought. Other factors, such as the child's own need to feel like a girl or a boy and peer influence, may play a far more significant role in gender stereotyping. The media, schools, and even language all play a role in shaping the formation of children's gender schemata, as will be discussed in a subsequent section of this chapter.

Yet, researchers maintain that parents do play a significant role in childhood gender socialization. Adults will often attribute dispositions to their children based on a number of factors, including logical inferences from the children's actual behavior, the parents' emotions, and preexisting beliefs influenced by class, culture, and personal values. In turn, these parental perspectives interact with the child's own perspective (Dix, 1993).

Many individual, cultural, and gender differences may stem from the way that adults understand the dispositions and competencies of their children. Subsequently, by expressing their views of the dispositions that they attribute to their children, parents directly influence children's views of who they are and how they should act. Children feel motivated to conform to these acquired self-attributions and to the expectations implied by these dispositional labels (Dix, 1993).

The Baby X experiment (Seavey, Katz, & Zalk, 1975) pointed to a marked difference in graduate students' interactions with a female infant according to whether they were informed that the infant was a boy or girl. Both male and female adults chose a gender-stereotyped toy (a Raggedy Ann doll) to interact with the three-month-old infant when the child was described as female. Males had significantly less contact with the infant than did females in the no-gender-information condition. Even though the infant was female, 57 percent of the male students and 70 percent of the female students thought the baby was male in the no-name condition. The subjects readily found cues to support their gender guess. Thus, those who said the baby was a boy noted strength of grip or lack of hair; those who said the baby was a girl referred to the infant's softness and fragility.

When replicated with both a male and female infant and undergraduate students as subjects, stereotyped behavior regarding toy choice was even more pronounced (Sidorowicz & Lunney, 1980). In this study, toy choice was greatly influenced by gender label. When the male or female infant was reported to be a boy, the vast majority of participants chose a football to interact with the baby. In contrast, regardless of the infant's sex, a doll was the overwhelming choice when the infant was labeled with a female

name. Attributions about the infant were similar to those in the earlier study in the gender-neutral condition. Clearly, adults' perception of infants' gender influences their interactions with the infant.

In general, parents tend to foster boys' autonomy and girls' dependence. While boys are socialized to take a more active, mastery-oriented stance toward their environment, girls are discouraged from taking new risks and from mastering new situations on their own. For example, parents have been found to encourage and reward boys' involvement in physically active games requiring large motor coordination while steering girls toward calmer, safer activities (Rosen & Peterson, 1990).

Parents play with boys and girls differently, tending to talk more with their daughters and engage in more active games with their sons. Parents also encourage gender-appropriate activities by providing children with gender-typed toys and clothing (Will, Self, & Datan, 1976). When interacting with their children, parents display a stronger tendency to assist girls with their endeavors, even when this help is not necessary. In addition, boys are subtly encouraged to roam away from parental supervision, but girls are discouraged from such independence-producing behavior. This is true even at the level at which chores are assigned: boys are usually responsible for taking out the garbage and raking leaves; girls attend to indoor duties (Denmark, Nielson et al., 1993). Thus, parents support high levels of dependency in girls (Denmark, Nielson et al., 1993; Rosen & Peterson, 1990).

Children often model their behavior after that of their parents. For example, household responsibilities relegated to one sex or the other in a particular family tend to be viewed as women's work or men's work by the children raised in that particular family. These perceptions are often distorted; for example, a child might assume that men are better drivers simply because the family's life-style has the father doing more of the driving.

Studies comparing the developmental outcomes of children reared in heterosexual homes and in homes with one or more lesbian parents suggest that, in large part, children in both homes progress similarly in major developmental categories (e.g., Patterson, 1992, 1994; Steckel, 1987). Interestingly, children in homes with one or more lesbian mothers appear to be less aggressive and more positive than children reared with heterosexual mothers (Steckel, 1987). Charlotte Patterson, who has done extensive work in this area, conducted a study in 1994 that compared grade school children living with heterosexual and lesbian mothers on a number of dimensions. Results from this research indicate that children living with lesbian mothers expressed their feelings, both positive and negative, more often than children in homes with heterosexual mothers. One interpretation may be that children who are in homes with lesbians as primary care-givers may be encouraged to recognize their affective states and to verbalize feelings and related experiences (Patterson, 1994).

Marital quality differentially affects parents' interactions with their daughters and sons. Fathers who are less satisfied with their marriage tend to behave and feel more globally negative toward their daughters, regardless of their daughters' behavior. Less satisfied married mothers are more likely to respond aversively to negative verbalizations from their sons. These mothers also negate their daughters when the daughters behave in an assertive manner inconsistent with a traditional feminine gender role (Kerig, Cowan, & Cowan, 1993).

Explanations proposed for these phenomena provide insight into the effect that parents might have on their children's gender-role socialization. It is possible that distressed mothers look to their daughters for emotional support, because nurturing is traditionally a feminine function. This family dynamic would have negative consequences for the daughter's relationship with her father. On the other hand, fathers may be more likely to transfer disappointment in a marriage to a female child. This is probable because a father's role as husband tends to influence his role as father. A third suggestion is that, because fathers usually withdraw emotionally from their wives in the face of marital distress, they may also withdraw from their daughters. Girls may develop an assertive and assiduous style to gain the attention of their emotionally distant fathers, which could have the unfortunate effect of fostering

their fathers' further negativity toward them (Kerig et al., 1993).

Sons of parents who are lower in marital satisfaction may not only be passive observers of the reciprocity of negative affect taking place between their parents, but may also become involved in, and socialized into, such interactions with their maritally distressed mothers. It is possible that this phenomenon provides a mechanism through which intergenerational transfer of marital dysfunction might take place. As for maritally dissatisfied mothers negating their daughters' assertive behavior, this tendency may reflect an attempt by these mothers to socialize their daughters into an interactional style that they themselves experience in the marital relationship (Kerig et al., 1993).

It is apparent that the emotional quality of the relationships between marital partners and their children affects parents' interaction styles with their sons and daughters. These differing interaction styles foster discrete notions of the social roles of females and males within the children's perceptions. When the mothers' and fathers' feelings about their marital partners affect the quality of the parent–child relationship, the significance of gender in the development of the family system begins to emerge (Kerig et al., 1993).

Single Parenting

Many children are raised in single-parent households, either due to death of a parent, divorce, or other circumstances. The parent responsible for the primary care of these children is usually hardworking and devoted to the children's welfare. However, single-parent homes have their own set of ramifications for children's gender-role attitudes. Because the absent parent is usually the father, and fathers tend to encourage gender-appropriate behavior more strongly than mothers do, one would expect that children raised in single-parent homes would display more androgynous behaviors. Consistent with this prediction, preschool-aged boys in female-headed households are typically less aggressive and less likely to engage in rough-and-tumble, stereotypically masculine play. This may result from single mothers' tendency to be more protective of their children than mothers with a partner in the home and the lack of a father to balance out the mother's caution by encouraging the son's independence and risk taking. Lack of a male role model may be another reason for this tendency (Leaper, Smith, Sprague, & Schwartz, 1991).

However, some boys in this situation may develop an exaggerated masculine style to compensate for feelings of uncertainty about their gender identity. These boys tend to have difficulty establishing close relationships, depend excessively on the male peer group, rebel against the authority of adult males, and avoid anything perceived to be feminine (Biller, 1981). Indeed, Stevenson and Black's (1988) meta-analytic review found support for this tendency in the literature: older boys in homes where the male caretaker was absent tended to demonstrate more aggressive and other stereotypically masculine behavior. This may be a reason why some impoverished, single, African American mothers described their male children as significantly more difficult than female children (Jackson, 1993). This may be a function of boys tending to be more active than girls and thus more difficult to socialize, especially when their mothers work full time. The characteristics enumerated above tend to preclude mothers' involvement with their own children. This may perpetuate a cycle in which many of these children, having suffered the emotional absence of a father and a mother, are unresponsive to their own children as adults. This is not unique to poor African American families; all impoverished families are potential candidates for this syndrome.

Girls, on the other hand, seem less directly influenced by father absence, possibly because the father is a less salient role model for them. However, in adolescence, girls from female-headed households have difficulty interacting comfortably with males. Although girls from homes where the mother was widowed seem anxious and inept around males, girls from divorced homes act more sexually assertive. A possible explanation is that girls from widowed homes are less exposed to men. Girls from divorced homes, on the other hand, may be more exposed to men because their mothers are more likely to date. They may see their mothers interacting with these men in a flirta-tious way and follow this example, generalizing this way of behaving as the way in which to socialize with all males.

While mother absence results in the reversal of traditional gender roles in the home, having a father as the primary care-giver has less effect on children's gender-role behavior. A possible explanation for this is the greater likelihood of children living with their fathers to come into contact with a female *parent figure* (either the child's own mother, a female relative, a nanny, or a babysitter) than of children living with their mothers to be exposed to a male parent-figure and role model. Children living with their fathers tend to have a more balanced experience in terms of male and female adult figures.

In Williams, Radin, and Allegro's study (1992) of adolescents raised primarily by their fathers, increased father participation in child rearing contributed to more nontraditional gender views of parenting. However, assessments of a role-reversed parenting arrangement differed for boys and girls. Sons tended to see more advantages than disadvantages, stating that their relationship with their fathers was enhanced. Daughters, on the other hand, regretted missing the contact with their mothers that they felt they needed.

Parents of each sex have distinct qualities and values to offer to their children. The next section will explore some of the differences between men and women as parents and how this affects children.

Effects of Parents on Children

It is interesting that several studies show that fathers tended to stereotype their children according to gender to a greater degree than mothers did (Maccoby & Jacklin, 1974). This is true as early as infancy, when the child does not yet display salient gender-typed traits. Fathers tend to view their newborn sons as "firmer, larger featured, better coordinated, more alert, stronger, hardier," while describing newborn daughters as "softer, finer featured, more awkward, more inattentive, weaker, and more delicate" (Rubin, Provenzano, & Luria, 1974). This trend continues as their offspring develop in childhood.

Lewis (1972) analyzed the behavior of mothers and infants and found additional evidence that parents do change their behavior measurably as a function of the sex of the child. For six months or so, infant boys have more physical contact with their mothers than do infant girls, but by the time boys are six months old, this relationship reverses, and girls receive more physical as well as nontactile contact.

Fathers may spend less time with their infants than mothers do, but father–infant interaction is more playful than mother–infant interaction (Clarke-Stewart, 1978; Parke, 1978). Fathers' play with infants tends to be more vigorous and physical than mothers' play. Mothers' play is often more intellectually oriented, possibly involving verbalization (e.g., nursery rhymes) and conventional games (e.g., peek-a-boo). Mothers are also more likely than fathers to use toys to stimulate their infants (Clarke-Stewart, 1978; Lamb, 1979; Parke, 1978).

Parents have been found to attend to, stimulate, and interact with infants of their own sex more than with infants of the other sex (Parke, 1978). This is especially true of fathers, who tend to make more trips to visit their male newborns in the hospital, engage their infant sons in more play, and display more physical affection with them (Belsky, 1979; Field, 1978; Lamb, 1979; Weinraub & Frankel, 1977). Mothers also display a tendency to imitate, talk to, and play with their infant daughters more than with their sons. The special interest that parents show their same-sex offspring may enhance the parents' attractiveness to their children, making it more likely that the children will seek out their same-sex parents as companions and role models.

The extra stimulation that boys receive from their fathers may have important consequences for male development. Boys may reciprocate their fathers' interest and affection, which may be the reason that boys typically prefer interacting with their fathers rather than their mothers by their second birthday (Belsky, 1979; Lamb, 1979). Fathers also provide a special sort of stimulation for their sons, which teaches them competencies that they are unlikely to learn from others. Indeed, research has shown that infant boys who were fatherless showed less interest in manipulating novel objects than did boys from intact families (Parke, 1978). Although girls also benefit from interaction with their fathers, father absence is typically associated with more negative consequences in male than in female children. This may be partially explained by the lack of a father figure, but another reason might be the difficulty encountered by mothers attempting to discipline their sons singlehandedly.

Fathers' tendency to reinforce gender differences in their sons and daughters is especially pronounced in the area of physical activity. Fathers involve boys in more active and physical play than girls (Rosen & Peterson, 1990). Fathers are also more likely to reward girls for positive, compliant behavior and to reward boys for assertiveness (Kerig et al., 1993).

A strong relationship exists between boys' masculinity and their fathers' personalities: boys who are masculine tend to have fathers who are both affectionate and powerful (Hetherington, 1967; Mussen & Rutherford, 1963; Payne & Mussen, 1956). But the converse does not hold true; there is very little evidence of a parallel relationship between mothers' personality and their daughters' femininity. In fact, paternal personality characteristics actually tend to influence girls' gender typing more than maternal traits.

Both parents express different views of their daughters and sons and treat them accordingly. Girls are viewed as more truthful, and parents relate to them with more physical closeness and warmth. Boys, on the other hand, are disciplined more harshly. Girls are attended to when they ask for help, whereas boys' attempts at assertiveness are reinforced by their parents (Fagot, Hagan, Leinbach, & Kronsberg, 1985; McDonald & Parke, 1986; Ross & Taylor, 1989).

In general, fathers see child care as the mother's primary responsibility and view their role as "helping out" and being the primary provider. They often use gender-specific excuses for spending less time with their children than their wives do, such as the fact that work keeps them away or that they are impatient with young children (LaRossa & LaRossa, 1981; McHale & Huston, 1985; McKee, 1982). Interestingly, fathers from the lower socioeconomic bracket tend to spend more time with their children than other fathers do (Cohen, 1998).

However, the U.S. father may play many roles in his family—that of provider, decision maker, nurturer, husband, and father (McAdoo, 1986). Contrary to popular belief, men can and often do fulfill their children's needs for emotional support and understanding. In fact, children in single-parent homes where the father heads the household rate their fathers as more nurturing than children in two-parent homes rate either parent. Fathers feel that they best express their love to their children by how well they take care of them, whereas children express their love by how well they cooperate and show deference to their father (Hanson, 1986).

It is clear that the father plays a highly salient role in a child's psychosexual development and sex typing, more so than the mother does. Johnson (1963, 1977) argues that, whereas mothers treat their sons and daughters more alike than do fathers, fathers develop distinctly discrepant styles of interaction with their male and female children that lead the children to develop masculine and feminine traits. According to Johnson, fathers teach daughters to be feminine by interacting with them in a warmly indulgent, protective, and mildly flirtatious way. With sons, on the other hand, fathers act demanding and critical, insisting that the boys display traditionally masculine behaviors and shun feminine ones. The father socializes both boys and girls toward independence, but in different ways—boys toward instrumental competence within the male peer group and girls toward eventual establishment of an expressive role within a new family context.

Why do men perpetuate gender roles more ardently than do women? Some claim that it is because men are concerned with maintaining the power and status advantages that they currently enjoy. Another explanation is that men are simply transmitting to others the stronger pressure that they themselves have experienced for conforming to the culturally prescribed male sex role.

However, besides parenting styles, other factors have an impact on gender differentiation. The next section will discuss the various socializing events that affect gender.

SOCIALIZING FORCES

Language

Language is not neutral; it differentiates women from men. **Linguistic sexism** refers to the perpetuation and reinforcement of sexist ideology through the content of a language (Nilsen et al., 1977). In addition to separating women and men, the English language strongly favors men, affording them greater power over women. Linguistic sexism in the English language takes one of three distinct forms, either ignoring women, defining women, or deprecating women.

The English language tends to *ignore women* by extending male terms to refer to humans as a whole. For example, when talking about the human species, people commonly refer to it as *man* or *mankind.* Yet, girls and women make up close to 52 percent of the human race, making them the majority.

The use of *he* as a generic pronoun referring to both men and women usually results in the listener or reader imagining a male as the subject of the sentence (Cole, Hill, & Dayley, 1983). In fact, most of the antecedents to the pronoun *he* in textbooks refer only to men, not to men and women (Bertilson, Springer, & Fierke, 1982). It is only natural that children's exposure to this form of linguistic sexism will affect their image of their own gender as well as that of the other gender. In fact, according to Hyde (1984), most elementary school children have learned to think of males when they hear *he* in a gender-neutral context and do not know that *he* can refer to both males and females. Because they are exposed to a constant stream of information using the masculine gender as normative, they learn to think of the typical person as male. This is an important step toward the cultural assumption that the male is normative and the female atypical or deviant.

Society also tends, through language, to *define women* in terms of their relationship to men. For example, a woman is often referred to as so-and-so's wife, widow, or daughter. In addition, the practice of women giving up their surnames for their husbands' names upon marrying stems from the ancient patriarchal tradition of viewing a woman as her husband's possession. Changing one's name implies that the person is changing or losing some aspect of his or her identity. Finally, language *deprecates women* and has done so throughout history. Misogyny is pervasive in classical literature. In addition, when we note the number of words indicative of sexual activity, we find well over 200 such words to describe a sexually active woman but just over 20 words to describe lustful men (Stanley, 1977). Even with parallel terms, the female counterpart of a male term often has a more negative connotation (e.g., bachelor–spinster, master–mistress, etc.).

Most of an individual's relations with the social world are mediated by language, and the learning of language is one of the first and most important tasks facing a developing child. Children's development of gender identity and gender role may be inextricably bound up with the acquisition of language (Constantinople, 1979). The labels that children learn (i.e., boy, girl, man, woman, daddy, mommy) help them to form the categories around which they build a fundamental understanding of gender and to guide their thinking about this concept. For this reason, linguistic sexism can have a pervasive influence on children's developing gender identity.

Play and Competition

A strong preference for one's own sex is exhibited when children are observed in play. This preference begins in the toddler period, continues through the preschool years, and increases during middle childhood (Fagot, 1991; Serbin, Moller, Powlishta, & Gulko, 1991). Girls' preference for members of their own sex as playmates appears as early as age 2, whereas this preference in boys is not as clear until about three years of age (Hayden-Thomson, Rubin, & Hymel, 1987). This preference for others of the same sex has been observed in many other cultures and seems to follow roughly the same time course, emerging in the toddler period and increasing through middle childhood (Shepard, 1991). In general, gender dominates children's decisions to play with or avoid another child, often overruling other characteristics such as race and ethnicity.

One reason children prefer their own sex is that they simply get along better with others who possess similar styles of interaction and similar interests. The key factor in compatibility seems to be the partner's social responsiveness, with girls being more responsive and cooperative, whereas boys are often more assertive and domineering. Boys also appear to enjoy rough-and-tumble play more than girls do and are therefore more likely to initiate it with each other (Rosen & Peterson, 1990).

Another reason for children's seeking out members of their own sex as playmates is their need to establish a gender identity. Once children become aware that they are members of one gender group, they are motivated to stick with that group. Shared gender membership is even more important to children than mutual interests and, as a result, children increasingly spend time exclusively with those of the same sex. Within their respective play groups, girls and boys socialize one another into traditional gender-role behavior by punishing those who deviate from gender-role-appropriate activities with critical remarks, abandoning play with the friend who persists in doing something that appears gender inappropriate, or trying to get the friend to do something else. Children are more careful to play with gender-appropriate toys when another child is present than when they are alone, even if the peer is not actually interacting with them (Serbin, Connor, Buchardt, & Citron, 1979). Apparently, children are anxious for their peers to view them engaged in only gender-appropriate behavior.

Research has found many gender differences in children's play. In addition to engaging in more rough-and-tumble play, boys are more physically aggressive than girls are and are more likely to display antisocial behavior. Boys also seem to be more impulsive than girls. There is strong evidence that boys engage in more exploratory and curiosity-seeking behavior. Boys also play outside more than girls and tend to play competitive and challenging games more often. Boys play in larger groups than do girls (Rosen & Peterson, 1990).

The games and physical activities of boys also serve as preparation for what they will do when they grow up. In competitive sports boys experience victory and defeat. Effort and experience become salient; they learn to try harder, to reach a bit higher each time, and gradually and steadily to improve the development of achievement skills and competitive behavior skills. They also learn that failures are commonplace and do not necessarily indicate that an individual is inadequate. For girls, on the other hand, at least until the last decade, both competition and winning have been fairly unfamiliar experiences. Box 5.2 describes the different types of toys commonly given to girls and boys.

In middle childhood, avoidance of the other sex increases and becomes quite salient. For example, boys may tend to run from girls, claiming that they

---

Box 5.2_____

Toys for Girls and Boys

Girls are more likely to get passive toys, such as dish sets, clothes, and coloring books. They may get toy ovens, irons, and sewing machines. The more elaborate models of these toy household appliances actually work, and so girls can start ironing and baking at an early age. Many of these toys are realistic representations of the things that girls may do later in life. Girls may also get dollhouses in which they can move furniture and play house. Their dolls can be handled like real babies: fed, diapered, and even bathed. These toys prepare girls for futures as mothers and homemakers.

Boys are more likely to get toys that encourage creativity and manipulation: chemistry sets, erector sets, toy trains, and tool chests. Boys are also more likely to get mobile toys, action toys, and sports equipment. The toys that boys get are often connected with action and exciting occupations, such as being a cowboy, a policeman, or an astronaut. For the most part, however, these toys do not represent occupations likely to be entered by most young men. Seldom does a boy get a toy briefcase and a bunch of papers to shuffle in an imitation of an adult's likely role.

Source: From *Masculine and Feminine: Gender Roles across the Life Cycle* (2nd ed.), by M. Richmond-Abbott, 1992, New York: McGraw-Hill.

---

have "cooties." Contact that does take place between the two groups is often tinged with romantic or sexual overtones (Adler et al., 1992). Such contact appears to be a prelude to the shift that takes place in the teenage years, when interest in members of the other sex becomes acceptable among one's peer group and may lead to dating.

Media

Television, which exerts a significant influence on children's attitudes toward gender, overwhelmingly stereotypes masculine and feminine roles. Prime-time shows tend to portray women as young, unemployed, family bound, and/or sexual objects. Even those shown in responsible roles are commonly searching desperately for a man. Prime-time males in the United States, on the other hand, are depicted as tough, cool men who are engaged in violent, mobile occupations and have numerous female admirers (Signorelli, 1989). Soap operas and comedy shows also tend to portray female characters as inferior to male characters.

Cartoons aimed at young children provide some of the most sexist depictions of males and females in the media. Male characters and male themes predominate in most cartoons. As a result, boys will rarely watch female-centered cartoons, and girls, in contrast, will be exposed mainly to male-centered cartoons.

A popular children's animated television show in the early 1990s depicted superheroes called the "Teenage Mutant Ninja Turtles." Elementary school children were asked to enact original episodes of these shows and they typically excluded girls from their stories. Although a girl was able to obtain a part after some negotiation, she was required to fit the specifications of the superhero script, which typically emphasized her desirability and did not place her on equal footing with the male characters. A more recent cartoon show about the "X-men" gave females a greater role in superhero play. Yet boys enacting episodes of this show continued to exclude girls from their play because of their romantic associations in the show; elementary school boys did not wish to be victims of teasing for this type of association with girls in the class (Dyson, 1994).

Children's Literature

In an analysis of five sets of primary readers cross culturally, all the countries' texts studied were found to subscribe to the traditional sex-role stereotypes. Almost all the texts (with the exception of the Swedish readers) were found to portray fewer female characters than male characters. At least until the 1970s, some Russian, Rumanian, and Swedish texts depicted women in less traditional roles, but only the Swedish text showed men or boys in the nurturant or nontraditional role (Denmark & Waters, 1977).

However, children's literature has improved greatly since then, when studies showed that males dominated the stories, titles, and illustrations in popular children's books (Purcell & Stewart, 1990; Sadker, Sadker, & Klein, 1991). In spite of these changes, some gender stereotyping remains; there are still more male supporting characters, female characters are more likely to need help than are male characters, and males are more likely to be the ones to assist them (McDonald, 1989). Classic children's literature, however, prolifically read to children by their parents and studied in school, is highly gender stereotyped.

A colleague who has been teaching a course on the psychology of women at the University of Manitoba in Winnipeg, Canada, conducted an informal study of college students' favorite fairy tales from childhood. She found that her students, primarily young women, overwhelmingly chose Cinderella as their favorite fairy tale of childhood. Distant second- and third-place choices were Snow White and Sleeping Beauty (Marianne Johnson, personal communication, 1998). It is striking that their most revered character from early childhood, Cinderella, is portrayed as a passive female who is powerless and must sit at home in anticipation of her prince's arrival. The fairy tales that pervade young children's lives broadcast highly stereotypic views of men and women.

Advertising

Children today, as never before in history, are bombarded with adult advertising of increasing sophistication and power. Advertisements in magazines, on billboards, and on television contain many subtle messages encouraging gender stereotyping. Much of advertising for women is directed at convincing them to purchase products that will make them more attractive. The message in these advertisements is that women who are natural are not good enough and can improve themselves by using the product in question. Many of these advertisements also suggest that older women are unnoticed and unworthy, and it is incumbent on women to stave off the aging process; if they do age, it is their own fault for not trying hard enough to stop the clock (Kilbourne, 1987).

Advertisements also tend to portray women as childish, cutesy, dumb, or uninformed. Ads for cleaning products depict housewives who are unable to clean successfully or overjoyed when they actually can. These childlike and trivializing portrayals of women make it difficult to take them seriously and may even convey the message that women are dumb and incompetent.

Men, on the other hand, appear dominant in most of the ads portraying men and women. Women are usually shorter in relation to men, often sitting or lying down while men stand. Women cling to men and look adoringly at them, usually smiling, while men are in control of the action and look aloofly off into space or into the camera. Women are often grabbed, tossed, or otherwise treated as childlike objects to be played with by a dominant adult male (Goffman, 1979).

Much of advertising relies on sexual appeals. It is especially here that women are placed in a disadvantaged position relative to men. These advertisements, regardless of whether they target men or women, portray women as scantily clothed sex objects, even though the ad may have nothing to do with sex. For men, the implication appears to be that the woman shown is the man's reward for using the product; for women, it may be one of identification; that is, the woman who uses the advertised product will succeed in appealing to men. Although recent decades have brought some improvement in the roles in which women in advertisements are portrayed (from family roles to occupational roles), these women continue to be depicted as concerned with personal beauty, household, and family, while the men are shown as cool, unemotional, and dominant (Courtney & Whipple, 1985).

School

Schools can also have a great impact on children's ideas about gender roles. Students are often separated by sex for both formal and informal events, such as lines for an assembly or separate places for girls and boys to hang up their coats (Delamont, 1990). A function of schooling is to socialize children into the world of adulthood by teaching them appropriate behavior, and this unfortunately can often include societally stereotypic gender-appropriate behavior. In addition, girls and boys have very different experiences within the classroom.

According to Alton-Lee, Nuthall, and Patrick (1993), pronounced gender bias exists in several social studies units. The few women mentioned in these units are characteristically marginalized or rendered invisible. Alton-Lee and Patrick also found that teachers were more likely to call on boys in class and criticize girls' responses to questions. Although their research was performed in New Zealand, strong gender bias has also been demonstrated in schoolchildren in the Philippines, Guatemala, and the United States (Gibbons et al., 1993). In the United States in particular, the educational system has been found to track girls toward traditional, sex-segregated jobs and away from areas of study that lead to careers in science and technology (American Association of University Women, 1992).

Recently, the issue of whether single-sex schools or single-sex classrooms in coed schools would better serve to educate females has been the subject of considerable debate. In a study of American schools done by the American Association of University Women analyzing the value of single-sex education, girls did not attain measurably better skills in math and science. However, many girls did report having greater confidence and better attitudes about these subjects, which are traditionally male areas of dominance (Lewin, 1998) (see also Chapter 6).

Box 5.3

Gender Bias in School

There is a direct link between high school courses chosen by girls and their subsequent career choices. Typically, girls opt for vocational classes in home economics, secretarial work, and health care. Boys tend to select courses that teach skilled crafts, such as woodworking and auto repair. When girls attempt to cross the gender barrier in their educational selections, they are met with many challenges. For example, note the difficulties experienced by this Vietnamese American high school student:

> I took a full-year shop class in high school. I was the only girl in the class, that is, the only girl by the end of the year. There was another girl, at the beginning, but the two of us were—well, I wouldn't exactly say harassed, but it's true. After just a few days, the other girl transferred out of the course. I'm quite stubborn, so I stayed in the course the entire year. The boys literally pushed me around, right into tables and chairs. They pulled my hair, made sexual comments, touched me, told sexist jokes. And the thing was that I was better in the shop class than almost any guy. This only caused the boys to get more aggressive and troublesome. . . . Throughout the entire year no teacher or administrator ever stopped the boys from behaving this way. (quoted in Sadker and Sadker, 1994)

Source: From *Race, Class, and Gender in a Diverse Society,* by D. Kendall, 1997, Boston: Allyn & Bacon.

In New Zealand, classroom dynamics tend to reflect a subtle negativity toward women. Social studies curricula overwhelmingly acknowledge the contributions of men and ignore, minimize, or derogate those of women. Thus, a message is conveyed about the relative cultural devaluing of women, which in turn affects the children's attitudes toward them. Teachers were observed to favor the participation of male children in class and evaluate the contributions of the females more harshly. The classroom arrangement in itself relegated the girls to the back of the classroom, while the boys sat in a semicircle in close proximity to the teacher (Alton-Lee, Nuthall, & Patrick, 1993).

Teachers in the United States tend to allow the girls to work independently as the teachers attend to the boys in the classroom. Whereas boys demand attention from the teachers, girls learn to quietly wait their turn. Teachers watch boys carefully and are quick to reprimand their misbehavior in public, while girls who misbehave are usually rebuked quietly as if to avoid embarrassing them (Serbin, O'Leary, Kent, & Tonick, 1973). Many boys enjoy the public attention that they receive for behaving badly, which serves as a reinforcer for misbehavior. Girls, on the other hand, do not receive this reinforcer and therefore tend to act out less than boys do. As such, typical female schoolchildren take on a more passive stance, whereas typical male children learn to behave assertively.

The extent to which boys and girls are differentially treated by their teachers is also affected by ethnicity and social class. Teachers pay more attention to children from middle- and upper-middle-class families than those from working-class families, and White children are expected to be higher achievers than children of color (Alvidrez & Weinstein, 1993; Sadker et al., 1991). Within each gender, White middle-class children receive more attention on the whole than do ethnic minority lower-class children.

Schools also provide children with a sadly representative view of the status of employed women. An overwhelming majority of elementary school teachers are female, whereas barely half of high school teachers are female (U.S. Department of Commerce, 1990). Often, high school science and math courses are taught by males, while English and foreign language courses are taught by females. Principals and superintendents, the major authority figures in the schools, are usually male. Research has demonstrated that this can affect children's perspective on gender roles; first graders in schools with female principals were found more likely to say that either men or women could be school principals than were children in schools with male principals (Paradise & Wall, 1986).

Peers

The peer group may be the most powerful socializing agent in an adolescent's life. Most teen-age boys and girls are more eager to earn the approval and acceptance of their peers than of their families. Therefore, the peer group will have a profound influence on gender-role conceptions at this stage of life. However, the pervasive influence of the peer group begins before adolescence; once children begin school, whatever nonsexist upbringing they have had is subject to interference from their classmates' attitudes (Katz, 1979). Peers abet gender typing by encouraging the segregation of boys and girls, expressing prejudice toward members of the other sex, and treating boys and girls differently.

At a young age, children show strong preferences for members of their own sex when selecting playmates. Students of various ages who were asked to rate certain traits as typical of boys or girls tended to assign more favorable traits to their own gender and more undesirable traits to the other gender (Etaugh, Levine, & Mennella, 1984). In addition, attractive female children receive more positive attention from their peers than do unattractive female children, whereas attractiveness is not a factor in the treatment that boys receive from their peers (Smith, 1985). Clearly, girls are taught from an early age that their level of attractiveness affects their treatment by their peers, but this standard does not exist for boys.

In adolescence, many of the peer expectations of gender behavior learned in childhood are reinforced and may take on new definition. Adolescent boys emphasize toughness as a masculine attribute, idealizing a strong, heavy, athletic body build, participation in sports, and even violence as an extension of competitive sports. "Coolness" is also a valued trait, requiring that males express little or no emotion. Adolescent males often experience homophobia and are therefore afraid to express emotions to other men for fear of appearing effeminate. A third ideal for adolescent boys is being good at something, preferably sports.

This extends to expressing high achievement motivation in terms of a future career, although academic success is not necessarily part of this equation. Other areas fall into this category as well, such as being a good driver and/or being sexually competent.

Female adolescents are less likely than male adolescents to gain self-esteem from concrete achievements that are within their control. They tend to emphasize physical appearance, often preoccupying themselves with their weight to the point of anorexia or bulimia (see Chapter 12). Sometimes, young women associate prettiness with being worthy as a person, and will therefore feel unworthy if they consider themselves less than attractive. Girls also base a good deal of their self-esteem on their popularity and interpersonal relationships (see Box 5.4). In terms of the future, although girls have become more career oriented, they continue to juggle their career expectations with their expectations of having a family. Whereas some girls anticipate adjusting their career plans for the sake of having children, many girls wish to have it all. In a recent survey, the issues that preoccupied a sample of 733 adolescent girls were not the traditional concerns of marriage and children; rather, the girls were primarily concerned with their future careers and financial responsibilities (Murray, 1998).

For adolescents who are physically disabled or are living with chronic disease, the challenges of this developmental period are certainly exacerbated. Teenagers of both genders are inundated with images heralding physical beauty and fitness. More studies are needed to explore how these youths' social and emotional development are affected. It is important to address whether girls and boys respond differently to their condition and, as a corollary, whether and how they are treated differently by peers and care-givers.

Peers and significant adults in these children's lives would do well to encourage and support interests and endeavors that reflect a range of values and abilities. It is especially important that these youth hear from important others that physical appearance and abilities are merely part of what is interesting and special in each individual. As we know, many disabled

BOX 5.4

Peer Pressure in Adolescence

During adolescence, females adopt strict gender roles as an attempt to fit in with a particular group. Peer cliques serve an important function in allowing an individual to feel acceptance. Often adolescents who are different from a peer group will be rejected, causing feelings of isolation, self-doubt, and depression. The following statements highlight the significance of establishing a peer group:

Unless you dress like everyone else, you are considered a neb.

You have to dress cool and act and behave accordingly, otherwise you are seen as weird.

Fitting in with my friends is important. Sometimes I don't feel like I belong and that makes me crazy.

The best thing about going to school is being with my friends and feeling like I am part of a group, where I matter.

Source: From "Adolescent Females' Perception of Autonomy and Control," by J. Kaufman, 1998, in *Females and Autonomy: A Life-Span Perspective* (pp. 43–72), edited by M. B. Nadien and F. L. Denmark, Boston: Allyn & Bacon.

individuals have healthy, accomplished, and fulfilling lives.

In sum, many socializing forces affect the development of gender typing in children and may pave the way for a gender-discriminate adult world.

PUBERTY AND ADOLESCENCE

As children move toward their teen-age years, both biological and social differences between boys and girls appear to increase. Biologically, hormonal processes catalyze internal and external bodily changes during the preteen and teen-age years. These changes have social ramifications as well. Both girls and boys show trends in the direction of gender-role intensification from grades 7 through 9, when *not* acting like the other sex becomes more important (Hill & Lynch,

1983; Simmons & Blyth, 1987). This finding has not changed even though the times have; gender-role stereotyping among boys and girls has not decreased significantly in the decades following the onset of the feminist movement (Lewin & Tragos, 1987).

Young lesbians face many added challenges to the normal crises of adolescence. Most are not privy to the correct information regarding their sexual and emotional development. They also face prejudice, intolerance, and possibly rejection from parents and primary support groups from their uninformed peers (Greene, 1997). As such, they often fail to seek out support at this developmental period—when they are most in need (Hersch, 1991). As you read the rest of this section, these issues should be kept in mind, because for all the reasons mentioned above and more, adolescence may be an even more intense developmental period for the lesbian or gay youngster.

Puberty is the period of most rapid physical growth that humans experience, excluding prenatal and early postnatal life. Not only do children's bodies change at puberty, but their cognitive capabilities expand and their relationships with family members change. Puberty involves physical events such as the growth spurt, changes in body composition, and the development of secondary sex characteristics. **Adolescence,** on the other hand, is defined by society as the period between childhood and maturity. (See Chapter 3 for a fuller discussion of puberty.)

The timing of puberty, which differs for girls and boys, influences much of an adolescent's social development. On the average, girls begin and end puberty approximately two years before boys do. Within this average, however, there are variations.

For the girl who begins to mature sexually earlier than her classmates, there are several disadvantages. For one, it has been suggested that fourth and fifth graders are disturbed about the loss of their childish bodies, choosing to camouflage breast development with sloppy big shirts and sweaters (Delaney, Lupton, & Toth, 1988). This self-consciousness is probably compounded for the girl who is one of the first of her peers to develop breasts (Lerner & Olson, 1997). In addition, while breasts are viewed as a prerequisite for physical attractiveness in a woman, women are usu-

ally dissatisfied with their breasts. For an early developing girl, the "imperfection" of her breasts is likely to serve as a source of severe self-consciousness.

Early maturing girls usually weigh more and are slightly shorter than their late maturing peers, even once pubertal growth is complete for both (Brooks-Gunn, 1987; Patlak, 1997). Perhaps this is a factor in early maturing girls' poorer body images and greater dieting concerns relative to late maturers (Attie & Brooks-Gunn, 1989).

In addition, early maturing girls have been found to date more than late maturing girls in middle and junior high school (Brooks-Gunn, 1988). They appear to be more involved with boys (Crockett & Petersen, 1987) and may engage in "adult behavior" such as smoking, drinking, and sexual intercourse (for which they are not necessarily ready) at an earlier age (Magnusson, Strattin, & Allen, 1985; Patlak, 1997). This may be a function of associating with chronologically older friends. Early maturing girls are more likely to be asked out by older boys, which may give them the message that their physical appearance is their major asset. This may take a toll on their self-esteem (Simmons, Blyth, Van Cleave, & Bush, 1979) and could be related to the poorer academic performance of early maturing girls (Simmons & Blyth, 1987). Early dating also takes a toll on girls' friendships with other girls (Katz, 1997), which may explain why girls tend to choose best friends who are at the same level of physical maturation as themselves (Brooks-Gunn, Samelson, Warren, & Fox, 1986).

Early maturing boys, on the other hand, appear to be at an advantage. Boys who mature early tend to perceive themselves more positively than boys who are either on time or late (Lerner & Olson, 1997). A boy who reaches puberty early is likely to have a size advantage over his peers and to be successful in sports, a major factor in social status for boys. Early maturation for boys is also associated with greater independence and decision making.

However, like their female counterparts, early maturing boys are more likely to get involved with older friends and to engage in activities for which they are not psychologically prepared. As a result, they have a higher rate of school problems, substance abuse, and delinquency. Boys who have a few extra years of childhood have more time to develop emotionally. In addition to being just as successful in adulthood as their early maturing peers, they also seem to be more creative and to enjoy life more (Steinberg, 1993).

For many girls, **menarche,** or the onset of the menstrual period, signals the beginning of womanhood. As such, it is a pivotal event in female puberty. Our society conveys mixed messages to girls about menarche, viewing it as both a positive and a negative event. Adolescent girls themselves feel ambivalent about menarche, expressing feelings of both happiness and fright (Petersen, 1983).

Menarche appears to focus the adolescent girl's attention on her body (Koff et al., 1978). In addition, postmenarcheal girls report thinking more about dating, marriage, and having children (Brooks-Gunn & Warren, 1988). Some girls feel that menarche means giving up the freedom of childhood (Peterson, 1983).

Younger and premenstrual girls appear to have very negative expectations about menstruation, expecting more severe symptomatology than do their postmenarcheal counterparts (Brooks-Gunn & Ruble, 1983). In general, adolescent girls view menstruation more negatively than their mothers do (Stoltzman, 1986). Girls will often not tell their friends that they have begun to menstruate for several months, even though menarche is a topic of discussion among them. They also appear to get more information about menstruation from the media and their peers than from their mothers. This makes it challenging, but even more important, for mothers to adequately prepare their daughters for menstruation. In fact, girls who are adequately prepared for these events have been found to experience less symptomatology (Brooks-Gunn & Ruble, 1983).

Some doctors and researchers consider **semenarche** (also called *spermarche*), the boy's first ejaculation, to be the marker of sexual maturity that is analogous to menarche in girls (Stein & Reiser, 1994). Like girls learning about menarche, boys get much of their information about this milestone from the media, rather than from their fathers (Brooks-Gunn &

Matthews, 1979). Another aspect of semenarche, which is paralleled by girls' reaction to menarche, is boys' reluctance to discuss the event with others (Gaddis & Brooks-Gunn, 1985).

While girls gain body fat during puberty, boys gain muscle. Both of these are normal physical changes, but girls tend to view their increase in fat as making them unattractive, whereas boys are proud of their bodies (Lerner & Olson, 1997). Girls tend to be less satisfied with their weight than boys are in general, and perceiving oneself as underweight was associated with the greatest amount of satisfaction for girls.

Social class tends to interact with girls' feelings about their weight. Young women from higher social classes are more likely to wish to be thinner, although the majority of young women in every social class wish that they were thinner (Dornbusch, Gross, Duncan, & Ritter, 1987). Interestingly, Black adolescent girls appear more well adjusted than White adolescent girls with regard to body image and in general (Freiberg, 1991; Ingrassia, 1995).

Parent–child relations change during puberty. For girls, menarche seems to cause parents to view them as more mature (Danza, 1983), whether menarche is early or late. In the first six months after menarche, however, daughters report more parental control (Hill & Holmbeck, 1987).

Mother–daughter interactions change both qualitatively and quantitatively as puberty progresses. Mother–daughter conflict is pronounced during early puberty (Brooks-Gunn & Zahaykevich, 1989). Premenarcheal girls use more aggressive, oppositional, and critical speech with their mothers. Postmenarcheal girls, on the other hand, use more passive communication styles, such as indifference and denial (Zahaykevich, Sirey, & Brooks-Gunn, unpublished). Mothers of premenarcheal girls tend to use more dogmatic techniques (such as reference to a fixed external rule system) to influence their daughters, whereas mothers of postmenarcheal girls used more projective methods (such as requiring the girls to put themselves in their mother's place). This may foster mother–daughter conflict, because young adolescent girls find it more difficult to take their parents' perspective (Smetana, 1988).

Some fathers are more reserved with their adolescent daughters, who behave more assertively or brusquely once they have reached menarche (Hill, 1988). They are reluctant to discuss body changes or sexuality with their daughters, and girls, in turn, are embarrassed by these topics in front of their fathers (Brooks-Gunn & Zahaykevich, 1989). This may be a reflection of the incest taboo, with fathers attempting to distance themselves from their sexually maturing daughters. And perhaps some fathers are less emotionally invested in their daughters to begin with and are therefore more willing to let go as the child moves into adolescence.

For boys, relationships with their parents change as well. Mothers report the highest levels of opposition from their sons (Hill & Holmbeck, 1987). Mothers appear to lose influence over their sons during adolescence (Steinberg, 1981) and usually end up giving in to them in arguments (Welsh & Powers, 1991). This is probably connected to the fact that teen-age sons of divorced mothers tend to do better in school when the mother remarries. The addition of a father figure provides increased monitoring, supervision, and support (Hetherington, 1989; Zimiles & Lee, 1991).

Fathers also yield to sons in some cases, possibly out of a desire to promote independence. However, as a rule, fathers have been found to become more controlling and competitive as their sons enter puberty, and the sons often yield to the fathers. Perhaps their sons' budding adulthood and strength is threatening to the fathers, who are concurrently reaching middle age and possibly feeling the onset of physical decline.

In general, however, parents of adolescents give boys more independence and autonomy than they give to girls. They are apparently worrying more over the possibility that their daughter will become pregnant than over the equally salient possibility that their son will impregnate someone else's daughter (Meyer, 1991). Unfortunately, both boys and girls are short-changed by this discrepancy. Adolescent boys suffer when parents give them too little discipline, attention, and support, rationalizing that boys need to learn to stand on their own feet. Girls, on the other hand, are likely to be excessively restricted (Dubow, Huesmann, & Eron, 1987; Leaper et al., 1989; Lempers,

Clark-Lempers, & Simons, 1989; Vaughn, Block, & Block, 1988).

In adolescence, the peer group begins to take on increasing importance while the influence of the family diminishes. Intimate friendships are formed earlier for teen-age girls than boys. These friendships are of central importance to girls, who will cultivate them by sharing secrets, asking for the friend's advice, complimenting the friend's popularity, and avoiding doing anything that would indicate that they feel superior to their friends (Buhrmester & Furman, 1987; Savin-Williams, 1979). Girls' friendships in adolescence provide them with emotional support as they cope with self-consciousness, change, and other adjustments. Girls who mature early and start dating ahead of their peers are likely to miss out on the benefits of friendships with other girls (Miller, 1993; Steinberg, 1993).

Although girls' friendships are stereotyped as being more valued by them than boys' friendships are by their male counterparts, evidence suggests otherwise. Boys have a strong capacity and need for same-gender friendships (Blyth & Foster-Clark, 1987); they may simply be more cautious about admitting that their friends are important to them (Berndt, 1992). This could be a function of societal gender expectations associating masculinity with autonomy.

As in childhood, boys' peer groups exhibit themes of status and dominance, especially in junior high school when the transition to a new school takes place. Girls as a group appear to be much more permanently affected than boys are by school transitions during pubertal years. The shift from elementary school to junior high school and then to high school has a strong detrimental impact on girls' self-esteem (Simmons & Blyth, 1987).

A possible explanation for the effects of school transition on girls' self-esteem is the shift in educational methods from elementary to secondary school. As children mature into adolescence, classes gradually shift from lectures and tests to seminars. In the former, quiet, conscientious work (i.e., taking notes and studying) ensures success; in the latter, confidence, assertiveness, and a willingness to take risks (i.e., participation in class discussion) prevails. As such, the type of academic work for which girls have been traditionally rewarded becomes less valued (Huston & Alvarez, 1990).

In sum, it appears that although boys may be subject to much turmoil in adolescence, girls are far more vulnerable emotionally. Their self-esteem is taxed by self-consciousness, poor body image, academic adjustments, and other changes. However, as one of the authors has pointed out, "Yet although adolescence represents an often difficult period in a young woman's life, for many teens, this is also a time of exploration, freedom to try new things, growing independence, and self-awareness. During this period, the adolescent girl begins to form her own unique identity" (Denmark, 1997, p. 377). In addition, they must deal with menarche and their mixed feelings regarding this milestone. It is interesting to note that Black girls appear to be better adjusted than White girls with regard to body image, and that girls of higher socioeconomic status have more difficulty dealing with weight issues. This attests to the significant influence of culture, ethnicity, and class.

ETHNICITY, RACE, CULTURE, AND CLASS EFFECTS ON GENDER DEVELOPMENT

Chapter 4 looked at culture, race, ethnicity, and class. In this chapter we are reviewing some of the effects of these variables on gender development. Recent literature suggests that race, class, and ethnicity all affect the study of child development and gender (Binion, 1990). However, studies of gender that take these variables into account have been rare. A complete understanding of the factors influencing developmental processes, including gender-role development, cannot be achieved without considering the effects of ethnicity and/or social class (Reid & Paludi, 1993).

Gender typing varies across race and ethnicity. For example, African American children appear to experience less gender stereotyping in their upbringing. Traditionally, African American women have worked outside the home and displayed independence and assertiveness in addition to nurturance. African American men, on the other hand, have often been more nurturant and expressive than their white

counterparts (Bardwell, Cochran, & Walker, 1986). African American children report that they see both parents as providing instrumental (provider) and expressive functions. This suggests that African American children are more immune to society's gender typing.

In school, both White and African American boys experience a conflict between their definition of masculinity and being a good student; however, this conflict is greater for African American boys (Reed, 1988). On the other hand, African American girls are probably free of some of the difficulties experienced by their White counterparts in this area. African American girls, having been encouraged by their community to be self-sufficient and assertive, are likely to be more independent in the school setting. As a result, although girls generally get less attention in the classroom, this lack of attention may not hurt African American girls' self-image as much as it does that of their White counterparts (Ogbu, 1982).

Some African American care-givers, particularly mothers, are very protective of their male children. This can create unique gender-role patterns that are not prevalent in other cultures. For example, older children in many African American families are responsible for caring for their younger siblings. This is particularly true of girls, but the role flexibility in African American families allows for *boys* to fulfill this function.

In Hispanic cultures, girls receive conflicting messages about their identity from an early age. On the one hand, women are considered morally and spiritually superior to men; yet they are expected to accept male authority. This is reinforced by the concept of **marianismo,** which considers women morally and spiritually superior to men and, therefore, capable of enduring male-inflicted suffering (Stevens, 1973).

Both boys and girls in Hispanic cultures tend to be close to their mothers and feel alienated from their authoritarian or uninvolved fathers. The mother's relationship with the son tends to be more dependent, sometimes to the point where the son protects his mother from his father. The mother's relationship with the daughter, on the other hand, is of a more reciprocal nature; mothers teach their daughters how to be good women and fulfill their eventual roles of wife and mother (Stevens, 1973).

In Native American culture, girls' education traditionally focused on domestic tasks and responsibilities once puberty commenced. However, in modern times, certain tribes teach community values to children without stressing sex differences. Native American girls can participate in active sports enjoyed by their male counterparts (Schlegal, 1973).

Asian American cultures vary in terms of their views of females. Many Asian cultures, particularly those built on Confucian philosophy, are particularly oppressive toward women. Girls are raised to be deferent to family, community, and the patriarchs. However, Filipino culture subscribes to a more egalitarian distribution of power between males and females. Japanese parents' attitudes and behavior toward their child differ according to the sex of the child. Girls in Japan are expected to conform to the traditional female gender role; males, on the other hand, who are not as strictly disciplined, are not constrained to conform to the traditional male role (Sukemune, Shiraishi, Shirakawa, & Matsumi, 1993). Although traditional Chinese society has a similar double standard for boys and girls, Hong Kong has juxtaposed these ideas with more modern and Westernized ideas of child rearing (Yu, 1993). Korea, as a Confucian society, tends to favor men (Kim, 1993).

The diverse parenting styles presented above indicate that Asian American children's ideas of gender will differ according to their (or their parents') country of origin. In general, however, it is clear that even among Confucian-based societies, increasing pressures to modernize and Westernize have mitigated proscriptions against women to some degree. This has had an effect on Asian American children's upbringing.

In Jamaican culture, gender roles are fairly stereotyped and rigid. Although girls are expected to embody traits such as obedience, femininity, and attractiveness, they are also required to be bright and educated. Yet, they must remain inferior to men in these areas. As such, Jamaican girls are exposed to a double standard that strongly encourages education as a means to economic stability, but discourages staying in school "too long" (Allen, 1988). Jamaican boys, on the other hand, are expected to be adventurous and less responsive to discipline. Masculinity is verified by the man's ability to father children and to earn a decent living. Thus, particularly in the lower classes, Jamaican boys are geared toward choosing employment that will enable them to support a family. Unfortunately, father absence is common and the boys are often socialized by their mothers. As a result, they are without an appropriate model of how to relate as a father and husband. This deficit may result in a sense of inadequacy that negatively affects their own child-rearing endeavors later. (Allen, 1988).

Within the U.S. classroom, girls of different racial backgrounds show a relative preference for same-race, same-sex playmates and a greater relative avoidance of White boys than of African or Asian American boys. Boys of various races showed a relative preference for White race, same sex playmates and least relative avoidance of same-race girls. This might be explained by White boys being perceived as having higher status, and same-race children being perceived as more attractive (Fishbein & Imai, 1993). It is interesting that classroom racial minority status (i.e., being in a classroom in which most classmates are of a different race) was associated with peer rejection of girls but not of boys (Kistner, Metzler, Gatlin, & Risi, 1993). This suggests that girls are more victimized by their peers' racism than are boys.

Socioeconomic status is another variable that can affect gender typing. For example, division between the sexes is more rigidly defined in the working class than in the middle class. Women expect men to provide a decent living for their families, while the home is considered the woman's responsibility, in spite of the fact that economic necessity has forced a large percentage of working-class women to seek employment (Rubin, 1980). Therefore, one might expect children from working-class homes to form more rigid gender stereotypes than do children from middle-class homes.

This is consistent with the fact that, although studies show that middle-class children with externally employed mothers are less sex-role stereotyped than those whose mothers are primarily housewives, these results are mixed for working-class children

(Cordua, McGraw, & Drabman, 1979; Gold & Andres, 1978; Marantz & Mansfield, 1977; Meyer, 1980). It is possible that middle-class mothers tend to be employed by choice in jobs that they find satisfactory, whereas working-class mothers are employed out of economic necessity and express less job satisfaction. Therefore, middle-class children are more amenable to the idea of women working than are working-class children. More information about the effects of maternal employment on children can be found in Chapter 7.

In a study of temper tantrum prevalence, boys who threw tantrums were more likely to be of an upper social class, whereas their female counterparts were more likely to be of a lower social class (Bhatia et al., 1990). In keeping with general behavioral theory, this suggests that boys' tantrums are reinforced among upper-class families and girls' tantrums are reinforced among lower-class families. The ramifications of this for gender upbringing among those of different socioeconomic status would be of interest for future study.

In preschool, girls appear to be more aware of social class cues than are boys (Ramsey, 1991). This may parallel the finding cited previously that girls who are the racial minority are more likely to be rejected by their peers than are boys who are the racial minority. Perhaps this can be explained by girls' emphasis on popularity and interpersonal relations as validating their self-worth and femininity. Girls might be afraid to make friendships that could jeopardize their social status and thus are far more sensitive to both social class and racial cues when choosing friends than are boys.

In general, little research exists that examines the interaction of race and class with gender. This area bears much study, and students of different demographic backgrounds are urged to devote their research to this highly important topic.

SUMMARY

Psychological theories of gender-role development include the psychoanalytic, social learning, and cognitive-developmental perspectives. Freud's psychoanalytic views emphasize intrapsychic forces and conflicts that result in children's identification with their same-sex parents. Social learning theory, on the other hand, focuses on external, environmental influences. The cognitive-developmental perspective discusses the role of the child in his or her own socialization.

While classic theoreticians assumed that girls were only capable of inferior moral development relative to boys, recent researchers such as Gilligan have suggested otherwise. Gilligan claims that girls' morality is merely different, not inferior, and studies suggest that it is based more on differential experiences than on innate personality differences.

Children's internalized images of gender play an important role in such areas as popularity in elementary school, conceptions of personal power, self-esteem, and motivation and personal goals for adolescents. Images of gender vary across cultures and are reinforced by the child's surrounding environment.

Gender schema theory suggests that children create knowledge structures that organize gender-related information in memory and are used to evaluate new information according to their gender. Children's gender schemas may be more or less flexible, and this flexibility or rigidity will affect their attitudes toward members of both sexes. Attitudes toward gender tend to be differentiated among children across cultures, with biases that usually favor men but sometimes favor women.

Parenting plays a significant role in childhood gender socialization. In general, parents tend to foster boys' autonomy and girls' dependence. Single-parent homes have their own set of ramifications for children's gender-role attitudes, however. Fathers tend to reinforce gender-typed behavior more than mothers do, so the absence of the father can result in more androgynous behavior. Children living with their fathers tend to have a more balanced experience in terms of male and female adult figures. Even in intact marriages, mothers and fathers parent differently.

Socializing forces that influence gender-role development after birth include language, play, media, school, and peers. Socialization into gender roles of girls and boys is also mediated by race and social class. However, far too few studies exist in this area. This topic would be an exciting one for future research.

KEY TERMS

Adolescence (p. 163)
Conventional reasoning (p. 147)
Gender identity disorder (p. 148)
Gender schema theory (p. 149)
Linguistic sexism (p. 156)

Marianismo (p. 166)
Menarche (p. 164)
Morality of constraint (p. 146)
Morality of cooperation (p. 146)
Postconventional reasoning (p. 147)

Preconventional reasoning (p. 146)
Puberty (p. 163)
Semenarche (p. 164)

DISCUSSION QUESTIONS

1. How are gender roles constructed for boys and girls before birth? What is the suggested connection between prenatal hormones, particularly the presence or absence of androgens in the womb, and the personality traits of boys and girls?

2. Compare the moral development of girls and boys based on the theories of Freud, Kohlberg, and Gilligan. Do you believe that moral reasoning lies on a continuum from lowest to highest? How does Gilligan's theory incorporate the experiences of girls into Kohlberg's male-based paradigm?

3. List the qualities and characteristics that you associate with femininity and masculinity. Compare the list of feminine items with the list of masculine items. Which list contains more positive traits? Which of these qualities do you personally embrace and which qualities do you reject? Why?

4. What role do cultural values and expectations play in developing gender attitudes in children? Identify the predominant roles of women and men prescribed by your own culture. How do these gender stereotypes resonate with the choices that you have made?

5. Describe the differences between men and women as parents. How do fathers perpetuate gender stereotyping of their children? How does the match or mismatch between the sex of the parent and the sex of the child influence the type of parent–child interactions that occur?

6. How does language contribute to the differentiation of males and females? Do you feel the adoption of gender-neutral language empowers women?

7. Spend a few hours viewing television programs and commercials. How are women and men portrayed differently? List all the innuendoes you see and hear that denigrate women. Translate all of them into insults aimed at disabled people. Would disabled people allow that? Would the FCC allow that? Would you allow this if you were disabled?

8. Girls and boys have been shown to adopt strict gender-role orientation during adolescence. To what extent is their adherence to traditional gender roles during adolescence due to the physical changes of puberty? What social forces operate during adolescence to explain this phenomenon?

9. Do you feel that your gender-role development has been strongly influenced by your race, ethnicity, and class? Can you think of experiences in which being a female transcends racial, ethnic, and class lines, and times when the reverse is true?

SUGGESTED READINGS

Crosby, F. (1991). *Juggling: The unexpected advantages of balancing career and home for women and their families.* New York: The Free Press.

Johnson, N. G., Roberts, M. C., & Worrell, J. (1999). *Beyond appearance: A new look at adolescent girls.* Washington, DC: American Psychological Association.

Pipher, M. (1994). *Reviving Ophelia: Saving the selves of adolescent girls.* New York: Grosset/Putman.

Reid, P. T., & Paludi, M. A. (1993). Developmental psychology of women: Conception to adolescence. In F. L. Denmark & M. A. Paludi (Eds.), *Psychology of women: A handbook of issues* (pp. 191–212). Westport, CT: Greenwood Press.

Sadker, M., & Sadker, D. (1994). *Failing of fairness: How America's schools cheat girls.* New York: Charles Scribner's Sons.

Thompson, B. W. (1994). Childhood lessons: Culture, race, class, and sexuality. In B. W. Thompson (Ed.), *A hunger so wide and so deep: American women speak out on eating problems* (pp. 27–45). Minneapolis: University of Minnesota Press.

_____ CHAPTER 6 _____

ABILITY AND ACHIEVEMENT

It is about as meaningful to ask "Which is the smarter sex?" or "Which has the better brain?" as to ask "Which has the better genitals?"
—Diane Halpern

Over the past 150 years, the most famous scientists of Europe have propagated scientific findings about sex and race. Virtually every claim that biological difference explains social inequality has turned out to be bogus. But hope springs eternal.
—Anne Fausto-Sterling

The day when, misunderstanding the inferior occupations which nature has given her, women leave the home and take part in our battles; on this day a social revolution will begin, and everything that maintains the sacred ties of the family will disappear.
—Le Bon as quoted in Gould

Although it is true that boys as well as girls benefit from an education, it seems that educating girls actually produces a greater return; in many parts of the world, it is the woman's schooling that is the crucial factor in lifting her family out of poverty. . . . Yet despite the long-term benefits of educating girls, parents in many parts of the world prefer to invest in educating their sons.
—Neft and Levine

It would be difficult to find a research area [than gender differences in cognitive ability] more characterized by shoddy work, overgeneralization, hasty conclusions, and unsupported speculations.
—Julia Sherman, as cited in Fausto-Sterling

Gender differences in intellectual abilities and achievements have preoccupied scientists in many disciplines for decades. To this day, few arenas of gender differences are more fraught with political minefields and emotional rhetoric than those involving cognitive abilities. For people all along the political spectrum, there is much at stake in the answer to this question: Who's smarter, women or men? Whether there are gender differences in intelligence and, if so, to what degree and for what reasons may have serious implications for males' and females' educational opportunities, academic achievement, career choices, occupational status, and lifelong earnings—for their standing as people in a society. This chapter reviews the evidence arising from gender comparisons in cognitive abilities, as well as gender issues in education, literacy, and overall achievement.

ISSUES IN COMPARING MALES' AND FEMALES' COGNITIVE ABILITIES

In Western society, where we attach great weight to mental abilities, asking which group of people is smarter is tantamount to asking which group is better. Behind this question is the lurking suspicion, if not the outright assumption, that such differences, if they exist, are biological in origin, immutable, and socially significant. As Fausto-Sterling (1992) has observed, at the crux of this question also lies important practical decisions about how to teach reading and mathematics, whether boys and girls should attend different schools, job and career choices, and how much men and women are worth in the job market. The disciplines of psychology, education, sociology, and biology have all contributed to the scholarship on this issue. There have been thousands of empirical studies on gender differences in intelligence and thousands more commentaries explaining, refuting, and complicating the existence of such differences. The media and public show a similar fascination with gender differences in this area, and it is not at all uncommon for a study trumpeting gender differences in brain functioning or cognition to make the front page of a newspaper or magazine, whereas a study of gender similarities or declining differences is more likely to be buried in the body of the text. This fascination is rooted in the histories of intelligence testing and the studies of gender and racial comparisons in the United States that evince preoccupation with finding and explaining individual and group differences.

The History of Gender Comparisons in Cognitive Ability

The study of cognitive differences in intelligence has a long history in psychology, driven largely by the presumed lack of women of recognized genius or high achievement. In 1903, James McKeen Catell, a psychology professor at Columbia University and then-editor of *Science,* the official journal of the American Association for the Advancement of Science and the leading scientific journal in the English language, studied the lives of eminent individuals and noted that few were women. He found a dearth of high-achieving women throughout the ages and only a tiny proportion of women among the top thousand scientists (Fausto-Sterling, 1992). Catell concluded that because there was not any social prejudice against women in science, he found it "difficult to avoid the conclusion that there is an innate sexual disqualification" (Catell, 1903). Catell's colleague at Columbia, the leading educational psychologist Edward L. Thorndike, who championed the use of statistics in educational research, was also impressed by the rarity of female geniuses. Thorndike concluded that it made little sense to squander educational resources trying to bring women into the ranks of the intellectual elite and that women were better off studying to become nurses and teachers where the "average level is essential" (Thorndike, cited in Seller, 1981). Profiled in Chapter 1, G. Stanley Hall, the father of child psychology and the first president of the American Psychological Association, argued against coeducation at the American Academy of Medicine in 1906 on similar grounds:

> It (coeducation) violates a custom so universal that it seems to express a fundamental human instinct. . . . girls . . . are attracted to common knowledge which all share, to the conventional, are more influenced by fashions, more imitative and lack the boys' intense desire to know, be, do something distinctive that develops and emphasizes his individuality. To be thrown on their own personal resources in sports, in the classroom, in nature study and elementary laboratory brings out the best in a boy, but either confuses or strains a girl. (Hall, 1906, pp. 1–2)

Catell, Thorndike, and Hall saw the differences between male and female intellectual achievement as rooted in biology, rather than in different socialization practices or severely limited educational, occupational, and social opportunities for women (Fausto-Sterling, 1992). They also believed that men were, by nature, more variable than women on a number of characteristics and that this presumably explained why, despite the fact that the mean (average) intelligence levels of men and women were the same, more men than women appeared at the highest levels of intelligence. According to the *variability hypothesis,* for biological reasons that are seldom made clear, males appear more frequently at both the lowest and highest levels of intelligence, with women clustered around the middle range. The work of these men has had a profound impact throughout this century on the study of gender differences in all kinds of traits, including intelligence. Indeed, as we noted in Chapter 1, pioneers in the first generation of women in psychology frequently devoted large portions of their careers to attempting to discredit notions like the variability hypothesis that in effect represent women as more ordinary and limited than men (Montague & Hollingworth, 1914). But versions of this hypothesis survive to this day, as we will see shortly.

The history of the study of cognitive sex differences closely parallels the history of the study of other "sex differences" in personality, aptitude, and achievement, in which characteristics that are presumed to be more common among males are valued precisely because they are male. An enduring belief in male superiority on important traits has led most researchers to search for explanations, preferably biological and thus natural, that might justify the continuing unequal positions of men and women in society.

UNDERSTANDING THE MEANING OF DIFFERENCE

Before weighing the evidence for the what and where of sex differences in cognition, it might be useful to consider whether and how males' and females' brains are different, how statisticians and psychologists find and interpret group differences, and what is the theoretical and social significance of group differences in cognition. We will discuss biological factors, methodological and statistical issues, and the meaning of cognitive differences in turn.

Sex and the Brain

The particular biological mechanisms by which men were thought to be superior to women have changed over time as each has been discarded for lack of scientific evidence and as technological advances have offered new possibilities. At various times, the seat of male superiority has been thought to be the size of the male brain, which is on the average larger than the female brain. As Fausto-Sterling (1992) explains, this explanation ran afoul of the "elephant problem": if brain size was the key to intelligence, then elephants and whales ought to rule Earth. Attempts to correct for this problem by dividing brain size by body size resulted in females coming out ahead of males, and this line of explanation and research has been subsequently abandoned. Interestingly, however, in what we will see is a theme of much biological research on gender differences in cognition, old ideas die hard and often resurface with modern twists. A much discussed front-page finding in 1997 was that men have about 5 billion more brain cells than women (although men's brain cells die faster!) (Angier, 1999). Other supposed female deficiencies in the brain include a smaller surface area of the corpus callosum (a mass of nerve fibers that connects the left and right halves of the brain) and the level of complexities of the convolutions of the brain, both of which have been largely discredited.

More recently, attention has been paid to the topic of hemispheric differentiation or **lateralization.** Functionally, humans have two brains, with the left hemisphere appearing to specialize in language analysis, computation, and sequential tasks and the right side hosting artistic abilities, and an emotional, nonanalytic approach to the world. Not long after the discovery by neurobiologist Roger Sperry that the supposedly symmetrical brain had different capabilities, some scientists have been using the asymmetrical brain to ex-

plain the different patterns of male and female abilities. Jerre Levy, a student of Roger Sperry, has hypothesized that the most efficiently functioning brains have the most complete lateralization: the most complete hemispheric division of labor (1969). Women and men appear to have different patterns of lateralization; that is, men have more highly specialized (more "efficient") brains, with the left side active in solving verbal problems and the right side in spatial ones. Some studies do suggest that there is more hemispheric specialization in males than females, but findings are inconsistent and the size of the gender difference appears to be small, with most males indistinguishable from most females.

Although many hypotheses have been raised and much research conducted, there is still no strong supporting evidence that the brains of males are more lateralized in general than those of females (Lips, 1997). There is some evidence, however, that the brains of females and males may differ in organization in some specific abilities; for example, the location of speech areas in the brains of females may be different from that of males (Kimura, 1987), but, again, there are broad variations across the genders.

Brain organization is evidently involved in cognitive ability, but the mechanisms that could mediate any sex differences have not been well elucidated. There is still little to no evidence of a clear relationship between hemispheric lateralization and gender differences in cognition. The origins, meanings, and size of this gender difference are still hotly debated, and, at present, it is reasonable to question why lateralization is framed in such positive terms.

The work of Doreen Kimura suggests a role for prenatal sex hormones on brain organization (Kimura, 1997). According to Kimura, androgens (a male hormone present to a greater degree in males than females) organize the male brain in ways that boost some forms of spatial ability throughout the entire life-span. Furthermore, Kimura reports that in adult men seasonal and diurnal (daily) fluctuations of testosterone are associated with changes in scores on tests of spatial ability on which men excel, but not on tests of abilities in which females excel, such as verbal fluency and verbal memory, or on tests of sex-neutral abilities. In women undergoing natural fluctuations of the menstrual cycle, high-estrogen periods are associated with enhanced performance on tasks in which females excel, such as fine motor skills and articulatory fluency, whereas low-estrogen periods correspond to enhanced performance in tests of spatial ability. Kimura (1997) uses evolutionary theory to explain her findings (see page 184).

As we consider biological evidence for sex differences, it is crucial to keep in mind that most studies in these areas are correlational in nature, meaning that they cannot and do not prove a causal role for factors like hormones. Such studies merely suggest an association between two factors that may be due to other factors not studied. Experimental studies, in which the effects of hormones are systematically manipulated and causal inferences can be made, are relatively rare for humans because of the ethical and practical issues involved in manipulating such variables. But recent experimental studies with humans in which hormone levels were manipulated support the argument that male and female sex hormones may play a role in cognitive ability. For example, when normal aging men were given testosterone to enhance their sexual functioning, they also showed improved performance on visual spatial tasks (Janowsky, Oviatt, & Orwoll, 1994). And when female-to-male transsexuals were administered high levels of testosterone in preparation for sex-change procedures, they experienced a dramatic improvement in their visual–spatial ability and a correspondingly dramatic impairment in their verbal fluency (Van Goozen, Cohen-Kettenis, Gooren, Frijda, & Van De Poll, 1995). The evidence in favor of hormonally induced increases and decreases in mathematical ability is less compelling. Experimental studies in which the presumed causal variables are manipulated rather than measured provide better evidence than correlational studies for a causal link between hormones and cognitive function, but such studies are uncommon, often involve specialized groups, and are frequently open to alternative explanations.

Recent experimental work with animals suggests that female hormones like estrogen can preserve and even improve some of the brain's highest mental functions. Investigators have found that estrogen may have a therapeutic effect in the prevention and possible treatment of Alzheimer's disease. Apparently, estrogen protects nerve cells and may have diverse positive effects on learning and memory throughout the lifespan (Luine, Rentas, Sterbank, & Beck, 1996; Luine & Rodriguez, 1994; Sherwin, 1998; Wickelgreen, 1997).

Keep in mind that the history of biological research in this area is replete with the practice of locating a morphological (physical) difference—any difference—between male and female brains and attributing important functional (behavioral) disparities between the sexes to this difference, with or without scientific justification. It is true that sex differences in brain morphology and function have been noted in many areas, including lateral asymmetry and anterior and posterior organization. The search for biological bases of sex differences in cognition has only heated up in recent years, along with improvements in computer technology such as positron emission tomography (PET) scans and magnetic resonance imagery (MRI) that enable us to better "see" the brain. Indeed, some studies have detected somewhat different patterns of brain activity among males and females when problem solving (Shaywitz et al., 1995). But, to date, none of these morphological differences or differences in patterns of activation has been conclusively related to the few and small differences in cognitive function that have been reliably observed. Moreover, the profound sexism that has pervaded the long search for biological explanations should render us cautious in interpreting research findings in this area. Because biological explanations sound more scientific than social or cultural ones, they are accorded more respect than other explanations. Some people confuse biological explanations with scientific ones. But what renders a study scientific is not its subject matter, but rather the quality of the methods it uses.

Making Comparisons and Evaluating Differences

As we will see, there are many cognitive areas in which the sexes, on average, differ, and many in which there are no differences. Some differences favor men and others women, although, overall, gender differences in cognition are typically small rather than large, with great overlap between the sexes. Obtained differences are the function of many features of a study other than true differences in male and female cognitive ability. This is discussed in the following sections on research methods and statistical issues.

Methodological Issues: Samples, Tests, and Context

Samples.   It is increasingly clear from the thousands of studies of gender differences that whether differences are obtained and the size of these differences depend on various features of the study. One critical feature appears to be how the samples of males and females were obtained. Many studies comparing males and females use convenience samples that are not representative of males and females and from which generalizations should not be made. Moreover, most gender comparisons are made of college students, who are certainly not representative of the general male and female populations on many dimensions, most notably age. Indeed, age of respondents matters a great deal in gender comparisons, as some differences appear early in life, others not until adolescence, and still others later in life (Halpern, 1997).

The fact is, however they are sampled, boys and girls and men and women are *nonequivalent groups,* and comparisons between them are fraught with difficulties. Males and females differ on so many dimensions—on the biological level, in genes, brains, and hormones, among others; on the psychological level, in life experiences of all types, attitudes, beliefs, emotions, and expectation levels, among others; and on the social level, in opportunities, discriminations, and stereotypes, among others—that it is virtually impossible to determine which of the many variables confounded or correlated with biological sex is responsible for a gender difference if one emerges. Scientists are people first, and just like laypeople, scientists often have psychological, social, or political preferences for different levels of explanation of gender differences, with some favoring biologically based explanations, such as evolutionary theory, and others

favoring more socially based explanations. What we need to evaluate is whether there is sound scientific evidence to support both the existence of and the explanation for the difference.

Tests.   Another crucial variable is the type of test or task used to measure cognitive differences. Increasingly, contemporary scholars are rejecting the old taxonomy that divides experimental results neatly into the areas of verbal, mathematical, and visual–spatial ability (Halpern, 1997). This is because these are not unitary constructs, and this categorization scheme has not proved useful in organizing gender-related findings. As we will see, females excel at some visual–spatial tasks and not others, whereas males excel at some verbal tasks and not others. There is no one, ultimate verbal or mathematical test or task that fully represents the constructs of verbal or mathematical ability. Even more basically, we may question why ability is so often discussed in terms of standardized test performance. Because we are frequently unsure of what tests actually measure, we should have a healthy skepticism about group differences on tests of ability.

Context.   Until recently, the importance of context surrounding the administration of the test was often overlooked. People do not come into testing situations "tabula rasa" or blank slates; they are profoundly affected by their values, beliefs, and expectations about the test and the meaning of their performance. As Eccles (1987) noted, the attributions people make for their successes and failures, their expectations for succeeding, their strategies for test taking, and their experience with tests all combine to affect their motivation and performance. Males and females are well aware of the different stereotypes that society holds about male and female abilities, and many people feel that "girls can't do math." Social psychologists Steele and Aronson have recently demonstrated the unconscious and powerful influences of negative stereotypes on vulnerable groups (Steele & Aronson, 1995). Steele (1997) found that, under instructional sets in which women feel that their mathematical ability was being tested, women performed more poorly than when the test was presented to women in a less threatening manner. How people interpret the meaning of the test and their scores on it appears to be quite relevant to their performance.

Some Basic Statistical Issues

Distributions.   Before we consider the vast and complex research on sex differences in cognition, it is crucial that we understand what the word *difference* means—and what it does not. Scores on tests are often represented in frequency distributions, which are graphs of how many people in a sample receive each score. Distributions vary in their shapes and means and the amount of variability of the scores. Most psychological traits, including intelligence and its many components, are normally distributed, with most scores clustered around the group mean and successively fewer scores as you move to the extremes in either direction (see Figure 6.1a).

Research shows that when most people think about group differences in any trait, they tend to exaggerate the size of that difference and to imagine essentially **nonoverlapping distributions,** as we see in Figure 6.1b, where virtually all members of group B score higher than virtually all members of group A (Fausto-Sterling, 1995). The fact is, with almost all group differences involving human traits, the frequency distributions are largely overlapping, with most members of the different groups being indistinguishable from each other, as we see in Figure 6.1c. The frequency distributions of male and female cognitive traits vary in their degree of overlap, but all of them look more like Figure 6.1c than Figure 6.1b. On virtually all psychological traits—certainly on intelligence—males and females are much more alike than they are different.

We have noted that a theme in the thinking of Cattell and Thorndike, which continues in various guises to this day, is that men are more variable in their cognitive abilities than women are: that while the mean measured IQ of men and women is about the same, the distribution or variation in scores is greater for men than for women. Obviously, it is possible to arrive at the same mean for two distributions despite

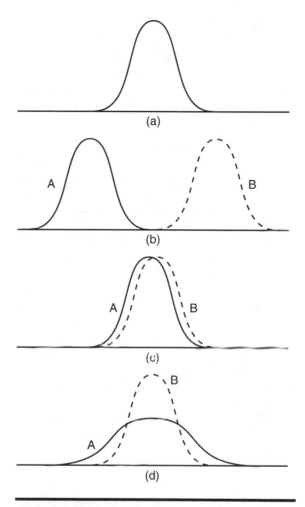

FIGURE 6.1   Distribution Curves
Line graph (a) presents a normal distribution curve. Line graphs (b) through (d) present three combinations: (b) two frequency distributions with no overlap, a very uncommon outcome when comparing groups; (c) two frequency distributions with a high degree of overlap, typical of most distributions of male and female traits of all kinds; and (d) two frequency distributions of scores with the same mean but very different variability.

very different patterns of scores: The mean of the scores 100, 100, 100, 100, and 100 is 100, and so is the mean of this distribution: 90, 110, 80, 120, and

100. In Figure 6.1d, you can see that the two distributions have the same mean of 100, but quite different variability, with distribution A showing considerably more variability than distribution B. A bit later we will review the contemporary evidence concerning whether male scores on cognitive skills are more variable than female scores.

Statistically Significant Differences.   When cognitive differences between men and women are evaluated, the findings are typically reported in terms of the mean differences and, less often, the variability of the distributions, or the percentage of very high scorers. Mean differences are either held to be *significant,* meaning reliable and not due to chance, or *not significant,* meaning possibly due to chance alone. If the differences are significant and the study meets methodological criteria, the investigator has a potentially publishable study and a potentially "sexy" finding: people pay attention to sex differences on important traits. If a difference does not achieve significance, the study is far less likely to be published, despite the importance of the research topic or strength of its methodology, and the finding of no difference will probably disappear into the investigator's file drawer.

Many people outside (and inside) psychology are confused about the meaning of **statistically significant differences,** and they often think that "significant" means more than it does. Whether statistically significant differences are achieved depends, among other things, on the size of the samples, with larger samples having a much greater chance of yielding significant findings than smaller ones. For example, a mean difference of 6 IQ points is unlikely to be significant if the scores of 6 men and 6 women are compared, but highly likely to be significant if the scores of 6000 men and 6000 women are compared. The variability among scores is another consideration, with larger mean differences needed to achieve significance the more variable the samples. Also, the mere fact of statistically significant differences says nothing about the size of the difference. A very tiny difference of just a few points on a 200-point scale may emerge as significant, given other features of the study. Throughout this chapter, we will sometimes refer to a newer statistic known as the **effect size** (Cohen's *d*), which gives us a better sense of how large a difference exists between groups (Cohen, 1969). In any case, it is important to remember that statistical significance is contingent on many factors and must not be confused with social significance. Relatedly, keep in mind that measures of variability and percentage of high scores depend critically on *which* men and women are in the study, that is, how the sample was constituted, as noted previously.

Meta-Analysis.   Would you drastically change your diet or begin taking a new drug on the basis of the results of a single study? Probably not, as you are undoubtedly aware that the results of multiple studies in any given area are often inconsistent. On virtually all important topics in psychology, there are literally hundreds of studies of an effect or phenomenon, and the results, taken together, are often inconclusive. This opens the door for much mischief, as some people selectively choose to cite only those findings that support their position and conveniently ignore the rest. But thanks to a new statistical technique called **meta-analysis,** we are now able to combine the results of different studies of the same research question. For each study included in the meta-analysis, the researcher computes the effect size noted above, Cohen's *d,* which measures not only the size of the difference between males and females, but also indicates the direction of the difference (which group scored higher or lower). The statistic *d* is comparable across studies and can be averaged across studies to tell us how large the average gender difference is and which group it favors. What often emerges from meta-analytic reviews is a clearer and fairer portrait of the state of knowledge in a given research area. Thanks to pioneers, such as Janet Hyde, in the application of meta-analysis to the study of gender issues, we are now able to summarize vast literatures on gender differences on various dimensions, and we will cite the findings of meta-analyses wherever possible.

Meaning Is in the Eye of the Beholder.   All scientific work takes place in a particular historical, cultural, and social context that gives it special meaning at the same time that it limits its generalizability to populations, settings, and times not studied. Scientific "facts" are always laden with the insights and blind spots of the times. It is easy to see the blatant sexism and racism in early research on gender and race differences, but it is always harder to see the forces that shape work in the present (Unger & Crawford, 1996). We can be sure that, when we study variables like gender, race, and class, forces like social characteristics and personal values are at work.

Finally, we need to remember that a mind—male or female—is a tough thing to change (Halpern, 1997). Most of us have been observing and making judgments about the abilities of males and females all our lives, and many of us have already formulated strong opinions about the nature and origins of gender differences. The evidence is that such opinions are not easily changed by scientific evidence and that people tend to dismiss findings and reinterpret conclusions when they do not support their preexisting views (Lord, Ross, & Lepper, 1979). Altering the information rather than changing one's model of the world is especially likely with "hot-button" topics like gender, race, and other group differences in intelligence.

The What, Where, When, and Size of Gender Differences in Cognition

Overall Intelligence.   There are no overall sex differences in general or global intelligence (Fausto-Sterling, 1992; Maccoby & Jacklin, 1974). As important as this statement appears to be, it is less than meets the eye, because the makers of IQ tests have discarded items on which males and females reliably differ. As Hyde (1996a) notes, saying that there are no gender differences in intelligence essentially means that the test constructors succeeded in their quest to eliminate gender differences. Nonetheless, it is clear that it is in patterns of specific abilities, rather than overall intelligence, that gender emerges as an interesting variable.

Gender Comparisons on Verbal, Mathematical, and Visual–Spatial Abilities.   In Maccoby and Jacklin's (1974) famous study of gender comparisons, they considered numerous possible dimensions on which males and females were thought to differ and concluded that the genders differed reliably on only four.

Three of those four dimensions were the cognitive areas of verbal, mathematical, and visual–spatial abilities (the fourth was in the area of aggression). It is now part of general lore that females excel in verbal ability and males in mathematical and visual–spatial abilities, but the real picture is considerably more complicated than that. In fact, the old taxonomy that divided abilities into the tripartite system of verbal, mathematical, and visual–spatial abilities has dissolved in the light of research that shows that different cognitive processes underlie abilities within each of these domains, and some of the same cognitive processes underlie abilities across these different domains (Halpern, 1997). In other words, verbal, mathematical, and visual–spatial abilities are each made up of very different kinds of tasks, and lumping the areas together is misleading. Research suggests that males reliably excel at some verbal tasks, just as females reliably excel at some mathematical and visual–spatial tasks.

As we see in Table 6.1, tests and tasks on which females obtain higher average scores than males are highly diverse and cross all three domains of abilities, including mathematical calculations, perceptual speed, memory for spatial location, reading comprehension and writing, and speech articulation. Similarly, tests and tasks on which males excel cover all domains, including tasks that require transformations in visual working memory, such as mental rotation, in which a figure is manipulated in space and requires correct identification from another angle, mechanical reasoning, verbal analogies, and motor tasks that involve aiming.

We can see that it is not accurate to make sweeping statements about broad areas of male and female abilities, and, indeed, that practice merely reinforces pernicious stereotypes about the sexes. "Math may be tough," as Barbie famously "said" in her first utterance, but it is in fact not harder for the average female than for the average male. We summarize the latest information on verbal, visual–spatial, and mathematical abilities in the section that follows.

Verbal Abilities.   In most areas of verbal ability, the gender differences are small and may be disappearing over time. Probably the largest remaining gender

TABLE 6.1 Cognitive Tests and Tasks That Usually Show Sex Differences

TYPE OF TEST/TASK	EXAMPLE
Tasks and Tests on Which Women Obtain Higher Average Scores	
Tasks that require rapid access to and use of phonological, semantic, and other information in long-term memory	Verbal fluency—phonological retrieval (Hines, 1990) Synonym generation—meaning retrieval (Halpern & Wright, 1996) Associative memory (Birenbaum, Kelly, & Levi-Keren, 1994) Memory battery—multiple tests (Stumpf & Jackson, 1994) Spelling and anagrams (Stanley, Benbow, Brody, Dauber, & Lupkowski, 1992) Mathematical calculations (Hyde, Fennema, & Lamon, 1990) Memory for spatial location (Eals & Silverman, 1994) Memory for odors (Lehrner, 1993)
Knowledge areas	Literature (Stanley, 1993) Foreign languages (Stanley, 1993)
Production and comprehension of complex prose	Reading comprehension (Hedges & Nowell, 1995; Mullis et al., 1993) Writing (U.S. Department of Education, 1997)
Fine motor tasks	Mirror tracing—novel, complex figures (O'Boyle & Hoff, 1987) Pegboard tasks (Hall & Kimura, 1995) Matching and coding tasks (Gouchie & Kimura, 1991)
Perceptual speed	Multiple speeded tasks (Born, Bleichrodt, & van der Flier, 1987) "Finding As"—an embedded-letters test (Kimura & Hampson, 1994)
Decoding nonverbal communication	(Hall, 1985)
Perceptual thresholds (large, varied literature with multiple modalities)	Touch—lower thresholds (Ippolitov, 1973; Wolff, 1969) Taste—lower thresholds (Nisbett & Gurwitz, 1970) Hearing—males have greater hearing loss with age (Schaie, 1987) Odor—lower thresholds (Koelega & Koster, 1974)
Higher grades in school (all or most subjects)	(Stricker, Rock, & Burton, 1993)
Speech articulation	Tongue twisters (Kimura & Hampson, 1994)

differences are in the areas of verbal fluency and writing ability, both of which strongly favor females and show up throughout the life-span. There are also small to moderate advantages for females in reading comprehension, with ds ranging from 0.18 to 0.30 (Hedges & Nowell, 1995). There is a slight male advantage in verbal analogies that emerges after adolescence (Halpern, 1997). But, overall, the sexes are far more similar in level of verbal skills than they are different, with similar mean scores and similar variances on most verbal tasks, with the important exceptions of writing and fluency.

Mathematical Abilities. The results of meta-analyses of mathematical skills generally suggest a very small overall advantage for males in average mathematical ability with ds ranging from about 0.05 to 0.19 (Hedges & Nowell, 1995; Hyde, Fennema, & Lamon, 1990). But the size of gender difference varies with the level of difficulty of the particular types of mathematical tests, ranging from the least difficult computational tasks, through understanding of mathematical concepts, to the most difficult: problem solving. Girls show an early advantage over boys in mathematical computation in grade school and middle school, but

TABLE 6.1   **Continued**

TYPE OF TEST/TASK	EXAMPLE

Tasks and Tests on Which Men Obtain Higher Average Scores

Tasks that require transformations in visual working memory	Mental rotation (Halpern & Wright, 1996; Voyer, Voyer, & Bryden, 1995) Piaget Water Level Test (Robert & Ohlmann, 1994; Vasta, Knott, & Gaze, 1996)
Tasks that involve moving objects	Dynamic spatiotemporal tasks (Law, Pelligrino, & Hunt, 1993)
Motor tasks that involve aiming	Accuracy in throwing balls or darts (Hall & Kimura, 1995)
Knowledge areas	General knowledge (Feingold, 1993; Wechsler Adult Intelligence Scale [Wechsler, 1991]) Geography knowledge (Beller & Gafni, 1996) Math and science knowledge (Stanley, 1993; U.S. Department of Education, 1996)
Tests of fluid reasoning (especially in math and science domains)	Proportional reasoning tasks (Meehan, 1984) Scholastic Assessment Test—Mathematics Graduate Record Examination—Quantitative (Willingham & Cole, 1997) Mechanical reasoning (Stanley et al., 1992) Verbal analogies (Lim, 1994) Scientific reasoning (Hedges & Nowell, 1995)

Source: From "Sex Differences in Intelligence: Implications for Education," by D. F. Halpern, 1997, *American Psychologist, 52*(10), p. 1102. Copyright © 1997 by the American Psychological Association. Adapted with permission.

Males are also overrepresented at the low-ability end of many distributions, including the following examples: mental retardation (some types; Vandenberg, 1987), a majority of attention-deficit disorders (American Psychiatric Association, 1994), delayed speech (Hier, Atkins, & Perlo, 1980), dyslexia (even allowing for possible referral bias; DeFries & Gillis, 1993), stuttering (Yairi & Ambrose, 1992), and learning disabilities and emotional disturbances (Henning-Stout & Close-Conoley, 1992). In addition, males are generally more variable (Hedges & Nowell, 1995). References provided are examples of relevant research. The literature is too large to attempt a complete reference list in this article.

this advantage evaporates by high school. The sexes are virtually indistinguishable on understanding of mathematical concepts throughout school. But in the area of problem solving, the sexes are similar throughout elementary and middle school, and a moderate difference favoring males emerges in high school ($d = 0.29$) and persists in college ($d = 0.32$). Some researchers report that the gender difference in mathematics has declined over time (Feingold, 1988; Hyde et al., 1990), whereas other researchers claim that the gender difference in mathematical ability has remained relatively constant over time (Halpern, 1997;

Hedges & Nowell, 1995). We will return shortly to the issue of what changes over time in gender differences might mean.

One critical issue in gender comparisons of mathematical ability has to do with the relative numbers of males and females in the very highest ability levels. It is well established that average gender differences in mathematical ability are modest, but it appears that many more males than females score in the mathematically gifted categories, with ratios ranging from 3:1 to 8:1 in favor of males. These findings are of concern because achievement in math and science generally requires very high scores on these kinds of standardized tests. There is evidence, for example, from occupational surveys in Project Talent that people who have careers in science and engineering are overwhelmingly more likely to have scored in the ninetieth percentile on mathematics tests in high school (Wise, Steele, & MacDonald, 1979).

Another important issue that emerges repeatedly in the literature is the relationship between mathematics performance on standardized tests and the amount of mathematics studied in school. The single best predictor of standardized test performance in mathematics is the number of mathematics courses previously taken. When course taking is controlled, that is, when the number of math courses is equal for males and females, the gender difference nearly disappears (Crawford & Chaffin, 1997). Recently, the sexes have become more equal in their enrollments in mathematics courses, with girls taking courses in algebra and geometry nearly as often as boys, although they still tend to avoid calculus and other advanced math courses (Sadker & Sadker, 1994). As Crawford and Chaffin (1997) note, however, we must keep in mind that, even when boys and girls take the same courses, they experience different worlds in the classroom, with boys, particularly white boys, receiving more encouragement from teachers than other groups. Moreover, boys are more likely than girls to participate in activities like chess, mathematics, and computer clubs and to attend science and computer camps in the summer. These activities supplement and enrich boys' experience with classroom mathematics in ways that encourage achievement, whereas the lack of these activities undermines girls' performance, self-confidence, and future possibilities.

Visual–Spatial Abilities. Of all the areas of cognitive gender comparisons, it is in the area of **visual–spatial ability** that some of the largest and most persistent gender differences emerge. Meta-analytic studies of gender differences in these areas have revealed three broad classes of visual–spatial tasks (Linn & Petersen, 1985). One is *spatial visualization,* which involves finding a figure that has been embedded (hidden) in distracting stimuli. On this task, there

is a very slight, near-zero gender difference favoring males ($d = +13$). In *spatial perception,* which requires one to locate a true vertical or horizontal line in the midst of distracting information, males enjoy a moderate advantage ($d = +0.44$). It is on *mental rotation* tasks, which ask the test taker to mentally turn a figure in space so that it can be correctly identified from a different angle, that males enjoy a relatively large advantage ($d = +0.73$). Examples of some of these items are presented in Figure 6.2.

As we can see, with visual–spatial abilities as with other domains, the size of gender differences

SPATIAL VISUALIZATION
Is figure (a) part of figure (b)?

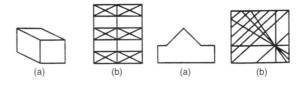

SPATIAL PERCEPTION
Which of the following four tilted glasses has a horizontal water line?

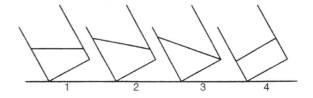

MENTAL ROTATION
Which two of the four choices below show the standard in a different orientation?

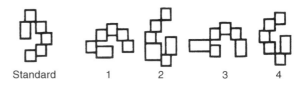

FIGURE 6.2 Test of Visual–Spatial Abilities
Source: Adapted from Yoder, 1999 and Rollins, 1996.

depends critically on the particular tests and tasks in question. There are other visual–spatial tasks on which females excel, for example, memory for spatial location (Silverman & Eals, 1992). It is also true that for most visual–spatial tasks only a small percentage of the variation in scores can be accounted for by sex; the other 95 percent of the variation is due to individual differences having nothing to do with being male or female. Nonetheless, as with mathematical abilities, the highest scorers on visual–spatial tasks are disproportionately male.

As Hyde (1981) has noted, many, if not most, occupations do not require especially high levels of visual–spatial ability, but in some occupations, for example, engineering and architecture, these types of skills are very important. Still, gender differences in visual–spatial test scores do not account for the huge disparities in the numbers of males and females who are engineers or architects. If the only factor standing in the way of an engineering career for women was visual–spatial ability, we would still expect to find about one-third of engineering positions filled by women. But only 1 percent of all U.S. engineers are women (Fausto-Sterling, 1992). Clearly, factors other than visual–spatial ability are depressing the numbers of women in areas like engineering, architecture, and mathematics.

Other Cognitive Abilities.   Gender comparisons have been made on other cognitive abilities that do not fall neatly into the categories of verbal, mathematical, and visual–spatial abilities. As Table 6.1 suggests, females excel at fine motor tasks and tests of perceptual speed, perceptual thresholds, and speech articulation. Males excel at tasks that involve moving objects, motor tasks that involve aiming, tests of mechanical reasoning, and tests of *fluid reasoning* (Halpern, 1997).

Conclusions.   In all domains of cognitive ability, men and women are more similar than they are different, and this is especially true of the vast majority (95 percent) of people who are in the middle of the distribution of scores. The largest gender differences appear to be in the areas of verbal fluency and writing, favoring females, and visual–spatial abilities, favoring males. The average effect size in these areas, about

one standard deviation, is of a magnitude that can be said to have social significance. That is, group differences of this size may have real-world consequences in the form of noticeably different proportions of males and females exhibiting a skill or scoring above a cutoff score for scholastic and occupational opportunities. In most other areas, cognitive gender differences are so small as to be virtually meaningless.

In part because of feminist scholarship and critique of existing research on gender differences in cognition, research on gender comparisons is today more sophisticated and methodologically sound than ever before. But sexism remains a serious problem in this research. Why is it, for instance, that the literature on the female advantage in verbal fluency is so much smaller than the literature on the male advantage in visual–spatial ability? We need to question why scholars seem always to be trying to explain male excellence in some visual–spatial abilities instead of female excellence in some verbal abilities. Are some abilities valued more in society precisely because they are "male" and others devalued precisely because they are "female"? It is by now well known that spatial abilities, like most other abilities, involve skills that can be taught (Vasta, Knott, & Gaze, 1996). If visual–spatial ability is as important as it appears to be and if girls are at a serious disadvantage relative to boys, why are there so few curricular programs to develop this skill in girls? Certainly, there are reading and math remediation programs for students struggling in these areas.

We need also to interrogate the frequently encountered and still robust assertions that males are "generally more variable" than females. As noted earlier, saying that males are more variable suggests that they are more special, more promising, and less ordinary than females. In fact, the variability hypothesis has an undistinguished history rooted in blatant sexism and questionable science. Even today it is inconsistently studied, found, reported, and interpreted, raising questions as to why variability is studied more often with some traits than with others. It remains unclear what being "more variable" means—and many investigators note it without attempting to explain it—but the connotation appears to be that level of variability is biologically based, even in the absence of any evidence of biological causation.

Finally, we should question the routine application of evolutionary theory to explain cognitive gender differences. According to these theories, the division of labor based on sex required early men to roam large areas and kill animals, which in turn required cognitive and motor skills like mental rotation and aiming missiles. Early women, on the other hand, were mainly preoccupied with pregnancy, nursing, child care, and gathering fruits and vegetables, which presumably did not call for nuanced spatial skills. We need to keep in mind that evolutionary theory explanations, while seemingly compelling, are untestable, explain everything after the fact, and ignore large bodies of data that do not conform to that explanatory framework. Moreover, such explanations fail to note that women have always engaged in spatial tasks and have played significant roles in hunting (Smuts, 1995).

GENDER ISSUES IN ACADEMIC ACHIEVEMENT AND THE EXPERIENCE OF SCHOOL

Education around the World

Education is probably the single most important factor in improving the lives of women and men. Although boys and girls obviously both benefit from an education, it appears that educating girls actually produces a greater return; in many parts of the world, it is the female's level of education that is the critical factor in lifting the family out of poverty (Neft & Levine, 1997). Throughout the world, it is generally the case that the more education a woman has, the brighter the future for her and her children. Educated women are more likely to use birth control, have smaller families with children spaced farther apart, and experience fewer complications of pregnancy. Educated women are not only better able to obtain a paying job, but they also are more likely to take good physical care of their children, educate them, and share their knowledge with them and community members. Yet despite the well-documented benefits of educating females, parents in many parts of the world, and some parents in

the United States, prefer to invest in educating their sons rather than their daughters, keeping their daughters home to help with the household chores and care for younger siblings. About two-thirds of all students who leave school before completing their first four years are girls, with the gender difference much larger in developing countries. Religious laws and customs also affect girls' access to education: in some Muslim societies, for example, girls are kept out of school because their parents do not want them taught by male teachers or sitting in classrooms with boys (Neft & Levine, 1997).

Whereas girls are severely disadvantaged educationally in the developing world, particularly in sub-Saharan Africa and parts of Asia, girls now stay in school longer than boys in most of the developed world. Over the past few decades, some countries have witnessed dramatic increases in the number of girls remaining in school through high school. In the United States, for example, 75 percent of girls now finish high school, compared to just 53 percent as recently as 1970. Similarly, in many of the developed countries women now outnumber their male classmates in colleges and universities. More women than men receive baccalaureate degrees in the United States (U.S. Bureau of the Census, 1993). Only in Switzerland and Japan, in which women account for 36 and 40 percent of the student body, respectively, do more men than women go to college (Neft & Levine, 1997). Women overtaking men in overall educational achievement in the United States and much of the West is a striking cultural development with a host of possible implications, but it is curious that this trend has gone largely unremarked in the media. Chapter 5 contains further information about the role of education in development.

Gender in the Classroom

Over the past two decades, much research attention has been paid to gender in the classroom. We will briefly review the research on how boys and girls perform in school, how teachers respond to boys and girls, and the potential effects of sexism in schools, from grade school to college.

BOX 6.1

Practical Implications of Cognitive Sex Differences

Psychologist Diane Halpern (1997) has extensively reviewed the vast literatures on cognitive sex differences and offers the following guidelines in drawing conclusions from this complex research:

1. Just because there are average differences in some cognitive abilities between males and females does not mean that one group is smarter or better than the other. Sex differences depend on numerous features of the study, including the particular test or task, the instructions, and the sample of males and females. They are not necessarily permanent. Do not misuse the data to advance a social or political agenda.

2. Research findings are based on group averages, and no one is average. The results cannot be generalized to any one individual. Group membership must not be permitted to make inferences about individuals or to limit talent development.

3. Beliefs about group differences, even without conscious awareness, exert powerful effects on thoughts and behaviors. Research suggests that people hold stereotypes about males' and females' abilities and that these stereotypes have negative effects on males' and females' performance. Research shows that instructions and other contextual factors affect performance and can exacerbate gender differences.

4. Be mindful that the hormonelike chemicals that are polluting our environment, particularly pesticides that mimic the action of sex hormones, may alter the intelligence of humans exposed to them, a hypothesis that remains untested.

5. Biologically based research on human cognition needs support. Research on the effects of estrogen and testosterone replacement therapy offer great hope to an aging society.

6. There are many implications of the fact that boys mature later than girls, and teachers should consider this when making assignments to low-ability groups in the primary grades, especially in reading.

7. We have remedial instruction in reading and mathematics, but spatial reasoning, in which boys far outperform girls, is virtually never taught in school, despite research suggesting that it is a skill that can be improved with training. All children need opportunities to develop these skills.

8. Most standardized tests used for admission to college, graduate, and professional schools and for scholarships underpredict or underestimate female performance and overpredict or overestimate male performance. Multiple measures of abilities must be used in decision making, including course grades and tests of writing.

9. There are no cognitive reasons to support sex-segregated schools, but there may be social reasons to support sex-segregated education. It is by now well documented that boys and girls have different experiences in schools. We need further research on the effects of sex-segregated learning environments.

10. Interpret all research results in the area of cognitive sex differences with a healthy skepticism and make sure that all conclusions are data based. People frequently have social and political preferences for different explanations. Be especially wary of simple-minded conclusions like "It's all in the hormones" or "It's all in the mother's attitude." No one study will settle controversial issues raised by this research, and no one explanation for differences is likely at this point to account for the complex patterns of findings in this area.

Source: From "Sex Difference in Intelligence: Implications for Education," by D. F. Halpern, 1997, *American Psychologist, 52*(10), pp. 1097–1099. Copyright © 1997 by the American Psychological Association. Adapted with permission.

Grades. Research is consistent in showing that girls get better grades than boys in all or virtually all subjects, including mathematics, throughout school (Stricken, Rock, & Burton, 1993). Many possible reasons have been put forth to explain why males do better on standardized tests and females do better in course grades or, alternatively, why standardized test scores underpredict later course grades for females but not for males. Until very recently, the kinds of tests on which females excel—written or essay tests—were rarely used by major crafters of tests, such as Educational Testing Service (ETS), the organization that brings us the SAT and GRE tests. ETS has recently incorporated a writing component into their exams. It has also been suggested that grades reflect other sorts of behaviors besides cognitive ability, for example, studiousness and neatness, that are unrelated to cognition (Bridgeman & Moran, 1996). Finally, it is possible that there is a grading bias against boys. In any case, the fact that girls outperform boys in virtually all subjects suggests that they are learning in school at least as well as boys and that factors other than ability to learn are keeping them from entering some fields.

Teacher Expectations and Behavior.   Research consistently shows that, from preschool through college and graduate and professional school, teachers give boys and men more attention than girls and women. In elementary school, teachers check boys' work more often, call on them more often, and criticize and punish them more often than they do girls (Brophy, 1985). This is in part because boys "demand more attention" from teachers than girls in the form of presenting more behavior problems, challenging the teacher's authority or information, and asserting themselves by asking questions without raising their hands. But as we read in Chapter 5, there is evidence of sexism in the classroom, with teachers treating boys and girls differently, for example, by directing more questions to boys than girls and asking boys higher-level questions than girls (Barba & Cardinale, 1991). Studies of teachers' attributions for boys and girls have found that teachers were more likely to attribute boys' academic successes to ability and girls' successes to hard work (Hunter College Women's Studies Collective, 1995), and that teachers have higher expectations of boys than girls (Sadker & Sadker, 1994). There are some exceptions to this trend, however: Teachers generally have higher expectations for the performance of African American girls than boys (Ross & Jackson, 1991).

Sexism in the classroom is not limited to teachers' treatment of boys and girls, and it would be unfair to characterize most teachers as sexist or blame

teachers for reproducing arrangements that were created by the larger society. A report called "Women on Words and Images" published in 1974, analyzed 134 elementary school readers with 2,760 stories and found that stories in which boys were the center of attention outnumbered stories about girls by a ratio of 5 to 2. Stories about male adults outnumbered stories about female adults by 3 to 1. Male and female characters in animal stories appeared in a ratio of 2 to 1, and in folk and fantasy tales, 4 to 1. There were 147 role possibilities for male characters compared with 25 for girls (Hunter College Women's Studies Collective, 1995). More recent examinations of gender-role stereotyping show a trend for girls to be portrayed as more active than they had been previously, but, overall, girls are still portrayed as less active and competitive than boys and boys as less nurturing and dependent than girls (Kortenhaus & Demarest, 1993).

Similarly, school textbooks, especially in math and science, are full of sexist references. Men are more likely to be portrayed in active roles and exciting occupations, with women portrayed as less active and successful (Federbush, 1974). Only recently have school textbooks started using nonsexist language and more sex-fair portrayals (Hunter College Women's Studies Collective, 1995).

The situation does not improve markedly for girls as they climb the academic ladder. As noted in Chapter 5, a well-known study entitled "How Schools Shortchange Girls" supported by the American Association of University Women (AAUW, 1992) cited the unequal treatment that girls receive in high school in a wide range of areas, including curricula, materials used in classrooms, testing, and teacher attention. Despite these disadvantages, high school girls get better grades than boys in all subjects, including math and science, and they like school better and drop out less than boys. During high school, girls outnumber boys in all extracurricular activities except sports and hobby clubs. Almost twice as many girls as boys participate in student government, band and orchestra, and drama and service clubs. More girls than boys work on the yearbook and school newspapers and are members of honors and service societies. Many more boys than girls participate in sports, but the gap is narrowing quickly.

Despite the gains made by girls in recent years, it remains the case that both overt and subtle factors affect adolescents in high school in ways that reinforce stereotypical choices in course selection and career preparation, with high school counselors in particular steering adolescents in gender-biased directions. At the highest levels of academic achievement, boys are encouraged to seek the most prestigious careers, and in vocational training, boys more than girls are guided toward higher-paying skilled craft jobs (Hoffman, 1972; Hunter College Women's Studies Collective, 1995).

On the college level, one report described the classroom climate as "chilly" for women (Hall & Sandler, 1982). Several patterns of behavior that harm women in the college classroom have been identified, including disparaging comments about women generally, seductive behavior toward women, calling more on male than female students, offering men more and better choice research opportunities, and ignoring the women in the class (Hall & Sandler, 1982). Women are conspicuously absent in college textbooks (Ferree & Hall, 1990). Even when women's contributions are cited, their gender often goes unremarked and they are taken for men, or they are presented as handmaidens to their male colleagues, sometimes their husbands. Even two-time Nobel prize-winning scientist Marie Curie has been characterized in print as her husband's "helpmate" (Basow, 1992, p. 150).

As we noted earlier, women now receive more undergraduate degrees than men, but they still do not receive an equal number of professional and doctoral degrees, and those who receive these advanced degrees do so in an atmosphere that is less supportive and hospitable than it is for men.

Achievement Motivation

Despite the facts that girls and women do better than boys and men in school, and are graduating from high school and college in greater proportions than men, women still enjoy considerably less occupational success than men. Psychologists, among others, have taken pains to explain why there is a gap between women's cognitive ability and their achievement. There are many possible explanations. For one thing, there has been and continues to be discrimination against women throughout all levels of schooling and in all the professions. At the end of the nineteenth century, for instance, almost all women physicians were affiliated with women's institutions, because men's medical schools would not admit them. Quotas restricting entry of women (and Jews and men of color) into medicine persisted well into this century. Similarly, a struggle was necessary in nearly all the states where women sought to become lawyers (Hunter College Women's Studies Collective, 1995).

Another possible explanation for women's lower levels of accomplishment may reside in their **achievement motivation.** As defined by the originator of this construct, David McClelland, achievement motivation is the desire to accomplish something of importance due to one's own efforts, the desire to excel at what one does (McClelland, Atkinson, Clark, & Lowell, 1953). McClelland and his colleagues tested achievement motivation using a projective technique that asked people to write a story about an ambiguous set of pictures that was designed to elicit achievement themes. They found that, under competitive conditions, men but not women showed an increase in achievement motivation. They concluded that women did not have the motivation to achieve and continued their program of research using only men.

Matina Horner revived interest in studying achievement motivation in women with a different kind of projective test (Horner, 1969). She asked her respondents to compose a story following this lead sentence, which differed only in the gender of the target person: "After first term finals, Anne (John) found herself (himself) at the top of her (his) medical school class." Female respondents wrote about Anne; males about John. Horner found that more than 90 percent of the men wrote happy stories about John that indicated satisfaction, dedication, and continued success for the character. But 65 percent of the female respondents wrote strange and conflicted stories about Anne that were full of negative imagery suggesting the belief that high academic success in women was associated with physical unattractiveness, social rejection, concerns about adequacy as a woman, and denial that Anne achieved her success. Horner dubbed her findings women's "fear of success," and the concept caught fire in psychology.

Subsequent research on **fear of success** has not consistently supported the notion that there are large gender differences in the motive to avoid success. Michele Paludi (1984) reviewed 64 studies on the fear of success and found about the same incidence of this fear in men as in women. Cherry and Deaux (1978) further refined our understanding of this construct by replicating the original Horner study (1969) with a new variable: how gender appropriate the occupation is for the target individual. They asked students to complete sentences about Anne and John, who were at the top of their classes in either medical or nursing school. They found high fear of success stories written about Anne in the medical school story and John in the nursing school story, suggesting that men and women may fear the negative consequences of deviating from societal norms that specify what is permissible for each gender. Meanwhile, despite a conspicuous lack of empirical support, research on fear of success as a personality defect in women continues to the present (Piedmont, 1995).

Some people have suggested that the key to explaining the achievement gap between men and women lies with their different motives to succeed: men achieve because of their desire to excel; women because of a desire to affiliate or win others' approval (Hoffman, 1972). There is not much evidence to support the notion that men and women achieve for entirely different reasons—indeed, research suggests the opposite. But gender role socialization and the internalized norm standards by which men and women judge themselves suggest that there may be different expressions of achievement motives for men and women. Societal norms for being a successful woman have always involved being a nurturant, devoted wife and mother, a socially adept and physically attractive person. Being a successful man in our society does not require excellence in so many disparate domains. Attempting to fulfill all these roles pulls women in different directions and makes it more difficult to

compete successfully with men in graduate and professional schools and in their occupations. As we note further in Chapter 9, there is ample evidence that high-achieving women often put their careers on hold to support their husbands' careers and begin families. For example, when graduate students marry each other, the woman is likely to undertake all the household tasks and, once they become mothers, many women are unable to continue their studies, citing reasons for dropping out like the emotional strain involved, pressure from husbands, and a belief that their professors did not take them seriously enough (Hunter College Women's Studies Collective, 1995). Women's achievement may take different forms throughout the life-span, with some women becoming quite ambitious for their husbands and children while their families are young and pursuing their personal ambitions by returning to school or entering the work force as their family obligations ease. We will discuss issues relating to returning or *reentry* women shortly. See Box 6.2 on men's and women's career patterns in science for a glimpse into some of the factors affecting the paths of elite women and men in science.

In conclusion, women and men are not very different in their overall fear of success or motive to achieve, although we need further research on the conditions that activate these motives in men and women. In any case, it is unlikely that these factors account for the large differences in occupational achievement between men and women.

Attributions for Success and Failure and Expectations for Performance

"I got an A." "She gave me a D."

We bet that at some point in your college careers you have heard students talking about their grades this way: taking responsibility for a positive outcome and distancing themselves from a negative one. Social psychologists have found that we make judgments all the time about the likely causes of outcomes in our lives and that these judgments have implications for how we feel and behave in the future. These judgments about the causes of our own and other people's behaviors are called **attributions** (Heider,

BOX 6.2

Achievement Patterns of Men and Women in Science

The impetus for much of the work in cognitive sex differences was the observation that women were severely underrepresented in the ranks of great scientists. Women have clearly made progress in science over the course of this century, with more women than ever before listed as members of the prestigious National Academy of Sciences, the main scientific advisory group to the government. The number and percentage of women recipients of the Nobel Prize for science have slowly increased over the past 30 years. Since its inception in 1901, the Nobel Prize has been bestowed on more than 650 recipients in the areas of science, economics, literature, and peace, but as of 1996 only 28 (about 4 percent) of all recipients were women, and fewer than half of women's awards were in science (Neft & Levine, 1997). The position of women in science today is a blend of undeniable progress and unfulfilled promise (Sonnert & Holton, 1996). Despite clear gains over the past quarter-century, a big gender gap in scientific achievement persists.

A recent large-scale study called Project Access researched the degree of gender disparity in career outcomes in science and examined possible causes for the gender differences. Project Access focused exclusively on an elite group of male and female scientists who had received prestigious postdoctoral fellowships in the areas of the biological, physical, and social sciences, engineering, and mathematics. About 700 scientists of different ages and stages of professional development participated in this study of career patterns.

As you would expect, the study found great variation in responses within each gender. But some clear gender differences emerged. For example, in most scientific areas, women's academic rank fell below that of men's, even after controlling for academic productivity (usually measured in terms of number of scientific articles). In fact, women published less than men, although their work was cited by other scientists more often, one clear indicator of scientific impact (Sonnert & Holton, 1996).

Other gender differences pointed to some of the obstacles that women face in science. Almost three-quarters of the women reported experiencing sex discrimination in science, compared with 13 percent of the men who reported reverse discrimination based on their sex. This discrimination included sexual harassment by colleagues, but also exclusion from collaborating on research projects as equal or senior partners and marginalization at scientific conferences. Many more women than men stated that their mentors treated them as subordinates rather than peers.

Gender differences in socialization and resultant gender differences in style may contribute to some of the differences in outcomes that were observed. Male scientists in the study expressed much more confidence in their scientific ability than women did, and men emerged as more combative, competitive, and self-promoting than comparable women. The competitive and aggressive style of male scientists is frequently noted by others in science (Sonnert & Holton, 1996). Relatedly, women were more likely than men to shun hypercompetitive areas in science and were more likely than men to carve out small niche areas to probe. There was no evidence in this study to suggest that women "did science" fundamentally differently from men; if anything they were more meticulous and perfectionistic in using traditional research methods.

The authors explained the differences in the way that men and women approach science in terms of different socialization patterns of males and females and the structural features of the scientific establishment. Women are taught from girlhood not to promote themselves or their ideas too forcefully, to back down when challenged, and to be conciliators and compromisers in groups of people. But beyond these gender-role explanations, we cannot ignore that gender differences in achievement in science also arise from a collegial environment that is hostile to women—putting them under the magnifying glass and denying them opportunities (Sonnert & Holton, 1996). Finally, while Sonnert and Holton did not find a negative effect of being married or having children on achievement in science for women or men in this elite sample, they did find that female scientists were far more likely to choose opportunities to be with their spouse than male scientists, and thus women sacrificed high-powered scientific careers for their families far more than men did.

In her recent book, *Why So Slow? The Advancement of Women*, Virginia Valian (1998) reviews the results of hundreds of studies on the status of women

(continued)

BOX 6.2   Continued

in the professions, science, and the academy, and amplifies these findings: women start out on roughly equal footing, but over time their careers diverge, with men getting more promotions and raises. In science and academia, even when productivity in the form of publications is held constant, men advance more quickly than women. Although men publish more papers than women, women's work is cited more often by other scientists: a sign that their work is regarded as valuable. Valian found, with Sonnert and Holton, that women emphasize quality over quantity in research. She makes the point that gender bias in science and academia is mild and subtle, but over time it profoundly affects women's outcomes.

1958). Some social psychologists have suggested that males and females make different attributions about their successes and failures in achievement situations and that females' patterns of attributions hurt their performance.

Psychologists have identified three dimensions of attributions about causality in achievement situations (Weiner, 1986). The first is whether the cause is internal to the individual, something the individual is or does, or external, something that happens to the person. The second is whether the cause is stable, an enduring characteristic of the person or situation, or unstable, a condition or situation that can be changed. The third is whether the cause is controllable by the individual or uncontrollable. According to Weiner (1986), success and failure in achievement situations can generally be attributed to one of four causes: a person's ability, effort made, task difficulty, or luck. These causes all differ in how internal, stable, and controllable they are. Generally, ability and effort are considered internal factors, and luck and task difficulty are external factors. Task difficulty and ability are regarded as stable, whereas effort and luck are unstable. Effort is seen as controllable, but ability level, luck, and task difficulty are usually not. There are exceptions to this neat division: for example, sometimes people can control task difficulty by choosing or avoiding demanding courses, curricula, or institutions. And, with enough practice, we can often change our level of ability in many areas.

Early research in the 1970s comparing the kinds of attributions that men and women make for success and failure found an interesting and disturbing pattern of results: men tended to attribute their successes to their ability, whereas women tended to attribute their successes to luck. In an interesting observational study, Kay Deaux and her colleagues noticed that, at amusement parks, men more often played games of skill like tossing a ring around a bottle, whereas women tended to play games of luck, like bingo (Deaux, White, & Farris, 1975). They then designed a laboratory study to test under controlled conditions the notion that men more than women prefer tests of skill. They found that 75 percent of the men chose a game of skill over a game of luck, compared with 35 percent of the women. The problems with this gender difference are clear: attributing your success to your ability, an internal and stable characteristic, means that you may be more likely to pursue challenges in this area in the future, to say to yourself, for example, "I'm good at math; maybe I'll be a math major." But if you attribute your success to luck, an external and unstable factor, you may not wish to press that luck by taking any more math classes. The gendered pattern of attributions is replicated when people are judging others as well as themselves: Deaux and Emswiller (1974) found that when people are judging the performance of others they attribute men's successes to their abilities and women's to good luck.

In the 1980s, meta-analytic reviews of the studies on gender differences in attributions show essentially no gender differences in how people make attributions for successes and failures (Frieze, Whitley, Hanusa, & McHugh, 1982). Current research on gender comparisons has complicated the picture, however. Gender differences in attributions have appeared inconsistently, taking on a "now you see them, now you don't" look (see Mednick & Thomas, 1993, and Swim & Sanna, 1996, for extensive reviews). For example, it has been found that, when men and women score high in instrumentality, women make ability attributions at the same rate as men. More recently, Hill and Augoustinos (1997) failed to find the traditional pattern of female-derogating, male-favoring attributions for achievement in Australian college students. They explained their findings in terms of attitudinal, political, and social changes over the last 20 years and note the possibility that contemporary sexism is more subtle and expressed in more socially acceptable ways. Ongoing research is looking to the personal and situational factors that affect how men and women make attributions, for example, age and level of achievement of respondents and type of task.

Research on attributions for success and failure may show inconsistent gender patterns, but research on different expectations for success by gender paints a clearer portrait: in elementary school and especially in the earliest grades, girls are more likely than boys to see themselves as smart and express confidence about their abilities to succeed, although boys already begin predicting that they will do better on certain tests, such as mathematical tests, in the earliest grades. By eighth grade, however, girls start to lose their confidence and begin to perceive themselves as increasingly less intelligent and less likely to succeed. By high school and throughout college, girls have less confidence in their abilities to succeed than boys. In college, females asked to estimate their college grades predict lower grades than males do, even though their grades still tend to be higher than males' (Crandall, 1969). This tendency to underestimate their performance occurs especially on tasks and tests considered masculine, such as mathematics, visual–spatial ability, and unfamiliar tasks (Beyer, 1990). This trend is especially disturbing because research in psychology consistently shows that people who expect success are more likely to achieve it, and low expectations are a drag on performance (Crandall, 1978).

Teachers' and parents' expectations for girls' achievements in mathematics and science decline as girls progress through high school, and may account in part for girls dropping out of the most challenging curricula in those areas. In turn, girls' and women's lowered expectation for success may indeed explain why they achieve less than their male counterparts.

We need further research on the situational factors that affect expectations for success for men and women. We already know that instructional sets that stress competition lower women's expectations for success (House, 1974) and that evaluative feedback that offers an accurate assessment of their performance is particularly helpful to women (Roberts, 1991). Roberts points out that, because of socialization factors that encourage competition among boys and men and provide frequent evaluative feedback to them, boys and men are at an advantage relative to girls and women in receiving regular information about their abilities. As opportunities to compete and obtain feedback increase for girls, their expectation for success may also increase.

SPECIAL TOPICS IN ABILITY AND ACHIEVEMENT

Gender and Computers

At the same time that the gender gap is closing in on so many important areas in education, it is large and growing in a key area—technology, specifically computers. The late 1990s witnessed a puzzling drop of enrollment in higher-skill computer classes and in the numbers of bachelor's and master's degrees awarded in computer science for both men and women. But enrollment of women in computer classes and degrees in computing awarded to women are dropping much faster than is the case for men. Thus, women are becoming a smaller proportion of people in academic computer science and the computing industry. For example, in the early 1980s, 37 percent of graduates with computer science degrees were women, whereas in 1995 only 28 percent were women (Neft & Levine, 1997). There is mounting evidence that many women expressing early interest in computing careers drop out of the academic pipeline and pursue other careers. This information comes at a time when many scholars are noting that girls from grade school to high school are also losing interest in computing.

We live in an age of high technology in which facility with computers is helpful in many disciplines and occupations and essential in others. Many people are concerned that we have created a hypermasculine "computer culture" that is hostile to girls and women and discourages their entry into certain career paths. Why has the use of computers become so gendered, and how can society foster more and better computer use among girls?

Some scholars argue that the lack of a formal computer science curriculum in most middle and high schools and the dearth of required courses in computers at these levels spells chaos in computer classrooms, where the most aggressive students, typically boys, hog the machines. Leslie Klein, instructor of information systems at Pace University in New York City and computer teacher of middle-school children, described the typical computer classes this way: "The computers are always consumed by the boys who rush in, desperate to continue where they left off the day before in Oregon Trail, Karateka, or Carmen San-diego. An occasional girl wanders in, but would practically need interference from the heavens to gain access to these monopolized computers" (Klein, cited in Frankel, 1990, p. 36). She adds that boys are more likely to use pirated software, whereas girls follow the rules and subsequently have fewer and less interesting programs with which to work.

Others have pointed to sexist educational software as a cause for different computer use by boys and girls and men and women. In their book on sex bias in educational software, Huff and Cooper (1987) presented evidence to suggest that software designers virtually always used male as the "default" value of student and designed gamelike programs featuring missiles, violence, and other metaphors and fantasies that were very exciting for boys, but were anxiety-producing and unappealing to girls. Less sexist software that is as attractive and interesting to girls as current software is for boys may increase girls' and women's interest in computers. As late as 1999, however, companies that tried to market computer games for girls that depict girls in nonstereotypic ways struggled to succeed (Harmon, 1999). In 1998, six of the top ten computer games for girls had Barbie themes, and the other four featured Madeline, the French heroine of children's books. Nonetheless, there is evidence at the turn of the millenium that girls' attitudes about

technology and the software industry's attitudes about girls and technology are becoming more progressive (Harmon, 1999).

Relatedly, observers note that males and females use computers differently, with males more likely to see them as toys and females more likely to see them as tools for solving problems and doing tasks. Obviously, a competitive nation cannot afford to foster the notion that technology is a largely male domain. Developing and marketing more software aimed at helping females to accomplish their academic, career, social, and personal goals would be a step in the direction of increasing computer use among females.

Issues in Evaluating Single-Sex and Coeducational Institutions

Do boys and girls and men and women learn better in schools and classes that are separated by sex? This question has captivated scholars in recent years (AAUW, 1998). It seems like a simple one, but in fact it has many complicated answers. For one thing, we need to consider college men and women separately from students in grades K through 12. During the 1960s and 1970s, most women's colleges either closed or became coeducational, seemingly ending a long and distinguished tradition in the United States of single-sex education for women. Around the same time, most remaining single-sex colleges for men, with the important exception of military academies, threw open their doors to women, who indeed now predominate on most college campuses. But recently there has been renewed interest in single-sex education, particularly for women, and single-sex women's schools are experiencing a surge in applications (AAUW, 1998). How do women benefit from single-sex schools? Are there disadvantages to women of single-sex schools?

Early studies on the effects of single-sex colleges for women appeared to show that such schools produced a disproportionate number of high-achieving women (Tidball, 1973). Tidball investigated the college backgrounds of women whose achievements were listed in *Who's Who of American Women* and whose college experience occurred between 1910 and 1960. She found that women's colleges produced more high-achieving women than did coeducational institutions in each of the five decades and attributed this to the greater number of women faculty and administrators who serve as role models in women's schools. It is also the case, as Rice and Hemmings (1988) noted, that the kinds of women who applied to women's colleges before the 1970s were a self-selected and special group—brighter, better prepared, and more socially and economically advantaged than female students who went to coeducational schools. Today, with so many options for top female students, it is not necessarily true that the most competitive women attend women's colleges. Still, it remains the case that in women-only colleges women experience fewer distractions and gain self-confidence to further develop themselves, especially to exercise leadership (AAUW, 1998).

The American Association of University Women (AAUW) Educational Foundation recently commissioned a major study of the broad effects of single-sex classes and schools on students in grades K through 12. This study found many shortcomings in the existing research on single-sex classes and schools, but found evidence for the value of such schools in helping girls to establish comfortable places to explore the world and to consider issues of gender identity, especially around early adolescence. A more recent study compared the effects of sex-segregated and coeducational high schools on boys and girls. Evidence for the effects of such classes and schools on academic achievement is mixed, with some studies showing clear advantages for single-sex settings and some not (AAUW, 1998).

One particularly large and complex recent study investigated how socialization to gender operates in three types of independent high schools: boys' schools, girls' schools, and coeducational schools (Lee, Marks, & Byrd, 1994). Observational data were collected in 86 classrooms in 21 schools. These investigators found similar amounts of sexism in all three types of schools, although the forms of sexism varies, with gender domination (either boys dominating discussions or teachers recognizing boys more often than girls) overwhelmingly more common in coeducational schools and sex-role stereotyping more common in

single-sex schools. Explicitly sexual incidents, for instance, sexually objectifying the other sex, was found only in boys' schools. The severest forms of sexism overall were found in boys' schools. Within coeducational schools, chemistry classes were the site of the most frequent and blatant forms of sexism: male domination of discussions and teachers favoring boys and humiliating girls. The authors concluded that, although girls' schools were the most gender fair of all three types of schools, they also perpetuated a pernicious form of sexism: academic dependence and nonrigorous instruction in some areas, including chemistry. There is other evidence that single-sex settings have more positive outcomes for high school girls than boys.

The spotlight has been placed on single-sex schools at all levels in the past few years. We have witnessed dramatic, less-than-successful attempts to integrate all male preserves such as the Citadel and Virginia Military Academy. In inner cities, educators are struggling to solve problems of learning and discipline by attempting single-sex public education for boys and girls. Given the reality that most students attend schools with both males and females, we need to focus on how coeducation can be made more gender equitable for the ultimate good of both males and females. At the same time, evidence suggests that we need more and better information on how to preserve and improve a single-sex option for students who want and might benefit from such a choice. Clearly, we need further research on how to develop the aspirations and goals of adolescent girls in coeducational institutions. For example, we have seen how, within coeducational schools, the presence of adult women in positions of leadership and the formation of a committee to monitor gender equity may be advisable (Lee & Marks, 1990). Although sex segregation is prohibited by law (Title IX) in public schools, providing sex-segregated math, science, and computer classes may have merit under some circumstances.

Finally, we need to look beyond test scores as outcome measures in this research and instead look at measures of leadership, confidence, feelings of community, empowerment, and a sense of what is possible. We are just beginning to understand the complex effects of single-sex and coeducational schools on males and females at the primary, secondary, and college levels.

Diversity Issues in Education

There is no one male or female student: males and females come only in different ages, ethnicities, social classes, and other demographic categories. There has been a great deal of research in recent years on how ethnicity, class, and other factors vary with measured cognitive ability and academic achievement. A full discussion of these issues is beyond the scope of this chapter, but see Chapter 4 for additional perspectives on diversity issues. It is crucial to note here that failure to take these variables into account impedes our understanding of achievement and shortchanges women. For example, at this time Latinas in the United States are significantly less well educated than most U.S. women, with less than 53 percent of Latinas completing high school as of 1993 (U.S. Bureau of the Census, 1994). College educations and professional careers are at odds with traditional concepts of women's family roles in many Latin cultures. Among African Americans, on the other hand, achieving in school is highly compatible with the notion that women pass on their advantages to their children, and African American women experience less conflict in combining roles of family and career than white women. African American girls and women outperform African American boys and men in all levels of schooling. Asian Americans, especially those from China and Japan, are exceptionally high achieving in the United States. Until recently, Asian American women lagged somewhat behind Asian American men in their academic achievement, but the evidence is that they are catching up fast. Still, it is the case that many Asian cultures remain traditional, with prescribed roles for women that require them to subjugate their career goals to family roles.

The past two decades have witnessed large numbers of women, called reentry or returning women, who finish their education after many years away from school, usually to raise families. Increasingly, these women are self-supporting (Hunter College Women's Studies Collective, 1995). Able to focus on their personal goals, often for the first time in their lives, many reentry women are especially strong students. The point is that cultural factors interact with gender and other factors to produce striking effects among different kinds of women.

There is recent disturbing evidence that some women, particularly disadvantaged women, believe that they must hide who they are in order to succeed. A fascinating qualitative study explored the educational experiences of women who were academic high achievers and were disadvantaged as children (LePage-Lees, 1997). In this study, disadvantage was described as having all three of the following characteristics: coming from a poor family, being a first-generation college student, and experiencing at least one type of familial dysfunction or traumatic childhood stress. The article described how participants managed their disadvantage in a system that rewards silence about such matters. It explored whether there needs to be a separation between the personal and the professional for people who are disadvantaged and how a connection between education and life experiences can be forged. Investigations like this point out the need to consider class and other background factors in understanding achievement.

Violence: A Developing Issue in Our Schools

The surge of violence in our schools has created a climate in which children and adolescents have been physically threatened and harmed as well as emotionally traumatized. The victims and witnesses of violent acts often suffer a range of psychological consequences after such incidents, including post-traumatic stress disorder (PTSD) (described more fully in Chapter 11), which includes a variety of symptoms such as anxiety, loss of appetite, sleep disturbance, and nightmares. Violence and its emotional consequences are not only severe problems in and of themselves, but they also profoundly affect students' ability to achieve in school.

The disturbing increase in the number of violent incidents in middle schools and high schools in the late 1990s in the United States and other countries challenges us to consider a broad range of noncognitive factors affecting the learning and development of students.

SUMMARY

There are no easy answers to questions such as, who's smarter, men or women? In fact, women and men are more alike than they are different, and any differences that exist between men and women are subtle variations in patterns of abilities. Indeed, what we call sex differences are better regarded as gender differences because we do not know what biological, psychological, social, or cultural factors are at the root of these variations. What we do know is that many of these differences are disappearing with time and are affected by practice.

Many noncognitive factors have been studied in an attempt to understand girls' and women's achievement and, in particular, the achievement gap between men and women. Some of these include achievement motivation, fear of success, attributions for success and failure, and expectations for success. Research

evidence for gender differences in these areas is generally inconsistent with the exception of expectations: girls and women expect to do less well than boys and men, and girls and women tend to underestimate their performance on many different kinds of tasks. Given the importance of expectations for performing well, we need to find ways to raise the confidence level of girls and women, and research is pointing to the importance of factors like specific, accurate feedback about performance.

There are fascinating issues that currently concern scholars who are interested in gender and achievement. These include computers in the classroom, sex-segregated versus coeducational schooling, and diversity issues. We need to consider how gender equity can be achieved in testing and education, and beyond.

KEY TERMS

Achievement motivation (p. 187)
Attributions (p. 188)
Effect size (p. 178)
Fear of success (p. 188)

Lateralization (p. 174)
Meta-analysis (p. 178)
Nonoverlapping distributions (p. 177)

Statistically significant differences (p. 178)
Visual–spatial ability (p. 182)

DISCUSSION QUESTIONS

1. Let us imagine that the cognitive differences that are currently understood to exist between men and women were found to be innate. What would be the practical implications of such a finding? What would change about the educational and career opportunities and outcomes for men and women?

2. Ask your friends about their understanding of cognitive sex differences? In what areas do they see differences? How large do they think they are? How do they explain them?

3. What are some of the gender differences and similarities in the ways that boys and girls and men and women use computers? Consider word processing, programming, e-mail, Internet use, computer games, and the like. What are some of the implications of the ways that males and females use computers?

4. What are some of the advantages and disadvantages of single-sex schools? Do these differ for males and females? Why or why not?

5. Ask your female friends about their experiences with math and science in school. Were they encouraged or discouraged to pursue these areas? To what do they

attribute their successes and/or failures in math and science (talent, effort, luck, difficulty of the material)?

6. Females now outnumber males in higher education. Why do you think this is so, and what are the implications of this trend?

SUGGESTED READINGS

Fausto-Sterling, A. (1992). *Myths of gender: Biological theories about women and men* (2nd ed.). New York: Basic Books.

Fox, M. F. (1989). Women and higher education: Gender differences in the status of students and scholars. In J. Freeman (Ed.), *Women: A feminist perspective* (4th ed., pp. 217–235). Mountain View, CA: Mayfield.

Hare-Mustin, R. T., & Maracek, J. (Eds.). (1990). *Making a difference.* New Haven, CT: Yale University Press.

Valian, V. (1988). *Why so slow? The advancement of women.* Cambridge, MA: MIT Press.

CHAPTER 7

THE WORLD OF WORK

Women constitute half the world's population, perform nearly two-thirds of its work hours, receive one-tenth of the world's income and own less than one-hundredth of the world's property.
—United Nations report

When we abolish the slavery of half of humanity, together with the whole system of hypocrisy that it implies, then the "division" of humanity will reveal its genuine significance and the human couple will find its true form.
—Simone de Beauvoir

Somewhere out in this audience may even be someone who will one day follow in my footsteps, and preside over the White House as the President's spouse. I wish him well.
—Barbara Pierce Bush, remarks at Wellesley College commencement

This chapter discusses the changing role of women in the workplace. We will explore and critically examine the myths that prevail regarding women's alleged limitations and discuss how these myths have shaped societal attitudes regarding women. Gender-based segregation within the workplace will be examined, with specific examples from both the white- and blue-collar worlds, describing experiences of women in both traditional and nontraditional occupations. Women experience a variety of discriminatory practices in the workplace based on gender, race, class, and sexual preference. Yet women do more than simply survive in the workplace. They and their families thrive on the economic advantages that work provides to women and their families. This chapter discusses women's multiple roles, suggesting ways in which women (and men) can attempt to deal effectively with the often conflicting demands of their personal and professional lives. Examples of gender discrimination, both in hiring practices and on the job, are explored, along with other obstacles that impede the progress of women in the work force. Finally, this chapter deals with cross-cultural issues, the exploitation of women, and the very human need for women to have access to meaningful work outside the home as a part of their lives.

THE CHANGING ROLE OF WOMEN IN THE WORLD OF WORK

According to one estimate, approximately 60 percent of all women presently work outside the home and comprise 45.3 percent of the U.S. labor force (Hunter College Women's Studies Collective, 1995). These figures reflect a steady increase in working women over the past several decades. However, these proportions represent a major increase in the labor force participation rate of White women and a lesser increase in the rate among African American women (Higginbotham, 1997). African American women's work experience is uniquely rooted in slavery (Jones, 1985), and their participation in paid employment is long established (Davis, 1981). Table 7.1 shows women's occupational and labor participation rate by ethnic category.

Not only are women working in more significant numbers than ever before, but they are also taking on far more significant roles within the work force, training for and assuming positions of leadership in the worlds of business, medicine, and other realms that were once considered exclusively male (Iglitzen & Ross, 1986; United Nations, 1991). Just as women were once considered bad business risks and/or not worth training for executive positions, because it was assumed that the responsibilities of home and family would soon usurp their loyalty to their professions, today's antidiscrimination legislation has declared such thinking both archaic and illegal. Moreover, the trend toward allowing women (and men) more generous maternity (paternity) leave and providing on-site day care has opened doors for working mothers, whose numbers have increased more than tenfold since 1940 (Russo & Denmark, 1984), and has also helped to secure the future for women who wish to pursue meaningful, productive, lifelong careers. Before proceeding to the next section, take a moment to answer the questions in Box 7.1.

TABLE 7.1 Women's Occupational and Labor Participation Rate by Ethnic Category

CHARACTERISTIC	TOTAL UNITED STATES	WHITE AMERICAN	AFRICAN AMERICAN[a]	ASIAN AMERICAN[a]	HISPANIC	MEXICAN AMERICAN	PUERTO RICAN	CUBAN AMERICAN
Total Females 16+	100,654	77,270	11,684	2,550	7,842	4,726	883	480
In civilian labor force[b]	57,558	44,682	6,803	1,502	4,072	2,348	408	232
Percent in civilian labor force	57.2	57.8	58.2	58.9	51.9	51.6	46.2	48.4
Employed females	53,997	42,456	6,119	1,439	3,617	2,168	363	216
Percent unemployed	6.2	5.0	10.0	4.2	11.1	11.1	11.0	7.3
Occupation (%)								
Managerial/professional	28.8	30.9	18.8	27.9	15.4	13.6	18.5	18.4
Technical/sales/ administrative support	42.8	43.9	39.7	43.3	40.9	40.7	48.4	49.0
Service	18.0	16.0	27.0	15.7	24.6	24.9	19.9	20.1
Farming/forestry/fishing	0.8	0.9	0.3	0.2	1.8	2.8	—	—
Precision production/ craft/repair	1.9	1.7	2.3	3.0	2.5	2.8	2.4	2.0
Operators/fabricators/ laborers	7.7	6.6	12.0	10.0	14.8	15.2	10.8	10.6
Females with earnings	62,050	48,613	10,944	1,606	4,240	2,542	424	251
Less than $10,000	37.9	37.0	54.0	36.0	32.7	49.6	35.9	33.3
$10,000–19,999	—	—	—	29.3	—	—	—	—
$10,000–24,000	37.9	37.7	24.1	—	38.1	36.7	42.3	42.0
$20,000–29,000	—	—	—	17.2	—	—	—	—
$25,000–49,000	21.1	22.0	11.6	—	14.5	12.7	20.8	23.7
$30,000–39,000	—	—	—	8.7	—	—	—	—
$30,000 or more	—	—	7.3	—	—	—	—	—
$40,000–49,000	—	—	—	4.8	—	—	—	—
$50,000 or more	3.1	3.3	—	4.0	1.4	1.0	1.0	0.9
Median earnings ($)	13,675	14,241	9,623	14,122	10,813	10,098	14,200	14,117
Mean earnings ($)	16,745	17,141	—	—	13,587	12,588	15,656	16,456

Source: For total United States, Whites, Hispanics, Mexican Americans, Puerto Ricans, and Cuban Americans, U.S. Bureau of the Census (1993d, 1994c); for African Americans, U.S. Bureau of the Census (1991, 1993c); for Asian Americans, U.S. Bureau of the Census (1992).

[a]Includes Hispanic origin.
[b]All numbers are in thousands.

Box 7.1_____

True or False? Test Your Ideas about Women and Work

1. _____ T _____ F Most women in the United States seek employment in order to earn money for little luxuries that their families could not afford with one income.

2. _____ T _____ F There is clear evidence that a woman is more likely to be employed if her mother was employed.

3. _____ T _____ F High-school career counselors have different aspirations for female and male students.

4. _____ T _____ F Women earn less than men on the average, but the difference between their salaries can be attributed to the fact that men have more experience, work more hours, and so forth.

5. _____ T _____ F American women spend about the same amount of time on housework now as in the 1920s.

6. _____ T _____ F Men and women in the same profession, such as business administration, are fairly similar in their personality characteristics.

7. _____ T _____ F The best explanation for the absence of women in nontraditional fields is that they lack the appropriate personality characteristics and skills.

8. _____ T _____ F When women are employed, their husbands perform substantially more household chores than when women are not employed.

9. _____ T _____ F Children of employed women have normal intellectual development, but they are often socially maladjusted.

10. _____ T _____ F Role strain, which women experience when they combine employment and home responsibilities, often leads to poor mental health.

Answers: (1) F; (2) T; (3) T; (4) F; (5) F; (6) T; (7) F; (8) F; (9) F; (10) F.

MYTHS OF THE WORKPLACE

Popular mythology would have the world believe that women are governed by their emotions, their lack of physical prowess, and their menstrual cycle. If they venture forth from "women's work"—not very many notches above "child's play" in difficulty or significance—they are not natural women. They are shrews, castrating females, and worse. Moreover, women's very presence in the work force, the myth makers assert, tends to distract their stronger, more rational male colleagues, lowering productivity and morale. Never mind that women have proved themselves more than capable at managerial and executive levels; never mind that they have successfully executed jobs that call for great physical strength and discipline. Popular mythology would have the world believe that women are, at best, inferior workers for the reasons cited above; at worst, they are a hazard—a jinx. Ancient superstition, for example, has it that the very presence of a woman aboard a sailing vessel guarantees disaster.

The myths that abound regarding women in the workplace tend to echo society's myths regarding the limitations of women and how these so-called limitations should dictate the positions to which they aspire. In academia, for example, women are perceived as nurturers and likely candidates for teaching positions, rather than for the more prestigious and highly compensated research positions (Pease, 1993). Women are seen as capable of taking on positions that are interactive, responsive, supportive, and labor intensive, such as teaching low-level, large classes that call for an enormous amount of preparation, paper work, and individualization. Men, on the other hand, are perceived as capable of doing work that is described as solitary, dominating, controlling, and unilateral (Fowlkes, 1987). Their work is objective and dispassionate. Thus, just as housewives are expected to play enabling roles in home and family while their husbands assume jobs that remove them from family life, teachers, usually women, are expected to play featured roles on campus, motivating students to succeed in both curricular and extracurricular activities, while researchers, usually men, remove themselves from all contact with students. The researcher works to satisfy her- or himself; the teacher, and others. Furthermore, just as housewives and mothers are lauded with great sentimentality for efforts that go largely unpaid, so too are teachers more readily compensated sentimentally than financially.

Similarly, women living on a kibbutz in Israel, where egalitarianism among the genders is a philosophical ideal, tend to associate continuing education and pursuing a career with masculinity. Some Israeli women, according to a study by Lobel, Agami-Rozenblatt, and Bempechat (1993), are likely to aspire only to "women's" occupations, such as teaching and social work, nurturing roles that are extensions of motherhood. Nonetheless, despite their tendency to choose "feminine" jobs, these women consider themselves more masculine than their less educated counterparts on the kibbutz, who perform such traditionally feminine tasks as cooking, cleaning, and tending children. This attitude is entirely consistent with our own society's image of a corporate woman as less than feminine, as though ambition, assertiveness, and self-reliance were gender-related traits. Indeed, whether a woman breaks with society's norms by continuing her education, by becoming an engineer or astronaut, chances are that society, and in the case of the working women of the kibbutz, the woman herself, will see her nonconformity as a masculine trait. For a brief questionnaire on discrimination, answer the questions in Box 7.2.

CONTEMPORARY SOCIETAL ATTITUDES TOWARD WORKING WOMEN

Economic and Personal Outcomes

Despite the strides that women have made, social attitudes and expectations regarding women are slow to change. Economic reality notwithstanding, there are many critics of working women, just as there are receptive audiences for these harsh comments. Such criticism grows more intense if a woman is also a mother and more intense still if she is perceived as a woman who is working to realize her professional ambitions. Society's attitudes toward working women play an important role in the way that grown women perceive themselves as workers and the way that adolescent women perceive themselves as prospective workers.

Box 7.2 _____

Discrimination Questionnaire

Discrimination has become a fact in society and permeates our lives. If we seriously examine almost any situation, we can usually find evidence of some unequal disadvantage. Answer each of the following questions:

1. Overall, how much discrimination do you think women experience in the United States?
   _____ None   _____ Some   _____ Moderate   _____ A Great Deal

2. Overall, how much discrimination do you think women experience in your community?
   _____ None   _____ Some   _____ Moderate   _____ A Great Deal

3. Overall, how much discrimination do you experience?
   _____ None   _____ Some   _____ Moderate   _____ A Great Deal

Source: Adapted from "The Denial of Personal Disadvantage among You, Me and All the Other Ostriches," by F. J. Crosby et al., in *Gender and Thought: Psychological Perspectives,* edited by M. Crawford and M. Gentry, 1989, New York: Springer-Verlag.

Cross-Cultural Perspectives

A 1993 study of Guatemalan, Filipino, and U.S. adolescents' images of women as office workers and homemakers (Gibbons et al., 1993) reveals that a great many pan-cultural similarities exist in the traits differentially attributed to women and men. Their findings corroborate earlier research by Williams and Best (1982, 1990), Offer, Ostrov, Howard, and Atkinson (1988), and Schlegel and Barry (1991), with Williams and Best and Offer and colleagues approaching the question from an **etic** (universal) and Schegel and Barry from an **emic** (culturally specific) perspective. Their conclusions, which support the notion of a *universal adolescent* (similar across cultures), are consistent with the report by Gibbons and her colleagues as noted earlier in this chapter.

Gibbons and her group worked with adolescents in Guatemala, the Philippines, and the United States. These three nationalities were chosen because they represent three different continents, cultural traditions, and sets of conditions for women in the home and workplace. The researchers approached adolescents within these groups and had them interpret drawings that were executed by other adolescents within their respective groups. These drawings depicted ideal women within both the home and workplace. The results demonstrated the greatest degree of individualism among U.S. respondents and the greatest degree of collectivism among Guatemalan respondents. Filipino respondents were intermediate in their collectivism–individualism scores.

While a number of significant differences characterized responses in the three settings, a number of universal perceptions also emerged that attest to adolescents' views of women and work, a view that shapes the way adolescent females perceive themselves as they mature and the roles to which they intend to aspire as adults. The women who were cooking, for example, were seen by respondents from each of the three countries as mothers; that they were cooking for others and not preparing their own meals was a given. Thus, the adolescents in this study echo the widely held belief that women are more relational than men, a notion encountered earlier in Pease's study, which reported the tendency to offer teaching positions to women, who are seen as nurturers and enablers, and research positions to men, who are considered better suited to this isolated task.

In all three samples, the women who were engaged in office work were perceived as hardworking and in pursuit of an end. In Guatemala this end was the betterment of self or family, but in the United States and the Philippines this end was the realization of a dream. These responses are consistent with other responses that point to a very traditional view of women among Guatemalan youth and a more modern view of women among adolescents in the United States, with Filipino youth falling somewhere in between. The Guatemalan adolescents, who live in a male-dominated society and see women in the work force as something of an innovation, tended to interpret the desire for women to work within the context of tradition; that is, their desire to work was viewed by participants as an extension of the women's desire to better their families. The U.S. respondents, however, tended to see working outside the home as a norm for women and a means through which they might realize personal ambitions; nevertheless, the U.S. respondents acknowledged that this has not always been the case.

THE PERSISTENCE OF DISCRIMINATION: CONTEMPORARY OCCUPATIONAL SEGREGATION

Just as popular mythology has shaped societal attitudes regarding women in the workplace, so have these attitudes shaped the roles that different women are permitted to play therein, a phenomenon called **occupational segregation** (Blau & Ferber, 1987). Occupational segregation occurs when specific occupations are overwhelmingly either female or male. Many researchers use a quantitative rule to determine if an occupation is segregated, such as 70 percent. That is, if an occupation is more than 70 percent male, such as auto mechanics, then that occupation is considered to be segregated. Such segregation is observed at every level of employment, ranging from the most menial, entry-level positions in supermarkets or fast-food chains to the highest levels of corporate management. It both reflects and perpetuates the social norms from which it springs. (See Box 7.2.)

The workplace, not unlike the home, is unofficially divided into women's work and men's work (Reskin & Hartmann, 1986). In fact, according to Reskin and Padavic (1994), full gender integration would require 53 percent of women (or men) workers to change their occupations. Studies indicate that, although the degree of occupational differentiation between the genders dropped nearly 23 percent between 1940 and 1980, it decreased by only 3 percent between 1980 and 1988 (King, 1992). Many women continue to find themselves in female-dominated occupations, that is, jobs that offer lower pay, status, and responsibility than jobs in male-dominated fields (Tomkiewicz & Hughs, 1993). Table 7.2 summarizes the top ten occupations for men and women. The data of the table demonstrate the continued resistance of many occupations to integration. Reskin and Padavic (1994) point out that if the occupations of typist, office clerk, and stenographer were added to a job category with secretary, that one category would account for about 10 percent of all women workers!

Denmark and her colleagues (1996) summarized work showing that women of color (African

TABLE 7.2 Top Ten Occupations for Each Sex, 1990

OCCUPATION	NUMBER EMPLOYED
Women	
Total Labor Force	56,487,249
Secretary	3,966,179
Elementary school teacher	2,372,174
Cashier	2,259,316
Registered nurse	1,777,885
Bookkeeper, accounting clerk	1,721,202
Nurse's aide	1,621,981
Salaried manager, administrator, nec[a]	1,585,636
Waitress	1,197,485
Salaried sales supervisor, proprietor	1,050,658
Men	
Total Labor Force	66,986,201
Salaried manager, administrator, nec[a]	3,355,970
Truck driver	2,733,620
Salaried sales supervisor, proprietor	1,964,716
Janitor, cleaner	1,700,984
Carpenter, except apprentice	1,337,544
Sales representative, mining, manufacturing, wholesale	1,179,380
Construction laborer	1,103,482
Cook	1,085,895
Supervision, production occupation	1,069,504
Automobile mechanic	936,977

[a]The Census Bureau uses the abbreviation *nec* for miscellaneous occupations that are "not elsewhere classified."

Source: From *Women and Men at Work* (p. 53), by B. F. Reskin and I. Padavic, 1994, Thousand Oaks, CA: Pine Forge Press. Copyright © 1994 by Pine Forge Press. Reprinted by permission of Pine Forge Press.

American, Latina, Asian American, and Native American women) experience racial discrimination along with gender discrimination. Racism has placed African American women at the lowest rung of the labor market. A study of professional Latinas (Mexican American, Puerto Rican, Cuban, and women from other Latino groups) shows that 82 percent report discrimination. Asian American women enjoy higher labor participation, education, and economic status than Latinas, but highly educated Asian American women are rarely rewarded equitably. Native American women are the most economically disadvantaged group in the United States (Hunter College Women's Studies Collective, 1995).

Disabled women comprise another group vulnerable to workplace discrimination. Although the Civil Rights Act of 1964 explicitly prohibits this type of discrimination, the reality for disabled women does not always conform to the law. A study of disabled women and men highlighted the need for retraining programs and additional employer education workshops. Disabled women who were employed had a significantly better outlook on their health status than disabled women who were not employed (Kutner, 1984). This finding suggests that employment may improve the physical and psychological well-being of disabled women.

Although it has been 30 years since the passage of the Equal Pay Act, men are still favored as candidates for more prestigious jobs, and they also earn higher salaries than their female counterparts in the same jobs. For every dollar that men earn, women earn only 74 cents (U.S. Census Bureau Statistics, 1998). In a *Washington Post* article, Mann (1997) wrote, "With all of the educational and professional progress women have made in the last 20 years, the wage gap has proven the most intractable barrier to economic equality" (p. E3). Rosenberg's (1993) comment that women lawyers are at greater risk of discrimination within the private sector than they are within the public sector holds true for professional women across the board. Mann (1997) quotes Susan Bianchi-Sand, who addresses the problem of the information gap. Since salaries in the public sector are made public, less of a wage gap exists there. "It's time to close the wage gap," she proclaims. "We don't fully value women's work" (p. E3). Figure 7.1 humorously depicts the wage gap that persists between women's and men's work.

If major inequalities still persist for women, for example, crowding women into fewer "acceptable" occupations than men, there are some differences among women when considering race and ethnicity. Table 7.1 also demonstrates that White women are far more likely to be employed as managers and professionals than any other group except Asian American women. Service jobs, which are among the poorest paying, are disproportionately held by African American women.

Some would argue that a certain degree of occupational segregation may be appropriate. Tomkiewicz and Hughes (1993), who studied the differences be-

" OH! THAT EXPLAINS THE DIFFERENCE IN OUR WAGES "

FIGURE 7.1   The Wage Gap

tween those women who choose business administration and those who choose administrative services, concluded that it would not be wise to "impetuously" integrate women into higher-echelon jobs in business. Tomkiewicz and Hughs set out to understand why it is that more women who attend business schools choose to prepare for careers in administrative services, training for careers that the U.S. Bureau of Labor Statistics classifies as "administrative support" (e.g., office supervision), rather than opting for the study of business administration, which would prepare them for career opportunities that the U.S. Bureau of Labor Statistics classifies as "executive, administrators, and managerial." This is a puzzling phenomenon in light of the fact that the latter yields greater prestige and higher earning power, while both fields call for equivalent amounts of training and expense.

Their study reveals that the women who pursued the respective study tracks differed in their attitudes toward feminism. Not surprisingly, those who chose the administrative service track that prepared them for occupations that have traditionally been held by women were less pro-feminist than those who chose the business administration track, which prepared them for executive and managerial positions. Also, the female administrative service majors differed from their counterparts in business administration in their attitude toward management. The former were significantly more amenable toward unionization and strike activity than the latter. This would indicate a labor (as opposed to management) orientation on their part. Thus, Tomkiewicz and Hughs (1993) conclude that the more traditional women cannot be considered equivalent to their feminist counterparts in the business administration program. The major thrust of this research is that, even when women share many occupational characteristics and pursuits, they are not necessarily homogeneous. We should bear this in mind when we discuss "women"; it is a highly varied category of individuals who do not necessarily share common values, aspirations, or goals. If we discuss women as if they are a unified group, we may, in fact, be contributing to some stereotype of women that is less complex and nuanced than it should be (see Chapter 1).

To conclude, many researchers point to the fact that much, if not most, occupational segregation stems from anything but a logical core. Even as early as 1978, Krefting, Berger, and Wallace noted that gender imbalances in a particular trade may well be self-perpetuating. Often an employer favors a particular gender when interviewing candidates merely because that gender dominates the field. Thus, work may be defined not so much by gender traits as by demographics. Men's work is not necessarily work that is suited by job content or personality to men rather than women; men's work is nothing more than work that has been traditionally performed by men, as Table 7.2 clearly demonstrates.

Affirmative Action

The Equal Employment Opportunities Commission (EEOC) was created to administer Title VII, enacted in 1964, which outlawed job discrimination on the basis of sex, age, and race in hiring and promotion. The term *affirmative action* is a legal expression with historical grounding in the labor laws of the first part of the twentieth century. "In general, affirmative action consists of extra steps taken to ensure that a legally required result is actually produced" (Lindgren & Taub, 1993). Affirmative action emerged as the result of a set of presidential executive orders in the 1960s and 1970s (Reskin & Padavic, 1994). Initially, affirmative action was meant to change the employment practices of contractors who did business with the federal government so that White women and minority women and men would have the same access that White males have traditionally enjoyed. As Reskin and Padavic point out, since all taxpayers foot the bill for government contracts, all taxpayers should have a shot at the jobs that result.

Affirmative action has been recommended as a means by which to correct job-related gender inequities at the hiring level. A *USA Today*/CNN/Gallup Poll taken in March 1995 showed that 55 percent of women favor affirmative action programs both for women and minorities. A *Los Angeles Times* poll indicated that, while 52 percent of Americans supported affirmative action for minorities, 60 percent supported affirmative action for women. However, Jeffe (1995) reports that women cannot be expected to represent a united front regarding affirmative action. Unlike sexual harassment, which women oppose in a single voice, affirmative action evokes some ambivalence. Not all women, Jeffe claims, care to break through the **glass ceiling;** some do not aspire to CEO positions. Affirmative action threatens them because they fear for their husbands' or sons' professional positions. Interestingly, this filial regard on the part of mothers corresponds to similar emotions expressed by men in the business world. According to the *New York Times* (Barringer, 1992), men advocate day-care and parental leave reforms in the interests of their daughters whom they have educated and prepared for productive professional lives.

The Need for Two Incomes: Contemporary Trends

The growing presence of women in the work force not only reflects personal ambition but also economic realities of the present time. No longer can the ideals of the 1940s and 1950s—large, single family dwellings,

multiple cars, and so on—be maintained on a single income. Indeed, at every social and economic level we find a need for two incomes in order to sustain a desirable standard of living. The cost of living rose dramatically in the latter half of the twentieth century, but income levels did not keep pace. Thus, the percentage of working mothers with children younger than one year old rose from 31 percent in 1976 to 53 percent in 1990. Overall, women with young children are increasingly found working outside the home. Figure 7.2 shows that in families in which there is a spouse and a child under 6, women in 1996 were three times more likely to work outside the home than similar women in 1960. These women are driven by economic need, as well as by changing attitudes toward self-fulfillment (Eckholm, 1992). In fact, the dual-earner model, a pattern in which both partners work outside the home for income, now dominates. In 1997, 60 percent of married couples were two-earner couples, a dramatic increase from 1970 when only 36 percent of couples were dual earners (Jacobs, 1998). Unlike the families of the 1950s, dual-earner families of the 1990s did not rely on one income. Two incomes per family mean not only greater economic stability,

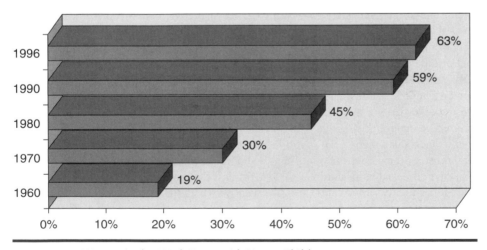

FIGURE 7.2   Women in the Work Force with Young Children
Source: U.S. Department of Labor, 1998.

especially during job losses and illness, but also the potential for a family life-style that models cooperation among all its members in maintaining a household (Barnett & Rivers, 1996).

Just as families are increasingly voting for the economic and psychological rewards associated with all its members working, however, employment relations in the United States are rapidly changing. Whereas the dominant twentieth-century model of employment encouraged long-term attachment to an organization and provided career-ladders for promotion, these rules are being tested and, in many instances, rewritten (Barker & Christensen, 1998; Spalter-Roth et al., 1997). The rise of the **contingent** (or "nonstandard") **worker,** an individual who is working part-time as a "temp" or on a per diem basis, does not resemble the permanent and full-time employment pattern we frequently associate with work. Furthermore, the rapid advance of technology and corporate downsizing has threatened the security of white- and blue-collar workers alike. These multiple trends, including changing employment relations, downsizing, and new technologies, plus the need for two incomes in many families, create a dilemma for many workers. On one hand, the rainy day looms as a very real prospect for all workers, male and female alike. Thus, workers are wise to hold on to their jobs and whatever seniority and security these positions offer. On the other hand, many workers question whether employers are committed to long-term employment relations, given the evidence of corporate downsizing and the rise in the use of temporary hires (Bennett, 1989; Uchitelle, 1996). Therefore, both men *and* women need to continuously develop their skills and abilities and seek new ones so that they can negotiate a changing landscape of employment expectations and opportunities over the course of their lives.

Given these changes, one can well understand the emergence of women as a vital and vibrant part of the work force throughout the latter half of the twentieth century. This emergence has not occurred without a significant amount of controversy and stress, and the many issues that women face—the "double shift" of working a shift at work and another shift at home, family members' lack of contributions,

and employer discrimination—have yet to be resolved for all women.

SEGREGATION: A MATTER OF ASPIRATION, DISCRIMINATION, OR CHOICE

What, then, came first, the need for "manly" traits to implement men's work, or the predominance of men in that field, dating back to a time when women did not work outside the home? This chapter has discussed a number of job-related gender inequities affecting pay and prestige. Gottfredson (1981) attributes these inequities and other aspects of occupational segregation to differences in the career aspirations of men and women. That is, men and women are in different careers because of preference, not discrimination. An early review of the research, however, indicated that sex discrimination in hiring plays a more important role than any differences that may exist in aspiration (Safilios-Rothschild, 1979). A more recent review has confirmed this pattern (Valian, 1998).

Sex Discrimination in Hiring

Masculine Chauvinists.   Peter Glick (1991) argues that those who wish to explain the difference in prestige and salary between men's and women's jobs and the existence of sex discrimination in hiring fall into two camps: those who stress gender-typed personality traits associated with a particular job and those who suggest that sex discrimination in hiring exists regardless of the traits that applicants are thought to possess. Glick calls the former theorists *masculine chauvinists,* individuals who value prototypically masculine personality traits over feminine. He cites Eagly (1987) who suggests that masculine traits tend to be instrumental or agentic and are therefore the kind of traits required in most jobs, whereas feminine traits cluster around the home-oriented trait of nurturance. Thus, jobs associated with masculine traits will naturally bestow greater prestige on those who perform them and demand higher pay.

Glick adds that, although particular jobs may seem to call for masculine traits, women may still be hired to fulfill them. Nonetheless, those who discriminate because of preconceived notions regarding gender traits tend to favor applicants whose gender predicts success in a particular role. Women are favored only for positions such as administrative assistants—positions that offer neither high pay nor prestige—whereas men are favored for executive positions. It may be, Glick points out, that because society as a whole seems to value masculine traits over feminine traits, lower prestige and pay are accorded those occupations that call for feminine traits.

Leidner (1991) argues that traditionally masculine and feminine traits take on flexible definitions within the context of the workplace. That is, the skills that are required to perform one job (for instance, a job dominated by men) may not be different from the skills that are needed to perform a different job (one dominated by women). But these same skills may be socially constructed to be vastly different. For example, she noted that the skills needed to perform effectively as an insurance agent, in a field that is dominated by men, do not differ substantively from those required to work at the window of a fast-food restaurant, a female-dominated area. Like all interactive service jobs that rely on forming relationships between the salesperson and client, both of these jobs are often scripted, both call for achieving a tone of friendliness and urgency, and both require tact when dealing with difficult customers. And yet, whereas men perceive themselves as unnatural candidates for the fast-food window, because they are convinced that they would be too likely to respond inappropriately to customers who are rude, they consider themselves the primary—indeed, the only—candidates for insurance sales. For all that, the impartial observer would imagine that insurance sales personnel are far more likely to meet with rejection by their clients. When it comes to selling hamburgers, it seems, men feel that they should not be expected to exercise tact; when it comes to selling insurance, however, only men ("real" men) can be expected to properly "seduce" their clients and, if necessary, take defeat "like a man." The fast-food worker, a woman, who smiles at an impolite customer exercises *deference;* the insurance agent, a man, who does the same exercises *control.*

Leidner stresses that the insurance agents in her study, all of whom were men, interpreted their work as suitable only for men, emphasizing the aspects of their jobs that they consider manly, whereas the women who worked at fast-food windows did not seem to invest their sense of femininity in their job descriptions. This is most probably related to the notion that society tends to value traits that are typically ascribed to men, and therefore masculinity is more highly valued than traits associated with femininity. This will be discussed again when we examine women's attributions for success. The important point is that women's opportunities for employment in the workplace are limited by the social construction of gender (e.g., what is a male trait and what is a female trait) and its relevance for any one job.

Male Chauvinism.   In contrast to masculine chauvinism, *male chauvinism* is the preference for hiring men over women regardless of the gender traits that are required by the job. This notion states that since men predominate culturally, they are more highly valued. Therefore, those jobs that attract a large proportion of men will be more highly valued and will offer both higher prestige and more pay. Finally, jobs may be defined as man's work or woman's work simply by the existing ratio of men to women in the field. Krefting, Berger, and Wallace (1978) purport that once a job is dominated by one sex, that job takes on a male or female identity. Thus, if one is accustomed to seeing men driving buses, then one would not expect a woman to perform this job successfully; if one is accustomed to seeing women teaching preschool, one would not expect a man to function effectively in that role. This reality makes it difficult to distinguish whether discrimination in hiring is based on a preference for masculine or feminine traits or is simply a reflection of the status quo. There is every reason to believe that the roots of discrimination consist of a complex combination of these factors.

Job Prestige: A Matter of Sex Typing

Glick's study of trait-based and sex-based discrimination demonstrated that masculine traits are more highly valued than feminine traits in the workplace. The best predictor of job *prestige* is the degree to which that job is associated with masculine traits. Although feminine traits are not regarded as being without value, they do not carry the importance of masculine traits. Glick notes that masculine, rather than male, chauvinism is responsible for the prestige associated with certain jobs. He suggests that what appears to be male chauvinism in the reduction of status of particular fields as they begin to attract greater numbers of women is not so much a reflection of the fact that women have joined the ranks. Rather it is a reflection of a fear that womanly *traits* will begin to characterize the fields while masculine trait requirements will be reduced. Male chauvinism was, however, a distinct and important factor in wage discrimination. Glick notes that the tendency to pay men higher salaries, while it may have originated because men were assumed to be the primary breadwinners in the family, continues even when they are *not* sole breadwinners. Men, the study shows, receive more pay not for any perceived masculine traits, but simply because they are men.

Along with gender discrimination, women must also deal with discrimination based on appearance. Attractive women have been evaluated more favorably for feminine jobs, but not for masculine jobs. Attractive men, on the other hand, are generally evaluated more favorably for both types of jobs (Cash, Gillen, & Burns, 1977). Thus, even when applying for "feminine" jobs, attractive women lose their edge when competing against attractive men, and their appearance does not help them at all if they are competing for jobs that are not female dominated. The notion of discrimination based on appearance is part of **Heilman's lack of fit model** (1983), which postulates that gender biases stem largely from an incongruity between an applicant's perceived attributes and the requirements of the position.

To conclude this section, it should be noted that the devaluation of women's work is a truism that holds up historically and universally. Women's work, whether paid or unpaid, skilled or unskilled, is both underpaid and undervalued, regardless of where on the planet it is being done. This attitude is slow to change, although some progress has been made, as noted when comparing the responses of students in the United States, Philippines, and Guatemala to drawings of women at work. In addition, in his study of gender differences in work values and personality characteristics among Indian executives, Singh (1994) discovered that, compared to men, women seemed "more interested in making money, more involved in their work, more enthusiastic, more socially bold, more opinionated, and somewhat more tense" (p. 700). They also seemed to derive more satisfaction from performing well at their jobs. These differences are also echoed, to some extent, in the United States (see Jeffe, 1995). The gender gap, however, seems to be closing regarding professional ambition as more women climb the corporate ladder—but not without some ambivalence on the part of women.

TURNING THE TIDE: ISSUES OF COMPETENCY, ACCESS, AND SOCIALIZATION

Despite the barriers of occupational segregation and discrimination in hiring and pay, women continue to press forward and advance at most levels in the workplace. Is this advance due to a slow change in attitudes toward women and the jobs they are suited for? Is it due to women's continued success in higher education? If stereotyping does remain, how pervasive and damaging is it to women as they continue to make inroads in domains that were once male? An examination of how women's success is characterized and how women are faring in nontraditional professional schools provides both some encouraging and some discouraging insights.

Aversive Sexism

In 1978, Cherry and Deaux studied a group of undergraduate men and women, having each of them write a story about a female (Anne) or male (John) target who was at the top of her or his class in medical school or nursing school. The ensuing stories indicated that men and women alike evaluated both targets negatively when they excelled in nontraditional occupations. Yoder and Schleicher (1996) sought to replicate this study, allowing for the changes in attitudes that have evolved since 1978, such as the fact that attitudes and stereotypes regarding both men's and women's work have changed with the introduction of greater numbers of women into the work force (Kelley & Streeter, 1992). In addition, they noted, the gender composition of medical schools has changed in the past two decades, with women today constituting 33 percent of the student body (Reis & Stone, 1992), as opposed to a mere 13 percent in the mid-1970s (Taeuber, 1991). Enrollment in nursing schools has remained stable, with women constituting 95.4 percent in 1974–1975 (*Digest of Educational Statistics,* 1976) and 94.7 percent in 1988–1989 (*Digest of Educational Statistics,* 1992). For this reason, Yoder and Schleicher added a number of options for "Anne" and "John," including electrical engineering school, where the gender composition (8.5 percent women) parallels that of medical school in 1978. Their results support those of Cherry and Deaux—eighteen years later, occupational gender stereotypes still existed.

Although one might predict that, given today's more egalitarian ideals, the study would indicate a substantial diminution of occupational gender stereotypes, this is not entirely the case. Overt attitudes may have changed, but more subtle forms of stereotyping persist. Dovidio and Gaertner (1986) discuss **aversive racism,** a process in which covert forms of discrimination prevail even among those who loudly proclaim their egalitarianism. Yoder and Schleicher's review and research attest to the aversive sexism that is alive and well within the working world. Citing studies performed in the mid-1970s (Hagen & Kahn, 1975) and mid-1980s (Hodson & Pryor, 1984), which indicate that successful women are rejected socially and professionally, Yoder and Schleicher suggest that successful women suffer work-related costs as well as personal costs in today's workplace. Furthermore, studies that focus on the attributions that underlie women's successes show that these are seldom perceived as stable dispositional traits, such as ability (Deaux & Emswiller, 1974; Feather & Simon, 1975; Weiner, 1974). Instead, their successes are generally ascribed to good luck (Deaux & Emswiller, 1974), easy tasks (Feather & Simon, 1975), or hard work (Feldman-Summers & Kiesler, 1974; Yarkin, Town, & Wallston, 1982). In many cases, women's achievements are viewed as having been enabled by their male colleagues or mentors (Paludi, 1992). Finally, a study by Greenhaus and Parasuraman (1993) reveals that the effective performance of most highly successful women managers is less likely to be attributed to ability than is the performance of their male counterparts. Egalitarianism notwithstanding, aversive sexism and the double standards that nourish it are very real factors in today's workplace.

For all that, though one can applaud the fact that overt stereotyping regarding men and women in nontraditional occupations has been interrupted, it is clear that the road to gender equality has yet to be paved. While demographics reflect a change in gender balance within the world of medicine, for example, such occupations as day care, electrical engineering, and nursing remain skewed. Moreover, the aversive sexism that shapes attitudes toward individuals in nontraditional occupations seems to be especially severe for women targets (Yoder & Schleicher, 1996). Women, it would seem, are less territorial about their traditional occupations than their male counterparts. Perhaps one may ascribe this lack of territorialism to Leidner's (1991) belief that women do not offer proof of their femininity by citing their job, regardless of the nature of their work, because adult female identity is not usually viewed as something that is attained through paid work. Men, on the other hand, have traditionally believed that the performance of manly work supports their male identity. Thus, as Williams (1989) discovered, women nurses do not feel threatened by men who join their ranks, whereas male marines attempt to exclude women from the corps. Moreover, although male nurses attempted to assert their masculinity by distinguishing their work from that of their female counterparts, female marines felt no such need. Leidner's findings that women at fast-food windows do not invest their feminine identity in their occupation tends to hold true for working women across the board, at least in the United States.

Discrimination against Lesbian Women

While much has been written on the career development of heterosexual women, less attention has been paid to the experiences of lesbians in the workplace (Morgan & Brown, 1993). We will learn that many women enter educational and career paths that were originally based on the "male-as-normative" model of development. But does this model apply to all women, including women with same-sexual orientation? At least two different opinions prevail on the issue of the career development of lesbians, and these opinions are not always necessarily exclusive of one another.

The first position is that lesbian women experience vastly different workplaces, different from and more hostile, for the most part, than do heterosexual women. Lesbian women's needs in terms of their work experiences should not be "subsumed under the study of the general female population" (Morgan & Brown, 1993, p. 267). Like other women, lesbian women earn 74 percent of what men earn, but unlike some heterosexual women, they do not live with a male wage earner who earns substantially more. Lesbian women may experience discrimination based on their sexual orientation. Homophobia may influence hiring, promotion, and firing. Yet, Morgan and Brown also indicate that little empirical data on lesbian workers are available, and even the data that are available are based on nonrandom samples of lesbians who are willing to identify themselves.

Janis Bohan (1996), another scholar long involved in the psychology of lesbian, gay, and bisexual research, has recently reviewed the literature on gender and sexual orientation. She concluded, in contrast to Morgan and Brown, that

> Gender is a more significant determinant of behavior and experience than is sexual orientation. Gender role socialization appears to result in gay men being more like straight men and lesbians more like straight women than gays and lesbians are like each other. We have seen this in the research on developmental tasks, on relationships, on sexuality, on the nature of community. . . . It is a profound commentary on the oppressive nature of heterosexuality and the gender roles

> that undergird it that people would choose an identity that is so pervasively denigrated rather than accede to heterosexist norms. . . . In all these areas, the profound impact of gender is highlighted, and new directions for psychology emerge from the shadows. It is not sexual orientation per se that represents so great a challenge to established systems, but the coercive weight of socially constructed notions of gender. It is toward this coercion that psychology might well direct its energies, for it appears that gender rather than sexual orientation is the culprit. . . . It appears that in all this, sexual orientation is fundamentally a vehicle for incursions of gender. (pp. 233–234)

Further research is needed to probe and explore the issues of discrimination based on sexual orientation.

Becoming "Gentlemen": The Tolerance of Inequities in the Legal Profession

Whereas research shows that most women may not perceive *themselves* as more or less feminine because of the demands of their occupations, social stigma targeting working women persists. Citing a survey conducted by Shaffer and Wegley (1974), Yoder and Schleicher (1996) report that women and men rated a target woman as least attractive as a work partner when she combined competence with high career orientation and *masculine* preferences [emphasis added]. Thus, research indicates that social stigma and negative stereotyping play a far greater role in the perpetuation of occupational segregation than personal identity issues. At issue, however, is that certain occupations may be especially hostile to women because they have a long history of male incumbency and, to be successful in these occupations, a woman needs to demonstrate both a high career commitment and behavior that is stereotypically associated with men. One such profession is law.

Rosenberg, Perlstadt, and Phillips (1993) undertook a study of women lawyers and the discrimination, disparagement, and harassment that they experienced at work. Their study bears out the patterns that we have discussed previously and is relevant to this chapter's discussions of women in various workplaces, ranging from higher education, to fast-food restaurants, to coal mines. Compared with male colleagues, women lawyers tend to occupy lower-status positions. In private practice they are concentrated in lower-paying specialties (Heinz & Laumman, 1982) and are less likely to be made partners than their male counterparts (Curran, 1986). They earn approximately two-thirds the salary of men (Chambers, 1989; Hagan, Zatz, Arnold, & Kay, 1991).

Studies suggest that, although hiring practices have grown less unfair, women lawyers continue to face on-the-job discrimination (Acker, 1990). Rosenberg et al. (1993) suggest that women may be less than forthcoming about reporting instances of sexual harassment for fear of rocking the boat and appearing to take a too staunchly feminist position, one that would jeopardize their relations with their colleagues and superiors. They consider themselves newcomers to the playing field and feel an overwhelming pressure to conform to professional norms and defer to authority. It is easy to see how this pressure can inhibit their ability to see discrimination for what it is. But when does this pressure begin? What values are female attorneys conforming to?

In 1994, a comprehensive study of women's experiences at an Ivy League law school was published (Guinier, Fine, Balin, Bartow, & Stachel, 1994). Guinier, herself a law professor at the law school, and her colleagues paint a disturbing picture in which female law students were excluded from the formal educational structure of the school and also excluded from the informal educational environment.

Within the formal structure of the institution, alienation and a decline in academic performance were linked. For example, although both men and women had exactly the same credentials upon admission to the law school (college GPA and LSAT scores), men received better grades by the end of their first year. Importantly, men retain this advantage, as gender differences in GPA are consistent across the three years of school. These disproportionate low rankings for women have far-reaching effects, ranging from nonelection to the school's *Law Review* and moot court to lower employment status offers at grad-

uation. If women and men are so similar in capabilities upon entering a law school, why are women performing so poorly?

Guinier and her colleagues uncovered a series of problems that women encountered in the formal education system. First, law professors, who are primarily male at this law school, prefer the Socratic method—the use of a particularly challenging form of questioning—of teaching in the classroom. Many legal educators assume that learning is most effective when accompanied by stress and pressure. However, many women reported being uncomfortable and anxious with this methodology, and the hierarchy implicit in many law classrooms. "Many students, especially women, have simply not been socialized to thrive in the type of ritualized combat that comprises much of the legal educational method" (Guinier et al., 1994, p. 62). Students perceived that White men are encouraged to perform in the classroom much more than women and students of color. Many students, primarily women, withdraw from the classroom, choosing silence. This silence, however, is also imposed on women vis-à-vis a type of peer hazing to which the first-year women are subjected. Women who spoke up in class reported being laughed at, being called "man-hating lesbians" (the latter from a woman who was married), and hissed at within and outside the classroom.

Given the chilly quality of the classroom, it is not surprising that women begin to withdraw from or not be encouraged to participate in the school's informal educational structure. Guinier and her colleagues believe, as most educators do, that a substantial amount of learning takes place informally out of the classroom. In their study, they found that male students reported being more comfortable interacting with faculty outside the classroom than female students, who tried to determine by indirect cues whether a professor would be open or friendly to them. Women reported that the hazing that took place in the school forced them to seek intellectual and emotional support from female peers, not their professors. Thus, it is not surprising that when awards are granted at graduation, the basis of which is often subjective, a mostly male faculty bestowed a disproportionate number of awards on their male students. Thus, a failure to thrive within the institution because one feels a lack of competency in "thinking like a lawyer" justifies a lower sense of self-esteem, a feeling that one's place is at the bottom of the hierarchy.

The studies conducted by Guinier et al. (1994) and Rosenberg et al. (1993) demonstrated that, ironically enough, the very legal and social developments that have created opportunities for women have reinforced patterns of gender stratification and inequality, indirectly and directly. Women who study law face disparagement, risk harassment, and are compelled to deal with situations in which ideas are road-blocked, their advancement impeded, and their identities are "zippered" as they learn to enact a lawyer's role, or "become gentlemen."

It should come as no surprise that **tokenism** is widely practiced among lawyers, who well know the consequences of exercising overt discrimination. No less predictable are the results of Rosenberg et al.'s (1993) study, which indicate that women who occupy token positions in law firms are more frequently the object of discrimination and harassment than their counterparts in firms where women are employed in greater numbers. Women who seek employment in the private sector are at greater risk of discrimination, both in hiring and on the job, than those in the public sector, where they are protected somewhat by rules and regulations governing fair hiring. Nonetheless, Curran (1986) notes that women are being recruited into the private sector in greater numbers than before. The question for many women remains: How far can I go?

THE GLASS CEILING

Occupational segregation is not only manifested in the types of employment readily available to women; it also plays a role in the level of advancement to which they may aspire, the so-called "glass ceiling" that prevents women from rising beyond a given point in a particular corporate ladder. The Glass Ceiling Commission, set up by the federal government in 1991, reported in 1995 that, while the work force was 57 percent female, women held a mere 5 percent of senior management jobs (Stead, 1996). Attempts to ameliorate this imbalance are often perceived as a threat to men, who feel that any change in the status quo reflects an unfair bias favoring women (Orenstein, 1995). This perception reflects an entitlement that men have claimed and that, until recently, women have conceded. In an interview reported in *USA Today* (Cauchon, 1991), Katharine Graham, chairman and CEO of the *Washington Post,* admits that she did not consider herself equal to her male colleagues in the boardroom when she inherited her position from her husband a quarter-century ago. "I was brought up in the old-fashioned world," she told Dennis Cauchon. "We were as much of a problem as the men. We did not view ourselves as equals. . . . When the women's movement started, it had a lot to tell me as well as men" (p. 9A).

It seems that much remains to be told, not only to men and women, but to boys and girls as well. Orenstein (1995) tells of a particular grade-school teacher who, in an attempt to correct an imbalance, consciously called on the girls in her class exactly as often as she called on the boys, keeping track in her roll book. The boys began to complain that the girls were called on more frequently than they, when in reality the teacher had simply begun to give girls equal time. It is clear that work must begin from the ground floor up if society hopes to shatter the glass ceiling for good.

Just as the glass ceiling has inhibited the professional growth of women within the corporate world, it also serves to suppress them within the blue-collar work force in workplaces that have traditionally been dominated by men. Reskin (1993) reports that, among the women who entered nontraditional blue-collar occupations some two decades ago, many have remained in entry-level positions. Antidiscrimination regulations notwithstanding, men still dominate the channels of upward mobility and hold higher-salaried positions of authority.

In her study of gender relations and the division of labor in coal mines, Tallichet (1995, p. 698) cites Reskin and Roos (1987, p. 9), who contend that **gendered**

division of labor is "grounded in stereotypes of innate sex differences in traits and abilities" and that through "various social control mechanisms" these divisions continue to function. Women are perceived as posing a threat to the privileges that men feel entitled to enjoy by virtue of their masculinity. For this reason, men will stress women's alleged incapability of performing "man's work." If women are allowed, grudgingly, to participate in this work, they are expected to remain "in their place," occupying subordinate positions and deferring to the men in charge. Thus, men are able to tolerate women who work in male settings provided that they continue to perform "women's jobs" and do not attempt to take on traditionally male roles (the reverse does not hold true when men invade women's professional territory).

Kanter (1977a, 1977b) documented that women's presence in workplaces from which they had been barred led to men's exaggeration of the differences between them. This results in what Enarson (1984) calls "sexualization of the workplace." What should be an asexual, professional domain suddenly takes on a dimension of sexuality, with the introduction of sexual harassment and bribery, particularly on the part of foremen and others who wield power, as well as an increase of gender-based jokes and profanity in an attempt to "separate the men from the boys" or, rather, the boys from the women (Enarson, 1984; Gruber & Bjorn, 1982; Swerdlow, 1989). Enarson adds that these behaviors can be considered abusive and that they reflect "a cultural tradition which sexualizes, objectifies, and diminishes women" (1984, p. 109).

It is this objectification of women that lays the groundwork for discrimination and occupational segregation in the coal mines, according to Tallichet. Women are expected to assume "womanly" roles and, for this reason, they are assigned low-level tasks, requiring little skill, if any. Their successful completion of these tasks tends to reinforce their employers' (male) opinion that they have been well assigned, rather than suggesting that they might be capable of rising to greater challenges. Thus, as Schur points out

(1984), objectification and work-related trivialization are mutually reinforcing processes. The trivialization that women experience is, to an extent, self-perpetuating as well, since many women will fatalistically accept the boundaries that men have placed on them, their self-esteem having been eroded by their treatment on the job. Not unlike Graham, whom we quoted previously, the blue-collar female worker stands to learn a great deal from the women's movement and *must* do so if she hopes to realize her potential as a worker. As one woman miner in Tallichet's survey said, "For the past ten years I felt like I was the underdog, that I shouldn't be stepping on their toes. *I haven't felt like I was a person.* . . . If there was a top-paying job, if I thought I could do it, most of the time I'd say let him do it" (Tallichet, 1995, p. 708 [emphasis added]).

Just as women's positions in the white-collar world mirror their traditional roles in society, with women serving as teachers but not researchers, pediatricians but not cardiologists, so, too, the women in the blue-collar world are expected to perform tasks that correspond to their duties at home, chores that service and support men. Tallichet (1995) quotes a female miner who complained that her job consisted of carrying cinder blocks and rock dust behind the male miners, "cleaning up after them." Another said that no matter what section she was assigned, she was expected to clean the "dinner hole."

Tallichet points out that women miners who wish to advance in what has long been a male-defined workplace have, on an individual level, maintained a continued effort to demonstrate their competency in spite of the obstacles set before them (Tallichet, 1995). Laudable though these efforts may be, they cannot adequately address what is a collective problem. As long as sexualization of the workplace is tacitly promoted or dealt with at the managerial level in reactive rather than proactive ways, advancement of women miners will continue to be unnecessarily difficult.

Whether they choose to work or they are compelled to do so for financial reasons, whether they are single or married, whether or not they have children, all women confront a variety of obstacles in the workplace. Even before they enter the workplace, they are likely to meet with such disagreeable challenges as sexual harassment while they are training for eventual employment in male-dominated areas. On March 11, 1997, *USA Today* reported that the Citadel dismissed a male cadet and punished nine others who hazed, harassed, and assaulted two female cadets (Kanamine, 1997). The article pointed out that this behavior was part of a broader treatment of women in the military, noting that a recent sexual harassment scandal has brought "a torrent of complaints" from young female recruits, who claim that they have been treated unfairly and subjected to sexual harassment, bribery, and other forms of sexualization of the workplace. Women complain about a **brass ceiling,** the exclusion from combat, which prevents their advancement. Still, the article notes, opportunities for women have increased both in number and in variety. Although women feel that they have too few female mentors and complain of loneliness on the job, those interviewed expressed overall happiness with the range of opportunities offered.

Women miners and military women, like their white-collar counterparts, must join forces, forming support groups and presenting their grievances regarding pay, advancement, and sexual harassment in an assertive and meaningful way. Only through solidarity and the understanding that they do not have to accept the notion that they are subordinates or intruders in a man's world, will women succeed in effecting positive change (Tallichet, 1995), whether they are in mines, on military bases, or in office suites high atop Madison Avenue.

DENIAL OF PERSONAL DISADVANTAGE

Given the preceding findings, one could expect that women are especially resentful of limited career choices and opportunities; recent research by Faye Crosby, however, indicates otherwise. Crosby and colleagues have conducted a number of studies (Crosby, 1982; Crosby, 1984; Crosby, Clayton, Alkinis, & Hemker, 1986; Crosby, Pufall, Snyder, O'Connell, & Whalen, 1989) that asked women and men to consider the issue of discrimination as it affects women in general and, more specifically, their personal experiences of discrimination. Reasoning that movement toward gender equality has been glacial, Crosby was the first to document and investigate a very durable finding: Individuals acknowledge that others can be disadvantaged, but deny that they *themselves* have been the victims of discrimination. In other words, although women will acknowledge that, in general, women experience disadvantages, they consider themselves to be personally privileged, or exempt, from similar disadvantages. Crosby has termed this an **ostrich effect,** by which sex bias is agreed to operate in society, "but not for me."

Crosby has speculated on some of the reasons for the durability of this particular form of denial. First, it is difficult, if not impossible, to constantly confront bias and prejudice on a minute-to-minute and day-to-day basis. Few individuals are capable of sustaining the resentment that would result from such constant vigilance, never mind the poor mental health that can emerge from chronic dissatisfaction. Living the "personal is political" may not always be possible or optimal. Another reason for the observed denial is that individuals do not always have aggregate data with which to compare their situations with others. For example, most workers in nonunion settings do not know what others are earning. A manager may be pleased with her salary of $40,000, knowing that two other managers, Fred and Juanita, make slightly less. What she does *not* know is that her information is anecdotal, not systematic. If she has all the data for her firm, she might learn that Fred and Juanita are the exceptions and that she earns substantially less than the average earnings of male managers with comparable skills and experience.

The lesson from these investigations is perhaps best summarized by Crosby and her colleagues: "We must not measure the need for social reform by how upset people feel with their personal situations in life. Karl Marx was right about false consciousness: those who are oppressed or disadvantaged rarely have a well-developed sense of their own disadvantage" (Crosby et al., 1989, p. 94).

COPING WITH STRESS

Even though a woman may not categorize herself as one who is discriminated against, she may still experience a substantial amount of stress. (For a full discussion of stress and health, see Chapter 13.) Some of this stress may be due to her working conditions, whereas other stress may arise due to home-related conflicts. Traditional occupations for women, such as sewing machine operators, maids and cleaners, and cashiers, produce stress because they are routine and low-paying "women's work" (Epstein, 1986). Women who choose to pursue nontraditional professions also expose themselves to a great degree of pressure. Much of this pressure relates to the external factors discussed earlier, such as the continuing need to prove their competency, the need to combat (or tolerate) sexual harassment, and the frustration that comes with being the object of discrimination, to name a few. Working women who also manage homes and families cope with many pressures that are part of those roles as well.

Internal versus External Stress

Research supports the notion that women and men react differently to stressors, with women reporting more symptoms than men (Gerdes, 1995). Men apparently predominate when it comes to substance-abuse disorders and personality disorders, while women are predominantly diagnosed with more anxiety and affective disorders, particularly depression (Thoits, 1987b). Women also consistently demonstrate higher levels of anxiety, depressed mood, and demoralization (Thoits, 1987b). Although some believe that this difference may be attributed to their differing *exposure* to stressors within their social roles (Barnett & Baruch, 1987; Gore & Mangione, 1983), others hypothesize that the two groups differ in their *vulnerability* to stressors (Newman, 1986; Thoits, 1987a).

As Gerdes (1993) notes, the research regarding work-related stress has, until recently, concentrated on specifying the dangers of work for men. If one were to accept that women are more vulnerable to stress than men, one would expect to find women's mental health

at risk when they enter the work force. This hypothesis, which was put forth by Waldron (1976), has not been supported. In fact, research indicates that women who are employed outside the home demonstrate better physical and psychological health than their nonemployed counterparts (Aneshensel, Frerichs, & Clark, 1981; Baruch, Beimer, & Barnett, 1987; Thoits, 1987b). Moreover, studies by Los Cocco & Spitze (1990) and Barnett, Marshall, Raudenbush, & Brennan (1983) show that relationships between job experiences and distress are similar for men and women.

Nonetheless, a study conducted at Bucknell University (Gerdes, 1995) in which nontraditional women and traditional women were observed showed that, although men and traditional women differed in their *response* to stress on the job, no significant difference was found between women with traditional aspirations and women with nontraditional aspirations. Female students were more susceptible than their male counterparts to psychosomatic symptoms, physical illnesses, psychological disorders, and anxiety. The women preparing for traditionally male professions reported more chronic stress than men, whereas women preparing for traditionally female professions did not. However, the symptoms that they demonstrated did not differ qualitatively.

Some differences were observed among the two groups of women regarding the relationship between stressor and symptom. Although the two groups did not differ when exposed to average levels of stress, nontraditional women reported higher levels of anxiety, depressed mood, and physical illness when exposed to higher levels of stress. Also, nonwork stress (home events) predicted greater anxiety for nontraditional women. Gerdes (1995) suggests that women who seek to compete in male-dominated fields are more threatened by home events because of the potential conflict between family and professional demands.

Gerdes's (1995) study concludes that, at a high level of work stress, nontraditional women report more job tension than both men in the same fields and traditional women. She suggests that these greater vulnerabilities may be attributed to such factors as personality, coping styles, choice of career, or gender.

Finally, she notes, one must also consider the social pressures and discrimination that loom ahead for those women who choose nonnormative careers.

Sexual Harassment

The term *sexual harassment* did not even exist until 1976, when it was used in connection with a legal suit filed by Carmita Wood, the first woman to seek unemployment compensation after leaving a job in which her boss made sexual advances toward her (Fitzgerald, 1996). As Catherine MacKinnon, law professor and leading advocate for women's rights, noted in 1979, "The unnamed should not be taken for the nonexistent" (MacKinnon, 1979, p. 28).

In the workplace, a few predictors of sexual harassment have emerged. For instance, research suggests that men who harass women tend to be older than their victims and less attractive than women who harass men (Hemming, 1985; Tangri, Burt, & Johnson, 1982). Moreover, women are more often harassed by men of equal or greater power, whereas men report the greatest amount of unwanted sexual attention from less powerful women (Bingham & Scherer, 1993). In several studies, peers have emerged as the most frequent source of harassment, followed by supervisors, subordinates, and clients (Lafontaine & Tredeau, 1986).

In the study of attorneys by Rosenberg et al. (1993), it was found that, although as a rule younger women tend to be victims of harassment more often than older women, the numbers change when working in the private sector. There, older and younger women alike were subject to harassment. However, whereas a woman's marital status did not seem to affect the likeliness of harassment overall, married women suffered less harassment in the private sector than did single women. Rosenberg et al. suggest that this indicates that the harassment is based not so much on sexuality as on an aggressive need on the part of the men involved to demonstrate dominance. For this reason, married women would be protected by the fact that other men have established a claim upon them.

Surprisingly, women who define themselves as "careerist" rather than feminist in orientation may be more vulnerable to sexual harassment and disparagement. Since they claim to believe in the system and consider the schedule of promotions within their firms to be based on meritocracy, they are less likely to complain about discrimination. To do so might indicate that they are bad sports. As a result, they will go along with whatever behavior seems normative, even if this behavior is disparaging and/or discriminatory in nature. Feminists, on the other hand, put forth a clear message that they will not stand for sexual games of any sort. Although their stridency may not win them a great many fans among potential harassers, it may well save them the discomfort of having to put up with them.

Various contextual or situational factors have been explored in connection with the incidence of harassment. One major variable to be studied is the sex-ratio or gender composition of the occupation. Generally, sexual harassment is more common in male-dominated occupations like fire fighting and construction work and in female-dominated occupations like nursing and secretarial work than in sex-integrated occupations in which there is an approximately equal number of men and women (Konrad & Gutek, 1986).

Several investigators have attempted to explain why sexual harassment occurs at work. Tangri, Burt, and Johnson (1982) offered three explanatory models: the *natural biological model,* which stresses males' greater sex drive; the *organizational model,* which sees harassment as the abuse of power in formal hierarchies; and the *socio-cultural model,* which views harassment as the result of gender inequalities throughout society.

Based on their three models of sexual harassment, Tangri et al. (1982) made predictions and tested them using data from the U.S. Merit Systems Protection Board (1981). Whereas none of the models received clear-cut empirical support, stronger support was found for the organizational and sociocultural models, both of which conceptualize sexual harassment as an abuse of power, than for the natural/biological model (Saal, Johnson, & Weber, 1989).

In their explanatory model, Terpstra and Baker (1986) identified three *causal factors* in sexual harassment: gender, power, and perceptions of work climate. They predicted and found that women are more likely to be harassed than men, that people with less institutional power are more likely to be harassed than people with more institutional power, and that sexual harassment is more common in organizations that are perceived as tolerant of harassment. Other tests of their model have generally garnered some support (Bingham & Scherer, 1993).

Another model attempting to explain sexual harassment was proposed by Gutek and her associates (Gutek, 1985; Gutek & Morasch, 1982). They propose that sexual harassment of women at work is a product of sex-role spillover. *Sex-role spillover* is the carryover into the workplace (or academy) of gender-based expectations for behavior. Several aspects of the female-sex role are often carried over to work. One is the "stroking function" of women, in which women are expected to be more nurturant, supportive, sympathetic, or complimentary than men in the same work roles. According to Gutek and Morasch (1982), "Projecting a sexual image and being a sex object are also aspects of the female sex role: sex-role spillover occurs when women, more than men in the same work-roles, are expected to be sex objects or are expected to project sexuality through their behavior, appearance, or dress" (p. 58).

Gutek and Morasch (1982) claim that *sex-role spillover* is a potential cause of sexual harassment when the sex ratio is skewed in either direction, that is when women are in male-dominated or female-dominated occupations. There is some empirical support for Gutek's model, just as there is for the other models discussed. It is important to note that these models are not contradictory and in many cases make identical predictions about the conditions under which harassment is most likely to occur.

All the models reviewed so far are helpful in explaining sexual harassment, but no one model entirely explains why sexual harassment exists. Most recent conceptual frameworks see sexual harassment in all its forms in the workplace, academia, and public

sphere as being rooted in the combination of sexual interest and unequal power between the sexes. Whereas power is often defined as one's position within an organization, power may stem from any of several sources other than formal authority, such as work-group alliances, personal characteristics like physical size, and control of valued resources (Bingham & Scherer, 1993). In this way, sexual harassment is used as a tactic of social control, a means of keeping women in their place, especially in work and school settings that are traditional male preserves, such as the firehouse or military academy.

Relatively few studies have examined the relationship between occupation and harassment. Tangri et al. (1982) found no overall differences in level of harassment between or within white- and blue-collar jobs. Lafontaine and Tredeau (1986) found higher levels of reported harassment in management and engineering than in professional careers in the sciences, computers, higher education, and public administration.

Organizational climate with regard to sexual harassment—the perception that workers have about how organizations respond to sexual harassment—has received some research attention. Working environments differ in the degree to which sexual harassment is a problem, and employees frequently describe their workplace in terms of tolerance of sexual harassment (Bingham & Scherer, 1993; Booth-Butterfield, 1986). Some research supports the idea that perceived organizational climate is related to the prevalence of sexual harassment (Bingham & Scherer, 1993). For example, Lafontaine and Tredeau (1986) found that the percentage of women reporting sexual harassment was higher among those who rated their company low on the equal-opportunity scale than among those who rated their company high on this scale. More research is needed on the effects of organizational climate on sexual harassment. See Chapter 11 for additional information about sexual harassment.

Coping Strategies

Along with the social pressures faced by working women, one must take into account the inner conflicts that they face, particularly those represented by combining their roles at work with their life roles. Kibria, Barnett, Baruch, Marshall, and Pleck (1990) reported that the quality of the homemaking role has important associations with the psychological well-being of women. Women who devote themselves exclusively to homemaking often feel socially isolated and suffer from low self-esteem related to the low social status of homemaking (Berk & Berk, 1979; Bose, 1985; Lopata, 1971; Nilson, 1978). Kibria and colleagues, however, discovered that women who combined their homemaking with outside employment derived greater satisfaction from their roles within the home. Thus, they conclude, one can compensate for the negative aspects of a particular role by engaging in another that provides stimulation or gratification.

According to Amatea and Fong-Beyette (1987), most professional women employ *problem-focused* coping methods when dealing with conflicts between their work and life roles. The methods they choose include reactive role behavior (i.e., working harder to meet all demands, attempting to meet all demands in a beleaguered way), external role redefinition (i.e., delegating tasks to others), increased planful role behavior (i.e., trying to work more efficiently in order to meet all demands), and internal role definition (i.e., purposefully modifying standards and overlooking certain role demands).

Professional women use *emotion-focused* coping methods less frequently, usually when stressors are health related rather than work related. They are more likely to take an active role in solving problems related to parenting and a more passive role when dealing with the demands of self and spouse or lover. Varying coping devices meet with varying degrees of success, with the most consistent rates of success attributed to social support strategies that involve others in the solution of personal problems.

McLaughlin, Cormier, and Cormier (1988) conclude that women who cope most successfully with stress are those who take an active approach to their problems. Too many women are prepared to accept stressors as the price they must pay for the opportunities that have now come their way. This acceptance,

they point out, acts as yet another stressor. Denmark, Novick, & Pinto (1996) advocate "reframing" problems, a three-part process consisting of changing the standards by which a woman measures herself, viewing problems as solvable rather than inevitable, and seeing problems as part of a particular situation, rather than as an indication of a personal deficit.

Carol Gilligan (1982) has emphasized that women must begin to develop self-interest, recognizing their personal validity and nurturing themselves along with the many others with whose care they are involved. This form of self-centeredness should not be perceived as a character flaw; rather it is a necessary survival skill worthy of cultivation. They should seek out support groups and enlist the encouragement of bosses, mentors, professional counselors and therapists, as the dictates of particular situations require.

Multiple Roles: Myths and Realities

When considering the stressors that affect working women, one cannot overlook female workers with family obligations. The induction of women into the work force and their ascension up the corporate ladder have given rise to a new character in popular mythology, the "Super Mom." Her life runs like a well-oiled machine. She comes to work each day, meticulously groomed and dressed, having shipped her 2.5 children off to school no less well dressed, carrying nutritious lunches that she prepared the night before. She projects a totally professional image from 9 to 5—working overtime, if necessary—and somehow arrives home with the energy to prepare dinner and deal with the children's homework, the careful delegation and implementation of household chores, which she shares with her Super Dad husband, the soothing of hurts and minor traumas that may have plagued her perfect children, the reading of bedtime stories and singing of lullabies, preparation for tomorrow's work as a high-power executive, and the next chapter in her vibrant and exciting sex life. The only problem here is that our Super Mom is no less a mythological character than Athena, Venus, and Juno—all of whose qualities she is alleged to possess.

In reality, women who manage career and family do so only if they have strong support systems. Even older school-aged children must be cared for after school hours, and mothers must have effective back-up plans for when their children are ill. The notion of dividing household chores equally does not hold up in reality. In fact, according to Coltrane (1997), overall, men perform five to eight hours of household chores a week, or about one-third of what their spouses perform. Similar findings have been reported for dual-earner African American families (Hossain & Roopnarine, 1993). Even among young, dual-career couples, people in their twenties and early thirties with no children, the men spent only half as much time as the women doing housework (Denmark, Shaw, & Ciali, 1985). Moreover, the onus of responsibility for child care and household chores falls on the woman, regardless of any arrangements that she and her spouse may have made to the contrary. Roxanna Diaz, a Miami-based social worker, notes that if her husband does 50 percent of the child care "that's a lot more than is expected of him. . . . If I do 50 percent, it's a lot less than is expected of me" (Stead, 1996).

Overall, women retain the responsibility for arranging and supervising labor-inducing services, such as child care and cleaners (Hochschild, 1997), responsibilities that are time consuming. An acquaintance of one of the authors of this volume, a woman in her sixties who combined a career as a teacher with duties in the home at a time when this was all but unheard of, admits that she considered herself obliged to serve meals no less varied, healthful, and attractive than her stay-at-home friends, in spite of the hours spent teaching, preparing her work, and grading papers. To her mind, greater demands are being made of women. They have not so much exchanged their household chores for professional duties as they have increased their burden by adding professional duties to the long list of household chores from which they have not been exempt. This woman's critique notwithstanding, the number of mothers in the work force has increased more than ten times since 1940 (Russo & Denmark, 1984) to include 62 percent of all mothers (Bianchi, 1995). By 1996, six out of ten mothers with children under age 6 were in the labor force.

This raises an issue of some controversy: Do children of working mothers suffer at the expense of their mothers' careers? According to Eyer (1994), there is no scientific evidence that women shortchange their infants and toddlers by working outside the home. Not only are the much-touted negative effects of day care questionable at best, but studies usually show that working mothers spend close to the same amount of time with their children as do the so-called stay-at-home mothers (Eyer, 1994).

One might expect that the stressful demands of job and family would be difficult for a mother to juggle and that she would experience overload. Were this the case, the toll on the mother's mental health would make it difficult for her to be an adequate, let alone good, mother. Fortunately, a review of the literature concludes to the contrary that the effects of multiple roles on women's mental health vary, and that for many women, working actually has a positive impact on self-esteem and life satisfaction (Denmark et al., 1996; Hyde, Klein, Essex, & Clark, 1995). We have already seen that women employed outside the home, whose interests are varied, derive more satisfaction from the routine chores of homemaking than their nonemployed counterparts (Kibria et al., 1990).

The population of women with children under three years of age who are in the work force has been growing steadily in recent years, reaching 55 percent in 1993 (U.S. Department of Labor, 1993). The wisdom of the mother's decision to leave her infant or toddler to go to work is not uncontested; in fact, the subject has evoked such controversy as to inspire several federal studies. One such study, coordinated by Sarah Friedman, of the National Institute of Child Health and Human Development, involved 1,364 children from the time that they were six months old through age 3. The results, published in *USA Today* (Elias, 1997, p. 1A, 11A), indicated that language and cognitive development and the relationship with mother are linked more directly to family qualities and the child's temperament than to whether that child has been in day care. Nonetheless, the quality and quantity of care are important factors. The study also demonstrates that children who receive higher-quality care will have better language development and more positive social skills. However, if the mother's working hours are such that she spends very little time with the child, the less socially engaged the pair is likely to be and the less sensitively the mother will relate to the child. This failure to bond adequately at an early age is likely to be a harbinger of greater problems to come.

So, working mothers face a double dilemma. Not only must they secure day care of high quality, but they must also determine how many hours of day care are advisable so as not to jeopardize the bonding process and their relationships to their children. At the same time, their own mental health is likely to be more secure if they do participate in some work outside the home. The result is often a juggling act.

We have already noted that women in multiple roles exhibit greater levels of self-esteem than those who identify themselves as homemakers and do not work, either for pay or as volunteers, outside the home. This is true of working women even after they have retired. Studies show that women who identify themselves as retirees as well as homemakers demonstrate greater levels of self-esteem than those who identify themselves only as homemakers (Adelmann, 1993). Lower rates of depression and higher self-esteem were noted among older women who kept busy with do-it-yourself projects and volunteer activities that provided concrete and social rewards, as well as a sense of personal accomplishment. Traditional household chores, on the other hand, were not related to self-esteem. Child care was negatively related to self-esteem. Adelmann points out, however, that this refers to primary care for a child living in the home, not the typical care associated with being a grandparent. In conclusion, we find that traditional women's work to the exclusion of work that provides intellectual and social stimulation is not enough to generate self-esteem and promote good mental health at any phase of a woman's life.

THE TIME BIND

Many individuals still think of home as a sanctuary from the hubbub of day-to-day life. In this view, home is an escape from the pressures of modern life and provides an individual with opportunities for privacy,

leisure, and pleasure from interaction with household members. But is this home-as-sanctuary model true today and, if so, for whom? Increasing levels of education and career attainment result in, supposedly, the benefits of job security and enough affluence to enjoy travel and other activities. However, companies have increasingly downsized their workforce. At the same time, they have implemented empowerment programs, such as quality circles, in which employees are expected to be serious players and demonstrate their commitment to a firm through long hours. These same firms have also initiated family-friendly policies that permit workers to request job-sharing, part-time schedules or reduced workload. In this section, we will consider the competition workers feel between family obligations, career commitments, and the issue of *time*—whose is it and how should it be used—in the modern workplace.

Part-Time Work and Flex Time

Thirty years ago, it was commonplace for women to reduce or abandon their jobs during their childbearing years. Today, however, women's work patterns more closely resemble men's patterns of continuous workforce attachment (Spalter-Roth et al., 1997). Women want and need full-time permanent work. According to Moen (1992), women recognize the disruptive effects of discontinuous jobs and careers in terms of earnings, job stability, and advancement. However, as noted earlier, men have not stepped forward to assume an equal share of household responsibilities when their spouses work. At the same time, many women recognize and appreciate the social benefits and psychological rewards associated with paid employment. The dilemma for women is how to juggle these activities, a feat even more onerous when a couple is not "collaborative" (Barnett & Rivers, 1996) in sharing the work load at home. For some women, nonstandard work arrangements, such as part-time, temporary, on-call, home-based work or independent contracting and self-employment, promise a reconciliation between home and work. A key research question, however, is whether these actually help in managing work and family. Research indicates that some women may be swapping one set of problems for another when they enter these arrangements.

Barker (1993) was concerned that women who selected part-time work, no matter what their occupational status (i.e., attorneys, bankers, nurses, professors, or clerks), were penalized in the workplace. Many women select part-time employment to cope with child-care and home-related activities. Yet, a part-time work status, in distinction to the male normative work status of a full-time work schedule, is not neutral. For example, the social history of part-time work demonstrates that it was relegated to immigrants, freed slaves, and women because they were deemed by employers as "inferior" (Morse, 1969). Yet contemporary occupations have also historically varied in their traditions regarding the availability of part-time work. Therefore, Barker examined women working full and part time in male- and female-dominated professions (primarily attorneys and nurses) and clerical occupations.

Within occupations, Barker found that part-time women consistently reported less inclusion than full-time colleagues. Greater inclusion in the workplace was most often associated with those in the professions. The feelings of exclusion were greatest for those in clerical occupations. In general, part-time workers were more apt to report that they were unlikely to be promoted, felt they were off track, and were perceived to be less committed than they really felt they were. Perceived vulnerability to layoff was significantly greater for part-time professionals compared with full-time colleagues.

A second broad area of inquiry in the Barker study addressed career goals. If various employment schemes confer differential rights and benefits (Christensen & Murphree, 1988), and women working in part-time jobs reported less career satisfaction than full-time peers (Hall & Gordon, 1973), it was reasoned that the greater exclusion reported by part-time workers would be related to their lower levels of career motivation. Barker found that both full- and part-time groups uniformly reported that they worked because it brought personal satisfaction.

Finally, in terms of the juggling of work and family responsibilities, Barker also wanted to know if women working part time would report lower role conflict and overload than would full-time working women. She found that part-time work did not contribute to lower role conflict or overload. Occupation did, however, predict role conflict. Women working in female-dominated professions reported lower amounts of role conflict than women working in male-dominated professions. Control over work schedule appeared to be more important than the actual work itself. When women were involuntarily working in their schedule, they were more likely to report role overload than women working voluntarily in their schedules. Single mothers can face an even more dramatic home work load in addition to being the sole income provider for their families. These women cannot consider leaving the work force for even a brief period, nor do they freely choose alternative work arrangements that reduce earnings or are inherently unstable, such as temporary or seasonal work.

Perhaps the most important consideration for women thinking about nonstandard work versus regular arrangements has to do with earnings and benefits. Nonstandard workers receive fewer benefits than workers in regularized employment. Only 23 percent of women and 16 percent of men in nonstandard arrangements receive health and pension benefits compared with 80 percent of full-time women and men workers (Kalleberg & VanBuren, 1996). Considering that women live longer than men, the absence of pension benefits in most nonstandard jobs points to a long-term vulnerability that women bear in coping with work–family conflicts. When women opt out of the workplace, they do not contribute to separate social security benefits, and when women work part time, their social security benefits upon retirement may be much less than if they had worked full time (DuRivage, 1992). The message is clear that women *pay* in multiple ways for coping with work–family responsibilities.

Maternal and Paternal Leave

Many couples who hope to combine dual careers with raising children will decide to engage in some form of a reduced work schedule, at least while their children are small. There is, however, no reason to assume that it is the woman who will have to cut back on her career. Many individual decisions need to be carefully weighed before and after a child enters a dual-career working couple's life. Options such as on-site day care, job sharing, working in the home, and flextime enable more parents to combine child rearing and career. Many couples find that through careful time management, judicious use of nannies and housekeepers, and compartmentalization of their work and home lives they are able to enjoy the economic and psychological benefits that come with pursuing a meaningful career along with the intense emotional satisfaction that comes from raising children.

A related issue of debate to the problem of combining career and family is the amount of postpartum parental leave to which mothers (and fathers) are entitled. The notion of parental leave is relatively new in the United States. Until recently, postpartum leave was confined to mothers and was generally aimed at allowing women to recover from childbirth (Hyde & Essex, 1991). However, recovery from childbirth should not be viewed as physical recovery alone. As Hyde, Klein, Essex, and Clark (1995) point out, when an employed woman takes on the role of mother, she can be expected to experience physiological and psychological stress and distress. Adding this role may well overload her system, according to the **scarcity hypothesis,** which states that human beings have a set amount of time and energy (Goode, 1974).

Parental leave takes into account more than a woman's recovery from childbirth; it refers to time allowed to either parent for child rearing. In January 1993, President Clinton signed the Family and Medical Leave Act, providing for up to 12 weeks of parental leave with job security following birth or adoption of a child. Although this has apparently been in an effort to consider the needs of the infant, Hyde et al. (1995) maintain that the emotional needs of mothers must also be addressed. Their study found that short parental leave is a risk factor for psychological distress when combined with other factors such as unfulfilling work or a rocky marriage. Another finding was that women employed full time display increased anxiety, emphasizing the importance of workplace

policies that permit part-time work, job sharing, and incremental (rather than immediate) return to work for women during the first postpartum year. A more recent study, reported next, however, focuses on the failure of many parents, both women and men, to pursue flexible workplace policies.

Evading the Time Bind

In a study of one major corporation with such family policies, Hochschild (1997) found that most workers did not avail themselves of progressive workplace policies even when they had supervisors who were flexible, because the firm still managed to pressure its employees to be more work centered. The result was that working parents experienced a time crisis. She wondered why these parents were not engaged in a "culture of resistance" (p. 34), fighting for more time with their families and less time at work. Rather than asking for shorter hours, for example, parents found ways to avoid or deny that the problem existed. Hochschild described a cultural reversal under way in which the workplace and the home traded roles, with work serving as a retreat from pressures at home. In one organization, Hochschild reported a number of disturbing findings in her survey of mostly middle- or upper-middle-class parents in their 30s: 89 percent considered themselves workaholics, 89 percent reported experiencing a problem termed *time famine* or lack of sufficient time, and half of those who reported a time famine also reported feeling guilt about not spending enough time with their children. Only 9 percent reported that they felt that they could balance work and family.

Hochschild then wondered whether these working parents were tolerating their situation because they found work more rewarding than family life. She asked, "Does it sometimes feel to you like home is a workplace?" Eighty-five percent said yes. She also asked, "Is it sometimes true that work feels like home should feel?" and 25 percent answered "very often" or "quite often" and 33 percent answered "occasionally." The remainder, 37 percent, responded "very rarely." Hochschild concluded that in her study of employees at two corporations "working parents feel more at home at work because they come to expect that emotional support will be more readily available there" (p. 200). At one firm, 49 percent of the workers reported being more relaxed at work than at home. For these workers, shortened family hours are burdened with the sort of stress that once characterized the workplace. Hochschild says that more and more workers practice "emotional asceticism" as a coping device, denying themselves the fun and support that normal family relations provide. This perpetuates the growing phenomenon of *workaholism*. Indeed, studies show that women who are workaholics, devoting 50 hours or more each week to their professions, are more likely than men to pay for this behavior with divorce and fewer deep, personal relationships. Some 35 percent of these women never marry, as compared to 9 percent of their male counterparts. Their devotion is not always rewarded with greater prestige or higher salaries (Elias, 1984).

As more and more women enter the work force, few can envision a return to the time when women were primarily in the home. Yet, women's emergence in the workplace occurred without a challenge to the normative working week—35 to 40 or more hours—that dominated the model of full-time work in the twentieth century. Despite the coping strategies that women develop, some investigators forecast tremendous personal costs due to time famine. Writers such as Hochschild (1997) foresee that time famine will continue to accrue and perhaps worsen unless society engages in a debate on the organization of work, including flexibility, and the competition between the emotional investment in personal relationships and America's "love affair with capitalism" (p. 249).

CONCLUSION: LOOKING BACK WHILE LOOKING AHEAD

We have seen that exploitation of women continues, not only on the job, but in the home as well. The tasks that have traditionally defined women's roles culturally and socially continue to define their activities within the work force. They are seldom credited with their accomplishments within the home, but quickly and harshly condemned for falling short of their duties

as mothers. One has but to recall Marcia Clark's experiences when prosecuting O. J. Simpson for an example of the cruel judgmentalism that threatens a successful, high-profile woman. Her professionalism was called into question when she responded to her children's needs, and her competence as a mother was called into question when she demonstrated an appropriate level of commitment to her profession. The defense attorney, Johnnie Cochran, was held to no such personal standard.

Good news for women comes not only from the United States, where such women as Katharine Graham, publisher and owner of the Washington Post, and Sheila Widnall, Secretary of the Navy, have blazed trails for women within the worlds of journalism and the military, respectively. Good news also comes from South Africa, where Mamphela Ramphela serves as the first Black president of the University of Cape Town, as well as from studies of workers performed in the former Soviet Union that declared men, not women, "the weaker sex" (Shlapentokh, 1984). The progress that women have made across the world should not be overlooked in the face of the work that remains to be done. For example, when compared with women in the United States and Europe, Japanese women suffer far greater obstacles to equal opportunity. "Thus, even though nearly 40 percent of the Japanese work force consists of women, most of them work in insecure jobs without benefits accorded to men" (Sukemune, Shiraishi, Shirakawa, & Matsumi, 1993, p. 180). Feminist researchers in Japan believe that there is a lack of fundamental respect for women's human rights in Japanese society. Japanese women are far less likely to be elected to policy-making arenas, such as parliament, or have distinguished positions in the public sector, such as posts in government. As access to all levels of society is impeded, so too is Japanese women's progress in the workplace.

Ours has traditionally been considered a man's world. Important tasks were carried out by men; important decisions were made by men; the mundane and routine stuff of life was the domain of women, their sole domain. The emerging role of women in the work force has shattered the long cherished myth of male entitlement, not without resentment on the part of men and not without suffering on the part of women. Occupational segregation, unequal pay, unequal distributions of work and family obligations, and sexual harassment—all these testify to the challenges to which women must continue to rise so that collectively they will eventually realize their considerable worth, not only within the home, but also within the professional world.

SUMMARY

Women have always worked, but in the past few decades increasing numbers of women are working outside the home in paid employment. Economic forces are the primary reason for women's increasing profile in the workplace. Yet, myths regarding women's role in the workplace, such as their lack of physical prowess and negative concomitants of the menstrual cycle, are referred to in stereotypes regarding the limitations of women workers. Some of the more intense criticism of women concerns their dual roles as mother and worker. Unfortunately, society's ambivalence toward women workers affects women's views of themselves as workers and mothers.

Occupational segregation within industrial societies continues at overwhelming rates. "Women's work" and "men's work" remain divided, with women crowded into fewer and lower-paying jobs than men. Women receive 74 cents for each dollar that men earn. Furthermore, women of color experience additional discrimination due to race and ethnicity, with fewer African American women and Hispanic women working as managers and professionals than White women. Studies of the differences in political views of women with different career histories point to fears regarding integration of women in high-level positions. Some women may have feminist viewpoints that threaten traditional managerial or corporate perspectives. Women are not a homogeneous group, and this is especially true when querying women about their perspectives on workplace justice, such as affirmative action.

Post-World War II ideals were the foundation of many boomers born during the 1950s. These ideals collided with the economic realities that greeted their generation: stagnant wages and downsizing. Many women raised during the rhetoric of the 1960s and 1970s women's liberation movement sought outside employment. A major revolution accompanied the rise of women in the workplace. Women sought empowerment through education and work, and many families benefited. Yet, even as many women were seeking a collaborative couple approach to work, contingent work in the United States began to erode prior gains for many workers, men included. The collaboration between the sexes that is needed at home to nurture family members is still not apparent in the workplace, because the distribution of women in jobs that pay well falls far short of that of men. In fact, researchers note that what is perceived to be a necessary trait for a job is based on highly stereotypical assessments of both the job and gender. Skills required to perform one job (e.g., appliance sales*man*) may not be different from those required to perform a job dominated by women (e.g., cosmetics sales*woman*). Yet, many employers simply hire men for jobs because men are preferred by the employer. Furthermore, if a job attracts more women, incumbents begin to fear that womanly traits will come to characterize a job, demeaning men's skills and masculinity. Extensive research demonstrates that men are paid more simply because they are men, not because of special masculine traits. The endurance to keyboard all day at a computer is considered equal to the endurance and physicality required to be a truck driver. Unfortunately, however, so-called women's work has been traditionally devalued, regardless of the cultural or social context.

Whereas some people would once have easily reported that women's proper work was in the home, these individuals now suppress such comments. It is not that they want to be *politically correct* as much as they do not want to reveal their deeply held sexist or racist beliefs and therefore be *incorrect*. Aversive sexism, a covert form of discrimination, continues unabated in the arena of workplace discrimination. Women not only experience a work-related penalty (salary), but a personal cost (stress) from discrimination. Enforced heterosexuality in the workplace extracts a penalty from lesbian women workers, although preliminary evidence supports the notion that the primary discrimination that they face is gender based and not due to sexual orientation (Morgan & Brown, 1993). The very legal and social development that created opportunities for women has reinforced patterns of gender inequality. Such inequality in the workplace results in an unearned male privilege that men take for granted and women concede. When women do not conform to the stereotypes that define working women, they may experience a penalty and need to be put in their place through sexual harassment or bribery. The effect is to confer special privileges and status on male workers, such as those in the mines or military schools. Women who describe themselves as *careerist* tend to believe in the meritocracy of the workplace and are less likely to interpret sexual aggression as a function of male social dominance.

Although many people do not want to recognize their own disadvantages vis-à-vis others, women in nontraditional professions expose themselves to greater health risks. Women in both traditional and nontraditional jobs have similar responses to stress, however. Married women are less subjected to sexual harassment in private firms than single women. Women who cope most successfully with their stress are those who take an active approach to their problems—Super-Moms excluded. Women who manage careers and family successfully do so only if they have strong support systems. However, even women who think that they have good family support systems would be surprised to learn that male spouses, on average, perform less than half of the housework that women perform. Yet, given the obstacles women face at work and at home, children of working moms are no different psychologically than children of nonworking moms, perhaps due to the higher self-esteem that women in multiple roles exhibit.

Employment arrangements, such as nonstandard or contingent work, may ameliorate some work–family conflicts, but part-time work is not possible for single mothers who need income to support their families. Nonstandard work is less likely to offer benefits, such as health care or pensions, and such employment may affect women in retirement. Alternatively, some parents choose to work full time and withdraw from the home, practicing an emotional asceticism as they live a workaholic life-style.

Despite the multiple problems and issues that women confront in the workplace and the challenges of balancing work and family, women continue to enter and stay in the work force over the course of their lives. Movement to a more progressive society may be perceived as occurring at a glacial rate. Women continue, however, to press for greater equality in the home and family, and change is occurring, however slowly it appears.

KEY TERMS

Aversive racism (p. 210)
Brass ceiling (p. 215)
Contingent worker (p. 207)
Emic (p. 202)
Etic (p. 202)

Gendered division of labor (pp. 213–214)
Glass ceiling (p. 206)
Heilman's lack of fit model (p. 209)
Occupational segregation (p. 202)

Ostrich effect (p. 215)
Scarcity hypothesis (p. 223)
Tokenism (p. 213)

DISCUSSION QUESTIONS

1. Researchers have found that boys travel farther from home without an adult and are more familiar with and are more manipulative of their environment than girls. How might these early different experiences with the environment later influence one's relationship to choices of jobs and career?

2. To facilitate one's awareness of career options and eliminate the consequences of occupational sex typing, some researchers suggest that the socialization process of

young girls must be changed. How might this occur? What may be the long-term effects of the change? When should it begin?

3. Considering occupational segregation, what are the similarities and differences among White women, Black women, Latinas, and Asian women?

4. What are the paradoxes for women working part time? For which women is part-time work an entitlement; for whom is it a privilege? If part-time work is not a permanent solution to work–family conflicts, what is a solution, taking into account the emerging growth of contingent work?

5. What are the paradoxical effects of attractiveness for women in the workplace? Do you think that this paradox is true for all jobs, some jobs, certain jobs? What characteristics of a setting have to be present in order for Heilman's results to be generalizable? Consult research articles to support your position.

6. Would you choose to enter an extremely male dominated field? Why or why not? What would be the pluses and minuses after reading this chapter? Ask a 5-year-old girl what she intends to do with her life. How does she explain her choices?

7. Women today have a variety of career options from which they can choose. Ask an elderly aunt or grandmother what she would do if she had to do it all over again. Why would she make that particular choice? Was her choice congruent with your expectations? Why or why not?

SUGGESTED READINGS

Barker, K., & Christensen, K. (1998). *Contingent work: American employment relations in transition.* Ithaca, NY: ILR/Cornell University Press.

Barnett, R. C., & Rivers, C. (1996). *She works/he works: How two-income families are happier, healthier, and better off.* San Francisco: Harper San Francisco.

Franz, C. E., & Stewart, A. J. (1994). *Women creating lives: Identities, resilience, & resistance.* Boulder, CO: Westview.

Morgan, K. S., & Brown, L. S. (1993). Lesbian career development, work behavior, and vocational counseling. In L. D. Garnets & D. C. Kimmel (Eds.), *Psychological perspectives on lesbian and gay male experiences* (pp. 267–286). New York: Columbia University Press.

CHAPTER 8

SEXUALITY

Sex is not, of course, the only biological activity to be overloaded with social meaning; both eating and defecating spring to mind. However, it does appear to be the primary and principal act in most human societies.
—Tamsin Wilson

The most intense way we relate to another person is sexually. . . . Sex is not simply a matter of frictional force. The excitement comes largely in how we interpret the situation and how we perceive the connection to the other. . . . What is exciting is interpersonal; how the other views you, what attitude the actions evidence.
—Robert Nozick

Female sexuality is turned inside out from birth, so "beauty" can take its place, keeping women's eyes lowered to their own bodies, glancing up only to check their reflections in the eyes of men.
—Naomi Wolf

Perhaps the best we can do in a bad situation is to speak the truth of both sides of the reality that we live in by speaking the truths about female sexual desire—both the pleasures and the dangers—and voicing the real experiences that girls and women have in their bodies.
—Deborah Tolman

There is no one right pattern of sexual response. What works, what feels good, what makes us feel more alive in ourselves and connected with our partners is what counts.
—Boston Women's Health Book Collective, *Our Bodies, Ourselves* (1992)

It is hard to imagine a topic in which gender matters more than sexuality. If, as we have argued throughout this book, gender affects so many aspects of people's lives, then inevitably it influences people's patterns of sexual desire and arousal, their responses to sexual imagery, and their sexual attitudes and practices. Sexual behavior is a response to a complex mix of sociocultural, psychological, and biological forces and cannot be adequately understood in terms of any one force alone.

In this chapter, we consider physical aspects of sexuality, research on the prevalence of sexual behavior, sexual orientation, responses to sexual imagery (erotica and pornography), sexuality among the disabled, sexual dysfunction, and contraceptive use. But we begin with a discussion of how female sexuality has been socially constructed—how social realities affect how we identify, describe, classify, and ultimately experience sexuality.

SEXUALITY IN A SOCIAL CONTEXT

We take a social constructionist perspective on sexuality that focuses on the historical and the cultural context in which sexuality is learned and practiced. This view argues that all societies organize sexual desires, behaviors, and identities into approved (encouraged), permitted (tolerated), and tabooed (stigmatized and

punished) patterns (Lorber, 1994). These patterns are internalized by individuals, who often come to view them as natural and inevitable, even biological, in origin.

Both male and female sexuality are shaped and limited by society and culture. To be sure, societal messages to males about sex are value laden and conflicting and may pose many emotional and sexual difficulties for them (Kilmartin, 1994). But in most societies throughout history, sexuality is made problematic for females in ways that it is not for males (Gagnon, 1977; Gagnon & Simon, 1973). Some of these problems are due to the biological fact that sexual intercourse is far more consequential for females than males, because females alone bear children. But others result from social realities that, throughout history, males have defined sexually, including female sexuality, from their own perspective. Because of their greater physical, social, and economic power, men have been in positions to define when, how, with whom, and under what circumstances sex is appropriate, and they have often done so in ways that are disadvantageous to women. For example, the very definition of what constitutes sex reveals a deeply androcentric (male-centered) and heterosexist bias (see Box 8.1). In Western societies, "having sex" usually refers exclusively to vaginal intercourse: male penetration and ejaculation. Hugging, touching, and kiss-

BOX 8.1

Heterosexist Bias in the Study of Sexuality and Intimacy

Defining sex as vaginal intercourse reveals a heterosexist as well as androcentric bias. Many authors have recently challenged what they perceive is a deep and widespread heterosexist bias in the literatures of sexuality and intimate relationships, a bias that has contributed to gender inequality. Adrienne Rich (1980) forcefully criticized heterosexist bias in the social sciences in her influential and provocative essay "Compulsory Sexuality and Lesbian Existence." In this essay, she challenges the notion that women are "innately sexually oriented toward men" and that lesbian experiences are deviant, abhorrent, or insignificant. She argues that heterosexuality has been forcibly imposed on women as a means of assuring male rights of physical, economic, and emotional access. According to Rich,

> Women have married because it was necessary, in order to survive economically, in order to have children who would not suffer economic deprivation or social ostracism, in order to remain respectable, in order to do what was expected of women because coming out of "abnormal" childhoods they wanted to feel "normal" and because heterosexual romance has been represented as the great female adventure, duty, and fulfillment. (p. 82)

Rich challenges feminists to examine heterosexuality as an institution maintained by a variety of forces, including physical violence, and to question the extent to which it represents a choice or preference for women. One of the many ways that heterosexuality is made compulsory for women, according to Rich (1980), is the "rendering invisible of the lesbian possibility" (p. 78). Just as African American women have historically been deprived of a political existence through inclusion in the discourse on African American men (hooks, 1981), lesbian existence has often been yoked with, and eclipsed by, the gay male experience. Gay males receive much more attention from science and society than lesbians. Rich recognizes the shared experiences and common cause of gay men and lesbians, but insists on the acknowledgment of the differences between them, including men's economic and cultural privilege relative to women. Rich's analysis invites us to revisit the assumption that certain forms of sexual behavior are more "natural" than others and to consider, for example, whether we should question the causes and meanings of heterosexuality as well as homosexuality.

---

ing (which for some women are more stimulating than vaginal intercourse) do not count as having sex in this formulation. If they are considered at all, it is as *foreplay,* a preliminary, secondary, and ultimately dispensable set of activities.

As we shall see, males and females have been seen by scientists and lay people alike as representing very different modes of sexual behavior, attitudes, and feelings, with females generally seen as less sexual and more variable in their sexual desire, behavior, and responses than men. In many textbooks on the psychology of women, there are no chapters devoted exclusively to female sexuality, although there are often chapters on the sexual victimization of women (rape,

incest, and sexual harassment) and/or reproductive issues (pregnancy, menstruation, contraception, and sexually transmitted diseases)—the complications that sex presents for women.

We see the distinctions in the constructions of male and female sexuality quite clearly in the *double standard* by which the sexual feelings and behaviors of men and women are judged differently. We will discuss the double standard at length, because it is the lens through which virtually all aspects of female and male sexuality are seen and distorted. The double standard has several related strands, including the Madonna–whore dichotomy, the prizing of female virginity and fidelity, the differential socialization of boys and girls, and the relationship between physical attractiveness and sexuality in females. We will consider how such variables as race, class, and ethnicity affect sexuality. We will discuss these topics in turn, focusing on how they contribute to profound ambivalence about female sexuality among males and females alike.

The Double Standard: A Historical Perspective

It is important to note that the long-standing notion that women are less sexual than men has not always prevailed. Several of the ancient myths and images of women discussed in Chapter 2 depicted women as sexually desiring as well as desirable. In some preliterate societies, women's capacity for multiple orgasms so threatened men that they physically confined women to control their sexuality (Lorber, 1994). In Europe from the sixteenth through the eighteenth centuries, it was believed that women's orgasms were as necessary for conception as men's (McLaren, 1984).

We can trace modern sexual norms in the United States and Europe to the Victorian era in Great Britain, roughly the middle and later parts of the nineteenth century. During this time, science and medicine bolstered the prevailing Judeo-Christian ethic in actively discouraging the pursuit of sexual pleasure. Sexual intercourse was seen as physically and spiritually harmful to women, and good women were thought to lack interest in sex. Men, whose sexual passions were never questioned, were cautioned to be gentle and restrained with their virtuous wives. Apparently, many thought that they were doing their wives a favor by indulging their lustful feelings with the "other kind of women"—readily available prostitutes (Wade & Tavris, 1994). One estimate holds that there may have been as many as one prostitute for every 12 London men (Tannahill, 1980). Women were depicted in medical textbooks at that time as rarely interested in sex and often frigid and sexually dysfunctional. William Acton, an influential English physician, observed in 1857 "that the majority of women (happily for society) are not much troubled with sexual feeling of any kind" (Acton, as cited in Nevid, Fichner-Rathus, & Rathus, 1995, p. 18). The double standard of sexual

behavior and desire, a historic feature of Western civilization, was reinforced with religious, medical, and even legal backing.

During the early twentieth century, a number of forces acted to change sexual attitudes and behavior in the United States and Europe. Two world wars caused tremendous social upheaval and, with this, more sexual permissiveness. The revolutionary writings of Sigmund Freud put sexuality squarely at the center of personality development. Freud not only recognized female sexuality, but saw a link between taboos on women's sexual expression and constraints on their thinking (Wade & Tavris, 1994). Scientific advances in birth and sexually transmitted disease control removed many of the barriers to sexual activity. The sexual revolution of the 1960s and 1970s further eroded barriers to a wide range of sexual behaviors. During this time of relative economic affluence, political liberalism, and increased permissiveness, traditional prohibitions against casual sex collapsed. In the 1980s and 1990s, stagnant economic prospects, political conservatism, and the threat of AIDS and other sexually transmitted diseases brought with them a return to more conventional sexual behavior, at least among some groups (Centers for Disease Control, 1990). But some aspects of the sexual revolution have endured: a greater willingness to discuss sex openly, increasing tolerance of premarital sex, especially among younger teens, and the liberation of female sexuality, bringing female levels of premarital and even extramarital sexual behavior closer to that of males (Rathus, Nevid, & Fichner-Rathus, 1997). But even with the general decline of sexual repressiveness for men and women and increasing equality between the sexes, evidence abounds that the double standard of sexual behavior is still alive and well.

The Madonna–Whore Dichotomy. Perhaps nowhere is the double standard more stark than in the way in which women are divided into *Madonnas,* sexually chaste, desirable but not desirous women who "just say no" to sex, and *whores,* sexually wanton, promiscuous women who like sex and have many sexual partners (or just one under the wrong circumstances). These conflicting representations of women date back at least to the Middle Ages, the period in Western history from about 476 to 1450 to the present. The Roman Catholic Church, which dominated medieval Europe, regarded women as tainted by the sin of Eve, the seductress who used her sexuality to tempt men to their downfall. In the Eastern Church of Constantinople, the cult of the Virgin Mary flourished, which depicted Mary as the ideal image of womanhood: chaste, loving, pious, and saintly (Nevid et al., 1995).

The schism between the Madonna and the whore suggests a profound rejection of female sexuality in Western thought. There is no middle ground in this model, no way for a woman to engage in sex, especially outside of a committed love relationship, and still be a "good woman." Many writers have noted the large number of derogatory slang terms for women who like or have sex too much: sluts, tramps, pigs, and bimbos, to name a few. In both everyday and scientific usage, sexual women are often regarded as promiscuous, sex addicted, or nymphomaniacs, terms that imply moral turpitude, abnormality, even illness. There are no comparably pejorative terms for men who have sex outside of committed relationships or who like or have sex a lot. Indeed, such men are often admired and praised with names like Romeo, stud, playboy, stallion, and player.

Prizing of Female Virginity and Fidelity. Throughout most of the history of Western civilization, women have been regarded as the property of men. A female belonged first to her father and later to her husband. She was an item of exchange among men, valued chiefly for her worth as a sex object and reproducer. The influential anthropologist Lévi-Strauss (1969) suggests that the institution of marriage arose through the reciprocal exchange of women by tribal leaders to enlarge and strengthen kinship systems. The practice of trading women for other valued objects and influence has been credited for spawning the *ideology of virginity,* the notion that a woman is more valuable as a bride if she has never belonged to another man.

Virginity before marriage has been highly prized, but only for females. We can find evidence for this valuation in disparate times, places, and peoples, in myths, proverbs, and ancient and modern history. In Christianity, the virginity of Mary, the mother of God and central female figure, is an article of faith. In most European countries until modern times, a family's honor depended on the virginity of its unmarried females, and death was preferable to dishonor.

David Buss, a leading evolutionary psychologist, recently conducted a major survey of over 10,000 participants from 37 cultures on six continents about the characteristics that they sought in mates (Buss, 1989, 1994). He found that the value that people currently place on chastity, defined as premarital abstinence from sex, in prospective mates ranges from "indispensable" in China to "irrelevant" in Sweden and the Netherlands. In 62 percent of the 37 cultures, males valued chastity in mates more than females, and there was no culture in which the reverse was true.

Today, a woman's virginity can enhance her value in institutions ranging from marriage to prostitution. The long-standing African practice of female genital mutilation exists in large part to ensure virginity and improve marriageability (Toubia, 1993). The worth of virgins can be seen in the burgeoning sex trades of Asian countries like India, where virgins command three times the price of sexually experienced girls and women in part because of a common belief that sex with a virgin cures venereal diseases (Serril, 1993). The saying to the effect that "why buy the cow when you can get the milk for free" crudely captures the notion that "giving away sex" compromises a woman's worth and marriagability (Unger & Crawford, 1996).

If virginity before marriage has been (and in many cultures still is) valued in females, female fidelity after marriage can be a matter of life and death. Throughout most of history and in almost all cultures, adultery has been tolerated in men, but punished—sometimes by death—in women. Suzanne Frayser, an anthropologist, has studied sexual behavior in 62 different cultures. She found that in 26 percent of the cultures the husband alone is permitted sex outside of marriage, whereas there is no society in which only the wife is permitted extramarital sex (Frayser, 1985). More than half of the 48 societies for which data were available allowed the husband to kill his unfaithful wife. In modern societies, the price of even suspected infidelity for women is too often battering and even death.

While precise figures are impossible to determine and the gap between men and women has narrowed over recent years, almost all surveys of extramarital sexual behavior suggest that men are more likely to be unfaithful in marriage than women (Kinsey, Pomeroy, & Martin, 1948; Kinsey, Pomeroy, Martin, & Gebhard, 1953; Laumann, Gagnon, Michael, & Michaels, 1994). There is also recent evidence to suggest that men feel more justified in engaging in extramarital sex than women and feel less guilt and remorse about it (Margolin, 1989). Men's permissiveness with respect to their own extramarital behavior does not extend to their wives. In recent U.S. surveys, men place fidelity in marriage as the number one desired characteristic in a potential spouse. This finding has been replicated in other Western societies like Germany and the Netherlands (Buss, 1994). Women's attitudes toward extramarital sex appear to be more conservative and reflect an acute awareness of the double standard. A 1994 nonscientific sample of 7,000 female readers of *New Woman* found that the vast majority of both faithful and unfaithful wives believed that infidelity is morally wrong and that more than 90 percent of all wives believed that adulterous wives are judged more harshly than adulterous husbands.

Both sociobiological–evolutionary and learning theories have been advanced to explain why males seek to control female sexuality both before and after marriage. Social learning theories tend to focus on differing sexual socialization of boys and girls (to be discussed later), greater taboos and societal sanctions against adultery for women than for men, and historically fewer opportunities for women, especially homemakers, to have outside relationships. Sociobiologists argue that female monogamy is central to males because, unlike females, males can never be certain that they are the parents of offspring. Because males do not want to rear and support someone else's children, it is essential to them that their female mates do not stray. Whatever the explanation offered for the greater importance of female fidelity, there can be little question that males have sought to control the sexual behavior of females through the premiums placed on female chastity: virginity before marriage and fidelity within it.

Socialization in the Double Standard

Girls face the trials of exploring their sexuality in the shadow of realistic fears of pregnancy, interpersonal violence, and sexually transmitted diseases. Rates of adolescent pregnancy are higher in the United States than in virtually any other developed country (Jones, 1985). Girls and young women are more likely to be victims of rape than any other age group (Koss, Heise, & Russo, 1994). Females are much more likely—perhaps up to 15 times more likely—than males to contract AIDS through heterosexual sexual intercourse (Rodin & Ickovics, 1990). Young women, especially young women of color, are becoming the fastest growing segment of people infected with HIV (Ickovics & Rodin, 1992). Realistic fears of violence, victimization, pregnancy, and sexually transmitted diseases take on important social and psychological overlays through the processes by which boys and girls learn about sex.

From early childhood, traditional socialization encourages very different goals and roles for males and females in sexual relationships (Allgeier & McCormick, 1983; Lottes & Kuriloff, 1994). Compared to little boys, the names that little girls have for their sex organs are often vague (e.g., "down there" and "private parts") and are unlikely to inspire pride. During adolescence, boys are socialized to enjoy their sexuality, initiate sexual relations, and take pride in their sexual development, prowess, and experience. Girls, on the other hand, receive more complex, ambivalent, even negative messages about sex. Most girls learn to view the physical changes that occur during adolescence and the attention that these changes bring from boys and men with a mixture of pride, excitement, fear, and mistrust. The message that "good girls" don't want or have sex is not lost on girls, as research with diverse populations of girls and young women shows. In her interview study of 52 young women aged 16 to 24, Woodhouse (1982) found that many feared being seen as sexually promiscuous by their boyfriends. These girls equated femininity with the absence of sexual behavior, understanding that they were expected to display sexuality but "not use it directly." Tolman (1992) reports similar findings with samples of urban and suburban adolescent girls from middle to low socioeconomic classes.

With a different population, McCormick (1987) found that having sex was a male goal, whereas avoiding sex was a female goal. Subsequent studies have found that a young woman described as sexually experienced received less positive evaluations than a less experienced woman (Garcia, 1986) and that promiscuity is shameful only for women (Preston & Stanley, 1987). In a recent survey of high-socioeconomic status students enrolled in an elite private college, where the likelihood of sexual equality is relatively high, men reported more permissive sexual socialization than women from both parents and peers (Lottes & Kuriloff, 1994). Combining the results of many studies of gender differences in sexual attitudes using meta-analytic techniques (explained in Chapter 6), Oliver and Hyde (1993) found greater acceptance by males than females of all categories of sexual behavior, including casual premarital sex, sexual permissiveness, premarital sex in a committed relationship, and extramarital sex. Even in the 1990s, 30 years after the much vaunted sexual revolution, there is strong evidence of differential sexual socialization of males and females.

The Missing Discourse of Desire. Where is the good news for girls about sex in a society that tells them that sex, at least for them, is bad? Fine posed this and other related questions in a ground-breaking article in which she identified the "missing discourse of desire" in discussions of female, especially adolescent female, sexuality (Fine, 1988). Fine describes the extent to which schools, parents, and religious institutions unwittingly conspire to scare girls and young women away from sex by equating sexuality entirely with negative outcomes—violence, victimization, pregnancy, disease, immorality, and low-class behavior. What females hear most often from authority figures is that all males are out to take advantage of them sexually, with dire social, psychological, and physical consequences. It is their job to put the brakes on boys' behavior and, better yet, to gain their love and respect.

This is a heady assignment for girls and young women, and it is hardly surprising that there is so little room for desire in the discourse on female sexuality.

That sex is portrayed so negatively to girls obviously does not prevent them from having sex, as recent surveys consistently show (Zeman, 1990). But many girls experience a wide gulf between their sexual desire, intimacy needs, peer and media influences, and actual experience of sex on the one hand, and the profoundly negative messages about sex from authority figures on the other hand. According to Fine (1988), messages that acknowledge female desire and the attractions of sexual relationships while warning of realistic dangers might be more successful.

Sexual Scripts. What happens to female desire when it is shrouded in so many social, psychological, and physical dangers? From all directions and in many different ways, girls learn that the only way to have sex and still be a "good" girl is to fall in love and enter the romance and marriage market. Recent surveys suggest that today a majority of men and women endorse premarital sex in the context of long-term relationships or when the partners are described as being "in love" (Oliver & Hyde, 1993). The message to girls is that sex and love are inextricably intertwined, and love makes sex right. Debold, Wilson, and Malave (1993) write "Good girls have sex when it is 'true love.' As many girls and women come to find out, this is one of the biggest manipulations that boys and men figure out. 'Tell them that you love them and you can do anything.'" (p. 72).

Many boys hear a distinctly different message; that is, sex and love are contradictory, so they cannot love someone with whom they are sexual and cannot be sexual with someone whom they love (Kilmartin, 1994). We recognize this as a by-product of the Madonna–whore dichotomy discussed earlier. Many studies have shown that men are considerably more comfortable than women in viewing sex as a purely physical release or adventure, unconnected to relationships (Carrol, Volk, & Hyde, 1985).

In 1977, Laws and Schwartz coined the term *sexual scripts* to denote the unspoken, informal, but nonetheless critical rules and guidelines that men and women follow in their interactions with each other. The rules are backed by substantial social rewards for following the scripts and punishments for failing to follow them. In Western societies, at least for the dominant (white) subculture, women gain power and status through attracting and marrying a man of higher socioeconomic status. Her lures, or "weapons of weakness," are her innocence (expressed by her virginity, sincerity, and reasonableness), youth, and beauty (Debold et al., 1993). These scripts are taught literally from infancy by countless fairy tales and the cartoons and images that they inspire, and are reinforced later in the soap operas, romantic movies, and romance novels that are marketed so successfully to adolescent and adult women.

Nowhere are sexual scripts so transparent as in romance novels, whose authors literally follow a formula that permits few variations (Debold et al., 1993). Romance novels account for almost 40 percent of all mass-market paperback sales. The leading romance publisher, Harlequin Enterprises, has sales of 200 million books worldwide. They now appear in many languages, including Japanese and Greek, and have begun to appear in Eastern Europe (Linz, 1992). The readership for romance novels is almost exclusively women.

Sexual scripts specify that men choose whom they will ask for dates and initiate sexual contact, and women act as gatekeepers who accept or reject dates and forbid or permit sexual activity. If women forbid sex, men are encouraged to press their case and not take no for an answer, to overwhelm or ravish women. If sexual activity is permitted, men are scripted to take active, even aggressive, stances, whereas women are scripted to be passive, submissive, receptive, and, at most, "responsive."

Sexual Objects and Sexual Subjects

> *Beauty pornography . . . claims that women's "beauty" is our sexuality when the truth goes the other way around.*
> —Wolf, 1991, p. 136

A gendered perspective on sexuality requires that we consider physical attractiveness and body image in conjunction with female sexuality. Research suggests that, unlike most men, many women bring to their sexual relationships strikingly negative feelings about their looks generally and their bodies particularly (Debold et al., 1993; Wolf, 1991). Appraisals of female beauty, her own and others', play an important role in a woman's sexual desire, expression, and behavior and can profoundly affect her self-esteem and self-confidence.

A vital, nearly invariant part of sexual scripts in Western societies is that interesting, wonderful adventures and opportunities for romance and riches happen only to young, beautiful women. In myths, fairy tales, movies, and romance novels, even great works of literature, girls and women learn that heroes risk their lives only for beautiful women, and men learn that beautiful women will be their rewards for bravery and success (Debold et al., 1993).

Several lines of research consistently show that men value physical attractiveness in potential mates more than women do (Coombs & Kenkel, 1996; Hatfield & Sprecher, 1986). Attractiveness matters more to men in evaluating a prospective date, and especially a prospective sexual partner, than it does to women (Nevid, 1984). An interesting way of comparing the relative importance of physical beauty for men and women is to examine what qualities they seek and offer in personal advertisements, which are a particularly valuable source of information for researchers because, in them, advertisers make very explicit the qualities about themselves that they think others will find attractive and the characteristics about others that are most important to them. In almost all studies of personal advertisements, across time, geographic location, and social class of advertisers, researchers have found that, regardless of sexual orientation, men are more likely than women to seek physical attractiveness in their partners, and women are more likely than men to offer physical attractiveness to their partners (Deaux & Hanna, 1984; Harrison & Saaed, 1977).

From an evolutionary perspective, Buss's large-scale cross-cultural study of mating preferences and selection looked at gender differences in sexual attraction (Buss, 1994). Buss and other evolutionary theorists believe that how people select sexual partners is of great scientific importance because it reveals ancient, ancestral selection pressures on men and women and affects other components of the mating system, such as how women and men compete within their own sex for access to attractive mates. He found that in each of the 37 cultures studied, men placed a greater premium on physical attractiveness than did women. He concluded that "Contrary to thinking in the social sciences, it is now known that our desires in a mate are neither arbitrary nor infinitely variable across cultures" (p. 40). In other words, Buss (and other evolutionary theorists) believe that gender differences in mate selection leading males to prefer beautiful females are natural and biologically determined, rather than learned and culturally determined.

Buss's research has spawned a number of studies from an evolutionary perspective on what specific female characteristics men desire. Singh (1993) found that men particularly prize a low waist-to-hip ratio, which is regarded as an key indicator of fertility, and symmetrical body features, which is interpreted as a sign of good health. Other studies have found that facial features such as clear, smooth skin, clear eyes, lustrous hair, full lips, and an absence of sores or lesions are widely seen as attractive in females (Symons, 1979). Perrettet, cited in Brody (1994), studying British and Japanese men, found that female faces characterized by large eyes, high cheekbones, full lips, and narrow jaws were ranked as most attractive. Evolutionary theorists argue that these preferences are tied to disease resistance, health, fertility, and youth. It is important to note, however, that some evolutionary theory predictions about preferences for physical characteristics have not been borne out. For instance, the hypotheses that people would find most appealing those faces that displayed gender-appropriate characteristics was not supported in recent research. Whereas it was predicted that men with traditional hallmarks of male dominance, such as a big jaw, square face, and heavy brow, would favorably impress men and women, people of both sexes preferred feminine facial features in men as well as women (Angier, 1998). In fact, the significance of research on preferences for various facial and body features has not been established.

Whatever the source of male preferences for various physical attributes in females, females from childhood onward are bombarded with the message that their power and worth lie in their physical attractiveness and that they need to invest time and money in improving their looks. And they do not have to look hard to see how female beauty is defined. Media images have never been so available or explicit, and the standards of beauty that they promote have never been so high. Current images of beautiful female bodies, for instance, portray women as thin, tall, and athletically fit, with large breasts, a constellation of characteristics that is rare in any one individual. Today's women have omnipresent, graphic images of perfection against which to measure themselves and find themselves wanting. It is hard to overestimate the various effects of these standards on female sexuality, as we will see later when we consider the cases of physically disabled women.

Sex, Race, Ethnicity, Religion, and Class

If sexuality is socially constructed, we would expect to see a wide variety of sexual beliefs, attitudes, and practices around the world and within the United States, which is a nation of hundreds of different ethnic and religious groups. Indeed, there has been an explosion of recent research documenting a rich variety of sexual expression throughout the world and in the United States. This research confirms that there is no one male or female sexuality. People only come in different ethnicities, religions, races, and classes, and these variables interact with gender (and each other) to affect how sexuality is experienced and expressed.

Much recent research has focused on race in the study of sexual behavior and outcomes in the United States (Wyatt, 1994). Our society has long been preoccupied with race as it is defined in the popular culture, and has had an abiding interest in emphasizing racial differences in sexual practices. Historically, studies have compared African and European sexual practices (cf. Vontross, cited in Wyatt, 1994) and, more recently, Asian, African, and U.S. sexual practices (Chan, 1990). Because of widespread racial myths and stereotypes, along with real subcultural differences among broadly defined racial groups, many researchers have found it worthwhile to explore race as a variable in research on sexuality.

Recent studies of sexuality and ethnicity suggest that Asian American and Hispanic American teenagers are more sexually conservative than either their White (non-Hispanic) or African American counterparts. Among Chinese American college students at the University of California at Berkeley, Huang and Uba (1992) found that only 40 percent reported engaging in premarital intercourse. Research suggests that Mexican American women also initiate sexual intercourse later than their White (non-Hispanic) and African American peers (Slonim-Nevo, 1992) and that Mexican American male and female college students report having sex less frequently and with fewer partners than comparable Anglo students.

Race is a troublesome variable in sexuality research, as it is in so many other areas, in part because racial biases and stereotypes often affect the research questions asked and the findings reported. African American males and females are often stereotyped as being "more sexual" and "promiscuous" than White males and females, even by African Americans (Wyatt, 1994), despite the lack of good research evidence to support these stereotypes. For instance, research suggests that White women are more likely than minority women to reject religious teachings about contraception and adopt a recreational rather than procreational model of sex, to plan sexual activity in advance, and to engage in a wider variety of sexual practices (Laumann et al., 1994; Wyatt, 1994). White women also report having sex more often than minority women (Laumann et al., 1994). Clearly, what constitutes promiscuity is in the eye of the beholder.

Undoubtedly, some of the reasons that such myths and stereotypes persist have to do with the different consequences of sex for White and some minority populations. Larger percentages of African American than White teenagers become pregnant and have babies outside of marriage (U.S. Department of Health and Human Services, 1992). Minority women in the United States have higher rates of abortions than

White women (Henshaw & Silvurman, 1988). African American women are more likely to contract AIDS than White women (U.S. Department of Health and Human Services, 1992b). Minority and poor women are also more at risk than White women for other sexually transmitted diseases, including syphilis, gonorrhea, genital herpes, pelvic inflammatory disease, and chlamydia.

In interpreting these findings, it is critical to note that race is usually correlated (or confounded) with other major variables, most notably social class indicators, such as education level, occupation, and income. In the United States, most racial minorities are disproportionately poor. Wyatt (1994) notes that the differences in the ages of first sexual intercourse between White and African American girls disappear when social class is taken into account. Similarly, racial differences in unintended pregnancies, sexually transmitted diseases, and abortions may be more properly attributed to social class, life experiences, religious beliefs, and ethnic–cultural values than to race. For instance, it is Catholic doctrine that the purpose of sex is procreation, and contraceptive use for any reason is itself sinful. The low rates of contraceptive use among Hispanic and African American girls relative to White girls may be due not to lack of knowledge or concern about birth control, but rather to traditional religious beliefs and conservative value systems.

Moreover, when racial differences in sexual behaviors or outcomes are found, the assumption may be that there is something inherent in racial group membership that causes these behaviors or outcomes. Often, little consideration is given to how or why gross racial categorizations, which identify a superficial common dimension of people who vary along so many important dimensions, can explain something as complex as sexuality. Finally, a focus on racial differences inevitably risks exaggerating the differences and downplaying the similarities, perhaps even suggesting that the races are more different in their sexuality that they are similar. In fact, within-group variation is much larger than between-group variation. Moreover, recent surveys suggest that the races and ethnic groups in the United States are more similar than different in their sexual behavior and are becoming more similar over time.

SCIENCE STUDIES SEXUALITY

Until the middle of this century, sexuality was considered an inappropriate topic for scientific study, and there was little research into the nature and extent of human sexuality. Since the publication of Alfred Kinsey's first survey of sexual behavior, entitled *Sexual Behavior in the Human Male,* in 1948, followed by *Sexual Behavior in the Human Female* in 1953, the study of sexuality has become respectable and indeed quite popular in recent years.

Researchers in human sexuality use the same panaply of research methods that all scientists use. As in all areas of research, the choice of research methods depends on the research question and hypothesis (if any). Much of the research in human sexuality to date has focused on one of two areas: (1) determining the prevalence of various sexual practices and desires among different groups and (2) studying patterns of sexual arousal. Prevalence has most often been studied in the field by means of the survey, and arousal by means of physiological measures in the laboratory. We will consider the prevalence issue first.

Sex by the Numbers: United States Sex Life from World War II to the Present

The first major survey of sexual behavior was conducted from 1938 to 1949 by Alfred C. Kinsey, a biologist. Kinsey and his colleagues interviewed 5,300 males and 5,940 females about their sexual behavior, including premarital and extramarital sex, masturbation, responses to erotica, incidence of orgasm, and homosexual activity. Kinsey's was not a scientific survey, meaning that there was no attempt to gain a sample that was truly random or representative of the people in the United States as a whole. He recruited what is known as a convenience sample—volunteer members of a variety of organizations and institutions (such as college fraternities and sororities, boardinghouses, and

prisons) who were willing to discuss their sex lives in detail. Certain groups of people, such as the elderly, ethnic and religious minorities, and those living in rural areas, were underrepresented. People who were especially sexually permissive and adventurous may have been overrepresented. In addition, Kinsey's respondents, both males and females, were all interviewed by male interviewers. Women and other subgroups may not have felt comfortable reporting certain kinds of information to male interviewers.

It is generally accepted today that Kinsey's survey methods were quite flawed. Nonetheless, Kinsey's was a heroic first effort to understand human sexuality, and his surveys had several methodological strengths. For instance, he was sensitive to research concerns such as reliability and validity of reports. Furthermore, whereas his sample was not representative of the U.S. population, it was broad based and included many people of different ages, socioeconomic groups, and geographic localities.

What did Kinsey find? The Kinsey studies shocked America in mid-century by describing a sexually permissive society in which masturbation and homosexual acts were far more common and fidelity in marriage less common than most people believed. With a few notable exceptions, Kinsey's results have been supported by several more recent surveys using different populations and methods and conducted by university researchers (see, for example, Janus & Janus, 1993; Wyatt, 1989), research foundations like the *Playboy* Foundation, and such magazines as *Redbook* and *Cosmopolitan*.

The first large-scale *scientific* survey of sexual behavior in the United States was published by University of Chicago scientists Laumann, Gagnon, Michael, and Michaels in 1994. This recent survey, in which all respondents were both interviewed and administered questionnaires, is the first major survey of the sexual practices of adults in the United States to use a form of probability or random sampling, meaning that every individual (within certain restrictions, such as ages between 18 and 59) had an equal chance of being selected to participate. Almost 80 percent of all people contacted agreed to be interviewed and to fill out the questionnaires, a remarkably high return rate for any kind of survey, particularly one that measures private behavior such a sexual practices.

With some important exceptions, this recent study of 3,432 cases paints a picture of a far more sexually conservative United States than Kinsey, *Playboy,* and most other earlier surveys (Laumann et al., 1994). What do sex surveys from Kinsey et al. to Laumann et al. suggest about sexual behavior in the United States, from mid-century to the present?

Overall, surveys of sex in the United States show a trend over 40 years toward a higher incidence of all kinds of heterosexual activity, in virtually all age groups, especially younger ones, and a greater variety of sexual activity. With only minor variations across race and ethnicity, religious affiliation, and level of education, U.S. adults between the ages of 18 and 59 fall into three groups: about one-third have sex at least twice a week, one-third a few times a month, and one-third a few times a year or not at all.

Sex before marriage, once uncommon in females, has become the norm for both sexes, and attitudes toward premarital sex are generally permissive. Still, as measured by the number of sex partners that men and women have over a lifetime, sex has not become much more casual or "promiscuous"; the average woman in the United States reports two sexual partners over a lifetime and the average man, six. Overwhelmingly, Americans' favorite sex act is vaginal intercourse, with 96 percent reporting this as "very or somewhat appealing." Watching one's partner undress is rated second, and oral sex is listed as a distant third (Laumann et al., 1994). The trend is also toward more permissive attitudes about homosexuality, but not a greater incidence of homosexual activity itself. In fact, recent surveys have failed to support Kinsey's often repeated finding that one in ten men is homosexual. The general increase in sexually permissive attitudes apparently does not extend to extramarital sex, although it may be particularly difficult to measure the incidence of this almost universally proscribed behavior. Estimates of the incidence of extramarital sex vary widely from survey to survey and are regarded as particularly suspect.

Sex in and out of Marriage

Premarital Sex.   Perhaps nowhere was the sexual revolution of the 1970s more obvious than in the increased rates of premarital sexual intercourse, especially for girls and women, from the time of Kinsey's work to the present. Kinsey found that 77 percent of single men but only 20 percent of single women had experienced intercourse by age 20. Among those still single at age 25, 83 percent of men and 33 percent of women had engaged in sex. In the early 1970s, the *Playboy* survey found that, among people under 25, 95 percent of men and 81 percent of women reported having premarital coitus, a striking increase for women (Hunt, 1974). Rates of premarital sex have continued to climb since the *Playboy* survey (Janus & Janus, 1993), although there is some evidence that sexual activity is beginning to decline among unmarried women on college campuses in response to fears of AIDS and increased political conservatism (Gerrard, 1987).

Not only has premarital sex become the norm for men and women in the United States, but people are also having sex at younger ages. At the time of the Kinsey surveys, only 7 percent of White females had sex by age 16, but in 1988 Zeman found that 27 percent of females had sex by age 15 (Zeman, 1990). Estimates of the average age of first intercourse today are put at 16 for girls and 15.5 for boys (U.S. Department of Health and Human Services, 1992b). Some surveys suggest that African American adolescents begin having intercourse about two years before White adolescents (Brooks-Gunn & Furstenberg, 1989; Laumann et al., 1994).

Several investigators have recently tried to identify some of the factors associated with premarital sexual intercourse, especially among young teens. One consistent finding is that adolescents whose parents are separated or divorced engage in sex earlier than their peers from homes with both parents present (Coles & Stokes, 1985). Several explanations have been offered for this finding. It is possible that parents whose own relationships have dissolved lack the authority to restrict their children's sexual behavior. Perhaps some divorced parents, themselves sexually active, convey more sexually permissive attitudes to their children. Finally, single parents may supervise their children's behavior less closely due to many other demands on their time (Nevid et al., 1995). Other factors associated with early sexuality among adolescents are poor academic performance and low career aspirations, father absence, and permissive attitudes about sexuality (Keith et al., 1991).

Marital Sex.   Sexuality in marriage has itself undergone something of a transformation since the Kinsey surveys of the 1940s and 1950s. In general, recent research evidence suggests that the frequency, duration, and kinds of sexual activity have increased in marriage. For example, Kinsey reported that married couples between the ages of 16 and 25 had the most frequent sex (2.45 times per week), with the frequency of relations steadily declining to the oldest category of respondents, between ages 55 and 60 (0.50 times per week). In 1974, the *Playboy* survey estimated frequency among the youngest group at 3.25 times per week, with those 55 and older reporting having sex once per week (Hunt, 1974). Regardless of the couple's age, the frequency of sexual intercourse appears to decline with the number of years married (Blumstein & Schwartz, 1990).

Sex in marriage is rated as highly pleasurable by men and women. The *Playboy* survey found that, depending on age, from 94 to 99 percent of men rate marital coitus as very or mostly pleasurable (Hunt, 1974), with ratings dropping off very little with age. Using reported incidence of orgasm as a measure of sexual satisfaction in marriage, satisfaction has increased from the time of Kinsey's survey to the present, with more married women now reporting always having orgasms during coitus and fewer women now reporting never having orgasms during coitus.

One of the most dramatic changes in marital sex from the Kinsey to the *Playboy* surveys was in the duration of marital coitus, from about two minutes (Kinsey) to ten to thirteen minutes (*Playboy*). Women are more likely to experience orgasm during marriage than during premarital sexual activity. In the *Redbook* survey, over one-third of respondents said that they never had orgasms during premarital intercourse,

about a third reported achieving orgasms most of the time, and less than 7 percent said that they experienced orgasm all the time. Among married women, only 7 percent reported never experiencing orgasm during coitus, 48.2 percent reported achieving orgasm most of the time, and 15 percent reported experiencing orgasm all the time.

The increased sexual interest and pleasure that couples, especially women, apparently now find in marriage have been variously attributed to better birth control methods, more information about how to obtain sexual satisfaction, and freer attitudes about sex, especially about women's sexual expression (Hunt, 1974). Sexual pleasure in marriage consistently correlates positively with overall marital satisfaction, with wives' open communication about sexual needs and feelings, and with their taking an active role in sex (Tavris & Sadd, 1977).

Extramarital Sex.   Unquestionably, one of Kinsey's most surprising and provocative findings was that more than 50 percent of all married men and about 26 percent of all married women reported engaging in sexual intercourse at least once outside of marriage (Kinsey et al., 1948, 1953). Most of the more recent surveys suggest that the rates of extramarital sex are not as high as Kinsey indicated. In fact, extramarital sex may be the type of sexual relation that has been least affected by the sexual revolution. In the Lauman et al. (1994) study, nearly 75 percent of married men and 85 percent of married women reported that they have never been unfaithful. These figures are comparable to those obtained with probability samples in surveys in the late 1980s by the National Opinion Research Center (NORC), which report that 96 percent of the married respondents were faithful in the preceding year, suggesting that married men and women have particularly high rates of monogamy (Laumann et al., 1994). Blumstein and Schwartz (1990) found that among married couples 11 percent of husbands and 9 percent of wives reported at least one extramarital relationship within the past year.

Magazine surveys, which use convenience samples of interested readers, tend to show somewhat higher levels of nonmonogamy among women. In the *Redbook* magazine sample, which polled 100,000 married women, 29 percent admitted having at least one extramarital experience (Tavris & Sadd, 1977). More recently, *Cosmopolitan* magazine surveyed female sexuality and reported that 39 percent of married women admitted to infidelity, most with just one man.

It is important to keep in mind that regular readers of most magazines like *Playboy, Redbook,* and *Cosmopolitan* are often younger, better educated, and more affluent than the general population and may have more liberal attitudes toward sex. Moreover, volunteer respondents to a magazine sex survey may be more sexually permissive and adventurous than a random sample of respondents. It is also worth noting that, unlike premarital and marital sex, extramarital sex is still considered highly undesirable behavior, especially for women. Given the strong taboos against extramarital sex, it is unclear to what extent women (and men) answer truthfully even anonymous, confidential survey questions about infidelity. Most investigators in this area caution that actual rates of extramarital sexual intercourse are probably underreported to an unknown extent.

Taken together, what the surveys suggest about extramarital sex in the United States is that it is relatively uncommon and that, unlike premarital and marital sex, it has not increased among most groups since Kinsey's time. The one exception may be younger married women, especially those employed outside the home, whose rates of infidelity are approaching those of men. Nonetheless, all surveys show that extramarital sexual activity is still more common among men than women, and, as we noted in the section on the double standard, it is more accepted for men by both men and women. In Kinsey's survey, despite the fact that twice as many men admitted being unfaithful, women's infidelity was more likely to be cited as the reason for divorce. Among divorced respondents in that survey, 27 percent of women compared to 51 percent of men reported that their spouses' infidelity was grounds for the divorce.

What are the factors related to extramarital activity? People who are unfaithful report being less committed to and less satisfied with their marriages. They are also more likely to have friends who have had affairs (Nevid et al., 1995). Among women, extramarital activity is related to employment outside the home (Tavris & Sadd, 1977).

People engaged in extramarital sex have offered many reasons for their affairs. Some report that they are not fulfilled by their marital relations, and others cite boredom, curiosity, or strong attraction to another. For others, nonsexual motivations like retaliation for past injustice or hostility are given (Nevid et al., 1995). Men and women offer different reasons for engaging in extramarital sex. Men (75 percent) are more likely than women (55 percent) to offer a desire for sexual excitement as a justification for the affair, whereas women (77 percent) are more likely than men (43 percent) to offer "falling in love" as a reason for extramarital sex (Glass & Wright, 1992). It is possible that men and women offer different reasons for their affairs because they have been socialized to explain their actions differently: it is more socially acceptable for men to cite sexual motives and for women to invoke romantic love to justify sexual relations.

Sexual Orientation

Sexual orientation is usually defined as the focus of one's sexual and romantic desires and behaviors toward members of one's own gender, the other gender, or both. The past two decades have seen a surge of scholarly interest in the questions of sexual orientation and sexual identity: why are some people gay, straight, or bisexual? Is sexual orientation learned or is it inborn? Once established, can it be changed? What defines sexual orientation: behavior and/or desire? Do people fall into discrete categories that differ qualitatively from each other, or is sexuality on a continuum, with people possessing degrees of "straightness" and "gayness"? What proportions of men and women fall into each category? Are certain orientations healthier than others?

Obviously, complete discussions of these issues go beyond the scope of this chapter. But one's sexual identity and orientation are such central parts of one's self-concept that they merit some treatment here. We explore the position that sexual orientation and identity, like all of sexuality, is socially constructed. To say that sexual orientation is socially constructed is not to deny a role for biological factors in influencing sexuality (see Chapter 3 for a discussion of biological correlates of sexual orientation). All it means in this context is that defining heterosexuality, homosexuality, and bisexuality is itself complex because the definitions will vary with cultures, communities, and situations. Sexual acts that in some cultures and at some times will be labeled homosexual will not be labeled as such in other cultures and at other times. For example, there is an initiation rite among Sambians of the New Guinea highlands in which adolescent boys perform fellatio on the adult men of the village because of a belief that young boys grow into adulthood only through the ingestion of semen (Money, 1990). Would it be correct to regard these as homosexual acts? Heterosexual men who have been separated from women for long periods of time, as in prison, sometimes engage in sex with men. Have these men turned gay? If a woman has sex with men but fantasizes about having sex with women, what is her sexual orientation? Among some ethnic groups, men who are the insertive partners in sexual intercourse with other men do not identify themselves as homosexual. How should they be identified? As these examples suggest, the relationship among sexual acts, sexual identity, and sexual community is variable and complex. The chief advantage of a constructionist perspective on sexual orientation is the new questions it encourages us to ask.

Most surveys that have probed sexual orientation have grappled at least to some extent with these issues of definition and identity. Not surprisingly, the first to do so was Kinsey, who yet again shocked the nation with explosive findings on sexual orientation from his surveys of men and women. He found that, among males between the ages of 20 and 35, 18 to 42 percent had at least some homosexual experience. Between 3 percent and 16 percent of males in this age group had exclusively homosexual experiences (Kinsey et al., 1948). For women, the figures were somewhat lower, with 11 to 20 percent of the women between the ages of 20 and 35 reporting at least some homosexual experience, and 2 to 3 percent of females in this age category reporting exclusively homosexual experiences

(Kinsey et al., 1953). It has long been suspected that biases in Kinsey's samples, especially of men, accounted in part for the strikingly high level of homosexuality. For example, a higher proportion of male prisoners served as respondents than exist in the general population (Nevid et al., 1995). But even correcting for this bias, the proportion of homosexuality reported by Kinsey was considered startling.

Prevalence of Gay, Lesbian, and Bisexual Sexual Orientation.   In his surveys, Kinsey and his associates went against the prevailing views of the day, that homosexuality and heterosexuality were discrete categories, by measuring sexual orientation on a seven-point continuum, with heterosexual and homosexual at the poles. He also recognized that how people were defined depended on what particular questions were asked. For example, asking people if they had ever reached orgasm with a member of the same sex might exaggerate levels of homosexuality, because many more people have a few same-sex encounters in adolescence than identify as homosexual in adulthood.

More recent surveys, including one by the Kinsey Institute, tend to report a lower incidence of homosexuality among both males and females, especially if single or sporadic episodes of adolescent experimentation are excluded. Several recent, large-scale studies of sexual orientation in the United States, Britain, and France put the estimates of adult male homosexuality in the range of 1 to 4.1 percent (Barringer, 1993; Billy, Tanfer, Grady, & Keplinger, 1993). The researchers in the recent Laumann et al. study (1994) divided their questions about sexual orientation into what they believe are three basic underlying dimensions: sexual behavior, sexual desire, and sexual identity. Over 4 percent of the women and 9 percent of the men reported engaging in some type of sexual activity with a member of the same sex. When asked about sexual attraction to same-sex others and the appeal of sex with a same-sex partner, about 5 percent of men and women reported some same-sex attraction and finding the idea of sex with a same-sex partner somewhat appealing. But less than 3 percent of the men and 1.5 percent of the women surveyed reported some level of homosexual or bisexual identity. Clearly, these numbers are well below Kinsey's figures. But they do suggest that estimates of gay and bisexual identity depend, among other things, on whether behavior, desire, or identity is explored. And depending on how bisexual is defined, there are at least between 1.5 to 7.5 million bisexual people over the age of 18 in the United States, between 1 percent and 4 percent of the adult population.

Bisexuality.   Recent research suggests that **bisexuality** may be understudied and underreported in surveys (Garber, 1995). In part, this is because bisexuality is particularly complex and fluid, with sexual orientations changing over time and attraction to both sexes often unequal. Furthermore, people may be reluctant to embrace the label of bisexuality in surveys because bisexual individuals have often been rejected and stereotyped by both gay and straight people. Bisexuals are seen by some as straight people who are indulging their taste for the exotic and forbidden and by others as gay people without the courage to reveal their sexuality openly. Since the AIDS epidemic, the term *bisexual* is used more often and has taken on special meaning because bisexuals are seen by many as the conduits by which AIDS can spread, particularly from gay men to heterosexuals. This concern on the part of society, and the scapegoating of bisexuals in its wake, has had the effect of politically mobilizing bisexuals, resulting in new visibility and new, more positive images.

The new scholarship on bisexuality takes a more affirmative approach to this sexual orientation. Ronald Fox (1996) attributed this new willingness to acknowledge bisexuality as a valid sexual orientation to the elimination of homosexuality as a clinical diagnostic category, which led to the development of lesbian and gay identity theory, and to a critical reexamination of the dichotomous model of sexual orientation, which led to the articulation of a multidimensional model of sexual orientation.

Causes of Sexual Orientation   What causes sexual orientation? Of course, as Box 8.2 makes clear, this question typically interrogates the causes of homosexuality, not heterosexuality. Most researchers today believe that sexual orientation is determined by a com-

plex interplay of biological—genetic and hormonal—and psychological and social factors (Rathus et al., 1997). Biological theories of sexual orientation are discussed in Chapter 3. In this chapter, we consider nonbiological theories and some of the research that they have inspired.

An important class of psychological theories of sexual orientation are psychoanalytic theories. Freud believed that infants' sexuality is undifferentiated and that children are open to all forms of sexual stimulation, a condition he called *polymorphously perverse* (Rathus et al., 1998). Freud posited the existence of a "bisexual disposition which we maintain to be characteristic of human beings" (Freud, 1931, p. 255), a disposition that he believed manifested itself more commonly in females than males. Thus, in Freud's view, we all have the potential to be heterosexual, homosexual, or bisexual in our sexual orientation.

As noted in Chapter 3, under the normal course of development, a child is expected to develop a heterosexual orientation. According to Freud, gay sexual orientation is the result of problematic psychosexual development, specifically failure to resolve the Oedipus complex by identifying with the parent of the same gender, with resulting fixation at the phallic stage of development. For males, unresolved castration anxiety is also believed to play a role in gay male sexual orientation. Freud's view of female homosexuality is less well developed. Essentially, he theorized that girls become envious of boys' penises when they discover they do not have penises of their own. In Freud's view, if a girl fails to resolve her *penis envy* by supplanting her desire for a penis with the desire to marry a man and bear children—the ultimate penis substitute—she will develop a lesbian sexual orientation.

Generally, psychoanalytic theories of sexual orientation tend to focus on the family dynamics in "causing" gay, especially gay male, sexual orientation. For example, the classic pattern fostering gay male sexual orientation features a dominant, possessive mother and a distant, aloof father. The parallel pattern supposedly fostering lesbian development is a rejecting, unconcerned mother and a distant or even absent father. Some retrospective interview studies, such as

BOX 8.2

The Heterosexuality Questionnaire

The purpose of this questionnaire is to examine the manner in which heterosexual norms and assumptions affect how gay men and lesbians are studied and represented. You may recognize these items from the questionnaire as parodies of the ones that gay men and lesbians are asked all the time about their sexual orientation and lives.

THE HETEROSEXUAL QUESTIONNAIRE

Instructions: Heterosexism is a form of bias in which heterosexual norms are used in studies of homosexual relationships. Gay men and lesbians are seen as deviating from a heterosexual norm, and this often leads to marginalization and pathologizing of their behavior.

Read the following questionnaire with this definition in mind and respond to the questions.

1. What do you think caused your heterosexuality?
2. When and how did you first find out that you were heterosexual?
3. Is it possible that your heterosexuality is just a phase that you may grow out of?
4. Is it possible that your heterosexuality stems from a neurotic fear of others of the same sex?
5. If you have never slept with a person of the same sex, is it possible that all you need is a good gay lover?
6. Do your parents know that you are straight? Do your friends and/or roommate(s) know? How did they react?
7. Why do you insist on flaunting your heterosexuality? Can't you just be who you are and keep it quiet?

8. Why do heterosexuals place so much emphasis on sex?
9. Why do heterosexuals feel compelled to seduce others into their life-style?
10. A disproportionate majority of child molesters are heterosexual. Do you consider it safe to expose children to heterosexual teachers?
11. Just what do men and women *do* in bed together? How can they truly know how to please each other, being so anatomically different?
12. With all the societal support that marriage receives, the divorce rate is spiraling. Why are there so few stable relationships among heterosexuals?
13. Statistics show that lesbians have the lowest incidence of sexually transmitted diseases. Is it really safe for a woman to maintain a heterosexual life-style and run the risk of disease and pregnancy?
14. How can you become a whole person if you limit yourself to compulsive, exclusive heterosexuality?
15. Considering the menace of overpopulation, how could the human race survive if everyone were heterosexual?
16. Could you trust a heterosexual therapist to be objective? Don't you feel she or he might be inclined to influence you in the direction of her or his own leanings?
17. There seem to be very few happy heterosexuals. Techniques have been developed that might enable you to change if you really want to. Have you considered trying aversion therapy?
18. Would you want your child to be heterosexual, knowing the problems that she or he would face?

Source: From *Sex and Gender: Student Projects and Exercises* (pp. 35–36), by C. A. Rickabaugh, 1998, New York: McGraw-Hill. Copyright 1998 by The McGraw-Hill Companies. Reprinted with permission.

those of psychoanalyst Irving Bieber in 1962 with gay men and of psychiatrist Charlotte Wolff in a rare early study of lesbians, have been interpreted as supporting such theories (Wolff, 1971). But these studies are fraught with methodological problems, and evidence

for this view is generally not strong. It cannot be determined, for example, whether a son's sexual orientation alienated the father or whether the father's hostile behavior engendered gay sexual orientation. Moreover, gay men and lesbians come from a variety of family backgrounds exhibiting many different kinds of patterns (Rathus et al., 1997).

Sociological theories of sexual orientation emphasize how social structures and forces in society influence our sexual desire and behavior. Conceptions and definitions of heterosexuality, homosexuality, and bisexuality are the products of particular cultures and have been shown to vary widely across different cultural groups and shape their behavior. In exploring the social origins of same-sex attraction, sociologist Reiss suggests that the power and dominance hierarchies in society influence patterns of sexual orientation. In this view, male-dominant societies with highly rigid gender roles should show the greatest prevalence of gay sexual orientation. For a variety of reasons, some young boys may find it difficult to observe, learn, and/or embrace such a narrow, highly defined role. In such societies, there will always be a certain number of males who either do not like such roles or cannot completely conform to them and who will reject aspects of the role, including heterosexual behavior. Societies with less rigid roles are more flexible and indulgent about the expression of different types of sexuality (Hyde, 1996b; Reiss, 1986).

Learning theories have traditionally focused on the role of reinforcement in the development of sexual orientation, especially the important determining role of pleasurable early experiences with the same or the other sex. But many people have early pleasurable experiences with the same sex and go on to have heterosexual sexual orientations. Moreover, many gay people report that they were aware of their attraction to same-sex others before their first sexual encounter.

Recently, social psychologist Darryl Bem offered a provocative developmental explanation for same- and other-sex sexual orientation in a gender-polarizing society like ours, based on the importance of biological and experiential variables. Bem's (1996) theory proposes a developmental sequence that begins with genes and prenatal hormones, which do not code for sexual orientation per se but for childhood temperaments, such as aggression or activity level. The child's temperament predisposes him or her to enjoy some activities more than others, to prefer gender-conforming or gender-nonconforming activities and same-sex or other-sex playmates. Gender-conforming children will feel different from other-sex peers, whereas gender-nonconforming children will feel different from same-sex peers. These feelings of dissimilarity or unfamiliarity produce heightened autonomic arousal, which is then transformed in later years into erotic–romantic attraction. In this way, "the exotic becomes erotic." Bem's hypothesis, that a mediating personality variable might account for the observed correlations between biological variables and sexual orientation, is intriguing. It is consistent with some of the existing evidence generated by both the biological theorists, who can point to empirical links between biology and sexual orientation, and the social constructionists, who can point to historical and anthropological research suggesting that sexual orientation is a culture-bound notion. It is as yet unclear whether the theory will generate new research that supports its predictions, but the theory has already come under fire for failing to clearly define key terms such as exoticism, to present new data to support the theory, and to consider evidence that does not support the theory. Moreover, Bem's claim that his theory applies equally to both sexes has been questioned, and it has been argued that the theory particularly neglects and misrepresents women's experiences (Peplau, Garnets, Spalding, Conley, & Veniegas, 1998). One psychologist expresses her views on the origins and meanings of sexual orientation in Box 8.3.

In short, it is not at all clear that there is a single cause of sexual orientation. Sexual orientation, comprising as it does a complex array of desires, behaviors, identities, and commitments, is an unlikely candidate for a simple explanation. For example, one study of bisexual individuals suggests that different components of an individual's sexual orientation need not coincide; for example, some bisexual respondents reported that they were more erotically attracted to one sex and more romantically attracted to the other (Weinberg, Williams, & Pryor, 1994). There is not one kind of lesbian or gay man, or straight man or woman, or bisexual man or woman, and the complexity and variability of our sexual orientations need to be better reflected in research.

BOX 8.3

Sexual Orientation: Fixed or Fluid?

Of course public debate has raged in recent years, driven largely by contentions of the Religious Right that homosexuality is an immoral behavior that an individual can choose not to engage in. On the other hand, gay/lesbian/bisexual rights activists have claimed that sexual orientation is not a choice, and persons of diverse sexual orientations should not be condemned or denied civil rights on the basis of their orientation. Thus, in the public arena, the debate has revolved around the question of choice.

In my opinion we don't fully understand the forces that shape sexual orientation, though they are undoubtedly complex. Questions about the fixedness or fluidity have not been given much scientific consideration, but it appears that for some individuals sexual orientation is somewhat fluid. There appears to be some gender difference here, with sexual orientation being somewhat more fluid among some women than among men in general. Some have suggested that this means that biological variables may play a more important role in the etiology of sexual orientation for men than for women. This is not necessarily the case. We know that gender roles are generally more fixed for males

than for females and that females are afforded more flexibility in terms of gender-role behavior than are males. In fact, for developing males, there is more negative social judgment for gender-inappropriate behavior than there is for females. It is possible that some of the same mechanisms at work for gender-role development also impact the development of sexual orientation, and this could explain the apparent gender difference in fluidity of sexual orientation.

Many questions remain: Is it possible that there are multiple paths to diverse sexual orientations and that individuals may vary greatly in the fluidity of their sexual orientation? Might there be clear gender differences in how sexual orientation develops and is expressed? How can we explain the phenomenon of women who have led heterosexual lives electing in their later years to adopt a lesbian or bisexual orientation? What, if any, is the relationship between scientific questions, such as whether or not sexual object preference is a choice, and the social treatment of diverse individuals?

—Maryka K. Biaggio

Source: Printed by permission of Maryka K. Biaggio. Piece not previously published.

Sexual Practices

In this section, we consider the role of gender in the appeal and practice of various sex acts. A summary of the percentages of respondents reporting various sexual activities in three prominent sex surveys spanning almost 50 years is presented in Table 8.1.

Masturbation. The word **masturbation** comes from the Latin *masturbari,* which combines the roots for "hand" and "to defile" (Nevid et al., 1995). Masturbation is solitary sexual activity, practiced by means of manual stimulation of the genitals, with or without the aid of artificial stimulation. Masturbation, like all forms of nonprocreational sex, was denounced by

Jews and Christians, at least in part because it did not lead to an increase in their numbers at a time when fecundity was an issue of survival of communities. The ancient notion that masturbation is defiling oneself through one's hand and warrants condemnation on moral, religious, and medical grounds persisted until very recently. Even today, masturbation is considered such a sensitive issue that all information in the Laumann et al. (1994) study pertaining to masturbation was gathered using a self-administered questionnaire, with no questions about masturbation asked during the face-to-face interviews. In 1994, Surgeon General Jocelyn Elders was forced to resign after the uproar that attended her suggestion that sex education in the schools should aim to destroy the myths and guilt

TABLE 8.1 Percentage of Participants Reporting Sexual Activities in Three Sex Surveys

SEXUAL ACTIVITY	KINSEY SURVEYS (1948, 1953)		PLAYBOY FOUNDATION SURVEY (1974)		NATIONAL OPINION RESEARCH COUNCIL (1994)	
	Men	*Women*	*Men*	*Women*	*Men*	*Women*
Masturbation to orgasm	92.0%	58.0%	94.0%	63.0%	—	—
Masturbation before age 13	45.0	14.0	63.0	33.0	—	—
Masturbation during marriage	40.0	30.0	72.0	68.0	57.0%	37.0%
At least one homosexual experience	37.0	28.0	—	—	7.1	3.8
Primarily homosexual orientation	13.0	7.0	2.0	1.0	4.1	2.2
Premarital intercourse	71.0	33.0	97.0	67.0	93.0	79.0
Extramarital sex	50.0	26.0	41.0	18.0	<25.0	<10.0
Sexual abuse during childhood	10.0	25.0	—	—	12.0	17.0

Source: From *Gender: Psychological Perspectives,* by L. Brannon, 1999, Boston: Allyn & Bacon.

associated with masturbation in adolescents. Her endorsement of masturbation as a technique that can provide sexual satisfaction without the risk of pregnancy and sexually transmitted diseases was widely regarded as irresponsible.

Despite these condemnations of masturbation and the guilt that half of all men and women report feeling about masturbating, survey results show that most people have masturbated at some point in their lives. Laumann et al. (1994) state, "Masturbation has the peculiar status of being both highly stigmatized and fairly commonplace" (p. 87). Probably the largest known gender difference in sexual practice exists for masturbation. All studies show that more men masturbate than women (e.g., Hunt, 1974; Kinsey et al., 1948, 1953; Laumann et al., 1994), that men begin masturbating at younger ages than women (Leitenberg & Henning, 1995), that men masturbate more frequently than women (Leitenberg & Henning, 1995), and that men are more likely to experience orgasm while masturbating than women (e.g., Kinsey et al., 1948, 1953). In their meta-analysis of gender differences in a wide variety of sexual practices and attitudes, Oliver and Hyde (1993) found that the largest gender difference of all was in the incidence of masturbation, with males

much more likely to masturbate than females. We do not know why gender differences are so pronounced in these areas. Women's lower rates of masturbation have variously been explained in terms of their lower sex drive, their greater tendency to tie sex to love relationships, and the socialization pressures that teach women not to explore their own bodies and that sex for its own sake is not really acceptable for them.

Recent research shows that masturbation is strongly related to level of education, with more educated men and women reporting higher levels of masturbation. Race, decade of birth, and age are three other factors related to masturbation. Whites tend to masturbate more than other groups (Laumann et al., 1994). There is a decade-of-birth effect for masturbation as well, especially for women, with those born more recently more likely to report masturbating (Oliver & Hyde, 1993). Masturbation tends to decline with age for both men and women, although it increases when people lose partners through death and divorce (Hegler & Mortensen, 1977).

It is commonly assumed that people who have stable sexual relationships with available partners seldom masturbate. However, research since the time of Kinsey has failed to support this assumption. Although married people masturbate less frequently than their single counterparts, most married people, especially when young, masturbate at least occasionally (Tavris & Sadd, 1977), and unmarried, cohabiting men and women masturbate quite frequently (Laumann et al., 1994). This research has gone a long way toward dispelling the unfortunate myth that people who masturbate are lonely, sex-starved individuals incapable of maintaining stable, intimate relationships with others.

Indeed, masturbation is emerging from recent research and clinical practice with a new, more benign image. It is now understood that people masturbate for many different reasons, ranging from achieving tension release in order to go to sleep to attaining self-knowledge (Dodson, 1987). We now know that women experience orgasms more reliably through masturbation than through sexual intercourse and that the experience of masturbating serves as a means for women to explore their bodies and learn more about what arouses them (Dodson, 1987; Masters & Johnson, 1966). Masturbation does not supplant or eclipse partnered sex for women (or men); if anything, people who masturbate are more sexual and sexually aroused during sex with others. In fact, many sex therapists recommend directed masturbation programs as the treatment of choice for women who have trouble reaching orgasms with their partners.

Sex with Partners.   Obviously, there is an almost infinite number of possible sexual expressions between two people. It is important to keep in mind that the very definition of what constitutes a sex act is socially constructed. The impeachment trial of President Clinton in 1999 began a public debate in the United States about what counts as sex. That same year, a highly publicized survey of college students' attitudes about what constitutes having had sex was published (Sanders & Reinisch, 1999). Results showed that 59 percent of respondents indicated that oral sex was not having "had sex," and 19 percent said that anal sex was not having "had sex." These findings support the view that, at least at the present time in the United States, there are widely divergent opinions about what having "had sex" is.

Kissing is completely absent in some cultures as an act with erotic overtones. In other cultures, it is practiced very differently from the way it is in Western countries and takes the form of partners sucking each others' lips and tongues (Nevid et al., 1995). In our own culture, where kissing is almost universally practiced, kissing techniques vary widely, and many forms of kissing are loving without being erotic.

Kissing can be regarded as a type of foreplay. Like kissing, **foreplay,** the general name given for a variety of acts that are intended to be sexually arousing and a prelude for later intercourse, is also present in some cultures like ours and absent in others (Frayser, 1985). The kinds of acts that are construed as erotic and therefore part of foreplay differ among and within cultures. Some acts, such as kissing and breast stimulation, may be considered foreplay in some circumstances by some people, but are considered ends in themselves by others.

Interestingly, the kinds of sexual acts in which there are cultural differences in frequency and appeal are often the ones in which we find gender differences in frequency and appeal. Masters and Johnson (1979) discussed gender differences in preferences during foreplay, noting, for example, that women are less genitally oriented than men and tend to favor relatively long periods of foreplay, with overall body kissing and caressing before direct manual, oral, or genital contact with their genitals is made. Men, who are more quickly aroused than women, are more likely to desire direct genital stimulation early in foreplay. Surprisingly, watching a partner undress, a behavior not ordinarily considered a sex act at all (and not typically measured by researchers even as a form of foreplay), has recently emerged as the second most sexually appealing act to both sexes (Laumann et al., 1994). Interestingly, this is one of the few forms of foreplay rated more appealing by men than women.

As noted earlier, only vaginal intercourse is rated more appealing by heterosexuals than watching a partner undress. Oral–genital sexual activity, called **fellatio** when performed on men and **cunnilingus** when performed on women, was rated the third most appealing sexual activity. It appears that the prevalence of oral sex has increased dramatically from Kinsey's time to the present. Kinsey found that the educational level of respondents was a major predictor of whether or not they had engaged in oral sex, with 60 percent of married college-educated couples reporting having engaged in oral sex, 20 percent of those with a high school education, and 10 percent of those with a grade school education. Age is another factor related to the incidence of oral sex, with younger people more likely to give and receive oral sex than older people. This may be as much a *decade-of-birth* or *cohort effect* as an age effect: in more recent generations, oral sex has become a regular part of many couples' sexual repertoire. In the Laumann et al. (1994) survey, 75 percent of the men and women surveyed reported experiencing oral sex in their lifetimes, but only about 25 percent report it as a "current activity."

Apparently, anal sex is not widely practiced among heterosexual couples. About one-quarter of all heterosexual men and one-fifth of all heterosexual women reported a lifetime incidence of anal sex. Only 2 percent of men and 1 percent of women reported engaging in anal sex in their last sexual encounter (Laumann et al., 1994).

Many heterosexual people express puzzlement about how gay men and lesbians, particularly lesbians, "have sex." With the obvious exception of vaginal intercourse, gay and lesbian couples have as many modes of sexual expression as heterosexual couples. Sexual activities like hugging, kissing, caressing each others' bodies, oral and manual stimulation of the breasts, and mutual genital stimulation are common in all couples, regardless of sexual orientation. Whereas the types of activities engaged in by heterosexual and gay couples tend to be more similar than different, the frequency of various sexual practices certainly differs between heterosexual and gay and lesbian couples. Mutual genital stimulation is a very common sexual technique among gay men and lesbians and may be the single most common technique among lesbians (Bell & Weinberg, 1978). Active and passive oral sex is also a common activity among both gay men and women, characterizing over 80 percent of gay-identified respondents in Laumann et al.'s (1994) survey.

The incidence of anal sex among gay men is significantly higher than in the heterosexual population, with about 75 to 82 percent of gay-identified men reporting engaging in this activity at least once since puberty (Laumann et al., 1994). Most men who practice anal sex alternate between the insertive and receptive roles at various times. The frequency of anal sex, which has been associated with the spread of AIDS/HIV infection, may be declining among gay men (Centers for Disease Control, 1990).

Aside from oral and manual genital stimulation, lesbian couples commonly engage in "humping" or *genital apposition,* whereby partners position themselves so as to rub their genitals together (Nevid et al., 1995). Lesbian women, like heterosexual women, tend to be less genitally oriented and focused on achieving orgasms than gay or heterosexual men. More than heterosexual lovemaking, lesbian lovemaking, especially in its early stages, involves hugging, caressing, kissing, and other forms of nongenital contact before direct stimulation of the breasts and genitals. Lesbian sexuality, like so many other aspects of lesbians' lives, has received far less research attention than gay male sexuality or heterosexuality. Even the recent, ambitious, Laumann et al. (1994) survey studied too few of the sexual activities in which lesbians engage (construing homosexual behavior in male-centered terms of masturbation, oral, and anal sex), and located too few lesbian-identified women to present a picture of what lesbian sex looks like.

Human Sexual Response

The groundbreaking laboratory research of William Masters and Virginia Johnson in the 1960s has been indispensable in understanding the *sexual response cycle,* the series of bodily changes that occur as males and females become increasingly sexually aroused. Masters and Johnson (1966) measured and photographed the physiological responses of 382 women and 312 men. Single respondents participated in studies that did not involve intercourse, such as various forms of autoerotic behavior, whereas married couples engaged in intercourse. They developed specially designed machinery, such as a transparent artificial penis containing photographic equipment, to measure female sexual response. One of the most important products of their research is the finding that the sexual responses of men and women are surprisingly similar, with men and women passing through the same four stages of physiological responsiveness: excitement, plateau, orgasm, and resolution. The stages of sexual arousal are depicted in Figure 8.1.

Four Stages of Sexual Arousal

Excitement Phase.   In men and women, sexual feelings can be aroused by a variety of stimuli, from internal stimuli like fantasies or memories to external stimuli like reading erotic material or the caress of a lover. In the early stages of arousal, increased blood flow to the sexual organs, known as **vasocongestion,** occurs. This causes a penile erection in the male and a *sweating* reaction in the female, in which fluid seeps from the vaginal wall and lubricates the vagina. Vaginal lips and the clitoris, which is densely packed with nerve endings and highly sensitive, begin to swell. At the same time, muscles throughout the body contract, which is known as **myotonia.** For example, the nipples of both men and women may become erect. Breathing, heart rate, and pulse may all increase.

Plateau Phase.   A plateau is an elevated but level plane, and the plateau phase refers to a time when vasocongestion and myotonia reach a peak level and men and women are highly sexually aroused. In men, the testes become elevated, and Cowper's glands, which are located at the tip of the penis, may secrete a few droplets of clear fluid. In women, the outer third of the vagina becomes engorged with blood and the vaginal opening narrows, thus grasping the penis more tightly if this occurs during intercourse. Other physiological changes in the female are the elevation of the uterus and the retraction and shortening of the now extremely sensitive clitoris.

Orgasmic Phase.   Orgasm in the male consists of two stages of involuntary muscular contractions. The first stage causes seminal fluid to collect in the urethral bulb at the base of the penis. In the second stage, five to eight contractions of muscles surrounding the urethra and urethral bulb propel the seminal fluid through the urethra and out of the body. The contractions tend to occur at intervals of 0.8 seconds, with the first few contractions faster and more intense.

In women, orgasm is a series of anywhere between 3 to 18 involuntary rhythmic contractions of the vagina and uterus and, in some women, of the rectal and urethral sphincter muscles as well. The first few contractions occur at a faster pace, in about 0.8-second intervals, with later contractions occurring at a more variable pace.

Women generally reach orgasm more slowly than men, because a greater level of vasocongestion is required in women for orgasm to occur. In both men and women, orgasm is accompanied by peak levels of blood pressure, heart rate, and respiration. Subjectively, it is also associated with feelings of sexual pleasure and release of sexual tension.

Resolution Phase.   This phase describes the body's return to its prearousal state. After orgasm, blood is released from the engorged blood vessels in the penis and vagina. In the male, the swelling of the penis diminishes and the erection is either partially or totally lost. Some men are capable of continued intercourse after ejaculating. Following orgasm in the female, the clitoris emerges from its retracted position and begins to lose its erection. Decongestion of the female organs proceeds at a slower rate than male organs, and in the presence of continued stimulation, females may become rearoused and may experience multiple orgasms within a short period of time. Men, on the other hand, experience a **refractory period** during which they are physiologically unable to experience erection and orgasm. The duration of the refractory period varies with a man's age, physical health, and various psychological factors, and can last anywhere from a few minutes to 24 hours.

Masters and Johnson's model of sexual response has not been immune from criticism, nor is it the only model of sexual responsiveness. Some have criticized this model because of the total absence of cognitive and affective or emotional factors in sexual response. An alternative model of sexual response was developed by Helen Singer Kaplan, who proposed three

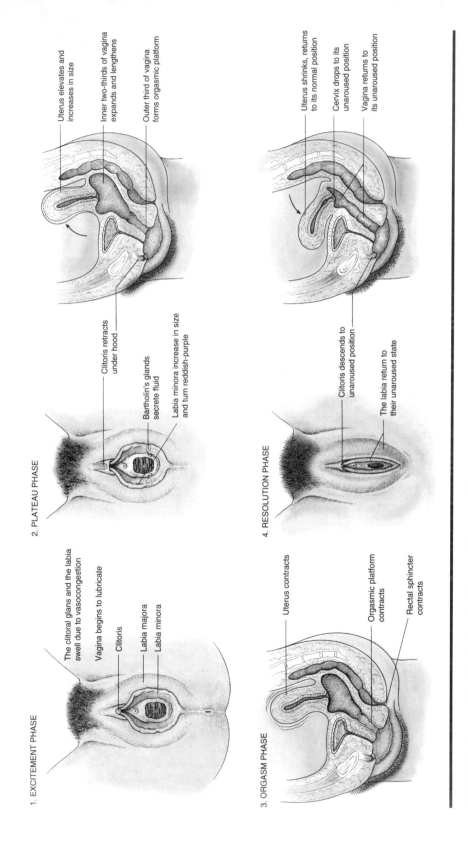

FIGURE 8.1   Female Genitals during the Phases of the Sexual Response Cycle

Source: From *Human Sexuality in a World of Diversity* (pp. 150–151), by S. A. Rathus, J. S. Nevid, and L. Fichner-Rathus, 1997, Boston: Allyn & Bacon. Copyright © 1997 by Allyn & Bacon. Reprinted by permission.

1. EXCITEMENT PHASE

The clitoral glans and the labia swell due to vasocongestion

Vagina begins to lubricate

Clitoris

Labia majora

Labia minora

2. PLATEAU PHASE

Uterus elevates and increases in size

Inner two-thirds of vagina expands and lengthens

Outer third of vagina forms orgasmic platform

Clitoris retracts under hood

Bartholin's glands secrete fluid

Labia minora increase in size and turn reddish-purple

3. ORGASM PHASE

Uterus contracts

Orgasmic platform contracts

Rectal sphincter contracts

4. RESOLUTION PHASE

Uterus shrinks, returns to its normal position

Cervix drops to its unaroused position

Vagina returns to its unaroused position

Clitoris descends to unaroused position

The labia return to their unaroused state

stages of response: desire, excitement, and orgasm (Kaplan, 1979).

Factors Related to Orgasm.   One by-product of the sexual revolution and women's movement of the 1970s was the recognition of female sexual potential and, particularly, the focus on women's orgasms as a topic of interest. It has been noted that female sexuality is more variable than males, and one of the areas that best exemplifies this variability is the experience of orgasm. Some adult women have never experienced an orgasm, whereas others regularly have several orgasms in a single sexual encounter. Some women reliably experience orgasms under certain circumstances (for instance, when masturbating with a vibrator or receiving oral sex) and seldom have them under other conditions (e.g., when having vaginal intercourse). Some women's orgasms consist of 3 to 5 contractions; others' orgasms involve 12 to 15 contractions. The male experience of orgasm appears to be less variable with respect to the percentage of those who have reached orgasm, the likelihood of achieving orgasm during any given sex act, the number of orgasms achieved during a single sexual encounter, and the number of contractions during an orgasm.

Generally, males reach orgasm more consistently than females. The Laumann et al. (1994) study found that about three-quarters of the men reported always having an orgasm during sex with their primary partner compared to about one-quarter of the women. These percentages did not vary much with age, marital status, education, or religion.

What are the factors associated with experiencing orgasm in women? It appears that the variability in orgasmic capacity in women is not related to differences in physiological capacity, but rather to their amount of sexual experience, opportunities for sexual expression, and sexual values, beliefs, and practices. Research suggests that orgasmic capacity is correlated with age, with many women reaching their peak in their thirties and forties (Kinsey et al., 1953), and with level of intimacy, with more women achieving orgasm in the context of committed relationships, especially marriage, than in casual sexual relationships (Lau-

mann et al., 1994). Women who reach orgasm have also been found to be better able to communicate with a partner regarding the need for direct clitoral stimulation and to have greater sex knowledge, less sex guilt, and less negative attitudes about masturbation (Kelly, Strassberg, & Kircher, 1990).

Like female sexuality generally, the female orgasm has long been a topic of controversy. Among the issues debated are whether there are two (or three!) kinds of female orgasms and whether one is superior to the other(s) (Singer & Singer, 1972); whether there exists in the vagina a **G-spot,** short for **Grafenberg spot,** that, when stimulated, produces a distinct and powerful form of orgasm, accompanied by vaginal ejaculations (see Box 8.4); and whether women's orgasmic capacity (in terms of number and intensity) is more likely to be realized during masturbation than vaginal intercourse. Some people wonder whether women who do not have orgasms at all suffer from a "sexual dysfunction" or whether women who have just one orgasm during a sexual act are missing out and should be seeking more.

BOX 8.4

The G-Spot

In 1950, a gynecologist named Ernest Grafenberg identified what he believed was a highly sensitive spot in the vagina, situated about two-thirds of the way up the vagina toward the cervix, along the front or anterior wall. According to Grafenberg and others (e.g., Perry & Whipple, 1981), women in whom this area is sufficiently stimulated by stroking experience unusually intense and pleasurable orgasms, which may be accompanied by a gush of milky discharge, similar to the release of semen in men. There is considerable controversy about whether the G-spot exists, as it cannot be seen and apparently requires continued stimulation to be felt. Moreover, the nature and source of the ejaculate remain mysterious. More research is needed on the nature of the female orgasm and the possibilities inherent therein.

Clitoral versus Vaginal Orgasms.   No less a figure in twentieth-century Western thought than Sigmund Freud argued that females can experience two distinct orgasms, the clitoral orgasm and the vaginal orgasm. According to Freud, orgasms due to oral or manual clitoral stimulation are immature, representing fixation at the phallic stage of development, and are inferior to the vaginal orgasm, which results from deep penile thrusting. Freud's view, supported by psychoanalysts and psychiatrists over decades, has had the effect of glorifying the vaginal orgasm and making women who require direct clitoral stimulation feel that they are sexually inadequate. Research conducted by Masters and Johnson (1966) showed that, physiologically speaking, there is only one kind of orgasm. In fact, all female orgasms require some clitoral stimulation, however indirect. The clitoris is the only sex organ whose sole function is sexual pleasure; it develops from the same fetal tissue as the penis and, like its male counterpart, is richly endowed with nerve endings that are exquisitely sensitive.

Is there evidence then for the vaginal orgasm? Research is inconclusive, and researchers remain divided on this issue. Women in other cultures who have had their clitorises entirely removed in procedures like clitoridectomies or infibulations (a procedure that is even more mutilating, involving not only the complete removal of the clitoris, but also the removal of the inner and outer lips of the vagina) still report experiencing orgasms during vaginal intercourse (Toubia, 1993). (See Chapters 4, 11, and 13 for more information on female genital mutilation.) The vagina, which has the important reproductive function of serving as the birth canal, contains relatively few nerve endings and is more sensitive to pressure than touch. It may be that deep penile thrusting that distends the vagina may cause sexual pleasure to the point of orgasm.

Multiple Orgasms.   Another of Kinsey's most exciting and controversial findings had to do not with the nature of the female orgasm and its vaginal or clitoral origins, but the extent of the female orgasm. It was Kinsey who first reported that a small percentage of women (14 percent) reported regularly experiencing

multiple orgasms (Kinsey et al., 1953). This finding was met with much skepticism, and many of those who accepted the results derogated the women who reported multiple orgasms, regarding them as nymphomaniacs (Nevid et al., 1995). Masters and Johnson's (1966) laboratory research later confirmed that many women do indeed experience multiple orgasms, which they defined as the occurrence of one or more orgasms after the first within a short period of time, before the body returns to the prearoused state. In fact, Masters and Johnson found that most women were capable of experiencing multiple orgasms if they continued to receive stimulation in the resolution phase of the response cycle. In their laboratory, some women had between 5 and 20 orgasms during masturbation and even more with a vibrator, where fatigue is less of an issue. According to Masters and Johnson it is not possible for men to experience multiple orgasms: a refractory period, however short, is necessary after each orgasm. However, more recent evidence suggests that some men do not enter a refractory period and apparently are capable of multiple orgasms. These can take the form of one or two dry orgasms—orgasms without ejaculation—followed by orgasm with ejaculation, or several dry orgasms following ejaculation (Dunn & Trost, 1989).

Although women can experience multiple orgasms through masturbation, petting, and coitus, masturbation, especially with a vibrator, tends to be the most reliable method of achieving multiple orgasms (as it is the most likely method for achieving any orgasms for women). Furthermore, Masters and Johnson (1966) found that for both men and women orgasms achieved through masturbation are more physiologically intense than orgasms obtained through sexual intercourse. They note that physiological intensity is not the same thing as subjective pleasure and that most men and women greatly prefer sex with a partner to the solitary act of masturbation.

What are the factors correlated with the experience of multiple orgasms in women? There is not yet a great deal of research on this issue. One survey of female nurses found that 42.7 percent reported having multiple orgasms (Denney, Field, & Quadagno, 1984).

Compared to those who had single orgasms, multi-orgasmic women began masturbating earlier and were more likely to use sexual fantasy and erotic material, to give and receive oral sex, and to have sex partners who stimulated their breasts. Multiorgasmic women had less sex guilt and seemed overall to be less constrained by society's constructions of female sexuality.

Orgasms and Sexual Dysfunction.   One unfortunate and unintended consequence of the tremendous amount of scientific attention devoted to the female orgasm in recent years is that many women have come to feel sexually inadequate. Especially vulnerable are women who have never had orgasms or only experienced them during masturbation and those who have never experienced multiple orgasms. For these women, females' legendary biological capacity for multiple orgasm sometimes becomes a burden and a reproach.

The fact is that many women are not orgasmic not because they are dysfunctional, but because they have never received the type and amount of stimulation that arouse them to the point of orgasm. As we have noted throughout this chapter, female sexuality is poorly understood by both men and women. Moreover, many women are socialized to be passive and accepting during sex and not to verbalize their own needs and desires. After a long history of not experiencing orgasms, some women understandably develop anxiety and negative attitudes about sex. Concerning the number of orgasms, many women are happy to have just one in a sexual encounter.

Sexual Dysfunction

The term **sexual dysfunction** is often applied to women in ways that reveal deeply sexist and androcentric conceptions of sexuality. Two of the most common categories of sexual dysfunction among women are primary and secondary orgasmic dysfunction. *Primary orgasmic dysfunction* is defined as the inability to experience orgasms under any circumstances, including those characterized by high levels of stimulation. *Secondary orgasmic dysfunction* describes a failure to

achieve orgasm under many circumstances, for example, during vaginal intercourse. Another sexual dysfunction commonly ascribed to women, *inhibited sexual desire,* refers to a general lack of interest in sex.

Without in any way minimizing the distress that many women feel when they cannot achieve orgasms or feel sexual desire, we question whether women with these conditions are dysfunctional. Men with inhibited orgasm or desire who cannot achieve penile erections are dysfunctional in the real sense that they cannot have vaginal intercourse or (naturally) impregnate women. On the other hand, women with these conditions can and do have vaginal intercourse (sometimes with considerable pleasure, even if not to the point of orgasm) and are able to conceive children.

Models of sexual dysfunction that define orgasms as the goal and mark of success of every sexual encounter are more appropriate for men than women. Women are not as fixated on orgasms as a sign of their sexual health or satisfaction as men are. As we have seen, women do not experience orgasms with anything like the regularity that men do, requiring types and levels of stimulation that their partners, for whatever reason, often do not provide. Many women arrive at inhibited desire or orgasm after childhood sexual encounters, experiences with forced sex or sexual violence, or years of frustrating, even painful sexual intercourse. What is often overlooked by sexologists is how often women continue to function sexually despite low levels of desire or orgasms, usually to please their partners.

Sexual pain disorders like vaginismus and dyspareunia can render women truly sexually dysfunctional: unable to have sex (or unable to have sex without great pain). *Vaginismus,* which can be traced to either psychological or medical factors, is defined as contractions of the outer third of the vagina, which can constrict the vaginal opening to such an extent that intercourse is impossible. *Dyspareunia* refers to a medical condition such as pelvic inflammatory disease that makes sexual intercourse very painful. Other physiological or medical conditions can contribute to sexual dysfunction in both men and women (Hyde, 1996b; Master et al., 1995).

Sexual Fantasy

By **sexual fantasy** we mean any mental imagery that people find sexually arousing. Until recently, the study of sexual fantasy has been regarded as frivolous and barely scientifically respectable. After all, descriptions of people's fantasies are titillating, and collections of fantasies in books and magazines have an obvious erotic function. However, the last decade has witnessed an explosion of scientific research on this topic, because it is increasingly recognized that fantasy is a central aspect of human sexual behavior. In an important review of the work in this area, Leitenberg and Henning (1995) note:

> Certainly it is by now a truism that one's brain is at least as important a sexual organ as one's genitals. What humans think about can either enhance or inhibit sexual responsivity to any form of sensory stimulation, and, in the absence of any physical stimulation, sexual fantasy alone is arousing. (p. 469)

Leitenberg and Henning (1995) also consider sexual fantasies potentially important for many other reasons. For instance, they are almost universally experienced. They may affect future sexual behavior as well as reflect past sexual experience. Unlike sexual behavior, sexual fantasies are relatively unconstrained by societal and legal restrictions and thus may be more revealing of people's sexual desires than their behaviors are. Some researchers find that fantasies may play a significant role in the commission of sexual offenses like child sexual abuse (Hall, Shondrick, & Hirschman, 1993). From our perspective, they are also interesting for what they reveal about men, women, and gender differences.

Sexual fantasies have been studied in terms of the context in which they occur, their frequency, and their content. The three contexts in which fantasies are typically assessed are during masturbation, during intercourse, and during nonsexual activity. Research consistently shows that most people have sexual fantasies while they masturbate, with men significantly more likely than women to fantasize during masturbation. Studies of gender differences in sexual fantasies during intercourse present a somewhat different

picture. Again, studies find high levels of fantasizing during intercourse, with many studies reporting about 90 percent of all respondents expressing such fantasies (Knafo & Jaffe, 1984; Price & Miller, 1984). But there are no consistent gender differences in sexual fantasies during intercourse; women are as likely to fantasize during intercourse as men are. Gender differences reemerge in the incidence of fantasies during nonsexual activity. Laumann et al. (1994) found that 54 percent of men compared with 19 percent of women thought about sex every day or several times a day. Cameron and Biber (1973) found that men thought about sex more often than women in all age groupings. Men also report having a greater number of different kinds of sexual fantasies than women.

Interesting gender differences have also been found in the content of sexual fantasies. In fantasy, men more than women imagine doing something sexual to a partner, and women more than men imagine something sexual being done to them. Women are more likely than men to fantasize about someone they are currently or have been involved with and to focus on the personal and emotional aspects of the partner and their own and the partners' physical and emotional reactions. Men's fantasies are more impersonal and sexually graphic, with a focus on visual images and body parts, specifically genital features of their imagined partners. Men are more likely than women to fantasize having sex with multiple partners, including partners whom they desire but have never had a relationship with. Finally, and perhaps most controversially, women are more likely than men to have submission fantasies, whereas men are more likely than women to have dominance fantasies (Leitenberg & Henning, 1995).

In all the literature on sexual fantasy, the finding that women commonly (but by no means universally) have fantasies of being overpowered or forced to have sex is probably the most controversial. This appears to reinforce the pernicious "rape myth" that women want to be raped and enjoy being raped. As Leitenberg and Henning (1995) show, nothing could be further from the truth. Women who have these fantasies emphasize that they have no wish to be raped in reality. Moreover, in women's submission fantasies, women and not men are in perfect control of the situation, the imagined violence is very little, the women know that they are safe, and they do not experience any physical pain. In the typical rape fantasy, the woman perceives herself to be so sexually desirable that the man cannot resist her and so ravishes her. One of the most common explanations of submission fantasies is that they are actually fantasies of a woman's sexual attractiveness and desirability—her sexual power over men, rather than her weakness with respect to them (Hariton & Singer, 1974). It has also been suggested that, in a society that restricts female sexuality, submission fantasies allow a woman to feel blameless for engaging in sex, especially in sexual acts that are socially unacceptable or prohibited (e.g., anal sex, sex with a spouse's best friend, etc.) (Leitenberg & Henning, 1995).

Psychologists have attempted to account for overall gender differences in the incidence, frequency, and content of sexual fantasy with explanations based on learning theories, evolutionary theories (Udry, Billy, Morris, Groff, & Raj, 1985), and sociocultural theories (Wincze, Hoon, & Hoon, 1977), which have all been used to explain gender differences in sexual fantasy.

Research on sexual fantasies may illuminate gender differences in response to pornography. (For further discussion of pornography, see Chapter 11.) Like men, women become physiologically aroused by watching X-rated videos, but it is well known that many women have negative reactions to such videos and do not seek them out (Wincze et al., 1977). Men are overwhelmingly the primary consumers of X-rated videos and all other forms of hard-core pornography, whereas women are overwhelmingly the primary consumers of romance novels. According to Leitenberg and Henning (1995), that is precisely because the videos and novels capture the essence of the male and female sexual fantasies, respectively:

> If one examines the typical X-rated movie, one immediately sees naked bodies engaged in sexual activity without much story line, gradual build-up, affectional–emotional ties, and so forth. The fantasy being portrayed is primarily the male fantasy of multiple female sexual partners ever ready for sexual activity of any kind without any chance of the man being rejected. On the other hand, the primary fantasy of the typical romance novel is a woman who inflames the passion and lifelong love of a desirable man under difficult circumstances. . . . The sex, however fervent, is subsidiary to the love story. (p. 484)

Sexuality among the Disabled

For too long, the sexuality of disabled people, especially disabled women, has been ignored or dismissed by science and society. The underlying assumption appeared to be that "disability is not sexy"—that disabled people, especially disabled women, were not sexually desiring or desirable. What research exists is largely done on males, and successful sex is defined in male terms, such as intromission and sustained erection. In areas like spinal cord injury, disabled women's reproductive capacity to sustain pregnancies and deliver babies has been studied more than their sexual capacity, possibly because of the underlying belief that women play a passive role in sexual relations (Fitting, Salisbury, Davies, & Mayelin, 1978). The women's movement of the 1970s and the more recent political organization of people with disabilities in the 1980s and 1990s have begun to focus much needed scientific and clinical attention on the sexuality of women with disabilities.

The sketchy portrait that emerges from studies of sexuality and disability is interesting indeed. In important early calls for attention to concerns of disabled women, Fine and Asch (1981, 1988) note that disabled men are much more likely to marry than are disabled women, and women who are already married at the time that they are disabled are more likely than men who become disabled to get divorced. A study of sexuality of women with spinal cord injuries found that fewer than 10 percent of the women who had a sexual relationship prior to injury maintained that relationship postinjury (Fitting et al., 1978). Several investigators report that physical disability renders a woman more vulnerable to abuse of all kinds (Nosek et al., 1994). These findings are sobering, suggesting that disabled women are strongly devalued by others as sexual beings, treated to what Fine and Asch (1981) refer to as "sexism without the pedestal" (p. 233). Fortunately, these findings do not make up the whole picture.

While the onset of a disability may break up pre-existing sexual relationships, there is evidence from at least one study that most women with spinal cord injuries began new intimate relationships after injury and described their sexual relationships as very enjoyable. Some women continued to have orgasms after their injuries (although the orgasms were experienced differently). Importantly, all women involved in a sexual relationship after becoming disabled perceived themselves as very or somewhat attractive (Fitting et al., 1978). A more recent study of women with mobility impairments found that after injury women felt that their bodies were only half as attractive as before, despite the fact that although physical function had decreased, overall physical appearance had not changed markedly. Sexual self-esteem was lower among women whose disabilities occurred later in life. Sex and even orgasm (for about 50 percent of respondents) remained possible and enjoyable, but both were more difficult and occurred less frequently (Mona, Gardos, & Brown, 1994). One interesting finding of this study is that women surveyed did not expand their repertoire of sexual behavior after their injuries, but continued to express themselves sexually as they always had. Perhaps more intimacy and pleasure for these women and their partners would be possible with open communication, education, counseling, and sexual experimentation.

There are now many organizations, books, and educational materials available for disabled people who wish to explore their sexual options. In the popular sex manual *More Joy of Sex,* Comfort (1974) had these words for disabled people before offering them sound practical advice about lovemaking:

> *Minor disability may only limit your choice of positions, etc. Major disability will mean that you may have to carve out a whole special form of sex for yourself. Virtually nobody is too disabled to have some pleasure from sexuality—with a partner if you can, without one if you must. Generations of disabled people have been hocused out of this by other people's*

> *embarrassment, the pattern of institutions, and the desire of society to suppress any sexual expression which was suppressible. . . . Your big problem, after that of getting well people to treat you as a person, will be in getting it through their heads that you have the same needs as they have. . . . Above all, get rid of the idea that nobody can love, or have pleasure with, a disabled person. Thousands can and do. . . . (p. 202)*

Birth Control and Safe(r) Sex

It is a fact of life that sex is far more consequential for women than it is for men, and this is mainly (but not only) because women bear children. Few events have the potential of changing women's lives as much as bearing and rearing children. Given these realities, it is hard to overestimate the effects of readily available, relatively safe, and effective forms of birth control on the sexual revolution in the 1960s and 1970s. For many women, the ability to control their fertility is fundamental to their sense of themselves as free, autonomous, and sexual people. Many of the changes in women's sexual behavior that we have noted from the time of Kinsey's surveys to the present are directly attributable to the widespread use of birth control methods over the past 30 years. At the same time, birth control remains a highly charged issue in the United States and elsewhere. Artificial means of controlling birth are vigorously opposed by the Catholic Church and orthodox Jewish groups, among others. However, they are even more vigorously *promoted* among women in China, where the "one child per family" policy is enforced in some cases by involuntary sterilization, the public tracking of menstrual cycles, and even more draconian measures.

Reproductive health and birth control are political as well as physical and mental health issues. Decisions about birth control do not take place in a political or social vacuum. Reproductive research and services are sometimes as responsive to perceived needs of society, such as the desire to reduce the welfare budget, as they are to women's needs and realities. It cannot be assumed, for example, that every woman wants to use birth control or that every woman is able to use birth control when she wants to, and models of birth or sexually transmitted disease (STD) control that fail to take social and psychological factors into account may be doomed to failure.

This section considers those social and psychological factors that enter into contraceptive use and discusses some of the variables that predict contraceptive use. We also consider when and how people try to prevent the spread of STDs. Since the onset of the AIDS epidemic in the 1980s, there has been increased attention to and practice of safe(r) sex. Obviously, birth control and STD control are not the same thing: some methods of birth control offer protection against STDs and others do not. For further discussion of STDs, including treatment and prevention, see Chapter 13.

Contraceptive Use. Throughout the world, most men and women appear to assume that women, who have much more at stake than men in preventing pregnancy, bear the responsibility for birth control. This places an enormous burden on women, in part because there is no such thing as a perfect contraceptive and in part because sexual pressures from men can make it difficult for women to control their fertility.

Nevid et al. (1995) have listed a number of factors that affect the use of **contraceptives.** For example, contraceptives differ considerably in how convenient they are to use. Generally, a technique or device is more convenient if it does not have to be purchased in advance and does not require a visit to the doctor or a prescription. Cost is another factor affecting use. Some contraceptives are relatively cheap, like condoms, whereas others, like intrauterine devices (IUDs), may cost several hundred dollars. Safety (or perceived safety) is an important variable in determining contraceptive use. The use of the birth control pill and IUDs has fallen off among some women because of side effects: weight gain, headaches, and dizziness in the case of the pill (Shapiro, 1988) and perforation of the uterine or cervical walls with IUDs (Reinisch, 1990). Reversibility, that is, the ease with which fertility can be regained, is a critical factor; most methods are reversible, but others, notably sterilization, are not. Obviously, effectiveness and perceived effectiveness are important predictors of contraceptive use, and techniques vary widely in effectiveness. Most pregnancies in the United States are

unplanned, and most techniques are not used consistently and correctly. Much of the research on the effectiveness of different techniques compares failure rates with *perfect* (correct and consistent) use to failure rates with *typical* (less than perfect) use and find the latter considerably higher. Approximate failure rates of various methods of birth control are presented in Table 8.2. For example, overall, the contraceptive sponge has a high failure rate of 20 percent even when used perfectly and a still higher failure rate of 36 percent when used typically. Condoms have a relatively low failure rate of 3 percent when used perfectly and a considerably higher rate of failure of 12 percent with typical use (Hatcher et al., 1994).

Contraceptives differ widely as to whether they offer protection against STDs, and this is another factor affecting their use. The resurgence of the popularity of condoms in recent years can be directly traced to the protection they offer against AIDS and other STDs. Many adolescents who use condoms today do so more to protect themselves against AIDS than against unwanted pregnancies (Lewin, 1991).

Other more psychological variables come into play in choosing contraceptive methods. Some methods require more sharing of responsibility between partners than others, and for some couples this sharing is a positive feature, whereas for others it is not. The use of the pill and the IUD require no sharing of responsibility, whereas alternating the use of condoms and a diaphragm involves both partners (Nevid et al., 1995). Some men like to use condoms because they have some control over the likelihood of impregnating their partners and contracting STDs from them. Other men believe that it is the women's responsibility alone to control fertility and do not wish to use condoms. The perceived effects of a birth-control method on one's own and one's partner's sexual pleasure are understudied variables in birth-control research, but they are potentially very important variables. It is well documented that women have more positive attitudes about condom use than men do, and more men than women report that condoms diminish their sexual pleasure (Campbell, Peplau, & DeBro, 1992). The perception that condoms reduce male pleasure is one of the reasons that some men refuse to wear condoms,

TABLE 8.2   Approximate Failure Rates of Various Methods of Birth Control

| METHOD | WOMEN EXPERIENCING AN ACCIDENTAL PREGNANCY WITH FIRST YEAR OF USE (%) | | WOMEN CONTINUING USE AT ONE YEAR[3] |
	Typical Use[1]	*Perfect Use*[2]	
Chance	85.00	85	
Spermicides[4]	21	6	43
Withdrawal	19	4	
Cervical Cap[5]			
Women who have borne children	36	26	45
Women who have not borne children	18	9	58
Diaphragm	18	6	58
Condom Alone	12	3	63
Pill	3		72
Progestin Only		0.5	
Combined		0.1	
IUD			
Progestasert T	2.0	1.5	81
Copper T 380A	0.8	0.6	78
LNg 20	0.1	0.1	81
Depo-Provera	0.3	0.3	70
Norplant (6 capsules)	0.09	0.09	85
Female sterilization	0.4	0.4	100
Male sterilization	0.15	0.10	100

Source: From *Contraceptive Technology 1992–1994* (16th Rev. ed.) (p. 113), by R. A. Hatcher et al., 1994, New York: Irvington. Copyright © 1994 by Irvington Publishers, Inc. Reprinted by permission.

[1]Among typical couples who initiate use of a method (not necessarily for the first time), the percentage who experience an accidental pregnancy during the first year if they do not stop use for any other reason.

[2]Among couples who initiate use of a method (not necessarily for the first time) and who use it perfectly (both consistently and correctly), the percentage who experience an accidental pregnancy during the first year if they do not stop use for any other reason.

[3]Among couples attempting to avoid pregnancy, the percentage who continue to use a method after one year.

[4]Foams, creams, gels, vaginal suppositories, and vaginal film.

[5]With spermicidal cream or jelly.

and some women are reluctant to ask their male partners to use them. The use of condoms also requires that the couple interrupt lovemaking long enough for the man to put on the condom. Some people find that this interruption "breaks the mood" or reduces spontaneity and passion.

Different contraceptive techniques vary in how morally acceptable they are to potential users. The *rhythm method,* in which the couple has sexual intercourse during the times in a woman's menstrual cycle when she is unlikely to be fertile, does not involve artificial means and is the one method of birth control that is sanctioned by the Catholic Church. Women who are opposed to abortion may find that oral contraceptives that prevent fertilization from taking place are acceptable, whereas those methods that allow fertilization to occur but prevent implantation of the fertilized ovum in the uterus are not. Methods of birth control that involve planning ahead, such as taking the pill or having an IUD inserted, require that a girl or woman admit to herself (and her physician) that she is having or intends to have sex. Many adolescents and young women find it difficult to admit this to themselves or others, because they feel, or others have told them, that it is wrong to have sex.

Most of the research on the characteristics of different contraceptive users has focused on teen-age girls and young women. Many people find the focus on girls and women to the virtual exclusion of boys and men to be deeply sexist and misguided (Amaro, 1995). Scientific researchers, like society generally, tend to ignore how gender, women's social status, and women's roles affect contraceptive behavior and women's ability to control their fertility, and we will consider these factors shortly. Females' role in contraceptive use is exaggerated by science and society not because they are in fact more responsible for birth control, but rather because they are the ones who become pregnant.

More than 1 million adolescent girls in the United States become pregnant each year, and 90 percent of these pregnancies are unplanned (Rathus et al., 1997). Overall rates of teen pregnancies have been increasing in recent years. Today, two of three adolescent mothers are unmarried, compared with just 15 percent in 1960 (National Research Council, 1993). The consequences of these unplanned pregnancies for the teen-agers, their babies, families, communities, and society can be disastrous. Babies born to teen-age mothers are at greater risk of physical, emotional, and intellectual problems and are much more likely to live in poverty and to suffer maternal abuse and neglect.

In the United States, the percentage of sexually active teen-age girls is no different from the percentage of sexually active girls in other developed countries, but U.S. rates of adolescent pregnancy are between two and five times higher than in the rest of the industrialized world (Rathus et al., 1997). It is difficult to explain why U.S. teens are at such a high risk of pregnancy compared to their peers, although some investigators point to the profound ambivalence toward teen sexuality in the United States, as manifested in the lack of sex education in the schools, poor access to services that provide cheap or free contraceptives, and relatively low use of birth control pills, a highly effective form of birth control, among young women in the United States (Rathus, Nevid, & Fichner-Rathus, 1997). The United States is also home to one of the Western world's strongest antiabortion movements, which has not only affected girls' acceptance of and access to abortions, but has also affected attitudes about and impeded access to other family planning services, including birth control.

We cannot overlook the fact that, although most teen-age pregnancies are unplanned and unwanted, some teens want to become pregnant or become mothers. Some believe that becoming pregnant will cement a shaky relationship or win independence from their parents. Others believe that having a baby is the best of a limited set of options that they perceive for themselves (Nevid et al., 1995). Many conceptual models that have recently been developed to explain contraceptive use ignore the fact that in some ethnic groups women use a model of sexuality that is based not on recreation but procreation, where sex includes a possible, even likely, outcome of conception and pregnancy. When the intent of sex is conception, a couple will obviously not use a condom, even though the condom also protects against STDs (Wyatt, 1994).

Finally, it is clear that many girls and women resent being made increasingly responsible for ensuring birth control. This may be especially true for women of color, who are frequently criticized by society for their high rates of teen pregnancies and who are the regular targets of birth-control efforts. There are few programs and little research attempting to encourage boys and men who are involved with girls and women to take responsibility for unintended pregnancies. Women's socialization encourages them to let men take the initiative on matters pertaining to sex, including contraceptive use. The assumptions that women do all or most of the sexual and contraceptive decision making in relationships, that women make decisions about sex or contraception in isolation of their partners, or that women talk to partners in advance about the sexual practices in which they will engage do not correspond with reality for most women, especially for poor women of color. Clearly, we need more research aimed at increasing responsible sexual and contraceptive practices among men as well as women, and at understanding, rather than controlling, contraceptive use in diverse populations.

Safe(r) Sex. Ever since it was recognized in the mid-1980s that *acquired immunodeficiency syndrome* (AIDS) can be a sexually transmitted disease, the terms **safe sex** and **safer sex** have become commonplace in the discourse of our society. As most sexually active Americans know, the terms refer to sexual practices that eliminate or substantially reduce the chances that the human immunodeficiency virus (HIV) will be transmitted from an infected to an uninfected individual. Some sexual practices are far more efficient transmitters of HIV than others. For example, the chances that HIV will spread through oral sex is quite low, whereas the likelihood that HIV will spread through unprotected anal sex is relatively high.

As we discuss further in Chapter 13, in the United States, AIDS is a disease that predominantly affects intravenous drug users and men who have sex with men. But recent research suggests that heterosexual transmission accounts for the largest proportionate increase in AIDS cases. Heterosexual transmission occurs mainly through unprotected vaginal intercourse without a condom. (Unprotected anal intercourse is another, less common route among heterosexuals and the major route of transmission among gay men.) While it is possible for men to contract HIV through vaginal intercourse, presumably through vaginal secretions that contain the virus, it is much more likely that women will contract the virus from men than men from women. This is apparently because more of the virus is contained in men's ejaculate than in women's vaginal secretions. Thus, unprotected vaginal inter-

course puts women at considerably higher risk of HIV infection than men.

After abstinence, condom use* is the most effective means of protecting oneself and one's partner from sexually transmitted HIV. While condom use has increased in recent years in response to the AIDS epidemic, condom use among sexually active adolescents and adults is alarmingly low. Most sexually active people do not use condoms consistently. A recent survey of condom use among sexually active college students found that only 20 percent reported using condoms all the time (Caron, Davis, Haldeman, & Stickle, 1993). In a national survey of HIV risk factors among the general population, Catania et al. (1992) found that only 17 percent of those with multiple sex partners, 13 percent of those with high-risk partners, and 11 percent of untested transfusion recipients used condoms all the time. This study also found that Hispanic women were the least likely group to report using condoms. In a survey of adolescent and adult residents in a high-risk urban area of Philadelphia, one-third of respondents reported using condoms all the time, one-third some of the time, and one-third never used condoms (Geringer, Marks, Allen, & Armstrong, 1993). In this study, women were more likely than men to identify themselves as responsible for condom use decisions, but were less likely than men to use a condom with a new partner. Heterosexual couples often do not consistently use condoms even when one partner, usually the man, is known to be infected with HIV (Lollis, Johnson, Antoni, & Hinkle, 1996).

Recent surveys suggest that knowledge about AIDS in the general population is increasing rapidly. The vast majority of Americans now know that AIDS can be transmitted through heterosexual intercourse (Geringer et al., 1993). Despite massive educational efforts by the media and other sources to inform people about how AIDS is transmitted and to encourage condom use to prevent the spread of AIDS, many

---

*Given the paucity of female condom use as of 2000, these remarks all pertain to the male condom.

people continue to engage in unprotected sex. Why do so many heterosexual people consistently fail to protect themselves against AIDS/HIV? Many reasons have been suggested for the high prevalence of risky sex in all age groups, but especially in young people. For one thing, for most people, sex is not primarily a future-oriented, cognitive experience involving purposeful planning and thinking about the consequences before it occurs. For many people, especially those who are poor, sexual encounters are not anticipated, nor are the consequences of unprotected sexual encounters (Wyatt, 1994). The act of having sex is highly complex, affected by various thoughts and feelings, diverse personal histories, cultural backgrounds, fleeting circumstances, relationship characteristics, and the like. It is naive to think that simple information about transmission patterns will greatly influence such a complex, multidetermined behavior or that concerns about the threat of AIDS are uppermost in people's minds when they contemplate—or are confronted with—sexual situations.

Other factors identified by researchers as predictive of risky sex include perceived low risk of infection among heterosexual individuals and the belief that one can identify high-risk individuals by the way they look and act. People sometimes form informal personal theories, known as *implicit personality theories,* that they use to categorize others as safe or unsafe. Once people have established a stable relationship with someone, they are more likely to regard that person as safe and to stop using condoms with them. Many of us subscribe to the myth of personal invulnerability: the false belief that AIDS happens to "other people" (Rathus et al., 1997). Tragically, research shows that some minority populations who are at highest risk for AIDS/HIV infection are most likely to report believing that they have "no chance at all" of contracting AIDS (Amaro, 1988; Rodin & Ickovics, 1990).

Just as with the topic of general contraceptive use in avoiding unwanted pregnancies, far too little attention from science and society has been given to men's roles in low and inconsistent condom use. Several dilemmas are at the heart of this issue. Even though it

is men and not women who must wear condoms, women are the targets of condom-use programs. It tends to be men and not women who resist condom use, and they resist on several grounds. For some adolescent boys with traditional attitudes toward masculinity, pregnancy among female partners validates masculinity (Pleck, Sonenstein, & Ku, 1993). Condom use seems too premeditated, clinical, or "unnatural" to some men, especially poor men and men of color, and robs them of their masculinity (Amaro, 1995). Some men interpret the request to use a condom as a sign that they are regarded as diseased or unclean or that their women have other sexual partners. Others believe that a woman's preference for condom use signals that she is not very committed to the relationship. Finally, many men believe that condom use reduces their sexual pleasure.

Unlike the birth control pill, IUD, diaphragm, and many other contraceptive techniques, the use of a condom requires male cooperation. Women generally do not have equal power with men in their relationships. Many women, whether because of financial dependence, cultural tradition, fear of violence, rejection, or abandonment, do not perceive that they are in positions to insist on condom use (Amaro, 1995). Exhorting women to assure using condoms more consistently, like educating people about how AIDS is transmitted, does not go far enough in promoting safe(r) sex. Just as we need to increase boys' and men's responsibility for contraception, we also need research and prevention efforts designed to increase their responsibility for safe(r) sex. As things currently stand, women have even less control over condom use than over the use of other contraceptives, and this situation will not change until women have a contraceptive of their own that prevents STDs as well as conception. The goal of maximizing the sexual health of our diverse population will not be easily attained. It requires, for example, that we understand the underlying social conditions that facilitate STDs and work for improvements that seek to change unjust aspects of society that cause these conditions (Amaro, 1995). But it is essential that the research community begin the hard work of achieving this goal.

SUMMARY

In this chapter, we have attempted to show how male and female sexuality is strongly influenced by historical, cultural, and social forces. The social constructionist perspective challenges the belief that any one form of sexuality or any one sexual behavior is solely determined by biological mechanisms. Sexuality and sexual behaviors have been and continue to be subject to historical and social conditions, and thus to change.

In the first part of the chapter, we use the double standard of sexuality as the lens through which to view gender differences in a variety of sexual behaviors. We discuss how gender differences develop and are maintained through socialization in the double standard. We explore how racist, ethnocentric, and heterosexist biases can affect our judgments of sexual behavior.

In the second section of the chapter we review scientific research on sexuality, from the groundbreaking work of Kinsey and Masters and Johnson to the present. Issues and methods of research in sexuality are presented, and research on sexual practices is summarized. The human sexual response is described.

In the final sections of the chapter, selected topics in human sexuality are treated. We describe common sexual dysfunctions and question possible sexist biases in the use of that term. We discuss recent research and thinking about sexual orientation and consider how culture and society construct categories of heterosexual, homosexual, and bisexual. We review the rapidly growing literature on sexual fantasy and consider various theories about gender differences in this area. Sexuality among disabled people, a grossly understudied area of research, is briefly discussed. Finally, we present current research and thinking in the important areas of contraceptive use and safe(r) sex practices, exploring the critical role of gender in these areas.

In conclusion, sexuality generally and female sexuality particularly remain understudied and poorly understood. As we have seen, gender inequalities abound, and 30 years after the sexual revolution, sex remains far more problematic for females than males. Fortunately, science and society have begun to acknowledge some of the biases and gaps that have hampered their efforts. There is increased recognition that sex and sexuality always occur in a context and must be described and studied with that awareness.

KEY TERMS

Bisexuality (p. 244)
Contraceptives (p. 259)
Cunnilingus (p. 249)
Fellatio (p. 249)
Foreplay (p. 249)

Grafenberg or G-spot (p. 253)
Masturbation (p. 247)
Myotonia (p. 251)
Refractory period (p. 251)
Safe sex (p. 262)

Safer sex (p. 262)
Sexual dysfunction (p. 255)
Sexual fantasy (p. 256)
Sexual orientation (p. 242)
Vasocongestion (p. 251)

DISCUSSION QUESTIONS

1. Think about your first conversations with your parents about your sexuality. What were their issues and concerns? Did they attend to the positive as well as negative aspects of sexuality?

2. List some of the terms we use to indicate sexual activity. Many of these terms indicate harm. Why do you think this is so? In describing heterosexual intercourse, the man is usually the grammatical subject and the woman the grammatical object. What does this convey about sex between a man and a woman?

3. What counts as having sex? To what extent are genital contact, penetration, and orgasm important to your definitions of sex?

4. Men typically report many more sexual partners in their lives than women do. What are the possible explanations for this finding?

5. Some people regard masturbation as a dirty little secret, only tolerable among teens, the very old, and the lonely. Why are there so many taboos about masturbation?

6. One of the largest, most consistent sex differences has to do with prevalence of masturbation, with many more men reporting having masturbated than women. Why do you think this is so?

7. Women are far less likely than men to experience orgasm during vaginal intercourse, and some women fake orgasms during vaginal sex. What are the implications of these facts for how men and women think about intercourse?

8. Bisexuality is becoming more visible in our culture. Some people say that we are in a *bisexual moment* in which more and more people are being experimental about their sexuality, but others doubt that bisexuality really exists. What do you think, and why? To what extent do you think that sexual orientation is shaped by culture and is fluid in the sense that it can change throughout a lifetime?

9. Many men and women report sexual fantasies that are not "politically correct." That is, they represent such themes as overpowering or being overpowered by others, multiple partners, and so on. What does this reveal, if anything, about the nature of men and women and about our culture?

10. Research suggests that more men than women want to avoid using condoms during vaginal intercourse. What are some of the strategies that men use to avoid wearing condoms? How can a women deal with these strategies? What are some of the strategies that a woman can use to persuade a man to wear a condom?

11. If you use contraceptives, what factors are important to you in choosing them?

12. Despite the fact that most people know that STDs such as AIDS are spread through unprotected sex, most people continue to have unprotected sex. Why do you think this is so?

SUGGESTED READINGS

Angier, N. (1999). *Woman: An intimate geography.* Boston: Houghton Mifflin.

Boston Women's Health Book Collective. (1998). *Our bodies, ourselves for the new century: A book by and for women.* New York: Simon & Schuster.

Dodson, B. (1987). *Sex for one: The joy of selfloving.* New York: Crown.

Fine, M. (1988). Sexuality, schooling, and adolescent females: The missing discourse of desire. *Harvard Educational Review, 58,* 29–53.

Oliver, M. B., & Hyde, J. S. (1993). Gender differences in sexuality: A meta-analysis. *Psychological Bulletin, 114,* 29–51.

Rich, A. (1980). Compulsory sexuality and lesbian existence. *Signs: Journal of Women in Culture, 5,* 647–650.

Wolf, N. (1991). *The beauty myth: How images of beauty are used against women.* New York: Morrow.

CHAPTER 9

INTIMATE RELATIONSHIPS

Genuine love ought to be founded on the mutual recognition of two liberties; the lovers would then experience themselves both as self and as other: neither would be mutilated, together they would manifest values and aims in the world.

—Simone de Beauvoir

. . . the inarticulateness of love is not its flaw but its essence; not its lack of insight but its insight. If we could ascribe our feelings to the attractiveness or virtue of the loved one, our love would be attached to this attractiveness or that virtue rather than to the love object itself. Love is precisely the sense that we are acting far beyond the call of any particular external qualities, that we are creating or generating value from deep within ourselves.

—Phillip Brickman

The idea of there being more than one body's worth of substance, will, and wit lined up behind one's projects has its appeal. As one woman said, after going through the reasons, "My God, who wouldn't want a wife?"

—Marilyn Frye

Mothering, like everything else in life, is best learned by doing. I think that the mothering that women have done has taught many of us skills of listening to what is said and to what is not said. I think in mothering we hone our empathic abilities, learn to understand the vulnerability in others without profiting from it. I think that the experience of mothering teaches people how to be more emotionally and intellectually nurturant, how to take care of each other. It is not the only way to learn that lesson, but it is hard to mother and not learn it.

—Barbara Katz Rothman

There is no question that the dominant society has said, men will do the important work; women will tend to the "lesser task" of helping other human beings to develop. At the outset, this dichotomy means that our major societal institutions are not *founded on the tenet of helping others to develop. All people need development at all stages, but it is made to appear as if only children do. This casts both women and children under a pall, with many psychological consequences for children of both sexes. The person most intimately involved in their development is seen as a lesser figure performing a lesser task, even though she is of preeminent importance to them.*
—Jean Baker Miller

Only connect.
—E. M. Forster

LOVE
   Who Dates Whom, and Why?
   What's Love Got to Do with It?
   Falling in Love
MARRIAGE
   Why Do People Marry?
   When Marriage Takes Place, Who Marries, and Who Marries Whom?
   Types of Marriages
   Division of Labor
   Happiness and Psychological Well-Being in Marriage
   Gay Marriage
   Conflict in Marriage
COHABITATION
   Who Cohabits?
   Money, Work, and Sex among Cohabiting Couples

   Which Cohabitors Marry?
   Gay and Lesbian Couples
GENDERED PARENTING
   Why Do People Become Parents?
   The Motherhood Mandate
   The Motherhood Mystique
   Enforcing Motherhood
   The Experience of Mothering
   Fatherhood
   Taking Care: Women's Other Relationships
SUMMARY
KEY TERMS
DISCUSSION QUESTIONS
SUGGESTED READINGS

For most people, the personal relationships that they have with others—being mothers, grandfathers, lovers, sons, wives, and close friends—represent their most cherished identities, their strongest feelings, and their deepest commitments. We might think that intimate relationships have long been a major focus of psychological research, but in fact, as we shall see, scientific research in many types of intimate relationships is sparse indeed. Until recently, psychology has ceded the study of many of these relationships to sociology and social work. Within psychology, intimate relationships have often been studied in a clinical context, involving couples and families that are distressed or troubled. And, for the most part, research on intimate relationships in the United States has taken place with the White middle class. Such research may not be generalizable to a broader range of people.

There are probably several reasons for mainstream psychology's relative lack of interest in intimate relationships, including psychology's long-standing biases against probing topics associated with relational as opposed to individual processes, "feminine" interests as compared with "masculine" ones, and the home and personal sphere relative to work and the public sphere. But psychology's late entry into the study of intimate relationships also reflects how difficult it can be to study close personal relationships scientifically. By their very nature, such relationships are long-term, dynamic and everchanging, and intensely complex and private. For ethical and practical reasons, they resist most forms of experimental and laboratory study. Research on intimate relationships relies heavily on self-report surveys and is vulnerable to the kinds of problems inherent in such data, for example, people misremembering information or trying to "look good."

The last decade has witnessed an explosion of psychological research in personal relationships. Most treatments of close personal relationships in gender texts concentrate only on love and marital relationships, with occasional portrayals of motherhood. The present chapter brings together research from psychology and numerous related areas to represent the rich variety of intimate relationships that men and women have: romantic love, marriage, and parenting relationships, to be sure, but also other vital relationships like friendships and care-taking relationships. First, we will discuss dating and cohabiting relationships and then marital relationships, with a focus on heterosexual couples. Next, we will consider special issues faced by gay couples, particularly lesbians.

Parenting, with an emphasis on mothering through the life-span, comprises the next major section. Then we look at other family relationships, including what it means to be a female and a male in a family. In our final section, we consider the research on other important personal relationships in the lives of women and men that are too often overlooked in treatments of intimacy: friendships and care-taking relationships. Throughout our discussion on close relationships, we braid in issues of race, ethnicity, culture, and social class and call for more and better research on the diverse experiences of women and men in intimate relationships.

LOVE

Who Dates Whom, and Why?

Why do people date? Who dates whom? What are the implications of dating patterns for sexual and marital relationships? Theories about pair bonding in dating, romantic, and sexual relationships can be classified into three basic categories. The first focuses on the importance of *physical attraction* on the partnering process (Feingold, 1991). Much of this work attempts to explain the consistent finding, among both dating and married couples, that the physical attractiveness of partners is moderately positively correlated (about 0.50) (Laumann et al., 1994): we tend to date people who are roughly as attractive as we are. As Laumann et al. explain, this finding may indicate that people intentionally choose partners similar in attractiveness to themselves, or as Kalick and Hamilton (1986) suggest, this finding may also result from people choosing the most attractive partner available, with those who are most attractive choosing each other early on and dropping out of the market. As we have discussed in Chapter 8, both evolutionary and social learning theories predict gender differences in the importance placed on physical attractiveness in prospective mates by men and women. In an influential survey of the characteristics considered important in prospective partners for sexual and meaningful relationships, Nevid (1984) found that men were much more likely than women to emphasize physical attributes like figure and facial features when considering sexual relationships. But both men and women rated attributes of personality and character as more important than physical characteristics when considering what was important in long-term, meaningful relationships.

A second approach to understanding how people select partners focuses on the importance of *similarity* in certain social attributes, like race, religion, age, and education level. There are several reasons why people may seek similar others or "matches." People may be better able to communicate with those with whom they share cultural background, tastes, interests, and attitudes, and they may view interactions with similar others as more validating and gratifying (DiMaggio & Mohr, 1985). Moreover, people may be stigmatized and punished by friends, family, and the larger society for dating outside their ethnic, racial, religious, and class groups. Expectations of disapproval by others can serve as a powerful disincentive for romantic involvement with dissimilar others (Parks, Stan, & Eggert, 1983). In fact, recent evidence indicates that even among sexual partners who are unmarried and noncohabiting, there is a strong tendency for people to seek out similar others, especially with respect to race and ethnicity, and for certain groups—Catholics and evangelical Protestants, for example—religion as well. Here again there is a gender difference, with attitudinal similarity being a more important determinant of attraction for women than men (Feingold, 1991).

The third approach to explaining how romantic partnerships are formed construes relationships as a *form of exchange,* in which people pursue those partnerships for which the perceived value of the resources that they will receive from their partner is greatest relative to the value of the resources that they can offer in return. It has been suggested that, when selecting a prospective husband, a woman exchanges her attractiveness and homemaking skills for a man's earning potential. Thus, exchange theory stands as one explanation for the consistent research finding that women tend to marry men who are more educated than they are, even after taking into account gender differences in educational attainment (Laumann et al., 1994). Exchange theory is often invoked to explain the consistent patterns of seeking and offering traits found in studies of personal advertisements, where it appears that heterosexual men are offering financial security in exchange for women's youth and beauty, and vice versa (Davis, 1990; Deaux & Hanna, 1984). A key motive for seeking matches seems to be fear of rejection by more attractive partners. So strong is the notion of exchange in relationships that when people see a couple who are mismatched on a salient characteristic, like physical attractiveness, they assume that the less attractive partner has compensating features that even out the exchange. Thus, Bar-Tal and Saxe (1976) found that people judging mismatched pairs in which the woman was more physically attractive than the man ascribed greater wealth, success, or intelligence to the man.

As interesting as the theories of dating partnerships are, they tend to exaggerate the extent of individual choice and ignore the actual social processes by which real-world relationships are initiated and maintained. We do not pick people off a shelf as we do sweaters. Instead of selecting partners from the population according to our own criteria, we are limited to those with whom we come in contact. The findings of Laumann et al.'s survey (1994) suggest that in the case of dating relationships that end in marriage, almost 50 percent of people report meeting their partners through friends and family members, with another third reporting self-introductions as the source of contact. In the case of short-term sexual relationships, family members were much less likely to introduce the couple, and self-introductions accounted for almost half of all cases. Relationships that lead to marriages, cohabitations, and other long-term partnerships are more likely to begin at school, work, and places of worship, whereas those that end in short-term sexual pairings often begin at private parties and bars. These and other survey findings raise more questions than they answer about how people meet and mate, but suggest that our choices of dating and sexual partners are actually quite constrained, and the social context in which an introduction occurs is an important predictor of the course of a romantic relationship.

What's Love Got to Do with It?

Romantic Love as the Basis of Relationships.   Our culture recognizes many kinds or styles of love, but the notion of romantic love, distinct from companionate love or lust, is a powerful one in Western culture. For all of our familiarity with the concept, **romantic love** is difficult to define. It is generally understood as strong physiological or sexual arousal paired with an idealized image of the beloved. Although most societies throughout history show evidence for the existence of romantic love, its centrality in Western culture, particularly contemporary Western culture, is hard to overestimate. More than 80 percent of U.S. college men and women report believing that being in love is a prerequisite for marriage (Berscheid, 1988). Not only is love the basis for marriage in our culture, but it also justifies extramarital affairs in the eyes of many men and women, and the lack or loss of love is seen as just cause for divorce (Glass & Wright, 1992). Romantic love provides the theme for much of our great art and literature and for most forms of popular entertainment. Concepts of romantic love are introduced very early in Western countries by means of fairy tales, myths, and legends that explain and give meaning to human experience. Cinderella, Sleeping Beauty, Beauty and the Beast, and numerous other fairy tales are powerful showcases for romance stories. Later, countless books, songs, movies, and advertisements embody romantic notions of heterosexual relationships. Indeed, "love makes the world go 'round."

Romantic love is a powerful concept for both men and women. More than 95 percent of both U.S. men and women, for example, report in nationwide surveys that romantic love is important to them (Janus & Janus, 1993). And, as we shall see, the question of which gender is the more "romantic" is far from settled and depends on specific definitions and various components of romance, as well as the stage of the relationship. But romantic love is a very gendered concept in the sense that it has quite different meanings and consequences for boys and girls, men and women.

> For men, the cultural story-to-live-by is the hero legend. For women, it is the romance story. . . . On entering adult society, men must sacrifice intimacy, emotional vulnerability, and community. Women must sacrifice their public life, voice, and power, as well as their trust in other women. As children, we take in these stories as important prescriptions for our lives. Eager to learn how to live in the world, children grab hold of these stories as guides and as a balm that soothes the pain of the sacrifices made to fit into Western culture. (Debold, Wilson, & Malave, 1993, p. 66)

The representations of boys and girls in the "stories we live by" differ sharply. Boys and men are invariably the heroes of myth and legend. Theirs is the world of action and adventure. For their sacrifices, courage, and daring, their lack of emotional connectedness, they are rewarded with "the run of the place"—entitlement to act as they please in the public world and in their private worlds to have access to and power over the most beautiful and virtuous women. As Debold et al. (1993) point out, women fit into only one chapter of the hero story: the romance story, where, as long as they are young, pretty, sweet, and innocent enough, they are the heroes' reward for bravery and sacrifice. The romance story in its various guises encourages girls and women to put their ambition and hopes into the narrow search for the perfect relationship, to look outside themselves—to boys and men, and later, their children—for their deepest fulfillment, to confuse sexual desire with love, and to equate finding a mate with securing a rosy economic future: "living happily ever after." It even encourages women to view relationship violence, extreme jealousy and possessiveness, and other oppressive aspects of gender relations as more tolerable. It should not be surprising that the romance story—the notion that love defines a woman's existence—has profound effects on heterosexual dating, cohabiting, and marital relationships.

Several scholars have remarked on how society writes the script for boys and girls and young men and women in their dating behavior. It falls to males to ask for the date, arrange transportation, plan the activities, pay for the date, and initiate any sexual activity. Girls and women are the gatekeepers of activities: they respond to male initiatives. Lest readers think that dating scripts have changed much since the sexual revolution, they should read *The Rules,* a mid-1990s restatement of the traditional dating script (Box 9.1).

Falling in Love

If women are culturally scripted to be the more romantic ones in a heterosexual relationship, are they more likely to fall in love than men and to hold

BOX 9.1

Do You Follow *The Rules*?

Don't meet him halfway or go Dutch on a date.

Don't open up too fast.

Don't call him and rarely return his calls.

Don't expect a man to change or try to change him.

So begins the best-selling book of the mid-1990s, *The Rules: Time-Tested Secrets for Capturing the Heart of Mr. Right,* by Ellen Fein and Sherrie Schneider (1995). The Rules are 35 prescriptions for attracting and marrying the right kind of man. As the authors admit, the Rules may sound familiar—indeed, you may have heard them from your grandmothers—but, according to the authors, that does not mean that they are ineffective in forming committed relationships in the modern age. The Rules operate on the principle that women are more desirable when they play "hard to get." Thus, women are cautioned not to accept dates for Saturday after Wednesday, to end phone calls and dates first, to be mysterious, aloof, and unavailable. This notion that we

value people and things more when we "suffer" for them is a basic tenet of cognitive dissonance theory (Festinger, 1957) in social psychology. Cognitive dissonance theory holds that we act to reduce the discomfort (dissonance) we feel when two of our thoughts (cognitions) are inconsistent by changing one of our thoughts. When someone acts in a cool way toward us or is hard to attract, we often come to feel that they must be worth the trouble. Evolutionary theory is another theoretical pillar of *The Rules* because it suggests that it is in men's deepest biological interest to pursue many women, whereas it is in women's interest to be coy and selective.

The Rules caused quite a stir when it was published, with some feminist thinkers protesting their sexist assumptions. And it inspired other critiques, parodies, and sequels, for example, *The Sistahs' Rules: Secrets for Meeting, Getting, and Keeping a Good Black Man* (Millner, 1997) and *The Real Rules: How to Find the Right Man for the Real You* (De'angelis, 1997). The authors wrote a sequel to the book in 1997 entitled *The Rules 2: More Rules to Live and Love By* (Fein & Schneider, 1997).

---

romantic notions about true love overcoming obstacles and lasting forever? It depends. At least in the early stages of dating, research consistently shows that men are quicker to fall in love and express more attraction to and passion for their partners (Hatfield & Sprecher, 1986; Hill, Peplau, & Rubin, 1981). Moreover, men are more likely than women to subscribe to romantic ideals like the idea that true love lasts forever and can overcome obstacles like race and class. However, there is some evidence that these gender differences level off as the relationship progresses (Hatfield & Sprecher, 1986), and, in fact, women may become more emotionally involved than men over time. Women report more emotional reactions to falling in love, like the inability to concentrate, than men do (Peplau & Gordon, 1985). In a nationwide survey, slightly more single men than women described

themselves as romantic, whereas among married respondents, more women than men self-identified as romantic (Janus & Janus, 1993). Women are more likely than men to initiate breakups, and men are more likely than women to report depression after breakups.

How can we explain these disparate findings about men's and women's romanticism? Peplau and Gordon (1985) offer some possible reasons. Men, more than women, depend on physical attributes in forming attractions, and these can be quickly determined. Women may be more cautious in falling in love because they have to take a more pragmatic orientation to relationships. Traditionally, in choosing a mate, a woman was also choosing her social class and other life circumstances. Women, who have more at stake in sexual relationships than men do, may feel more pressure to define their feelings as love, at least after the relationship has become sexual. Moreover, women are permitted the expression of a wider range of most emotions than men, and it is more socially acceptable for women than men to disclose the emotional symptoms of love.

Some psychologists have offered theories of different styles or components of love. Thus, Hendrick and Hendrick (1986) developed a love-attitude scale that measures six distinct styles of love: romantic, game playing, friendship, logical, possessive/excited, and selfless love. They have found that, at least among college students, most people in love experience several of these styles simultaneously, but that men and women differ somewhat in their dominant styles of love. College men more often reported romantic (idealized) and game-playing (uncommitted) styles, whereas college women more often reported friendly, logical (practical), and committed styles. Another theory of love offered by Sternberg (1988) suggests that love consists of three components: passion, intimacy, and decision/commitment. He predicts that different combinations of these three components result in different kinds of love. For example, he defines romantic love as an experience characterized by passion and intimacy, but without the decision/commitment component. Consummate love, on the other hand, is the complete measure of love and involves the combination of all three components. Partners are well suited to each other to the extent that their "triangles" are congruent. Sternberg has developed a scale to measure the three components of love (see Box 9.2). How useful are these theories in explaining romantic love? Research evidence in support of these theories to date is somewhat mixed, and it is clear that we need more study of ongoing love relationships.

MARRIAGE

Despite regular laments about the decline of the family in years, adults in the United States and elsewhere overwhelmingly continue to form long-term social and sexual relationships. Most recent statistics suggest that by their late twenties 85 percent of U.S. women and 70 percent of U.S. men have formed a stable two-person partnership, either through marriage or cohabitation (Laumann et al., 1994). By the time they turn forty, 93 percent of women and 90 percent of men in the United States marry at least once (Kammeyer, 1990). Nonetheless, as several scholars have recently noted, the U.S. family has changed more in the last 40 years than in the previous 250, and many of these changes are attributable to changing patterns of marriage and divorce, particularly since World War II and the sexual revolution of the 1960s and 1970s (Blumstein & Schwartz, 1983). Since the 1960s, we have witnessed a fall in the rate of marriage and a rise in the average age of first marriage, an increase in the rate of divorce, a decrease in fertility, and an increase in the rate of cohabitation. These social trends have enormous implications for the meaning of marriage and family today.

As we have noted, both men and women ascribe to our society's notions of romantic love and say that they marry for love. But marriage generally and the wedding day in particular are idealized for women in ways that they are not for men. In the cultural "story-to-live-by," the wedding day is the goal, mark of success, and end of story for girls. Like the princesses of myth and fairy tale, great emphasis is placed on brides and brides-to-be in our society, as in most others as well, with grooms playing decidedly subordinate roles. It is to brides that all attention is turned. Advertisers pitch their appeals to brides in the many successful magazines targeted specifically at them. (A magazine aimed at grooms in the early 1990s produced a single, obviously unsuccessful issue.) Indeed, in most households of all social classes, the wedding validates an enormous expenditure by the bride and her family that is rarely exceeded by any other purchase over a lifetime except a house.

As Debold et al. (1993) note, few stories are ever written about the princess after the wedding day.

> *Reading between the lines of other stories, we can sketch out her "happily ever after": The princess gets pregnant and hopes for sons. As long as she is faithful and bears sons, she is considered to be a good wife. We don't hear whether or not she's a good mother, unless something goes wrong with her children. She's*

BOX 9.2

Sternberg's Triangular Love Scale

According to psychologist Robert Sternberg (1988), all kinds of love relationships can be conceptualized as a mix of three elements: intimacy, passion, and commitment. He represents his model as a triangle, with intimacy, passion, and commitment as the vertices of the triangle, with the shape of the triangle determined by the way that the elements are balanced. Different kinds of love involve varying degrees of these elements. For example, maternal love is a mixture of commitment and intimacy, whereas romantic love consists of passion and intimacy. What Sternberg calls consummate love, the highest and most desired form of love, is represented as an equilateral triangle, the "perfect balance" of all three elements.

How do you know the combination of elements that describes your love relationship? Take Sternberg's *Triangular Love Scale* and consult the scoring key.

TRIANGULAR LOVE SCALE

Instructions: To complete the following scale, fill in the blank spaces with the name of one person you love or care about deeply. Then rate your agreement with each of the items by using a 9-point scale in which 1 = "not at all," 5 = "moderately," and 9 = "extremely." Use a point in between to indicate intermediate levels of agreement between these values.

Intimacy Component

_____ 1. I am actively supportive of _____'s well-being.

_____ 2. I have a warm relationship with _____.

_____ 3. I am able to count on _____ in times of need.

_____ 4. _____ is able to count on me in times of need.

_____ 5. I am willing to share myself and my possessions with _____.

_____ 6. I receive considerable emotional support from _____.

_____ 7. I give considerable emotional support to _____.

_____ 8. I communicate well with _____.

_____ 9. I value _____ greatly in my life.

_____ 10. I feel close to _____.

_____ 11. I have a comfortable relationship with _____.

_____ 12. I feel that I really understand _____.

_____ 13. I feel that _____ really understands me.

_____ 14. I feel that I can really trust _____.

_____ 15. I share deeply personal information about myself with _____.

Passion Component

_____ 16. Just seeing _____ excites me.

_____ 17. I find myself thinking about _____ frequently during the day.

_____ 18. My relationship with _____ is very romantic.

_____ 19. I find _____ to be very personally attractive.

_____ 20. I idealize _____.

_____ 21. I cannot imagine another person making me as happy as _____ does.

_____ 22. I would rather be with _____ than anyone else.

_____ 23. There is nothing more important to me than my relationship with _____.

_____ 24. I especially like physical contact with _____.

_____ 25. There is something almost "magical" about my relationship with _____.

_____ 26. I adore _____.

_____ 27. I cannot imagine life without _____.

_____ 28. My relationship with _____ is passionate.

_____ 29. When I see romantic movies and read romantic books, I think of _____.

_____ 30. I fantasize about _____.

Decision/Commitment Component

_____ 31. I know that I care about _____.

_____ 32. I am committed to maintaining my relationship with _____.

_____ 33. Because of my commitment to _____, I wouldn't let other people come between us.

_____ 34. I have confidence in the stability of my relationship with _____.

_____ **35.** I could not let anything get in the way of my commitment to _____.

_____ **36.** I expect my love for _____ to last for the rest of my life.

_____ **37.** I will always feel a strong responsibility for _____.

_____ **38.** I view my commitment to _____ as a solid one.

_____ **39.** I cannot imagine ending my relationship with _____.

_____ **40.** I am certain of my love for _____.

_____ **41.** I view my relationship with _____ as permanent.

_____ **42.** I view my relationship with _____ as a good decision.

_____ **43.** I feel a sense of responsibility toward _____.

_____ **44.** I plan to continue my relationship with _____.

_____ **45.** Even when _____ is hard to deal with, I remain committed to our relationship.

Source: From "Triangulating Love," by R. J. Sternberg, in *The Psychology of Love* (pp. 119–138), edited by R. J. Sternberg and M. L. Barnes, 1988, New Haven, CT: Yale University Press. Copyright 1988 by Robert Sternberg. Reprinted with permission.

---

safe and cared for in the castle. Occasionally, something might be written about the good deeds she performed, acts of charity and the like. But by and large, she's not heard from again. (p. 64)

Why Do People Marry?

In the United States today, as in the past, romantic love is the basis of marriage. As Blumstein and Schwartz (1983) note in the introduction to their volume on the U.S. couple:

> *Marry someone handsome and wealthy and you will be congratulated, but say that you are not in love with that person and your cynicism will earn you the censure of all around you. At the same time it is clear that people accrue great benefits by the marriages they contract. "Marrying up" is applauded as long as one does not consciously admit to having made this the foundation for choosing a mate. We, as a people, still firmly believe that arranged marriages and marriages of convenience are un-American. (p. 28)*

It is often noted that marriage is both a personal relationship with individualized characteristics and a universal institution that is highly culturally scripted. On the personal level, marriages serve deep emotional needs for sex, companionship, intimacy, and security, and strong practical needs for tangible benefits like financial support, housekeeping, and child care. On the

cultural or societal level, marriages serve many critical functions as well, including the legitimization and restriction of sexual relationships and the provision of economic responsibility for children, the maintenance of stable family life, and the orderly transmission of property and wealth from one generation to another (Nevid et al., 1995). Of course, most married people most of the time do not conceive of themselves as "living in an institution" subject to laws about their marital rights and responsibilities, but rather as making a unique relationship as they go along. The culturally scripted, prescribed nature of marriage tends to come to the fore during relatively unusual circumstances, as when we need medical or legal assistance, for instance, during marital separations, divorces, serious injuries, and deaths. Marriage, with its substantial privileges, is not yet legally permissible in the United States for people seeking same-sex unions. And, as we shall see shortly, the institution of marriage prescribes certain roles for husbands and wives.

When Marriage Takes Place, Who Marries, and Who Marries Whom?

When Does Marriage Take Place? As noted earlier, most people in the United States, as in Western nations generally, marry: 93 percent of women and 90 percent of men have married at least once by age 40.

These high percentages suggest the durability of marriage as an institution, at the same time that they mask important changes in how and when people enter marriage and large differences in the rates of marriage of people of different races and ethnicities.

Throughout the West, there has been a dramatic increase in the age of first marriage among men and women in the last 25 years. The mean age of first marriage for women is 24.4 years, and for men, 26.5 years, up about 3 years for both since 1975 (Saluter, 1992). Many reasons are offered for this trend. Men and especially women are attending college in increasing numbers, and the pursuit of education has traditionally postponed marriage. Relatively stagnant wages and high unemployment along with high prices for lodging have made it hard for young couples to set up housekeeping and start families. The sexual revolution of the 1960s and 1970s has meant that marriage is no longer a prerequisite for sex. With the decline of the stigma against premarital sex has come a sharp increase in the number of cohabiting couples. In recent years, almost 50 percent of individuals reported living with a partner before marrying, compared with only 11 percent in 1970 (Bumpass, Sweet, & Cherlin, 1991).

Who Marries?   In the United States, race–ethnicity is an important predictor of marriage rates. It is a consistent research finding, for example, that African American women are less likely than White women to marry. There are several possible reasons for this racial disparity, many rooted in economic conditions related to racism and discrimination. It is often noted that there is a shortage of marriageable African American men for African American women to marry, contributing to what has been called a "marriage squeeze" for African American women. This shortage is due largely to structural factors like relatively high rates of migration, incarceration, unemployment, poverty, and interracial marriage among African American men in the United States (McLaughlin & Lichter, 1997), and to patterns of educational attainment among Blacks in which women are more highly educated than men, reversing the usual gender difference in educational levels. Almost a third of the Black women who go to college remain unmarried by age 30 (Staples, 1993). Traditionally, marriage has not afforded Black women the same economic and social benefits that it has conferred on White women, and having children and primary romantic relationships outside marriage has not carried with it the same stigma in African American communities than it has, at least until recently, in White communities.

It is clear that the White U.S. family is moving in the same direction as the African American family with respect to rates of cohabitation and out-of-wedlock births, but changes have been far greater for Black Americans. Some have noted that Blacks have come full circle to the period of slavery, when marriage was denied them (Staples, 1993). After slavery, Blacks married in record numbers, and by the beginning of the twentieth century, most Blacks were members of nuclear families. Even more recently, Black women over 65 had higher marriage rates than comparable White women (Staples, 1993). Today, many unmarried African American men and women are in stable partnerships. This suggests that the relatively low rate of marriages among African American couples is not rooted in lack of interest in forming nuclear families, but rather in structural factors: the result of political, economic, and social forces that make it difficult to support families adequately.

As marriage rates drop and society expresses mounting concern for the future of the family, there is a need for more study of the causes and consequences of different marriage patterns among people in the United States and elsewhere and, possibly, a reexamination of marriage itself.

Who Marries Whom?   It should come as no surprise that people marry others similar to themselves on important characteristics. After all, people are attracted to and date similar others. Given the obvious importance of practical factors in a lifelong partnership, there are several key categories within which people seek others like themselves.

The notion of like marrying like people, called **homogamy,** extends to physical and psychological characteristics, but is especially dramatic with respect to demographic characteristics. In more than 99 percent of cases, people marry within their own race (U.S. Bureau of the Census, 1994), although intermarriage rates vary within different ethnic groups and by gender. For instance, Asians, especially Asian women, have relatively high rates of intermarriage, whereas White men have relatively low rates. Black men are more likely to marry outside their race than are Black women (U.S. Bureau of the Census, 1991), and Hispanic women are more likely to intermarry than Hispanic men (U.S. Bureau of the Census, 1992). More than 90 percent of the people in the United States marry within their own religion, although, again, rates vary within subgroups (Berger, 1988). In our culture as in other Western cultures, people tend to marry others within their social class and general geographic location (Ember & Ember, 1990). We also tend to marry people within our age range, at least for first marriages. On the average, men tend to be two to five years older than their wives (Buss, 1988). In later marriages, the age gap between men and women tends to widen.

Aside from demographic characteristics, we marry people who resemble us in height, personality traits, attitudes, intelligence, overall physical attractiveness, and even specific physical characteristics like the thickness of the lips. Opposites may attract, but in dating and especially marriage patterns, birds of a feather flock together. There are exceptions to this rule, of course, and one of the most common is known as the **marriage gradient.** This refers to the tendency for men to *marry down* in age, social and economic terms, and for women to *marry up.* Thus, it is not uncommon to see a male boss marry his female secretary, but the opposite scenario is less likely. As we have seen, the marriage gradient is well explained by **exchange theory,** which suggests that men exchange their socioeconomic resources for women's youth and physical attractiveness.

Why do we seek similarity so pervasively in our marital relationships? People who are similar to us in background, experience, and general appearance are more likely than others to share our interests, values, attitudes, and goals. Indeed, happily married couples frequently cite these areas of similarity as the reason for the success of their marriages (Lauer, 1985). Cou-

ples who are similar to each other may experience less conflict over the kinds of things that couples fight about: rearing children, religion, and money, to name a few. We should not assume, however, that similarity guarantees happiness or that dissimilar couples are doomed to be unhappy. Dissimilar couples can and do work to resolve the issues that divide them, developing shared interests and goals and creating in their households respect for diversity and richness of experience. Increasingly, people are crossing the borders of race, ethnicity, and religion in their formation of love relationships, and marriage across frontiers is bound to increase. Indeed, there is evidence that this is already happening across the variables of religion and ethnicity (Laumann, Gagnon, Michael, & Michaels, 1994).

Types of Marriages

Marriages have universal and unique elements that make them at once like all other marriages and like no other marriages. Obviously, marriages can also be classified into particular types. One common way to classify marriages is according to how conventional or traditional they are, based on the division of power in the marriage, how husbands' and wives' roles are defined, and the quality of the relationship between the spouses (Peplau & Gordon, 1985; Scanzoni & Scanzoni, 1976).

In **traditional marriages,** the husband is the dominant partner and the wife submissive. The husband is better educated than his wife, his source of income is the sole source of money for the family, and his career dictates where the family lives. The roles for the husband and wife are specific and rigid: for instance, the husband initiates sexual activity and makes major purchasing decisions, whereas the wife takes care of the children and the house. In traditional marriages, the couple does not live together before marriage, and the wife takes the husband's last name. The emphasis in such relationships is on ritual traditional roles rather than friendship and shared interests. Husbands' friends are male peers; wives' are other women. Husbands and wives do not often socialize or share leisure interests together.

Traditional marriages have been in decline over the past two decades, largely because of economic conditions, which have meant that most women must work to help support the family, and the women's movement of the 1970s, which challenged traditional roles for women. But traditional marriages are by no means a thing of the past. According to surveys, the percentage of households in which women stay at home while their husbands support the family stands at about 16 percent (Hochschild, 1989). This situation, while increasingly uncommon, continues to represent the ideal family scenario for some couples. The form of traditional marriage varies by class and ethnicity, although the stereotype of this type of marriage is probably a working-class couple with fixed views of gender roles. But traditional marriages are found in every social class and among all ethnic groups.

Modern marriages have been characterized as "senior partner–junior partner" relationships (Unger & Crawford, 1996). This captures the notion that the wives and husbands are almost equals in most respects, but in important matters such as whose career will be given priority or who will make a major family decision, the husband's will predominates. Marital roles are not so rigidly prescribed in modern marriages: wives often do work outside the home, but their income is less central to the household and their careers are often interrupted for child rearing. The emphasis in relationships is on companionships and sharing leisure activities; husbands and wives in modern marriages often describe themselves as "best friends."

Many marriages of dual-career couples today can probably be characterized as modern marriages and, at a glance, they appear reasonably equal and fair. But studies of dual-earner couples find that, even when women work full time outside the home, husbands do not adjust their work around the house or with the children accordingly. Berardo, Shehan, and Leslie (1987) found that, whereas dual-earner wives devote less than half the hours on household chores as full-time housewives, they continue to spend triple the amount of time that their husbands spend on household tasks. Moreover, Burn (1996) found that husbands' understanding of their households did not change when their wives became employed. Employed wives are still primarily responsible for the care of the house and the children, which means that many of them put in "second shifts" at home after working full time outside the home (Hochschild, 1989).

Finally, in **egalitarian marriages** the husband and wife are partners in the truest sense of the term. Neither spouse is dominant or submissive; education is considered equally important for both spouses; the breadwinning role is shared, and the career of either spouse may determine the location of the family residence. The parents share child-rearing chores, and both spouses have flexible roles. Egalitarian couples may live together before marriage, and the wife may choose to keep her maiden name. The emphasis in this kind of marriage, as in the modern marriage, is on companionship and sharing.

Division of Labor

Egalitarian marriages have become a kind of ideal to which many couples, especially women, now subscribe. People generally want to think of their relationships as fair and equal and overestimate the extent to which their relationships are truly egalitarian. But despite the reevaluation and redefinition of gender roles over the past two decades, very few couples can be described as egalitarian at the present time, especially after the birth of children. Even with strikingly unequal division of domestic labor in most households, many women apparently perceive their marital relationships as fair and equal. Researchers in recent years have struggled to understand how and why women maintain these perceptions of fairness in the face of continued unequal division of labor. Some have suggested that women feel less entitled than men to value their own labor (Crosby, 1982). Women may describe the division of household labor as fair even when it is not because they feel that their husband's time is more valuable than their own. Other researchers note that men who help around the house are credited for crossing traditional gender lines, doing "women's work," and their behavior is more salient and more likely to be considered "fair" (Thompson, 1991). Furthermore, research has found that women tend to compare their husbands' household contribution with that of men who do less, which permits them to think of their situation as fair even when it remains unequal (Burn, 1996). What these various explanations have in common is the importance of gender-role attitudes and the unequal power relations between men and women in the development and maintenance of perceptions of fairness. The mental and physical health consequences of the unequal division of labor for women may be profound, as we will see in the following section.

What can be done to reduce the inequity in the division of household labor? Burn (1996) offers a number of worthwhile suggestions. One is to reduce the gap in earnings between men and women, as this would eliminate the rationalization that women need to do more at home to offset their smaller financial contributions to the household. Another suggestion, one that is apparently already underway, is that women should consider lowering their standards for cleaning house, entertaining, and maintaining the family's social life. She further recommends that parents teach their male children how to perform household tasks, just as men should allow themselves to be tutored by women. Finally and importantly, Burn cautions that women need to be clear in their requests for men's participation in work around the house. She notes that women are often ambivalent about asking men to do more, and they couch their requests for help in indirect terms that are easily misconstrued. Burn (1996) notes "They may, for example, say something like 'Boy, this laundry really piles up quickly. I'm having a hard time staying on top of it,' when what they really mean is, 'Please do a couple of loads of laundry this week'" (pp. 172–173).

Happiness and Psychological Well-Being in Marriage

Many writers and researchers have noted a central irony surrounding gender, marital happiness, and psychological well-being: Women are the ones typically thought of as seeking marriage and commitment, defining themselves in terms of their marital and family relationships, and fulfilling their deepest emotional needs through these relationships. But in fact it is men who appear to reap more varied and substantial benefits from married life. As sociologist Bernard (1972) noted, there are two marriages in every relationship—his and hers—and his is better.

The literature on the relationship between marriage and psychological health and happiness for men and women is inconsistent. Early studies showed that married women have more psychological problems than married men, whereas single women have fewer psychological and physical problems than single men (Bernard, 1972). More recent studies seem to show that marriage "works for women, too." Still, it appears that married men are less depressed and more satisfied with their relationships than married women (Fowers, 1991; Steil & Turetsky, 1987). These gender differences emerge most clearly in dissatisfied marriages. One study of long-term marriage found that wives had poorer physical and psychological health than husbands in dissatisfied marriages, but not in satisfied marriages (Levenson, Carstensen, & Gottman, 1993). Recent research suggests that marriage brings considerable benefits to both men and women. Specifically, marriage changes people's behavior in ways that favor physical and mental health: it is associated with much lower illegal drug use, more active sex lives, less violence in the home, and better health care. It is also associated with higher incomes (Marano, 1998, p. C1). Married men and women live longer than single people. But married women more often than married men make sacrifices for the sakes of their marriages and families that depress marital happiness for women.

Why are married women less happy, less psychologically well adjusted, and even less physically healthy than married men? This question has intrigued many scholars and inspired a great deal of research in recent years. There are probably many reasons underlying this consistent gender difference in marital satisfaction and well-being. The key to understanding this difference may lie in examining satisfaction levels in different kinds of marriages (Unger & Crawford, 1996). For example, research has found that employed men exhibit the highest levels of psychological adjustment, employed women an intermediate level, and full-time housekeepers the lowest level of adjustment (Steil & Turetsky, 1987). Although there are several possible interpretations of this finding, one suggestion is that something about being "just a housewife" contributes to unhappiness and dissatisfaction in women. Even for people who enjoy keeping house, housework is frequently boring, repetitive, and physically demanding. It often involves serving other people and taking their needs, tastes, and perspectives into account. It receives practically no recognition or respect from people outside the home and, all too frequently, little from those within the home who benefit from it most directly. It is unpaid and never ending. Historically, housework is the work of women and the poor, people with little power and status.

Research suggests that when women work outside the home for pay, the bulk of housework and child care remains their responsibility. This is even true for those who earn as much as or more than their husbands (Steil, 1997) although, generally, women with higher incomes have more power and influence in marriages than women with lower incomes (Blumstein & Schwartz, 1983). The general mental health benefits of working outside the home for women (discussed more fully in Chapter 7) are greatest when their husbands share more equitably in household tasks. One study found that employment was associated with greater psychological well-being for wives only if their husbands shared household tasks (Krause & Markides, 1985). Similarly, another study found that wives whose husbands shared in child-care responsibilities reported lower levels of depression than wives whose husbands did not (Ross & Mirowsky, 1988).

The unequal division of household labor, a clear sign of power imbalance due to gender-role inequality, stands as a strong possible explanation for women's greater dissatisfaction and psychological distress in marriage. But research reveals many other possible explanations as well. Perceptions of social support by one's spouse are strongly related to marital satisfac-

tion and well-being, and wives tend to be more supportive, caring, and communicative than husbands (White, Speisman, Jackson, Bartis, & Costos, 1986). Women have been found to be more sensitive to problems in a relationship than men are, and this may be a source of greater marital dissatisfaction.

Although it is interesting to ponder gender differences in marital satisfaction and well-being, it is important to note that many factors that predict happiness in wives are associated with happiness in husbands as well. These include high level of education, lack of financial problems, long acquaintanceship prior to marriage, and good communication and conflict resolution skills (Antill, 1983; Birchler, Fals-Stewart, & Herson, 1996). Intriguingly, physical attractiveness in a partner is negatively correlated with relationship satisfaction (Howard, Blumstein, & Schwartz, 1987).

Gay Marriage

As of the time of this writing, gay men and lesbians could not legally marry in the United States. The 1990s have witnessed tremendously increased interest in securing the rights and benefits of legal marriage for gay people. The state of Hawaii, for example, unsuccessfully sought to legalize same-sex marriage in 1996. As recently as 1998, the states of Alaska and Hawaii reaffirmed this position against gay marriage. Early social science research suggests that most gay people strongly favor the right of gay people to marry legally and that straight people are largely mixed in their feelings about extending the rights and privileges of marriage to gay couples.

Many gay people feel that by denying them the right to marry, society refuses to recognize the magnitude and importance of their love for each other and undermines the stability and respectability of their relationships. Moreover, married people enjoy many rights and benefits that unmarried couples, even those in domestic partnerships, do not have. Halvorsen (1998) has documented many of the benefits denied same-sex couples: reducing their tax liability by filing joint tax returns; Social Security and other retirement funds for surviving spouses and dependents; health, life, and disability insurance and other spousal benefits from employers; automatic inheritance and rights of survivorship; immunity from subpoenas requiring testimony against a spouse; next-of-kin status in medical and legal decisions; and numerous others. Obviously, these benefits are of enormous practical and tangible importance in and of themselves, but they also serve to reinforce the personal aspects of relationships.

Aside from the illegal status of gay marriages, the major religions practiced in the United States also forbid gay marriage. But, increasingly, some ministers and rabbis are performing formal marriage ceremonies for same-sex couples. While these marriages are not recognized by the state or by the mainstream factions of Protestantism or Judaism, they are often seen by gay people as an important step in the process of becoming recognized for their love and commitment.

Conflict in Marriage

Even under the best of circumstances, blending two lives is difficult. On a daily basis, married couples need to make decisions for themselves, each other, and others, leaving much room for disagreement and conflict. Moreover, the ideology of and societal support for marriage enable a marital relationship to absorb a great deal of conflict without collapsing, and this permanence and security affords couples great latitude to express unhappiness.

In their landmark study of U.S. couples, Blumstein and Schwartz (1983) intensively interviewed heterosexual married and cohabiting couples and gay and lesbian couples about three major areas of life that concern couples today: money, work, and sex. This survey was not scientific; that is, like most surveys of its type, its sample was not randomly drawn from the population and its respondents were volunteers and not necessarily representative of the four types of couples. But the researchers made a strong effort to include a diverse sample of respondents in all categories and reduce selection biases. And it is one of the few studies that compares heterosexual married and cohabiting partners and gay male and lesbian partners

on a number of dimensions. Unlike many studies of relationships, it explored relationship processes. We will draw from this important study throughout the sections on marital, cohabiting, and gay and lesbian relationships.

Most conflict in marriage is centered on money (both the amount of money available and the management of money), working lives, especially women working outside the home, and sex, both within and outside the relationship. We will briefly consider the nature of marital conflict in each of these three domains.

Unlike the cohabiting heterosexual and gay and lesbian couples we will discuss shortly, married people operate within an institution that offers guidelines for money acquisition and management. In traditional marriages, the husband makes (at least most of) the money and makes decisions about major expenditures, whereas the wife makes day-to-day household purchases. It is assumed that the couple shares everything, despite different levels of contributions or individual attitudes about sharing. But Blumstein and Schwartz (1983) found that married couples fought more about money than other kinds of couples and more about money management than about income. Typical conflicts arise when a husband does not respect a wife's ability as a household manager or when one partner feels that the other is spending improperly on himself or herself. When the wife works outside the home, too, she expects to exercise more control over financial decisions, and this may be another source of conflict. With married couples as with other kinds of couples, partners who feel that they have equal control over how money is spent experience less conflict than those who do not feel that they are participating equally in financial decisions.

Because of profound changes in the participation of women in the work force, the inability of one paycheck to support a family in an increasing proportion of families, and recent trends in the U.S. economy that have made employment for men and women less secure than it used to be, work has emerged as a major source of conflict in marriage. Couples disagree a great deal about whether wives should work full time outside the home. There is sometimes disagreement about whether wives should work outside the home at all, especially wives who are the mothers of young children. When such disagreement occurs, it is usually because wives want to work and husbands want wives to stay home. Many men—and women—feel that a wife's first duty is to her home and children. Indeed, many women who work outside the home describe frequent feelings of guilt and anxiety about the home and children that working men do not report. When women work outside the home, especially when they work full time, the balance of power within their relationship shifts toward equality. Men and women have both been socialized to appreciate the skills and discipline, the stresses and competitions involved in work outside the home. And in this as in many other societies, money is power and the ability to earn it confers respect. Married couples who disagree about the wife's right to work are less happy than couples who don't.

Even among couples who agree about a woman's right to work as she wishes, work may be a significant cause of conflict. Working wives still bear the brunt of the responsibility for housework and child care no matter how much they earn, although in affluent households hired help relieves some of this burden. Unlike the case of *Mr. Mom* in the movies, where an initially reluctant househusband becomes a Superdad in short order, in the cases of real-life husbands who do a lot of housework, there is often a great deal of resentment and marital conflict. And when wives work, couples fight more about how the children are being raised (Blumstein & Schwartz, 1983). Nonetheless, for wives, a good marital relationship and a good job can be mutually enhancing. With work, women gain status in the household and have a stronger voice in all decisions than they would have otherwise.

Sex inside and outside the marital relationship poses rich possibilities for conflict. Couples may fight over how and how often they have sex with each other and may experience conflict over real or suspected extramarital relationships. The quality and quantity of a couple's sex life is important to the overall well-being of the couple. Married people who reported infrequent

sex experienced dissatisfaction with their entire relationship. Obviously, it is hard to disentangle whether a poor sexual relationship leads to problems in other domains in a marriage, or troubles in nonsexual aspects of a marriage sour the sexual relationship, and certainly the causal arrow can point both ways. Blumstein and Schwartz (1983) concluded from their survey that the more likely causal path is that conflicts in other areas of the relationship, particularly conflicts over housekeeping, income, and expenditures, spill over to the sexual relationship. They note,

> *It is hard to know whether an unsatisfactory relationship leads to less frequent sexual activity and reduced sexual pleasure or whether the problems begin in the bedroom and eventually corrode the entire relationship. From our vantage point it looks as if other problems come into the bedroom and make it less likely that the couple will want to have sex together. The low frequency then becomes a source of dissatisfaction in and of itself. (p. 201)*

Dissatisfaction with marital sex and fighting about sex, but not the frequency of sexual relations, are associated with breaking up.

Couples have strains over issues surrounding initiating and refusing sex. Generally, in most marriages, husbands initiate sex more often than wives and wives refuse sex more often than husbands. Equality in sexual initiation and refusal is related to a happier sex life (Rathus et al., 1997).

Physical attractiveness, especially of wives, continues to exert an influence on couples' sex lives throughout the marriage. Some people view a partner's weight gain or other physical changes in marriage as a loss of interest in sex. Even when beauty is not especially important to people, the couple is more likely to prosper if both partners are about equally attractive. If one partner becomes much more or less attractive than the other, the balance of power in the relationship shifts perceptibly.

As we note in Chapter 8, it is difficult to establish the frequency of nonmonogamy, or extramarital relationships. Whether or not it actually occurs, nonmonogamy occupies a big place in people's imaginations. Many studies suggest that monogamy is a strongly held moral ideal even when people do not live up to it (Nevid et al., 1995). Many married people are jealous or possessive of their spouses and wonder and worry about their partners' straying. And many married people are at least occasionally tempted to have an affair. People offer several motives for having affairs, including retaliation and hostility toward a spouse, a need for sexual excitement and variety, the desire to boost one's self-esteem or prove that one is still attractive to others, and a need for emotional closeness that is missing in the marriage (Glass & Wright, 1992). Men are more likely than women to have extramarital affairs, and they have more extramarital partners than women, but married women have more emotional attachments to other men than married men have to other women. In general, the more powerful person in the marriage (often, but not always, the man) is more likely to have an affair than the less powerful partner.

Interestingly, research suggests that married people who have extramarital affairs do not have less sex or lesser quality sex within their marriages and are not less happy with their marital relationships than people who do not have affairs. But people who have affairs are less certain that their marriages will last than other people. Thus, they may be less committed to the future of their marriages. Couples in which a partner has had extramarital affairs are in fact more likely to break up than are other couples. Today, about half of all marriages end in divorce. Divorce is discussed more fully in Chapter 10.

COHABITATION

The term **cohabitation** refers to unmarried people who live together. Over the past two decades, cohabitation has been increasing in popularity and visibility. The Census Bureau of the U.S. Government keeps statistics on the number of unmarried people of the other sex who share the same household (though not necessarily the same bed) and found that this number increased 80 percent from 1980 to 1990, from 1.6 million couples to 2.9 million. Subsequent studies have shown that the percentage continued to increase throughout the 1990s (Rathus et al., 1998; Saluter, 1992).

The dramatic increase in cohabitation over the past 20 years has caused many people to worry that cohabitation is a dangerous new form of relationship that will replace marriage. But, as we noted earlier, there is little evidence to date that marriage is being supplanted by cohabitation, despite recently declining marriage rates and the rise in the average age in marriages. At least up until now, about half of all cohabitations end within a year, and another 40 percent end in formal marriage (Laumann et al., 1994). At this time, it is not clear whether higher levels of cohabitation simply mean more trial marriages, leading either to formal marriages or breakups, or more people adopting cohabitation as a permanent life-style.

Kammeyer (1990) has distinguished three styles of cohabitation: (1) part-time or limited cohabitation, (2) premarital cohabitation, and (3) substitute marriage. In the first type, limited cohabitation, a dating couple progressively finds themselves spending more and more time at one partner's residence until eventually the couple are practically living together. In this case, a conscious decision to live together is often never made. Rather, the couple drifts into cohabitation. In premarital cohabitation, the couple expect to get married but live together first. One variation of this arrangement is the trial marriage, in which living together is a test of compatibility or commitment. Finally, in the type of cohabitation that is substitute marriage, the couple makes a long-term commitment to each other but, for one of a variety of reasons, does not expect to marry. For example, a widow may not wish to sacrifice her deceased husband's pension to a new marriage, or a person who has experienced a very messy divorce may be reluctant to enter another marriage.

Who Cohabits?

Typical images of cohabiting couples include liberal college students and well-to-do professional people. It is true that most cohabitors are younger than 35.

Cohabitation is much more likely among younger people than older people, although it is not clear whether this represents an age effect (as people grow older, they are less inclined to cohabit) or a cohort effect (people born more recently are more likely to cohabit than people in previous generations). But most cohabitors are not particularly well educated or well off financially. And the cohabitation rate is about twice as high among African American people as White people (Nevid et al., 1995). Taken together, this information suggests that people may cohabit at least in part because they cannot financially afford to be married, with all that being married entails in modern day society.

People whose parents were divorced before they turned 14 and who had sexual partners before age 18 are more likely to cohabit than other people. Church attendance is negatively correlated with cohabitation rates (Laumann et al., 1994).

Money, Work, and Sex among Cohabiting Couples

One of the most comprehensive studies of cohabiting couples was Blumstein and Schwartz's (1983) survey of U.S. couples. They compared cohabiting couples with heterosexual married couples and gay and lesbian couples on attitudes and behaviors related to money, work, and sex. Overall, they found that cohabiting couples use money to achieve equality in their relationships. That is, for cohabiting couples, unlike married couples, the impact of income differentials on the balance of power in the relationships is substantial. The male is not cast as the provider and the female as homemaker. Cohabitors believe strongly in each partner's contributing his or her share. The partner with the larger income exerts the most control over financial matters and even recreational activities. Since the relationship is not regarded as permanent, the questions of trust and pooling assets are tricky ones for cohabiting couples, who often consciously design their relationships to avoid the economic entanglements of marriage. Blumstein and Schwartz (1983) found that cohabiting couples shy away from pooling if they doubt the durability of their relationship and are far less dependent on each other in financial matters. In doing so, they prevent themselves from forging a bond that could sustain them through troubled periods.

As a group, cohabitors more than married people feel that both partners should work outside the home. This is especially true of female cohabitors, who are more concerned than married women about the power that working outside the home and making an income provides. More than married couples, cohabiting couples feet strongly about having time away from their partners. They are more likely to see friends and enjoy other recreational activities separately. They are more independent than married couples in their expenditure of time as well as money, and these factors direct their energies away from the relationship.

Cohabiting is generally seen as a sexier relationship than formal marriage. No matter how long they are together, cohabiting couples report having more sex than married couples. The institution of marriage acts to preserve a married couple's relationship even when sex occurs infrequently. Cohabitors do not enjoy the protection of the institution, so sex functions differently in cohabiting than married relationships. Sex becomes a more important bond for cohabitors than for married people. Still, cohabitors are less likely to be monogamous than are husbands and wives, and this is especially true for males.

Which Cohabitors Marry?

Only about 40 percent of cohabitors eventually marry. Blumstein and Schwartz (1983) found that the cohabitors in their study who married were very different from those who did not. First of all, they were more traditional in their attitudes about gender roles and relationships. They were possessive about each other and wanted to spend more time with each other. They were more likely to pool their resources from the very beginning. They tended to see each other in flattering ways; for instance, male cohabitors saw their partners as sexy. Both male and female partners saw the other as ambitious and successful.

It should not be surprising that cohabiting couples are much more likely than married couples to break up. After all, as we have argued, they have fewer ties that bind them during the inevitable tough periods of any long-standing relationship. What may be more surprising is that cohabitors who eventually marry are significantly more likely to break up than are people who did not live together prior to marriage. Researchers generally explain this finding by pointing to the selection factors that lead some people to marry and some people to cohabit in the first place. Cohabitors are more concerned than others with personal independence and autonomy, and are less religious and conventional than people who marry. Thus, it may be the attitudes of cohabitors, rather than the fact of cohabitation itself, that lead to marital dissolution (Nevid et al., 1995). In any case, cohabiting before marriage does not appear to strengthen the marital bond.

In conclusion, it seems that cohabiting is not yet an institution that takes a predictable form. Cohabiting is an unstable way of life, not supported by society in any of the usual ways. For example, other than the expression *common-law marriage,* there are few generally accepted terms for people who live together without marriage. Rules of law and etiquette designed for married couples do not always apply to cohabiting couples. Families and other communities frequently do not know how to treat cohabiting partners. The lack of societal support for cohabitation makes staying together through difficult times a daunting challenge for these couples. There is, however, increasing evidence that cohabitation has become more socially acceptable, with fewer references these days to "living in sin" and "shacking up" than there once were (Rathus et al., 1997).

Gay and Lesbian Couples

Most work on romantic relationships has been done with heterosexual couples. For a variety of reasons, information about heterosexual couples cannot be generalized indiscriminately to gay and lesbian couples. Scientific information about same-gender couples is limited to date, but the past decade has witnessed new interest in psychology in studying gay and lesbian couples. Despite the many serious gaps in our knowledge, some research findings appear to be consistent across studies, and new theoretical models

are being developed that provide a framework for understanding and generating research (Kurdek, 1994).

Gay and lesbian couples differ importantly from heterosexual couples in at least three ways. First, given the nature and extent of gender socialization in most societies, the fact that gay and lesbian couples are composed of two people of the same gender may have profound effects on attitudes, feelings, and behaviors within relationships. Second, unlike heterosexual relationships, gay and lesbian relationships develop without the support of economic and social institutions and often without the support of families and communities of origin. Finally, Kurdek (1994) argues that because sexual activity in same-sex relationships does not have procreative intent, issues such as monogamy and fidelity may play out differently than in heterosexual relationships.

Stereotypes about Gay and Lesbian Couples. Gay men and lesbians grow up in a heterosexist world that stereotypes them or renders them invisible. By and large, this world does not provide role models to guide their relational behavior or safe spaces for them to get to know themselves and others. Peplau (1991) notes a variety of commonly held and uniformly negative stereotypes about gay and lesbian couples. These include the notions that gay men and lesbians are incapable of forming lasting relationships and that their relationships are inferior imitations of heterosexual relationships. Other pervasive stereotypes are that gay men and lesbians do not like children, pose a sexual threat to children, do not make good parents, and adversely affect their own children's development. Most people in the United States consider gay men and lesbians to be immoral, unhappy, and harmful to others (Rothblum, 1994). Gay men are often portrayed as "sex machines," overly concerned with physical appearance, whereas lesbians are depicted as physically unattractive women who do not like men (Rothblum, 1994). Obviously, it is not easy to develop a sense of oneself as a worthwhile person and maintain caring and rewarding relationships in light of such pejorative portraits. In fact, given the many obstacles placed in the way of gay and lesbian youth and adults, D'Augelli (1994) has suggested a model of gay and lesbian development that takes as its premise the idea that lesbians and gay men lead exceptional lives:

> *Women and men who express their needs for closeness and intimacy more consistently with people of the same gender have evolved within their own life histories and have departed from heterosexual socialization patterns. Continued growth and personal fulfillment as a lesbian or gay man in our culture at this time demands unusual competencies and special strengths. By starting with the assumption of exceptionality, efforts can be made to discover these adaptive coping talents. (p. 120)*

Despite profoundly negative images and stereotypes and lack of social support, gay men and lesbians do indeed shape their own development and form successful relationships. Peplau and Cochran (1990) found that between 40 to 60 percent of gay males and between 45 and 80 percent of lesbians are involved in steady relationships, and many gay and lesbian couples form lifelong relationships. Moreover, they found that reports of relationship satisfaction and love among lesbian and gay couples is similar to that found among heterosexual couples who are matched on age and other relevant characteristics.

These core similarities are not to suggest that there are no differences between heterosexual and same-sex couples. As D'Augelli (1994) notes, because of historical need, over time distinctive social institutions have evolved to structure the socialization and intimate relationships of lesbians and gay men. The primary meeting place for urban gay men has been the gay bar and, to a lesser degree, the gay bathhouses that have largely disappeared since the onset of the AIDS era. On the other hand, lesbian socialization often takes place in small, private, informal groups or in women's communities. According to D'Augelli (1994), these very different contexts have shaped highly distinct behaviors and stereotypes: the gay man as "sex machine" and the lesbian as "relationship bound" (p. 127). In recent years, the number and variety of social opportunities have increased for both gay men and lesbians, with more nonsexual options for gay men and more expressive options for les-

bians. Young gay men and women who are coming of age today will have a different developmental history and be socialized under different circumstances than earlier gay and lesbian cohorts. In D'Augelli's (1994) words, they will be "different persons" (p. 127).

How Money, Work, and Sex Are Negotiated among Gay and Lesbian Couples.

As noted earlier, Blumstein and Schwartz's (1983) major study of U.S. couples included volunteer samples of gay men and lesbians as well as heterosexual married and cohabiting couples. Although the sample was not randomly selected or scientific, and generalizations across all gay and lesbian couples cannot be made, it nonetheless gives us a glimpse of how major issues are negotiated in same-sex relationships.

Concerning the earning and expenditure of money, Blumstein and Schwartz found that money establishes the balance of power in all relationships except among lesbians. Since women in this society are not socialized to judge their own worth by their income, they tend not to judge their female partners by this standard. Gay men, on the other hand, gain significant control and power advantages over their partners when they earn substantially more than them. Because earning power is a central part of a man's identity, having more money gives a man symbolic and real advantages. For all kinds of couples, partners who feel that they have equal control over how the money is spent have a more tranquil relationship.

Gay couples, like an increasing proportion of married couples, have to deal with the stresses of making a living, dealing with competition, allocating housework, and finding time to be together. The great majority of same-sex couples believe that both partners should work, and in most same-sex couples, both partners do work outside the home. Gay men tend to be more competitive with each other about work than lesbians, probably because of the meaning of work to men's self-esteem (Blumstein & Schwartz, 1983). Interestingly, same-sex couples appear to enjoy an advantage over heterosexual couples when it comes to juggling the conflicting demands of work and home. Same-sex couples conserve more time than heterosexual couples because they share similar lives and interests by virtue of their gender roles.

Blumstein and Schwartz (1983) studied the sex lives of gay men and lesbians and found large and important differences between these couples in the frequency and variety of sexual expression. They found that gay men have sex more often in the early part of their relationship than any other type of couple, but after 10 years they have sex together less often than married couples. Sex with other men tends to balance the declining sex with the partner. Lesbian couples have sex less often than any other couples, and they do not have much compensating sex outside the relationship. Taken together with their data on heterosexual couples, these findings compelled the authors to make generalizations about men as a group and women as a group. That is, they found that husbands and male cohabitors were more like gay men in their sexual behavior and attitudes than they were like wives and female cohabitors, and wives and female cohabitors were more like lesbians than they were like husbands and male cohabitors. Regardless of sexual orientation, men generally are more likely to value physical attractiveness in their partners, to pursue sex within the relationship, and to be nonmonogamous than women are. Regardless of sexual orientation, women generally are more likely to link love and sex than men are. Thus, gender matters in shaping a person's sexual opportunities and choices.

Other issues that arose with respect to same-sex couples concern sexual competitiveness for the admiration of others and working out a sensitive ratio of initiating and refusing sex. These and several other issues relevant to gay and lesbian relationships need further research. For example, some theorists have suggested that gay men and lesbians have a tendency to idealize romantic relationships, believing that gender similarity precludes conflicts. This may render gay men and lesbians less likely to label battering appropriately. If lesbian and gay couples are out, their relationship may be challenged or ridiculed, and if they are not out, they may suffer the strains of secrecy, deception, and lack of acknowledgment (Greene, 1994c). Relationships in which gay men and lesbians are involved with people who self-identify or are seen by others as bisexual also need further study.

GENDERED PARENTING

Parental love and commitment can attain a peak of intensity that has become proverbial. The bonds that tie parent to child are widely understood to be the strongest and most enduring of most people's lives. For parents, especially mothers, in modern-day Western society, the costs, sacrifices, and inconveniences of rearing children are profound and far outweigh any material benefits that people can reasonably hope to realize through having offspring. The evidence that people appreciate this is that fewer people today are choosing to have children at all, and most others are having many fewer than they might. Nonetheless, most adults become parents, and those who cannot conceive children frequently endure remarkable hardships to become parents. Why do so many people, particularly women, "choose" sleepless nights; drastically reduced flexibility and freedom in career choices and social life; the financial and emotional burden of care, feeding, housing, and education; and the general and continuing costs of socializing unwilling recruits to civilization (Brickman, Janoff-Bulman, & Rabinowitz, 1987)? Psychologists have long sought to explain the ferocity of parental love, the reasons that people want children so much, and, because parenting is perhaps the most gendered of all human endeavors, the different meanings and significance of motherhood and fatherhood for women and men.

Why Do People Become Parents?

Not surprisingly, there are a variety of biological, psychological, and social explanations for the complex behaviors involved in wanting and having children. Before briefly reviewing them, it is important to note that such explanations seemed quite unnecessary when children had greater economic value than they do now. Romanticized views of parenthood, particularly motherhood, and of children are quite modern notions. Throughout most of human history, children were far less costly and more materially valuable to their families as workers and sources of support in old age than they are today. In eras when children had greater material value to parents, parents took a more instrumental or pragmatic orientation toward their children (Aries, 1962; Shorter, 1975). By drastically reducing the economic value of children, other explanations for wanting children stand out in sharper relief.

On the one hand, the answer to the question of why men and women want to be parents may seem quite obvious: in order for the species to survive, it is necessary for men and women to procreate. The pleasure involved in sexual reproduction is in service of this necessity on the species level. But, although it is to the obvious benefit of the species that men and women have offspring, it is not obviously beneficial (at least in modern-day Western society) to individual men and women to reproduce. Indeed, as we noted, when one considers the potential costs to one's freedom, social and career options, emotional and financial independence, and physical health and safety, especially for women, the decision to have children hardly seems rational. Major theories of behavior, such as evolutionary theory, suggest that it is the largely irrational and unconscious desire to pass on one's genes through having children that is the central motivator of all human action. In these theories, the desire to become parents is instinctual for both sexes, but especially for women, giving rise to the frequently invoked *maternal instinct* (Bernard, 1975). There is little dispute that women are more likely than men to nurture children and appear more skilled at it. The question is whether such nurturance is the expression of an innate biological drive or a learned behavior. The idea that women are biologically programmed to be more nurturant than men is an extension of the observation that femaleness in humans and other mammals is defined by the manner of reproduction: gestation and nourishment in the womb followed by nursing infants after birth.

In her social history of parenting, Lorber notes that, whereas it makes evolutionary sense for a mother to bond with her newborn, whether she actually does has always depended on the social worth of both the mother and child (1994). Lorber reviews the historical

evidence, which suggests that the strong emotional bond that we take for granted as part of parenting is a luxury that many men and women throughout history could not afford. The abandonment, neglect, and murder of infants has always been prevalent among parents of children who had too many to feed or too many of one gender (usually female) or whose children were called "illegitimate." In early modern Europe, 10 to 40 percent of the children registered as born were abandoned, even in prosperous times (Boswell, 1988). In England, infant mortality rates were not recorded until 1875, and registration of births was not compulsory until 1907. In fact, as Lorber notes, the lines between stillbirths, accidental deaths, neglect, and infanticide have never been clear, and how an infant's death is classified, today as in the past, depends on society's judgment of the mother's social and moral worth.

In the late 1990s, a series of news stories about discarded newborns, some alive, some dead, riveted the nation's attention. These incidents signaled to some the lack of morality and humanity in the modern world. But rather than a new sign of troubled times, the abandonment, neglect, and murder of infants, by mothers as well as fathers, were once much more common in the West than they are today. In any case, history relates that the social and emotional value of children to parents is not fixed biologically, but fluctuates widely from time to time and place to place, and with it the fortunes of children. In fact, there is little evidence to date to suggest the existence of a biological instinct to parent, and, more specifically, to mother.

Closely related to the biological–evolutionary theories about parenting are the psychoanalytical theories positing an innate psychological need on the part of women to have children. Certainly the most famous or infamous of these is Freud's, postulating that women want to bear a child, preferably a male child, as a penis substitute (Freud, 1925/1961). In fact, research suggests that, despite clear societal preferences for boys and frequently their husband's own preference for sons, most women do not prefer sons to daughters (Steinbacher & Gilroy, 1996) before their children are born. Moreover, there is no evidence that women seek fulfillment through their sons more than their daughters. In fact, research suggests that mothers' relationships with their daughters occupy a more central place in their lives than their relationships with sons throughout the life-span (Forcey, 1987). In a more recent formulation that combines psychoanalytic theory with a feminist orientation, Chodorow (1978) has suggested that women's nurturing orientation derives from girls' early childhood experiences of closeness to their mothers. According to Chodorow, little girls, unlike little boys, do not have to distance themselves from their beloved primary care-giver in order to identify with a powerful same-sex adult. Thus, girls' development emphasizes relatedness and connectedness with others, whereas boys' requires separation from others, rejection of things feminine, and mastery of the outside world. Having babies presumably satisfies women's deep-seated relational needs.

But the emotional closeness between most (but by no means all) mothers and their children is at least as likely to be the result as the cause of the fact that women are the primary care-givers of children in most societies. Studies suggest that becoming a mother changes women in the direction of becoming more mature, responsible, tolerant, warm, and vulnerable—more feminine (Helson, Mitchell, & Moane, 1984). Furthermore, when fathers are the primary care-givers, they experience more intimacy with their children and exhibit more stereotypically female characteristics like nurturance and expressivity than traditional fathers (Risman, 1987). In short, when men must mother, they behave more like mothers.

Until recently, women often became mothers simply because they had little or no control over their sexual and reproductive lives or few other ways to feel valued in their communities and to function as respectable adults. With advances in reproductive technologies and increases in women's rights and life options, many women in industrialized societies have more choices, and an increasing proportion of them are choosing not to have children at all, or to have many fewer than women typically had just one or two generations ago. And, as we shall see, there is very little evidence to suggest that women who do not have children are less happy or fulfilled than those who do. In fact, there is evidence to suggest the opposite: women without children are happier than those with

children. These findings suggest that factors beyond innate biological and psychological forces support motherhood.

Many surveys have been conducted asking people, often college students, why they want to be parents. In one study of college students, the most frequently endorsed motives for having children, in descending order, were the desires to expand oneself and have someone to follow one, to achieve adult status or social identity, to provide a family for oneself, to experience the fun and stimulation of children, and to be able to influence or control someone (Gormly, Gormly, & Weiss, 1987). The only significant gender difference emerged in the rating of one item, to achieve adult status or social identity, which was much more frequently endorsed by women than men. Another study of undergraduates compared motivations in 1977 and 1986 for having children (Morahan-Martin, 1991). This study found an increase in emphasis on positive factors cited by both genders over time, with a corresponding decrease in emphasis on the negative aspects of parenting. There were, however, gender differences in the rated importance of traditional reasons for having children, with men more likely than women to cite reasons such as continuity, tradition, security, and role motivations. Responses to such surveys are interesting in and of themselves, not so much because they reveal people's actual needs and motives, but because they reflect the culture's constructions of parenthood. Psychologists have long known that the processes that govern people's actions and the processes that govern how they explain their actions to themselves and others are quite distinct. People are especially unlikely to invoke unconscious motives, such as a desire to pass on one's genes or fulfill one's deep-seated emotional need for closeness, or socially undesirable motives, such as a desire to produce an heir and inherit money or raise one's status in the family, in a straightforward survey.

The Motherhood Mandate

There may be little direct evidence for a biological imperative to have children, but there can be little doubt of a social imperative. Russo has labeled the enormous social pressure to have and raise children as the

motherhood mandate (Russo, 1976). This mandate refers to the pervasive belief that in order to be a real and complete woman, a woman must have children, preferably more than one, and raise them successfully. No other accomplishment by a woman, no matter how unusual or significant, can compensate for the failure to mother. Speaking for generations of women, former First Lady Jacqueline Kennedy once remarked that "There is no more important job for a woman than to be a good mother. If a woman bungles that, then it doesn't much matter what else she does."

Training in the **motherhood mystique** starts early for girls, who are given baby dolls as toys and praise for expressing the desire to be mommies when they grow up. In contrast, boys who play with dolls, especially baby dolls, are often the source of great concern for parents. In the uncommon event that boys claim ambitions to be daddies, they are likely to be asked what else they want to be, with the clear implication that being a daddy is not enough of an ambition for a boy. But being a mother is supposed to be the major preoccupation of adult women, and this mandate is enforced, like most successful societal imperatives, by idealization of the role on the one hand and stigmas and punishments attached to failing to fulfill the role properly on the other hand. We will now discuss how motherhood is alternatively romanticized, regulated, and devalued in modern Western society.

The Motherhood Mystique

The word *mother* simply denotes a woman who has borne (or raised) a child, but few words in the English language connote greater depth of positive feeling. Phrases ranging from "motherhood and apple pie" to "a face that only a mother could love" suggest the unquestioned good that is motherhood and its incomparable potential for unconditional love. As sellers of greeting cards, telephone operators, and restaurateurs know all too well, Father's Day is not a close second to Mother's Day in the sentiment—or business—that it invokes.

The images of motherhood that we cull from religion, myth, fairy tale, and the mainstream media are stunningly similar and idealized portraits of young,

well-groomed, usually slim and conventionally beautiful women. They are virtually always heterosexual, married to the fathers of the children, White, and middle class. In personality and orientation to their children, they are usually gentle, patient, loving, devoted, and self-sacrificing. They are basically asexual; in fact, they have few personal needs and desires of any kind and certainly no negative proclivities. These qualities are reified by the Latin American mestizo cultures in an ideal known as *marianismo,* based on the qualities symbolized by the figure of the Virgin Mary. According to Stevens (1993), *marianismo* is a ubiquitous stereotype prescribed for all social classes. Among the characteristics of this ideal are "semi-divinity, moral superiority, and spiritual strength. This spiritual strength engenders abnegation, that is, an infinite capacity for humility and sacrifice. No self-denial is too great for the Latin American woman, no limit can be divined to her vast store of patience with the men of her world" (p. 485).

Recently, scholars have studied so-called "myths of motherhood"—how the ideology of patriarchal cultures supports and maintains women in the incredibly demanding, low-status, uncompensated work of mothering—and how they affect real mothers' feelings and behaviors (Weseen, 1999). These myths include the seemingly natural and common-sense notions that only women can be loving and nurturing enough to raise a child; that men are vocationally superior to women; that good parenting requires that one parent, virtually always the woman, regularly subordinate personal goals to the children's and family's needs; that motherhood is uniquely joyous and fulfilling for women; that a good mother is invariably kind, unselfish, and loving; and that motherhood is the ultimate way for women to gain esteem and support as adults. Research has largely dispelled each of these myths, and these myths hurt women, because when women and their families do not live up to them, they frequently feel that they have failed as mothers and thus as women, as people (Weseen, 1999). Yet they persist in the minds of women and men. Why?

Feminist analyses of mothering have pointed to the ways in which such myths, widely held to as sacred and beyond question, control and constrain the behavior of women in ways that support patriarchy and the prerogatives and privileges of men. Polatnick (1993) has reviewed the many ways in which "bread-winning beats childrearing." These include, first and foremost, the ability to achieve in the workplace as the major source of money and social status in Western societies. Breadwinning power translates into power within the family, with studies showing that the more money a man (or woman) makes, the greater the decision-making power in the family. With the ability to make money comes the right to exercise control over its use and a corresponding lack of dependence on others. However it idealizes motherhood, society attaches greater value to the role of wage earner than parent, and earning wages legitimizes power-wielding inside and outside the family. In working outside the home, one accrues many tangible and intangible benefits that can affect the balance of power within relationships. To name a few, wage earners gain organizational experience; social contacts, including contacts with potential sexual and romantic interests; knowledge of the world; and feelings of independence and confidence. Aside from wanting and benefiting from the increased power due to their wage earning, men gain from women staying home in countless other ways as well. When women are home, they are not competitors for jobs, and this ensures continued male domination in the occupational world. While women are consumed by domestic duties, men are building careers and consolidating resources in the outside world; by the time women complete their full-time child-rearing tenure, most women cannot catch up occupationally and recoup their losses (Polatnick, 1993). All the while, women who stay at home minister to husbands' everyday needs of laundry, cooking, cleaning, and keeping the social calendar, just as they do to their children's, thus making husbands' careers and life-styles possible.

This brings us to the issue of the nature of child-rearing tasks themselves. Not only are these tasks not a significant source of power, money, or prestige in the larger society, but they are also inherently onerous. They involve tremendous responsibility, constant demands, deprivation from other identities, isolation from other adults, disappointment with unhelpful spouses, and guilt about not measuring up to the ideal. They do not confer power on people, and people with power do not perform them. We know that few men do these tasks with or without pay, and women do not perform them for pay when they have other options. Whatever rewards there are in mothering, and as mothers, the three authors know them well, the fact is that child rearing is not regarded as a desirable job for those who are not the mothers of the children. Hollingworth made this point as early as 1916, in her groundbreaking and myth-exploding early study of mothering, in which she cited the long years of exacting labor and self-sacrifice, and also the

> drudgery, the monotonous labor, and other disagreeable features of childrearing are minimized by "the social guardians." On the other hand, the joys and compensations of motherhood are magnified and presented to consciousness on every hand. Thus, the tendency is to create an illusion whereby motherhood will appear to consist of compensations only, and thus come to be desired by those for whom the illusion is intended. (pp. 20–21)

Enforcing Motherhood

The motherhood mystique is invaluable in maintaining the status quo, which so clearly benefits men at the expense of women. But it is not through rewards alone that society supports motherhood. The flip side of idealization of motherhood is punishment and devaluation of "bad" women: women who do not mother or mother differently from the cultural ideal. In this section, we will consider how society constructs women who have no children by choice or who are lesbian mothers, single mothers, noncustodial mothers, mothers on welfare, or simply mothers who work too long or at dangerous jobs.

Women Who Choose to Remain Child Free. Most recent surveys show that, overwhelmingly, women still expect to become mothers. One survey of undergraduates found that fewer than 3 percent wished to be child free (Baber & Allen, 1992). When child-free couples are asked why they do not want children, they frequently cite the cost of rearing a child today, the fear that they will not be good parents, and concerns about interference with flexible life-styles and vocational and educational plans (Cowan & Cowan, 1992; Ireland, 1993). Research on women who do not have children shows that they are often White, urban, well educated, and professional (DeVellis, Wallston, & Acker, 1984), suggesting the importance of career considerations in remaining child free. Yet, in contrast, professional men often have families with two or more children and do not have to choose between having careers and families, but professional women have to make that choice and often have no children or one child. In some cases, women choose not to have children because they themselves had unhappy childhoods or distant relationships with their parents and do not wish to repeat these patterns (Houseknecht, 1979).

A stigma is attached to women who do not have children, whether by choice or not. The terms applied to child-free women, such as *childless* and *barren*, reflect this negative bias. At least until recently, they have been seen as more selfish, unhappy, and neurotic than other women (Peterson, 1983). People wonder why they did not have children, frequently ask them about the decision not to have a child, and question whether they feel that they are missing something essential in life, questions that arise far less frequently with men. Research consistently shows that women without children are, at least in early adulthood, basically happier, more satisfied with their marital relationships, less conflicted, and more successful in their careers than women with children. Only widows between the ages of 60 and 75 with children report being more happy and less lonely than comparable women without children, but the differences between groups were quite small (Beckman & Houser, 1982). Of course, these correlational findings do not suggest that children cause unhappiness in women, and most women who have children are very happy with their choice and report that they would make the same choice again. But these findings explode the myth of the miserable barren woman.

"Bad" Mothers: Falling Short of the Ideal. Given the narrow stereotype of the ideal mother, it is not surprising that so many women fall short of the ideal and incur society's disapproval and even rejection and punishment. Lesbian mothers risk losing their children in custody battles, despite the fact that research shows that the children of lesbians are indistinguishable from the children of heterosexual mothers on numerous psychological and behavioral characteristics (Flaks, Ficher, Masterpasqua, & Joseph, 1995; Hoeffer, 1981). Stepmothers are among the most hateful and hated characters of myth and fairy tale, so much so that one of our daughters at age 5, on seeing an attractive and pleasant stepmother interviewed on television, marveled that a stepmother could be pretty and nice. The image of stepmothers so prevalent in our culture may contribute to the resistance and resentment that some stepchildren feel toward stepmothers.

Single mothers, especially those who are sexually active, are frequently seen as "loose," immoral, and unfit, whereas the fathers of these children frequently escape our gaze altogether, even if they shun all responsibility for their families. Society is especially disapproving of the single "welfare mother," who is often depicted as using her fertility to enrich herself while defrauding the tax-paying public. We have only to consider how seldom we hear the devalued terms "single father," "unwed father," or "welfare father" to realize how harshly society judges women by their mothering. Women who have only one child are frequently criticized for that choice (Russo, 1976), and women who have "too many" children are seen as foolish and irresponsible. Mothers who "lose their children"—who do not seek or obtain custody of their children in divorce proceedings, for example—are viewed as stunning failures, often stemming from a lack of understanding about how mothers become noncustodial and from the common belief that only mothers can be good parents (Grief, 1979). Mothers whose jobs are demanding are frequently blamed for their absence from home, their use of day care or baby-sitters, and their concentration on their careers, in a way that fathers almost never are. Mothers whose jobs are possibly dangerous, for example, police officers, firefighters, or soldiers, are often viewed as irresponsible and self-indulgent parents for risking their lives, whereas fathers who have such jobs are viewed differently, even heroically. After her death, Christa McAuliffe, the teacher who was aboard the space shuttle *Challenger* when it exploded in the disaster of 1986, was roundly criticized for putting her interests in being part of history ahead of those of her children, but the male astronauts who were fathers were not similarly judged. Mothers who smoke, drink, or use other drugs, especially while they are pregnant or breast-feeding, face extremely harsh disapproval, criminal prosecution, and even the loss of their children in some cases.

Along with blaming women for mothering that diverges from the ideal, mothers have traditionally been blamed for all kinds of problems in their children and the family generally. This pattern of mother blaming in psychology dates back at least to Freud, in whose theory of psychosexual development all mothers walk a tightrope between overindulging and underindulging the child at each stage of development, leading to lifelong unresolved problems for the child. A content analysis of articles published in mental health journals across the disciplines of psychoanalysis, psychiatry, psychology, and social work found strong evidence of a tendency to blame mothers for the myriad problems of clients, ranging from arson to frigidity to minimal brain damage (Caplan & Hall-McCorquodale, 1985). Except when fathers clearly physically or sexually abuse their children, they are strangely immune from blame for their children's physical, psychological, and social problems, and even in those cases, mothers are still blamed for not better protecting their children from their fathers. The point is that all mothers fall short of the "ideal mother" to which most aspire. Mothers are often made to feel guilty and inadequate for that failure, and are blamed by society for "deficiencies" in themselves and their children.

The Experience of Mothering

Pregnancy.   Most women who become mothers do so as a result of a biological pregnancy (as described in Chapter 3). For many women, the lived experience of mothering begins with the recognition that they are expecting a child. Pregnancy is a period of enormous change: Being pregnant creates a critical new relationship in one's life, and the announcement or recognition that a woman is pregnant changes her relationships to the important people in her life, her community, and the larger society. All cultures mark pregnancy as a special event and shape individual women's attitudes and behaviors toward it (Seegmiller, 1993).

Seegmiller (1993) has extensively reviewed the vast literature on the experience of pregnancy. She notes that women receive information about pregnancy from a variety of sources that affects their views about their own pregnancy throughout their entire lives. With pregnancy, women often enter into a "society of women" through which the folklore, prescriptions, and taboos of pregnancy are communicated both transgenerationally and among peers. Folklore touches on virtually all aspects of pregnancy. We are all familiar with some of the ways in which people in our culture predict the sex of the fetus using signs like heart rate, the amount of fetal kicking, how a women's weight is distributed, or whether the woman is carrying the fetus high or low. Prescriptive actions are recommended to ensure easy or successful pregnancy and birth. For instance, some Puerto Rican and Mexican women drink certain teas to prevent morning sickness, whereas Anglo women ingest saltines or Benedictine for the same purpose. Taboos, usually surrounding food but often about action and sex, derive from fears of causing harm to the mother, fetus, or others. In her fieldwork among Jamaican women, Kitzinger (1978) found many rules for pregnant women: do not cork bottles or one will not "open up" and have an easy birth, avoid looking at disabled or ugly people or things lest the baby will be similarly marked. In the United States today, many women are fearful that baby showers and baby gifts before the birth may jinx the baby's chances of survival or that sex during pregnancy will harm the fetus (Brown, 1981).

Most investigators of pregnancy have identified a series of stages as the major tasks of pregnancy. In the first stage, the woman adjusts to being pregnant, becoming more preoccupied with herself as she becomes aware of and focused on the subtle changes occurring in her body. The next stage is incorporating (feeling that the fetus is a part of one) and accepting the fetus, which is facilitated by becoming visibly pregnant or experiencing ultrasound procedures and hearing the heartbeat. Forming an attachment to the fetus, the third stage, often begins with sensing fetal movement or "quickening" in the second trimester. It is around this time that many women begin talking to the fetus, with references to "we." This is when the woman tends to bring her partner further into the pregnancy by encouraging the partner to talk to and about the fetus, feel the fetal movements, and attend prenatal classes (Sherwin, 1987). During this period of attachment to the fetus and with increasing identity as a mother-to-be, a woman frequently becomes more concerned with her relationship with her own mother, reconciling differences, drawing closer, and forming a new relationship based on shared identities and experiences. The final stage, during the third trimester, is marked by differentiating and separating from the fetus and internalizing the identity of "mother." It is then that the woman often names the fetus and engages in "nesting behaviors" (e.g., decorating the baby's room, buying clothes for the baby, cleaning the house). In the last trimester, the woman's body size is a constant reminder that the baby will soon separate. Most women focus closely on the delivery date in the last trimester and are eager to give birth. The culmination of this process is a new sense of self, the baby, one's own mother, and one's partner (Seegmiller, 1993).

Obviously, the development and intensity of attachment to the fetus vary widely from woman to woman and depend on many factors. A consistent finding is that a woman's relationship to her fetus is associated with her feelings about her own mother, particularly her early experience of having been mothered. Women who have positive experiences of being mothered—who view their own mothers as warm, empathic, and satisfied with their maternal role—have an easier time adjusting to pregnancy and show greater ego strength and less anxiety during pregnancy (Liefer, 1977). Many other physical, psychological, and social factors are associated with adjustment to

pregnancy. Some of these concern the pregnancy itself: whether the pregnancy was wanted and planned, whether the pregnancy is easy or difficult physically, the woman's reactions to the physical changes of pregnancy, especially weight gain, and expectations and hopes about the sex of the baby (Seegmiller, 1993). Personality factors such as strong coping ability and ego strength, high self-concept and level of growth motivation, nurturance, and independence are associated with positive experiences of pregnancy.

Social, relationship, and other contextual variables have also been correlated with adjustment to pregnancy. The amount and quality of social support that a pregnant woman receives is a critical determinant of the lived experience of pregnancy. Strong social support from one's partner and others can buffer the inevitable stresses and anxieties of pregnancy. Increased social support has been cited as one reason that first pregnancies are experienced more positively than subsequent ones. The finding that women of low socioeconomic classes do not show poorer adjustment to pregnancy than more privileged women, despite suffering a greater incidence of physical problems during pregnancy, birth, and the neonatal period, has been linked to the beneficial effects of social support (Seegmiller, 1993). Women of color and ethnicity, who comprise a disproportionate share of the poor, tend to have more extensive and reliable networks of social support for pregnant women than other women (Stack, 1974).

Pregnancy changes women's relationships to individuals and communities. We have discussed its potential to change women's relationships with their mothers, often but by no means always for the better. For many women, their first pregnancy is a time of increased sharing, more open affection, and recognition and acceptance of their adult status. For some, however, the mother–daughter relationship degenerates when the mother fails to accept the daughter as an adult and attempts to control the daughter or to prove that she is a better mother (Seegmiller, 1993).

Women's relationships with their partners affect and are affected by their pregnancies. Most studies of women's relationships with their partners during pregnancy are of married heterosexual couples, and the results may not be generalizable to other kinds of partnerships. These studies tend to show that the pregnancy is associated with decreased relationship satisfaction, especially for husbands (Leifer, 1977). But some studies show that pregnancy is associated with a positive response from husbands and wives when the couple perceives the pregnancy as a common goal (Seegmiller, 1993).

Women's experiences of pregnancy vary enormously. Some women describe pregnancy as one of the happiest and most hopeful times in their lives, whereas others describe it as a time of constant sickness, stress, and anxiety. Factors like cultural and family background, psychological makeup, physical circumstances, and social and relational contexts interact to produce different reactions in every woman (Seegmiller, 1993; Unger, 1979). Of course, it is important to remember that not every woman who becomes a mother does so intentionally, in the context of a sexual relationship, or even by becoming pregnant. Some women who become pregnant choose to terminate their pregnancies (see Box 9.3).

Pregnancy, like motherhood generally, remains an understudied phenomenon by psychologists, despite the fact that most women consider their pregnancies to be among the most significant events in their lives. We do not yet have sufficient research on the topics covered here, let alone psychological responses to the use of reproductive technologies and the process of adoption, although these are becoming vital areas of research.

Giving Birth. As we saw with the experience of pregnancy, the experience of giving birth, one of the central events in a mother's life, is undervalued and understudied in psychology. This is largely because giving birth in the United States has been treated as a medical event that was, until recently, primarily managed by men to a degree unparalleled in the world. The medicalization of childbirth in the United States and, to a lesser extent, elsewhere in the industrialized West, inevitably colors how women perceive themselves, their babies, and the experience of childbirth.

A brief history of the medical management of childbirth reveals a struggle between male and female practitioners. In the preindustrial United States, babies were delivered by midwives and community women. When complications arose, women called upon barber–surgeons, usually male, who used forcepslike instruments and hooks to extract babies. A formal training period was deemed necessary for the surgical removal of babies, and the subspecialty of obstetrics, the first subspecialty to be taught in medical schools in the United States, was born. During the Victorian era, male doctors gained control of childbirth in the middle and upper classes, aided by new prosperity and increased respect for education, science, and technology among these social classes. Once entrenched, obstetricians waged an aggressive campaign against midwives, stereotyping them as ignorant, dirty, and irresponsible. As medical boards and state legislators suppressed midwifery, women had little recourse but to turn to doctors and hospitals for childbirth. In 1900, 5 percent of babies were born in hospitals; by 1935, 75 percent, and by 1970, 95 percent (Boston Women's Health Book Collective, 1992; Ehrenreich & English, 1979).

Childbirth has always involved a natural fear of things going wrong, the unknown, pain, and the risk of death of the mother and baby. But insensitive medical attitudes and practices may foster doubts and intensify fears of something going wrong. At its worst, the hospital experience for women about to give birth may be frightening and isolating, as the following quote illustrates:

> *Hospitals reduce labor and birth to a medical, debilitating event. As healthy strong women, we enter these places for sick people and our strength is systematically depleted. Often we are put into wheelchairs. Our personal effects are taken away. We are cut off from our friends and the people closest to us, isolated among strangers and made dependent and anonymous. . . . (Boston Women's Health Book Collective, 1992, p. 438)*

The authors of the quote perceive that there had been little continuity of care, with unfamiliar doctors and nurses hovering over the pregnant women for short

BOX 9.3

Abortion

Many women who become pregnant decide not to become mothers. Reliable figures on the number of abortions performed each year are not available, but estimates are that about 1.6 million abortions are performed each year in the United States and about 50 million annually worldwide (Neft & Levine, 1997). Of the 50 million abortions, about 20 million are illegal, with most of these performed in developing countries. In some countries, especially those with highly restrictive abortion laws, illegal abortions may terminate as many as one-quarter of all pregnancies (Neft & Levine, 1997). Illegal abortions are much more likely to be unsafe than legal ones and may result in many problems, including infections, infertility, and death.

About 38 percent of the world's population lives in countries where abortion is available on request; these include the United States, Canada, China, and Russia. Another 46 percent lives in countries where abortion is available under certain circumstances, such as Argentina, Brazil, and Mexico, where abortion is still quite restricted, and Australia, France, and Italy, where there are many more permissible grounds for abortion. Grounds for abortion, aside from saving the life of the woman, are preserving her physical and/or mental health, conditions of rape or incest, and fetal impairment. Finally, the remaining 16 percent of the population lives in countries where abortion is legal only to save the woman's life. The great majority of these countries are overwhelmingly Islamic or Roman Catholic, as these religions strictly forbid abortions. Ireland, a very Catholic country, is the only developed country in the world where abortion is permitted only to save the woman's life. Only a handful of countries, most notably Chile, do not permit abortion under any circumstances at all (Neft & Levine, 1997).

Within the United States, women of color have proportionately more abortions than White women (Centers for Disease Control, 1992). There are approximately 55 abortions per 1000 women of color reported annually in the United States, compared with 23 for White women. More than half of all women having abortions are in their twenties, with another quarter between the ages of 15 and 19. Contrary to stereotypes, almost half of the women having abortions are already mothers with significant family responsibilities (Henshaw & Silverman, 1988).

Just as policies about abortion vary enormously throughout the world, attitudes about abortion differ widely among individuals within societies. In 1973, the U.S. Supreme Court legalized abortion nationwide in the landmark *Roe* v. *Wade* decision, which held that a woman's right to an abortion was protected under the right to privacy guaranteed by the Constitution (Nevid et al., 1995). Yet abortion remains one of the most controversial of all social issues in the United States, with a capacity to divide families and other social groups like few other topics. In the United States, there is a strong right-to-life (pro-life) movement, which takes the position that human life begins at conception and abortion is the murder of an unborn child. People endorsing this position sometimes favor permitting abortion to save the woman's life or when the pregnancy results from rape or incest. There is also an active pro-choice movement, which contends that abortion is a matter of personal choice and that the government has no right to make laws restricting access to abortions (Nevid et al., 1995). Other countries where abortion is still a contentious issue include Canada, France, Germany, and Ireland (Neft & Levine, 1997).

Not every woman who has an abortion freely chooses this outcome. In China, where the government has instituted a policy of one child per family, some women are coerced into aborting fetuses by agents of the government if they have already borne a child. Others feel enormous pressure from their husbands or others to bear a son and abort female fetuses.

In countries like the United States, individual women may also be coerced by others—parents, lovers, husbands—to have abortions that they do not want. But more often, women choose to have abortions for many reasons. Some women become pregnant because their birth control fails. Others become pregnant and want a child, but find that their personal or social circumstances change. Others find out through prenatal screening that their fetus has serious problems. Still other women become pregnant because of rape, incest, or other forms of sexual coercion (Boston Women's Health Book Collective, 1992).

But even when a woman wishes to end her pregnancy, she does so against a backdrop of moral, social, and political forces that deeply affect the decision to have an abortion and the experience of abortion. Some women, including many, but not all, Catholics, Muslims, and Orthodox Jews, believe that abortion is murder. Even those who do not see abortion unequivocally as murder often experience a spiritual quandary about taking away the potential for human life. Indeed, few people are "pro-abortion." For other women, it is compulsory pregnancy and enforced motherhood that are morally wrong (Boston Women's Health Book Collective, 1992). Some people view abortion as a tool of population control, especially as a way of eliminating Third World peoples. Within the United States, some women of color are skeptical about the possibly racist motives of the pro-choice movement and link abortion to genocide. At the same time, many women of color choose to have abortions, and some advocates for women of color argue that accessible, affordable, safe, and legal abortions are essential for these as for all women. In recent years, there has been a spate of illegal and increasingly violent acts against abortion clinics and providers, and many people are increasingly concerned about the erosion of women's access to abortions because of these trends: less judicial support for legal abortion, new restrictions such as parental consent and notification laws in many states, reinstating spousal consent laws, and prohibitions against the use of public facilities and federal funds for abortion services, including providing information and making referrals about abortions (Boston Women's Health Book Collective, 1992).

Given the social context in which abortions take place, what are the effects of having an abortion on women's mental health? It is commonly believed that abortion causes severe guilt and depression, but a vast literature on the effects of abortion reveals this to be a myth (Adler et al., 1990; Russo & Green, 1993; Schwartz, 1986). Schwartz (1986) reviewed 32 scientifically sound studies on the psychological consequences of abortions and found that psychiatric problems were rare in women, on the order of 1 or 2 percent. When they did occur, they were related to pre-existing psychiatric problems and pressure to have an abortion against one's own judgment. A review of well-controlled empirical studies documented relatively minor risks to women's psychological well-being due to abortion (Adler et al., 1990). This review found that the predominant response to abortion is relief. Although some feelings of guilt, depression, and regret may be experienced after the procedure, these feelings are usually mild and transitory (Russo & Green, 1993). When compared with other significant reproductive-related events, like childbirth and miscarriage, abortion held no greater risk for depression (Wilmoth & Adelstein, 1988). Repeatedly, studies show that most women respond well to abortions. The predictors of negative responses to abortions are a history of emotional disturbance, not expecting to cope well with the abortion, feeling coerced to have the abortion, difficulty in deciding to have the abortion, abortion in the second trimester of pregnancy, and limited or no social support (Adler et al., 1990; Russo & Green, 1993).

Research on responses to abortion has been plagued with a number of problems, including an emphasis on finding negative outcomes to abortions and a reliance on clinical samples, that is, women who are experiencing some kind of psychological distress. Even with these negative biases, however, research has failed to link abortions with psychiatric or other serious disturbances of any kind. Unwanted pregnancy is unquestionably distressing for many women, yet most who seek abortions are reportedly relieved to have had access to the procedure and do not regret the experience. Adoption, often proposed as an alternative to abortion for the resolution of an unwanted pregnancy, poses psychological difficulties for many women, who show evidence of distress even decades after the adoption and who frequently initiate searches for their surrendered children (Russo & Green, 1993). Clearly, we need more research on how women make pregnancy-related decisions and on the psychosocial outcomes of those choices, given their importance in the lives of so many individuals.

---

periods of time, and then there may have been no one with the laboring woman for some periods of time. Women were often wheeled from room to room as they progress through labor. By the time a woman gave birth vaginally, she was on her back with her feet in stirrups, often drugged, and isolated from all familiar faces except possibly, in recent years, her partner. Many scholars have noted that such a position is unnatural for childbirth as it defies gravity. Increasingly, women do not deliver babies vaginally, but have cesarean sections in which babies are surgically re-moved. In 1968, the average rate of cesarean section in the United States was 5 percent, and by 1987 it had risen to 25 percent, where it still stands today (Lagrew & Adashek, 1998). This significant increase, the high-est in the world, has been attributed to several factors, including physicians' practice of defensive medicine, having had a previous delivery by cesarean section, trends in obstetrical training, changing indications for cesarean section, and economic incentives for surgery (Boston Women's Health Book Collective, 1992). These medical practices and the ideologies behind them cause doubts and raise fears, disrupt the physi-ology of labor, and distort the experience of giving birth.

It is important to note that cesarean sections are sometimes medically necessary. Advances in repro-ductive technology have enabled many women who could not conceive or carry a fetus to term, including older women who wish to become mothers, to have successful pregnancies. With the increase in the num-ber of high-risk pregnancies in both these groups, there may be greater need for careful medical man-agement, including cesarean sections.

An increasing number of women are choosing more natural ways of giving birth at home, in birth centers, and even in hospitals. Over the past 20 years, women have made substantial gains in their efforts to exert control over one of the central events of their lives. More partners attend childbirth classes and are present at births, more births are attended by mid-wives, and more decisions are in the hands of birthing women. The effects of these experiences are under-studied and insufficiently understood to date, but they appear to be promising:

> These women who gave birth confident in their own birthing powers, at home, in birth centers and in hos-pitals, show us that giving birth can be richer than we ever imagined. They speak of excitement, doubt, de-termination, effort, learning about themselves; of mo-mentary lapses and pulling themselves together; of hard work and giving in; of contentment, amazement, ecstasy, and exaltation. They listen to their bodies, re-main open to their attendants' encouragement to relax and renew themselves. (Boston Women's Health Book Collective, 1992, p. 436)

The Postpartum Experience.   Postpartum literally means "after birth" and denotes a period of time rang-ing from the first days to the first year following de-livery, when women are adjusting to what it means to be the mother of a baby. It is sometimes divided into three phases: the first phase, during which women make the transition from pregnancy to motherhood; the second phase, during which the focus is on learn-ing what it means to have a baby in their lives; and the final phase, when women begin to face some of the long-term issues that motherhood poses for them (Boston Women's Health Book Collective, 1992). As we review these phases, it is important to keep in mind that the **postpartum experience** varies widely from woman to woman depending on the physical, psycho-logical, and social landscape of her life.

The first phase, transition to parenthood, is a time of tremendous physical and emotional upheavals for many women. Depending on the circumstances of the birth, women may feel exhilarated and jubilant, proud of giving birth and of their new issue. But they may also feel disappointed or ambivalent about many as-pects of the birth, ranging from their experience of labor or delivery to the responses of their partner to the health, sex, or appearance of the baby. A few days after birth, many women experience "the baby blues," a brief period of inexplicable sadness. A small percentage of women experience a full-blown depres-sion that is incapacitating. Hormonal shifts are at least partly responsible for these reactions, which often appear just as mothers' milk comes in. But many woman are also saddened by frustrations with breast-feeding, problems with the newborn, fear of the awe-some responsibility of motherhood, or sheer physical exhaustion.

During the second postpartum phase, from a week to about six months after birth, women learn to adjust to life with their baby. This period, especially the early part, is often experienced as fragmented and disorga-nized. Probably the most common stressor is fatigue, caused by nights of interrupted sleep and the experi-ence of being on 24-hour call. Some mothers experi-ence loss of interest in sex and physical discomfort. Others struggle to cope with the monotony of long hours spent alone with an infant and isolated from the society of adults. In this stage some mothers experience postpartum depression that is more serious and longer-lived than the baby blues experienced right after birth. Almost one in three women experience some mild form of recurring depression after they give birth, and up to two in a thousand women experience such debilitating depression that they require hospitalization. Just a few decades ago, women who experienced postpartum depression were seen as mentally ill or unconsciously rejecting the responsibilities of motherhood. Today, the causes of postpartum depression are not completely understood, but two types of stressors may be involved. Physical-stress theories cite the dramatic reduction in estrogen and progesterone as causing depression. Oakley (1980) studied postpartum mothers living in London and found that the likelihood of postpartum depression increased with low levels of help with child care from the partner, unrealistic views of motherhood, few interests outside of child rearing, high levels of isolation, low levels of social support, and low levels of control over what happened during pregnancy and childbirth. Other studies have shown that those most likely to suffer from postpartum depression are having a first baby, have had previous bouts with postpartum depression, have experienced a move or change of life-style that has separated a woman from her family, or have a family history of death of a parent during childhood or childhood experiences of desertion, abuse, or traumatic divorce (Gordon & Gordon, 1967). If the new baby was premature or ill, had to remain in the hospital after the mother's discharge, or has ongoing health problems, postpartum depression is more likely. Often overlooked in studies of postpartum depression is infant temperament. Individual differences in behavior are present from early infancy, and mothers of infants who are irritable, unadaptable, and difficult to console are in fact more likely to be depressed (Hopkins, Campbell, & Marcus, 1987).

For many new mothers the experience of fatigue, loneliness, and loss of self during this period is outweighed by the wonderful aspects of mothering a new baby: the pleasures of holding and kissing the baby and watching the baby develop intellectually and emotionally and become more responsive each day. Many mothers are overwhelmed by the intensity of their feelings of love, connectedness, and protectiveness.

In the third and final postpartum phase, the period between 6 and 12 months, some of the chaos and uncertainty subside, and mothers feel more relaxed, energetic, and confident. By now, most babies begin to sleep through the night, eat solid food, and take predictable naps. With the welcome routine, however, some troubling long-term issues may come to the fore. With the birth of the baby, mothers' lives are irrevocably changed. Some women struggle with changes in their bodies that are not easily reversible; others mourn other losses: of their sense of self and their former interests and activities. Still others worry that they are not as effective at or as satisfied with being a mother as they had expected to be. If women live with partners, these relationships are changed. Studies of married couples consistently show that relationship satisfaction declines sharply with the birth of the first child (Etaugh, 1993; Hackel & Ruble, 1992). Partners may resent that sexual relationships change as women have less time, energy, and privacy. Women are often disappointed in the share of housework and child care taken on by their partners and are surprised at how easily they have slipped into traditional gender roles now that their daily lives differ so much from their partners' in their routines, social opportunities, tasks, and rewards. As difficult as it is to renegotiate relationships after the birth of a baby, women without partners experience even more difficulties and more depression than women with partners (Hopkins et al., 1984). Feelings of fatigue, isolation, and loneliness are especially high in single mothers during the postpartum period.

An increasing proportion of women face the prospect of working full or part time during the postpartum period. Working while one has very young children is complicated practically and emotionally:

We have to find child care and juggle the double demands of home and workplace. We love and miss our children; we are afraid of being replaced in their affections; we want to know that other caregivers will care deeply, too. These kinds of anxieties and questions are normal signs of caring. However the deep doubts and guilt that many of us feel in making and carrying out the decision to work are not a necessary part of being a working mother. These doubts are our response to being raised as females in a culture that insists that nurturing, and especially child care, is "women's work." (Boston Women's Health Book Collective, 1992, p. 492)

More than 60 percent of U.S. women with preschool-age children are now in the workplace, a percentage that has increased steadily in recent years. Yet, the United States remains the only major industrialized country not to have governmental policies and institutions that recognize parents' need for high-quality child-care options. Because men have been spared the stresses involved in trying to make a living and caring for families at the same time, they are not, by and large, highly motivated to transform the workplace to provide supports for working parents (Silverstein, 1996). Obviously, we need to question whether motherhood necessarily means constant child care and how we might restructure society—its policies and practices—to help to support children and those who care for them. Combining motherhood and work is also discussed more fully in Chapters 7 and 10.

Motherhood beyond the First Year.   Like pregnancy, childbirth, and the postpartum period, motherhood through the life-span is little studied by psychologists. There is a renewed empirical interest in the study of motherhood, largely fueled by the influx of women in psychology, and much of it concerns how women combine child care and work (a major preoccupation for psychologists who are mothers). Motherhood, like other major life experiences, remains difficult to study because it is embedded in psychological and social variables like social class and ethnicity that are themselves large and complex. There is no "all-purpose mothering experience": mothers come only in different social classes, races, and ethnicities, with different family backgrounds and family constellations, and different personalities and social realities. As children age and families take different shapes, women's experiences of mothering diverge all the more. This makes it difficult to generalize about the experience. We will briefly discuss two of the themes that emerge in research and writing about mothers.

Motherhood as the Central Identity and Commitment of Women's Lives.   As Rich (1976) aptly noted, motherhood is both an institution and a relationship.

Despite the constraints and commonalities of the stereotypes about motherhood, there is no one way to mother, no simple set of stages through which all women progress, no classic patterns of problems and solutions for all mothers. What most mothers share is the reality that having children has changed their lives forever and that being a mother is one of their most central identities. It is also their largest and most cherished commitment: mothers report overwhelmingly that if they could relive their lives they would have children again (Yankelovich, 1981). Despite the substantial costs of mothering so often noted in this chapter, most mothers find the positive aspects of mothering far more intense and compelling, and yet much harder to describe, than the negative aspects, which are plentiful and easily listed. When people name the advantages of mothering, that it is challenging; confers adult status; can be a source of fun, pleasure, and pride; carries on the family line, and the like (Gormly et al., 1987), the list often seems trite and beside the point. Like other ultimate values, for example, romantic love and religious faith, maternal love is difficult to explain and justify in rational terms, by appealing to external qualities of the child or rewards like fun, challenge, or societal respect. Indeed, maternal commitment is precisely the sense of acting beyond the call of any particular external qualities or rewards, and the profound rewards of maternal commitment come through the simple acts of loving and caring.

Motherhood Is Constantly Changing as Both Mother and Child Develop over Time.   It seems obvious that the experience of mothering is quite different with babies than it is with elementary school-age children, adolescents, and adult children. As children age, they become less physically demanding, and this frees mothers from the fatigue and isolation that mark the earlier postpartum period. School-age children are frequently seen as "easiest" on mothers, although mothers continue to be constrained by school schedules and the round of after-school activities—soccer, scouts, dancing or piano lessons—that figure prominently in the lives of many middle- and upper-class children today and keep many women from pursuing careers or full-time jobs. Rearing adolescents is widely seen as the most difficult period of motherhood after rearing infants. As the old saying goes, "Little children, little problems; big children, big problems." Adolescence is a particularly difficult time for the mothers of daughters, who often rebel by asserting themselves or withdrawing as a way of detaching from their mothers (Fischer, 1987). But mothers are closer to their adult daughters than their adult sons, with the turning point often being when the daughter herself becomes a mother. And daughters play a key role when mothers become elderly and the daughter is often the one to become the care-giver (Walker, Pratt, & Wood, 1993). Strong emotional relationships between mothers and children last a lifetime, enduring many changes in circumstances (Unger & Crawford, 1996). More research is needed on the experience of mothering—how mothering changes women and how women change as mothers—over the life-span.

Mothering under Difficult Circumstances. It has been a theme of this section that under the best of circumstances mothering is difficult work, but it is especially taxing under the less than best conditions in which many people find themselves. As we have noted, mothering can only take place in a context. When the family is poor or children (or parents) are seriously ill, mothering is complicated still further. Nearly one in five children in the United States lives in poverty today. Poverty rates for children in single-parent (mostly mother-headed) households is 50 percent, a figure that has changed little in more than 30 years (Schatz & Bane, 1991). Most of us who were reared or are rearing children in middle-class households can only imagine the dreariness and terror of living in substandard housing in unsafe neighborhoods, being unable to afford a variety of nutritious foods, having inadequate access to decent medical care and educational systems, being hassled by creditors, or humiliated and disrespected by agents of society like teachers and social service workers. In a consumer society like ours, in which all children are bombarded by images of great wealth and glamour, it is heartbreaking to have to say constantly to your children "no," to deny them the products, experiences, and opportunities that so many other children enjoy (Lott,

1991). It is especially difficult for mothers to be competent and nurturant when, being poor, they themselves are more likely to be ill, poorly educated, single, with a history of abuse or neglect. Throughout the 1990s, the United States has moved in the direction of espousing a moral model of poverty and reducing aid to the poor: tightening welfare eligibility and cutting benefits. We need to consider how women and children will be affected in the twenty-first century by the harsh and sweeping welfare policy changes of the mid-1990s and how a wealthy nation like the United States can tolerate such a high percentage of poor children.

Mothers of children who are chronically ill or disabled also face special challenges that deserve more research and societal attention than they currently receive. A society that worships the healthy, able-bodied, and good looking and renders others invisible makes it difficult indeed to rear children who do not conform to the ideal. Mothers rear ill and disabled children in a context that subscribes to the notions that health and vigor are moral virtues for everyone, and that the body can be controlled if only one tries hard enough. We also live in a society that prizes individual solutions for problems and holds that individual families are responsible for providing all the resources that ill and disabled children need, often at enormous personal sacrifice (Wendell, 1993). Moreover, in the United States, the only major industrialized society without some kind of national health care policy, families without Medicaid or an excellent private insurance plan quickly spend all their money trying to secure adequate medical help for their children.

Sick and disabled children often require more care and resources than other children, and this strains the entire family physically and emotionally, as well as financially. Mothers may feel guilty that their healthier children are burdened and neglected because of the attention devoted to the ill or disabled child. Fathers frequently work overtime or take extra jobs to make ends meet. Parents and children could be significantly helped by policies—and a construction of illness and disability—that did not impoverish, isolate, shame, and blame families for children's problems. We now understand that some of what is ill or disabling about a physical condition is a consequence of social arrangements and attitudes. These arrangements and attitudes can be changed in ways that can support families in their struggles and enable affected children to participate more fully and productively in society.

Infertility.   *Infertility* is defined as the failure to conceive after one year of vaginal intercourse without the use of contraceptives (Benson, 1983). In the United States, approximately 10 percent of couples in which the woman is of child-bearing age are infertile: almost 20 percent of all couples without children. About 50 to 60 percent of infertile couples eventually conceive, but the remaining 40 to 50 percent will remain infertile (Abbey, Andrews, & Halman, 1991). In about 70 to 80 percent of the cases, infertility is due to one individual: about 40 percent of the time, the woman, and in 30 to 40 percent of the cases, the man. In 10 to 20 percent of the cases, the cause is unclear. Some major factors that cause infertility are *sexually transmitted diseases* (STDs), which can lead to permanent damage to the reproductive system, intrauterine devices (IUDs), which sometimes contribute to infertility by causing *pelvic inflammatory disease* (PID) after insertion, women's delay of childbearing until the late thirties or early forties, when women are less fertile, and the increase in environmental and industrial toxins, which can damage both men's and women's reproductive systems. Infections following abortions, if untreated, can sometimes cause infertility (Boston Women's Health Book Collective, 1992). Regardless of which member of the couple has the physical problems that cause infertility, most of the tests and treatments focus on the woman's body and require her to take an active role (Abbey et al., 1991). STDs are discussed further in Chapter 13.

Infertility is almost always unexpected and is experienced by most people as a life crisis. Many investigators have documented the negative psychological, behavioral, and social effects of infertility. These include depression, anxiety, guilt, anger, frustration, and helplessness. Infertile individuals report feeling like defective or failed men or women, with predictable effects on self-esteem and body image (Menning, 1977).

Infertility puts enormous strain on a marital relationship. The partners who are infertile frequently tell their partners that it is understandable if they leave the relationship and then worry about desertion (Andrews, 1984). As people are unlikely to confide this particular problem to others, the two partners are often each other's only source of emotional support. Sex becomes a chore rather than a joy as it becomes routinized and prescribed.

There are consistent gender differences in response to infertility, with women experiencing much more negative affect than men. One study found that half of the infertile women, compared to only 15 percent of infertile men, described their infertility as one of the most upsetting experience of their lives (Freeman, Boxer, Rickels, Tureck, & Mastroianni, 1985). Infertile women perceive having children as more important than their husbands (Abbey et al., 1991). Women's greater infertility-related stress and depression probably have several causes, chief among them the centrality of the parenting role and identity for women and the fact that other people typically regard infertility as being the "woman's fault," thus stigmatizing the woman. Women tend to cope more actively with the infertility, take more responsibility for it, and work harder to control it. Infertile men experience a somewhat different set of problems. They sense that their wives experience the prospect of not having children more negatively than they do, and they struggle to cope with their wives' distress (Abbey et al., 1991).

Fatherhood

Fatherhood is a central commitment and identity to many men, our fathers, husbands, and many friends among them. Yet there is a long tradition of ignoring the father's role in parenting. In the first edition of *Dr. Spock's Baby Book,* he devoted only nine pages to fathering. Many current textbooks on men do not feature chapters or even separate sections on fatherhood but, sadly, do have sections on "father absence" (Kilmartin, 1994). The fact is that fatherhood is only recently getting the attention it deserves from psychologists and others. There are many reasons for the relative absence of fatherhood as a topic for study in psychology. One is surely the androcentric (male-centered) bias within psychology that devalues the study of all relationships, especially family relationships. Another is the implicit belief (and, at least in the past, too often the reality) that for many men being a father was a less central identity than others, for instance, being a worker. As Silverstein (1996) notes, "late 20th century fatherhood ideology continues to reflect the belief that active participation by mothers in the daily care of children is obligatory, whereas nurturing and caretaking by fathers is discretionary" (p. 11). This ideology generally rendered fathers invisible, with the curious exception of when they *were* invisible, that is, absent from the family. Father absence is blamed for a grab bag of pathologies in children, especially African American children, even though why father absence is so problematic is rarely addressed. Still others see the new emphasis on fatherhood at this point in history as a ploy to reassert the essential significance of men's paternal rights at a time when men's power and control over women is declining (Silverstein, 1996). With the rise of the new discipline of men's studies, in which men are studied *as men* rather than as exemplars of all humanity, fatherhood is finally attracting scholarly attention.

Much of the psychological research on fatherhood can be organized around a few themes: (1) Must mothers be the primary parent? Can fathers nurture? Can fathers mother? (2) Does father absence really matter? and (3) How much do and how can fathers participate in child care? We will very briefly consider the empirical research on each general question.

To the question of whether fathers *can* nurture children in ways similar to mothers, the answer appears to be yes. In her excellent review of fathering, Silverstein (1996) notes that, historically, fathers were responsible for the religious, moral, and vocational education of their children. The introduction of mandatory formal education, along with industrialization and the separation of home life and work life, contributed to the demise of fathers as teachers and moral leaders in the family. Early research suggesting that fathers and mothers parent differently is being reevaluated. As Silverstein notes, despite cultural beliefs to the contrary, research findings with humans and animals do not suggest sex differences in the ability to care for infants. Rather, the extent to which fathers in human and other mammalian species actively care for infants depends on a complex array of ecological, demographic, and temperamental variables. When fathers are thrust into the primary caretaking role, they act like mothers.

The question of whether fathers freely choose to nurture their children is another matter. Studies show that the amount of time that fathers spend in direct interaction with their children each day averages between 12 and 26 minutes (Silverstein, 1996). Lamb (1987) found that mothers continue to shoulder about 90 percent of the care of young children. Hyde, Essex, and Horton (1993) found that the way that fathers increase their contributions to their young families is by working harder on the job, not by spending more time with the children. Despite the media attention in recent years on the "nurturant" father, paternal involvement in child rearing has not changed much in the past 30 years. Even in countries that are more supportive of parental child care than the United States, for example, Sweden, fathers do not appear to take on significantly more of the child-rearing duties than fathers in the United States (Silverstein, 1996).

How important is involved fathering anyway? Is father absence a devastating blow to children? In her review of the relevant literature, Silverstein concluded that the active involvement of responsible, nonabusive fathers was indeed beneficial to the entire family in several domains. Active father involvement in the household is one of the major determinants of decreasing stress for working mothers (Hoffman, 1989) and contributes to fathers' sense of competence, self-confidence, and self-esteem as fathers. The bulk of the research suggests that neither a male or female parent is necessary for positive developmental outcomes or gender identity formation. What is needed is loving and caring *adults,* rather than mothers or fathers *per se.* Silverstein (1996) argues that the many studies consistently showing that children who grow up in mother-headed households fare more poorly than children who are reared by both biological parents cannot be adequately explained by father absence. The general pattern of findings suggests that father absence is confounded with numerous other variables. With two loving and responsible adults in the home, the family experiences a higher income, an additional attachment figure and role model, more adult supervision, and some relief for the primary caregiver.

Women now contribute a substantial amount to the family income in over half of the households in the United States. They are in the workplace to stay. Overwhelmingly, men and women continue to want to have children. It seems that, as we begin the twenty-first century, mothering and fathering will increasingly involve both earning money and nurturing children. We need as a society to figure out how the workplace can be reorganized to accommodate the new realities (Silverstein, 1996). Moreover, research suggests that we need to acknowledge and reinforce men's capacity to nurture. Finally, there is much research yet to be done on fathering. We do not know enough about how fathering differs for boys and girls, although research suggests that fathers are involved more with their sons than with their daughters (Crouter, McHale, & Bartko, 1993). We have too little information on fathers of color, although new research is exploding some myths about irresponsible young African American fathers. For example, McAdoo, cited in Silverstein (1996), found that many poor and working-class African American men who do not live with their families do play a role in their children's lives. McAdoo also cited data suggesting that young African American teen fathers were more likely to contribute to their children's support than White teen fathers. We need more information on gay fathers. Also, we need further work on how fathering changes men and their constructions of masculinity, and how we might strengthen the identity and commitment of fatherhood.

Taking Care: Women's Other Relationships

Women have many key relationships in their lives other than those with lovers, spouses, and children. These relationships are central to most women's sense of well-being and happiness. Until recently, psychology had almost completely overlooked the study of women, gender, and close relationships outside of romantic and parental bonds, but interest in these areas is rapidly expanding.

Women are widely seen as the relationship experts between the sexes. Certainly, gender stereotypes suggest that women are more socially skilled, agreeable, emotionally sensitive, expressive, and concerned with personal relationships than men are (Eagly, 1987). Research consistently shows that women are more likely to seek and receive social support from others than men are and that women have more extensive, effective, and satisfying social support networks than men (Barbee et al., 1993). In families generally, middle-aged women carry out most of the care-giving and support functions needed by younger and older members, including in-laws. It is often noted that families are linked through their female members, who have closer ties with each other than with male family members. Middle-aged and older women are more likely than men or younger women to worry about other family members and to experience more family-related conflicts and stresses (Etaugh, 1993; Green & Russo, 1993). Overwhelmingly, the direct care of the sick and elderly in our society, as in others, is in the hands of women. By virtue of their gender role, cultural expectations, and social power, women are the care-givers of society. This role can obviously be enormously demanding and debilitating, as the substantial literature on care-giver burden suggests (Etaugh, 1993; Green & Russo, 1993). But it is also a role that many women cherish, and new research is uncovering some of the rewards of, for instance, daughters caring for their elderly parents.

Grandmothering, discussed in Chapter 10, is a central identity for many women and a critical function in many families. Psychologists are only now beginning to study grandmothering in a systematic way. As little as we know about grandmothers, we know even less about women as sisters, daughters, daughters-in-law, mothers-in-law, and aunts. Indeed, given their importance in the lives of women, all the roles women play in families need and deserve more research.

Friendships.   Friends who share our interests, help us in time of need, enjoy our company, and value our opinions enrich our lives (Veniegas & Peplau, 1997). For many groups of people today, friends have replaced family as their most cherished and reliable support networks. Friendships are complicated relationships, varying in depth, closeness, and conflict. Like all other intimate relationships, they are poorly understood but increasingly the focus of empirical research.

People have long noticed a gender difference in friendship patterns. For one thing, at least until now, our closest friends are people of our own sex. Male friendships tend to be based on shared interests, whereas female friendships are more often based on disclosure (Reis, Senchak, & Solomon, 1985). Not so long ago, male friendships, sometimes called *male bonding,* were extolled in literature and film as more noble, loyal, and deep than female friendships, which, when they were portrayed at all, were depicted as shallow, trivial, and competitive. But today, *Butch Cassidy and the Sundance Kid* has given way to *Waiting to Exhale.* Many factors have combined to change the view of what friendship is and might be and the valuation of male and female friendships. For instance, with the feminist revolution came a more positive reassessment of female qualities like expressivity and nurturance. Empirical research in psychology over the past 20 years has consistently documented the positive effects of social support and self-disclosure on physical and mental health and, alternatively, the negative effects of "keeping things in" and suppressing emotions. Moreover, women's greater willingness to talk about their feelings and ask for help means that they are more likely to get the help that they need than men are.

Research on diverse samples of people consistently finds gender differences in the quality of same-sex friendships, regardless of how quality is measured: Women rate their friendships higher than men on meaningfulness, intimacy, nurturance, enjoyment, and satisfaction (Veniegas & Peplau, 1997). We do not yet understand why women's friendships appear to be closer, more meaningful and satisfying, but several possible explanations have been offered (Kilmartin, 1994). Many of these are rooted in aspects of the masculine gender role that inhibits the formation of close relationships between men. For instance, men are socialized to believe that other men are competitors and

that the establishment of intimacy rests on revealing one's weaknesses. This leads to an atmosphere of distrust among men. The gender-role demand for independence also inhibits self-disclosure in men because it keeps them from asking for help or comfort. According to Kilmartin (1994), homophobia is probably the greatest barrier to friendships between men. Some men may have difficulty making a clear distinction between sexual and nonsexual intimacy and may be concerned that getting close to another man is tantamount to being sexual with him.

It is true that the style of intimacy associated with female friendships has many benefits and the style associated with male friendships some drawbacks, but it would be a mistake to exaggerate the differences between male and female friendships or to disparage the different forms that friendships might take. Men and women's friendships are more alike than they are different (Veniegas & Peplau, 1997) and may become more similar as boys (and girls) are socialized differently in the future. Shared interests and activities and instrumental acts of helping others, mainstays of male friendships, are obviously valuable, and talking or ruminating about problems in the absence of action can keep women stuck in bad jobs and relationships.

Although they are not nearly as common as same-sex friendships, cross-sex friendships are vital sources of satisfaction for many adults. Men as well as women seek out women with whom to talk about their feelings, and, like women, men report feeling more emotional closeness to female than male friends (Wheeler, Reis, & Neslek, 1983). Cross-sex friendships are complicated by the fact that men and women have different interactional styles (Tannen, 1990), with men generally less egalitarian and more directive than women in their communications, which some women find aversive (Kilmartin, 1994). Cross-sex friendships are sometimes made difficult because of sexual tension. Studies show that men are more likely to sexualize a relationship than are women, and to perceive sexual interest or flirtation where women see friendliness (Abbey, 1982). More cross-sex friendships are found in young adulthood than in any other developmental period. In later adulthood, especially after marriage, it is difficult to maintain these relationships, partly because of concern by potential friends and spouses about the sexual possibilities in the friendship (Kilmartin, 1994). The fact that cross-sex relationships have been inhibited in the past does not mean that they will be uncommon in the future. As traditional gender roles break down, there may be more possibilities for rich, egalitarian relationships between men and women.

SUMMARY

In this chapter we have considered the major topics explored by social scientists in attempting to understand intimate relationships in their richness and complexity. As you can see, psychologists have raised and attempted to answer some interesting questions but have barely scratched the surface of these intriguing topics. What is clear from this chapter is that intimate relationships are particularly important to women, that men, women, and children depend critically on women for social support, and that most problems that people face in their relationships may be improved substantially with social support. We need to shine a spotlight on the new relationships that women are forging with other women as mentors of other women. We may need new lines of inquiry to capture the changing nature of relationships in the context of continually evolving social structures, gender roles, attitudes, beliefs, behaviors, and values. And we are challenged with the task of illuminating those factors that cause problems for men and women in their most important relationships, that contribute to distress and conflict, and that stand in the way of contentment and fulfillment.

KEY TERMS

Cohabitation (p. 283)
Egalitarian marriages (p. 278)
Exchange theory (p. 277)
Homogamy (p. 276)

Marriage gradient (p. 277)
Modern marriages (p. 278)
Motherhood mandate (p. 290)
Motherhood mystique (p. 290)

Postpartum experience (p. 298)
Romantic love (p. 270)
Traditional marriages (p. 277)

DISCUSSION QUESTIONS

1. Do you believe that behaving according to *The Rules* works for women in establishing long-standing, committed relationships?

2. Do you think that romantic love is a good basis for marriage or lifelong commitment? Why or why not? Compare it with an alternative, for example, arranged marriages?

3. Should heterosexual women pay their own way on dates? Why or why not? Have you ever felt obligated to someone who was paying your way? What does it mean for a man to pay for a date? What does it mean for a woman to pay for a date?

4. Is there any reason to think that same-sex couples cannot achieve the same levels of love and commitment that heterosexual couples do? What is your position on gay marriage? Why do you support or oppose it?

5. Do you think that there should be two forms of marriage, one for childless couples that is relatively easy to dissolve, and another for couples with children that is more difficult to dissolve than marriages today?

6. How are dating and marriage possible under conditions of economic scarcity?

7. Discuss the relationship of power to the household division of labor. How was labor divided in the house in which you were reared, and how would you like it divided in your household?

8. Do you feel that fatherhood is as important as motherhood? If not, can it be? What changes would need to be made for this to be so?

SUGGESTED READINGS_____

Blumstein, P., & Schwartz, P. (1983). *American couples: Money, work, and sex.* New York: William Morrow.

Debold, E., Wilson, M., & Malave, I. (1993). *Mother daughter revolution: From betrayal to power.* Reading, MA: Addison-Wesley.

Russo, N. F. (1976). The motherhood mandate. *Journal of Social Issues, 32,* 143–153.

Seegmiller, B. (1993). Pregnancy. In F. Denmark & M. Paludi (Eds.), *Psychology of women: A handbook of issues and theories* (pp. 437–474). Westport, CT: Greenwood.

CHAPTER 10

GROWING OLDER

I have enjoyed greatly the second blooming that comes when you finish the life of the emotions and of personal relations; and suddenly you find—at the age of fifty, say—that a whole new life has opened before you, filled with things you can think about, study, or read about. . . . It is as if a fresh sap of ideas and thoughts was rising in you.
—Agatha Christie

The older I get, the greater power I seem to have to help the world; I am like a snowball—the further I am rolled the more I gain.
—Susan B. Anthony

I've been in the twilight of my career longer than most people have had their career.
—Martina Navratilova

In Chapter 5 we noted developmental issues through adolescence. This chapter will deal with the phenomenon of adulthood and aging. Some of the issues have been taken up in other chapters, such as Chapters 7 and 9. Therefore, we devote the first part of this chapter to choices confronting younger adults, including whether to marry, whether to combine marriage and career, and whether to have children. Having survived adolescence, young adults find themselves at the threshold of the rest of their lives. During this transition period, they may be taking college courses that will eventually lead them down a career path of their choice. They may be looking to find someone to marry, move in with, or simply date casually without any plans for commitment.

Young adults growing up today differ from their parents' generation at this stage. This chapter considers some of the evolving patterns, such as more single people choosing to remain single and many more committed couples opting to cohabit rather than marry. Even couples who have followed the more traditional route of marriage may prefer not to have children or to have children in their thirties or forties. As the years of young adulthood pass, individuals suddenly find themselves at another transitional point of life—mid-life. Women and men are confronted with the social stigmas of aging. A number of these stigmas are found to have surprisingly little validity when examined against the actual events in question. Menopause, once viewed as an earth-shattering end to a woman's youth and purpose, can actually be a positive event. The empty nest syndrome, when children leave home, rather than being a depressing period of purposelessness for middle-aged women, provides many of them with the opportunity to discover new talents and interests as reentry women. These women, bravely returning to school or work, are increasing in number.

As the aging process continues, new difficulties arise for women and men, such as spousal bereavement, retirement, and psychological and cognitive changes. Yet, just as in the middle years, some events of later adulthood are unfairly stigmatized. Spousal bereavement, while certainly an unfortunate and sometimes tragic experience, may provide older people with the opportunity to form new social circles, especially if relieved of caring for an ill spouse or partner. Retirement is not only the end of a career, but may be the beginning of an exciting new period as older people find themselves with more free time to engage in new pursuits and enjoy their grandchildren, another satisfying transition.

In addition, older members of the population may feel freer and less bound to conform to traditional gender-role expectations. Older women may "feel their oats" and be more assertive and outspoken, and older men may discover a gentler, more affiliative side to their personalities. Whether this is the result of their no longer being bound by traditional gender roles or not, the change is a positive one that seems to be correlated with growing older.

One may not be able to escape the almost inevitable physical and/or cognitive decline brought on by increasing age. Yet, many elderly people enjoy life in a way that they never had before this point. They no longer feel the pressures of earning money and raising a family and are able to relax and do things that they always wanted to do.

This chapter should provide the reader with a comprehensive overview of the developmental changes of early, middle, and later adulthood. Many of the myths surrounding aging should be dispelled by the information contained herein, in particular, those myths that are gender biased and present women or men in an unfair light.

ERIK ERIKSON

Erik Erikson's theory of life-span development brought increased realization that important cognitive and psychosocial changes occur not only in childhood, but throughout the adult years as well. His paradigm of psychosocial development is comprised of eight stages that begin in infancy and culminate in late adulthood. (See Table 10.1 for a complete listing of Erikson's psychosocial stages from infancy through adulthood.) According to Erikson, the establishment of love relationships was a key facet in early adulthood, and the major task of young adults was resolving the conflict between intimacy and isolation. Erikson maintained that the development of the capacity for intimacy depended on the successful formation of a stable psychosocial identity in adolescence.

TABLE 10.1   Erikson's Stages of Psychosocial Development

PSYCHOSOCIAL STAGE	TASK
1: Trust vs. Mistrust	If their needs are consistently met, infants learn to trust their environment. The failure to meet an infant's needs results in the development of mistrust.
2: Autonomy vs. Shame and Doubt	Toddlers who learn to regulate their bodily functions gain a sense of independence and autonomy. Toddlers who fail to achieve control over their bodies experience shame and doubt.
3: Initiative vs. Guilt	As preschoolers experiment with their developing physical and mental skills, they must learn to control their impulses.
4: Industry vs. Inferiority	Children aged 6 to 11 years learn to take pride in their emerging skills and abilities. Negative comparisons with other children often lead to feelings of inferiority.
5: Identity vs. Role Confusion	Adolescents combine their various roles to form one coherent self-identity. The failure to integrate different aspects of the self leads to role confusion.
6: Intimacy vs. Isolation	Young adults develop the capacity to form intimate relationships with others. Failure to develop interpersonal attachments leads to social and emotional isolation.
7: Generativity vs. Stagnation	During middle adulthood, individuals take an interest in fostering the development of younger generations. Preoccupation with one's own needs leads to stagnation and self-absorption.
8: Integrity vs. Despair	During late adulthood, individuals reflect on their lives, searching for meaning. If they find meaning in their lives, they experience integrity. If they fail to glean meaning from their lives, they experience despair.

According to Erikson, the main task of middle adulthood was the resolution of the conflict between generativity versus stagnation. During this stage, adults must take an active interest in guiding younger generations or they risk becoming preoccupied with themselves and self-absorbed. Successful middle age involves being productive workers, spouses, parents, mentors, and guides for new generations of family members, students, and apprentices.

Finally, Erikson claimed that the main psychosocial task of late adulthood is to resolve the crisis of integrity versus despair. Reflecting on their lives, older adults struggle to find meaning in their lives. Integrity results from looking back on one's life as important and successful, whereas despair arises from regret, meaninglessness, and social isolation.

Carol Gilligan (1982) has criticized Erikson's theory because it describes the developmental trajec-

tory of males better than females. Since Gilligan contends that female development emphasizes attachment to others and interdependence, many females must first achieve intimacy prior to the development of stable identity. Erikson's placement of identity formation prior to the development of deep relationships in his sequence of psychosocial development reflects the traditional pathway of male development in which independence is highlighted as the primary goal.

MAKING A CHOICE: TO PARTNER OR NOT TO PARTNER

In contrast to the intimacy of relationships detailed in Chapter 9, this chapter takes a developmental perspective on the choices faced by adults in terms of staying single versus marrying and staying married versus obtaining a divorce. In her book *Passages,* Gail

Sheehy describes "the trying 20s" as a time of leaving the safety of home behind and beginning to search for a partner and a role in life. The following decade, "the catch 30s," is meant to be a time of making, breaking, or deepening life commitments (Sheehy, 1974). Clearly, early adulthood is a time of cementing the structures that will define one's life. As such, marrying and starting a family is considered a pivotal objective for women and men who have reached this time of life. But is it?

Female and Male Singles: Desperately Seeking . . . or Not

An increasing number of individuals in their twenties are choosing to remain single. According to the 1997 current population survey, 14 million or 34.5 percent of adults between the ages of 25 and 34 have never been married (U.S. Census Bureau, 1998b). However, among people in their mid- to late thirties, the number of individuals remaining single has not increased as much (Glick, 1986), suggesting that the above trend reflects a decision to postpone marriage, but not necessarily indefinitely. Cherlin (1981) estimated that 90 percent of those who were young adults in the 1980s will marry. However, according to Norton and Moorman (1987), the number of people who *are* choosing to remain single indefinitely is also on the rise.

Several factors may explain this shift. Women's increased career opportunities and financial independence allow them to be self-sufficient, and the need to "find a man to take care of you" financially is obsolete. Today's more permissive attitudes make sex more available for the single woman or man and allow couples to postpone commitment by living together without officially marrying. In addition, the availability of contraceptives, as well as the growing awareness and acceptance of single motherhood as an option, decreases the likelihood of an unexpected pregnancy forcing a shotgun wedding. Knowledge of the increase in the divorce rate may also play a role, causing young women and men to think twice before accepting the risks involved with marriage.

Are single people happier than married people? According to a study by Wu and DeMaris (1996), they

are not. Unmarried women and men and married women report higher depressive symptoms than do married men. However, married women were found to be happier than unmarried women. Perhaps, although singles may be put off from marriage by the rising divorce rate, the decision to remain single is not necessarily optimal for their happiness.

Staying single longer has ramifications for gender-role behavior. Women who stay single longer are more able to grow as individuals and move ahead in their careers, acquiring more education and greater financial independence. These women are likely to be more assertive and to possess the means of finding fulfillment outside marriage. Men who have lived alone, on the other hand, are likely to be more domestic and to have developed friendships with other women and men that might have been precluded by marriage. This may account for part of the general shift in society from prescribed gender-role identities to more androgynous modes of being (Vannoy, 1991).

Whether or not a twenty-something person chooses the traditional route of marriage, most individuals in this **cohort** are seeking a romantic partner. For some, a purely sexual liaison with this partner is satisfactory, whereas for others a meaningful long-term relationship is what is sought. In recent times, dating has become less focused on mate selection (Rice, 1990).

It is interesting to note that women's and men's criteria are quite similar for the ideal long-term significant other but differ somewhat for the fleeting sexual partner. Women and men seeking long-term companions both value similar traits, including honesty, fidelity, warmth, and personality (Buss et al., 1990). However, women seeking sexual partners emphasize warmth and personality as well, whereas men omit these traits, focusing on figure or build and facial features (Nevid, 1984).

One might expect a woman or man seeking a romantic partner to want a strongly gender typed individual. However, this will depend on how strongly one identifies with one's own traditional gender role. "Hyperfeminine" women tend to prefer "macho" men who approach sexuality more aggressively. Conversely, less "hyperfeminine" women do not express this preference (Maybach & Gold, 1994). While non-traditional college-aged men preferred androgynous females, traditional college-aged men expressed an equal preference for androgynous and stereotypically feminine females (Orlofsky, 1982).

Much information as to what men and women seek in a partner is revealed in a look at personal advertisements. Personals written by men and women are surprisingly similar, and both men and women tend to request a partner who is sensitive, warm, or romantic. However, men are more likely to seek physical attractiveness in a partner (Koestner & Wheeler, 1988). This is consistent with findings that men seeking partners are more motivated by the possibility of sexual activity (Peplau, Rubin, & Hill, 1977; Roscoe, Diana, & Brooks, 1987). Men are also more likely than women to describe their own financial status in an ad, whereas women are more likely to include financial status among their specifications (Goode, 1996; Koestner & Wheeler, 1988). The personal ads in Box 10.1 have been modified from a newspaper in a large metropolitan area and illustrate the preceding comments.

Interestingly, the demands may differ when a personal ad is placed for a same-gender partner. For instance, in a study of 800 personal ads placed by heterosexual and gay adults (Deaux & Hanna, 1984), men seeking other men were similar to men seeking women in that they requested information about physical attractiveness and sexual characteristics and offered their own financial status as a lure. Of the four groups in Deaux and Hanna's (1984) study, lesbians were the least likely to request information regarding physical attractiveness and to offer information about their own looks. Lesbians seemed more focused on personality traits, sincerity, and the potential of a long-term relationship than the other three groups. Based on this information, it can be argued that those seeking relationships with men (i.e., gay men and heterosexual women) must place emphasis on their physical characteristics—indeed, that may be what is demanded. On the other hand, lesbians attend to other, less concrete characteristics, which reflect different role demands and expectations (Deaux & Hanna, 1984).

While we might prefer the more romantic view of dating as a spontaneous and natural event, courtship

---

BOX 10.1

Personal Ads: A Reflection of Gender Stereotypes

WOMEN

Sexy and Strikingly Attractive—Woman, 33, two children. Affectionate, funny, vivacious. Interests include opera, art museums, literature. Seeks single man, 35–45, financially secure, professional, to share romantic possibilities.

Head-Turning Blonde—cute, shapely young lady, 20s, enjoys fitness and the arts. My man is educated, generous, stylish, and very accomplished CEO, investment banker, or lawyer in his 30s or 40s. We will enjoy friendship and romance together, and possibly children.

MEN

Self-Made Millionaire—Male, 48, Harvard MBA, successful entrepreneur. Interested in mountain biking, travel, dining out, and exercise. Seeks attractive, slim (110 lbs. or less), physically fit female with good sense of humor and common interests.

MD—36, 6 ft, 200, good-looking athletic male. Loves being spontaneous, the outdoors, good books, and good company. Seeks bright, beautiful blond female in her 20s without kids. Missing that special person to share life with. Must include photo.

---

and related activities such as flirting and initiating or advancing sexual intimacy are actually highly scripted for members of both genders (McCormick, 1987; Pryor & Merluzzi, 1985). Women are expected to be concerned about their appearance, maintain conversation, control sexuality, and play a nurturing and emotionally supportive role (see Sprecher, 1985); men are responsible for planning, paying for, and organizing the date (Shulman, 1980). However, these role prescriptions are becoming more flexible (Rice, 1990). Many women, especially feminist women, report initiating and paying for dates at least some of the time (Korman, 1983; Korman & Leslie, 1982), and many males are comfortable with this (Goodman, 1982).

One might expect, intuitively, that since lesbians are not in romantic relationships with men, the importance of standard appearance is lessened. This is not always the case, however; lesbians are often reared by and work with heterosexuals and are thus socialized to place a high premium on their physical appearance. The pressures to be beautiful are many (Rothblum, 1994). So, although lesbians may not be competing for men's attentions, the fact that they are often not "out" means that they face many of the pressures to present themselves in a way that is appealing to men (Rothblum, 1994).

Once the relationship between a man and a woman has progressed, more gender differences become apparent. For example, although the actual amount of self-disclosure that takes place is about equal, women *prefer* to reveal more personal information than men do (Cozby, 1973; Morton, 1978). This phenomenon may be culturebound, however; studies of Chinese Americans do not find these gender differences in self-disclosure (Wheeler, Reis, & Bond, 1989). Interestingly, both women and men are more comfortable revealing themselves to a woman than to a man (Derlega, Winstead, Wong, & Hunter, 1985).

When conflicts arise, men and women tend to communicate differently. Consistent with traditional gender roles, men will urge women to "calm down" whereas women wish men would "warm up," a situation that can eventually jeopardize the couple's relationship if it becomes a regular pattern (Levenson & Gottman, 1985). Women and men's modes of verbal expression also reflect this pattern (Tannen, 1990). In order to be satisfied with the relationship, couples need the ability to appreciate the other partner's perspective (Long & Andrews, 1990). Conflict has the potential to break up a relationship but can also strengthen it and increase the partners' commitment to each other.

Lesbian relationships progress along similar developmental lines, with the initial idealizing period in which only the partner's positive qualities are perceived. With same-gender couples, however, this idealizing period may persist because many women may fantasize that their gender similarities preclude any differences that may exist (Greene, 1994c). This idealized period is followed by the introduction of reality-based concerns, such as finding ways of dealing with conflict and power struggles (Kurdek, 1994) and in some cases spousal abuse (Greene, 1994c). Lack of support from the larger society means that lesbians in abusive or otherwise unsatisfactory relationships have fewer resources available when they need them the most (Greene, 1994c). Finally, lesbian couples settle into a trust-based relationship in which each party balances autonomy yearnings with their commitment to the relationship (McWhirter & Mattison, 1984, cited in Kurdek, 1994).

Marriage

The social institution of marriage evolves with the times and has changed somewhat in recent years. In the past, when traditional gender roles were more prominent, marriages were **symbiotic** in the sense that women provided expressiveness and men provided instrumentality. In this way, each needed the other in order to experience the full spectrum of human emotions. With the advent of women in the workplace, however, both partners now play an instrumental role. As such, a more ideal framework for contemporary marriage would be the **mutual marriage,** in which each spouse provides both instrumentality and nurturance (Vannoy, 1991).

The increasingly instrumental role of women in their marriages creates other dynamic shifts as well. While the woman was once responsible for every detail of household maintenance, this is no longer practical for today's working women. As such, **role overload** is a common problem for married women (Benin & Agostinelli, 1988), especially if they have children. Although many husbands assist their wives with housework, their attitudes often remain traditional in contrast to their behavior (Hardesty & Bokemeier, 1989). Box 10.2 illustrates how marital roles are changing for women in other cultures.

A major issue in marriage is where the power in the relationship lies. According to Scanzoni and Szinovacz (1980), the power balance depends on several

Box 10.2

Evolving Marital Customs in Other Cultures

Some marriage customs are starting to change from a traditional form to a modern one. For example, in the People's Republic of China the Marriage Law was passed in 1980. This marriage law abolished the feudal marriage system, which deprived women of the right to choose their spouses. This law has established a democratic marriage system, one that gives women free choice of partners, and mandates monogamy and equal rights for both sexes. It also protects the lawful interest of women and children and outlaws bigamy, concubinage, child betrothal, interference in a widow's remarriage, and the extraction of money or gifts in connection with marriage (Yu & Carpenter, 1991).

Among the changes in Taiwan today are those that permit women to retain their family names after marriage. Women are also allowed to inherit property and to retain property and income in their own name. But in order for a woman to gain ownership of any property, a special contract must be drawn up. If this contract is not drawn up, all property acquired before and during the marriage will go to the husband (Yu & Carpenter, 1991). On the other hand, women are held responsible for their husband's debts (Diamond, 1973).

Source: From "Autonomy in a Cross-Cultural Perspective," by L. L. Adler, in *Females and Autonomy: A Life-Span Perspective* (p. 14), edited by M. B. Nadien and F. L. Denmark, 1999, Boston: Allyn & Bacon. Reprinted with permission of Lenore Loeb Adler, Ph.D.

---

factors, including the couple's gender-role preferences. According to **traditional gender-role ideology,** the dichotomy between the husband–breadwinner and wife–homemaker is emphasized and the power distributed accordingly. According to nontraditional or **modern gender-role ideology,** on the other hand, both partners participate in both of these roles (Amato & Booth, 1995). If both partners are traditional, the wife is likely to defer to the husband in congruence with her view of her role. If the husband is more modern,

the traditional wife will act according to his wishes (Scanzoni & Szinovacz, 1980).

If both partners are modern, roles are more flexible and the power may alternate between them in different situations. However, conflicts may arise because neither partner is clearly delineated as the head of the household. Perhaps the most at-risk couple would be the one in which the wife is modern and the husband is traditional, because the wife will resist her husband's wishes, and the husband will find this particularly difficult in light of his views on marriage (Amato & Booth, 1995). Research shows that modern women married to traditional husbands tend to be more dissatisfied with marital choices while their husbands are more avoidant (Haber & Austin, 1992).

Happiness in marriage depends in part on the congruence of husbands and wives' gender role ideologies. The highest levels of adaptation and marital satisfaction are reported by older couples with at least one spouse who believed in modern gender-role ideology and younger couples whose partners both adhered to modern gender-role ideology (Weigel & Weigel, 1990). In contrast, marriages found to have the lowest marital quality levels were reported by younger couples with at least one traditional partner and older couples whose partners both adhered to traditional gender-role ideology (Weigel & Weigel, 1990).

The shift in gender-role ideology and women's increasingly nontraditional role over the past few decades have taken a toll on marital satisfaction (Lye & Biblarz, 1993). Women with a contemporary view of gender roles are less likely to express happiness with their marriage (Amato & Booth, 1995), and fewer married women described themselves as happy in 1986 than in 1972 (Glenn & Weaver, 1988). Age, education, and work status do not appear to affect these findings. This may be because men continue to express more conservative views than women do on issues such as employment for wives and mothers and the wife's role in family decisions (Thornton, 1989). On a more positive note, however, husbands who adopt more egalitarian views report more marital satisfaction and fewer conflicts (Amato & Booth, 1995).

Many of today's married women may be dissatisfied with marriage because they experience role overload. Even wives who work full time, not to mention those who do not, report responsibility for twice as many household chores (Kamo, 1991; Shelton, 1992) and child-care–related activities (Douthitt, 1989). Contrary to popular belief, this is also true of ethnic minority marriages, even though the wife may contribute more financially (Wyche, 1993). This has negative effects on women's well-being (Lennon & Rosenfield, 1992).

Whether or not the partners are satisfied, the rising divorce rate may overshadow the fact that many marriages last for decades. Schlesinger (1982) found several common factors among couples with enduring marriages. The top ten factors cited by husbands and wives were mutual respect, mutual trust, loyalty, loving each other, depending on each other, considering each other's needs, providing each other with emotional support, commitment to making the marriage last, fidelity, and give and take. Wives, more than husbands, added recognizing one's own needs, positive relationships with children, sharing feelings and emotions, similar goals in life, and a sense of humor. Financial security was also rated high among factors said to contribute to a marriage's staying power.

Divorce

In the United States, the divorce rate was low and rather constant throughout the 1950s and early 1960s. It started rising dramatically around 1966, doubled over the next decade, and then leveled off at the higher rate, with a very slight decline more recently (Laumann, Gagnon, Michael, & Michaels, 1994). Today, about half of all marriages end in divorce, with about half of those ending in divorce breaking up within the first seven years (U.S. Bureau of the Census, 1987c). The United States has the highest divorce rate of any industrialized country. The latest census report reveals that 19.3 million adults, or 10 percent of the adult population, were divorced at the time of the survey (U.S. Bureau of the Census, 1998b). Remarriages are even

more likely than first marriages to end in divorce (Lown & Dolan, 1988).

Why has the divorce rate risen so sharply in this country over the past 30 years? Many explanations have been offered for this trend, including relaxation of legal restrictions on divorce, especially the introduction of the no-fault divorce. No-fault divorce was first instituted in California in 1970 and was followed by a 46 percent increase in the number of divorces within three years (Wheeler, 1994). It quickly spread to the other 49 states. Prior to no-fault divorce, the only legal grounds for divorce were adultery, extreme cruelty, and desertion. Now, no charge of marital misconduct is necessary for petition of divorce. In fact, the most frequently cited reason for divorce in recent years is lack of communication and understanding (Kitson & Sussman, 1982), rather than adultery or other misconduct. Since the introduction of no-fault divorce, about 90 percent of divorces are uncontested; that is, there is no dispute about the existence of grounds.

Other reasons for the rising divorce rate include the rise in women's incomes, which makes leaving bad marriages more feasible, higher expectations for marital relationships, less tolerance for unsatisfying relationships, and a decrease in the stigma attached to divorce.

What Risk Factors Are Associated with Divorce?
Social scientists have identified a variety of demographic, personality, and relationship characteristics related to divorce. As we review these factors, it is important to keep in mind that these factors are merely associated (correlated) with divorce rates; they do not necessarily cause divorces.

Several demographic attributes are associated with higher levels of divorce. These include age of marriage, with younger couples more likely to divorce than couples who were older at the time of marriage. Less educated people are more likely to divorce than more educated ones, although among the very highest levels of educated women (women who attend graduate and professional schools), divorce is relatively common. Catholics and certain denominations of

Protestants are less likely to divorce than other people. People whose parents lived together until they were at least 14 years old are less likely to divorce than those from families in which divorce occurred sooner. People who are of the same religion, race–ethnicity, educational level, and age level (within three years of each other) are less likely to be divorced than people who differ from their partners on these important dimensions (Laumann et al., 1994).

Other demographic variables that predict divorce rates are race and socioeconomic class, which are confounded, meaning that they occur together so that one cannot tease apart the effects of either alone. African Americans are about twice as likely as White people to get divorced, but this is largely because they tend to be in lower socioeconomic classes, which have higher divorce rates (Laumann et al., 1994; Price & McKenry, 1988).

Other risk factors for divorce include having sex before age 18, having children prior to marriage, and cohabiting before marriage. Regular church attendance is associated with a low rate of divorce (Laumann et al., 1994). Wives who hold nontraditional jobs for women like engineer and architect are more likely to get divorced than women who hold traditional jobs (Philliber & Hiller, 1983).

Some studies have looked at attitudinal and personality correlates of conflict in marriage and divorce. Different expectations about women's work outside the home and the division of labor within the home predict marital strife and divorce (Blumstein & Schwartz, 1983). Although the evidence for this is not completely consistent, several studies suggest that women who hold nontraditional sex-role attitudes are more likely to get divorced. Personality traits have not received the same research attention as attitudinal variables, but there is some evidence that anxiety is a risk factor for divorce.

The Social and Psychological Costs of Divorce.
Even when the decision to end a marital relationship is mutual, there are almost always feelings of profound disappointment by both parties. In some religions, notably the Roman Catholic religion, divorce is a sin, leading to excommunication from the sacraments. Many people view divorce as a tremendous personal failure. Research consistently shows that divorce is a highly complex social and personal phenomenon and one of life's chief stressors, akin to experiencing the death of a spouse or other loved one.

Divorce is complex because it is multifaceted: there are many legal, personal, and community aspects to divorce, all of which have the potential to cause enormous stress. Legally, money and property must be divided. If there are children, custody, visitation, and support arrangements must be made. Personally, people, especially women, commonly struggle with feelings of guilt, anger, hostility, regret, sadness, and loneliness. Many people report continuing feelings of attachment to their ex-spouses and a long struggle to regain individual autonomy (Bohannon, 1970). Divorce affects people's social lives and relationship to the community in countless ways, particularly for women. Many women report a loss of friends and social activities when they are no longer part of a couple. Demographic and other factors make single men, especially single older men, more socially valuable than single women, and many divorced men find themselves highly prized in their social circles. Indeed, divorced men are significantly more likely than divorced women to remarry (Richardson, 1988), a gender difference that increases as people age.

For divorced women who consider a lesbian lifestyle after divorce, a significant concern is the fear that if their homosexual identity is divulged they will lose the right to raise their biological children (Greene, 1994c). This fear is pervasive and, says Greene, justifiable, given the courts' history of denying or restricting gay men and lesbian women custody in divorce settlements. In their review of the literature in this area, Patterson and Redding (1996) found that, despite popular stereotypes, children raised with parents who are lesbian or gay by and large have positive developmental outcomes. That is, their parents are just as likely to provide an environment conducive to healthy development as are heterosexual parents. Thus, sexual orientation alone should not be the deciding factor in whether to grant custody (Patterson & Redding, 1996).

Another problem that disproportionately affects women is the economic crunch that often accompanies divorce. When a couple breaks up, legal expenses mount, two households are formed, and resources are often strained to the limit. Women, especially mothers of young children, do not make as much money as men. Women who have stayed home to raise their children often find that they cannot compete in the marketplace with younger, better trained, more mobile and flexible employees. Divorced fathers may find that it is difficult for them to pay child support and alimony, if awarded, while setting up a new household and adopting a new life-style.

The consequences for children whose parents divorce can be serious. Research on the effects of divorce on children is deeply flawed, because it is difficult to disentangle the effects of divorce per se from those of growing up in a household where there is serious marital strife. Most large-scale studies on the effects of divorce on children do not survey the children before the divorce occurs and thus cannot compare these children with matched control groups of children who continue to live in households with marital problems. Although the evidence to date is far from conclusive, it suggests that most children have problems adjusting to the divorce for at least the first year following the divorce. These problems include plummeting grades and behavior problems at school, especially for boys, and increased anxiety and dependence (Hetherington, Cox, & Cox, 1982). Regrettably, adjustment problems may endure throughout early adulthood. Wallerstein and her associates have found that 40 percent of children of divorce show evidence of academic underachievement, decreased self-worth, and anger even ten years after the divorce. Moreover, people whose parents divorce have more difficulty than others in trusting romantic partners and forming commitments in adulthood and are themselves more likely to get divorced than are people whose parents did not divorce (Wallerstein & Blakeslee, 1989; Wallerstein & Kelly, 1980). New research by Wallerstein ties higher rates of alcoholism

and other substance abuse to children of divorced parents (Wallerstein, 1997).

As much as divorce is an immense personal problem, it is also a problem for society, especially when the couple has minor children. Many ills of present-day society—the impoverishment of families, teen-age pregnancy rates, the violence of youth, consumerism, even lower SAT scores—have been attributed to high rates of divorce, and particularly to growing up in fatherless homes. Over one-third of all children at any one time live in homes without their fathers, and before they reach the age of 18, more than half of all children will spend some time living apart from their fathers. Approximately 85 percent of single-parent children live with their mothers (U.S. Bureau of the Census, 1998c). Individuals and institutions are increasingly exasperated with what they see as the decline of the family and the ills in its wake and are proposing a variety of solutions to the problem of high divorce rates. These range from restigmatizing divorce and single parenthood to restructuring economic and social policies to help people form marriages and keep them together. There are currently nationwide movements to rewrite or repeal no-fault divorce laws. Recently, the Louisiana legislature became the first in the nation to approve a law allowing a new and more binding form of marriage contract, called a *covenant marriage*, one that would permit divorce only in narrow circumstances like adultery or desertion (Pallitt, 1997). The new law would require engaged couples to choose between the current no-fault marriage contract or the more binding covenant marriage before they declared their vows. Clearly, the framers of the law expect that the new legislation will force couples to consider seriously their compatibility and prospects before getting married and starting families.

Few people would deny that divorce is a painful and unfortunate event or that children are better off when raised by both parents. Virtually everyone would prefer a loving and solid marriage to a divorce and two caring, cooperative adults in the home sharing the responsibilities of parenting to a single parent struggling alone. But this is not the choice for people in bad marriages. Most people contemplating divorce are not throwing away good relationships for selfish and frivolous reasons. Studies on the long-term consequences of divorce are few, but they suggest that only about 20 percent of divorced people believe that the divorce was a mistake five years later (Wallerstein & Kelly, 1980). Many people experience positive feelings after divorce, including enhanced senses of autonomy, independence, strength, and courage. Most people eventually start dating again, and four out of five remarry (Glick & Lin, 1986). Unfortunately, for women particularly, problems adjusting to divorce are too often complicated by tough financial circumstances. Only about one-half of the women in the United States who have been awarded child support are receiving the full amount of their award (Waldman, 1992). When parents cooperate with each other after the divorce, contribute fairly to the support of children, and continue to play active roles in their children's lives, there is evidence that children's adjustment to the divorce is eased considerably.

As discussed above, several factors affect the staying power of a marriage. Making decisions about whether to have children, how to rear them, and other issues can place a financial, physical, and emotional burden on couples. The quality of marriage has been found to decrease somewhat once there are children and to increase after the children have left the house (Rollins, 1989). In the next section, we will explore the experience of parenting for members of both genders.

Parenthood

Parenthood, once practically a given, is now an option chosen by fewer and fewer couples. In fact, one out of ten couples in their early twenties are choosing not to have children (Blake, 1982). Even couples opting to have children are having fewer these days; thus the birth rate is declining. According to a report from the U.S. Department of Health and Human Services (1996), the birth rate in 1996 was the lowest since 1987, the lowest in two decades. Moreover, this trend is not merely confined to the United States, but can be seen in Europe, Japan, and some developing countries.

Recently, Italy has become the first country in history where there are more people over the age of 60 than under the age of 20 (Specter, 1998).

Late marriage may be one explanation for this because couples have fewer childbearing years together. The increase in women working outside the home may preclude their deciding to have many children. Finally, many young couples prefer to use their resources to enhance the quality of their own lives rather than to raise a family (Swidler, 1983).

For many couples, the decision to have children results in a move toward more traditional gender roles in the family (Rossi, 1979). Perhaps this is because motherhood is viewed by a major part of society as the ultimate fulfillment of womanhood. After all, it is the woman who carries the baby for nine months of pregnancy. Until recently, women were expected to stop working once they discovered that they were pregnant and become full-time housewives.

These expectations have changed somewhat (Wallach, Matlin, & Young, 1992). Although mothers are viewed as more necessary than fathers to children's development (Silverstein, 1996), research demonstrates that fathers who play an active role in their children's development have children with more positive qualities, such as more empathy toward their peers and higher intellectual capacity (Lamb, 1987). Concurrently, these fathers display greater satisfaction with the fathering role, higher self-confidence in their parenting abilities, and higher self-esteem in general (Lamb, Pleck, & Levine, 1987). In addition, fathers who share household and child-care responsibilities with their wives enjoy greater marital stability (Gilbert, 1994).

In spite of this, even couples with a more egalitarian relationship are likely to become more traditional with respect to gender roles once they become parents (Silverstein, 1996). For practical reasons, the mother is more likely to remain home at least part time with the baby once it is born (Carter, 1992), especially if she is nursing and if she has maternity leave while the father has no paternity leave. This perpetuates a cycle in which the mother wakes up at night with the child because the father must go to work the next day. As a result, for many couples, possibly in spite of efforts to the contrary, the wife's career is taken less seriously than the husband's once parenthood ensues. By default, women often end up managing the family's emotional life, seeing to the children's everyday needs, keeping in touch with relatives, and worrying about the state of their marriage (Demo, 1992; Hochschild, 1989; Rubin, 1983).

However, this trend may be changing somewhat. Day care is becoming more and more popular as an option for working women. In addition, women from the previous generation who stopped working to raise their children, as was once the norm, are returning to work in their middle years (as will be discussed in a subsequent section). Yet, parenthood tends to demand more from women than from men. Women invest more emotionally in their children (Rubin, 1983). Working mothers, even those who have child care, often cannot escape the conflicting demands of their jobs and their children, which can affect negatively their mental health (Simon, 1992).

In a single-parent family, the parent living with the child is usually forced to take on both gender roles. Single parenthood is becoming more and more common these days (Green & Crooks, 1988). The large divorce rate plays a major role in this. Also, some spouses are widowed. An increasing number of mothers, however, have never been married (Dornbusch & Gray, 1988). According to Wines (1992), there is a small but growing trend to have babies without marrying, a trend reflected by the popular sitcom persona Murphy Brown. In fact, in 1997 the number of never married mothers with children under the age of 15 surpassed the number of divorced mothers with children under the age of 15 (U.S. Bureau of the Census, 1998c).

Single parents are confronted with a unique set of difficulties. Single-parent mothers, subject to the same discrimination in the working world as all other women, are in a double bind because they are solely responsible for the family's economic survival. Custodial mothers and fathers may experience role overload, because their chores include earning sufficient income, managing the finances, housework, child care, carpooling, and so on. Single mothers' difficulties are compounded by the fact that the workplace is still suited to the needs of men whose wives manage household duties and child care. Workers are expected to be wholly committed to their jobs and not to experience the conflicting needs of home life (Silverstein, 1996). Socially, it is difficult for single parents to fit in. Single parents may also be excluded from couples' gatherings, while finding it difficult to meet singles of the other sex who are not put off by the fact that they are parents.

Silverstein (1996) highlights a bias against mother-headed households that stems from societal misogyny. Citing a number of sources, she comments that, although children raised in mother-headed families have been found to show poorer developmental outcomes than do those raised by both biological parents (e.g., Bronstein, Clauson, Stoll, & Abrams, 1993; Dawson, 1991), it is not necessarily the absence of a father per se that is responsible for this. Rather, circumstances such as a lack of sufficient income affecting mother-headed households play a role (Krantz, 1988; Wilson, 1992, in Silverstein, 1996).

Yet, the picture for single parents may be improving. As the population of parents who are single grows, it is becoming easier for them to meet one another and form support networks. Many single mothers enjoy their autonomy and independence, and some divorced women express feelings of accomplishment and fulfillment (Richmond-Abbott, 1984). Single-parent fathers with custody of their children make taking care of them an important priority (Keshet, 1980). In general, single parenthood provides parents with the opportunity to experience both gender roles. Although this may be difficult when the obligations of both are thrust on the parent, the bonuses of being in the male or female role are provided equally as well.

As the years pass, new issues and adjustments arise for both couples and single parents. The fortieth birthday approaches and adults suddenly find themselves in the period known as *middle age*. This era of life is stigmatized, often unfairly, as one of crisis and negative changes. In the coming section, we will review the changes wrought for women and men by mid-life, as well as the contrast between expectations and reality for adults entering this period of life.

Gay and lesbian parents, single or in committed relationships, face a multitude of problems; some are unique. Amid negative stereotypes about their ability to serve as effective role models for children, gay and lesbian couples are opting in ever increasing numbers to have children, either through adoption or other means, namely, *in vitro fertilization* and *surrogate motherhood.* The struggles are many because these couples or single individuals face pervasive societal beliefs that they cannot raise emotionally healthy heterosexual children. They strive to protect their families from negative public opinion and to provide adequately for their children. As their children grow older, lesbian and gay parents are faced with the particular problem of deciding when and how to disclose their sexual orientation (Greene, 1994c).

MID-LIFE

This section of the chapter discusses a rarely emphasized but important facet of gender—women and men as they grow older. It will cover such areas as double standards of aging; the middle years; mid-life crisis; gender differences; reentry women; later life; changes in roles, options, and motives; and physical and cognitive changes. With advances in medicine and technology and increased health awareness in the United States comes increased longevity, a trend that is sometimes referred to as the **graying of America.** With these advances comes a shifting definition of what middle age is and when it begins. (See the section entitled "A Traumatic Transition?" for additional discussion of this topic.) Until recently, older adults were frequently neglected in research. However, the proportion of older people in our population is increasing and, as such, the body of knowledge pertaining to them is inadequate. Psychologists examining gender as a variable that influences the human experience are well advised to study its interaction with aging. Aging affects men and women differently in its various realms, including both the physical and the socioemotional domains. In addition, middle-aged men and women are viewed differently by our society, a topic that the first section of this chapter explores.

Double Standards of Aging

Our youth-oriented society stigmatizes aging in general, but particularly for women. One study found that 57 percent of monitored television ads promised "youth, youthful appearance, or the energy to act youthful." By contrast, seniors in the same ads were shown dealing with backaches, loose dentures, and constipation (Richmond-Abbott, 1992). Women suffer more from losing the beauty that is associated with youth. As women age, they are perceived as less physically attractive and desirable, and their reproductive and nurturant functions are no longer relevant. Women's most socially valued qualities, the ability to provide sex and attractive companionship and to have children and nurture them, are expressed in the context of youth. This stereotype holds true for aging lesbians as well. According to Pearlman (1993), although lesbians are not actively competing for men's attention, as middle age approaches they may experience some ambivalence about no longer being acknowledged as sexual beings by men. This loss in self-esteem is furthered by their often unrequited attraction to younger women (Pearlman, 1993).

For men, on the other hand, the wrinkles, gray hair, and extra pounds viewed as unappealing on the female body are euphemized and even glorified by terms such as *character lines* or adding character. Masculinity is identified with competence, autonomy, and self-control, qualities that the disappearance of youth does not threaten. Unfortunately, women are not traditionally encouraged to develop those qualities that often improve with age, such as intellectual competence. Thus, the same wrinkles and gray hair that may enhance the perceived status and attractiveness of an older man may be seen as diminishing the attractiveness and desirability of an older woman (Etaugh, 1993).

The Academy Awards are a case in point. Markson and Taylor (1993) found that women over the age of 39 have accounted for only 27 percent of all winners for Best Actress since 1927, while their male counterparts have accounted for 67 percent of the Best Actor awards. It is apparent that female film actresses, considered "older" by the time they are 35, find their careers winding down at the same time that male actors' film careers pick up. The biased images provided to movie viewers by this double standard are noteworthy. Where does the media provide positive role models for aging women?

Even television shows apparently designed to portray older women in a better light fall prey to stereotyping. "The Golden Girls" was a popular television series featuring three bright, attractive, and articulate women over 50. In spite of these women's *joie de vivre* and spunk, they were still depicted as preoccupied with finding men and maintaining relationships with them.

Such cultural values influence the way in which older women and men perceive their bodies. A study of gender and body image perception among senior citizens showed that older men assessed by the Draw A Person technique drew figures that were larger, taller, and more centered than those of women, suggesting more positive self-image on the part of the men (Janelli, 1993).

Double standards of aging extend beyond women and men's physical appearances and do not only victimize women. Older women are actually viewed as more personally acceptable and active in the community than are older men (Kite, Deaux, & Miele, 1991; O'Connell & Rotter, 1979). On the other hand, an elderly woman who comes across as lacking competence will be judged more harshly than will an elderly man also lacking in competence (Walsh & Connor, 1979).

In general, typical older women are perceived as less self-centered, more nurturant, and more sensitive than typical older men. Typical older women are also perceived as exhibiting more cognitive decline and being more passive and dependent than typical older men. This may be a function of women's increased longevity, however, whereby the greater number of older women results in greater visibility for women's cognitive decline and dependence (Canetto, Kaminski, & Felicio, 1995). Older women are viewed as

requiring costly institutionalized care (Lott, 1987), probably for the same reason.

Women, who live longer than men and comprise the majority of the elderly population, are more subject to **ageism** than are men. Older men are usually cared for by women, and the impact of ageism on older men is often buffered by their female caregivers. Women, on the other hand, have no such buffer (Kimmel, 1988). The fact that jokes about elderly people poke fun at old women three times as often as old men (Palmore, 1971) attests to this.

Another area where the double standard is poignant is in choosing a partner. Although it is socially acceptable for men to marry women as much as 20 years younger than themselves, older women–younger men combinations are rare (Bell, 1989). The stigma of aging is so much greater for women than for men that in the official membership directory of the American Psychological Association women are ten times as likely as men not to list their age (Bell, 1989).

Language is an important area of double standards for aging men and women. Metaphors about women's aging emphasize loss, such as vaginal atrophy and degenerative changes (Kitzinger, 1983). Men's age-related changes are not described in a parallel fashion, and men who receive hormone therapy (e.g., testosterone) are described as attempting to increase libido rather than preserve their youth (Reitz, 1981). As a result, many women view mid-life changes pessimistically, seeing them as inescapable and debilitating (Ussher, 1989).

Ageist stereotypes of women and men originate in the middle years. Middle-aged women, whose primary duties have been child rearing and child launching, are considered to be at the tail end of responsibilities and accomplishments. Middle-aged men, on the other hand, are supposed to be at the prime of life, having built their careers in their youth and now holding top jobs and accomplishing much. For this reason, a thorough examination of the aging process and gender must begin with a look at the middle years.

A Traumatic Transition?   As stated earlier and depending on the writer, middle age might be pinpointed as being anywhere from the age of 35 to 65 (Barbanel, 1990). However, many people place the start of the aging process at approximately the ages of 40 to 50, or *mid-life*. This stage of life involves many personal and social changes that affect women and men in different ways. Women in particular are affected by adjustments required of them in the middle years, such as caring for elderly parents, death of parents, illness or death of a spouse, unemployment, children leaving home, mid-life crisis of a spouse, divorce or separation, and moving (Rollins, 1996). According to Laura Barbanel (1990), members of this cohort comprise the **dominant generation.** This generation, also called the sandwich generation, is responsible for caring for both the young and the old.

As they move through mid-life, both women and men begin to lose their physical vitality, but only women are viewed as diminishing in sex appeal. While both women and men fear the changes wrought by this stage in life, men appear to fear dying in particular, whereas women fear the general aging process (Barbanel, 1990).

Middle age for women, according to Pearlman (1993), might be construed as a developmental crisis, with the potential to disrupt one's sense of self and create feelings of heightened vulnerability, shame, and severe loss of self-esteem. Pearlman describes a developmental transition called **late mid-life astonishment.** Typically beginning in a woman's fifties, this passage is marked by a sudden cognizance of the onset and stigma of aging. It is characterized by feelings of amazement and despair at the changes wrought by and/or occurring with increasing age, such as diminished physical and sexual attractiveness and other losses.

Thus, the fiftieth birthday for women may precipitate an emotional crisis. This crisis is usually worked through eventually once the woman has been in her sixth decade for a few years (Niemela & Lento, 1993). In a comparison of women aged 49 to 51 and 52 to 55, the older women were found to be better adjusted and were experiencing their lives and relationships more positively. In addition, they were less concerned about health and the prospect of illness and were more accepting of death (Niemala & Lento, 1993).

Some women in their forties and fifties may be starting a family, returning to school, beginning new love relationships, or peaking in their careers (Gilbert, 1993). In fact, many U.S. women actually view the early fifties as a new prime of life. Some aspects of this age period reported by informants include more empty nests, better health, higher income, and more concern for parents. Women in their early fifties showed confidence, involvement, security, and breadth of personality (Mitchell & Helson, 1990).

Despite this, middle-aged women are often viewed negatively and ridiculed by society. Clearly, cultural myths about these women are far removed from the realities of women's lives and experience. Specifically, two major areas of women's mid-life experience subject to much stereotyping are menopause and empty nest syndrome.

Menopause. Although the **climacteric** is the appropriate term for the entire aging process in men and women between the ages of 45 and 65, menopause is considered the pivotal event in women's aging and is therefore the most discussed topic. In fact, an examination of articles listed on Psych Lit and Medline (electronic databases) revealed that only a small percentage of articles written about women at mid-life did *not* discuss menopause (Rostovsky & Travis, 1996). Menopause is the cessation of the menstrual period, occurring in most women between the ages of 45 and 55. It is defined as having occurred when a woman has not menstruated for one year. See Chapter 3 for details on the biological aspect of menopause.

Menopause is viewed as bringing with it both physically distressing symptoms and psychological discomforts. Some of these symptoms include profuse sweating, headaches, increased weight, insomnia, aches and pains, dryness and thinning of the vaginal walls, irritability, and hot flashes (Dan & Bernhard, 1989; Weidiger, 1975). Hot flashes are the best known of menopausal symptoms, and most women experience the same progression. During a hot flash, the blood vessels in the woman's skin dilate and her skin conductance increases so that she feels extremely hot (Israel, Poland, Reame, & Warner, 1980). For many years, women were told that the hot flashes they complained of were "all in their heads" (Kronenberg, 1990, p. 52) but they are now considered to be a biological phenomenon. While low estrogen levels are associated with hot flashes, other evidence suggests involvement of temperature control mechanisms (Kronenberg, 1990; Masters, Johnson, & Kolodny, 1995). It is important to remember that the woman's social context will affect her experience of menopause. Thus, personality, life events, and culture will all have an effect (Dan & Bernhard, 1989).

Menopause's physical ramifications have been exaggerated by medical personnel. Many physicians tend to view all types of women's health problems as connected with female hormones when, in fact, problems occurring around menopause are more often a function of the aging process (Dan & Bernhard, 1989). In addition, physicians and nurses' experience with menopausal women tends to be limited to those whom they have treated for excessively severe symptoms. Women who seek treatment for menopausal symptoms tend to view menopause more negatively (Ussher, 1989). The vast majority of articles on menopause in medical and/or psychological literature promote the image of a deficiency disease that will be troublesome for most women. These articles are often replete with methodological flaws (Rostovsky & Travis, 1996). Such factors may help explain medical personnel's tendency to view menopausal symptoms as more severe and pathological than menopausal women see them (McElmurry & Huddleston, 1987).

Menopause is also mistakenly connected with vague illnesses (Bush, 1990) and with emotional disturbance (Busch, Zonderman, & Costa, 1994). The "menopausal woman" is stereotypically perceived in Western culture as ailing and in need of medication (hormones and tranquilizers), emotionally unstable, and having lost her purpose in life. Her discomfort is depicted as unique to her stage in life, even though symptoms from hot flashes to cessation of menstruation can happen at any stage in a woman's life and be attributed to factors other than menopause, such as surgical removal of the ovaries in premenopausal women (Kaufert, 1982; Neugarten & Kraines, 1965). While menopause is a biological phenomenon, the

social and cultural beliefs and attitudes toward menopause have structured women's responses to it as well as society's attitudes. As such, stereotypes are easily formed and individual variation summarily dismissed or ignored (Rostovsky & Travis, 1996).

This negative stigmatizing of menopausal women is part of many cultural traditions in which older women have been portrayed as sorceresses or witches in anthropological literature (Evans-Pritchard, 1937; Fortes, 1962; Harper, 1969). Base motivations are ascribed to these women, such as the "evil eye" or witchcraft (Fuller, 1961). The idea of fertility representing good power and, conversely, infertility representing malevolent power has been a pervasive one (Kincaid-Elders, 1982), which might explain this view of menopausal women. Current anthropological research demonstrates that this notion still exists today across several cultures. Cultural images of menopause stress deterioration, decline, regression, and decay (Van Keep, 1976). This affects the menopausal women's self-image.

In fact, Mansfield and Voda (1993) conducted a survey of middle-aged women in the United States and found that most of the perceived benefits of menopause were not benefits in and of themselves, but rather represented cessation of current, unpleasant conditions (i.e., termination of the menstrual period and its various difficulties). In addition, many participants in this survey expressed fears of becoming a "typically . . . bitchy menopausal lady," which may be a reflection of society's negative stereotypes of the aging woman. It is telling that the majority of the women surveyed obtained their information about menopause from friends and from the media (including television sitcoms), rather than from medical sources. Overall, women's views of menopause in this study lacked any sense that achievement or attained status could be associated with being menopausal. The negativity surrounding menopause may have unfortunate implications for women's adjustment to this transition (Mansfield & Voda, 1993).

Stigmatization of the changes wrought by menopause is very likely culturebound and based in accepted societal custom rather than in fact. In other cultures, for example the Giriama of Kenya, post-menopausal women are custodians of the central, ritual objects of a female cult that is believed to enable reproductive health. The Giriama see the life course as a continuum of hot or cool states and focus on maintaining harmony and social order. Because of its creative potential, the entire fertile period of women's lives is considered one of *heat*. The *cool* aspect of the older woman's postfertile state makes them ideal for counteracting the heat created through the required rituals (Udvardy, 1992). Another group, the Winnebagos, view menopausal women positively as well, perceiving them as being "just like a man" (Comas Diaz & Greene, 1994). An increase in women's status following menopause is common to several non-Western societies (Brown, 1982). This may explain findings that suggest that women in non-Western societies seem to suffer fewer physiological and emotional difficulties during menopause than do Western women (Kaiser, 1990).

Even in the United States, however, where menopause is believed to be a difficult, troublesome, confusing, and depressing period, psychologists and sociologists are beginning to offer a different view. Many women are happy and relieved to reach the finish of the stage in their lives marked by menopause. In a physical sense, menopause actually presents few problems for women and is frequently viewed as a nonevent, or even as a positive body change by women after the fact (Gilbert, 1993). Clearly, menopause is not the crippling life event it once was portrayed.

Older women who have experienced menopause view it more positively than do younger women who have not yet reached the age of menopause (Dan & Bernhard, 1989). Apparently, dramatic myths about menopause are more pervasive than the anticlimactic reality. However, a small but significant minority of women do actually experience emotional difficulties during menopause. This may be correlated with low self-esteem and life satisfaction before menopause (Bart & Grossman, 1978). These and other women's menopause-related troubles may actually be a function of psychological factors, rather than of biological events at their stage in life (Greene & Cooke, 1980).

In support of this hypothesis, one cross-cultural study found that women in cultures with fewer positive roles (or more demeaning roles) available to them experienced menopause more negatively (Griffen, 1979).

Psychologically, adolescence appears to be a more difficult adjustment for women than menopause. Menopausal women and adolescents reported the highest level of symptomatology, with adolescents reporting more psychological symptoms and menopausal women reporting more physiological ones. It is interesting that postmenopausal women reported the lowest level of symptoms, suggesting that once this milestone has passed women's well-being improves and exceeds their state at any other time of life (Neugarten & Kraines, 1965).

The physical symptoms of menopause can be ameliorated by taking replacement estrogen. However, it has been suggested that estrogen replacement therapy may increase a woman's risk of developing uterine or breast cancer, blood clots, liver tumors, and other problems (see Adami, 1992; Persson et al., 1989; Satyaswaroop, Zaino, & Mortel, 1983). On the other hand, estrogen therapy may significantly reduce the risks of cardiovascular disease and osteoporosis (Ettinger, 1993; Lindsay, 1993; Seed, 1994). In addition, there is evidence that, rather than remediating the symptoms, estrogen therapy merely postpones them: Hot flashes may return when estrogen is stopped. Some menopausal symptoms may be relieved with nonestrogen treatments, such as creams or jellies for vaginal dryness or a high calcium diet, exercise, and avoidance of cigarette smoking and heavy drinking, which all help decrease the risk of osteoporosis. Finally, women who are in good physical shape experience fewer symptoms (Wilbur, Dan, Hedricks, & Holm, 1990). See Chapter 13 for additional information.

Empty Nest Syndrome. **Empty nest syndrome** results from the departure of children, which has been said to leave middle-aged women feeling lonely and deserted (Mantecon, 1993). The point at which the empty nest is experienced is relative. Some women feel it when their youngest child reaches adulthood;

others may feel it when their youngest child enters kindergarten (Black & Hill, 1984).

Just as the starting point of empty nest syndrome varies from person to person, so too do its effects. Mid-life women who work can enjoy benefits such as a sense of self independent of one's family, professional development, financial autonomy, intellectual stimulation, and an expanded social group. Many couples report greater marital satisfaction after the children have left the house (Rollins, 1989).

Empty nest syndrome may be becoming obsolete. A review of the literature (Troll, 1989) suggests that many mothers (and fathers) view their children's departure as a positive event, albeit with mixed emotions. The empty nest catalyzed a crisis mainly for those women whose lives revolved around their children to the exclusion of a career. This may suggest that in today's day and age, with more than half of U.S. women working and building their own careers, empty nest syndrome is becoming less and less common.

Men at Mid-life.   Middle-aged men may experience negative stereotyping about their declining health, strength, power, and sexual potency. A gradual drop in libido is actually a common change among middle-aged men (Davidson, 1989). For men, the middle years often bring the first markers of inevitable physical decline (e.g., minor hearing loss, eyeglasses, graying or receding hair). Men's testosterone level and sperm production gradually decrease from the age of about 30 onward. For men over 40, enlargement of the prostate gland is a common change. This enlargement causes urinary problems and may be related to changes in hormone levels, but is correctable by surgery. See Chapter 13 for further discussion.

Yet, age-related changes taking place for men in their middle years appear to be more connected with changes in family status, social position, career, or health than with physiological processes. Some of these changes might include changes in workplace status (e.g., becoming a mentor or senior partner) or children moving out of the house. Men at mid-life may become aware that they will never achieve their ambitions of earlier years and may feel disappoint-

ment or the need to redefine their goals. For some men, youth-oriented masculine traits define their gender identity, and these changes force them to rethink this definition (Rybarczyk, 1994).

Couples may undergo several changes during mid-life. As relationships mature, tender feelings of affection and loyalty tend to replace passion and sexual intimacy as a main focus (Reedy, Birren, & Schaie, 1981). Some marriages that were more turbulent in early adulthood turn out to be better adjusted during middle adulthood (Rollins, 1989). One explanation for this might be that as marital partners grow older many of their earlier incompatibilities brought about by differences in religion, ethnicity, social class, levels of education, family backgrounds, and personality patterns have either been eliminated or adjusted to or have contributed to the breakup of the marriage (Golan, 1986).

Friendships change for both men and women who have reached mid-life. Whereas younger men tend to emphasize empathy and altruism in friendship less, middle-aged men appear to be more concerned and thoughtful about friendship. Middle-aged women seem to be more tolerant and less confrontational than younger women. Both women and men were found to describe themselves as eager to hold on to their friends. Gender-typed behavior exists in this realm, however; men tend to be negative about too much dependency in friendships and express an instrumental concept of need (i.e., concrete assistance) in contrast to women's more expressive emphasis (i.e., the need to talk, share, and be comforted) (Fox, Gibbs, & Auerbach, 1985).

One change of middle adulthood for both men and women is that of children becoming adults and replacing their parents as the present generation, with their own children as the second generation. When children and their parents are both within the adult age range, their relationships undergo an adjustment. Because the middle generation maintains contact with both their older parents and their growing children, similarities and differences across generations may be noticed. Gender role, however, is one area in which parent–child similarity is most noticeable (Elder, Caspi, & Downey, 1986).

Middle-aged women are often forced to deal with a conflict between the needs of their aging parents and those of their husbands, children, and employers. As daughters, middle-aged women serve as the primary source of care-giving for their frequently widowed mothers. However, many of these women do not experience this as a conflict on a regular basis, and those who do often have poorer relationships with their mothers (Walker, Pratt, & Wood, 1993).

Middle-aged women who are expected to tend to their elderly parents and to their children are often forced to cut back on their own private time in order to fulfill their responsibilities. In addition to providing physical assistance, both men and women also attempt to advise both their parents and their children, although men focus more on their children. Clearly, in spite of the much-touted generation gap, adult parents and children maintain contact (Troll, 1989).

Another challenge faced by middle-aged mothers, but seldom addressed in the literature, is the conflict that arises when a daughter is lesbian. Mothers most often have a difficult time reconciling that their daughters' life-styles are not in keeping with society's norms and may resort to self-blame, in keeping with society's tendency to blame mothers for their children's outcomes (Pearlman, 1992).

Surprisingly, middle-aged women are not caught between their parents and their children as often as one might expect. The majority of older people are in good health, suggesting that they are not forced to rely on their daughters. In addition, ages of women with elderly parents vary; a 65-year-old woman may still have a living parent that she is tending to (Stueve & O'Donnell, 1984) while her daughter is in her late thirties or early forties. Research is needed to examine the actual dynamics of intergenerational relationships.

Mid-Life Crisis

In the 1970s, society became fascinated with the idea of a male *mid-life crisis.* Popular opinion maintained that this crisis was universal and an automatic stage for men who reached a certain age. "Normal" men who reached 40 were expected to be making drastic changes in their lives (Rybarczyk, 1994) and experi-

ence intense emotional turmoil and despair (Levinson, Darrow, Klein, Levinson, & McKee, 1978). Middle-aged men are stereotyped as having heart attacks, which frighten them with the prospect of their mortality. The stereotype suggests that in reaction to this they abandon their families and marry **trophy wives,** highly attractive women who are far younger than they are. The image of a man going through mid-life crisis also includes aging men buying sports cars, dressing in clothes usually worn by younger men, and flirting with women half their age. Donald Trump's marriage to Marla Maples was viewed by many as a classic example of male mid-life crisis.

Mid-life crisis was originally described in a psychoanalytic framework as being a function of a mid-life man's awareness of his mortality. During this time, the middle-aged man experiences a struggle between his life instinct of Eros and his pull toward destruction and death, or Thanatos. He equates his loss of youth with loss of life and experiences inevitable psychic angst (Jaques, 1965). Subsequent theoreticians of various orientations support the idea of a crisis surrounding the middle-age transition (Pearlman, 1993; Yalom, 1980).

In reality, empirical research fails to support the idea that this crisis is universal and age-related. Research does show that men in their forties show higher depression scores and more alcohol and drug use than other adult men; however, they are similar to other men in anxiety, life satisfaction, and happiness (Tamir, 1982). Mid-life crisis is actually viewed as a myth by one researcher based on his survey of the literature (Kruger, 1994). If it does exist for a man, it appears to be related to career and/or family life rather than the aging process (e.g., children moving away from home and leaving their parents alone together for the first time in years; women returning to work or school and developing new interests, thus forcing adjustments in the couple's relationship). Men can usually adapt to it without making vast changes in several areas of their lives (Rybarczyk, 1994).

Mid-life crisis is a social construction, according to Markson and Gognalons-Nicolet (1990). Their research on French, Swiss, and U.S. samples concludes that cultural and historical factors influence one's conceptualization of mid-life crisis. While certain mid-life events, such as the departure of children and concern about elderly parents, are common to all industrialized nations, reactions to these events might be altered by factors such as age cohort and age structure of the population (Markson & Gognalons-Nicolet, 1990).

Reentry Women

An increasing number of women are returning to college or work or are beginning college for the first time in middle or older adulthood after years of devoting their lives exclusively to their families. Several possible reasons for this have been suggested, such as reduction in family responsibilities or divorce. In fact, divorced women are overrepresented among adult students and are also more dedicated as students and/or workers (Alington & Troll, 1984).

Middle-aged women who have chosen this course of action, known as **reentry women,** face a number of problems. Those entering or reentering college must deal with feeling unable to relate to their much younger classmates, convincing their colleges to accept their transfer credits from several years earlier, and, in particular, the institutional barriers, such as lack of evening courses or minimum course-load requirements (Schlossberg, 1984). In addition, reentry women must make a successful transition from housekeeper to college student or worker. Men, and perhaps even younger women, experience this transition in a more traditional way (i.e., high school to college to graduate school to career) than do these women, who transform their roles later in their adult lives. Thus, reentry women are at a disadvantage because mentors are less likely to want to invest in their careers, and they may be socially isolated from their colleagues, who more closely resemble the typical college student (Doyle & Paludi, 1991).

While women going back to school in their middle or later years are commonly viewed as attempting to occupy their newfound leisure time, many women choose to continue their education at this point out of necessity. Women's economic, social, and personal resources are more vulnerable than those of men in the later years as a function of gender-related limitations (such as lower salary and fewer job opportunities) experienced across their life-span. These women may confront this bias upon returning to school in later life (Harold, 1992).

In spite of such obstacles, reentry women do extraordinarily well. In college, they work hard and participate actively in their education. They participate fully in the workplace, in politics, and in organized efforts for social change. In fact, activism on the part of older people is a topic that has been underresearched but has much significance. Older adults have been instrumental in forming organizations to improve their position, such as the Gray Panthers, the Older Women's League, Senior Action in a Gay Environment (SAGE) for older gay men and lesbians (MacDonald & Rich, 1983), and others. Older women have also become active in other social causes, and many view their efforts as connected to feminism (Garland, 1988).

Life begins at 40 for many women, and it is not uncommon for women at mid-life and even later to discover new talents and interests and employ them successfully (Alington & Troll, 1984). In addition, women who attend college at an older age were found to be more assertive and thus expected and received more spousal support (De Groot, 1980). This would bode well for their success.

The population of reentry women is likely to increase as life-spans grow longer and good health care continues. In fact, women in their early fifties rated their lives as better than either older or younger women (Mitchell & Helson, 1990), attesting to the possibilities and opportunities arising during mid-life.

LATER LIFE

It is important to remember that research on women who are older today applies to women who grew up several decades ago, before the women's movement. Research on middle-aged or older women in the future may yield dissimilar findings, because women who are growing up today are exposed to and shaped by very different social norms. Thus, currently available research may not be applicable to mid-life or older women of the twenty-first century (Grambs, 1989). A person's cohort, or group of people born within the same year or years, provides a more accurate prediction of her or his ideals and actions than does chronological age.

The middle and later years have been commonly stigmatized as a depressing era of decreasing physical well-being and life satisfaction. Yet, these years can actually be a happier and more contented time than the much-glorified era of early adulthood. Elderly women in particular are falsely stigmatized as being unhappy with their lot in life, although no conclusive evidence points to systematic gender differences in later life satisfaction. In several studies, older women proved to be just as satisfied as their same-age male and younger female counterparts (e.g., Liang, 1982). Individual factors such as health, finances, and family relationships pertain more directly to individual differences in life satisfaction than does gender (Matlin, 1993). In fact, the later years are a time of self-discovery for older women as they pick up new interests and redefine their self-image.

For non-White elderly women in the United States, aging is a unique experience. On the one hand, they are forced to contend with the quadruple burden of being old, often poor, female, and of minority status. Black and Hispanic women are worse off economically than White women, and the majority of elderly Black women are in "poor" or "nearly poor" categories (Grambs, 1989).

On the other hand, women from minority groups are often equipped with adaptive advantages for dealing with aging. For example, in African American culture, grandmothers play a significant role in child rearing and, as such, women's importance and status within the family is enhanced with age (Comas-Diaz & Greene, 1994). Despite the fact that African Americans are significantly more disadvantaged socioeconomically than are Whites and that African Americans perceive their health as worse than Whites do, African Americans express significantly more contentment with their lives than do Whites (Johnson, 1994).

In Native American Indian societies, older women's age and wisdom are revered, and their knowledge of tribal history, herbal medicine, and sacred matters is valued. Despite living in poverty in large numbers (LaFromboise, Berman, & Sohi, 1994), in general, Native American Indian women report more satisfaction with their lives and greater enjoyment in spending time with old people than do their European American counterparts (Comas-Diaz & Greene, 1994).

In comparison with men, however, women may have less positive attitudes toward aging. A cross-cultural study comparing both Swedes and Turks found that in both cultures women were more negative about aging and expressed higher feelings of personal loneliness (Imamoglu, Kuller, Imamoglu, & Kuller, 1993). Negative stereotypes of older women in the United States presented by the media (as discussed earlier) suggest that this is probably the case in the United States as well.

The gradual changes that begin in the middle years become increasingly apparent as the aging process continues, and new changes take place as well. In terms of activities of daily living, dependence and mobility impairment have been found to increase in prevalence with old age, while functioning decreases (Strawbridge, Kaplan, Camacho, & Cohen, 1992). Older people must also contend with pivotal life events such as retirement and spousal bereavement. As is true of mid-life, much of one's personal well-being in later life depends on one's perspective, an important aspect being one's feeling of autonomy and personal control. Perception of personal control is an important factor in one's psychological well-being and one especially relevant to the elderly. One's locus of control (i.e., the perception that one's life is internally controllable by one's own efforts) may significantly affect life adjustment throughout the lifespan and influence one's ability to cope with changing life circumstances that occur in later life, such as retirement (Hollis, 1994).

Although much of the research with older adults has been conducted with heterosexual elders, Reid (1995) speculates that the distinctive issues faced by aging lesbians and gay men enable them to more successfully negotiate this developmental stage. However, for the aging lesbian, her sense of well-being and ability to accept all aspects of her self and reality depend in large part on the social context in which her lesbianism is framed. Many of these women are unable to publicly or personally acknowledge their lesbian identity since the environment has not allowed for public discourse. Thus, they are often invisible to the larger society (Thorpe, 1989). Shenk and Fullmer (1996) found that when public acknowledgement is not available, the older lesbian is often unable to acknowledge that aspect of her identity.

The normal changes of aging can include physical disabilities and medical problems (Cole & Cole, 1993). For example, visual and reflex impairments may prevent elderly people from driving, resulting in increasing dependence on others. (Additional physical health issues pertaining to women are discussed in Chapter 13.) These and other setbacks experienced by aging people on physical, mental, and social fronts can result in a decreased sense of personal control over one's life. These life experiences can blur gender roles, impede sexual creativity, and/or have a desexualizing effect on self-esteem and libido (Cole & Cole, 1993). Negative stereotypes of old age, when internalized, can also perpetuate a self-percept of helplessness.

A decline in functional capacity, possibly resulting from physical disabilities, has been found to greatly increase the likelihood that an elderly person will move in with others or become institutionalized. Women who suffered declines in functional capacity were found to be somewhat less likely to live alone two years later than were their male counterparts. African Americans who suffered declines were more likely than their White counterparts to continue living alone (Worobey & Angel, 1990).

While men are more likely to have acute and fatal diseases, women are more likely to suffer from functional impairment due to chronic diseases (Barer, 1994). Thus, women experience disability and the use of personal assistance to a greater extent than do men. For men, reliance on others or on devices for assistance is associated with feelings of reduced well-being. Reliance on devices brings about the same

feeling for women. For women, the use of devices may also be accompanied by feelings of frustration, embarrassment, and stigma, rather than increased independence. Yet, reliance on personal assistance does not evoke these responses in women according to Penning and Strain (1994).

However, another study (Stoller & Cutler, 1992) found no gender differences in the source of extra-household assistance for either activities of daily living or instrumental activities of daily living. In addition, husband care-givers were more likely to incorporate extra-household assistance than were wife care-givers. This may be a function of women feeling more comfortable in the care-giving, nurturing role than do men. People's association of women and domesticity includes older women as well (Eagly & Mladinic, 1998), which probably results in the above disparity between men and women's self-perception as care-givers. It is interesting, however, that this view of older women implies an expectation that women devote themselves to others consistently (Eagly & Mladinic, in press).

After the age of 80, death rates for males are higher, but surviving females appear to decline more than do surviving males. Females tend to survive longer with incident disability than do males (Strawbridge et al., 1992). For this reason, older women are widowed far more often than older men. One-half of the women over the age of 65 are widows and 70 percent of these women live alone (U.S. Bureau of the Census, 1998c). Within the elderly population, a high proportion of women were found to be unmarried, living alone, functionally impaired, and financially limited. Men, in contrast, had fewer decrements, were more financially independent, and exercised more control over their environment (Barer, 1994).

Spousal Bereavement

Spousal bereavement is a frequent change that profoundly affects older people, especially women. A husband's pension usually ends with his death, and the couple's savings may have been exhausted during his final illness. In addition to the financial burden and emotional hardship incurred by this event, many widows also endure diminished social status and increased isolation. This occurs if the spouse's death lessens or ends interaction with his family (Lopata, 1973) or if the widow is dropped from her network of married friends, a condition that occurs when married friends view her continued presence as a threat to them or to their network's gender balance (Babchuk & Anderson, 1989).

It was once thought that spousal bereavement was a pivotal tragedy of old age. Recent studies of spousal bereavement in the elderly have shown that older people tolerate this so-called worst life event surprisingly well, showing few intense symptoms even in the first few months after a spouse's death (Breckenridge, Gallagher, Thompson, & Peterson, 1986, cited in Belsky, 1992). This applies to both men and women. In fact, for a sample of middle-class women, widowhood was seen as a mixed experience—not just as a trauma but as a chance for self-expansion and self-discovery.

However, spousal bereavement and the death of friends can make loneliness a central part of an older person's existence. Research suggests that loneliness expressed by older persons is related to gender, health status, and economic condition; needs for affection and security and the desire to be part of a social network; and the existence of a set of friends (Mullins & Mushel, 1992). In a study of gender effects on elderly life-styles, Arber and Ginn (1994) found that, although elderly women's opportunities for making and maintaining friendships are constrained by their having fewer material and health resources than do elderly men, the relationship skills that women acquire earlier in life are an asset. Women are less likely than men to have relied entirely on their spouse for friendship, and women seem more adaptable to changed circumstances.

For lone elderly women, friendships act as a buffer, alleviating the effects of their considerable disadvantage in material and health resources. Mental health among the elderly in general is facilitated by regular social interactions (O'Connor, 1992). Although old age is a time of losing friendships through death, the majority of elderly women make new friends (Rollins, 1996). Men, on the other hand, are less likely than women to have close friends and confide intimate matters to them (Grambs, 1989; Lewittes, 1988).

Friends may actually be more important than grown children in alleviating an elderly widow's loneliness. Friendships, unlike family members, are voluntarily chosen and based on common interests. Friends are also viewed as desiring to help out in order to contribute to the friend's welfare, whereas family members might feel obligated to do so (Arling, 1976a). Even women who are physically limited maintain and widen their social networks via the telephone (Hochschild, 1978). It is interesting to note that African American widows are even more likely than are White widows to be actively involved with friends and neighbors (Arling, 1976b). In addition, their families provide them with more social support (Jackson, 1987). A review of the literature recommends that older women maintain a support system of friends, become more knowledgeable regarding finances, and seek professional help for physical and psychological problems. Advice to older men includes lessening dependence on their wives for companionship, making social contacts, and participating in community and other activities. Suggestions for therapeutic intervention with both aging women and men include helping elderly women to deal with problems related to sexuality and relationships with adult children and helping elderly men to find ways to replace lost status, activities, and contacts (Jacobs, 1994).

Research is needed to examine racial and class differences in the impact of spousal bereavement. The institution of marriage appears to be relatively less central to Black women's existence; Black women appear to be more independent than White women in this respect (Brown & Gary, 1985). This may be a function of poorer health among Black males, which causes Black women to rely less on male support in later life (Spurlock, 1984).

Sexual orientation may also have an effect on one's reaction to losing one's partner in life. Lesbians, whose relationships with their lovers may not be publicly acknowledged, might not receive the same social support provided to widows. Even people who are aware of the relationship might not understand the depth of the loss involved (see Doress et al., 1987). In addition, lesbians who have lost their lovers may suffer the same economic repercussions as widows, but without the same legal financial provisions.

Retirement

Like spousal bereavement, retirement is also traditionally viewed as an emotional trauma for aging people. However, since the 1970s, studies have shown that most men and women look forward to retirement; retirement is far from the emotional trauma it is supposed to be (Palmore, Burchett, Fillenbaum, George, & Wallman, 1985). Apparently, retirement and widowhood have a much more multifaceted meaning to people than we might think, symbolizing not just leaving something but entering a new stage of life.

Retirement can contribute to psychological difficulties though, particularly for the man whose identity is wrapped up in his work role. Men often experience themselves and their status as an extension of their occupational success, because a man's work role is closely tied to his job as the family provider. Once this is gone, a man sometimes experiences a loss in status and a loss of relationships and contact with former friends and associates. He must often develop a new identity, with new relationships, particularly with his wife and family, that may require him to be more intimate and vulnerable. Leisure time is yet another new experience that is often quite difficult to adjust to, particularly for the man whose life was his work (Denmark, Nielson, & Scholl, 1993).

Women may take longer to adjust to retirement than men, possibly because women are not under the same social pressures to be employed as men are. Those women who have chosen to work, whether out of financial need or commitment to their job, therefore may find it more difficult to stop working. In addition, retired women are more likely than retired men to report that their incomes are inadequate. This reflects the fact that women's retirement income typically is only about one-half that of men's. Women's

concentration in low-paying jobs and their often interrupted or delayed work careers can result in smaller retirement benefits. In addition, women are less likely to receive pensions than are men as a function of women's lesser years in the work force and lesser affiliation with unions, segregation in low-wage occupations, and discrimination involving training, promotion, and raises. Preretirement planning could help alleviate some of women's serious financial problems (Rollins, 1996).

The vignette in Box 10.3 illustrates the complex decisions faced by women who feel torn between early retirement and remaining at work.

On the positive side, retired women, particularly unmarried ones, are more involved with friends and neighbors than are retired men or lifelong housewives. For both sexes, a high level of life satisfaction in retirement is generally associated with having good health, adequate income, a high activity level (Etaugh, 1993), and, specifically for widows, support networks (Hong & Duff, 1994). However, whereas older females did not necessarily express less life satisfaction than elderly males when surveyed, interviewed female retirees appeared to be significantly less well adjusted psychosocially than their male counterparts (Hollis, 1994).

Adelmann (1993) found that women who described themselves as both retired and homemakers had higher self-esteem and lower depression than did women who identified themselves with a single role. Lower depression for older women was also associated with higher levels of education, marriage, good health, age, and engagement in hours of do-it-yourself activities. Higher self-esteem for older women was associated with age, education, health, do-it-yourself activity, and volunteer activity. On the whole, it appears that involvement in a number of activities and roles is beneficial for older women.

Reactions to retirement vary across cultures. One study (Yee, 1990) highlights the importance of careful cross-cultural research in the area of aging. In this study of Native American, Native Alaskan Eskimo, Asian and Pacific Islander, African American, and Hispanic families, it was concluded that there is di-

Box 10.3_____

Early Retirement

Imagine Alice, a healthy 62-year-old, faced with the possibility of early retirement from her position in a large communications firm. Her career has been successful and she has received many steady pay increases. However, she has not been promoted to a higher position in the last 12 years. She feels that the company is waiting for her to announce her retirement so that they can fill her position with a younger employee. The firm is offering a desirable early retirement package that is starting to look tempting to Alice. Also, the company recently paid for Alice and other employees in their late fifties and early sixties to attend a retirement seminar. She attended several seminars led by psychologists that emphasized the benefits of early retirement. One psychologist noted, "Early retirement will leave you free to pursue your interests while you still have your health." The sessions were compelling and offered some interesting views on early retirement. What should Alice do?

Alice derives immense satisfaction and pleasure from her job. She is competent to handle the demands of her job and makes valuable contributions to the firm (although she feels these efforts are not always appreciated). Alice feels she is just as sharp as the younger employees in her department. In fact, her experience and expertise in communications have proved invaluable on many occasions when critical decisions were made. Aside from slight arthritis, Alice is in perfect physical condition. She has not missed a single day of work in 10 years. Why should Alice retire early?

---

versity within each minority group and that the subgroups in each ethnic category share more similar life experiences with each other than with White, middle-class families.

Although men are stereotypically viewed as becoming less productive as they lose or surrender their competitive and aggressive "instincts," elderly men have actually made significant achievements in our culture. Many U.S. men continue to hold powerful positions well past the age of 65, sometimes hitting career peaks in "old age." These men continue to base their self-esteem on the success ethic (i.e., you are what you produce or achieve) and are not daunted by their advancing age in this respect (Rybarczyk, 1994).

Becoming a grandparent is a common role change among aging people. For most women, becoming a grandmother is a positive event because it does not bring with it the stress that motherhood entailed. This is especially true today as grandmothers take less responsibility for child care (Doress et al., 1987). Yet, economic factors may necessitate the grandmother's becoming a baby-sitter for her grandchildren, because her children may live with her (Long & Porter, 1984). Should the child's parents become ill or die, it may even fall to the grandmother to raise the child in some cultures.

An interesting phenomenon in gender issues among the elderly is the idea that the sexes become more like one another or even trade personality traits as they age. This was a basic finding in the Kansas City Studies of Adult Life (Neugarten & Gutmann, 1964), the idea that women become more assertive and men softer and less stereotypically masculine in the second half of adult life. Similarly, Fischer and Narus (1981) found that older women view themselves as more autonomous and competent than younger women, and older men view themselves as more communal and expressive than younger men. These self-descriptions run counter to gender stereotypes. While other studies find an increase in the number of feminine women and masculine men in the oldest age category (61 and older) (Hyde, Krajnik, & Skuldt-Niederberger, 1991), this possible gender-role flexibility of old age bears further investigation.

A possible implication of this finding is that earlier in life these more androgynous people may have had to suppress their real selves in order to conform to what Gutmann (1987) would call the **parental imperative;** that is, parental roles force female and male adults into relatively powerful or less powerful positions consistent with their respective gender roles. The onset of the postparental era at around age 50 may have provided them with the opportunity to express their true personalities.

However, the results of a study on elderly people in an Israeli kibbutz setting (Friedman, Tzukerman, Wienberg, & Todd, 1992) countered the parental imperative as an explanation for this shift in gender roles. Although parenthood did increase the power of the male and decrease the power of the female, as Gutmann argued, this was only true among urban families. Kibbutz couples experience the reverse: parental status actually increased power for the female and decreased power for the male. Apparently, the parental imperative described by Gutmann (1987) is affected by culture in terms of its ramifications, not biology as Gutmann suggested. Furthermore, older women in the kibbutz were found to use traditionally feminine power strategies, such as indirect power or manipulation, personal resources (e.g., friendliness and emotional support as opposed to concrete resources like money or strength), and helplessness (Johnson, 1976). Yet, their behavior was evaluated as more powerful than the same behavior in younger women. Thus, it is not the behaviors but rather people's evaluation of the behaviors that changes across the life-span (Friedman et al., 1992).

A possible explanation for observed shifts in gender-typed behavior among older people is that as men age the social roles available to them change. Men may engage in more domestic activities once retirement affords them the free time to do so. The gender-role expectations for older males may be less rigid, causing older men to feel freer to engage in less gender-stereotypical behaviors. They may view themselves as equally masculine but have less concern about maintaining their outward appearance (Rybarczyk, 1994).

Although the shift in gender-typed behavior may occur in the realm of personality, it does not necessarily extend to choice of activities. On the contrary, older women of various ethnic groups have been found to engage more in traditionally female sex-typed activities such as housework and cooking. Although older men engage more in hunting, farming, or working to support themselves, this difference was not significant (Harris, Begay, & Page, 1989). This lends some basis to the common stereotype of older women as nurturing, cheerful "grandmother" types (Brewer, Dull, & Lui, 1981). Typical older women are viewed as less self-centered, more nuturant, and more sensitive than typical older men (Canetto, Kaminski, & Felicio, 1995), possibly as a function of this stereotype.

Cognitive Changes

One of the most greatly feared aspects of growing older for both women and men is the decline in cognitive ability that often accompanies aging. For example, significant changes in everyday memory, memory capacity, processing speed, and depression have been found to occur with age. Gender differences were found as well, with older males showing a decrease in memory problems and females showing an increase in memory problems (Agrawal & Kumar, 1992). However, a longitudinal study of male and female senior citizens tested twice over three years found that, upon retesting, females were better at prose recall and list recognition performance than were men (Zelinski, Gilewski, & Schaie, 1993). More research is needed here.

Memory decline actually begins in middle adulthood, when it is more common with long-term than with short-term memory (Craik, 1977). Memory is also likely to decline at this stage if memory strategies such as organization and imagery are not used (Smith, 1977). In addition, memory for recently acquired information or infrequently used information begins to worsen in the middle years (Riege & Inman, 1981). Finally, in the middle years, recognition is better than recall (Mandler, 1980).

Intellectual decline in the later adult years is a subject of much debate and controversy. Although some maintain that the aging process results in cognitive deterioration universally (Wechsler, 1972), others argue that some abilities decline while others do not. For example, Horn and Donaldson (1980) agree that *fluid intelligence* (i.e., one's ability to reason abstractly) declines steadily from middle adulthood, but *crystallized intelligence* (i.e., one's accumulated information and verbal skills) actually increases with age. On the other hand, Schaie (1994) found that mental abilities do not decline until the age of 74, but when perceptual speed is removed, the actual decrement is significantly reduced.

However, the speed of processing information has clearly been found to decline in late adulthood (Sternberg & McGrane, 1993). Other cognitive changes supported by the research include decreased ability to retrieve information from memory (Sternberg & McGrane, 1993) and to efficiently use mental information in memory (Baltes, Smith, & Staudinger, 1991).

Do age-related cognitive changes differ according to gender? Recent magnetic resonance imaging (MRI) data suggest that men show more rapid age-associated atrophy of the left hemisphere than do women. However, data suggest that this does not translate into differential functional decline in simulated everyday verbal memory (Larrabee & Crook, 1993). In a study of memory for visual–spatial arrays in young and elderly adults, absolute errors increased with age. This is consistent with decreased antero-grade memory and visuospatial skills in the elderly. The writers speculate that "components of the complex mechanisms underlying visuospatial processing may be differently affected by gender" (Jue et al., 1992, p. 236), since elderly women outperformed elderly men on a spatial array memory test, and the reverse was true when the groups were tested on the judgement of line orientation.

Age-related cognitive decline has emotional effects as well. Fuhrer, Antonucci, and Dartigues (1992) examined the co-occurrence of depressive symptomatology and cognitive impairment in female and male elderly adults. Co-occurrence was found to be associated with age, little or no education (women were at a higher risk than men when this predictor was involved), functional impairment, and dissatisfaction with social support (for the latter two factors, men were at a higher risk than women). Women over the age of 85 were at an increased risk, and marital status was associated with co-occurrence for men but not for women.

SUMMARY

Clearly, development for both genders does not end with the onset of adulthood. Young adults who have finished adolescence are confronted with Erikson's classic conflict of intimacy versus isolation. Although in the past it was conventional to choose intimacy in the form of a formal commitment to marriage, the options today are much more varied, from the traditional course of marrying, to cohabitation, to simply remaining single. Even those who choose the former two may wait longer before settling down with a partner.

Single people usually choose to socialize with members of the other sex, whether they are motivated by the desire to find a partner or are simply dating casually without any serious intentions in mind. Here, too, social norms are changing. Whereas women used to play a more passive role in the courtship, they may now initiate and even pay for the dates. However, some gender differences persist, with women being more willing to self-disclose than men are. Women and men also communicate differently when they are in relationship conflicts.

Marriage, too, has changed with the times. Traditional marriage, in which both spouses adhered to traditional gender-role ideology, is now only one of several types of marriage. With women playing an increasingly instrumental role in their marriages and being more occupied with financial concerns, men should be taking on more household responsibilities. Unfortunately, this is often not the case. Role overload is a contributing factor to women's decreased satisfaction with marriage in recent times.

More couples today are deciding to delay having children, or not have children at all. Once couples do become parents, they often revert to traditional gender roles for practical and/or emotional reasons. Single parents are confronted with the unique challenge of taking on both gender roles with respect to their children. Gay and lesbian parents also face unique challenges brought on by negative beliefs about their ability to rear healthy, well-adjusted children.

Older adults face a double standard as they approach mid-life. Men are more often viewed as being in their prime and reaping the benefits of career building in young adulthood. Women, on the other hand, face ageism that is perpetuated by a society that disparages the physical changes that come with growing older (e.g., menopause, graying, wrinkles) and are viewed as worthless because their children have assumed independent lives. Many of these women, how-

ever, are responsible for providing emotional support for their adolescent and adult children and their own aging parents.

Both genders experience cognitive and physical decline as they approach retirement age. These changes may combine functional impairment with psychological difficulties as those suffering struggle to adjust to decline in abilities. This decline may be more evident in women; they live longer than their male counterparts and may require more social support.

KEY TERMS

Ageism (p. 322)
Climacteric (p. 323)
Cohort (p. 312)
Dominant generation (p. 323)
Double standards of aging (p. 322)
Empty nest syndrome (p. 325)

Graying of America (p. 321)
Late mid-life astonishment (p. 323)
Modern gender-role ideology
 (p. 315)
Mutual marriage (p. 314)
Parental imperative (p. 333)

Reentry women (p. 328)
Role overload (p. 314)
Symbiotic marriage (p. 314)
Traditional gender-role ideology
 (p. 315)
Trophy wives (p. 327)

DISCUSSION QUESTIONS

1. What constitutes a family? Which, if any, of these components are crucial to the establishment of a family: cohabitation, marriage, children? Why or why not? How does society's definition of a family compare with your own?

2. In your opinion, what are the primary roles of wives and husbands in a marriage? Compare your views on the roles of wives and husbands with those roles filled by your parent(s) or caretakers. Are they the same or different? Why do you think this is so?

3. Discuss the significance of power in female–male relationships. How does the power differential between women and men in marriage affect their roles in society?

4. What are some of the advantages of combining marriage with a career? What are some of the disadvantages? Are these the same for women and men? If not, what are the differences?

5. What are the physical and psychological changes that occur during mid-life for women and men? How do changes in physical appearance during mid-life affect women and men differently? What are your own beliefs regarding aging women and men?

6. How do women's responsibilities change as they grow older? What options open up for women? What additional tasks are relegated to women? In your opinion, do women gain or lose options in society as they age?

7. It has been shown that, on average, women live longer lives than men do. What are the positive and negative consequences of longevity?

SUGGESTED READINGS

Etaugh, C. (1993). Women in the middle and later years. In F. L. Denmark & M. A. Paludi (Eds.), *Psychology of women: A handbook of issues and theories* (pp. 213–246). Westport, CT: Greenwood Press.

Babladelis, G. (1999). Autonomy in the middle years. In M. B. Nadien & F. L. Denmark (Eds.), *Females and autonomy: A life-span perspective* (pp. 101–129). Boston: Allyn & Bacon.

Nadien, M. B., & Denmark, F. L. (1999). Aging women: Stability or change in perceptions of personal control. In M. B. Nadien & F. L. Denmark (Eds.), *Females and autonomy: A life-span perspective* (pp. 130–154). Boston: Allyn & Bacon

CHAPTER 11

GENDER, VIOLENCE, AND EXPLOITATION

It pays men to be aggressive, hasty, fickle, and undiscriminating. In theory, it is more profitable for females to be coy, to hold back until they can identify the male with the best genes. . . . Human beings obey this biological principle faithfully.
—E. O. Wilson

Alone and in isolation, the person who has been hit must struggle to regain broken trust—to forge some strategy of recovery. Individuals are often able to process an experience of being hit mentally that may not be processed emotionally. Many women I talked with felt that even after the incident was long forgotten, their bodies remained troubled.
—bell hooks

This is my weapon
This is my gun (points to groin).
This one's for killing
This one's for fun.
—Old Marine Corps chant

Among the more than 600 families surveyed in Southern Asia, 51 percent reported having killed a baby girl during her first week of life.
—N. Neft and A. D. Levine

THE NATURE AND SCOPE OF GENDERED VIOLENCE AND EXPLOITATION

Wherever they occur, from the family to the workplace to the street, experiences of violence and exploitation define and limit women in sexual and gender-specific terms. Sexist responses to women, ranging from putdown humor and insults to physical abuse and murder, are shockingly common in U.S. society and around the world. Why are women so often violated and exploited by men? No doubt the answer is complex and multifaceted, involving biological, psychological, social, and cultural factors. But it seems likely that the most important causes of violence and exploitation of women by men lie in gender inequality: women's lack of power relative to men. Whenever people are categorized into polarized groups such as male and female and one group has more power than the other, as men have more power than women, differences between groups are usually transformed into disadvantages for the less powerful group. We have seen these disadvantages in the many negative stereotypes and hurtful myths that exist about girls and women. These myths and stereotypes devalue women in their own and others' eyes. They make it more likely that women will construct identities, personalities, and sexualities around deference to men, and this in turn makes it more likely that women will be mistreated and abused by men (Bem, 1994).

This chapter addresses central questions of how gender inequality creates personal and social conditions conducive to exploitation of and violence against women and girls. The intersection of gender and violence is a particularly problematic area for a number of reasons. As we consider the many different forms that gendered abuse may take, we confront several hard questions. Chief among them is what it is that constitutes violence and exploitation. For example, few people would deny that incest, sexual assault, and the rape of a stranger constitute clear-cut examples of the abuse of women. But more people have difficulty classifying sexual harassment, date rape, and spousal and parental abuse as serious problems for women. And there is widespread disagreement and lively debate about whether and how pornography and prostitution harm women. Where possible, we discuss the gender, ethnic, cultural, and social class variations in the perceptions of different behaviors as violent or exploitative.

Men as well as women are targets of violence and exploitation. In fact, men are more often the targets of most forms of violence than women (Kilmartin, 1994), and heterosexual men are sometimes the victims of sexual assault, as in cases of prison rape. Although the perpetrators of violence against men are overwhelmingly other men, women sometimes abuse and even murder men. Violence against and exploitation of heterosexual men and boys are obviously serious problems, but they will not be treated extensively in this chapter because they are not regarded as cases of *gendered* abuse. That is, heterosexual men are privileged in society relative to other groups and are not abused and exploited because of their lack of power or status as a social group.

The most common and salient forms of gendered violence and exploitation are the abuses of women and girls by men, but these are not the only forms. This chapter also discusses the abuse of gay men and lesbians as in gay-bashing, gay-baiting, domestic abuse among gay male and lesbian partners, and other acts of violence and intimidation against people rendered vulnerable because of their gender or sexuality.

The present chapter considers the following classes of behaviors as instances of gendered violence or exploitation: sexual harassment, rape, partner abuse, child sexual abuse, pornography, prostitution, anti-gay violence, female infanticide, female genital mutilation (FGM), and elder abuse. While some scholars attempt to order forms of violence against women on a continuum of severity of abuse, we do

not do so. We wish to emphasize that all forms of abuse and exploitation engender a range of consequences in women, depending on a variety of background, situational, and personality factors. Moreover, in this chapter, the term *sexual assault* is not used synonymously with rape. We define sexual assault more broadly, to include any physical attack upon the sexual parts of a woman's body—pinching, grabbing, and the like. So defined, sexual assault can occur in many forms of violence against women. For each form of violence and exploitation, we will address issues of definition and prevalence, explore its cultural significance, review relevant theories and research about its origins and consequences, and discuss a range of individual and social responses to the problem.

SEXUAL HARASSMENT

Few forms of gendered abuse have posed more problems of definition for lay people and psychologists alike than sexual harassment. The term **sexual harassment** did not even exist until 1976, when it was used in connection with a legal suit filed by Carmita Wood, the first woman to seek unemployment compensation after leaving a job in which her boss made sexual advances toward her (Fitzgerald, 1996). As Catherine MacKinnon, law professor and leading advocate for women's rights, noted in 1979, "The unnamed should not be taken for the nonexistent" (p. 28). Sexual harassment has been a fixture of women's lives in the street, the workplace, and the academy for as long as women have appeared there. After the naming of sexual harassment in the mid-1970s, the closely watched confirmation hearings of Clarence Thomas in 1991, in which accusations of sexual harassment were made by Anita Hill against then U.S. Supreme Court Justice nominee Thomas, put the spotlight on a social problem of enormous proportions. More recently, the U.S. Navy Tailhook scandal and the resignation of U.S. Senator Robert Packwood after multiple accusations of sexual harassment by aides have increased awareness of sexual harassment. The last 20 years have witnessed an explosion of interest, research, and litigation in sexual harassment. In this chapter, we deal with issues relating to all forms of harassment, wherever it occurs, but topics particularly relevant to workplace harassment are covered more extensively in Chapter 7.

Definitions and Prevalence

There is no widely agreed upon definition of sexual harassment that is both broad enough to encompass the variety of experiences to which the construct refers and yet specific enough to be of practical use in identifying harassment (Fitzgerald, 1996). Basically, definitions of harassment can be classified into two categories: (1) general or theoretical statements that focus on the nature of the behavior and (possibly) the status of the individuals involved, and (2) those that list specific classes of behaviors that constitute harassment.

In the first category are most legal and regulatory definitions and some theoretical statements on harassment offered by psychologists. Catherine MacKinnon's early definition has been most influential: "Sexual harassment . . . refers to the unwanted imposition of sexual requirements in the context of a relationship of unequal power" (1979, p. 1). The Equal Employment Opportunity Commission defined harassment as unwelcome sexual advances, requests for sexual favors, and other verbal or physical conduct of a sexual nature when (1) such behavior is made explicitly or implicitly a term or condition of employment, (2) submission to such terms is used as the basis for employment decisions affecting the individual, or (3) verbal or physical conduct of a sexual nature has the purpose or effect of creating an intimidating, hostile, or offensive work environment. In an academic setting, sexual harassment has been defined as "the use of authority to emphasize the sexuality or sexual identity of the student in a manner which prevents or impairs that student's full enjoyment of educational benefits, climate, or opportunities" (Till, 1980, p. 7).

The second category of definitions of harassment is much more concrete and focuses on the specific classes of behaviors that constitute harassment (Fitzgerald, 1996). One particularly thorough catalogue classified the responses of a national sample of college women into five general classes of harassing behaviors (Till, 1980):

1. Generalized sexist remarks and behavior. This behavior, sometimes called **gender harassment,** is not necessarily designed to obtain sexual favors, but to convey insulting, degrading, or sexist attitudes about women.
2. Inappropriate and offensive, but essentially sanction-free sexual advances. This category, sometimes called **seductive behavior,** includes unwanted sexual advances for which there is no penalty attached to a woman's noncompliance.
3. Sexual bribery. This is the solicitation of sexual activity by the promise of reward.
4. Sexual coercion. This is the solicitation of sexual activity by the threat of punishment. With category 3, this category is sometimes called *contingency* or **quid pro quo harassment.**
5. Sexual crimes and misdemeanors. This category includes gross sexual imposition, sexual assault, and rape.

Whichever type of definition of harassment is used, problems arise that affect issues of measurement, incidence, and theories of harassment. One problematic feature of defining harassment lies in whether the conduct occurs in the context of unequal power relations between the victim and perpetrator. According to many legal and theoretical definitions, in order to be labeled harassment, the sexist or sexualized behavior must take place within the context of uneven power relations, that is, when the harasser has power over the victim's outcomes and can use that power to reward or punish. Can someone be sexually harassed by a peer or even a subordinate? Many scholars take the view that people can be harassed by peers and, indeed, that this form of harassment is very common (Hughes & Sandler, 1988). In societies in which men are pervasively privileged, where they have more freedom, autonomy, authority, credibility, education, money, status, and the like, men in general have greater power than women and sometimes abuse that power.

Probably the greatest difficulties in defining and labeling conduct as sexual harassment lie in the differing judgments that people make about the meaning of behaviors. As we will see to some extent with date rape, pornography, and prostitution, there is lively disagreement about the intentions of men and the harm done to women by various forms of sexual harassment. Individuals differ widely in their perceptions of sexist or sexualized conduct as harassing. Conduct that is extremely offensive to some people is not at all objectionable to others. Some scholars believe that, because all women are invariably oppressed by sexist and sexualized encounters in a society stratified by gender, all sexist and unwelcome sexualized behavior in settings like the workplace should be regarded as harassing, regardless of the victim's judgment of it as problematic (Fitzgerald, 1996; Lafontaine & Tredeau, 1986). For others, the perceptions of the victim are particularly critical to the label of harassment: the conduct in question must be unwanted, unsolicited, nonreciprocated, offensive, or repeated.

More than most forms of violence against and exploitation of women, appraisals of sexual harassment depend on various personal and situational factors. Many variables shown to influence perceptions of sexual harassment have already been identified. None is more consistently related to perceptions of harassment than gender. In study after study, women have been more likely than men to view behaviors as harassing and offensive (Fitzgerald & Ormerod, 1991; Powell, 1986). This is probably because women, far more than men, have experienced unwanted sexual attention in their lives. We will discuss the implications of these consistent gender differences later.

Other variables influencing perceptions of harassment include the status of the harasser. Behaviors initiated by supervisors or others with a substantial power advantage are more likely to be judged as harassment. The degree of coercion represented by the behavior is also important: requests for sex linked to threat of punishment or promise of reward (quid pro quo) are viewed more negatively than sexist remarks or jokes (gender harassment) or seductive behavior. Whereas *quid pro quo* behaviors are virtually always

seen by both women and men as sexual harassment, gender harassment and seductive behavior elicit considerably more disagreement (Fitzgerald, 1996). For example, in one survey of college students, only 30 percent of the male but 47 percent of the female students regarded sexist comments as sexual harassment (Adams, Kottke, & Padgitt, 1983).

The above definitions of sexual harassment raise some important questions with theoretical and practical significance. Is it possible for women to harass men? What about consensual sexual relationships between supervisors and subordinates? Isn't is possible for people with unequal power within an organizational setting to enter into a loving, mutually satisfying, long-lasting relationship devoid of coercion and exploitation?

In the early 1990s, Michael Crichton wrote *Disclosure,* a best-selling novel that was made into a major motion picture, about a woman who harassed a male co-worker. In fact, some males are harassed at work, school, and in the street, but the usual harassers of males are not women but other men. Women are not socialized to initiate sexual relationships in most societies, and sexually aggressive women are often stigmatized and punished. Moreover, women are much less likely to hold the organizational power that would permit them to offer rewards and punishments to men (Fitzgerald & Weitzman, 1990). Women sometimes do make unwanted sexual overtures to men, and these may be inconvenient or even painful to some men. But research evidence suggests that men suffer significantly less harm from sexual harassment than women (Bingham & Scherer, 1993). Given the relative power and threat of women and men in most societies, such unwanted overtures are probably better viewed as private hassles rather than sexual harassment (Dziech & Weiner, 1984), because men generally have the power to control the problem.

The issue of seemingly consensual sexual relationships between people in the context of unequal power remains a problematic and controversial issue for scholars who study sexual harassment. In fact, many people who enter into sexual relationships in which there is unequal formal power are convinced that there is equal power within the relationship, that both parties are equally free to enter into or terminate the relationship, and that neither party is at risk to be harmed by the relationship. Bosses dating secretaries, professors falling in love with students, and employers marrying housekeepers or nannies are common story lines in books, television programs, and movies and are not uncommon scenarios in real life. Some of these couples do indeed end up living "happily ever after." So what is wrong with this picture?

On the one hand, some scholars have argued that to regard all consensual relationships between people of formally different statuses as inherently unethical or harassing limits the power, control, and freedom of all people, including the powerless (Hoffman, Clinebell, & Kilpatrick, 1997). On the other hand, others believe that "truly consensual relationships are probably not possible within the context of unequal power, and thus may be generally inappropriate" (Fitzgerald, 1996, p. 42). Fitzgerald et al. (1988) noted elsewhere that while not always unethical, sexual relationships among people of unequal power within an organization are almost always unwise.

The prevalence of sexual harassment has been notoriously difficult to study because of the lack of a commonly accepted definition and, relatedly, of any standardized survey instrument that could provide comparable results across studies (Fitzgerald, Shullman et al., 1988). But since the early 1980s, the results of several large-scale studies in academia and the workplace suggest that sexual harassment is a widespread phenomenon. Probably the best-known study of the prevalence of sexual harassment is a national survey using a random sample of almost 24,000 male and female employees working for the federal government (U.S. Merit Systems Protection Board, 1981). The response rate to this survey was a very high 83.8 percent. Forty-two percent of all women respondents reported that they were the targets of sexual harassment within the previous two years. A wide range of harassing behaviors was reported, with repeated sexual remarks (33 percent) and unwanted physical touching (26 percent) the most common complaints.

The incidence of sexual harassment has been studied extensively in colleges and universities. The academy is an important place to study harassment because for many it is the repository of the best that society has to offer its members: it is an "ivory tower" or "safe haven" from the corruption of the workplace. Values are an important part of education, and colleges communicate values in many ways, including in the kinds of relationships between men and women and faculty and students that it promotes on campus (Hughes & Sandler, 1988). Moreover, the relationship between a professor and a student is held by many to be a special one with unique ethical responsibilities, and sexualizing that relationship is regarded as a particularly problematic betrayal of trust.

In fact, most surveys of sexual harassment on college campuses show that levels of sexual harassment by both professors and peers (other students) is shockingly high. In one survey of students in two large public universities, about 50 percent of the undergraduate women at one university and 76 percent of the undergraduate women at the second university reported experiencing at least one incident that meets the definition of sexual harassment (Fitzgerald, Shullman et al., 1988). In both settings, the most frequently reported situations involved either gender harassment or seduction. Between 5 and 8 percent reported being propositioned and another 5 to 8 percent reported unwanted attempts by professors to touch or fondle them. Nearly 5 percent at both universities reported being subtly bribed by professors with some sort of award to engage in sexual activity. Despite the severity of many of these behaviors (touching, fondling, propositions, etc.), only 5 percent of the female sample believed that they had been sexually harassed. Other surveys of college students variously put the incidence of sexual harassment at between 15 and 50 percent, with higher estimates occurring when situations involving gender harassment are included in the survey (Dziech & Weiner, 1984; Reilly, Lott, & Gallogly, 1986).

Street harassment—from whistling, to sexist and lewd remarks and verbal come-ons, to obscene gestures, to following, to men exposing themselves, or to grabbing and sexual assault—is often regarded as relatively trivial and has received far less research attention by psychologists and other social scientists than either workplace or academic harassment. But, in fact, street harassment may be more common than either of the other two types. A cross section of female respondents in New York City estimated that the average woman is harassed on the street about seven times a week, and male respondents guessed slightly larger numbers (Packer, 1986). Street harassment is not trivial, often restricting women's movements, autonomy, and sense of control, and sometimes causing great pain, fear, and humiliation.

Theories of the Origins of Sexual Harassment

As we have noted, recent surveys suggest that sexual harassment is probably one of the most common forms of abuse of women, with most women having experienced some forms of harassment at school, on the job, or on the street. Why do men harass women? There is relatively little literature that specifically addresses the origins of sexual harassment, but most theorists believe that we cannot understand sexual harassment without placing it within the context of gender inequality and sexist oppression.

Some models of sexual harassment trace a proclivity of sexual harassment to the conventional male gender role, especially the socialization of males to dominate and control others, to restrict emotional expression, to actively seek sex whenever possible, and, to avoid "feminine" behavior and feelings and define themselves in terms of achievement and success. Traditionally, males are not socialized to take an interpersonal orientation: to empathize with others or consider how others interpret an act. Sexual harassment is often a matter of whether the intended target feels uncomfortable, attacked, offended, or intimidated—what some people call the "eye of the beholder criterion." Kilmartin (1994) notes, "Many men are wondering, at what point does 'normal' flirting, sexual discussion, or complimenting cross the line into harassment?" (p. 241).

Kilmartin suggests that men harass women at least in part because their socialization offers them little experience in making judgments about what others, especially women, are thinking and feeling, and many men are unaware of their effects on women.

There is ample research suggesting that men and women do have different perceptions of some of the behaviors that constitute sexual harassment, especially the less severe forms of harassment. Generally, men are far less likely to view a behavior as harassing than women are. In the U.S. Merit Systems Protection Board (1981), women were more likely than men to regard sexual teasing, jokes, or remarks to be sexual harassment. Gutek (1996) also found that women who encounter sexual comments, looks, gestures, and unnecessary physical contact in the workplace are more likely than men to consider such behavior sexual harassment. These findings are consistent with those of Abbey (1982) and Abbey and Melby (1986), which suggests that men tend to perceive women's friendly behavior as a sign of sexual interest or availability. Men may initiate some behaviors that they do not believe to be offensive but are viewed as harassing by some women. Differences in the way men and women view social exchanges in the workplace are important components of any useful model of sexual harassment.

Using previous research, court cases, and legal defenses as their guide, Tangri, Burt, and Johnson (1982) proposed a theoretical framework of sexual harassment with three possible explanatory models. The *natural–biological model* suggests that men and women are naturally attracted to each other at work or in the academy, but that men simply have stronger sex drives than women and are thus more likely to initiate and maintain sexual behaviors. The critical aspect of this model is the absence of discriminatory or harmful intent on the part of the male perpetrator. The *organizational model* suggests that the hierarchical relations that exist within organizations create opportunities for sexual harassment. Various features of an organization, such as differential power, the numerical ratio of males to females, the norms of the organization, and the availability of formal or informal grievance procedures may all affect the incidence of sexual harassment. Finally, the *sociocultural model* describes sexual harassment as a result of the gender inequality that exists throughout society. In this formulation, sexual harassment on the job is a mechanism for maintaining male dominance over women in the workplace and in the larger society. None of these models has received clear-cut empirical support in organizational settings, but stronger support has been found for the organizational and sociocultural models, both of which conceptualize sexual harassment as an abuse of power, than for the natural–biological model (Saal, Johnson, & Weber, 1989; Tangri et al., 1982).

Terpstra and Baker (1986) offer a different explanatory model that identifies three "causal factors" in sexual harassment: gender, power, and perceptions of work climate. They predicted and found that women are more likely to be harassed than men, that people with less institutional power are more likely to be harassed than people with more institutional power, and that sexual harassment is more common in organizations that are perceived as tolerant of harassment. Other tests of their model have generally garnered some support (Bingham & Scherer, 1993). As we saw in Chapter 7, the notion of **sex role spillover,** the carryover of female gender role to work and school settings, has also been proposed to explain sexual harassment (Gutek, 1985).

All the models reviewed are helpful in explaining sexual harassment, but no one model entirely explains why sexual harassment exists. Most recent conceptual frameworks see sexual harassment in all its forms in the workplace, academia, and public sphere as being rooted in a combination of sexual interest and unequal power between the sexes. In this way, sexual harassment is used as a tactic of social control, a means of keeping women in their place, especially in work and school settings that have been traditional male preserves, such as the firehouse or military academy.

Research on Sexual Harassment: Who Harasses and Who Is Harassed?

Theories on what causes and maintains sexual harassment have inspired a great deal of empirical research in the past two decades. Research suggests that there are no typical harassers or victims of harassment, but certain individual and social characteristics are correlated with the incidence of sexual harassment.

Who Harasses?   Studies consistently find that men harass women far more often than women harass men (Bingham & Scherer, 1993; Gutek, 1985; U.S. Merit Protections Board, 1981). Remarkably little empirical literature bears on the social and psychological characteristics of men who harass women. The reasons for this omission are obvious. How does one study sexual harassers? Men who harass women are understandably reluctant to volunteer as participants for research. They do not declare themselves publicly. They are not found in self-help groups because they do not judge their behavior to be symptomatic of a personal problem (Zalk, 1996). Unlike rapists or child abusers, they are not found in jails.

The little research that has been done on male harassers finds few reliable predictors of harassment. Attitudes consistent with the traditional male gender role have been associated with the likelihood of sexual harassment. Pryor (1987) found that men who see women as sex objects first and human beings (or co-workers) second are at risk for sexual harassment. Men who hold adversarial sexual beliefs—that sexual relationships are a matter of exploitation and manipulation—are more likely to harass. In these ways, as we will see, the characteristics of sexual harassers are similar to those of acquaintance rapists in that feelings of masculine inadequacy and misogyny appear to fuel the behavior (Kilmartin, 1994). The psychological dynamics of male harassers in the academy and the profiles of different types of harassers have been explored in depth by Dziech and Weiner (1984) and Zalk (1996).

In the workplace, a few predictors of sexual harassment have emerged. For instance, research suggests that men who harass women tend to be older than their victims and less physically attractive than women who harass men (Hemming, 1985; Tangri et al., 1982). Moreover, women are more often harassed by men of equal or greater power, whereas men report the greatest amount of unwanted sexual attention from less powerful women (Bingham & Scherer, 1993). In several studies, male peers have emerged as the most frequent harassers, followed by supervisors, subordinates, and clients (La Fontaine & Tredeau, 1986). But, by and large, the search for individual predictors of sexual harassment has not borne fruit (Tangri et al., 1982)

Who Is Harassed?   The best predictor of being a victim of sexual harassment is gender: women are more likely to be victims of harassment, to be victims of the more severe forms of harassment, and to suffer a variety of negative consequences of harassment.

Aside from gender, position of power within an organization has been studied in its relationship to sexual harassment. People are much less likely to be harassed if they are supervisors than if they are not. For all types of harassment behavior, lower-status service workers are more likely to be harassed than higher-status professionals (Fain & Anderton, 1987). Within academia, some studies show that graduate students are more likely to be sexually harassed by their professors than faculty members or undergraduate students (Fitzgerald, Shullman et al., 1988). Given that graduate students have more status than most undergraduates, this may seem surprising. But graduate students, who rely on their relationship with a particular mentor for guidance, success in the program, and career opportunities, have more at stake than undergraduates and are in fact more dependent and vulnerable than the typical undergraduate student.

The relationship between marital status and all types of sexual harassment has been explored. In the workplace, divorced, separated, and widowed women are most likely to be harassed and married women the least likely (Fain & Anderton, 1987; Lafontaine & Tredeau, 1986; U.S. Merit System Protection Board, 1981). Similar findings with respect to marital status have been found with students (Dziech & Weiner, 1984). One possible explanation for these findings is that, traditionally, women are perceived as the property of their husbands and are off limits to other men.

Age is another variable that is strongly associated with being sexually harassed: younger women are more likely to experience sexual harassment than older women (Dziech & Weiner, 1984; Fain & Anderton, 1987). Of course, age is correlated with other variables (marital status, power within an organiza-tion, less education, more conformity to societal standards of beauty) that may be related to the incidence of harassment.

Recent research has focused on the effects of a victim's race or ethnicity on the likelihood of being sexually harassed (DeFour, 1996). What little research exists suggests that minority women are more vulnerable than White women to at least some of the less severe forms of harassment (Fain & Anderton, 1987). Sexual harassment of women of color can be viewed not only as a form of sex discrimination but also as a form of race discrimination (Murrell, 1996). Clearly, more research is needed on the interaction of race and ethnicity on sexual harassment.

Consequences of Sexual Harassment

A distressing portrait has emerged from research on the harmful effects of sexual harassment on its targets. The most obvious costs of sexual harassment are job and school related. Working women who are subject to harassment quit their jobs and show evidence of decreased morale and job satisfaction, greater absenteeism, poor job performance, and damaged interpersonal relationships at work (Fitzgerald, 1993; Gutek, 1993; Gutek, 1985; U.S. Merit Systems Protection Board, 1981). As we saw in Chapter 7, there is strong and consistent evidence that the job-related consequences of sexual harassment for women are far more negative than those for men.

Similar negative consequences have been found among victims of sexual harassment on college campuses. The relatively subtle, sophisticated form of sexual harassment that occurs in an academic setting commonly engenders in its student victims confusion and embarrassment, doubt, self-blame, and a desire to flee the situation rather than confront it (Rabinowitz, 1996; Till, 1980). Ninety percent of harassed female graduate students surveyed by Schneider (1987) reported negative reactions, with two-thirds worrying about actual and potential consequences to their careers. Dziech and Weiner (1984) conclude that sexual harassment often "forces a student to forfeit work, research, educational comfort, or even career. Professors withhold legitimate opportunities from those who resist, or students withdraw rather than pay certain prices" (p. 10). Women who have been harassed by their professors commonly stop coming to class, drop courses, change majors or educational programs, and even change their career goals as a result (Rabinowitz, 1996). Consequences tend to be more severe for graduate students, who have more invested in their career paths, and for women who have entered into what they believed were consensual sexual relationships, who may feel particularly compromised and betrayed (Rabinowitz, 1996).

In addition to job- and school-related consequences, women who have experienced sexual harassment sometimes suffer severe consequences to their physical and emotional health. Psychological outcomes reported in the literature include anxiety, depression, headaches, sleep disturbances, gastrointestinal disorders, weight loss or gain, and sexual dysfunction (Fitzgerald, 1993). In particularly severe cases, clinically significant depression or posttraumatic stress disorder (PTSD) may result. Of course, individual responses to academic and workplace sexual harassment vary as a function of the victims' personal style, the severity of the harassment, and the availability and quality of social support after the harassment (Paludi, 1996).

Personal and Societal Responses to Harassment

Personal Responses. Women who experience sexual harassment are often faced with choices so aversive that they hardly qualify as choices at all. They may go along with their harassers and feel guilty and compromised or resist and face a host of negative outcomes for their careers and feelings of well-being. They may report the harassment and be ostracized, transferred, demoted, or fired or be silent and endure (Fitzgerald, 1993). Whatever choices women make and whatever the outcome of the harassment, sexual harassment frequently shatters women's assumptions about their world and changes their lives (Koss, 1990).

In fact, there are relatively few empirical studies of how women cope with sexual harassment. A recent major study of men and women who experienced workplace harassment suggested that women and men generally responded similarly to harassment and that one of the most common responses, given by about half the respondents, was confronting the harasser directly and asking him or her to stop. For women, talking to friends and family about the problem was another common response. Consistent with findings from other studies, fewer than 5 percent of the respondents filed a formal complaint against the harasser (Bingham & Scherer, 1993).

Many studies have concluded that few women who are sexually harassed file formal (or even informal) complaints. This leads some people to mistakenly believe that sexual harassment is not a common or serious problem for women. But studies that have examined women's explanations for not filing complaints have uncovered a variety of reasons for this phenomenon. Many women are reluctant to file complaints because they have sympathy and concern for their harassers and do not want to destroy their families and careers. Some offenders are thought by their victims to need psychological or educational help. Some victims believe that they share some responsibility for the situation; that is, they sought or at least enjoyed the sexual attention they received. Others worry about not being believed in the first place, or, if they are believed, they fear social rejection for being a whistleblower. Many people are concerned with loss of privacy if their complaint becomes known. A substantial proportion of people, especially ethnic minorities, strongly dislike legal and other formal processes for the management of sexual harassment and attempt to deal with the problems privately (Rowe, 1996).

Societal Responses. The millions of women who suffer the many negative effects of sexual harassment every day are not the only victims of this problem. The organizational costs of sexual harassment in terms of lost productivity, turnover, and retraining expenses are huge. Sexual harassment has become one of the most frequently litigated issues in employment law (Fitzgerald, 1993; Terpstra, 1986). The burden on society of physical and mental health care costs are substantial (Quina, 1996). Fitzgerald (1993) has outlined a variety of needed societal responses to sexual harassment in the workplace and other institutions. She calls for legislative initiatives to require employers to develop and promote clear policies against harassment. She also recommends legal reforms that remove caps on damage awards, enable women who quit jobs due to harassment to collect unemployment compensation, extend the statute of limitations for filing sexual harassment charges, and ensure that the legal system does not revictimize harassment victims.

Finally, she notes that the only real solution to the critical problem of sexual harassment lies in primary prevention. Harassment grows out of women's inferior status in the workplace and academia and can be reduced by elevating that status. It has been consistently found that women who work in sex-integrated workplaces (where men and women work together in approximately equal numbers) experience less harassment than women who work in either female- or male-dominated workplaces. Fitzgerald advocates the widespread adoption of such policies as helping women to move into jobs traditionally held by men, eliminating discrimination in hiring and training, and instituting family leave and child-care assistance programs. Sexual harassment in the workplace is discussed further in Chapter 7.

RAPE

As this chapter attests, violence against women can and does take many forms. But to many people, rape is practically synonymous with violence against women. There is no form of gendered violence that women fear more than rape. In its threat or actual occurrence, it is unique in its ability to change women's lives.

As noted earlier, women are not the sole victims of rape. In the general U.S. population it has been estimated that 1 in 10,000 men is a victim of rape or attempted rape every year, with the incidence of prison rape being much higher (Kilmartin, 1994; Struckman-Johnson, 1991). Rape of men by other men also occurs in fraternity and military settings (Funk, 1993). Con-

trary to popular belief, these experiences are emotionally devastating for men (Kilmartin, 1994). Nonetheless, throughout the world, rape is overwhelmingly a problem of male violence against women.

Definitions and Prevalence

Like some other forms of gendered abuse, rape is notoriously difficult to define. Rape is a crime that occurs in a particular sociocultural context as well as an event with profound psychological consequences. Thus, there are legal definitions of rape that vary from state to state and across countries, and legal reforms continue to change the acts that define rape and the range of perpetrators (Estrich, 1987). To further complicate the picture, it is now known that people have private definitions of rape that differ from current legal definitions: Koss, Gidycz, and Wisniewski (1987) found that over 50 percent of the women who had experiences that met the legal definition of rape did not regard themselves as rape victims. The work of Mary Koss and her associates has succeeded in conceptualizing rape as a woman's health issue with long-term consequences for women's physical, psychological, and social circumstances (Koss, Heise, & Russo, 1994).

Although definitions of rape continue to vary, they share the essential element that rape is the lack of choice to have sexual intercourse. More specifically, **rape** is defined as vaginal, oral, or anal penetration by an object or body part, against consent and through force or threat of bodily harm, or when the individual is unable to consent (Searles & Berger, 1987). Current categorizations of rape often distinguish among stranger rape, acquaintance rape (including friends, co-workers, dates, etc.), and marital rape. Gang rape can occur in each of these cases.

Some scholars have also differentiated normative and nonnormative rape (Rozee, 1993). According to Rozee, **normative rape** is supported or at least tolerated by society. It includes rape by intimates, especially husbands, for which traditional notions hold that the marriage contract represents tacit agreement by the woman to provide sexual services on demand.

Punitive rape is a category of normative rape that involves raping women to punish them for gender-inappropriate behavior, that is, for behaving too much like men. Rape during times of war is another form of normative rape. Rape has been a frequent and particularly brutal weapon of war throughout history, including the present, as documented cases of widespread rape of Bosnian, Somalian, Rwandan, and Albanian women attest. Rozee (1993) also regards *exchange rape,* the bartering of female sexuality for male advantages; *ceremonial rape,* such as deflowering rituals; and *status rape,* which occurs because of role expectations between high-status men and the women over whom they have control, as examples of normative rape.

Nonnormative rape, which is not supported or tolerated by society, includes the kinds of rapes that come to mind most readily and conform to the stereotypic notion of rape: the "surprise attack on a virtuous women" (Koss et al., 1994). As Koss and colleagues point out, even in nonnormative rape, the wrongness of rape emanates not from the nature of the act against the woman, but from others' perceptions of her sexual history and standards, her behavior and attire around the time of the attack, her prior relationship with the attacker, and her marital status, among other things.

Obviously, it is hard to estimate the prevalence of something that cannot be clearly defined and takes so many different forms. National crime statistics on rape are notoriously poor guides to rape prevalence for several reasons, starting with the fact that many reported sexual assaults are not classified as rapes. For example, the sexual assault of children is typically regarded as incest if the perpetrator is a father or stepfather and child abuse if the perpetrator is not a family member. The FBI does not include marital rape in its rape statistics. Also missing from national crime statistics are cases of *statutory rape*—sexual relations with a person under the age of consent, variously defined, but usually involving having sex with a child between the ages of 12 and 16 (Lott, 1994).

But beyond problems of definition and official classification, it is nearly impossible to estimate the prevalence of rape because women throughout the world resist reporting rapes to authorities. Koss et al.

(1994), in an extensive review of the prevalence of rape worldwide, note that in community-based samples, fewer than 2 percent of rape victims in Korea and 12 percent of rape victims in the United States informed the police that they had been raped. Women not only resist reporting rapes to authorities, but they also usually resist telling anyone else about their victimization, especially if their attacker is someone they know. For a variety of reasons to be discussed later, most women in most societies are extremely reluctant to claim the dubious status of rape victim. This helps to explain why rape is the most seriously underreported of all major crimes in the United States and elsewhere.

Ethnographic (naturalistic observational) studies of nonindustrialized societies suggest that, depending on how it is defined, rape is found in between 42 percent and 90 percent of nonindustrial societies (Koss et al., 1994). Rozee (1993) examined the incidence of rape in 35 nonindustrialized societies and found some form of rape in 97 percent of them. Sanday (1981) examined the prevalence of rape in 156 tribal societies. She categorized societies as "rape-prone" if the incidence of rape is high or normative rape is common. Societies were regarded as "rape-free" if rape was extremely rare and not tolerated by society. Using these definitions, she classified 18 percent of the societies as rape-prone and 47 percent as virtually rape-free. Sanday found that rape-prone societies were the products of sexist and violent cultures where males and females were separated and unequal and sex roles were highly differentiated. In rape-prone societies, men were encouraged to be aggressive generally and warfare was common, whereas in rape-free societies gender inequality was reduced, interpersonal violence was uncommon, and women's roles and contributions were valued (Sanday, 1981).

The United States has the highest reported rate of rape of any industrialized country in the world (Gordon & Riger, 1989). Within the United States the prevalence of rape varies considerably by state, with Alaska suffering the highest rate and North Dakota the lowest (Baron & Straus, 1989). States with high rates of rape were found to have high levels of social disorganization (meaning high divorce rates, high percentages of female-headed households, and low rates of religious affiliation, among other things), high circulation of pornographic magazines, and high levels of gender inequality on economic and political measures (Baron & Straus, 1989).

Researchers interested in rape prevalence have found it more useful to rely on scientifically sound, anonymous sample surveys than official statistics. The majority of U.S. studies estimate that between 14 and 30 percent of all adult women have experienced rape or attempted rape (Koss, 1993). In studies of rape prevalence, college students have been the most extensively studied group of adult women, in part because of their availability, but also because they are in the age range of females who are most commonly sexually assaulted. In most recent methodologically strong surveys, women are not directly asked whether they have been raped, because, as noted previously, so few women regard themselves as rape victims. Rather, they are asked whether they have had specific sexual experiences involving threat or force, experiences that legally qualify as rape. One groundbreaking study using these types of questions was conducted by Mary Koss and her associates and was supported by the National Institute of Mental Health and *Ms.* magazine. They surveyed a random sample of over 6,000 college men and women at 32 different colleges and universities. They found that more than 15 percent of the women had experiences that met the legal definition of rape, and another 12 percent had experienced attempted rape, since age 14 (Koss et al., 1987). Using samples of college women, other surveys in the United States, Canada, the United Kingdom, and other industrialized societies have found similar results (Koss et al., 1994). Taken together, these surveys reveal that rape and attempted rape are much more common than crime statistics and popular thinking suggest, and that sexual coercion and assault are an alarmingly frequent part of women's lives.

Who Is Raped?

Are some women more likely to be raped than others? Many studies have attempted to answer this question with mixed results. Findings are inconsistent, suggesting generally that there is no typical rape victim

and that no one is immune from rape. But a few patterns have emerged. Recent surveys of rape prevalence from seven different countries commissioned by the World Bank (1993) reveal that a high percentage of rape victims are young girls: between 36 and 62 percent of rape victims were 15 years old or younger and between 13 and 32 percent were 10 years old or younger (Koss et al., 1994). Aside from youth, history of sexual victimization in childhood and higher-than-average alcohol use by the victim have also been associated with a likelihood of being raped (Koss & Dinero, 1989). Few other characteristics of rape victims have been reliably associated with rape, although there is some evidence that rape victims are more likely to be college students, poor, and African American than other groups.

Relationship of the Rapist and Rape Victim

Popular mythology has it that most women are raped by unknown assailants, loners, or psychopaths who are sexually frustrated and easily overcome by sexual enticement. Are most women raped by unknown assailants? Surveys of rape prevalence are consistent on this point as they are on few others: most girls and women are raped by men whom they know— dates, acquaintances, and family members, including spouses. In the seven surveys sponsored by the World Bank (1993), between 60 and 78 percent of rape perpetrators were known to their victims. Because a woman is less likely to label an experience rape if she knows her assailant and is especially unlikely to report the rape to the authorities if the rapist is a friend, boss, or family member, we can only assume that the percentage of perpetrators known to the victim is even higher than these numbers suggest.

Men Who Rape

Who are the men who rape? There are many elements of patriarchal and violent societies that support and maintain the rape of women by men, but it is nonetheless a fact that most men do not rape women and that personal and interpersonal factors are important. Again, research findings are inconsistent in this area, and it is clear that there is no one kind of rapist. In fact, rapists vary widely in their personal and background characteristics. Most of what we know about rapists has been learned from surveys, interviews, and other studies of incarcerated rapists. Trends that have emerged in this literature suggest that most rapists are not mentally ill or retarded. Most are not undersexed loners, but have had active and ordinary sex lives as adolescents and adults. Many are married or in other committed relationships (Lorber, 1994). These findings are interesting and important because they suggest that rapists are not apparently abnormal or easily identifiable. It is also worth noting that incarcerated rapists are not representative of rapists generally. Most rapists are not caught and convicted, and studies of incarcerated rapists invariably underrepresent acquaintance and marital rapists.

Anonymous surveys of college men suggest that men who rape are more hostile toward women, more aroused by depictions of forced sex, and subscribe more strongly to false beliefs that condone rape (rape myths) than men who do not rape. There is some survey evidence that sexually aggressive men are more likely to hold traditional sex-role attitudes, condone violence against women, and belong to peer groups, like college fraternities and sports teams, that encourage sexist behavior toward women (Koss, Gidycz, & Wisniewski, 1987; Malamuth, Sockloskie, Koss, & Tanaka, 1991).

Categories of Rape

Date and Acquaintance Rape. As we have noted, the overwhelming majority of rape victims know their assailants. One of the subcategories of acquaintance rape that has received a great deal of research attention in the past decade is **date rape** or courtship rape—rape that occurs in the context of a dating or romantic relationship. In the early 1990s, the highly publicized courtroom trials of celebrities like Mike Tyson and William Kennedy Smith brought the reality of date rape to the rapt attention of the U.S. public. For many people, date rape raises different issues than other forms of rape because, by virtue of the date, the woman has on some level expressed her interest in a

man and consented to a relationship with him. If the sexual relationship somehow gets out of hand, the problem is one of misunderstanding, miscommunication, or mixed signals, rather than sexual assault.

Research on date rape has identified several variables associated with its occurrence, many arising from the different socializing messages that boys and girls hear about masculinity and femininity and the relationship between the sexes. Males are generally reared to deny and control their emotions, with the important exceptions of sexual feelings, anger, and aggression. Like many societies, our society measures a man's worth by his deeds and results, rather than his feelings about himself or others. As Kilmartin (1994) notes, we admire men who "go after what they want" and "won't take no for an answer." As we have seen, boys are socialized to believe that when a girl says "maybe" she means "yes" and when she says "no" she means "maybe." Socialization of boys and girls in our society rarely includes training about sexual communication. Poor sexual communication characterizes most dating relationships, especially among young people. Few young couples are comfortable discussing sex between them before it occurs, and most are reduced to reading each others' unpracticed nonverbal signals under emotionally complex and ambiguous circumstances. This sets the stage for misunderstanding that can lead to unwanted sexual intercourse and rape. In fact, Blader and Marshall's (1989) research suggests that men who sexually assault acquaintances usually want consensual sex but are not deterred by women's resistance, often because they think that the resistance is an act or that the women will change their minds if they forcefully persist.

One factor that predicts date rape is males' permissive attitudes about rape, for instance, endorsement of the idea that rape is unimportant in society (Gillen & Muncer, 1995). Another factor is male peer support for aggressive sexual behavior. DeKeseredy and Kelly (1995) found that support for sexual aggression by male peers was one of the most important predictors of sexual victimization of college women. Drinking by men, women, or both consistently emerges as another precipitating factor in date rapes. In one study,

55 percent of the victims reported being drunk at the time of the sexual assault (Harrington & Leitenberg, 1994). In another study, drinking by men was associated with sexual violence (Frintner & Rubinson, 1993).

Marital Rape.   The very idea that a man could rape his wife is a relatively new one in our society. Traditionally, upon marriage, women became the property of their husbands, and husbands were seen as having a right to sexual favors from their wives. In the United States, it was not until 1977 that Oregon became the first state to criminalize marital rape, and, as of 1989, only 36 states specified that it was against the law to rape one's spouse (Pagelow, 1992). As late as 1992, marital rape was still legal in North Carolina and Oklahoma (Allison & Wrightsman, 1993), although now all states in the United States have laws prohibiting rape in marriage. Marital rape is still unrecognized as a problem in most countries.

The incidence of **marital rape** is even harder to estimate than other forms of rape because women are especially reluctant to label forced sex by their husbands as rape and to report marital rape to the authorities. As we will see again with women who are physically abused by their husbands, many women who are raped by their husbands feel that they have nowhere to go and no one to turn to when their own homes are not a safe place. Using survey methodology, Frieze (1983) estimated that between 10 and 14 percent of married women have experienced this form of rape, and a U.S. Congressional committee estimated that one in seven women is raped by her husband (Resnick, Kilpatrick, Walsh, & Veronen, 1991).

Even more than acquaintance and date rape, marital rape is not often taken very seriously and is regarded by many people as much less brutalizing and less traumatic than stranger rape (Sullivan & Mosher, 1990). In fact, marital rape can be among the most severe forms of rape, embedded as it often is in a generally violent and otherwise troubled relationship. A rape is more likely when the husband associates sex with violence, has extramarital affairs, and is unreasonably jealous of his wife (Frieze, 1983). Women who are raped by their husbands are as fearful for their health and their lives as women who are raped by strangers (Koss, 1993).

Just as with other forms of rape, motives for marital rape vary. Finkelhor and Yllo (1982) interviewed wives who had been raped by their husbands and identified three categories of marital rape. The first type is the "battering rape," committed by men who physically intimidate, beat, and rape their wives. Alcohol and drug use often accompany this form of rape. The second type is the "force only" rape, where violence is limited to the sexual relationship, and the husband uses sex to dominate his wife. Finally, the third and least common form of marital rape is the "obsessive rape," wherein the husband, obsessed with pornography and relatively unusual sexual practices, forces his wife to engage in activities, like anal intercourse or being bound, in which she is not interested.

Stranger Rape.   Stranger rape is committed by an assailant (or assailants) who is not previously known to the rape victim. It is this form of rape that most people think of as "real rape," that most readily comes to mind when people think of rape, and that women most fear. In fact, only about 20 percent of all rapes are stranger rapes. The typical stranger rapist is an opportunist who preys on women who seem particularly vulnerable—those who live alone, or are older, retarded, drunk, or asleep. After selecting a target, the stranger rapist seeks a safe time and place in which to commit the crime, a darkened street, an empty apartment, a deserted staircase, or the like (Nevid et al., 1995). More often than acquaintance rape, stranger rape is physically violent and involves a series of assaults by the same offender (Koss, Dinero, Seibel, & Cox, 1988). There is some evidence that rape by strangers is particularly psychologically traumatizing (Thornhill & Thornhill, 1991). Women who are raped by strangers are more likely than other rape victims to label the experience as rape and report the crime to the authorities.

Gang Rape.   Gang rapes involve two or more assailants and one rape victim. They are more frequent among strangers, but can occur among acquaintances and even within stable relationships. They are distinguished by their particularly violent and brutal nature. Men who rape in gangs tend to be younger than other rapists and to have criminal records. Alcohol use is common in cases of gang rape.

It is often noted that the exercise of power over women and feelings of anger and hostility toward women motivate gang rape. Social psychologists have identified a number of cognitive and behavioral processes that occur in groups that can contribute to mistreatment of outsiders and poor decision making (O'Sullivan, 1995). One cognitive process that may facilitate gang rape is the *outgroup homogeneity effect,* whereby all people not in one's own group (i.e., females) are seen as fitting one stereotype (i.e., "sluts"). Outgroup homogeneity often occurs with another cognitive process, *ingroup superiority,* the belief that one's own group (i.e., males) is better than other groups and more worthy of rewards and privileges. Finally, *groupthink* is the process by which groups, particularly elite groups (like sports teams), make faulty decisions because of an inflated belief in their own righteousness coupled with an exaggerated sense of other groups' unworthiness. It is easy to see how these cognitive processes can give men in groups the feelings of invulnerability and entitlement, as well as disdain for women, that make it easier to victimize them (O'Sullivan, 1995).

These cognitive processes operate along with other factors to promote gang rape. People are often more aggressive in groups, in which they are relatively anonymous and undifferentiated, than they are singly. This is especially true under conditions of drinking, partying, "wilding," and other forms of excitement. Male socialization to be independent, unsentimental, tough, and success oriented obviously contributes to group sexual aggression by men. In addition, male friendships often entail a combination of competition and camaraderie. Sexual success is an important arena for this competition, and it can be defined as having sexual access to a lot of women or getting women to do things that they don't want to do. Drinking and other forms of risk taking and breaking societal rules are also arenas for male competition and contribute to gang rape. On college campuses, the majority of gang rapes are perpetrated by fraternity men, followed by those who play team sports.

Cultural Significance of Rape and Sexual Assault

The notion of rape as a harm to or crime against a woman is a relatively recent phenomenon. For most of recorded history, rape, if it was regarded as a crime at all, was seen as a crime against a husband or father because of the damage and devaluation of his "property." Indeed, the only rapes that were considered crimes were the rapes of virgins. In both ancient Hebrew and Babylonian cultures, women who were raped, including married women and virgins, were routinely stoned to death because it was believed that they could have prevented the rape by crying out (Nevid et al., 1995). Today, violence against women is obviously not a problem of any one culture but is endemic throughout the world (see Box 11.1). Some scholars question whether rape is particularly "misogynist" or has a special status as a crime against women, as we see in this quote by philosopher Christina Hoff Sommers: "That most violence is male isn't news. But very little of it appears to be misogynist. . . . Rape is just one variety of crime against the person, and rape of women is just one subvariety" (1994, pp. 225–226). (Obviously, the authors of this text do not subscribe to this view.)

Why Do Men Rape Women?   There is no simple answer to this question. Sociobiologists, who see all behavior as motivated to pass on one's genes, view rape as an extension of "normal" male sexual behavior. According to sociobiological theory, males have stronger sex drives than women and are naturally more sexually aggressive. This theory posits that evolution favors males who are always alert for new female partners and are visually stimulated by physical attributes of prospective partners. Sociobiological theory suggests that, under certain circumstances, such as sexual scarcity or absence of punishment, many more men would rape women. In fact, Malamuth (1981) found that 35 percent of the college men that he surveyed reported that they would force a woman to have sexual intercourse if they knew that they could get away with it. In another survey, 51 percent of the men admitted at least some likelihood of committing rape if they were sure that they would not be punished (Malamuth, Haber, & Feshback, 1980). Given that

Box 11.1_____

Violence against Women around the World

In their important book *Where Women Stand: An International Report on the Status of Women in 140 Countries (1997–1998)*, Naomi Neft and Ann D. Levine chronicle how domestic abuse, rape, and other forms of sexual assault are universal problems that cut across geographic, cultural, religious, ethnic, and class boundaries. They note the specific forms that violence against women takes in various parts of the world. The following are adaptations of their reports on three selected countries, India, Nigeria, and Brazil, on three different continents.

INDIA

In India as in much of Asia, there is widespread preference for sons over daughters, and the killing of baby girls is common in some parts of India, with as many as 10,000 baby girls killed every year. Despite the fact that Indian laws ban infanticide and impose penalties of life imprisonment or death, few cases are brought to trial, and those that are rarely end in convictions.

Wife abuse is another terrible problem in India, with the most dramatic forms being physical abuse, torture, and even murder of young brides whose husbands or in-laws are dissatisfied with their dowries. Dowries are the lavish gifts and large sums of money that the bride's family must transfer to the groom's family upon marriage to compensate for the fact that daughters cannot inherit property from their parents.

Suttee, the centuries old custom by which the widow is burned alive on her husband's funeral pyre, has been illegal since 1829, but a resurgence of Hindu fundamentalism in the 1980s has led to renewed calls for the legalization of the practice. Meanwhile, widows in India have very low social status and are essentially treated like slaves.

NIGERIA

Though seldom reported, violence against women is common in Nigeria and cuts across all religious, ethnic, and regional boundaries.

The Nigerian penal code specifies that a husband can "correct" his wife as long as the correction does not leave a scar or require a stay of more than 21 days in the hospital. Women, especially those in polygamous marriages, commonly believe that physical abuse is a normal condition of marriage.

Although rape is illegal and punishable by life imprisonment, it is rarely reported in Nigeria.

Female genital mutilation is practiced throughout Nigeria, especially among the Christians in the South and the Muslims in the North. Almost half of all women have undergone some from of the procedure, ranging in severity from removal of the clitoral hood (clitoridectomy) to complete removal of the clitoris and the labia with the edges stitched together, leaving only a small opening for the passage of urine (infibulation).

BRAZIL

Violence against women is a major problem in Brazil, where the law and criminal justice system reflect deeply held cultural beliefs that women are inferior to men. As a result, many of the laws protect the assailants and not the victims. Domestic violence is a serious problem for Brazilian women, with more than half of all female homicide victims killed by current or former partners. Until 1991, a man could be pardoned for killing his wife if he even suspected that she had been unfaithful. Although this concept of "defense of honor" has been struck down, the courts are still reluctant to prosecute and convict men accused of assaulting their wives.

Rape is illegal and punishable by imprisonment in Brazil, but few rapists are brought to trial and convicted. If the rapist marries the victim, he is exonerated by law.

_____

people generally strive to avoid expressing socially undesirable intentions even in anonymous surveys, it is possible that the percentage of men who hold this view is actually much higher.

Clearly, sociobiological theory views rape as a sexually motivated act and all men as potential rapists. Other psychological theories attempting to explain rape take issue with one or both of these propositions.

Some challenge the view that sexual desire is the basic motivation for rape, and some look to individual pathology or social and cultural factors, rather than genetic and hormonal ones, to account for the prevalence of rape.

Sexual arousal and expression are obvious features of rape, but they are not necessarily the underlying causes of all or even most rapes. Groth and Birnbaum (1979), based on their clinical experience with more than 1000 rapists, concluded that there were three categories of rapes: *anger rapes,* which are particularly forceful and degrading rapes motivated by anger and resentment toward women; *power rapes,* which are less vicious and motivated by the desire to control and dominate women; and, finally, *sadistic rapes,* which are ritualized, humiliating, sometimes mutilating or murderous assaults that may be associated with individual pathologies. About 40 percent of rapes were categorized as anger rapes, 55 percent as power rapes, and 5 percent as sadistic rapes (Groth & Burgess, 1980). Other scholars contend that not all rapes are acts of aggression, control, or power and assign a larger role to sexual motivation in the commission of some sexual crimes (Hall & Hirschman, 1991; Leitenberg & Henning, 1995).

It seems clear that rape and sexual assault, like all human behavior generally, are complex and multiply determined by social, cultural, personal, and situational factors. Not all rapists are motivated by the same forces, and the extent to which sexual motives contribute to rape can be expected to vary considerably across individuals and categories of rape.

The importance of situational factors in supporting rape must not be underestimated. As noted above, it is well known that under circumstances that remove the usual constraints on sexual and aggressive behavior rape can become commonplace. During wartime, for example, women are traditionally considered "spoils"—the reward for conquering a people. The rape of women by soldiers has a long tradition in the military histories of many countries. It is considered one of the most effective means of demoralizing the enemy (Funk, 1993). The world witnessed this use of rape recently in Bosnia, Rwanda, and Kosovo. Cohesive male peer groups, such as gangs, sports teams,

and fraternities, sometimes use rape as a means of initiation into or bonding with the group. Finally, many studies suggest that drinking by men, women, or both is often associated with rape (Harrington & Leitenberg, 1994). About three-quarters of acquaintance rapes involve alcohol consumption on the part of the victim, assailant, or both (Koss et al., 1987).

How Does the Existence of Rape Change Women and the Relationships between Men and Women?

Rape affects all of us, men and women, even those whose lives are not directly touched by it. In a thoughtful article offering a male perspective on rape, Beneke pointed to what is missing when people contemplate rape statistics: the effects on women of the ubiquitous threat of rape (Beneke, 1993). In asking women how their lives would be different if rape were suddenly to end, he learned that the threat of rape is an "assault upon the meaning of the world" (p. 312). The threat of rape alters the meaning and feel of the night, for many women, transforming their cars into armored tanks and their apartments into fortresses. The threat of rape alters the meaning and feel of nature and women's ability to be alone in parks and wooded areas. It means that women need more money to buy security at the same time that it limits women's mobility and job options. Thus, the threat of rape seriously affects all women's freedom; it makes solitude and relaxation more difficult, inhibits women's expressiveness and freedom to be friendly, to make eye contact, and to dress the way they wish, among other things.

The threat of rape also makes women more dependent on men for protection. In this and other ways, the threat of rape benefits men as it diminishes women. It grants the night, the unknown, and the public sphere to men. It keeps women in a position of relative defensiveness and fear. It maintains male power and privilege by restricting women's freedom, independence, and opportunities. As Funk (1993) explains, the "rape culture" guarantees men an important position or role to play: that of protector of "his" women and "his" family. The more salient and constant the threat of rape is, the more justifiable male dominance over women is. In this way, as Funk states, "all men benefit from rape and the constant threat of rape" (p. 32).

The Role of Rape Myths in Supporting the Rape Culture. Of all the forces that support the existence of rape in societies like ours, **rape myths** are among the most subtle, pervasive, and important. Lonsway and Fitzgerald (1994) have defined rape myths as "attitudes and beliefs that are generally false but are widely and persistently held, and that serve to deny and justify male sexual aggression against women" (p. 134). Rape myths are best conceptualized as stereotypes that people have about behaviors, attitudes, and feelings surrounding rape. Some common myths include the notions that only certain kinds of women are raped, most women harbor an unconscious desire to be raped, women routinely lie about being raped, and women cannot be raped against their will.

Since rape myths were first named by Burt (1980) nearly 20 years ago, there has been a virtual explosion of research on rape myths and their acceptance. The single most consistent finding in this area is that men are more likely to accept rape myths as true than women. People with traditional sex-role attitudes and negative attitudes toward women are also more likely to subscribe to rape myths. Finally, men who report greater likelihood of raping women consistently demonstrate higher rape myth acceptance (Lonsway & Fitzgerald, 1994). As these authors note, the extensive research in this area holds immense potential for understanding what causes, maintains, and justifies sexual assault in societies such as the United States where rape is common and rape myths are widely believed.

Rape, Denial, and Blame. Two of the most consistently baffling and disheartening findings in all the rape literature concerns how often women attempt to deny even to themselves that they have been raped and how often they are held responsible—by themselves and others—for being raped.

As mentioned above, Koss et al. (1987) found that more than half of all women who had experiences that met the legal definitions of rape did not regard themselves as rape victims, even in an anonymous survey. Koss and her associates explain this finding by suggesting that to admit that one is a victim is to adopt the stance of a "loser," especially in our society, which so clearly values winning and success. One's losses in the case of rape are often severe and may include one's reputation, privacy, peace of mind, autonomy, feelings of control, and assumptions about the world. Contrary to a common rape myth, few women falsely accuse men of rape or seek the label of rape victim.

Even when women can admit to themselves that they have been raped, they frequently do not share their experience with others, especially when the rapist is a family member, date, or other acquaintance (Thornhill & Thornhill, 1990). We can only speculate about why women who have been raped by people whom they know are so reluctant to come forward. Some woman fear that the pain of accusation and possible trial is not worth the trouble. Others fear some form of retaliation or worry that they will harm the rapist or his family. But, clearly, many women fear that they will not be believed, and that in a society where women are held responsible for exciting and controlling men's sexual urges, they will be blamed for the rape.

Blaming the rape victim is part of a more general tendency people have to blame others for their misfortunes. According to Lerner's (1980) "just world hypothesis," we have a need to believe that people get what they deserve and deserve what they get. By believing that a rape victim somehow did something wrong to bring on her rape or that she is the type of person who deserves to be raped, people are able to maintain the position that this terrible fate will not befall them or the people that they love.

Studies of attributions of responsibility for date rapes consistently show that men, particularly traditional men who hold conventional sex-role attitudes, are more likely to assign responsibility to women for rape than women are (Bridges & McGrail, 1989). One study found that one in four men believe that rape is often provoked by the victim (Holcomb, Holcomb, Sondag, & Williams, 1991). Men have less empathy for rape victims than women do, are less supportive of rape victims, and are more lenient to rape perpetrators in courts of law (Kleinke & Meyer, 1990). There is ample evidence that some men do not take date rape seriously (Stacy, Prisbell, & Tollefsrud, 1992) and do not consider it "real" rape. Regrettably, society colludes in diminishing the seriousness of date rape in the rape myths that it perpetrates and the androcentric (male-centered) ways that rape law is written and enforced.

Effects of Rape and Sexual Assault on Women

Many studies attest to the fact that rape has significant emotional, behavioral, and health consequences for women. To date, most studies on the effects of rape have been conducted on Western women in peacetime who have experienced a single episode of rape (Koss et al., 1994). Thus, these findings may not be generalizable to women from other cultures, to women who are raped during times of war or other conflicts, or to women who have experienced multiple rapes.

Obviously, women differ in their responses to rape based on their family history, personality, experience of prior trauma, ethnicity, social class, and other variables. But some symptoms of psychological distress, including intrusive memories, attempts to avoid reminders of the trauma, depression, and anxiety, are experienced by almost everyone. In fact, these particular psychological effects are often conceptualized in North America as post-traumatic stress disorder (PTSD). In one study, 94 percent of rape victims exhibited the symptoms of PTSD an average of 12 days following sexual assault, and 46 percent met the criteria three months later (Rothbaum, Foa, Riggs, Murdock, & Walsh, 1992). For most rape victims, high levels of anxiety and depression gradually diminish over the course of the year following a rape, but fully 20 percent have continuing difficulties several years after the rape (Hanson, 1990). Burgess and Holmstrom (1974) have identified a particular form of PTSD called **rape trauma syndrome,** which is characterized by two phases. The first is an acute phase, usually lasting for several weeks, in which survivors exhibit severe disorganization in their lives and experience frequent bouts of crying and feelings of anger, shame, and fear. The second phase, long-term reorganization, may take several years. It is characterized by fears of recurrence, frightening dreams, and mistrust in interpersonal relationships.

Of course, not everyone experiences a variation of the rape trauma syndrome. Some women have a silent reaction to rape; that is, they tell no one about their experience, subtly avoid men or sexual situations, and quietly struggle with anxiety and loss of self-esteem, often for long periods of time. Others are somehow able to put the rape behind them with little outside assistance. Koss et al. (1994) suggest that what determines a woman's response to rape is not the actual event itself or her intrapsychic processes but rather an interaction between the two: her cognitive appraisal of the rape—her judgment of the experience arising from personal, cultural, and situational factors. In order to understand a woman's trauma and recovery process, one needs to know the personal meaning that the rape has for an individual woman. For instance, in societies where virginity is highly prized and the stigma of rape is profound, the greatest concern of unmarried rape victims in the aftermath of rape is getting their hymens reconstructed (Koss et al., 1994).

Aside from psychological reactions, girls and women often experience physical and sexual health consequences of rape. Many chronic conditions, including premenstrual syndrome and gastrointestinal disorders, occur disproportionately among rape survivors. In the United States, early sexual abuse is associated with a range of high-risk sexual behaviors on the part of victims, including unprotected sex and prostitution, and the use of alcohol and drugs. Koss and Heslet (1992) have found that sexually transmitted diseases are the result of rape in anywhere from 4 to 30 percent of the cases. If left untreated, as these stigmatized diseases often are, STDs can result in pelvic inflammatory disease and infertility or facilitate the transmission of HIV. The global, cumulative cost of sexual violence in terms of additional burdens on the health care system and healthy, productive years of life lost is staggering and is comparable to the burdens posed by HIV, cancer, and cardiovascular disease (Koss et al., 1994).

Personal and Societal Responses to Rape

As we have repeatedly stated, the personal tragedy of rape occurs within sociocultural, political, and personal contexts. An effective response to rape requires that we respond to rape on many levels.

Personal Responses. On the personal level, there are many steps that individual women can take to lessen the probability that they will become victims of rape. *The New Our Bodies, Ourselves* (Boston Women's Health Book Collective, 1984) lists several tips for women who seek to protect themselves and other women from stranger rape, including these suggestions to avoid being raped in one's own home (p. 137):

> *Keep lights in all the entrances; keep the windows locked and in place, have strong locks on every door; be aware of places where men might hide; don't put your full name on the mailbox; know which neighbors you can trust in an emergency; find out who is at your door before opening; say, "I'll get the door, Bill" when going to the door.*

Over the past decade, research has begun to address the question of what kinds of behaviors are most effective for women who are attacked by rapists. Regrettably, findings are inconsistent concerning the best ways for women to respond, and no single response is uniformly more effective than others. For example, some research shows that some of the less forceful and provocative forms of resistance, including pleading, begging, or reasoning with the assailant, can be dangerous strategies that actually heighten the probability of injury. Vigorous resistance by women makes it less likely that a rape will be completed, but it also makes it more likely that women will be physically injured during the attack (Nevid et al., 1995). Tactics that work in certain situations may not in others. For example, running away may be highly effective when there is a single assailant and an exit route, but is less likely to succeed when there are multiple assailants and nowhere to go. It appears that effective self-defense must be built on multiple strategies and an accurate appraisal of the options based on an assessment of the rapist, the situation, and a woman's ability to resist.

More recently, researchers have offered strategies for avoiding date rape. For instance, Powell (1991) advises women to communicate their sexual limits to dates, meet new dates in public places, be firm in refusing sexual overtures, be wary of their own fears of displeasing their partners, pay attention to their gut-level feelings about men, and be especially cautious if they are in new environments or have recently broken off a relationship with someone whom they don't feel especially good about.

The personal responses that women make to reduce the threat of rape are perhaps best construed as forms of rape deterrence, not rape prevention. Rape deterrence strategies protect individual women who use them (although with no guarantees), but do not reduce the vulnerability of women as a group. No one can be vigilant or respond effectively all the time. To the extent that there are men who will commit acts of sexual assault, women as a group remain vulnerable to rape. Obviously, personal responses do not address the major cause of rape—men's motivation (Lonsway, 1996).

Societal Responses. In recent years, there is increased recognition that personal responses to rape, however important, are not sufficient to combat what is a societal problem. To date, the most common societal responses to the problem of rape can be best characterized as environmental: installing better lighting or mirrors in elevators, trimming shrubbery for better visibility, and the like (Lonsway, 1996). But the past decade has also witnessed a sharp increase in the number of education programs aimed at men, women, or both, mostly on college campuses (see Box 11.2).

Scholars and advocates for women around the world are just beginning to unite around a global research agenda on sexual violence. This agenda calls for research into the sociocultural context of gender-based violence, the multiple consequences of rape for physical and mental health, the societal structures that promote rape, and the social networks through which people deal with sexual assault, as well as prevention and education efforts (Koss et al., 1994).

PARTNER ABUSE

Violence is a common feature in intimate relationships of all kinds. In this section, we focus on partner abuse—violence directed at spouses or lovers. It is clear from recent research that both men and women

Educational Programs
to Combat Rape

Educational programs to combat rape differ considerably in their assumptions and strategies. Programs aimed at women often incorporate elements of self-defense, assertiveness training, sexual communication strategies, debunking of rape myths, and assessment of risky situations. Programs for men also attempt to decrease rape myth acceptance and improve sexual communication, often by educating men about how male socialization affects men's capacity for violence and intimacy. Several include components that seek to increase empathy among men for rape victims. Rape prevention efforts designed for both men and women include many of these elements, along with general sexual education and feminist reconceptualizing of gender relations, often with a focus on common problems in cross-sex communication and dating expectations.

How well do such educational programs work in reducing rape? Evidence for their effectiveness is inconclusive to date. It appears that educational programs can reduce endorsement of rape-supporting attitudes among men and women, at least in the short run. But there is little evidence to date that such programs produce long-term attitude change or actually reduce sexual aggression and other rape-supportive behaviors (Lonsway, 1996).

Finally, rape prevention efforts aimed at men need to make clear the benefits *to men* of a rape-free society (Lonsway, 1996). As noted earlier, men as a group appear to benefit in many ways from the existence of rape. The payoffs for women of a sharp reduction in the incidence of rape are obvious, but the payoffs for men must be better articulated.

---

perpetrate violence in intimate relationships and that violence characterizes same-sex as well as heterosexual relationships.

Definitions and Prevalence

Like other forms of violence against women, partner abuse has only recently been widely regarded as a crime and a problem in society. Historically, a husband's authority over his wife extended to his right to hit her in order to keep her in line. Until quite recently, the criminal justice system in the United States viewed violence against women in intimate relationships as matters of "privacy" and "civil disturbances" not appropriate for criminal proceedings (Stahly, 1996). And like other forms of violence against women, partner abuse is hard to define. In all cases, hitting, punching, slapping, kicking, and shoving constitute abuse. Aborted attempts and threats to hurt a partner physically appear in most definitions. Many definitions of partner abuse contain elements of intimidation: controlling and limiting what a partner does, whom the partner sees and where he or she goes, and frightening a partner by smashing things or destroying property. Some definitions of partner abuse also include emotional and sexual abuse.

Obviously, variations in the definitions of abuse lead to differences in measurement and estimates of prevalence. But most estimates of partner abuse are based on some kind of physical violence. And these estimates suggest that nowhere is a woman in greater danger of becoming a victim of male violence than in her own home. In the United States each year, depending on the definition of physical violence used, between 2 and 6 million women are beaten by the men they live with, and about 1500 U.S. women die as a direct consequence of spousal abuse (Walker, 1979). Thirty percent of female homicide victims are killed by men with whom they have a family relationship (Arias & Pape, 1994). At any point in time, 40 percent of women treated in emergency rooms are victims of wife abuse (Dearwater et al., 1998; Stark & Flitcraft, 1988). Almost 30 percent of married couples in the United States admit experiencing at least one physically violent episode during their marriage (Straus, Gelles, & Steinmetz, 1980). Given the private nature of abuse in the home, the stigma attached to domestic abuse, and the fear in which most victims live, the actual incidence of abuse may be much higher. The American Medical Association estimates that nearly one-quarter of the women in the United States will be abused by a current or former partner at some point in their lives (Lawson, 1992). More U.S. women suffer injury at the hands of their partners than as a result of rapes, muggings, and automobile accidents combined (Stahly, 1996). When estimates of violence include instances of psychological abuse, they are much higher.

Unlike rape, which is virtually always committed by men (against women or other men), partner abuse is perpetrated by both men and women. Research shows that women are about as likely as men to start a fight or hit their spouses or dating partners (Ingrassia & Beck, 1994; O'Leary, Barling, Arias, Rosenbaum, Malone, & Tyree, 1989; Steinmetz & Lucca, 1988). A study of couples seeking psychological treatment for problems connected with marital aggression found that 86 percent of aggressive couples reported reciprocal aggression, and only 14 percent reported unilateral aggression (Cascardi, Langhinrichsen, & Vivian, 1992). There is little question that some women in violent relationships are themselves violent. But research evidence suggests that violence by women usually occurs in response to their partners' attacks, either in retaliation or self-defense (Gelles & Straus, 1988). And violence by men is far more likely to result in serious injury to a partner than violence by women.

The term *battery* is often used as a synonym for partner abuse, and abused women are commonly called **battered women.** But, as hooks (1993b) notes, the term *battered women* is problematic. While categories and labels can play an important role in drawing public attention to the seriousness of male violence against women in intimate relationships, labels like battered women can also be stigmatizing and inadequate. hooks states:

> *Most importantly, the term "battered women" is used as though it constitutes a separate and unique category of womanness, as though it is an identity, a mark that sets one apart rather than being simply a descriptive term. It is as though the experience of being repeatedly violently hit is the sole defining characteristic of a woman's identity and all other aspects of who she is and what her experience has been are submerged. (p. 207)*

hooks asserts that categorizing women's identity with this label strips women of their dignity and renders them silent and ashamed. It keeps the focus on their stigmatized identity rather than the behavior of the abuser.

Abuse in Lesbian Relationships.   As several scholars have noted, there is widespread belief that same-sex couples do not experience violence in their relationships at the same rates as heterosexual couples, because power imbalances due to gender differences do not exist (Browning, Reynolds, & Dworkin, 1991; Patterson & Schwartz, 1994). Furthermore, there is a cultural myth that lesbians in particular, because of their socialization as women and commitment to egalitarian relationships, do not encounter domestic violence (Browning et al., 1991). Although precise estimates are impossible, research suggests otherwise: levels of abuse in lesbian couples are comparable to heterosexual couples and actually exceed current estimates in gay male couples (Waterman, Dawson, & Bologna, 1989, cited in Patterson & Schwartz, 1994). How can we understand the surprisingly high rates of partner abuse among lesbian couples? Several explanations have been put forward. For one thing, women may be more sensitive to issues of abuse and more likely to label acts as abusive than men are. For another, the pressure of mutual dependence may itself be conducive to violence (Galvin & Brommel, 1991, cited in Patterson & Schwartz, 1994). That is, the high value that women place on making relationships work may render relationships involving women more tolerant of abuse than relationships involving men. It is also important to note that, simply because both members of a couple are of the same sex, we cannot assume that there are no power differences in the couple or that power differences between individuals are irrelevant to the abuse. We need further research on domestic abuse in same-sex couples and in the role that power plays in these relationships.

Theories of Partner Abuse

Is violence against women learned behavior? Are women masochists? Are all abusers of women substance abusers, psychotics, psychopaths, or just plain bullies? Are all men potential abusers of women?

These are some of the questions that have preoccupied those who have sought to understand the phenomenon of partner abuse.

Basically, theories of partner abuse divide into three categories: (1) those that focus on the role of women in causing and maintaining abuse, (2) those who see violence against women as the result of individual pathology in some males, and (3) those that see physical violence against women as arising from societal structures in which there is significant gender inequality.

Many scholars who have studied abuse against women have noted the curious emphasis in both the scholarly literature and the media on the questions of what are the characteristics of female victims and why abused women stay in abusive relationships. As we have noted in other contexts, this focus on the victim rather than the perpetrator suggests that the victim somehow causes her misfortune and deserves at least some of the blame for it. Blaming woman for physical violence against them can be traced back to Freud's theory of psychosexual development, in which Freud posits that *sadism* is an innate organizing feature of normal male development and *masochism* of normal female development (Shafter, 1992). Psychoanalyst Karen Horney asserted that social and cultural conditions rather than biological ones alone accounted for masochistic behavior in women. Contemporary psychoanalytic views discuss masochism in women as the outcome of the fear of separation or abandonment (Lego, 1992). However differently intrapsychic theories explain the origins of "female masochism," they all take the view that women have an unconscious need to be hurt and punished for their anatomic inferiority, sexual feelings, or other shortcomings.

Despite the long history of such theories, there is no empirical support for the notion that women are masochists, that they like being hurt by men, or that they stay in abusive relationships when they perceive that they have real alternatives. Women who are beaten by their husbands are less likely to initiate or enjoy sexual relations with them, less likely to regard their husbands as physically attractive, and more likely to report that they are staying in their relationships for financial reasons than are women who are not beaten by their husbands (Barnett & La Violette, 1993). Many women who stay in abusive relationships do so predominantly because they are afraid of leaving. Indeed, women are more likely to be hurt or killed at the point of leaving than at any other time in the relationship.

A second class of theories about the origins of women abuse takes the position that men who are violent against women are certain kinds of people: alcoholics and other drug abusers, psychotics, psychopaths, or just plain bullies. "Normal men" do not abuse their partners. In fact, as we discuss later, partner abuse is associated with certain characteristics of males, just as it is also related to some female characteristics and certain features of the relationship between men and women. But research is consistent in showing that partner abuse cuts across all socioeconomic, ethnic, religious, and age categories. While certain variables, particularly having witnessed or experienced abuse as a child, are good predictors of abusing a partner, there is no evidence that abusers are fundamentally different from normal men.

The third and final set of theories concerning the origins of partner abuse locates the sources of the problem of abuse in social and cultural factors that affect all men. These theories suggest that pervasive sexism and gender inequality in such institutions as marriage, formal religions, the economic and criminal justice systems, and the media support and maintain male violence. Historically, society has sanctioned a man's exercising his authority over his family by means of physical violence. The patriarchal tradition of treating women as property had granted men permission to do whatever they wanted with their wives. Research suggests that households in which there is domestic violence are more likely to be characterized by rigid, traditional divisions of labor by sex. Virtually all formal religions stress the primacy of the family and the virtues of remaining in marriage "for better or worse." Economic structures and conditions in which men make more money than women, about 30 percent more, render women, especially women with children, financially dependent and vulnerable. The law enforcement and criminal justice systems have long histories of treating domestic abuse cases as private, internal family matters instead of criminal offenses. Finally, male violence is glorified in cartoons, sports, Westerns, war, action movies, and "cop shows." These media depictions encourage modeling and provide vicarious reinforcement for male behavior in this society (Kilmartin, 1994).

Evidence supporting the sociocultural approach comes from research suggesting that domestic abuse thrives on patriarchal attitudes, rigid gender arrangements, and acceptance of male aggression and that it is a problem in all sectors of society. This sociocultural analysis suggests that domestic abuse will remain a problem for women generally as long as gender inequality exists.

Research on Partner Abuse: Who Abuses Women and Who Is Abused?

All three sets of theories about the origins of partner abuse have spawned research that focuses on the characteristics of men and women and the relationships and circumstances that are associated with partner abuse. It is important to bear in mind that because there are statistical correlations among groups of variables we cannot conclude that one set of variables causes another set of variables; for example, the fact that some women are more likely than others to be victimized does not at all mean that those women somehow invite their own victimization.

Increasingly, researchers have turned their attention to the social and psychological characteristics of male abusers. Probably the best single predictor of abusing a partner is having witnessed or experienced abuse oneself. Depending on the study, between 63 percent and 81 percent of men who abused their partners either experienced abuse as victims in their childhood or witnessed their fathers beat their mothers (Ewing, 1993). Partner abuse is also associated with low educational attainment and unemployment or low occupational status among males (Hotaling & Sugarman, 1986). Alcohol and illicit drug use also predict partner abuse. Most abusers tend to be young (under age 30) (Ingrassia & Beck, 1994).

The psychological profile that emerges from research on male abusers suggests that they tend to be overconforming to the traditional male gender role and the masculine culture of violence (Kilmartin, 1994). They have a high need for power and control over their partners. While their masculinity is tied to notions of dominance, they often do not have the economic status and resources to support a dominant stance (Lorber, 1994). Male abusers are more likely to have low self-esteem and show greater depression and emotional dependency than other men (Cascardi et al., 1992; Gondolf & Hanneken, 1987). In self-reports of reasons for spousal homicide, the most frequently cited justification given by men is sexual jealousy and/or the wife threatening to terminate the relationship (Cazenave & Zahn, 1992).

Empirically, characteristics of male partners are better predictors of women's risk of being victimized than characteristics of women themselves (Hotaling & Sugarman, 1986). But research suggests that some women are more likely to be abused by men than others. The most consistent risk factor for women is witnessing violence in their homes as children or adolescents (Hotaling & Sugarman, 1986). Women who are young, poor, and unemployed are also at risk for physical abuse by a partner. A history of alcohol and other drug use, dependency, isolation, and low self-esteem complicate the picture (Marano, 1993). Pregnant women are particular targets of abuse (Browne, 1993). Obviously, not all women fit this profile, and no woman, regardless of social class and life circumstances, is immune from this problem.

There are characteristics of couples or relationships that predict the incidence of physical abuse of women. As Lorber (1994) notes, paradoxically, abusive relationships often seem very romantic at first, because the man seems especially attentive. Over time, however, his interest appears increasingly possessive, controlling, and limiting. One study that compared women in violent and nonviolent relationships found that wives of abusive men were more likely than wives in nonviolent relationships to report that their husbands were jealous, did not trust them, and had them under surveillance (Barnett & LaViolette, 1993).

Violent men are more likely than other men to be pre-occupied with their intimate relationships and to have few outside friends or interests. As a result, they may be particularly emotionally dependent on, and fearful of the loss of, their relationships and are more likely to misinterpret neutral situations as threatening (Marano, 1993).

Consequences for Abused Women

Women suffer numerous physical and psychological outcomes from partner abuse.

Physical Consequences of Abuse. Epidemiological studies reveal that the kinds of aggressive acts that women report range from being slapped, punched, kicked, or thrown to being scalded, cut, bitten, choked, and smothered. Typical injuries range from bruises, black eyes, and broken bones to permanent problems, such as partial loss of vision or hearing and scars from burns or knife wounds (Browne, 1993). Research is consistent in showing that women sustain more injuries and more severe injuries from partner abuse than men and that nearly half of all women in emergency rooms seek treatment because of partner abuse (Cascardi et al., 1992). In addition, women who experience male partner abuse are at risk for a variety of other health complaints, including headaches, back and limb problems, frequent colds, fainting and dizziness, stomach and gastrointestinal problems, gynecological problems, heart and blood-pressure problems, lung and breathing problems, and/or skin problems (Follingstad, Brennan, Hause, Polek, & Rutledge, 1991). Physical abuse and the many problems it causes can shorten peoples' lives. Recent research on the mortality of older people (mostly women) who have suffered abuse at the hands of family members suggests that abused people may not live as long as similar others who are not abused (Lacks, Williams, O'Brien, Pillemer, & Charlson, 1998).

As noted earlier, it is a stunning and sad fact that pregnant women are particularly at risk of being abused by their partners. In the 1985 National Family Violence Survey of a representative sample, 154 of every 1000 pregnant women reported being assaulted by their partners during the first four months of pregnancy and 170 out of 1000 during the last five months of pregnancy (Gelles & Straus, 1988). Assaults around the abdomen may have devastating consequences, including placental separation; rupture of the uterus, liver, or spleen; and premature labor (Browne, 1993).

Hundreds of women are killed each year by their partners. As Browne (1993) notes, women are more likely to be killed by their partners than by all other categories of persons combined. Men are more likely—at least twice as likely—to murder their partners than women are (Browne, 1993). When women murder men, it is usually in self-defense or in response to threats or a long history of physical abuse. Women who murder their spouses are typically given more severe penalties than men who murder their spouses. (Browne, 1993). White and Kowalski (1994) note that a woman who murders her husband is likely to receive a sentence of 15 to 20 years, whereas a man who murders his wife is generally given only 2 to 6 years.

Psychological Consequences of Abuse. Women show a wide range of psychological effects of suffering physical abuse at the hands of a male partner. Because there are no truly representative surveys of the psychological responses of abused women and because so many abused women do not avail themselves of psychological treatments of any kind, it is extremely difficult to estimate the proportions of women who suffer various consequences.

Research suggests that abused women's psychological reactions to male violence closely follow the general pattern of responses that people have to a variety of traumatic events. Many of the psychological aftereffects of violence can be understood as conforming to the diagnostic construct of posttraumatic stress disorder (PTSD). During assaults, women's focus is on their own survival. They may react with a mixture of shock, denial, withdrawal, confusion, and fear (Browne, 1987). After the assaults, high levels of depression and anxiety are common (Browne, 1993). Other symptoms include chronic fatigue and tension, nightmares, and disturbed sleeping and eating patterns. After severe or chronic beatings, some women respond by abusing substances.

The severity and duration of the abuse are strongly related to women's psychological consequences. The more severe and repetitive the abuse is, the more likely the woman is to feel isolated and depressed and to consider committing suicide. As useful as the PTSD diagnosis is in characterizing the psychological consequences of violence as normal responses to abnormal events, it does not account for all the symptoms manifested by female victims of domestic abuse.

Personal and Societal Responses to Partner Abuse

Personal Responses to Partner Abuse: Why Don't Women Just Leave?

When the issue of partner abuse is raised, the single most frequently asked question concerns why abused women stay in violent relationships. This question appears to locate the cause of the problem with pathological behavior on the part of women who are abused. Instead, a more useful question concerns the social and psychological factors that constrain women from leaving.

Despite the popular portrayal of battered women as meek and passive, most women employ a variety of strategies to stop the violence or escape, especially early on in abusive relationships. They attempt to change the behavior that their partner criticizes, call the police for help, seek the counsel of clergy and family members, and turn to their doctors. These strategies, however reasonable, are often ineffective. Abusive partners find other things to criticize. The police may do little more than diffuse the current crisis. Clergy or family members may advise women to do whatever they can to "save their families," including being more submissive, accommodating, and accepting. Even medical doctors are limited in their responses to women and frequently treat the problem with tranquilizers, antidepressants, and sleeping pills. And many women do leave, at least temporarily, after beatings, only to be actively pursued by their partners with gifts and promises (and threats) and encouraged to go home by friends and family (Stahley, 1996). Studies consistently show that well over 40 percent of the women who seek aid from spouse abuse shelters return to live with their partners (Rusbult & Martz, 1995).

Over time, physical and psychological responses to abuse render many women depressed, dependent, helpless, and suggestible. Some abused women consider themselves failures because they have not succeeded in making happy homes. This makes it difficult for them to engage in long-range planning and take decisive action (Browne, 1993). Some investigators have found it useful to apply the "hostage syndrome" to the plight of abused women (Dutton & Painter, 1981). That is, when people feel that their survival depends on placating an unpredictable aggressor, a bond of sympathy and even affection often develops. Studies of animal and human behavior suggest that intermittent punishment and reward appear to strengthen the power of attachment (Stahly, 1996). Abused women often love their abusers and are committed to their marriages or relationships. They may depend on the abuser for shelter and other necessities of life. They have long histories of being blamed by their partners for the violence that they "provoke" and have learned to survive largely by seeing the world through their abusers' eyes. They find fault with themselves and make excuses for their partners.

Some psychologists are beginning to offer explanations for why women stay in violent relationships that go beyond women's personal dispositions (whether they precede or follow the onset of abuse). Rusbult and Martz (1995) use an investment model analysis to understand why women remain in abusive relationships that underscores the social and structural factors that constrain women from leaving. The investment model suggests that a woman's commitment to the abusive relationship level depends on the availability and attractiveness of alternatives to the relationship and the size of her investment in the relationship. Rusbult and Martz (1995) predict that commitment to an abusive relationship should be greater among women who have been involved with their partners longer, among women who are married rather than cohabiting or dating, and among women with a greater number of children with their partners. Empirical research on abusive relationships supports the investment model and suggests that, to understand the dynamics of abusive relationships, we must address the nature of an abused woman's relationship with her partner.

In addition to psychological and social variables, we need to consider the external realities that many women confront in deciding whether to stay in or leave an abusive relationship. Behaviors like failing to press charges against the abuser, which strike others as helpless or craven, may represent accurate and realistic evaluations of the abuser's potential for escalated violence and murder. The most likely time for a man to kill his partner is at the point when she leaves him or shortly afterward (Walker, 1979). Normal psychological responses to assault may well cloud a woman's thinking and lead to poor decision making. But even the clearest, most rational appraisals of threat and danger may induce a woman to stay with a violent partner (Browne, 1993).

Societal Responses. The problem of violence against women cannot be fully understood, let alone solved, by focusing exclusively on individual men and women (Goodman, Koss, Fitzgerald, Russo, & Keita, 1993). A lasting solution to the problem can only come with social and cultural change. As Goodman et al. (1993) note, many authors find the roots of male violence against women in women's efforts to escape their subordinate roles in the family, workplace, academy, and the larger society.

A variety of community-based services now exist for women who have been abused by their partners, many of them created by grassroots organizations and advocates for women (Goodman et al., 1993). These services include shelters for victims of violence and their children, crisis hotlines, support groups, and legal aid centers. As vital as these services are, they are underfunded and cannot meet the needs of all the women who need them.

On a larger scale, psychologists should work together with other social scientists and policy makers to bring about a fundamental change in social attitudes

and social institutions. Legislative efforts to treat gendered violence as civil rights violations, along with violence based on religion, ethnicity, disability, or race, exemplify how policy makers can attempt to shape society's attitudes toward women and reduce the social acceptability of abuse directed at them.

SEXUAL ABUSE OF CHILDREN

In the eyes of many people, child sexual abuse is among the most morally reprehensible of all acts. Indeed, it often has devastating effects on children that persist well into adulthood. It is a gendered crime in that most of the victims are girls and, overwhelmingly, most of the perpetrators are men.

Child sexual abuse was not even acknowledged as a serious social problem until the 1970s, when the women's movement and child protection legislation brought it to public attention. Feminists at this time noted that girls were vastly overrepresented as victims of child sexual abuse and that these problems were attributable to a patriarchal culture that exploited women and children (Cosentino & Collins, 1996).

Definitions and Prevalence

Sexual abuse of children is usually defined by researchers as any form of sexual contact that occurs before age 18, with a relative, a person at least five years older than the child, or someone who forces himself or herself on the child regardless of the age difference (Downs, Miller, Testa, & Parek, 1992). Sexual contact may range from invitations to perform a sexual act, to exhibitionism, fondling, and sexual touching, to anal or vaginal intercourse. By definition, any form of sexual contact between an adult and child is regarded as abusive, even if no threat is made or force used, and even if the child appears to consent or enjoy the sexual activity. Children are not capable of giving truly voluntary consent to have sex with adults. Voluntary sexual activity among children of similar ages is not considered child abuse (Nevid et al., 1995).

It is enormously difficult to estimate the prevalence of child abuse because the number of cases reported to authorities, fewer than 50,000 cases a year, is certainly a gross underestimation (Finkelhor & Hotaling, 1984). Most victims of child sexual abuse do not report their experiences because of feelings of guilt or shame, fear of retaliation or blame, or failure to label and remember their experiences as abusive. The closer the relationship between the child and the abuser, the less likely it is that the abuse will be reported to the police (Finkelhor, 1986). Surveys of adults that require people to reconstruct their childhood experiences, and thus are not highly reliable, have variously estimated the prevalence of child sexual abuse to be between 4 and 16 percent among boys, and between 16 and 30 percent among girls (Janus & Janus, 1993; Kohn, 1987).

Patterns of Child Sexual Abuse

Who Abuses Children?   There is virtual unanimity that most sexual abusers of both male and female children are male, with some estimates suggesting that 94 percent of girls and 84 percent of boys were molested by men (Finkelhor, 1984). Certainly almost all pedophiles—people who have persistent or recurring sexual attraction to children—are male. Some people have sexual contact with children only under conditions of unusual stress or lack of other sexual outlets and are not regarded as pedophiles.

There is currently increased research interest in women as perpetrators of child sexual abuse, with some researchers suggesting that it is more common than previously believed (Wakefield & Underwager, 1991). Female sexual abuse of children may be underreported for many reasons. Women can more easily than men mask sexually inappropriate contact through activities like bathing or dressing children. However, as Finkelhor and Russell (1984) note, female sexual abuse of children in which women act alone is rare. In most reported cases of child sexual abuse in which female perpetrators are named, females were complying with male child abusers.

There is no consistent personality profile of the child molester. But it has long been known that a disproportionate number of males and females who sexually abuse children were themselves sexually abused as children (De Young, 1982; Muster, 1992). In this

way, cycles of abuse may be perpetuated from generation to generation as children who are sexually victimized themselves become victimizers or partners of victimizers as adults (Nevid et al., 1995).

Contrary to the stereotype of the pathological stranger lurking in the schoolyard, the typical sexual abusers of children are people who are close to them— a relative, step-relative, family friend, baby-sitter, or other acquaintance. In one major study of child abusers, Gray (1993) found that noncustodial acquaintances made up the largest single group of abusers, with the victim's stepfather or mother's boyfriend the next largest group. Only about 20 percent of all child sexual abuse involves strangers (Waterman & Lusk, 1986).

Who Are the Victims of Child Sexual Abuse?   Approximately 80 percent of child sexual abuse victims are girls and 20 percent boys (Gray, 1993). The average age at which most children are first sexually abused ranges from 6 to 12 for girls and 7 to 10 years for boys (Knudsen, 1991). Girls are relatively more likely to be abused by acquaintances and family members, whereas boys are relatively more likely to be victimized by strangers and nonfamily members (Knudsen, 1991).

Context in Which Abuse Occurs.   Several other social variables have been found to be correlated with the incidence of child sexual abuse. Whereas children from all social classes are vulnerable to child sexual abuse, children from poorer, less cohesive families are more likely to encounter it than children from stable, middle-class families (Finkelhor, 1984), although father–daughter incest may be as likely in middle-class as in lower-class homes. It is more common in socially or geographically isolated environments, for example, rural areas, and in overcrowded living conditions (Finkelhor, 1979). But no race, ethnic group, or economic class is immune from this problem.

Incest

Incest has been defined as sexual relations between people (of any age) who are so closely related (by blood) that sexual relations are prohibited and punishable by law (Nevid et al., 1995). The law may also proscribe sexual relations between family members who are not blood-related—for instance, stepfathers and stepdaughters. Incest between adults and children by definition always constitutes child sexual abuse. As we have noted, incest is a highly gendered wrong: the typical pattern involves a male family member—father, stepfather, uncle, older brother—sexually abusing a young girl.

Sigmund Freud was the first to propose what is called **seduction theory,** the notion that women's neuroses were caused by child sexual abuse, based on his female patients' accounts of early sexual relationships with their fathers and other male family members. The idea that upper-middle-class Viennese men were molesting their daughters was so abhorrent to Freud's peers in the medical community that he later repudiated seduction theory and posited instead that the sexual relationships described by his patients were in fact their disguised wishes and desires to have sexual relations with their father, what he termed the Electra complex (Masson, 1984). Many scholars feel that if Freud had held to his original view, the terrible secret of incest would have emerged much sooner.

The focus in this section is on father–daughter and stepfather–stepdaughter incest. These are not the most common forms of incest, although they are probably the best known and are recognized as the most traumatic. In fact, brother–sister incest is by far the most common, with almost 40 percent of college women in one sample and 21 percent of college men reporting some sexual contact with a sibling of the other sex in their childhoods (Finkelhor, 1979). Siblings of the same sex rarely enter into sexual relationships. Mother–son incest is very uncommon, and mother–daughter incest is the most uncommon of all forms of incest.

Estimates of father–daughter incest are notoriously unreliable because parental abuse is the least likely form of abuse to be reported. Russell (1986), in a scientific survey of women in San Francisco, found that 16 percent of the women had been incestuously abused by age 18. Finkelhor (1979) put the estimate of father–daughter incest at 4 percent.

In its most typical form, father–daughter incest appears to emerge within a context of broader family dysfunction. Families in which incest occurs are characterized by alcoholism, strained marriages, and other forms of abuse (Waterman, 1986). They also tend to be socially isolated and rigidly religious (Storer, 1992). Marriages in incestuous households have been described as unequal relationships in which an authoritarian, punitive, and intimidating man dominates his passive, often incapacitated wife (Storer, 1992). Of course, incestuous families are not a homogeneous group, and no specific preexisting family patterns have been identified. The literature on father–daughter incest typically represents the father as religiously devout, under great stress, and sexually frustrated because of a withholding, unresponsive wife. Because of his strict religious beliefs, he does not seek sexual gratification in extramarital affairs, but rather looks within the family, usually to the oldest daughter, for the emotional and sexual support that he does not get from his wife. The daughter then becomes the "woman of the house," assuming many of the household responsibilities of her mother, who is often characterized as ill, alcoholic, mentally disabled, and so on (Waterman, 1986).

Traditional psychiatric analyses of the incestuous family frequently blame the mother in cases of father–daughter abuse, often portraying her as responsible for her husband's behavior by virtue of her incapacity, passivity, and refusal or inability to sexually satisfy her husband and protect her child. In fact, research on the mothers of daughters abused by their fathers suggest that in 75 percent of the cases the mothers did not know about the abuse, and in more than half the cases the mothers protected their daughters and rejected their husbands when the abuse became known (Myer, 1985). There is little evidence that mothers can be held responsible for maintaining a husband's behavior.

In the classic case of father–daughter incest, some stressful event in a father's life, coupled with alcohol use, triggers the first episode. This particular type of abuse often begins with cuddling and nonsexual touching and then escalates to teasing sexual play, kissing, masturbation, genital contact, and, when the child reaches adolescence, even penetration (Nevid et al., 1995). The average age at which father–daughter incest begins is ten years, and it usually lasts about three years. Father–daughter incest lasts far longer than other kinds of child sexual abuse. Few of these relationships involve violence and force because they often begin before the child can understand their meaning. Nonetheless, some form of coercion is usually present (Urbancic, 1987).

Consequences of Child Sexual Abuse

It is clear that incest victims must cope with multiple aspects of the experience: the physical and psychological trauma in the form of the actual sexual experiences, including violation of one's body, extended periods of fear, guilt, shame, and, in the case of incest, the loss of a trusted relationship with an emotionally significant person. Childhood sexual abuse often inflicts great psychological harm on its victims. It has many diverse, negative short- and long-term consequences for children.

Short-term effects, those occurring within two years of the abuse, include fear, anger and hostility, guilt, shame, depression, low self-esteem, physical and somatic complaints, sexual behavior disturbances, and poor social functioning (Browne & Finkelhor, 1986; Maltz & Holman, 1987). Abused children frequently either act out, that is, display aggressive, antisocial behavior in school, or withdraw, retreating into fantasy and isolation. Regressive behavior like bed-wetting and thumb-sucking also characterize some abused children.

Adolescents who have experienced incest tend to have many of these same problems, plus the additional ones of teen-age pregnancy, promiscuity and sexually aggressive behavior, truancy, running away from home, and drug and alcohol abuse. Benward and Densen-Gerber (1975) found that 52 percent of the girls who were sexually abused by relatives left home by age 16. They stress that a history of incest should be considered in all cases of adolescent runaways.

Long-term effects have included depression; behavioral and social problems, such as prostitution, alcoholism, and substance abuse; emotional disorders; suicide; somatic disorders; problems in interpersonal relationships; sexual disturbances; and revictimiza-tion (Browne & Finkelhor, 1986; Downs, 1993). For some victims, the negative effects of the abuse increase with time.

There is today great controversy about the validity of repressed memories of child sexual abuse: cases in which adults, usually in therapy, come to remember that they were abused as children. Some people have expressed great skepticism about the veracity of such memories, suggesting that they may be induced by therapists. Research suggests that it is certainly possible to induce false memories in people (Loftus, 1993). But research also shows that people are far more likely to shun victim status when it applies to them than to claim that status when it does not. Further research and debate will shed light on this controversial issue.

Obviously, individuals vary greatly in the severity and specific form of their responses to child sexual abuse. Researchers have found few consistent gender differences in response to abuse, with the most reliable difference being that boys more often than girls externalize their problems by becoming physically aggressive, whereas girls are more likely to internalize their problems by becoming depressed (Finkelhor, 1990).

Societal Responses to Child Sexual Abuse

Society is coming to recognize that childhood sexual abuse is a devastating and formative experience in the lives of countless women and men. As Cosentino and Collins (1996) note, significant progress has been made toward understanding some of the causes and effects of child sexual abuse, but we know too little about treatment of children and offenders. Given that research suggests that some victims are vulnerable to revictimization or to having children who are victimized later, we need to focus efforts on the psychological processes underlying intergenerational transmission so that we can reduce further victimization.

Society must help parents and schools better protect children against the likelihood of abuse. Obviously, children cannot prevent their own victimization in many cases, but they can be encouraged to tell about their experiences. Tighter controls in the hiring of people who work with children are necessary, as are educational efforts to help professionals at all levels to recognize the signs of abuse. Programs aimed at helping people who are sexually attracted to children before they commit abusive acts are also badly needed.

PORNOGRAPHY

Few topics covered in this chapter are more complex and controversial than pornography. As we will see, its very definition is widely disputed. Some people distinguish pornography from erotica, arguing that pornography harms women through its depiction of male dominance and humiliation of women, whereas erotica, which portrays consensual and mutually satisfying sex among equals, is not harmful to women. Others argue that all sexually explicit material is inherently harmful to women. Pornography is opposed by some people on moral or religious grounds because of its graphic sexual content and the casualness with which it presents sexual activity, and by others because it degrades women because of its violent and misogynist content. Some researchers have linked pornography to misogynist and aggressive behavior, attitudes, and fantasies in men; others have not. There are constant legal challenges to the dissemination of pornographic material; complaints against its spread to new outlets, such as music, cable television, and cyberspace; and calls for its censorship. Meanwhile, the sale and rent of pornographic materials is at an all-time high; pornography is one of the most profitable industries in the world, exceeding even the music and movie industries, earning billions each year.

What is pornography, and what important distinctions need to be made among forms of pornography? How common is exposure to pornography? Who uses pornography and how and why is it used? What are the attitudinal and behavioral effects of pornography on men and women and on male–female relationships? What are some constructive personal and social responses to pornography? These are some of the issues that we will treat in this section.

Definitions and Prevalence

Many psychologists, lawyers, politicians, and others have noted the difficulty of clearly defining pornography and erotica and distinguishing between the two. That so many people continue to struggle with these definitions and distinctions attests to the critical importance of differentiating explicit sexual content, on the one hand, from negative and harmful depictions of women, on the other.

The elusive term **pornography** comes from the classical Greek *pornographos,* meaning the writing (sketching) of harlots (Tong, 1982). Modern dictionaries tend to define pornography as materials specifically intended to arouse sexual desire. Generally, defining characteristics of pornography also include one or more of the following elements: its primary intention is to produce sexual arousal; it is usually produced for commercial (as opposed to artistic or educational) purposes; it objectifies people by reducing its targets, typically women, but also gay men, children, and animals, to their genitals and other body parts; it appears to condone or even endorse sexual desires and behaviors that are demeaning to or abusive of its targets; and it sexualizes power inequalities among people through sexist, racist, and homophobic depictions. *Erotica* is often defined as what pornography is not: it is seen as artistic expression with no specific intent to arouse sexual responses; it depicts the body or sexual acts with respect, portraying consensual and mutually satisfying acts among equals; and it is free of sexism, racism, homophobia, and other forms of discrimination.

It is an often repeated phrase that "one man's erotica is another man's pornography" (Russell, 1993), and indeed the distinctions between erotica and pornography can be problematic, especially when applied to particular cases. As Brod (1995) suggests, erotica and pornography are probably best seen as the poles of a continuum, with gray areas in between. Increasingly, however, there is recognition that the key to identifying sexually explicit material as pornography is its sexist or discriminatory stance toward its targets—its degrading or abusive portrayal of female sexuality.

In part because of the different definitions of pornography, the different ways questions are phrased, and the explosion of new outlets for pornographic material, such as the Internet and MTV, surveys of the use of pornography offer varying estimates of adult exposure. The *Hite Report on Male Sexuality* (Hite, 1981), a nonscientific survey, suggested that 89 percent of men report some involvement with pornography. A representative survey of 600 mid-western adults found that over 90 percent of the men and women had been exposed to pornographic magazines, with over 90 percent having seen at least one sexually oriented R-rated film and 69 percent of men and women having seen an X-rated film (Bryant & Brown, 1989). The readership of the six most popular pornographic magazines alone may be as high as 52 million people per year (Russell, 1993). All the evidence suggests that exposure to pornography among men and women is on the rise.

Cultural Significance of Pornography

On one level, the question of what makes pornography so popular among men and, increasingly, among women does not appear very complex. After all, people are sexually motivated, and yet societies throughout the world, historically and presently, have sought to restrict sexual expression. Even in relatively open societies like the United States and other Western countries, willing sexual partners are not readily available for many people, even for those in otherwise close and loving relationships. According to some scholars, widespread conditions of sexual desire thwarted by typical conditions of sexual scarcity give rise to the overwhelming popularity of pornography (Steinberg, 1993). While explanations of the sources of the gender difference vary, it is generally agreed that the experience of high sexual drive coupled with sexual scarcity describes men better than women. To explain why a much greater proportion of pornography is geared toward heterosexual males than females, sociobiological theorists appeal to the greater (inborn) sex drive of males. Sociocultural theorists explain this imbalance in terms of the different socialization messages that men and women receive about sex, with boys and men taught to pursue sexual success ("scoring") and girls and women taught to limit sexual accessibility to a single highly desirable and committed partner.

Several investigators have noted the similarities between the content of commercial pornography and male sexual fantasies. As Leitenberg and Henning (1995) have noted, the fantasy being portrayed in most pornography is primarily the male fantasy of multiple female sexual partners always ready for sexual activity of any kind without any chance of the man being rejected. According to Steinberg (1993), pornographic images that address the scarcity of sex partners and male desire for appreciation and reciprocation of desire, specifically those that convey female lust and female expression of male desirability, account for over 75 percent of all pornography.

Thus, currently available pornography, created overwhelmingly by and for males and most specifically for male masturbation and fantasy enhancement, casts a particularly male gaze on sexuality. It treats the sexes fundamentally differently and unequally. Women are more likely than men to be portrayed as victims of violence or aggression in pornography, as injured, tortured, bleeding, bruised, or hurt. Other forms of sexism are even more common. Women more often than men are depicted in scenarios of degradation, as inferior or debased. It is typical in pornography for male orgasm to be the mark of success—and end point—of a sexual encounter. Female orgasm is less commonly depicted and is rarely the point of sexual activity. Overwhelmingly, women featured in pornography are younger and more physically attractive than their male counterparts, more passive and sexually submissive, and chiefly valued for these characteristics.

Effects of Pornography on Men and Women

Many social, political, and legal commentators who have written about pornography have pondered whether it is either morally wrong or morally neutral or inherently harmful or not harmful to women. As scientists, psychologists empirically study the consequences of exposure to pornography on people's attitudes and behaviors.

Most of the psychological research on the effects of pornography to date has focused on its impact on the aggressive behavior of men against women. Malamuth, Donnerstein and their associates have conducted a series of carefully controlled laboratory studies on the effects of exposure to pornographic movies on college men. They have found it useful to distinguish between *aggressive pornography* or *sexually violent mass media images,* in which victims are often portrayed as deriving pleasure from a sexual assault, on the one hand, and nonviolent sexually explicit material, on the other, and much of their research compares reactions to these two broad classes of materials. Research by Malamuth and his colleagues (Malamuth, 1981, 1984; Malamuth & Check, 1983; Malamuth & Donnerstein, 1982) consistently shows that college men show evidence of increased sexual arousal to video images of rape, particularly when the female victim exhibits signs of pleasure and arousal. Aggressive pornography in which the female victim shows a positive reaction while being raped tends to change men's attitudes toward rape: that is, it produces less sensitivity to the harm in rape, more acceptance of rape myths (such as the mistaken idea that most women secretly wish to be raped), and an increase in men's self-reported likelihood of committing rape (Donnerstein & Linz, 1993). More than half of the college men who had been exposed to violent pornography expressed some likelihood of raping a woman if they knew they would not be caught (Donnerstein, 1983; Malamuth, Haber, & Feshback, 1980). In an important series of laboratory studies, Donnerstein and his associates demonstrated that exposure to violent pornography actually increases aggression against women (measured by willingness to shock a female student) (Donnerstein & Berkowitz, 1982).

More recent studies have examined more varied effects of repeated or long-term exposure to sexually violent mass media portrayals. One major study exposed college men in experimental groups to ten hours (five films over five days) of films that differed in their levels of violence and sexual explicitness. One significant finding suggested that over the course of five days, men exposed to aggressive pornography rated the material as less degrading to women and more humorous and enjoyable. They expressed greater willingness to see this kind of material again. These men were also more likely than those in a control group (that saw no film) to rate a rape victim as more worth-

less and her injury less severe. These kinds of effects were not found for men who were exposed to sexually explicit, nonviolent films (Linz, Donnerstein, & Penrod, 1984).

This research strongly suggests a potentially harmful effect of sexualized (and nonsexualized) aggression against women, but few harmful effects of merely sexually explicit material. In fact, more research attention is now being given to the effects of nonaggressive pornography. Zillman and Bryant (1982, 1984) have conducted some of the few studies of nonaggressive pornography that examine the effects of long-term exposure to material and the responses of women as well as men. They found that long-term exposure to nonaggressive pornography caused both undergraduate women and men to (1) express more tolerance of sexually violent pornography, (2) become less supportive of statements espousing sexual equality, and (3) become more lenient in assigning punishment to a rapist depicted in a newspaper account. Moreover, extensive exposure to nonaggressive pornography significantly increased men's sexual callousness toward women. Men's increased lack of sensitivity toward rape persisted for at least three weeks after exposure. It is important to note, however, that long-term exposure to nonviolent pornography did not increase, and in fact decreased, men's aggressive behavior (Donnerstein & Linz, 1993). The recent explosion of pornography on the Internet, with the attendant concerns of parents, policy makers, and other advocacy groups, adds urgency to this discussion. Box 11.3 highlights some of these issues.

Obviously, much research remains to be done on the effects of pornography. The critical question of whether pornography is a major cause of violence against women in the real world remains unanswered and hotly debated. The effects of long-term exposure to pornography in real-world settings need to be explored further. An increasing number of women are exposed to pornography and erotica, and there are too few studies of the effects of pornography on women and on couples. Teen-agers are another important understudied group.

BOX 11.3

Pornography on the Internet

On the global computer network known as the Internet, tens of millions of people in more than 150 countries are able to send and receive messages to thousands of news groups and bulletin boards. The exchange of sex-related material is one of the largest, if not the largest, recreational applications of users of computer networks like the Internet, Usenet, and the World Wide Web (Lewis, 1995). Computer networks represent an efficient, global distribution mechanism for extreme pornographic images that are not commonly available through other outlets, such as adult bookstores. One study suggests that the most popular forms of pornography in news groups and bulletin boards were the types considered most offensive— bestiality, bondage, incest, and encrypted pictures of nude adults and children (Durkin, 1997). Easy access to pornography over the Internet has raised a number of concerns among the public and policy makers, chief among them that pornographic material may be accessed by children and that pedophiles and child mo-

lesters will use chat rooms or web sites to locate and lure underage victims.

Increasingly, governments throughout the world are seeking means to stem the flow of pornographic material. Chinese and German officials have managed to cut off access to some pornographic material (Lewis, 1995). In the United States, there has been great debate about issues concerning free speech, censorship, and access to pornography, particularly child pornography, on the Internet. The Supreme Court recently ruled that the censorship on the Internet represents a threat to First Amendment rights and is therefore unconstitutional. This ruling has been met with anger and dismay by people who believe that by stopping obscenity in cyberspace we protect children. There will obviously continue to be discussion and debate on this topic for a long time to come. Psychologists can contribute to this debate by studying the uses and effects of pornography in cyberspace.

Educational efforts aimed at reducing the harmful effects of pornography need to be developed and evaluated. Special populations like judges, police officers, doctors, and lawyers, on the one hand, and men who rape and assault women, on the other hand, may require special research attention and intervention efforts. But it is clear that psychologists can add much to the debate in our society about the effects of pornography.

OTHER FORMS OF GENDERED VIOLENCE AND EXPLOITATION

In many other arenas, unequal power relations between the genders or among groups defined by their sexuality have harmful consequences for less powerful groups. In this section, we will briefly consider some

of these: prostitution, elder abuse, female infanticide, and gay bashing. For the most part, psychology has only begun to contribute to an understanding of the causes and effects of these cases of gendered violence or exploitation.

Prostitution

Prostitution, or the exchange of sex for money, gifts, and favors, was first brought into the public discourse in the United States and Europe in the eighteenth and nineteenth centuries. At that time, it became subject to control and regulation by the medical and legal professions. Prostitutes were widely condemned as sources of physical and moral disease and subjected to vice campaigns in which they were treated and examined for diseases and imprisoned as law breakers

(Lorber, 1994). To this day, prostitution remains a socially stigmatized activity and a sign of debased moral identity virtually everywhere. Although it is legal in some countries (e.g., the Netherlands), it is usually an illegal way of making money.

Most prostitutes are girls and women, but boys and young men also offer sex for money. Prostitution is a gendered problem because, overwhelmingly, the people who buy sex are men, and it is men who control the trade wherever it is practiced. That is, men working as pimps and traffickers often set the conditions of employment or inservitude, reap the profits, and maintain tight control over the lives of prostitutes.

Some feminists argue that the very word *prostitute* is problematic because of its moralistic and stigmatized qualities and advocate the substitution of the term *sex worker*. Margo St. James, for example, has campaigned to treat prostitution as freely chosen work (Lorber, 1994). Others suggest that prostitutes are not exploited by men, but rather exploit men's sexual interest in women. More commonly, however, the position is taken that prostitution is intrinsically sexually exploitative because it exists in societies in which women have less power and fewer resources, opportunities, and employment options than men.

Research strongly suggests that prostitution is not a freely chosen activity for the girls, boys, women, and men who engage in it. Studies show that prostitutes often begin their careers as adolescents, before meaningful choice is possible, and they are almost always manipulated if not coerced into this life-style by adults, often drug dealers, gangs, and pimps on whom they are dependent. Child prostitution is on the rise, especially in the third world and Eastern Europe, where poverty, chaos, and porous borders have turned prostitution into a global growth industry. Disproportionately, prostitutes are found to come from the ranks of sexually abused children, runaway and homeless children, and drug addicts (Graham & Wish, 1994; Yates, MacKenzie, Pennbridge, & Swofford, 1991). It is associated with multiple drug abuse, depression, suicide attempts, and dissociative disorders, including multiple personality (Ross, Anderson, Heber, & Norton, 1990; Yates et al., 1991).

As Overall concludes, it may make sense to defend prostitutes' entitlement to do their work and thereby earn more money than they would otherwise, but it makes less sense to defend prostitution as a practice in societies characterized by widespread gender inequality (Overall, 1992).

Anti-Gay Violence

Recent surveys suggest that roughly two-thirds of people in the United States condemn homosexuality or homosexual behavior as morally wrong or sinful. Many heterosexuals in the United States also reject gay people at the personal level, with only 45 percent stating that they "wouldn't mind" working around gay people (Herek, 1995). At the same time that there is widespread condemnation and avoidance of gay men and lesbians, people in the United States are increasingly reluctant to condone discrimination on the basis of sexual orientation and increasingly believe that gay men and women should have equal rights in terms of job opportunities (Colasanto, 1989). The brutal murder of a young gay man, Matthew Shepard, in Wyoming in 1998 brought the problem of *homophobia*—the intense and illogical fear of gay men and lesbians, along with negative and hostile reactions to gay people—into sharp relief. There were countless vigils for Matthew Shepard throughout the United States, bringing people of all ages, political parties, sexual orientations, and religious affiliations together in genuine grief and anger.

Despite survey evidence suggesting that men and women have become more tolerant about homosexuality, gay people still suffer discrimination, social ostracism, and physical violence because they are gay. A recent survey of 125 gay and lesbian college students indicated that 26 percent had been verbally insulted once and 50 percent twice or more, 26 percent had been threatened with physical violence, 17 percent had suffered property damage, and six respondents had experienced extreme violence. Most respondents reported that they expected harassment in the future and were driven to conceal their sexual orientation. Nearly half reported making specific life changes intended to decrease discrimination, harassment, and violence (D'Augelli, 1989).

Herek has offered a comprehensive model for understanding the causes of anti-gay violence and harassment based on a form of bias called *heterosexism* (Herek, 1995). **Heterosexism** is an ideological system that denies, denigrates, and stigmatizes any non-heterosexual form of behavior, identity, relationship, or community. It has two variations: cultural and psychological. *Cultural* or *institutional heterosexism* is pervasive in U.S. society and is seen in societal customs and institutions that render homosexuality invisible and, when it becomes visible, reprehensible. *Psychological heterosexism* is evident in individuals' attitudes and actions. Because of the interplay of cultural and psychological heterosexism, gay men and lesbians are frequently the targets of violence and exploitation. According to Herek, some people hold anti-gay attitudes and engage in anti-gay actions because they are functional; that is, they serve a purpose in people's lives. For instance, some anti-gay crimes serve an experiential function by enabling the attacker to make sense of negative past experiences with gay people. Others serve an expressive function by enabling attackers to feel better about their own groups and maintain status and affiliation with their peers. Anti-gay assaults are a means for some young men to affirm their heterosexuality or masculinity by attacking someone who represents an unacceptable aspect of their own personalities (e.g., homoerotic feelings or effeminate tendencies).

Herek believes that anti-gay attitudes and actions will diminish when they become dysfunctional, that is, when they no longer serve a purpose in people's lives, such as ego defense. This involves determining what psychological functions are served by a person's feelings or behavior and then intervening by helping individuals meet their needs in other, less destructive ways. Individual anti-gay attitudes and behaviors will become dysfunctional when they are no longer supported by religious and political institutions, when they are not reinforced by social norms, and when they are not integral to society's images of sexuality and gender.

Female Infanticide

Perhaps nowhere is the tragedy of gender inequality more evident than in the widespread practice of female infanticide: the killing of baby girls because they are girls. Throughout history, cultural, religious, social, and economic forces have served to devalue the lives of females. In almost all societies, including the United States, this devaluation has lead to the widespread preferences for male children. In some societies, the devaluation of females has led to more dire consequences for females: severe neglect of female babies relative to males and even murder.

Societies in which female infanticide is practiced vary in their characteristics but appear to have some features in common. In an exploratory study of female infanticide among the Kallar of Tamil Nadu, India, researchers identified the following reasons for the continuance of this practice: relatively low value placed on human life, perceived need for military strength against competing villages, marriage patterns that place heavy financial burdens on the bride's family, and a religious emphasis on the importance of sons (Krishnaswamky, 1984). Among the Canadian and North Alaskan Inuit (Eskimo) culture, it has been estimated that at various times between 15 and 50 percent of female babies are murdered (Schrire & Steiger, 1974). Female infanticide among Eskimos is commonly seen as economically based, with female children viewed as unproductive consumers who do not hunt and leave home to marry as soon as they reach an age at which they might be productive.

The sex ratios of men to women are deeply skewed in favor of men in today's China and parts of India. In China, economic practices and inheritance laws that strongly favor males and a traditional preference for sons, combined with China's restrictive one-child policy, have had devastating consequences for females. National surveys conducted in China indicate that 111 males are born for every 100 females, compared to a normal level of 106 males per 100 females (Hull, 1990). This means that more than 500,000 female babies are unaccounted for in China every year. There are probably several reasons for this reported sex imbalance, including selective abortions of female fetuses and the underreporting of females who were safely born and are still alive but are concealed from health care and school systems by parents who want sons. But a major factor in the missing females is infanticide (Herbert, 1997; Hull, 1990).

In northern India, the long-standing sex ratio imbalance in favor of males has been explained by several factors, of which female infanticide and selective abortion are major contributors. Other explanations include maternal mortality, suttee—the cultural practice of a wife immolating herself on her deceased husband's funeral pyre—murder, dowry murder, and forced suicide (Freed & Freed, 1989). All the explanations for the sex ratio imbalances in favor of males throughout the world imply important challenges to the life, health, safety, and welfare of girls and women.

Female Genital Mutilation (FGM)

An estimated 85 to 114 million girls and women throughout the world are genitally mutilated, that is, they have undergone a procedure in which their clitorises are removed (clitoridectomy) or, more radically, the clitoris and surrounding tissues of the labia minora and the inner layers of the labia majora are excised, and the labia majora, the outer lips of the vagina, are stitched together to cover the urethral and vaginal openings (infibulation), with a small aperture to permit the flow of urine and menstrual blood and to allow intercourse. Before or during delivery of a child, an infibulated woman is "opened" to allow the passage of the baby.

Most of these girls and women live in Africa, where FGM is found in at least 28 different countries (Abusharaf, 1998). Some live in the Middle East and parts of Asia. Increasingly, African immigrants migrate to the United States, Canada, and Europe, where they sometimes seek the procedure for themselves or their daughters (Toubia, 1993).

In the eyes of many scholars and activists around the globe, FGM is an extreme and outrageous example of efforts common in most societies to "suppress women's sexuality, ensure their subjugation and con-trol their reproductive functions" (Toubia, 1993, p. 5). After decades of commentary and debate, a consensus has been reached among scholars, medical practitioners, policy makers, and women's health advocates throughout the world about the need to eliminate this practice. We treat this issue in Chapter 4, which explores cultural aspects of FGM, and in Chapter 13, which discusses the historical use of clitoridectomy in England and the United States to control sexual impulses and other presumed mental disorders in women. We address it here because FGM is an important form of ongoing violence against women. Indeed, as an institutionalized form of violence against women that is tolerated by governments, encouraged if not enforced by culture, and represented—falsely—as sanctioned by religion, it is particularly problematic. As a practice, it is often brutal, conducted without anesthesia, in unsanitary conditions, using surgical implements such as knives, razor blades, or broken bottles wielded by people with no medical training. It leaves survivors vulnerable to numerous medical complications that can plague them throughout their lives, from recurrent infections to painful intercourse, infertility, and obstructed labor that can cause babies to be born dead or brain damaged (Abusharaf, 1998). As the Pulitzer Prize–winning African American novelist, Alice Walker, who decried the practice in her best-selling novel, *Possessing the Secret of Joy*, has noted, "torture is not culture" (Nevid et al., 1995).

Genital cutting is so entrenched in local customs and belief systems and is considered so essential to women's identity—a primary signifier of chastity, cleanliness, fertility, beauty, and marriagiability—that it cannot be meaningfully discussed without understanding indigenous cultures and showing sensitivity to its profound cultural, social, and psychological implications (Abusharaf, 1998). If the practice is to be eradicated, it will have to be done so with the cooperation of African, Middle Eastern, and Asian communities, and without the sensationalism, condescension, and other signs of cultural insensitivity sometimes exhibited by Western writers and advocates. Indeed, changes in the acceptability of this practice are already underway in Uganda, among other African countries (Kuka, 1998).

Elder Abuse

It is increasingly recognized that in old age both men and women suffer from neglect and maltreatment from their care-givers. The most vulnerable group of elders are those over age 80, the most rapidly expanding age group in the United States. Because 70 to 80 percent of abused and neglected elders are women, maltreatment in old age is largely a female issue (Nadien, 1996).

Nadien (1996) has identified three types of abuse and neglect that dependent elders may suffer. The most commonly reported of these is physical maltreatment, including abusive acts like assaulting, shoving, and grabbing and neglectful acts like depriving elders of the food or medicine that they need. Psychological maltreatment is believed to be the most common form of elder abuse, although it often goes unreported (Block & Sinnot, 1979). It includes abusive acts like verbal aggression, threats, coercion, and ridicule, whereas psychological neglect includes deprivation of needed social acceptance and stimulation. Finally, maltreatment can be material, financial, or legal. Abuses in these areas occur when care-givers misappropriate elders' property or money, and neglect occurs when the elderly are deprived of needed information, legal advice, representation, or social support.

Recent research suggests that elderly people who are abused, neglected, or exploited die sooner than same-age peers who are not mistreated, even when other relevant variables are controlled (Lacks et al., 1998).

Maltreatment of elders may be at the hands of adult children and grandchildren, spouses, more distant relatives, or paid home-care workers. In the case of institutionalized elders, there is the potential for maltreatment by members of the staff, usually nurses and aides, but sometimes doctors as well. Because of severe stigmatization surrounding this problem, and fear of retaliations and institutionalization, a conspiracy of silence is maintained by victims as well as perpetrators of maltreatment. For these reasons, the extent of elder abuse is not known (Kosberg, 1988). But if current demographic trends continue, an increasing proportion of Americans will be elderly, with growth most rapid among the "oldest-old"— those over 80. With these trends comes an increase in the number of elderly, particularly elderly women, requiring care-giving and vulnerable to maltreatment. As Nadien (1996) suggests, we need to sensitize people to the nature and effects of elder abuse, combat negative stereotypes about the elderly and other effects of ageism, and eliminate the conditions that foster elder maltreatment, including reducing some of the unavoidable sources of stress that accompany elder care.

SUMMARY

In this chapter, we have seen how sexual harassment, rape, partner abuse, child sexual abuse, pornography, prostitution, anti-gay violence, female infanticide, and elder abuse can be usefully viewed as gendered forms of violence or exploitation. Although there are many potential causes of each of these problems, we locate the root cause of the oppression of girls and women in their relative lack of power, status, and resources in most societies. This chapter addressed central questions of how gender inequality creates personal and social contexts conducive to exploitation of and violence against women and girls. As we argued, the

threat, fear, and reality of violence and exploitation change girls' and women's lives in countless ways, limiting their choices, opportunities, and possibilities.

Over the past 25 years, women throughout the world have joined in collective action against violence and exploitation (Boston Women's Health Collective, 1992). These actions range widely from the formation of consciousness-raising groups about domestic violence to public speakouts against forms of oppression. Women have established educational programs for thousands of law enforcement and health professionals. There are now thousands of organizations providing services around the country to women who have been raped or beaten by their partners. Neighborhood groups have formed networks of refuges, called safehouses or greenlight programs, where women attacked in the streets can find safety. Women have worked for legal reforms on many fronts, including changes in rape laws that make it easier for women to report crimes and obtain convictions. These efforts have been extraordinarily successful. But our analysis suggests that deeper societal changes are needed. As long as females are devalued in society relative to men, they will be victims of violence and exploitation by men.

KEY TERMS

Battered women (p. 361)
Date rape (p. 352)
Gender harassment (p. 342)
Heterosexism (p. 375)
Incest (p. 367)
Marital rape (p. 353)
Nonnormative rape (p. 350)

Normative rape (p. 349)
Pornography (p. 370)
Prostitution (p. 373)
Quid pro quo harassment (p. 342)
Rape (p. 349)
Rape myths (p. 357)
Rape trauma syndrome (p. 358)

Seduction theory (p. 368)
Seductive behavior (p. 342)
Sex role spillover (p. 346)
Sexual abuse of children (p. 366)
Sexual harassment (p. 341)

DISCUSSION QUESTIONS

1. Why is sexual harassment often so difficult to identify in specific situations?

2. Do you think that the context of unequal power relationships in which sexual harassment occurs is critical to identifying that conduct?

3. Do you think that there can be truly consensual sexual relationships between employers and employees, professors and students?

4. Men are generally far less likely to perceive a behavior as harassing than women are. Why do you think this is so?

5. Relatively few women who are harassed file formal complaints against their harassers. Why is this so?

6. Many women who are raped do not regard themselves as rape victims. Why?

7. What arc rape myths? Generate five or six rape myths, and explain how such myths support and maintain rape in a culture.

8. How does the existence of rape influence your thoughts, feelings, and behaviors? How do you think it affects the other gender?

9. Do you consider date rape as less serious or severe than other forms of rape? Why or why not?

10. Do you feel that there are circumstances in which a woman "deserves" to be raped? What are they?

11. Sexual harassment is common on college campuses. What is there about this environment and faculty and student relationships that makes harassment so common?

12. What is the difference between sexual harassment and sexual interest?

13. Why do you think so little pornography is targeted at women?

14. What images come to your mind when you hear the term *battered woman*? Do you find that you devalue women who have experienced abuse from their partners?

15. Why do you think that people are preoccupied with asking why abused women so often stay in their relationships?

16. Do you think it is possible for a person under the age of 18 to give meaningful consent to an adult at least six years older?

17. Do you consider pornography a form of sex discrimination? Why or why not?

18. If sex-selection procedures are improved, what do you think will be the likely effects on your society? How do you feel about that? Is there any restriction that should be put on its use?

SUGGESTED READINGS

Browne, A. (1993). Violence against women by male partners: Prevalence, outcomes, and policy implications. *American Psychologist, 48,* 1077–1087.

Funk, R. E. (1993). *Stopping rape: A challenge for men.* Philadelphia: New Society Publishers.

Herek, G. H. (1995). Psychological heterosexism and anti-gay violence: The social psychology of bigotry and bashing. In M. S. Kimmel & M. A. Messner (Eds.), *Men's lives* (3rd ed., pp. 341–353). Boston: Allyn & Bacon.

Koss, M. P., & Mukai, T. (1993). Recovering ourselves: The frequency, effects, and resolution of rape. In F. L. Denmark & M. A. Paludi (Eds.), *Psychology of women: A handbook of issues and theories* (pp. 477–512). Westport, CT: Greenwood.

Paludi, M. A. (1996). *Sexual harassment on college campuses: Abusing the ivory power.* New York: State University of New York Press.

CHAPTER 12

ISSUES IN MENTAL HEALTH

Doctors make the treatment of insanity not a leading part of their professional requirements. Those who have opportunity are often engaged in another line, and for want of time do not pay the due attention to this object. Others fear any innovation, and, from want of courage to exercise their own powers of reflection, follow the doctrines of their predecessors or of titled contemporaries.
—Dr. Spurzheim's Observations on Insanity

Live as domestic a life as possible. Have your child with you all the time. Lie down an hour after each meal. Have but two hours intellectual life a day. And never touch pen, brush or pencil as long as you live.
—S. Weir Mitchell to Charlotte Perkins Gilman

The bulimia started the week after we got engaged. He (Charles) put his hand on my waistline and said: Oh, a little bit chubby here, aren't we? That triggered off something in me. And the Camilla thing—I was desperate, desperate.
—From *Diana: Her True Story* by Andrew Morton

In 1892, a little more than a century ago, in "The Yellow Wallpaper," Charlotte Perkins Gilman described the treatment of a young woman for "temporary nervous depression." Both the illness and the prescribed treatment are understood by the physician—in this case the woman's husband—from a heavily gendered perspective. The patient is confined to a bedroom with a vertiginous yellow wallpaper, which has all the earmarks of a cell. There is a heavy, immovable bedstead, barred windows, rings on the wall, and a gate at the head of the stairs. Her therapy is the "rest cure," which consists of fresh air, rest, and, to build up her strength, cod liver oil and lots of tonics, to say nothing of ale and wine and rare meat. But perhaps its most important aspect is the incarceration and immobilization. All activity, including even reading, writing, and conversation, is severely curtailed. It is not surprising, then, that instead of achieving the intended remission of symptoms, the "cure" produces the opposite result: the patient experiences a slow descent into madness and becomes insane as all her forms of self-expression are taken from her by her paternalistic husband, also a physician familiar with Mitchell's "rest cure" (Gilman, 1892; Sechzer, Pfafflin, Denmark, Griffin, & Blumenthal, 1996).

This fictionalized account reflected Gilman's own treatment for depression years earlier by the most renowned U.S. neurologist of the time, Silas Weir Mitchell. A women's illness was, during that period, seen in the context of the social and cultural construction of women's "normal" and appropriate lives, which showed, according to the "scientific" evidence of the time, that the essential nature of a woman "was not to be strong and competent, but . . . to be a patient" (Ehrenreich & English, 1981). In Gilman's own account and in this story, mental health *is* physical health, conceived according to a male model and therefore by extension imperfect. The rest cure described by Mitchell in 1873 relied on seclusion, massage, immobility, and diet. It was a benevolent punishment for the **neurasthenia** so prevalent during the Victorian period; the severely imposed isolation became for some women a bitter medicine, and they were glad enough to accept the order to

rise and go about when the doctor issued a mandate (Mitchell, 1877).

A HISTORY OF MENTAL DISORDERS AND TREATMENT

The neglect and misinterpretation of women's mental health has had a long history. Brieger (1980) states that "according to them [Wood (1973) and Barker-Benfield (1976)], women's health care has always mirrored a male-dominated world" (p. 153). These authors perceived Victorian physicians as "maintaining a *status quo* by keeping women subordinate in domestic and maternal roles" (Brieger, 1980, p. 153). The history of the interpretation of women's mental health problems and their treatment is a reflection of the history of the enduring sociocultural attitudes toward women and the interrelated matters of race and ethnicity.

Even earlier, from the end of the eighteenth century to about 1865, in England and to some extent in the United States, the eighteenth-century sentimental novel concerned the love-mad woman. The representative figure of madness was no longer that of a madman in chains, but was supplanted by the woman whose insanity was assumed an extension of her female condition; the symbol of the mad or insane person shifted from male to female (Showalter, 1985; Small, 1996). In her book, *Love's Madness,* Small finds that the literature of the period abounded with tales of women becoming mad or insane and even driven to suicide by the demise or rejection and abandonment of their husbands or lovers. This view of femininity was a defined or ingrained part of the society and the culture that had already existed from the earliest times (see Chapter 2). Small has traced the fortunes of these love-mad women in fiction and medicine from the early 1800s, when two fields, literature and medicine, shared similar language and many of the same assumptions. In terms of literary interest, this period marked the emerging era of sensation fiction; in medical terms, it marked an important stage in the history of insanity. Medical reform in England began in the first half of the nineteenth century, and by 1865 the Medico-Psychological Association was formed, marking a separation of the fields of literature and medicine. Although medicine and literature did become distinct, attitudes toward women and their mental health problems persisted, especially as women's mental health began to show other characteristics in a male-controlled society (Showalter, 1985; Small, 1996).

The equation of femininity and insanity remained, and notions of gender continued to influence the definition and subsequently the treatment of mental illness, particularly in England during the late nineteenth century and early twentieth century. These concepts were not the conclusions of medical and scientific knowledge of the period, but "part of a cultural framework in which ideas about femininity and insanity were constructed" (Showalter, 1985, p. 5). Of great interest was the perceived difference in defining madness in females and males. Even though both men and women presented similar symptomatology, the male malady was associated with the economic and intellectual pressures on highly civilized men, whereas the female malady was associated with sexuality and the essential nature of women. Women were considered to be more vulnerable and to express insanity in particularly feminine ways (Showalter, 1985).

In England, people who were regarded as insane were confined to almshouses or even prisons and kept in chains or, later, straightjackets. Still later, asylums began to be built. Indeed, the brutal mistreatment of women in asylums triggered the lunacy reform movement. However, abuses continued over the next few decades (Showalter, 1985). In the United States, however, Americans were more tolerant of mental disorders. In the eighteenth century it was common to allow people with mental disturbances to move about freely. During episodes of madness, they were watched and cared for and then, when recovered, were allowed to rejoin the community and resume their jobs, even in highly responsible positions. However, tolerance in the community began to deteriorate with episodes of violence and the recurring fear in communities for individuals' own safety and for that of their families. In 1751 the first mental hospital,

Pennsylvania Hospital, was established. Hospitals and asylums for the mentally ill began to be common in the United States, England, and Europe just before and after the Civil War with the aim of moral treatment for the patients (Gamwell & Tomas, 1995).

Although asylum doctors claimed that their moral treatment was egalitarian, the implementation of their program varied with the patients' gender, class, and race. Men and women were housed in separate areas, and wealthy patients were permitted to bring their own furniture from home to decorate their rooms in the asylum. The program of activities also varied. For example, lawyers and bankers were encouraged to read and play games, but farmers and laborers were made to work in the kitchen, laundry, or gardens. Although women, regardless of class, performed household chores, their rank and education were considered in their assignments.

These class distinctions were meaningless when compared to racial discrimination. Black people were generally not welcome in "White asylums," although some did admit them, albeit reluctantly. Administrative officials assumed that the expense of hospital treatment was simply wasted on Blacks who were confined instead to jails where they received decidedly inferior care (Eckholm, 1994; Gamwell & Tomas, 1995). Some asylums in the South refused all Black patients; others took only free slaves (this was before the Civil War). Those that did accept Blacks placed them in separate and substandard quarters. As in the North, many Black people suffering from mental disorders ended up in jails or almshouses instead of hospitals or asylums. In many hospitals and asylums the public was allowed to visit and watch the activities and behaviors of the mentally ill. It served as a form of entertainment. Some hospitals and asylums actually charged an entrance fee, and visitors watched the patients much as they might watch animals in a zoo (Gamwell & Tomas, 1995).

In spite of positive reports of the proper and humane treatment of patients in the hospitals and asylums, many people suspected that terrible abuses were being committed. Reports circulated throughout the cities and towns in which these institutions were located. Crusades against abuse were to some extent successful, but even so there was little actual change in conditions.

In the late nineteenth and early twentieth centuries, science began to have an impact on perceptions of mental disorders. Physical causes of insanity and later brain anatomy began to be investigated. The brain was designated as the master organ of the body and results of studies on the brain were used to prove the superiority of the Euro-American culture. Data were falsified on brain size and capacity to further subordinate ethnic groups, non-Whites, and women. Blacks were considered to be "lowbrows" with smaller brains, while Whites were purported to be "highbrows" with larger brains and thus obvious intellectual advantages. The specialty of phrenology associated regions of the female brain with character traits and parts of a woman's body, usually with unfounded and denigrating conclusions. The brains of women were said to be smaller than those of men, making them less intelligent (Eckholm, 1994; Gould, 1980).

With the rise of neurology in the late nineteenth and early twentieth centuries, women came to be seen as especially prone to nervous disorders. As described in Chapter 13, all mature women were considered vulnerable to hysteria, with its causes sought in the uterus, and efforts continued to subordinate them. Women continued to be seen as responsible for the emotional and moral nurturance of husband and children. Religious authorities appeared to uphold this view by portraying family structure as biblically and biologically ordained. And physicians followed these specified gender roles, especially in assigning different reasons for mental disorders in men and women. For example, "uncontrolled passion" as a cause of insanity had a supposedly higher incidence in women.

As the twentieth century progressed, new technologies were developed and science made important strides in elucidating the causes and treatment of mental disorders with a somewhat more egalitarian approach. As urbanization and industrialization continued to grow, the position of women changed, especially after they won the right to vote. Women have made tremendous strides in realizing their effectiveness in education, the professions, and nontraditional workplaces. Young girls are now brought up with the knowledge that they can be anything that they desire. Yet, gender and racial bias still persist and are more extreme for the poor and elderly. We shall see the effects of these factors as the chapter reviews mental disorders.

The continually evolving roles as well as life-styles, particularly in developed countries, have been thought to result in changes in the incidence and prevalence of disorders in women and men. Differences between females and males are a consequence of biological endowment and psychological and social influences from the time of birth. However, changing roles and life-styles may override such influences and alter the vulnerability of one gender to disorders that have been assumed more predominant in the other gender (Blumenthal, 1996). The very things that lend women's lives such texture and richness—their jobs, families, and other caring relationships—may be significant sources of stress and conflict. Beyond this, the overall lower social and economic status imposed on women, including poverty or financial difficulty, the glass ceiling and other barriers to women's achievement, sexual harassment and discrimination, rape and sexual assault, and various other forms of physical and emotional abuse, are enormous sources of strain for many women. For ethnic minority and lesbian women, there are added stresses resulting from bias and discrimination.

This chapter addresses current mental health issues that are prevalent in our society today, how they affect females and males, and the variations in their prevalence for each gender, as well as the ages at which many disorders now appear. Biases in treatment as well as diversity issues are also considered. Because it is not possible to cover every aspect of mental disorders in this chapter, we have selected the most common mental disorders in which gender matters. Additional suggested readings at the end of this chapter provide information about other mental health issues not covered here. Many mental health issues not specifically addressed here are covered in chapters throughout the book.

THE DOUBLE STANDARD OF LABELING AND DIAGNOSIS

The labeling and diagnosis of mental disorders is not a neutral tool for treating women and men. Gender stereotypes shape what is considered normal behavior for women and men and can lead therapists to either trivialize women's problems, as when anxiety and depression are treated dismissively, or to exaggerate them, as when medications like antidepressants are over-prescribed for women. Over-diagnoses and under-diagnoses are the results of gender bias and may be used to control and oppress those who do not "fit in" by ensuring conformity to the social order and denying the connection between social inequities and psychological distress (Maracek & Hare-Mustin, 1991).

Diagnostic categories in medicine and psychology have traditionally provided the language and framework for therapists' judgments and actions. They have the effect of putting the spotlight on the individual with the condition rather than the social context in which the disorder is expressed. Using labels to identify the disorder within the person could foreclose an examination of the social context that may have given rise to the problem.

Diagnostic categories, however biased they can be in insulating individuals from the social/cultural context and blaming the victim, have been useful in organizing material on disorders. With these caveats in mind, we present some of the major diagnostic categories applied to women, recognizing that the source of the problems we discuss may well have societal rather than individual bases.

ANOREXIA NERVOSA: AN ALARMING EPIDEMIC

We eat in order to provide our bodies with the energy that they require to survive and function appropriately.

Eating is of concern to all of us. We usually derive great pleasure from eating our favorite foods and can recall with great detail particularly sumptuous lunches or dinners that we have had in the past. Yet, for some people, eating behavior grows out of control, often with profound consequences.

Anorexia nervosa has a long history. The first case reported was in England in 1694 by Dr. Richard Morton, but it was in the Victorian period that this disorder became well known. The name *anorexia* was given to it by Sir William Gull in 1868 (Halmi, Schneider, & Cooper, 1989).

Anorexia has now become an alarming epidemic, especially in Western countries, and it is being seen in younger and younger people. It represents an extreme effort to keep weight under control. Anorexia nervosa is considered a psychiatric disorder and is included in the *Diagnostic and Statistical Manual of Mental Disorders* (DSM-IVR) of the American Psychiatric Association (1994). The criteria for anorexia nervosa are shown in Table 12.1.

Anorexia is described in the following vignette of a young woman who had a rapid weight loss of almost 50 pounds.

Amy was 17 and a senior in high school. She was looking forward to attending college the following year and she and her friends spent hours talking about

---

TABLE 12.1 DSM-IVR Criteria for Anorexia Nervosa

1. Refusal to maintain body weight at or above a minimally normal weight for age and height.

2. Intense fear of gaining weight.

3. Disturbance in the way in which one's body weight and shape are experienced; undue influence of body weight on self-evaluation; or denial of the seriousness of current low body weight.

4. Amenorrhea (absence of menstrual cycle).

Source: Reprinted with permission from the *Diagnostic and Statistical Manual of Mental Disorders,* Fourth Edition. Copyright 1994 by the American Psychiatric Association.

the great social life they could look forward to. Amy, however, was concerned about her appearance and decided that she needed to lose about 8 to 10 pounds to really look fashionably slim. She began to diet and soon lost 10 pounds. Instead of concentrating on maintaining her new weight, Amy decided that she still looked "fat" and continued to restrict her food intake. After an additional loss of 15 pounds, Amy was still not satisfied with her appearance; she still felt overweight and continued to diet. By now her parents became alarmed and her schoolmates told her that she was too thin and didn't really look good. Amy then took to wearing bulky clothes to hide her extreme thinness and continued to diet, which now had entered the phase of starvation. Her breakfast consisted of a slice of diet bread with a small amount of jam and a cup of coffee. Amy usually skipped lunch or drank two to three cups of coffee. She refused to eat at the table with her parents and instead took a plate of food up to her room to eat or discard as she saw fit, usually to be flushed down the toilet so that her empty plate would be taken as evidence that she had eaten. She discarded most of her dinner in this manner, eating minimal amounts of foods or vegetables that were low in calories.

After school, Amy attended an exercise class and after her program spent 2 to 3 hours on the treadmill and stationary bicycle. Even though she was very thin, Amy had the high levels of energy typical of anorexia until later stages. Although people at the exercise club remarked on her thinness and encouraged her to gain some weight, she refused. As she continued to lose weight, Amy still did not consider herself too thin. She examined herself in her full-length mirror every morning and evening and still thought she was too fat. For some months her menstrual periods ceased; she was always cold and began to experience difficulty in concentrating. Now she began to fatigue easily. A fine covering of hair appeared over her body. By now her parents were truly frightened at what was happening to their daughter—Amy was below 90 pounds and at 5 feet 5 inches was truly in a state of **emaciation.** *She felt sick all the time and finally agreed with her parents to see their physician. She was about to be hospitalized.*

Anorexia nervosa is characterized by a pathological fear of obesity and intentional starvation. As described in the vignette, there is a rapid weight loss of at least 25 percent of total body weight and a reduction to about 15 percent below the normal weight for one's age, height, and gender. The morbid fear of becoming fat remains even with the extreme loss of weight. Anorectic people continue to see themselves as fat, and when asked to draw a picture of themselves, they will draw a picture of themselves as fat. Starvation may become so extensive that anorectics become seriously ill with heart disease, low blood pressure, or cardiac arrhythmias due to low body levels of electrolytes (e.g., sodium and potassium), which can result in death (Halmi, 1996; Penner, Thompson, & Coovert, 1991).

Incidence of anorexia is 15 to 20 times more frequent in females than males. It is higher in adolescent girls and usually declines in early adulthood. Studies in North America and Europe by Lacy and Birchnell (1986) and by Polivy and Thomson (1988) show that approximately 1 of every 250 adolescent girls is anorectic, that the disorder has been more prevalent in upper-class and upper-middle-class individuals, but that it is now appearing in middle- and lower-class women and appears to be increasing. Social class or race are no longer predictors of the development of eating disorders; it is seen in both White females and in other ethnic and racial groups (Garfinkel & Garner, 1982; Hsu, 1990). Dancers, models, and athletes are at an especially high risk for developing anorexia, as are dieticians who are constantly involved with food and calories (Halmi, 1996; Lacy & Birchnell, 1986; Werry, 1986).

BULIMIA NERVOSA: A DISORDER OF BINGING AND PURGING

Bulimia nervosa is a disorder characterized by alternating cycles of binge eating and purging and is apparently brought about in part by attempts to diet that are unsuccessful. One of the most publicized cases of bulimia is that of the late Princess Diana. Box 12.1 is an excerpt from Andrew Morton's book *Diana: Her True Story*; it identifies some of the problems that women face that may place them at high risk for eating disorders.

Box 12.1

Media Spotlight

BODY IMAGE

Princess Diana, who died in a tragic car crash in Paris in 1997, was regarded as one of the most beautiful women in the world. She blamed her body for the confusion, torment, and the apprehension she was experiencing in anticipation of her marriage to Prince Charles.

Even though Prince Charles reportedly ignored her throughout most of their engagement period and continued to send presents to Camilla Parker Bowles—his longtime lover, Diana blamed herself. She received little to no guidance for the royal role she would need to play as she was being catapulted onto the world stage. Even after their wedding, a royal worldwide extravaganza, Diana continued to blame herself and, believing that she was inadequate, allowed her body to become the victim of her poor self-esteem and self-doubts and perhaps even self-hatred.

Source: From "Body Image: The Last Frontier of Women's Rights," 1997 *Women's Health Advocate, 4*(10), p. 6. Copyright 1997 by the Women's Health Advocate. Reprinted with permission.

Bulimia was first considered a subtype of anorexia because weight loss was the ultimate goal, but achieved in a different way from starvation—by binging and purging. By 1979, it was finally recognized as a separate entity (Russell, 1979). The DSM-IVR criteria for bulimia are presented in Table 12.2. Bulimia, like anorexia, is seen primarily in females, but males do develop this disorder as well. Bulemics have also been separated into two subtypes: those who binge and purge with recurrent self-induced vomiting and those who binge but do not purge regularly and instead diet and exercise vigorously. The latter group seems to have less anxiety about eating and less body image disturbance (Halmi, 1996).

The typical binger–purger will gorge on food, sometimes ingesting more than 4000 calories at one time. Before the calories are absorbed into the body, vomiting is induced or laxatives are taken. These people continue to lose weight even though they spend hours gorging on food.

Surveys of dancers, including ballet dancers, have shown a high incidence of bulimia. Box 12.2 describes a fairly typical pattern of bulimic behavior that was told to one of the authors by a very young woman who was accepted into a ballet company in a large city.

Treatment of Anorexia and Bulimia

Anorexia is one of the most difficult disorders to treat since anorectics usually see nothing wrong with their continued dieting. Anorectics are resolute, resisting changes in their behavior. They respond negatively and with hostility to criticisms, appeals, and even warnings of the consequences of their behavior, especially from their families. They frequently drop out of treatment (Szmuckler, Eisler, Russell, & Dare, 1985).

A multifaceted program for anorexia is necessary to achieve any success. Such a program includes medical treatment and behavioral, cognitive, and individual as well as family therapy (Halmi, 1996).

TABLE 12.2   DSM-IVR Criteria for Bulimia Nervosa

1. Recurrent episodes of binge eating with a sense of lack of control.
2. Recurrent use of inappropriate compensatory behavior to avoid weight gain (self-induced vomiting, laxative abuse, diuretic abuse).
3. A minimum average of two episodes of binge eating and two inappropriate compensatory behaviors a week for at least three months.
4. Self-evaluation is unduly influenced by body shape and weight.
5. The person does not meet the criteria for anorexia nervosa.

Source: Reprinted with permission from the *Diagnostic and Statistical Manual of Mental Disorders,* Fourth Edition. Copyright 1994 by the American Psychiatric Association.

Box 12.2

Pressure to Be Thin

On pay day, a group of ballerinas would go to their favorite pastry shop and gorge themselves on rich pastries and coffee. On returning to the ballet theater, they entered the bathroom and, in each cubicle, faced forward over the toilet and induced vomiting by pushing their fingers down their throats. There was immediate relief that there would be no weight gain from their eating adventure. This same pattern was repeated week after week without any apparent concern or recognition of the seriousness of this behavior.

The young woman who related this story to me said that she was certain that many of these women did have guilt about their behavior, but felt it was an easy way to maintain their weight as was required, even mandated, by the ballet master. She was so astounded at this recurring practice and became so frightened about being vulnerable to this "seductive" method of weight control that she left the ballet and attended college. This young woman is now an architect and interior designer. In working out her interest in ballet, she frequently consults for ballet and opera companies on their scenic designs.

However, there is an immediate need to treat the patient's **emaciation** and restore her nutritional state. Until some measure of normal nutrient status is achieved, psychotherapy, regardless of the approach, is extremely difficult due to the patient's psychological symptoms from emaciation (15 percent to 25 percent underweight): irritability, depression, and continuing preoccupation with food and sleep disturbances. Severely anorectic emaciated patients almost always require medical treatment and should be hospitalized (Halmi, 1996).

Cognitive therapy for anorexia, first reported by Garner and Bemis (1982), is another approach to treatment. It involves assessing distorted cognition: the patient's feelings of being fat, her self-worth and body image, and the perception that the only way she can be effective is in dieting and losing weight. The need for and type of family therapy are determined by the therapist. A critical factor is that behavioral treatment in a hospital setting may not carry over to the family situation (Garfinkel & Garner, 1982). Age is important in this decision, since patients under 18 fare best in family therapy, but patients older than 18 have not been found to benefit. Medication may be needed as an adjunct to therapy (Russell, Szmukler, & Dare, 1987).

Multifaceted treatment has also been carried out with bulimics, who can usually be treated as outpatients rather than being hospitalized, as is so frequently necessary with emaciated anorectics. A combination of **cognitive–behavioral therapy** and medication (e.g., antidepressants) seems to be the most effective treatment, with the particular combination depending on the individual patient (Agras et al., 1992; McCann & Agras, 1990). In both anorexia and bulimia there are frequent relapses. Weight gained in the hospital is difficult to maintain. Decreasing the frequency of episodes of binging and especially purging requires constant self-monitoring, and for the recovering patient this is very arduous.

Changing Patterns of Eating Disorders

The fear of food and terror of gaining weight are not only affecting adolescents but also their little sisters. Anorexia and bulimia are seen now in younger and younger females. Adults' obsession with body weight has filtered down to children under 10 years of age. As children are growing up, they see their mothers' attempts to diet and exercise in order to remain thin, with notes about "fat" and "calories" attached to the refrigerator. Conversations about how not to gain weight and what foods are the lowest in calories are all too frequent. Many children today are brought up on diet foods (e.g., skim or 1 percent milk instead of whole milk, diet salad dressing, and fat-free cookies and ice cream). Such patterns serve as models for growing girls.

"There is evidence that the struggle for thinness that represents the prime acknowledged aim of the sufferers [anorectics and bulimics] represents an overvalued idea that emerges from a sense that bodily appearance is crucial for social acceptance, adult roles and evidence of self control" (McHugh, Moran, & Killilea, 1989, p. 7). Anorexia has unfortunately provided a model of chronic starvation and its consequences (McHugh et al., 1989). Booth (1989) continues this analogy: "The fashion mannequin has become the representative of an institution or ideology or the priest of a religion whose gods are slimness and youth. Her 'dry' bones come to life all too impressively when dressed in clothing" (p. 124). This standard of beauty and the inability to attain and maintain it have resulted in unhappiness and frustration with one's body. This provides the groundwork at a very early age for a poor body image and low self-esteem, which have been seen as the consequence of social pressures for girls who more and more have come to evaluate themselves in terms of their appearance (Heffernan, 1998).

Prevention. This changing pattern of eating disorders affecting younger and younger children is being seen as a new epidemic. It is critical to allow young girls to grow and develop at their individual rates. Parents must become more aware of the dangers of eating disorders to their children. Regulating food intake should not be an important focus in the home. Instead, the family should make every effort to eat together as often as possible. Parents should be more critical of accepting thinness as a standard of beauty and should encourage their daughters to develop healthy bodies through proper nutrition and physical activities rather than dieting.

DEPRESSION

Demographics

Depression is the most widespread psychological disorder. Chronic depression has become a major public health problem in the United States. It can be considered the common cold of mental illness. We have all felt some form of mild depression—feeling blue, sad, "down in the dumps," and unhappy. Today, we understand some of the causes of both mild and chronic depression and we can do something about them (Blumenthal, 1996; Rosenhan & Seligman, 1984).

Characteristics of Depression and Gender Comparisons

Although depression affects both men and women, it is generally regarded as a woman's disorder. Women appear to be more at risk than men for developing depression. The comparisons between women and men are significant: it has been estimated that 7 percent of U.S. women will be diagnosed with depression at some time in their lives, compared with 2.6 percent of men. This difference cuts across age, ethnic, and racial groups. The average age of onset of depression in women has decreased steadily and is now in the mid-twenties (Blumenthal, 1996; McLean & Woody, 1998).

Depression consists of both mood and cognitive components. Table 12.3 identifies the symptoms and criteria for a diagnosis of depression. Symptoms of depression differ in women and men. Women tend to report more emotional symptoms, such as crying and feelings of worthlessness; men report more physical symptoms, such as sleep disorders and loss of sex drive (Oliver & Toner, 1990). In men, depression can take a variety of forms. Substance abuse and aggressive behavior, even violence, have been attributed to depression in men (Fausto-Sterling, 1992).

The DSM-IVR classifies depression as a type of mood disorder and is found as a diagnosis on axis 1. The DSM-IVR identifies two subclassifications of depressive disorders: *major depression* and *dysthymia*. Symptoms of a major depression follow those in Table 12.3. Symptoms of dysthymia are much milder and tend to last for many years. Dysthymia presents with depressed mood as a chronic condition, with some loss of interest and some of the other symptoms of depression almost as a personality trait.

Depression can be *episodic* or *chronic*. An episodic depression, much more common, has less than two years' duration with a clear onset; in chronic depression, the symptoms are present for more than two years without any remission to normal functioning of at least two months' duration (Brannon, 1999; Rosenhan & Seligman, 1984).

There is also a distinction between **endogenous** and **exogenous depression.** Endogenous refers to biological causes arising from within the body; exogenous indicates causes coming from outside the

TABLE 12.3 Criteria for Depression

TYPE	SYMPTOMS
Mood Components	Loss of interest in activities and people
	An emotional emptiness or feeling of flatness
	A lack of responsiveness to the environment
Cognitive Components	Self-blame and reproach
	Guilt and self-depreciation
	Hopelessness and helplessness
Other Signs	Psychomotor retardation and/or agitation
	Loss of libido
	Sleep and appetite disturbances

Source: From "Depression in the Young," by D. Moreau in *Women and Mental Health: Annals of the New York Academy of Sciences* (pp. 181–190), edited by J. A. Sechzer, S. M. Pfafflin, F. L. Denmark, A. Griffin, & S. Blumenthal (1996). New York: The New York Academy of Sciences. Copyright 1996 by the New York Academy of Sciences. Reprinted with permission.

body. Perhaps women are more depressed than men because of endogenous factors (e.g., hormones), but it is also possible that they are more depressed because of exogenous factors such as their lower status in society, their lack of control over their lives, and because they are frequently the target of violence. There may be an interaction between exogenous and endogenous factors that work to complicate both diagnosis and treatment.

Race and Class

Racial stereotypes abound in the history of the treatment of mental disorders. Early in this century, G. Stanley Hall and others advanced theories that sustained racial stereotyping. One theory considered that Blacks were "innately happy-go-lucky" and therefore were immune to depression (Hyde, 1996a, p. 231). Such thinking is completely unfounded and no longer accepted. The incidence of depression in African American women is higher than for African American men and is in keeping with the 2:1 ratio generally found. Similarly, there is a higher rate of depression in Hispanic women than in Hispanic men (Canino, 1982). The incidence of depression in Asians and Asian Americans is difficult to estimate, especially

because of the different cultural and national groups here in the United States, yet it also appears to be higher in women than men. In studies of Asian Americans, Ying (1988) and Shum (1996) found that the higher the socioeconomic status, the less the rate of depression, and the lower the socioeconomic level, the higher the rate of depression among Asian American groups. The negative correlation between social class and rates of depression is found across all ethnic groups.

The **feminization of poverty,** regardless of race or ethnicity, has become associated with an increase in depression. The high proportion of single-parent households, primarily those of women, the inadequacy and deficiency of child-support payments to divorced women, and the lack of good and affordable child care that would enable these women to seek and hold higher-paying and more responsible jobs or to return to school to update and improve their education are all contributing factors to depression.

Bias in Treatment and Research

Treatment. Women and men diagnosed as depressed are treated differently by health-care professionals. Women are much more likely to have drugs prescribed for depression. Rodin and Ickovics (1990) have estimated that two-thirds of all prescriptions for psychotropic drugs are written for women. Ironically, although more women take these drugs, men are reported to be more responsive therapeutically to antidepressant medication (Rodin & Ickovics, 1990; Strickland, 1988).

Intervention for depression usually involves antidepressant medication for chronic patients. There are second and third generations of these medications that aim to achieve remission of depression with fewer side effects. Patients on medication need to be monitored by their prescribing physician as there are risks associated with such intervention. Many antidepressants are contraindicated for elderly patients and those with cardiac problems and other conditions. There have been reports, albeit few, of suicide with the drug Prozac, although it is not known whether these patients would have committed suicide without medication.

Individual therapy is the most common psychological intervention. Therapy by the psychologist may be combined with medication by a psychiatrist, and collaboration between psychologist and physician is important, as is collaboration with the patient's family. Psychotherapeutic intervention may be brief or prolonged depending on the patient's symptoms and progress. Exercise and relaxation training are also effective adjuncts in treating some forms of depression, as is strong social support by family and other groups.

In diagnosing and treating severe depression, there is always the risk of suicide. The therapist must at all times try to be aware of indications that the patient may attempt suicide either as a cry for help or to end suffering and be prepared to intervene.

Bias in Treating Depression.   In a discussion of the treatment of patients, Taylor (1995) cites reports showing that communication between physician and patient may be eroded when physicians encounter patients that they would prefer not to treat. Derogatory stereotypes of patients may contribute to problems in communication and subsequent treatment (Morgan, 1985; Schmelkin, Wachtel, Schneiderman, & Hecht,

1988). Studies show that (mostly White) physicians tend to provide less information, give less support, and demonstrate less proficient clinical performance with Black and Hispanic patients, and patients of lower socioeconomic class, including the elderly, compared with those of higher socioeconomic class (Taylor, 1995).

Sexism is also a factor in medical practice. Many male physicians do not communicate well with female patients. When patient and physician are gender matched, better rapport and exchange of information take place (Weisman & Teitelbaum, 1985). However, according to Hall, Epstein, DeCiantis, and McNeil (1993), both female and male physicians prefer male patients. In a study by Wilcox (1992), medical students heard an audiotaped patient portrayal of either a woman or man reporting symptoms typical of depression. The students perceived the female patient as less seriously ill than the male and less likely to need follow-up tests or laboratory tests, but as more likely to be recommended for psychotropic medication than the male patient. A nonpsychiatric consultation was more frequently suggested for the male patient. Unfortunately, such stereotyped attitudes can influence what a physician concludes and recommends in treating a patient.

Patients seeking treatment largely for depression, anxiety, or other types of psychological disorders elicit similar negative reactions from physicians. In such cases, physicians may provide cursory attention, and communication, especially with depressed patients who are passive, may be highly inadequate. Physicians seem to like healthier, not sicker, patients and prefer those with acute problems to the chronically ill, because chronic disorders pose uncertainties about prognosis that acutely ill patients do not (Butler, 1978; Hall et al., 1993).

Gender differences in assessing depression (prevalence, etiology, course, and treatment) are difficult to determine with certainty because they depend on the individual's willingness to get help and disclose personal information. Women are much more likely than men to seek help. As we have seen, diagnosis depends on the provider's interpretations of symptoms and behaviors and on her or his attitudes. Diagnoses of depression may well be linked to the ways in which women and men conform or fail to conform to traditional gender roles (Strickland, 1988). The differential labeling, acceptance, and treatment of similar symptoms in women and men exemplify how disorders, particularly psychological or behavioral disorders lacking clear and specific symptomatology, are socially constructed (Sechzer, Rabinowitz, Denmark et al., 1994).

Clearly, it has long been recognized that depression is a disorder in which sex–gender is a critical variable. Unger and Crawford (1996) have called depression "the disorder that has received the most attention in terms of sex and gender issues" (p. 562). With this in mind, let us look at another aspect of bias—how gender is studied as a variable in depression research.

Bias in Research on Depression. The authors of this text conducted a survey of published research on depression. The purpose of our study was to analyze patterns of subject use and to identify the gender of the subjects. Beyond this, we determined whether the findings of the studies were generalized to both females and males and whether such generalizations were appropriate, that is, scientifically justifiable. The journals we reviewed included the *Journal of Abnormal Psychology, Journal of Consulting and Clinical Psychology, American Journal of Psychiatry, Archives of General Psychiatry,* and *Journal of Affective Disorders.* All articles published in 1984 and 1991 relating to major depression were reviewed. The data were coded and analyzed; data from 1984 were compared with those in 1991.

As expected for both 1984 and 1991, many more females than males were studied. What was unexpected was the large percentage of subjects not identified as to whether they were female or male: 27.96 percent in 1984 and 23.19 percent in 1991. For both 1984 and 1991, there was adequate representation of women and men for those whose gender we could identify. With regard to generalizing findings to both genders, we found that such generalizations were ap-

propriate in only about 50 percent of the studies reviewed for both years. Included in the rating of appropriate or inappropriate was the question of whether gender differences were explored and tested. We found that gender differences were seldom hypothesized in the research and that there was actually a decline in the number of studies of hypothesized differences from 1984 to 1991. When differences *were* explored, they were found in more than half the cases and were always discussed. Although these findings were encouraging, the failure to identify the gender of the subjects was of concern, because it indicated insensitivity to gender as an important variable in research in a disorder with such evident gender differences.

It was not clear to us why so many investigators failed to identify the gender of the subjects and test for differences in results. We questioned whether some researchers believed that any differences that might emerge would be difficult to explain or whether some scientists believed that science should be sex or gender neutral. It was also of interest that the journal editors did not require sex or gender identification of the subjects, suggesting that at the very highest levels of science, sex and gender as variables in research remain undervalued and understudied. Now that there is a federal mandate to include males and females in studies of disorders affecting both genders, we are conducting a follow-up of current studies of depression and other disorders to determine the correct proportion of female and male subject use, as well as whether data are analyzed separately by gender.

PREMENSTRUAL SYNDROME

Premenstrual syndrome (PMS) is the name given to a group of symptoms known to begin a few days prior to the menstrual cycle. In the premenstrual phase, some women experience negative moods and cognitions as well as physical distress, with relief following the onset of menstruation (McFarlane, 1998). Symptoms may include tenderness and swelling of the breasts, headaches, acne, and back pain, as well as general discomfort. Premenstrual women can become depressed and feel tense and irritable, but also lethargic (Budoff, 1994; Matlin, 1996).

In 1987 the American Psychiatric Association (APA) included in the DSM-IIIR a *late luteal phase dysphoric disorder* (LLPDD) to cover these premenstrual symptoms and placed it in its appendix among disorders needing further study. Although this classification should have limited its use, LLPDD was used just as any other psychiatric diagnostic category in the DSM-IIIR. There was an outpouring of criticism because many felt that this would put untold numbers of women at risk for a psychiatric diagnosis. Instead, a similar diagnosis of *premenstrual dysphoric disorder* (PMDD) was proposed and was to be included in the new DSM-IVR as a mood disorder. Another controversy developed. Those endorsing placement in this category felt that women would be more likely to receive insurance coverage for treatment as a mood disorder; those against felt that a psychiatric diagnosis would stigmatize women as having a psychiatric disorder that is included in the same category as depression. Finally, after much argument, the APA placed PMDD in an appendix and not in the main text, but still in the section of disorders requiring further study (Brannon, 1999).

This controversy still continues because of the difficulty in defining PMS and what symptomatology to include in it. Some critics feel that all menstruating women have PMS; others say it is all in one's mind (Matlin, 1996).

Beyond that, many feminists are concerned that the labeling of this syndrome as a mental health problem diminishes all women and defines them as inferior because of their biology. The label suggests they are, at least for part of their cycle, less reliable and more emotional than men. This almost parallels the association of women with the cycles of the moon and "lunacy" as described in Chapter 2.

A recent review by McFarlane (1998) explores this controversy further and provides recommendations toward a solution. McFarlane points out that PMS has been recognized and written about for almost six decades and has been researched for about 40 of those 60 years. Some studies support the existence of PMS, whereas others have failed to do so, and in spite of all the studies carried out, no answers have been found. McFarlane feels that the reason for this is that the methodology used in the research does not provide for the social, cultural, psychological, biological, and other factors involved. The research has used a standard medical model that she feels may be inappropriate for studying PMS. McFarlane cites Walker, who has said that "before we begin to *explain* PMS, we must first *describe* women's experiences in detail" (McFarlane, 1998, p. 458).

McFarlane summarizes *essential* and then *important* criteria for research and diagnosis in her paper with Williams (McFarlane & Williams, 1994), as follows:

Essential Criteria: (1) Participants should be blind to the true (menstrual) purpose of the research; (2) all measurements should include both negative and positive aspects of menstruation in equal amounts; (3) given what is known about faulty and selective memories, participants should avoid giving retrospective reports in order to reduce stereotyped responses that do not match daily events; and (4) data should be collected at the same and equal intervals.

Important Criteria: (1) Data should be collected across two or preferably more cycles to help assure reliability; (2) both men and women should be included in the study because emotional cyclicity may not be unique to women; (3) researchers should study older participants since emotional distress across the menstrual cycle may increase with age. Cross-cultural studies should also be carried out; and (4) other cycles should be studied and compared with menstrual cyclicity (McFarlane, 1998).

McFarlane also reviews data from placebo studies, and concludes that placebos have been effective as a treatment. There may be special factors in the use of placebos that provide effective treatment, just as they have been effective in other treatments. It would be important to explore placebo effects to add to our understanding of PMS. Carrying out research with these caveats should be given high priority to advance our understanding of this syndrome. Rather than focusing only on those women who report symptoms of PMS, we should also study the many more women who do not report such symptoms.

ANXIETY DISORDERS

Anxiety disorders comprise several conditions, including agoraphobia, panic disorder, obsessive–compulsive disorder, and posttraumatic stress disorder (PTSD). Although some of these conditions are equally common in women and men, some, like agoraphobia, are much more frequently seen in women. Others, like PTSD, occur in both men and women but appear to have different causes for men and women. For example, PTSD is associated with war experiences for men and sexual abuse for women.

Agoraphobia literally means fear of the marketplace and is diagnosed when an individual has extreme anxiety about being in places or situations from which escape is difficult. Agoraphobics frequently fear leaving their homes, neighborhoods, or other familiar circumscribed places. Agoraphobia can occur with or without panic attacks—periods of intense anxiety accompanied by physical symptoms such as heart palpitations, profuse sweating, and shortness of breath. It is believed to be a learned response to stress, including marital difficulties, and it is about twice as common in women than in men. About 70 percent of people with agoraphobia are married women (Hafner & Minge, 1989).

Posttraumatic stress disorder (PTSD), discussed more fully in Chapter 11, was originally diagnosed in men returning from combat experiences, but has increasingly been diagnosed in women, many of whom are the victims of sexual abuse, assault, and other violent crimes and nonviolent crimes involving the abuse of power. (An example of the latter occurs when a therapist engages in sexual contact with a client. Although such behavior has been directly prohibited by the American Psychological Association since 1977, such misconduct still continues to be a problem.) Recent studies suggest that the prevalence of PTSD in women is surprisingly high, with about 12 percent of women reporting symptoms (Brannon, 1999).

TREATMENT OF MENTAL DISORDERS

Bias in Therapy

We have seen in the earlier section on depression how gender bias has played an important role in the diagnosis and treatment of depression. The diagnosis and treatment of other mental disorders can also be biased.

Most traditional types of psychotherapy involve a long-term relationship between patient and therapist in which the patient talks about his or her feelings, fears, attitudes, and behaviors. These problems are discussed and interpreted according to the theoretical orientation of the therapist and the type of therapy that she or he practices. Trust of the therapist is a major factor in the patient–therapist relationship. Often the therapist focuses on the early childhood of the patient as a determinant of the psychological problems presented. How adequately do these traditional therapies deal with the psychological problems of women and how do the attitudes of therapists toward women and men influence the diagnosis and therapy that their patients receive?

Thirty years ago, Broverman and his associates addressed these questions in a classic study of the clinical judgments of 79 female and male psychologists, psychiatrists, and social workers. They found that these therapists made clear-cut distinctions between who were healthy females and males. Broverman, Clarkeson, Rosenkrantz, and Vogel (1970) found no significant differences between standards for males and for adults, but found differences between standards for females and adults. Thus, the standards for mental health represent the male model, and females deviate from them. Broverman and his colleagues also found that more socially desirable personality attributes were assigned to men, with undesirable ones attributed to women. Of additional interest was the finding that there was no difference in the results whether the therapist was female or male, showing that women therapists may be just as biased as men (Broverman et al., 1970).

One important criticism of the study was that, although it measured therapists' attitudes, it failed to measure whether the therapists actually acted in a sexist way during the therapy session. Regardless of whether attitudes of therapists have changed, especially those of female therapists who made the same judgments as males in 1970, there still appears to be gender bias in diagnosis and treatment (Hyde, 1996a).

Types of Therapy

There are two broad categories of therapies, the traditional therapies and the new therapies for women. These are shown in Table 12.4.

Traditional Therapies

Psychoanalytic Therapy. In psychoanalysis the analyst works with the patient to bring repressed and unconscious material into consciousness. Psychoanalysis is based on Freud's theory, which was described in detail in Chapters 3 and 5. Briefly, Freud's theory emphasizes the importance of biological and anatomical factors and parental identification. The conflicts of the Oedipus and Electra complex, which the child usually resolves by the age of 5 or 6, is brought about by the realization that only boys have penises. Through this recognition, the child is motivated to identify with the same-sex parent. According to Freud, the child has incestuous desires toward the parent, which causes guilt and anxiety. The boy fears that his penis will be removed or "cut off," as in his mind this has already happened with girls, and comes to identify with his father. In the case of girls, they have already lost their penises and they develop penis envy. As a result, Freud theorized that a boy's gender identity is stronger than a girl's and that many girls never resolve the Electra complex. Identification with the same-sex parent is critical for the development of healthy feminine and masculine personalities. The

consequences of this for the negative attributes of females and the sexist aspects of his theory were described in Chapters 3 and 5. One problem with traditional psychoanalytic therapy is that women's achievement strivings may be interpreted as penis envy and treates as deviant.

Freud's theory and psychoanalysis have both been criticized extensively by feminists, who claim that it is profoundly sex biased. There has been a significant movement among some psychodynamic therapists to use basic tenets of psychoanalysis in an unbiased way (e.g., Nancy Chodorow, Karen Horney, Jean Baker Miller, Juliet Mitchell, Clara Thompson). For a more detailed review, see Women and Psychotherapy: An Assessment of Research and Practice, edited by Annette Brodsky and Rachel Hare-Mustin; Psychoanalysis and Women, edited by Jean Baker Miller; and the journal Women and Therapy.

Behavior Therapy. **Behavior therapy** is also known as behavior modification, or behavior mod. These therapies are based on the principles of Pavlovian classical conditioning, as well as those of operant conditioning techniques first developed by Skinner. They differ from psychoanalysis in that there is no in-depth analysis of the personality nor any attempt to uncover the patient's unconscious motivations. Behavior therapy concentrates on maladaptive behavior and seeks to modify behavior through the application of learning principles of reward and punishment, for example, rewarding the preferred behavior and either not rewarding or punishing the undesirable behavior.

Included in behavior therapy are techniques using **systematic desensitization** for the treatment of *phobias; positive reinforcement* techniques to reward behaviors; and *aversive learning,* in which an unpleasant stimulus, paired with the problematic behavior, is used to eliminate or decrease the problematic behaviors. *Assertiveness training* also uses *imitation and observational* techniques.

Concepts of behavior therapy are not inherently sexist and do not specify the need for gender differences. Nonetheless, in their focus on adaptiveness and appropriateness of behavior, some therapists may inadvertently reinforce gender-role stereotypes. Thus,

TABLE 12.4   Types of Treatment Therapies

TRADITIONAL THERAPIES	NEW THERAPIES FOR WOMEN
Psychoanalysis	Nonsexist therapy
Behavioral	Feminist therapy
Cognitive–behavioral	Relational therapy
Drug therapy	

an individual therapist may be sexist and introduce his or her bias into the therapy. Behavior therapists need to be aware of this so that any value judgments will be impartial for females and males.

Cognitive–Behavioral Therapy.   This approach has largely replaced behavior therapy, yet combines aspects of behavioral principles. Therapist and patient identify maladaptive or dysfunctional behaviors and maladaptive thought patterns. The cognitive approach is to focus on restructuring the patient's dysfunctional thoughts, and the behavioral approach applies principles of learning behavior to eliminate maladaptive behaviors and substitute adaptive and functional behaviors. As with behavior therapy, there is nothing inherently sexist in cognitive–behavioral therapy, although, as in behavioral therapy, a therapist could introduce gender schema bias into the treatment.

Drug Therapy.   Although this section is concerned with psychotherapies, it is necessary to include some mention of drug therapy, which is becoming an increasingly important part of the treatment of mental disorders. We know that even when women and men present the same symptoms and receive the same psychiatric diagnosis, women are still more likely than men to have medications (e.g., antidepressants) prescribed as part of their therapy. As critical as drug treatments appear to be in the management of psychiatric disorders, they have historically been viewed as paternalistic and as dismissive responses to women's distress. We need to guard against this practice and assure that medications are prescribed appropriately for women with mental disorders. (See Chapter 13 for additional discussion of the problem.)

Therapies for Women.   In light of the concerns about bias in traditional therapies and the consequent problems that they may have for women, feminist groups have made therapists and other concerned groups aware of the need to develop therapies that meet the specific needs of women. Three alternatives are currently available: nonsexist therapy, feminist therapy, and relational therapy.

Nonsexist Therapy.   The *nonsexist* approach contends that both women and men be treated alike. Indi-

vidual needs and abilities should guide a person's choices, rather than gender stereotypes (Worrell & Remer, 1992). According to Matlin (1996), nonsexist goals can be used with almost any therapeutic approach except for traditional Freudian analysis. From a variety of sources, Matlin (1996) has identified a group of the basic principles of nonsexist therapy. They are presented in Box 12.3.

Feminist Therapy.   For feminist therapy, the principles of nonsexist treatment, although necessary for therapy with women, are not enough. The feminist therapy approach contains two important parts: (1) inequalities perpetuated by society are responsible for shaping women's behavior, so the personal has also become the political, and (2) therapists should not be more powerful than their clients in the therapy relationship. These two basic components of feminist therapy have been used to develop additional major principles for feminist therapy (see Box 12.4). The first nine concern the relationship between society and the individual woman; principles 10 to 14 address the power relationships between the client and therapist.

Interest in feminist therapy has grown in the United States and has spread to England. It will surely increase in popularity as its theory and practice become more available in the literature. There is some evidence for the effectiveness of feminist therapy in diverse groups. Chaplin (1988) and Boyd-Franklin (1987) have reported the dramatic changes that feminist therapy can bring to individual women and how feelings of trust and sharing can develop in group therapy. McGrath, Keita, Strickland, and Russo (1990) and Johnson (1976) carried out studies of clients who had received feminist therapy. They found that the clients were as satisfied with their progress as those receiving traditional therapy. In another study by Marecek, Kravetz, and Finn (1979), feminist therapy was found to be just as effective for feminist and nonfeminist clients, in contrast to traditional therapy, which was judged to be less effective for feminist than for nonfeminist clients.

Feminist therapy has had a great impact on the therapists as well as on their clients. Other therapists consider possibilities of feminist therapy principles for therapy with men (Matlin, 1996). Mainstream psy-

Box 12.3

Principles of Nonsexist Therapy

1. Sexism is both pervasive and subtle in our society.
2. Therapists should be aware of their own values, particularly as they might relate to sexism.
3. Therapists should be aware of recent research on the psychology of women.
4. Clients should make decisions about their behavior according to what is best for themselves, instead of what is traditionally considered appropriate for members of their gender.
5. Clients should be viewed as individuals, rather than as men or women. Thus, marriage should not be considered better for women than for men, and women should not be expected to differ from men in characteristics such as assertiveness and tenderness.
6. Therapists should not use the power of their position to subtly shape women toward more feminine behavior.

7. Therapists should not use gender-biased testing instruments.
8. Therapists should not use language derogatory to women (including masculine generic terms such as "man" and "he," as well as infantilizing language).
9. Clients have the right to make their own decisions about sexual preference.
10. In general, nonsexist therapists do not explore how society often prevents clients from pursuing non-traditional choices.

(Maracek & Kravetz, 1977; Rawlings & Carter, 1977; Travis, 1988; Worrell & Remer, 1992)

Source: Excerpt from *The Psychology of Women* (3rd ed.) (p. 480), by Margaret W. Matlin. Copyright © 1996 by Holt, Rinehart and Winston. Reprinted by permission of the publisher.

chology journals frequently discuss gender issues in therapy, such as articles by Denmark, Novick, and Pinto (1996) about making psychology more sensitive to gender and diversity and by Ader and Johnson (1994) on reducing gender bias in research.

Relational Therapy. Members of the Stone Center at Wellesley College and the Jean Baker Miller Training Institute have worked together to develop another therapy model to help women recognize their relational needs. Relational theory is considered a source for the empowerment of women. This group began to look at the dependency of women in a new way. Instead of seeing dependency as a basis for their problems, they reevaluated it and gave it a new interpretation as relationship skills: sensitivity, empathy, and care of others. The group saw these skills as valuable not only to a women's development but also to society as a whole. These skills develop during child rearing, when "little girls are brought up to be like their mother, with a capacity for caretaking, empathy, and relationship built into their self-definition. Little boys

on the other hand, are taught to be as different from their mother as possible. Encouraged to be more autonomous and self-sufficient, men are discouraged from relating to others and become threatened by closeness" (Miller, 1976). The Stone Center group has demonstrated how empathy, mutual empowerment, and dependency can be valuable in treating several disorders. These include posttraumatic stress disorder, depression, anxiety, self-destructive behavior, and other problems that interfere with an individual's ability to function. Johnson and Ferguson, in their book *Trusting Ourselves: The Sourcebook on the Psychology of Women* (1990), expressed the opinion that the Stone Center's work was a comprehensive profemale psychological theory that could rival the promale perspective of Freud.

Relational therapy has been criticized on several grounds and questioned. There are reservations about glorifying a women's relational skills and creating a type of female chauvinism. Another criticism concerns placing such importance on women's nurturing and relational behaviors that it might reinforce the old

BOX 12.4

Principles of Feminist Therapy, 1–14

1. Feminist therapists believe that women have been assigned an inferior status because they have less political and economic power than men. The main source of women's problems is social rather than personal.
2. Clients learn that they have been taught "socially appropriate" behaviors, but these behaviors may not actually be ideal.
3. Society should be changed to be less sexist; women should not be encouraged to adjust to a sexist society.
4. Society may have encouraged the client not to value herself, but she has definite strengths that can be used to help her define and solve problems.
5. The focus on society as the root of women's problems should not be used as an excuse to escape individual responsibility; women must take charge of their own lives.
6. Women must work toward economic and psychological independence, and their relationship with other women and men should be marked by equality in personal power.
7. Inequalities with respect to ethnicity, age, sexual preference, economics, and disabilities should all be addressed; gender is not the only inequality.
8. Many clients experience the long-term psychological consequences of violence and sexual abuse.
9. Other women should not be seen as the enemy; they can often provide valuable emotional support. However, men are not necessarily the enemy either; if we label all men as villains, we simply reverse the discrimination.
10. Whenever possible, the power should be divided equally between the client and the therapist; if women clients are placed in subordinate roles in therapy, the situation simply echoes women's inferior status in society.
11. Throughout therapy, clients are encouraged to become more self-confident and independent and to develop skills to help themselves.
12. Feminist therapists share information about their own life experiences, further reducing the power differential.
13. The therapist believes that the client is her own best expert on herself; clients do not need to defer to the "authority" of the therapist.
14. Group therapy is often used to emphasize clients' power and to minimize the therapist's power.

(Brown, 1990; Maracek & Hare-Mustin, 1991; Maracek & Kravetz, 1977; Rawlings & Carter, 1977; Travis, 1988; Walker, 1990; Worrell & Remer, 1992)

Source: Excerpt from *The Psychology of Women* (3rd ed.) (pp. 481–482), by Margaret W. Matlin, 1996. Copyright © 1996 by Holt, Rinehart and Winston. Reprinted by permission of the publisher.

---

concept of separate domains for men and women. There is also the question of whether relational therapy is useful for women of color or different ethnic groups. On the other hand, Westkott (1997) supports this new model for women's psychology because it challenges widespread and standardized models of psychological functioning in which male bias is evident. The Stone Center relational model assumes a "distinct female psychology that has its own unique merits" (p. 366). Westkott argues that female attributes have been undervalued and neglected although they are positive human traits that all people need to develop.

The Stone Center is exploring the implications of this new therapy for clinical practice and how it will affect issues of power for women. Relational theory appears to be a new paradigm for women's psychological health and functioning. Jordan (1997) feels that the Stone Center model is not one of *self-development* but is about *relational-development*, which will succeed in empowering women. With more experience with different groups in the United States and other countries, we should be able to determine the effectiveness of relational therapy in revaluing women and as a source of empowerment.

DIVERSITY ISSUES, POVERTY, AND STRESSES OF IMMIGRATION

The new directions for women must be expanded to include the needs of racial and ethnic minority groups, as well as those of poor women. These groups have not had the access to mental health services that middle- and upper-class women have had and are invisible in models of mental health.

In addressing the needs of these women, the therapist must consider the extent of the identification of the woman with her racial–ethnic group, as well as how integrated she has become into U.S. society. Feminist therapists, as well as other therapists, need to learn more about the cultures that their clients come from and the degree to which their life-style is representative of the mores and philosophy of that culture. Clients may want to select a therapist of their own background with whom they will feel more comfortable, but at present there are few therapists of color. Although many therapists will work with women of color, there is often the problem of language. For ex-

ample, Asian clients may not be proficient enough in English to express their feelings and concerns; there are similar concerns for Latinas (Chisholm, 1996; Shum, 1996).

An additional consideration for training more therapists of color is to understand and help clients to cope with the stresses that are inevitable when people emigrate to another culture. Unless the new immigrant has relatives or friends in the United States, she will feel isolated, lonely, and often frightened, especially if she has difficulty with English. If she is a single mother and has children to support, the experience may well have profound psychological consequences. Even if the whole family immigrates, stresses are inevitable—new regulations to learn, fears about money and jobs, all contributing to internal conflicts as well. It is important that we encourage women of color to become psychotherapists. The need for these therapists will be even more evident as diversity in the United States continues to increase in the twenty-first century.

Author note: Many mental health issues not specifically addressed here are covered in chapters throughout the book.

SUMMARY

We began this chapter by reviewing the historical and cultural perceptions and biases of mental illness that have existed over time, especially toward women. Although many changes have taken place and others have been initiated, we should ask what progress has actually been made in the treatment of mental illness.

According to Blumenthal (1996), over the last six years the United States has finally begun to focus on women's health, on both mental and addictive disorders as well as physical health. There is no doubt that the media have played an important part in bringing health concerns before the U.S. public. Much credit, too, belongs to the women and men in the U.S. Congress who were seriously concerned about the lack of attention not only to health problems specific to women, but also to the sex and gender differences in

disorders that affect both women and men. Finally, the scientific community has started to study more rigorously the differences between women and men in mental health and addictive disorders, in addition to physical problems.

Eating disorders, which primarily affect women at all socioeconomic levels and across race and ethnicity, are also increasing in men. Eating disorders are increasingly the focus of epidemiological and scientific study. Such disorders are now considered to be a major public health problem. The death rates from eating disorders, especially anorexia, have doubled in the last 20 years and are now one of the highest reported for any mental disorder. We have also made progress in evaluating many of the psychological and cultural factors that are highly associated with the onset of anorexia and bulimia and some of the recent treatment modalities that are in practice. The U.S. government is working with several private agencies to organize a nationwide campaign to educate the public to recognize anorexia and bulimia and be aware of the avenues of help available, with the goal of significantly decreasing their incidence.

We have also begun to make some progress in treating depression. More data are now available to show that the incidence of depression is rising in younger people. Again, depression occurs across all socioeconoimic levels and across racial and ethnic groups, with more attention being paid to new immigrant groups with acculturation problems. Although, as indicated earlier, gender has long been recognized as a critical variable in depression, it, too, has not been rigorously studied. We have been involved in bringing the issue of sex and gender bias in depression to the forefront of research (Sechzer et al., 1994). Other groups have also studied gender in various aspects of depression and have made important contributions to progress in this area. Now that the U.S. government has mandated that both women and men be studied in disorders affecting both genders and that data be both compared and analyzed separately, we can look forward to more data about earlier recognition and appropriate treatment, both medical and psychotherapeutic, of women and men with this disorder.

The question of which therapies are appropriate for women, including women of different ethnic and racial groups, has also begun to be studied. The evolution of feminist, nonsexist therapy, and relational therapy is not only receiving much attention here in the United States, but is also being considered by therapists in other countries. More data are needed to evaluate the results of these therapies and compare them to the "standard" therapies that have been assumed to be appropriate for both men and women.

Finally, psychology has begun to focus on diversity, poverty, and stresses of immigration. Psychology has increasingly come to recognize the importance of knowledge by therapists about the different racial and ethnic cultures that compose an impressive proportion of the U.S. population. Although many more studies are needed, we have crossed an important threshold in this area.

Although psychology and affiliated disciplines have already made encouraging progress in the way that we study and care for women with mental health disorders, many more questions need to be answered. There is still an amazing lack of research by behavioral scientists on the effect of sex and gender in normal mental development. Coupled with this is the task of recognizing who is or who will be vulnerable to developing certain mental disorders and how to prevent their occurrence or reduce their severity. This is a huge task because it involves many interacting factors.

KEY TERMS

Anorexia nervosa (p. 385)
Behavior therapy (p. 395)
Bulimia nervosa (p. 386)
Cognitive–behavioral therapy (p. 388)
Depression (p. 389)

Emaciation (p. 388)
Endogenous depression (p. 389)
Exogenous depression (p. 389)
Feminization of poverty (p. 390)
Neurasthenia (p. 382)

Premenstrual syndrome (PMS) (p. 392)
Systematic desensitization (p. 395)

DISCUSSION QUESTIONS

1. Do you know anyone who is or was anorexic or bulimic? Did you observe any of the behaviors described in this chapter? What factors do you think were involved in their developing these eating disorders? What treatment was most effective for them?

2. Many people who are anorexic or bulimic do not understand the meaning of the behaviors that they are practicing, whether they are restricting food, binging, or purging. How would you go about helping someone that you suspected was anorexic or bulimic to realize that they had a serious disorder? What strategies would you use to help that person accept the problem and get help?

3. If you should need psychotherapy at some future date, have you thought about the kind of therapist that you would prefer, given the criteria for selecting a therapist in this chapter? Would you only see a therapist of your own gender? What do you think are the advantages and disadvantages of seeing a therapist of your same gender?

4. Discuss the characteristics of depression. What factors do you think would be important in predicting whether a woman or man will become depressed? Are these factors different for men and women?

5. It has been suggested that male physicians should not treat female patients because, for females, the psychotherapeutic relationship is just another power relationship in which the female must submit to the dominant male authority figure. Do you agree with this? If so, why? If not, why?

6. What kind of background and training do you feel a therapist will need to treat women of a different race or ethnicity? Must the therapist be matched with a client who shares the same race or ethnicity?

SUGGESTED READINGS

Blechman, E. A., & K. D. Brownell (Eds.). (1997). Behavioral medicine and women: A comprehensive handbook. New York: Guilford Press.

Brownell, K., & Fairburn, C. (Eds.). (1995). *Eating disorders and obesity: A comprehensive handbook.* New York: Guilford Press.

Mirkin, M. P. (Ed.). (1994). *Women in context: Toward a feminist reconstruction of psychotherapy.* New York: Guilford Press.

Nolan-Hoeksema, S. (1990). *Sex differences in depression.* Stanford, CA: Stanford University Press.

Pederson, P. (Ed.). (1985). *Handbook of cross cultural counseling and psychotherapy.* Westport, CT: Greenwood Press.

Tobach, E., & Rosoff, B. (Eds.). (1994). *Genes and gender series, Vol. 7. Challenging racism and sexism: Alternatives to genetic explanations.* New York: Feminist Press.

Ussher, J. M., & Nicolson, P. (Eds.). (1992). *Gender issues in clinical psychology.* London: Routledge.

CHAPTER 13

PHYSICAL HEALTH: ISSUES ACROSS THE LIFE-SPAN

[W]omen's health care has always mirrored a male-dominated world.
—Ann Douglas Wood and G. Barker-Benfield

As long as the course of scientific thought was judged to be exclusively determined by its own logical and empirical necessities, there could be no place for any signature, male or otherwise, in the system of knowledge.
—Evelyn Fox Keller

During the late eighteenth and nineteenth centuries the medical profession became organized as a profession along traditional masculine lines. This was particularly damaging to women healers and tended to undermine or exclude traditional "female" characteristics from "official" medicine.
—Ann Dally

The following issues are now undeniable truths: Women will constitute the larger population and will be most susceptible to diseases in the future; Overall, women have worse health than men; Certain health problems are more prevalent in women than in men; Certain health problems are unique to women or affect women differently than they do men.
—National Institutes of Health–Office of Research on Women's Health

Medical textbooks have presented a view of women as neurotic complainers, fostering the assumption in physicians that the symptoms a woman describes may be "all in her head" and handled, not with diagnostic testing, but with tranquilizers. This was to become deadly to women in the AIDS epidemic.
—Gena Corea

Whether we read a newspaper, browse through a magazine, or turn on the television, we will surely find a headline or report on a new advance or finding in medicine that will affect our health. For instance, a study of more than 22,000 physicians showed a beneficial effect of an aspirin every other day on coronary heart disease (Steering Committee of the Physician's Health Study Research Group, 1989). That sounds terrific! However, on reading the details of the report it seems that no women were included in the study, even though cardiovascular disease is the leading cause of death for both men and women (Wenger, Speroff, & Packard, 1993). Two years after the Steering Committee report, Manson et al., (1991) suggested that aspirin *may* have a similar effect on women. Finally, a more definitive study showed that aspirin does have a similar effect on women (Rich-Edwards, Manson, Hennekens, & Buring, 1995). Another study investigated the role of estrogen in prevention of heart disease, but only in men. Healy called this practice the Yentl syndrome (Healy, 1991; NIH, 1992). An earlier review of women's health issues by Rodin and Ickovics (1990) provided still another example. These authors pointed out that, even when women are the primary users of a particular class of drugs, the ma-

jority of research studies either did not include women or included them in small numbers. When women were included, it was often in the late stages of the study, so long-term effects could not be determined (Abramson, 1990; Palca, 1990).

Why have women been ignored in research on diseases or disorders that affect both genders? Why has it been, and often still is, assumed that there are no differences in etiology, symptoms, or treatment responses between men and women? This an extension of what we have already seen in other chapters in this book; women have generally been considered inferior to men and unimportant. In the case of health research, women have been understudied and sex and gender not considered important variables in the advancement of scientific and medical knowledge. Such gender stereotyping has permeated all phases of the life-span of both females and males and, as we will see, has affected the physical health of both. As described earlier in this book, these stereotyped attitudes toward men and women, derived from mythological, religious, or sociocultural constructions of women and men in many societies, have also strongly influenced medical research and the medical community's treatment of men and women. Moreover, medical care and treatment concerning health problems, whether developing during infancy, adolescence, adulthood, or old age, show marked differences for females and males, not only in physical health but also in mental health.

Why should psychologists be concerned about physical health? Is there really a mind–body relationship? Does the state of our health affect our mental processes and our behavior, and if so, how? Does the mind affect our health, and how? We will see that our state of physical health has psychological effects, many of which are related to issues of gender. We will also see that strategies for promoting health and well-being or for coping with physical problems involve behavioral changes in attitudes and practices.

In addressing these issues, we will define health and well-being and how gender stereotypes of men and women affect their health. We will explore the sociocultural background and history of these stereotyped attitudes, particularly by the medical profession, and how they have affected health research and the care and treatment of men and women. A review of research studies concerning major disorders affecting both men and women will highlight the extent of gender bias in research and practice and the importance of taking a gendered perspective on health. We will describe ongoing attempts to change medical care in Western societies, as well as preventive health strategies.

THE POLITICS OF ILLNESS

Victorian Times

A Male-Dominated World.   The neglect of women's health problems has a long history. In the last decade, many reviews of the literature on medical care and the diseases of women have appeared. This has come from the efforts of feminist groups, increasing interest in women's studies, and the efforts of women and men in the U.S. Congress. According to Wood (1973) and Barker-Benfield (1976), "women's health care has always mirrored a male-dominated world" (see Brieger, 1984, p. 153). They perceived Victorian physicians "as maintaining a *status quo* by keeping women subordi-

nate in domestic and maternal roles" (p. 153). Thus, two disorders that arose in the nineteenth century, *hysteria* and *neurasthenia,* have been thought to be the response to this male-dominated world.

Hysteria.   From the late 1800s to the early 1900s, a new disease appeared in England and the United States and was subsequently labeled *hysteria.* Affected women would faint or throw their limbs about without control, their backs would arch, and their entire bodies would become rigid. In many cases, paralysis of a whole body part, such as one hand, arm, leg, or foot, was common. Such hysterical people lost their voice and appetite, screamed, and at times laughed uncontrollably (Dally, 1991; Ehrenreich & English, 1981).

Hysteria spread throughout Europe and was reported to affect women almost exclusively. In England, it was an ideal disease for the doctors, for it was never fatal and required endless amounts of medical attention. Physicians began to suspect that these symptoms of hysteria were only a clever charade, because there were few reports of these attacks when women were alone. Doctors did insist, however, that hysteria was a disease of the uterus (hysteria is derived from the Greek *hystera,* meaning womb or uterus). As the prevalence of the disease rose, doctors came to label every incident of a woman's nontraditional behavior as "hysterical" (Dally, 1991; Ehrenreich & English, 1981).

Rich women in the United States routinely frequented health spas and saw elegant specialists like Silas Weir Mitchell for these problems. Women who were not as wealthy saw family physicians, took patent medicines like Lydia Pinkham's tonic or Swamp Root that were supposed to cure all manner of diseases (Fourcroy, 1994), and later resorted to popular advice books written by physicians on female health. The belief that held from the mid-nineteenth century to the early twentieth century was that the normal state for women was to be sick. "Even though women were treated for diseases of the stomach, liver, heart, etc., these diseases will be found to be sympathetic reactions or symptoms of one disease, a disease of the womb" (Dirix, 1869, pp. 23–24).

Neurasthenia.   While physicians struggled with attempts at understanding the symptoms of hysteria, another disorder, called *neurasthenia* (nerve weakness), appeared, with a vague syndrome of physical symptoms engulfing middle- and upper-class populations. Neurasthenia first appeared in the United States, and was described in 1868 by George Beard, but soon spread throughout England and Europe. In general, this was not seen as a disease in the medical sense, but actually appeared to be a way of life. It was the way these women were expected to live their lives, a way that predisposed them to continue to live as society demanded them to. Neurasthenia encompassed a wide range of symptoms, some of which included blushing, vertigo, headaches and neuralgia, insomnia, anorexia, and depression (Showalter, 1985). The delicate but wealthy lady, dependent on her husband, set the "sexual romanticist ideal of femininity for women of all classes" (Ehrenreich & English, 1981, p. 330). The problem was that marriage for these women had become a "sexuo-economic relation in which women performed sexual and reproductive duties [in exchange] for financial support" (Ehrenreich & English, 1981, p. 331).

Physicians treating affected women found that female functions were inherently pathological and concluded that menstruation was a serious hazard for affected women. Pregnant women were considered to be indisposed throughout their nine-month pregnancy. During pregnancy, a woman was cautioned to avoid sights that could shock her, any type of intellectual stimulation, anger, and lustful thoughts. She should not even smell alcohol or smoke on her husband's breath. These requirements were to be rigidly carried out to prevent the baby from developing a deformity or from becoming stunted during gestation. After childbirth and child rearing, all a woman could look forward to was her menopause, portrayed in the literature of the time as the "death of the woman in the woman" (Ehrenreich & English, 1981, p. 335). Physicians came to "establish" that women's sickness is innate and stems from the possession of a uterus and

ovaries. Furthermore, a woman's personality and her behavior were seen as dominated by her ovaries, which could then be blamed for all possible female disorders.

Medical Treatments for Women

Ovariotomy.   In the latter part of the eighteenth century, treatment for these female disorders gave way to drastic surgery such as ovariotomy or the surgical removal of the ovaries, and even clitoridectomy, the removal of the clitoris, the female organ analogous to the male penis (Dally, 1991). Ovariotomy (now known as oöphorectomy) was performed not only for gynecological symptoms, but also for the purpose of controlling psychological disorders. In 1872, Robert Battey, an American surgeon, performed the first ovariotomy in the United States on a 23-year-old woman for relief of her nervous (psychological) symptoms, menstrual dysfunction, and convulsions. This procedure would in a short time become the "cure" for epilepsy, as well as all kinds of insanity. By 1906, it was estimated that 150,000 women had been subjected to this procedure to treat more than just ovarian disease. After 1906, the purpose of the procedure for psychological disorders was finally discredited (Dally, 1991).

Clitoridectomy.   Although clitoridectomy is an old cultural rite in many African and Middle Eastern cultures, it came to be a new fashion in England and later in the United States during the late nineteenth century (see Chapters 4 and 11 for a further discussion of clitoridectomy—female genital mutilation). In England the prevailing attitude toward women was that the clitoris was a source of psychological disturbance, and the obvious solution was to remove it, hence this procedure. Clitoridectomy removed a woman's sexual pleasure and restricted her sexuality to reproduction. The procedure was first performed in the 1860s by Isaac Baker Brown, a prominent British surgeon. Clitoridectomy was performed to *cure* nymphomania, hysteria, epilepsy (then believed to be caused by masturbation), and insanity. The use of clitoridectomy increased for a time, but by 1867 Baker Brown was under attack. Although many physicians considered the surgery to be "quackery," the main complaint was not the procedure or the rationale for the procedure, but that Baker Brown performed it to excess and without suitable permission. It was then discredited in England, but Baker Brown came to the United States, where he found much support. Clitoridectomy to control sexuality became very popular in the United States until about 1925 (Dally, 1991). The last officially reported clitoridectomy procedure in the United States was carried out in 1948 on a five-year-old girl in order to cure her masturbation (Ehrenreich & English, 1981). In 1996, this procedure was made illegal in the United States but is still being performed because some immigrants from other countries adhere to this practice (see Chapters 4 and 11).

Health Status of Women

Certainly, women of the nineteenth and early twentieth centuries were considerably sicker than women are today. They wore heavy, tight-laced corsets in the style of the day, so tight that in some cases the pelvic organs and liver were displaced and the ribs fractured. Another risk for women, particularly young women, was tuberculosis. The death rate was very high. The health of women who were needy or impoverished received little to no attention from the medical community despite high rates of childbearing diseases and tuberculosis. Their general health was poor and they were therefore more susceptible to childbearing diseases and tuberculosis.

But the medical profession in general maintained that it was affluent women who were the most delicate and in need of special medical care. Attitudes of society had made the middle- and upper-class women sickly; working women, on the other hand, were supposed to be robust, just as they were supposed to be coarse and immodest. Similarly, Black women who worked in middle- and upper-class homes were also considered to be in good health. In an interesting comment, at odds with this position, Brieger (1980), who has reviewed the literature of this period, feels that some of this writing has "suffered from a feminist ideology based on a conspiracy theory of history"

(p. 153), for example, a conspiracy of male physicians against their female patients. However, she makes an important point that men too complained of the same neglect during the nineteenth century. This attitude toward working-class and poor women, both White and Black, was apparently generalized to working-class and poor men, so these groups also received little medical care.

With all these treatments for neurasthenia and hysteria, their real cause continued to elude physicians. While the conflict between hysterical and neurasthenic women and their physicians about the cause and treatment of these disorders and their symptoms remained unresolved, Sigmund Freud in Vienna was developing a treatment that would eventually remove the disease from the pelvis and reproductive system and from the gynecologist's control, to elevate it to a mental disorder. Freud's insight into hysteria and with it an understanding of women's resentment and rebelliousness about their forced way of life helped psychologists and psychiatrists replace medical specialists and gynecologists as the dominant experts in women's lives. Still, for decades, physicians would continue to view menstruation, pregnancy, and menopause as physical diseases and intellectual liabilities (Dally, 1991).

Although women's intelligence and abilities would begin to be accepted, many of these prejudices about women and their health status, engendered by the medical society's stereotypes, would remain and be sustained to the present day. These prejudices then became part of the medical and scientific research enterprise, which began to expand after World War II when the National Institutes of Health and other federal agencies were established.

WOMEN, MEN, AND HEALTH

Physical Health and Well-Being

Health Defined.   Health is a highly desired state. In 1973, Milton Rokeach began work on a study of values. Participants in the study were required to rank various states of being, such as wealth, power, and so on. Rokeach had originally planned to use health as one of these values. He found, however, that there was essentially no variance with regard to health since it was ranked first by almost everyone (Kaplan, Sallis, & Patterson, 1993). Even though health is such an important and cherished state, there have been many different approaches toward understanding precisely what health means. Many definitions are negative, such as health is the "absence of disease" or "not being sick." Other definitions have included only the physical aspects (Kaplan et al., 1993). Are physical health and well-being just the absence of a disease, disorder, or injury, or are there other components? Soon after the World Health Organization was established by the United Nations, it defined health as "a complete state of *physical, mental,* and *social well-being* and not merely the absence of disease or illness" (World Health Organization, 1948). This definition implies that being healthy involves various dimensions other than the absence of disease or infirmity. In considering the particular aspects of health, Antonovsky (1987) has suggested that, rather than viewing health and sickness as separate concepts, we should view them as overlapping ones and with degrees of wellness and illness. He has proposed a model of an illness–wellness continuum in which a *high level of wellness* is at one end and *premature death* at the other. Antonovsky feels that, rather than giving most of our attention to what makes people ill, we should instead give our attention to what makes people stay well. Thus, health indicates a *positive* state of physical, mental, and social well-being.

Gender-Role Stereotypes and the Consequences for Physical Health

There is an established relationship between gender and health. Stresses and pressures on a woman's and man's well-being are imposed by the general culture of which they are a product. Seventy years ago, Karen Horney wrote on the subject of a masculine civilization. Westkott (1998) has interpreted Horney's writing as referring to "the presumption within Western culture of male superiority and female inferiority" (p. 14) and the cultural assumptions and practices re-

sponsible for bringing these attitudes about. Even with the changes brought about across 70 years, the same concept of male superiority and female inferiority has persisted. Psychologists and other social scientists have chronicled the ways in which these attitudes and practices have affected girls' and women's mental and physical health regardless of their cultural backgrounds or race or ethnicity (Helstrom & Blechman, 1998; Westkott, 1998).

More women than men suffer from physiological and psychological disorders, with gender differences reported in the incidence of many specific disorders (for psychological disorders, see Chapter 12). On the other hand, even though life expectancy for both males and females has increased during this century, life expectancy still favors women. In fact, since 1900 this difference in life expectancy between men and women has consistently widened (Harrison, Chin, & Ficarrotto, 1995). How do we explain this?

Many of these differences have been associated with the perceived male gender role. The disparate life-styles may be an important component of these differences in physical health between men and women. Whereas women seek help frequently, men tend to delay seeking medical help in an effort to avoid being considered a "sissy" and to be stoic. Taking time off from work to recuperate or to see a physician may mean more financial loss for men than for women, because women's positions and salaries are generally inferior to men (Reddy, Fleming, & Adesso, 1992). In 1979, Scarf reported that about 60 percent of all medical appointments were made by women. This gender difference in medical visits does not appear in childhood, but increases in adolescence and then in adulthood. Even excluding physician visits for pregnancy and childbirth, women still have a higher incidence of physician visits. The reason for this difference is not clear. One explanation is that women may be more vulnerable and develop more diseases that not only require medical care but longer medical care. Although men show a higher incidence of fatal chronic disease, women have higher rates of prescription drug use and illness from acute disorders such as respiratory infections, infectious and parasitic infections, and chronic conditions, such as arthritis, disorders of bone or cartilage, anemias, or varicosities. There is also a small gender difference in medical service utilization with more women than men using such services (Reddy et al., 1992; Verbrugge, 1979).

However, there is a marked difference in diagnosis and treatment of the physical complaints of men and women. The evident sexism in society in general and in medical and other professions sustains this bias. Physicians may show gender bias in their treatment of women and attribute a woman's physical complaints to psychogenic rather than organic causes. The reverse appears true for men (Fidell, 1980, 1984; Wallston, DeVellis, & Wallston, 1983). This may be one reason that mood-altering drugs are prescribed for women more than twice as often as for men. The fact that these drugs do not ameliorate women's physical symptoms may result in more frequent visits to their physicians for the same unrelieved symptomatology. Regardless of the frequency of physician's visits, women may live longer but they will not be as healthy as men (NIH-ORWH, 1992). We shall see this in our discussion of bias in specific health problems for women.

Gender Comparisons in Morbidity and Mortality

The existing scientific paradigm that governs health research relevant to both men and women, including treatment, is based on a male model. The failure to recognize sex and gender as important variables in health research is a continuation of attitudes toward women by the medical and apparently now by the scientific community. Implicit in this male model has been the assumption that with the obvious exception of disorders affecting only women, there are no differences in etiology, symptoms, or treatment responses between males and females in disorders affecting both genders. Using this model, basic and clinical studies have usually been carried out with White males and results generalized to females as well as minority

groups, often without any rationale. The preference for male subjects in research is not limited to human participants; we see the same preference in animal studies, in which the predominant sex studied is also male. Data from male animal studies are also generalized to female animals of the same and different species and to humans. Findings from basic animal research frequently form the basis for human clinical studies (Sechzer, Denmark, & Rabinowitz, 1993; Sechzer, Zmitrovich, & Denmark, 1985; Sechzer et al., 1994). Until the end of the 1980s, the importance of sex and gender as significant variables in research was totally neglected. Because of the dire consequences of such neglect, this issue has now attracted the concerted attention of the public, government agencies, and the medical and scientific communities (Sechzer, Griffin, & Pfafflin, 1994).

By the end of the 1980s, national statistics pointed to a crisis in women's health. It was generally known that heart disease, cancer, and stroke were the major causes of death for men and women, but the number of women who die each year from these diseases was startling. According to Wenger, Spenoff, and Packard (1993), 500,000 women die annually of cardiovascular disease. By 1991, the number of deaths of women from cancer was more than 230,000 and still ranks first or second as the cause of death across age groups. Four types of cancer account for about 70 percent of all cancers in women: breast, colon–rectal, lung, and uterine (gynecological cancers) (Anderson, 1998). For women, cancer is the leading cause of death ranking first or second across all age groups. Breast cancer alone account for 32 percent of cancers. Breast cancer is higher for white women than black women, but survival is much lower for black women. Since 1980 there has been a "2% increase in incidence" (Anderson, 1998, p. 570). For these and other diseases relevant to both genders, the male was and still is the model because most biomedical data about causes, manifestation, and treatments of these diseases are derived from studies of males and the research generalized to females (Report of the National Institutes of Health: Opportunities for Research on Women's Health, 1991; Sechzer et al., 1992; Sechzer et al.,

1994). Box 13.1 presents additional data on the report of the NIH-Office of Research on Women's Health. The NIH report also describes the health problems of ethnic and racially diverse women and their children. Box 13.2 describes the findings.

STRESS

Stress and Stressors Defined

The ability to avoid, escape, or control stress is critical to the health and well-being of humans and animals. Sometime in the past we have all been in situations in

which we have experienced stress, whether preparing for a test, missing a train, or trying to handle job responsibilities and at the same time meeting the demands of one's teen-age children.

Stress has been defined as a negative emotional experience that is usually associated with physiological, psychological, environmental, and behavioral changes. How we respond to stress will indicate whether we adapt to some degree to the stressful event, alter it, or fail to adapt. Stress can also be defined as the effect produced by external (physical or environmental) or internal (physiological or psychological) *stressors* (National Research Council, 1992; Rice, 1987). Figure 13.1 on page 412 gives examples of potential stressors. Moreover, stress and an individual's response to it always involve the relationship between the individual and the environment. The individual then makes an assessment (sometimes unconsciously) as to whether she or he can meet the demands of the environmental stressor(s) and make a response. How an individual responds varies according to age, gender, physiological and psychological state, past experience, and genetic profile (Rice, 1987; Taylor, 1995).

As we have noted throughout this book, women are generally subjected to and experience more stress than men. In addition to illness, conditions for women that are particularly stressful include holding low-status jobs, receiving unequal pay for equal and comparable work, juggling careers, family, and household activities, and being the targets of harassment and violence.

Early Contributions

Cannon and the Fight or Flight Response. The historical work on stress will help to provide a basic understanding of this important topic. Walter Cannon and Hans Selye are the two scientists usually associated with early research that helped to elucidate some of the mechanisms of stress. Walter Cannon was the first to describe the **fight or flight response.** He proposed that when an organism perceives a threat (e.g., a woman facing an attacker), the body is rapidly aroused and changes in its internal environment take

Box 13.1_____

Gender Comparisons for Women's Health

Although women will live longer than men, they will be sicker, isolated, and will suffer more from chronic diseases.

In their 1992 report, the National Institutes of Health–Office of Research on Women's Health (NIH-ORWH) studied data from a different perspective and asked whether there were differences in the health of men and women. This group found that health problems specific to women were worsening and that currently science and medicine do not have enough knowledge to reverse this trend. The NIH-ORWH reported the following: (1) Women will constitute the larger population and will be more susceptible to disease in the future; (2) overall, women have worse health than men; (3) certain health problems are more prevalent in women than in men; and (4) certain health problems are unique to women or affect women differently than they do men. Among these findings and those of others are data showing that, throughout their lives, the quality of life for women lags behind that for men. Women's activities are limited by health problems by approximately 25 percent more days each year than are men's activities. Women are bedridden 35 percent more days because of infectious and parasitic diseases, respiratory diseases, digestive conditions, injuries, and other acute conditions. These findings have been upheld even when reproductive problems are removed from the calculations.

Box 13.2
_____

Ethnic and Racial Diversity in Women's Health

The NIH-ORWH 1992 report found that health status varies among the different subgroups of the U.S. population. Although data are lacking for many ethnic and racial subgroups for many health conditions, we know that many conditions and diseases occur with higher frequency in different groups of women.

Death from stroke occurs twice as often in Black women as in White women. The rate of death from coronary disease is higher for Black women than for White women, 172.9 versus 106.6 per 100,000 persons. The rate of death from complications of pregnancy and childbirth is 3.5 times greater for Black than for White women. Ectopic pregnancies are the main cause of pregnancy-related deaths among Black women.

Occurrence of adolescent pregnancies is highest among Blacks (23 percent) and lowest among Asian Americans (6 percent). Birth rate among Black girls under age 15 is seven times higher than for White girls. Systemic lupus erythematosus occurs three times more often in Black women than in White women.

The incidence of breast cancer is lower for Black women than for White women, but death rates from breast cancer are higher for Black women. Rates for lung cancer are higher for White women than for Black women. Black women have the highest incidence of gonorrhea and syphilis.

Although overall incidence of cancer is lower for Hispanic women, certain specific cancer rates are higher. The incidence of cervical cancer among Hispanic women is double that for non-Hispanic White women. Death due to stomach cancer is twice as high for Hispanics as for non-Hispanic Whites.

Among Hispanics, death rates from homicide, AIDS, and perinatal conditions are greater than for Whites. The incidence of tuberculosis for Blacks and Hispanics is four times that of non-Hispanic Whites.

The prevalence of noninsulin-dependent diabetes mellitus (NIDDM) is twice as high among Black women as White women. Hispanics have three times the risk of developing diabetes and greater metabolic severity than non-Hispanic Whites. Prevalence of noninsulin-dependent diabetes mellitus is two to five times higher among Native Americans than among other U.S. populations; 68 percent of Pima Indian women 55 to 64 years of age have noninsulin-dependent diabetes mellitus.

Obesity is a major risk factor for cardiovascular disease, stroke, and other diseases; 44 percent of Black women, 42 percent of Mexican American women, 40 percent of Puerto Rican women, 31 percent of Cuban women, and 24 percent of White women are overweight.

---

place. Heart rate increases; blood pressure, blood sugar, and respiration increase; blood circulating to the skin is decreased, while blood circulating to the muscles increases; and secretion of catecholamines (norepinephrine and dopamine) increases. This physiological response to a stressor mobilizes the organism to attack or to flee—the fight or flight response. Cannon concluded that the fight or flight response is an adaptive one because it enables the organism to respond quickly to the perceived threat. He also reasoned that stress can be harmful because it interferes with emotional and normal physiological functioning and could cause health problems over time. Cannon also proposed that, when the organism is incapable or prevented from making a fight or flight response and

stress is prolonged, its state of physiological arousal is sustained and can form the basis for health problems (Cannon, 1929; Rice, 1987; Taylor, 1995).

Selye and the General Adaptation Syndrome. Hans Selye also made major contributions to the field of stress with his concept of the **general adaptation syndrome.** While Selye was investigating the effects of sex hormones on physiological functioning, he became interested in the stressful impact that these hormones seemed to have. To explore this, Selye exposed rats to different and prolonged stressors, such as extreme cold and induced excessive fatigue. He measured their physiological responses to these stressors. All the stressors evoked the same pattern

FIGURE 13.1   Examples of Potential Stressors

CAUSES OF PHYSIOLOGIC STRESS	CAUSES OF PSYCHOLOGIC STRESS	CAUSES OF ENVIRONMENTAL STRESS
Injury Surgery } Pain[a] Disease Starvation Dehydration	Fear Anxiety Boredom Loneliness Separation	Restraint Noise Odors Habitat Ecology People Other species Chemicals Pheromones

Source: Reprinted, with permission, from *Recognition and Alleviation of Pain and Distress in Laboratory Animals.* Copyright 1992 by the National Academy of Sciences. Courtesy of the National Academy Press, Washington, D.C.

[a]Note that pain is shown as resulting from physiologic stressors. It could also result from environmental stressors (e.g., chemical) and be potentiated by psychologic stressors (e.g., fear).

of response in the rats. The animals developed enlarged adrenal glands coincident with increased amounts of corticosteroids from the cortex (outer layer) of the adrenal glands. The thymus gland and lymph nodes appeared shrunken, and ulcers were produced in the stomach and in the first part of the small intestine, the duodenum. From these observations, Selye (1956) developed his theory of the general adaptation syndrome. He explained that when an organism perceives a stressor, it mobilizes itself for some action. This is effected by increased secretion of corticosteroids by the adrenal glands, which results in activating the **sympathetic nervous system.** Regardless of the situation or the type of stressor, the response will be the same. Under conditions of prolonged stress, the system can become exhausted and physiological resources depleted (Levine, 1985; Selye, 1956; Taylor, 1995).

The importance and influence of both Cannon's and Selye's work is still evident today. They provided a way of defining stress, of identifying both internal and external stressors and the underlying mechanisms that established the foundation for a stress–disease relationship. Although it did not emphasize psycholog-

ical factors, the involvement and importance of psychological responses became evident as research in this field continued. We have learned much about different kinds of stressors, the stress that can result, and the types of responses that they may elicit.

Neutral Stress and Eustress.   Stress might not always be harmful to an individual; it might evoke responses that neither improve nor threaten an individual's well-being. This type of stress is called **neutral stress.** In some cases, environmental alterations or stressors (internal or external) that induce stress may also initiate adaptive responses that have potentially beneficial effects. Such stress is known as **eustress.** Some stress is probably necessary for well-being if adaptation to stressors occurs with a reasonable expenditure of physiological and psychological effort on the part of the individual (Breazile, 1987).

Distress Models and the Appearance of Maladaptive Behaviors.   If stress is prolonged and the individual is unable to respond or adapt adequately to the stress caused by physiological, psychological, or environmental stressors, as displayed in Figure 13.1, she or he may become severely distressed and begin to show **maladaptive behaviors.** However, if the stressors involved are short term and the individual cannot make an appropriate response (to avoid, escape, or control) and displays maladaptive behaviors, these responses do not usually, but may, result in long-term harmful results.

Two models of distress have been proposed. In the first, *distress induced by pain* (Figure 13.2), the relation is shown between the sensation of pain and the emotional or concomitant affect from the threshold of pain to the tolerance level of pain and then the point of intolerance. The individual can only adapt to a certain extent as pain increases and then will begin to show maladaptive behaviors. This can be seen in the column under "Behaviors" where the individual can adapt until the "Intolerance" level is reached.

The second model of distress is that of *distress not induced by pain.* As shown in Figure 13.3, stressors of various types (psychological, physiological, or environmental) will bring about a state of stress.

FIGURE 13.2 Model of Distress Induced by Pain
Note the relationship between sensory discriminative component and affective emotional component. Sensory component of pain ranges from threshold to tolerance and then intolerance. In affective components, intensity of pain can proceed from a state of comfort to distress. Arrow paths indicate flow from sensation to affect to behaviors. This is the normal case, but under some conditions, behaviors can influence affect and thus modify the sensation. Double arrows emphasize that behavior is primarily influenced by affect. (Direction of flow indicates schematized concept only, not neural pathways.)

Source: Reprinted, with permission, from *Recognition and Alleviation of Pain and Distress in Laboratory Animals.* Copyright 1992 by the National Academy of Sciences. Courtesy of the National Academy Press, Washington, D.C.

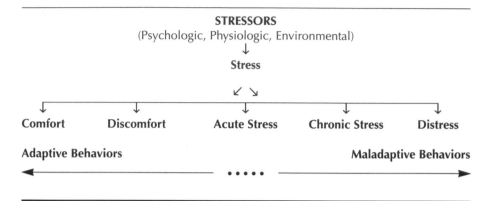

STRESSORS
(Psychologic, Physiologic, Environmental)
↓
Stress

↙ ↘

| ↓ | ↓ | ↓ | ↓ | ↓ |
| Comfort | Discomfort | Acute Stress | Chronic Stress | Distress |

Adaptive Behaviors   **Maladaptive Behaviors**

◄─────────────────── • • • • • ─────────────────────►

FIGURE 13.3   Model of Distress Not Induced by Pain
Stressors, leading to stress, can initiate various states in an individual ranging from
comfort to distress. Adaptative stress will not interfere with an individual's state of
comfort or well-being. When experiencing distress, maladaptive behaviors can result,
varying in range and severity with increasing distress.
Source: Reprinted, with permission, from *Recognition and Alleviation of Pain and Distress in Laboratory Animals.* Copyright 1992 by the National Academy of Sciences. Courtesy of the National
Academy Press, Washington. D.C.

Again, as in the pain model, results depend on the amount of stress that the individual can tolerate in an adaptive state with normal behavior. If the nature and duration of stress increase and become chronic, the individual may be unable to adapt any longer and enter a state of distress. At this point, he or she will begin to show maladaptive behaviors.

Reinforcement of Maladaptive Behaviors and Consequences for Health.   If the maladaptive behaviors that appear as a response to stress partially or temporarily reduce stress, these maladaptive responses will be reinforced or conditioned and will reappear not only under the same conditions but also in similar conditions. In this way, maladaptive behaviors can become a permanent part of an individual's repertoire. If these behaviors persist over a long-term period, they can seriously impair an individual's state of physical and mental health (National Research Council, 1992; Weissberg, 1983). Such behaviors may consist of undereating or overeating; excessive anxiety or fear; and depression and inappropriate so-

cial behaviors such as aggression, passivity or withdrawal, and, in some cases, alcoholism, drug abuse, emotional or physical or sexual child abuse, spouse abuse, father–daughter incest, and even suicide. Physical disorders may appear and can include headaches, gastric and intestinal ulcers, immunosuppression (an important risk factor for cancer), or hypertension (a serious risk factor for cardiovascular disease).

Coping with Stress.   Coping with stress can result in altering or removing the problem or ameliorating the emotional aspects of the problem. Behavioral or cognitive therapeutic approaches, increasing social support, enhancing aspects of personal control, and exercise may reduce stress and emotional responses to stress. Medication may also be necessary. Benzodiazopenes (i.e., tranquilizers like Valium and Librium) reduce physiological arousal and reduce anxiety (Serafino, 1994). Since benzodiazopenes can be addicting, they should only be used for short periods and under the strict supervision of a physician. Relaxation techniques, biofeedback, and modeling have also been shown to be effective in reducing stress.

Recent work on how women and men cope with a variety of stressful diseases and disorders, including rheumatoid arthritis and cardiovascular disease, points to the importance of examining sex and gender issues. For example, women more than men rely on emotion-focused coping. Men, on the other hand, tend to use coping strategies with a more instrumental approach. Women seek out and use social support more than men, and men are more likely to involve themselves with distracting activities. However, these are small average differences with considerable overlap.

Pain: A Major Stressor

Pain can be considered an important source of stress. We should also consider pain as a state of stress itself. Every day, millions of people are disabled by pain that interferes with their productivity at work and at home. It is the most common reason for medical visits. It is also the major and most consistent reason for absence in the workplace.

Definition and Measurement of Pain.   Pain occurs in humans and other animals. **Pain** was defined by the International Association for the Study of Pain as an "unpleasant emotional experience associated with actual or potential tissue damage" (Mersky, 1976, p. 249). Earlier definitions of pain only emphasized the physiological aspect of the pain experience, but more recent ones, recognizing the psychological impact of pain, now include the word *emotional* in defining pain. Pain perception depends on activation of a special set of nerve endings or receptors (nociceptors) by noxious or harmful stimuli (i.e., thermal, mechanical, or chemical) and subsequent processing in the spinal cord, the brainstem, the thalamus, and finally specific areas in the cerebral cortex. The perception of pain will vary according to site, duration, frequency, and intensity and can be influenced by psychological states, previous experience, innate differences, or the state of physical health. The perceived intensity of pain based on the state of the individual certainly influences the ability

to cope or adapt and, as discussed above, an inability to adapt and cope may well have dire consequences on the physical and mental health of the individual.

Hardy, Wolff, and Goodell (1952) and Wolff (1978) defined the threshold and tolerance for pain. The **pain threshold** is defined as the point at which pain is first perceived. According to Wolff (1978), the pain threshold represents only minimal pain and is not usually associated with stress. The pain threshold is essentially the same in humans and in warm-blooded animals (Hardy et al., 1952; Vierck, 1976). **Pain tolerance** is the upper limit or the highest intensity of pain that a human or animal will accept voluntarily. Pain tolerance varies with different conditions (anxiety, fear, health status, motivation, previous experience with pain, etc.) and within and between different species. The difference between the pain threshold and pain tolerance is known as the *pain sensitivity range* (Wolff, 1978).

Types of Pain.   As indicated above, nociceptive processing will ultimately reach areas of the central nervous system. These areas will then discriminate the degree of unpleasantness of pain, including its emotional and motivational qualities. Thus, there are two major components of pain perception, the sensory (physiological) and the affective (emotional or psychological) (Gracely, McGrath, & Dubner, 1978; Kaplan, Sallis, & Patterson, 1993; Price & Dubner, 1977). There are also two types of pain; *acute* and *chronic. Acute pain* is typically associated with an active disease state or traumatic injury (Chapman & Bonica, 1985). When the damaged tissue heals, pain disappears. Acute pain provides a signal that there is damage and that some evasive action is necessary. Thus, it usually stimulates a change in behavior in order to avoid further injury. When healing takes place but pain still persists, this pain is referred to as *chronic pain.* Chapman and Bonica (1985) identified three types of chronic pain: (1) pain that lasts after normal healing of a disease or injury, (2) pain associated with a chronic medical condition, and (3) pain that develops and persists in the absence of any identifiable organic problem.

Sociocultural Expressions of Pain.   Sociocultural studies have shown some evidence for cultural differences in behavioral responsivenesss to pain. A complete discussion of the studies conducted is beyond the scope of this chapter. However, Bloom (1988) has reviewed several of the studies carried out in the 1960s and 1970s that clearly established the point that pain is a psychological as well as a physical process. Zola (1966) compared a group of Italian patients with Irish patients admitted to a medical clinic in Massachusetts. The Italian group complained of significantly more pain of a diffuse nature than did the Irish patients. Zola suggested that the ways of expressing illness and pain was a reflection of traditional customs of managing problems in their specific cultures. Sternbach and Tursky (1965) and Tursky and Sternbach (1967) contrasted four different groups of women—all housewives: Americans of British descent, native-born Italians, Jews, and Irish. Rather than studying people who were ill, they brought the groups into their laboratory and studied their responses to electric shock. The differences found between these groups seemed consistent with cultural norms in the various groups. The American women adapted more quickly to shock and appeared to have a "matter-of-fact orientation toward pain" (p. 239); Italian women had a lower threshold for pain and desired pain relief; and Irish women were more anxious and showed unwillingness to express their feelings and tended to inhibit communicating their pain to others. Jewish women appeared highly concerned about the implications of their reactions and responses to pain. Similar to Zola, these investigators concluded that their findings were consistent with prevailing cultural norms. Obviously, such norms change over time and in different social contexts.

Zborowski (1969) studied a large group of men who were patients at a veterans' hospital in New York. The patients were representative of Italian, Irish, Jewish, and Anglo-Saxon Americans. Zborowski's findings were quite consistent with those of the studies described above. Italian and Jewish patients appeared more emotional than the Anglo-Saxon and Irish and more diffuse in their complaints about pain. They also were more apprehensive about their physicians. When Zborowski selected the patients with regard to the se-

riousness of their pain, he found that the Italian and Jewish patients expressed their pain more than the other groups. He concluded that, over a variety of illnesses, one's cultural background had an important, if not central, role in shaping responsiveness to pain and illness.

Later studies have focused on how societal factors appear to perpetuate pain, especially chronic pain. The long-term experience of pain involves processes that have important psychological components. Along with others, Steig and Williams (1983) have identified several societal factors that tend to increase the number of chronic pain patients seeking care. Some of these involve incentives provided by the medical and insurance professions, and such secondary gains from disability such as freedom from daily responsibilities and the elicitation of social support. In addition, job and economic stresses and changing family roles, including the division of household labor, all affect peoples' experience of pain (Bloom, 1988; Cohen, 1984; Steig & Williams, 1983).

Sex and Gender Differences in Pain Perception.   There are many sex differences in the perception of specific types of pain. Obviously, pain during labor and childbirth is unique to females. In diseases and disorders of both women and men, women experience a higher incidence of pain than men with arthritis, neuralgias, migraine headaches, and cystitis. Men, on the other hand, show a higher proportion of pain with back problems, cardiac conditions, and cluster headaches (Bodner, 1998).

There is recent evidence showing sex differences in pain perception and analgesia. In females who have not reached menopause, pain mechanisms and pain perception appear to depend in part on estrogen receptors, and pain relief may operate through distinctly different pathways in males and females. Mogil, Sternberg, Kest, Marek, and Liebeskind (1993) found that a pathway involved in pain and pain relief relies on the presence of estrogen. After ovariectomy in laboratory rats, pain mechanisms alter (Bodner, 1998; Touchette, 1993). Additional findings have also shown sex differences in response to different types of analgesic agents used to relieve pain in animals. In his review of this problem, Bodner feels it is imperative that physicians understand these sex differences so that appropriate treatment will bring about the most effective pain relief (Bodner, 1998). This should include an understanding of pain mechanisms in pre- and post-menopausal women. This may mean that under certain conditions (e.g., age, reproductive status) drugs designed to relieve pain in men might not necessarily be effective in women.

Treatment of Pain and Coping Strategies. Treatments for pain depend on the type of pain and the patient's responsiveness to pain. Drug treatment differs for acute and chronic pain, with concern for the patient becoming dependent or even addicted to the drug. Such drugs include peripherally (aspirin) and centrally (Percodan or Demerol) acting analgesics, local anesthetics (lidocaine or novocaine by injection or topical application), and indirectly acting drugs that affect the emotional response to pain that often contribute to the intensity of pain (sedatives, tranquilizers, antidepressants).

Surgery is the most radical treatment for controlling intractable chronic pain. Some surgical procedures disconnect part of the spinal pathways to prevent pain signals from reaching the brain. If successful, they produce numbness but can cause paralysis of the body part affected by the severed nerves. Pain is controlled, but not over a long period, and pain returns along with other sensations that have been reported to be worse than the original pain itself. Such procedures are rarely used today (Serafino, 1994). However, new techniques are being developed for implanting fine tubes or pumps into special areas of the spinal cord that can deliver pain medication on a controlled basis to avoid overmedicating the patient.

Behavioral and cognitive methods are being used to modify motivational and cognitive processes. These methods have been shown to help patients to cope with their chronic pain. Other techniques involve relaxation, biofeedback, imagery, hypnosis, exercise, physical therapy, visualization, meditation, tai-chi, and qi-gong (Bloom, 1988; Rice, 1992). Because of the difficulty in following these patients after treatment is completed, results are difficult to evaluate precisely.

Bloom (1988) cites several longitudinal studies of other investigators that do show substantial improvement of the pain experience with these methods.

ISSUES OF BIAS IN WOMEN'S HEALTH RESEARCH

The scientific paradigm that governs issues of women's health, including research and treatment, is, as we discussed earlier, premised on a male model. Such a model fails to recognize gender as salient in medical and scientific research. This neglect can be traced back to a historical exclusion of women from essentially all phases of the public domain. This practice extended into the sciences, where women were not only excluded from participation (in the behavioral as well as the biological and physical), but were all but ignored as subjects of research. Thus, male scientists, selecting male subjects, constructed a male research model for science and medicine (Sechzer, Griffin, & Pfafflin, 1994). According to Keller (1982), "As long as the course of scientific thought was judged to be exclusively determined by its own logical and empirical necessities, there could be no place for any signature, male or otherwise, in that system of knowledge" (p. 312). Yet, according to many findings, scientific thought has not been exclusively determined by these criteria, and our system of knowledge does sustain a male signature. This male paradigm for disease is not only biological and behavioral; it is, as we have seen, also sociocultural (Sechzer, Griffin, & Pfafflin, 1994).

Again, let us note that implicit in this male model has been the assumption that, with the obvious exception of disorders affecting only women, there are no differences in the etiology, symptoms, or treatment responses between males and females in disorders affecting both genders. Moreover, using this model, the results of basic and clinical sciences obtained with one sex, usually male, have been generalized to the other, frequently without justification. The pervasiveness of such bias and inappropriate generalization has been clearly evident in the research literature.

This section reviews diseases that occur in both males and females, but for which sex and gender bias are evident and for which a gendered perspective may be useful. Because space constraints prevent us from providing an exhaustive discussion of all diseases and disorders in which sex or gender bias is evident, we have selected those that we feel are of great concern to women: cardiovascular disease, lung cancer, and HIV/AIDS.

Cardiovascular Disease

Cardiovascular diseases are the leading cause of death in the developing world for both men and women. In cardiovascular disease, 50 percent of all women, but only 31 percent of men, suffering heart attacks die within a year. Approximately 90 percent of all heart disease deaths among women occur after menopause; and one in nine women between age 45 and 64 has some clinical cardiovascular disease, which rises to one in three at age 65 or older (NIH-ORWH, 1991). Although complete data are lacking for many ethnic and racial subgroups for many health conditions, it is known that many conditions and diseases occur with higher frequency in these different groups of women.

Stroke accounts for more deaths for White women than for White men, and deaths from stroke occurs twice as often in African American women as in White women. The rates of death from coronary disease are higher for African American women than for White women—172.9 versus 106.6 per 100,000 persons (NIH-ORWH, 1992).

These are startling statistics. Just what is cardiovascular disease and what are the conditions that contribute to its development in both women and men? Why do women with cardiovascular disease fare so poorly? Is it because they are misdiagnosed, diagnosed later, or not treated in the same way as men? And what research has been done in this area, and has it produced reasons for these striking differences?

Cardiovascular disease (CVD) appears to be a disease of highly developed countries. One way to explain this is that people in more highly advanced countries live longer; that is, they live long enough to fall victim to CVD. The stresses and other risk factors for developing CVD, such as diet and lack of exercise, seem to be much higher in modernized countries.

Kaplan et al. (1993) has provided a very clear description of this disease. CVD is a group of diseases with many components in common.

1. **Coronary artery disease** occurs when the small arteries that supply blood to the heart muscle become blocked, usually with atherosclerotic plaques. Three types of coronary artery disease result from such blockage: (a) Primary cardiac arrest, in which blood cannot be pumped through the body. This can result in sudden death before lifesaving techniques are begun. (b) Myocardial infarction (MI), commonly called a *heart attack,* occurs when a blockage in a coronary artery cuts off the blood supply to a particular part of the heart, which then dies. How large a part of the heart is affected determines the patient's recovery or death. Myocardial infarction is usually accompanied by a great deal of pain in the chest. (c) Angina pectoris is caused by restricted blood supply in the coronary arteries (not complete blockage) and manifests a type of pain similar to but not as severe as the pain experienced with MI.

2. **Cerebrovascular disease** is also known as *stroke* or a *cerebrovascular accident* (CVA). This disease occurs when blood flow to a part of the brain is altered either because of a blockage in an artery in the brain or a leak or breakage in a cerebral artery (an artery of the brain). When this occurs, that part of the brain dies. Consequences of stroke can vary widely, depending on the part of the brain affected. Disturbances may involve the ability to speak, other language abilities, motor function, memory, sensation and perception, or paralysis. Due to the redundancy of the brain, patients can often recover some or a great deal of function over a period of time. However, this too depends on the seriousness of the CVA. Stroke is often fatal and is the third largest cause of death in the United States.

3. **Peripheral artery disease,** often a complication of diabetes, is caused by diminished blood flow to the arms or legs. This results in pain and loss of function in the extremities. The reduced blood flow causes the affected tissue to die or in less severe cases to suffer a lack of oxygen. Function in the affected limb is severely curtailed and amputation may result.

Risk Factors   Genetic factors such as sex, age, anatomy of the heart and arteries, and inherited lipid and glucose metabolism all act to influence the risk of CVD. Lipid metabolism is the process by which fats and cholesterol are used and stored in the body. Glucose metabolism refers to how glucose is utilized in the body. In people with a genetic disposition to develop a disorder of glucose metabolism, these disorders may eventually show up as diabetes mellitus. Diabetes is not only a serious disease but also increases the risk of CVD. Behavioral and environmental factors are also extremely important.

Men are at greater risk for CVD than are women, at least until the time of menopause when estrogen levels start to decline and cease altogether. Women then catch up to men at an older age. High blood cholesterol, high blood pressure, and obesity are three well-documented physiological risk factors for development of CVD. Behavioral factors associated with CVD are cigarette smoking, diet, and physical activity. These factors are either direct risks or modify physiological processes. Stress is another important factor in CVD. Emotional components such as stress, anger, and hostility have also been implicated in the development of CVD (e.g., high blood pressure). The type of occupation (e.g., working as an air traffic controller), environmental conditions like living in a crowded apartment or neighborhood, or low socioeconomic status have been shown to influence the development of CVD. Type A behavior (e.g., competitiveness, hostility, aggression, impatience, and a sense of time urgency) has been implicated as a possible risk factor (Kaplan et al., 1993; Serafino, 1994).

Now that we know more about what CVD is and the associated risk factors involved, we can pursue the answers to the other questions that we asked by reviewing the research literature in this area and evaluating the results.

Bias Issues in Cardiovascular Research.

As indicated earlier, 50 percent of all women with CVD die within a year. According to Wenger, Speroff, and Packard (1993), this amounts to 500,000 women. One-half of these deaths are due to *coronary heart disease.* Wenger et al. (1993) state that there is insufficient information about prevention, diagnostic tests, responses to treatment, or intervention in women. One reason for this is because there are few studies of sex or gender differences in response to treatment, testing, or other therapies.

In 1994, the authors of this text began a comprehensive survey of the biomedical and behavioral research literatures in several key areas including CVD, cancer, depression, and AIDS. We analyzed patterns of subject use, representation of women and men, and the appropriateness of generalizing research findings to both males and females from either single-sex studies or from studies in which both sexes were included. We also evaluated whether patterns changed across an eight-year period from 1984 to 1992. Results of our survey of cardiovascular disease demonstrated exceptional gender bias across an eight-year period. We found that males were the predominant subjects in 1984 and 1992. Although women were included in most of the studies, they were included in small numbers. Data were not analyzed separately by gender, but combined, so evaluating responses to treatment by the women tested, as well as by men, was not possible. Moreover, in several studies, sex of the subjects was not even identified. These combined data were then generalized either implicitly or explicitly to both sexes. Little to no rationale for this practice was offered by authors of these studies. Unfortunately, there was little change across the eight-year period studied (Sechzer, Rabinowitz, & Denmark, 1994).

Why Should Gender Be Studied?   Johnson, Kayser, and Pedraza (1984) found that women and men with preoperative angina pain showed surprising differences after coronary bypass surgery was performed. Men experience better pain relief of their angina pain than women. In a Canadian study, Hung et al. (1984) concluded that much of the available technology for assessing coronary artery disease in men may not be sensitive enough to diagnose the disease in women, because women present atypical symptoms (symptoms that differ from those commonly presented by males). In 1992, Hannan, Bernard, Kilburn, and O'Donnel reviewed gender differences in mortality for coronary artery bypass surgery, with more women dying than men. This study reviewed problems of smaller coronary arteries in women, making them more at risk for surgery. This is especially important, for it seems that heart disease in women has not been taken seriously and, as a result, by the time that women are diagnosed they may be more seriously ill and thus at a greater risk than the average man of similar age.

Another recent follow-up study of men and women who had surgery (angioplasty or coronary bypass surgery) because of stenosis (blockage) in their coronary arteries was carried out by Faxon et al. (1992). This group of subjects had re-stenosed. However, more women were treated medically to reduce stenosis than men, who, instead, had repeat surgery for a second or third stenosis. These types of studies exploring gender differences in diagnosis, treatment, and outcome for women and men are too few in the research literature. Instead, as indicated earlier, data are combined so that we do not know the responses of men and of women to various treatments, including surgery and its outcome. Results are combined and generalized to males and females through a general statement in the conclusion of the study. Therefore, many of the generalizations made in these studies were rated as *questionable* or *inappropriate* (Sechzer et al., 1994).

However, things may be changing. More studies are being conducted to determine how women are doing with intervention. These show that women with CVD enter the studies older, sicker, and with a higher incidence of other disorders than do men. This is probably due to later diagnosis and referral for treatment (Legato, 1994). Data, when analyzed separately, show that women have more complications of surgery than men, perhaps due to late intervention. However, Legato (1994) feels that progress is encouraging in the area of gender bias and CVD, although women still tend to be treated differently than men not only in the United States, but also in the United Kingdom and other countries. Nevertheless, the greater attention being paid to gender bias in CVD and studies that not only evaluate CVD in women but also provide preventive education (e.g., the National Cholesterol Education program) indicate that progress is indeed being made. Such progress will be important for the health of women as well as the health of men. Nevertheless, there is still a long way to travel and many questions yet to be answered.

Treatment and Coping. Dietary strategies are used for weight control for obese CVD patients and for patients with elevated cholesterol levels and blood pressures (hypertension). If adhered to, they can be highly effective. Drug therapy to reduce blood pressure and cholesterol levels is initiated when diet is not effective. Diet usually involves salt reduction for the elevated blood pressure and a low fat diet to decrease cholesterol. Exercise is important in the control of weight and for reduction of hypertension. Relaxation therapy, biofeedback, and meditation are other strategies frequently used and can play an important role in reducing stress. Some programs address behavioral changes to improve the status of patients with CVD.

Over the last few years, the Ornish program, under the direction of Dean Ornish, has received much attention. The program includes an extremely low fat diet (10 percent of calories from fat) as well as caffeine-free beverages. It also emphasizes moderate exercise and helps smokers to decrease and hopefully eliminate cigarettes from their life-style. The Ornish program includes relaxation and yoga exercise as a daily part of the program's routine. Results of this program have been positive. Angina pain decreased and blockage in the coronary vessels decreased in the majority of patients. This was the first study to show that changing the behavioral life-style could lead to a reversal of blockage in coronary arteries due to atherosclerosis (Kaplan et al., 1993; Ornish, 1982; Ornish et al., 1990).

Individual or group therapy may also be necessary to help CVD patients to cope with and reduce stress. Anger and hostility must be dealt with in therapy to understand the source of these emotions and deal with them in ways that will not further compromise health.

Lung Cancer

Cancer is the second leading cause of death among U.S. women of all ages, accounting for more than 250,000 deaths each year. Approximately 160,000 cases of lung cancer are diagnosed each year. It is the leading cause of premature death (Bloom, 1988; NIH-ORWH, 1992). The five-year survival rate is only 13 percent, but survival is three times as high if the disease is discovered while it is still localized. However, in lung cancer the malignant cells begin to metastasize while still small and will usually have spread by the time the diagnosis is made. Although death rates for cancer in general have decreased, in lung cancer the death rate has not changed.

Until recently, breast cancer was the leading cause of death from cancer for women. However, death from lung cancer has now surpassed that for breast cancer. In 1991, 51,000 women died from lung cancer and 45,000 women died from breast cancer. This rate parallels the rate of increase in smoking among women. Although lung cancer rates in men are still higher than in women, they have begun to decline, while the rate of lung cancer in women has continued to increase. The lung cancer rates for African American women and White women are approximately equal. Five-year survival rates for African American and White women are relatively low, but comparable, and higher than for males (NIH-ORWH, 1992).

What Is Lung Cancer and How Does It Develop?
As in cardiovascular studies, some of the answers to these questions are to be found in the research literature. Cancer was certainly known at least as far back as the time of the ancient Greeks. The *Ebers Papyrus,* written around 1500 B.C.E. appears to be the first medical document to describe cancer, but it only characterized the swellings associated with some tumors. Hippocrates, in the third century B.C.E., gave the disease the name **cancer,** and several hundred years later in the second century C.E., the Roman physician Galen first used the word **tumor** (Brannon & Feist, 1992).

Cancer is a large group of diseases characterized by uncontrolled growth and spread of abnormal cells (American Cancer Society, 1991) that can affect any part of the body. Cancer cells may differ in different parts of the body, but they all have a common characteristic: the appearance of *neoplastic cells* (new and abnormal growth). In contrast to normal cells, neoplastic cells show new and unlimited growth and are

able to multiply uncontrollably and invade and overwhelm normal tissue. In this way, cancer cells spread or metastasize to other sites in the body. Once cells become cancerous, their growth and site in the body are no longer controlled by the same processes that control normal cells. Neoplastic cells can be **malignant,** neoplastic cells that can metastasize, or they can be **benign,** neoplastic cells that grow but are limited to a single tumor (Brannon & Feist, 1992).

Risk Factors. Lung cancer is almost entirely due to cigarette smoking (American Cancer Society, 1991; Centers for Disease Control, 1989), although other variables such as genetic factors, environmental carcinogens (air pollution), or cancer-causing substances that women and men encounter in the workplace (like asbestos and insecticides) may play a role in lung cancer (Taylor, 1995). Stress may also play a role in that it may decrease the functioning of the immune system, making the person more vulnerable to carcinogens.

Today, more young women become smokers than do young men. Recent evidence has also shown that smokers not only put themselves at risk, but also put others at risk who are exposed to *passive smoking* or second-hand smoke. Findings have suggested that women smokers are twice as likely as male smokers to develop lung cancer. This may be due in part to women's smaller lungs receiving a more concentrated dose of smoke with its carcinogens, which may make them more vulnerable (NIH-ORWH, 1992).

Bias Issues in Lung Cancer Research. In 1992, the Women's Health Initiative, under the aegis of the National Institutes of Health, was set in motion by Dr. Bernadine Healy, the then director of the NIH. The Initiative is a 14-year study and includes some 150,000 women at 45 clinical centers across the country. The purpose of this expansive study is to decrease the prevalence of cancer, especially breast cancer, cardiovascular disease, and osteoporosis among women. Yet, despite the fact that lung cancer is more lethal for women than breast cancer and the death rate may have already exceeded that for men, there is no comparable large-scale lung cancer study under way or even planned that is comparable to the Women's Health Initiative. Not only is the quantity of research in lung cancer insufficient, but in the research that has been carried out, inadequate attention is paid to gender (Denmark, Sechzer, & Rabinowitz, 1994, 1995).

As part of a study of sex and gender bias in science carried out to answer such questions, Denmark et al. (1994, 1995) reviewed studies of lung cancer research published in 1984 and 1992. Two leading cancer journals were examined, the *Journal of Clinical Oncology* and *Cancer.* For both years, although sample size was usually adequate, the gender of subjects was frequently unspecified. Just as in the cardiovascular studies, when gender was identified, male subjects predominated both in 1984 and in 1992. Moreover, even when gender was specified, there was little or no description of treatment responses by gender. Similarly, there was little or no identification of toxic effects of the drugs used on men or women; nor was there any indication of how many men and how many women died after a specific period of survival. In statements about the number or percentage of subjects who responded well to treatment and improved, again there was no indication of how many women and how many men responded positively. The typical study combined data for both males and females and then generalized the results, implicitly or explicitly, to both genders. This was usually found at the end of the discussion or in the conclusions at the end of the report. Generalizations of data from such studies were rated as *questionable* or *inappropriate.* Lung cancer studies did show somewhat more progress toward gender-fair research than cardiovascular studies. However, on reviewing animal studies cited as a basis for human research in some areas of lung cancer, we found that the animals used were either predominantly male or were unidentified as to their sex (Denmark et al., 1994, 1995; Sechzer, 1993; Sechzer et al., 1994).*

Of particular interest is that females generally have better immune systems than men. With the re-

cent focus on the relevance of the immune system in cancer and other diseases, exploration of gender differences should have been made, because this may be an important factor in treatment response. In addition to gender differences in immunity, males and females may also have different thresholds for toxicity in the drugs used for treatment. Milano et al. (1992) studied sex and age differences in the drug fluorouracil (5FU), one of the oldest anticancer drugs. These investigators found that, whereas age and 5FU were not correlated, clearance of the drug is slower in women. This raises questions of dosage and toxicity. If it takes longer for women to clear 5FU from their bodies than for men, then repeated dosage would increase the concentration of the drug in their system. This would place women at greater risk for developing toxicity to the drug and might affect their response and recovery. In some of the studies that involved 5FU treatment, toxicity was reported, but with no indication of the gender of the patients affected. An additional study by Waits et al. (1992) indicated sex differences in the drug etoposide, another drug used for lung cancer. In this study, women were found to be more responsive to the drug than men. Such differences might exist for other drugs, but sex differences would need to be explored and tested for such differences to be evident.

Although some progress has been made in this area of cancer research, it is still obvious that researchers prefer male subjects. Yet, as in cardiovascular studies, even when women are included, data are not analyzed separately for males and females and are generalized. We have seen in the cancer studies reviewed that there are differences between males and females in areas of drug toxicity and in the immune system that are based on biological differences. These findings underscore the need for sex or gender comparative studies. Learning about which drugs women and men respond best to, to determine dosage by gender, taking toxicity factors into account, should result in better treatment of the disease, with the patients suffering fewer side effects.

Treatment and Coping. Treatments for lung cancer include surgery, radiation, chemotherapy, and im-

---

*We found the same to be true for cardiovascular studies as well as for other studies of diseases and disorders using animals.

munotherapy. There are negative side effects to most of these procedures. The diagnosis of cancer always has a heightened psychological impact on the patient. When a person is told that she or he has cancer, it often seems like a death sentence, whether the patient knows little or a great deal about cancer. Fear and anxiety usually accompany cancer during the patient's illness. Helping patients to cope with the disease and the potential side effects of treatment, which are usually highly stressful, is an important task for psychologists and health-care providers. Many people with cancer become depressed, although levels of depression are varied. Sexual problems are not uncommon. Pain is also a frequent and severe problem for cancer patients, and proper pain management is crucial. In addition to analgesics (pain-relieving drugs), it is necessary to help the patient acquire coping skills to deal with the stressful effects of the disease. Some of these include individual or group therapy (which have been found to have positive effects on cancer patients and may improve survival) and relaxation training and meditation to reduce pain and to relieve some of the psychological effects of cancer. When patients are terminal, therapy and support are necessary to help the patient to accept the forthcoming death (Kaplan, Sallis, & Patterson, 1993; Serafino, 1994).

Prevention. Although it was previously believed that a diagnosis of cancer was a death sentence, we know that progress has been made in the length of survival rate of many cancers. Many cancers are thought to be avoidable through behavioral changes, most notably a cessation of smoking or a decision not to initiate smoking. Early and consistent screening with chest X-rays, particularly in low-income and minority groups, is another crucial preventive strategy.

Today's woman who smokes is at a greater risk of dying from a smoking-related disease than her counterpart in the 1960s, because it is highly likely that she began smoking at a younger age and therefore has more past years of smoking in her lifetime. Adolescent girls are beginning to smoke at a rate of 29 percent. It is also likely that today's woman smokes more cigarettes each day and inhales more deeply.

The most important issue in lung cancer is prevention. Tobacco smoke is generally recognized as the single most documented risk factor in lung cancer, but it is important for women to know that smoking is also a risk factor for cervical, bladder, and other cancers. To decrease smoking initiation and increase smoking cessation, research should focus on cigarette advertising, weight control without cigarette use, and social supports. Of special concern is advertising that specifically targets minority women such as African American and Hispanic women (NIH, 1992). Developing and implementing innovative smoking prevention and cessation programs will be an exceptional task.

Sexually Transmitted Diseases

Sexually transmitted diseases (STDs) are defined as those diseases that are spread by sexual contact. Today the main STD is HIV/AIDS. Other common STDs are syphilis, genital herpes, gonorrhea, chlamydia, and human papilloma virus (HPV).

STDs affect at least 6 million women in the United States each year, half of whom are teen-agers. Fifteen to 20 million women are chronically infected with either genital herpes or human papilloma virus (HPV). Women are now the fastest growing population with AIDS; intravenous (IV) drug abuse and heterosexual contact are the primary modes of transmission (NIH, 1992; Rathus, Nevid, & Fichner-Rathus, 1997).

AIDS/HIV Infection. The prevalence of the **acquired immunodeficiency syndrome (AIDS)** has now reached epidemic proportions, not only in the United States but globally. Cohen and Fauci (1998) report that as many as 30 million people worldwide are infected with the human immunodeficiency virus and (**HIV**) and that 90 percent of new infections are in developing countries. AIDS may be the most serious epidemic of the twentieth century and the beginning of the twenty-first century. Its high mortality rate is frightening. The growth of HIV/AIDS has been very rapid, accompanied by steady changes in its demographic distribution. In 1981, when we were just beginning to become acquainted with the terms HIV and AIDS and reports began to appear in the medical literature, less than 100 people died. By 1993, the Centers for Disease Control (CDC) estimated that there were more than 253,448 cases of AIDS (Cohen & Alfonso, 1994). By 1995, more than 74,000 new cases of AIDS were diagnosed in this country. And in 1996 alone, more than 548,000 Americans were diagnosed with AIDS and 338,000 died. AIDS is now considered to be the leading killer of Americans of ages 25 to 44. In 1998 it was estimated that approximately 1.5 million people living in the United States were infected with HIV (Centers for Disease Control, 1996; Rathus, Nevid, & Fichner-Rathus, 1997). The CDC (1998) also reported that between 1992 and 1997, the number of persons living with AIDS has increased. This was due to the expanded case definition of the disease and to the improved survival rate with new drug treatment. The number of women living with AIDS increased from 13.8 percent in 1992 to 19.1 percent in 1997; the number of Black people living with AIDS increased from 32.7 percent to 39.2 percent during this period, which is almost identical with the number of White people living with AIDS (CDC, 1998). There was a dramatic *decrease* in pediatric AIDS in the United States, due in large part to the Public Health Service guidelines for treatment with the drug *zidovudine* during pregnancy, which has reduced the perinatal transmission of HIV. There is little doubt that most of these infected people will go on to develop AIDS and most, if not all, will die, depending on such factors as the type of treatment available and their economic circumstances. In the beginning of the epidemic in the United States, it was believed that AIDS predominately affected men who have sex with men and intravenous drug users. But now HIV/AIDS is not limited to discrete populations and the incidence of HIV/AIDS from male–female contact is increasing. African Americans and Hispanics are among the fastest growing infected population in the United States. Of the number of Americans who have developed AIDS, approximately 46 percent of men but 75 percent of women are African Americans or Hispanic Americans (Rathus, Nevid, & Fichner-Rathus, 1997). Although AIDS/HIV infec-

tion was first observed in men, it is now the fastest growing disease for women in the United States and abroad. In 1990, 25 percent of all seropositive adults worldwide were women, and in 1992, 40 percent of all seropositive adults were women.

The CDC now estimates that in the United States, between 120,000 and 160,000 adult and adolescent women are infected with HIV. Thus, in just a little more than one decade, the proportion of all AIDS cases among adult and adolescent women nearly tripled from 7 percent in 1985 to 22 percent in 1997. In 1996, HIV/AIDS was the fourth leading cause of death among U.S. women aged 25–44 but the leading cause of death among African American women in the same age group. And, although AIDS-related deaths among women are decreasing as a result of advances in treatment, AIDS-related deaths among women are not declining as rapidly as AIDS-related deaths in men. Moreover, recent data for 25 states showed that a substantial number of women were newly diagnosed with HIV infection. There was a larger percentage of HIV cases diagnosed in women of color. African American and Hispanic women represent less than one-fourth of all women in the United States, yet they account for more than three-fourths of AIDS cases reported to data among U.S. women (CDC, 1998).

What is AIDS and why do most of the affected people die? Why is AIDS in women increasing? Has the research being conducted found anything different in women as compared with men in the development of AIDS?

What Is AIDS and How Do People Get It?   The human immunodeficiency virus is spread through sexual contact, through exposure to HIV-contaminated blood and blood products, and from mother to child through prenatal contact. Kaplan et al. (1993) has provided a clear understanding of how AIDS develops. These authors inform us that it takes at least eight weeks for the **antibodies** to HIV to develop and be identified on a blood test. However, upon contact, HIV rapidly enters the body. It attaches and enters cells in the host's body, usually CD4 helper–inducer **T cell** lymphocytes. These CD4 T cells are an important component of the white blood cells, a part of the **immune system.** Under normal conditions, when a virus (e.g., a cold virus) enters the body, the CD4 cells alert the immune system to this invasion by a foreign body, the cold virus. The normal response of the CD4 cells is to multiply on contact with the cold virus. However, when the HIV has already entered the body and is attached to the CD4 cells, HIV will multiply when the CD4 cells multiply, which is the normal response of the immune system. Thus, the life cycle of HIV contains a set of steps in which it uses the host's own cells to multiply and produces a tremendous number of new HIV viruses. As more and more CD4 cells become infected, the immune system becomes unable to respond to infectious agents. Individuals then die of other infections that the immune system cannot fight off. HIV also infects a number of other cells in the immune system, as well as in the skin, lymph nodes, and brain. As the body weakens, its immune system is no longer able to fight and opportunistic infections and tumors appear, which define full-blown AIDS. The final appearance of AIDS varies for different people.

Diagnosis in Women and Men. People with AIDS do not show any symptoms (are **asymptomatic**) until long after their initial infection with the HIV virus. Once infected, antibodies to the virus will be made, but may not appear until at least eight weeks or longer after exposure. The appearance of symptoms differs widely with the individual. Minor symptoms may include fever, sweats, fatigue, or nausea (Brannon & Feist, 1992). These symptoms are not characteristic of AIDS and frequently disappear before major symptoms manifest. The appearance of symptoms characteristic of AIDS can take years. Major infections will begin to appear when the immune system is severely compromised, and include Kaposi's sarcoma (cancer), *Pneumocystis carini* pneumonia (a parasitic infection), *tuberculosis* (a bacterial infection), and *cryptosporidium* (a parasitic infection), all of which deplete the body further. These infections when presented confirm the diagnosis of AIDS.

"Sex, drugs, infection, and death are inextricably linked with the spread of HIV infection" (Cohen &

Alfonso, 1994, p. 119). Transmission of the disease is of major importance to women, medically and psychologically. AIDS/HIV infection was first observed in men, and the definition (known as the *case definition*) was developed around the symptoms presented by men. The significant gaps in the case definition of AIDS/HIV seriously compromised women. Until 1994, the case definition by the CDC did not include medical illnesses frequently presented by women in the early stages of the disease, especially recurrent pelvic inflammatory disease and other pelvic infections. Therefore, by the time AIDS was diagnosed in women, they were more likely to be sicker than men, in whom the diagnosis is usually made much earlier. Thus, women diagnosed later than men died sooner than their male counterparts (Cohen & Alfonso, 1994). Whether this change has facilitated earlier diagnosis of AIDS in women remains to be determined. There are still a large number of physicians, especially gynecologists, who treat patients for medical problems that include pelvic inflammatory disease, rather than consider and test for HIV infection. But this practice is changing.

High-Risk Behaviors and Prevention. As a means of protection against exposure to HIV infection, everyone should know the high-risk behaviors involved. **High-risk behaviors** include any unprotected sexual intercourse; vaginal, anal, and oral forms are all unsafe without *barrier protection.* The risk seems to be highest for the receptive partner of anal intercourse. Sharing needles with intravenous drug users can transmit the HIV virus. This dangerous behavior may also expose an IV drug user's sex partner to the HIV virus. Women partners who are HIV positive and become pregnant may transmit the virus to their unborn or newborn infant. Women who are prostitutes and have been exposed to the HIV virus may then infect their male partners. Although abstinence is the safest way to avoid HIV exposure, this is not satisfactory or acceptable for many adolescents or adults. Use of condoms, especially those lubricated with the now available virucidal spermicide, can lower the risk. However, there is always the possibility of the condom leaking or breaking. Another way for protection is to maintain monogamous relationships. Information and general public awareness as discussed in Chapter 8 have not been adequate to change behavior to a safer life-style (Cohen & Alfonso, 1994; Grodsky, 1995).

Although now a more negligible risk in developed countries, contaminated blood products during transfusions should still be regarded as a potential source of exposure. Efforts should be made to use gloves and other protective garments, especially when there is a cut in the skin. In undeveloped countries where screening of blood donors is not routinely carried out, there is a high risk of contamination (Cohen & Alfonso, 1994; Kaplan et al., 1993).

Treatment: Medical and Psychological.   At the time of this writing, there is no medical cure for AIDS. The drug that has been continually in use is AZT (azidothymidine or zidovudine), which slows the progress of the HIV virus, but does not effect a cure. AZT does seem to prevent HIV infection of the brain (encephalopathy) and does lengthen survival considerably. Patients will still develop **opportunistic infections** associated with decreased immune function. Two of the most common opportunistic infections are *Pneumocystis carini* pneumonia and *Kaposi's sarcoma,* a form of cancer that was uncommon in the United States before the AIDS epidemic. Most of these infections can be treated successfully, but frequently allergies or hypersensitivity to the medication develops and then drug therapy is of no value. Even if patients survive bouts of infection, they still continue to deteriorate.

New approaches to treat HIV/AIDS have come about with the development of *antiretroviral drugs.* These drugs are protein inhibitors that act against HIV, which is a *retrovirus.* They suppress the viral load and increase T/CD4 cell counts. One combination of drugs (indinavir, zidovudine, and lamivudine) given simultaneously (not sequentially) showed a marked antiretroviral response in 78 percent of patients tested (97 patients were enrolled in the study), markedly suppressing HIV replication for long periods of time, up to 2 years. However, the duration of

HIV suppression varies among affected individuals (Gulik et al., 1998). The results of the study cited, as well as results from other studies, showed qualitative and quantitative changes in the immune system that were associated with improvements in immune responses. Although patients receiving antiretroviral drugs are not cured of HIV, they appear to have a great deal of protection against most AIDS-related opportunistic infections (Powderly, Landay, & Lederman, 1998). However, only in industrialized or developed countries is health-care funding adequate to treat the large number of people with AIDS (Cohen & Fauci, 1998).

Although antiretroviral therapy has significantly decreased the mortality rate for AIDS patients, the incidence of new HIV infections has not decreased as significantly in this country. In 1997, almost 6 million people worldwide became HIV infected and, importantly, more than 90 percent of these newly infected people live in developing countries. In these countries, the amount of money spent on health care is extremely small, and access to antiretroviral therapy is virtually nonexistent. These facts make the development of a vaccine a pressing need. Many vaccines are in development with some actually in clinical trials. But it will probably be years before an effective vaccine is developed given the many varieties of HIV subtypes (Cohen & Fauci, 1998).

Psychological interventions for AIDS patients have been developed. Cognitive–behavioral stress management with gay men after they were notified that they were **HIV positive** showed a decrease in depression and an increase in immune functioning (Antoni et al., 1991). Other encouraging programs include relaxation and stress management training, biofeedback, and visual imagery, some of which resulted in a decline of HIV-related symptoms (Taylor, 1995).

Psychological and Sociocultural Issues for Women with AIDS.   There are important sociocultural and psychological issues concerning women with AIDS. A large study of male and female heterosexuals showed a surprisingly low proportion of condom use, particularly for women with high-risk behaviors

(Catania et al., 1992). Catania concluded that women either do not understand the risks of HIV transmission or are in denial of their own personal risk. But this may also represent a lack of empowerment to enforce safe sex practices with their partner(s). Teen-agers are also among populations at particular risk because they frequently succumb to peer pressure not only to have sexual intercourse but also to use drugs. Women in all these groups need to understand that they have the ability to choose a method of contraception. But attitudes and beliefs often lead high-risk women to willingly avoid using contraception. The fear of loss of love, companionship, home, and financial support may influence their decision. Violence or even death may occur if some women insist on using barrier protection. **HIV-seropositive** women should be aware that there is a chance that their baby will be born infected with HIV if they do not choose to use contraception. Obviously, sexual behavior is not a cognitive activity and therefore does not lend itself easily to behavior change based on information alone. Efforts to educate and increase awareness about AIDS and its transmission have not been successful in altering behaviors (Cohen & Alfonso, 1994; Grodsky, 1995).

Compounding the devastating illness caused by AIDS, which results in profound emaciation, weakness, depression, pneumonia and other immune disorders, pain, disfigurement, and untimely death, there is now a form of discrimination called *AIDSism* (or AIDS-related stigma). This type of discrimination appears to be more devastating for HIV-infected women than for infected men. Discrimination against people with AIDS is well known; homophobia and fear of contagion are severe. Once the diagnosis has been made, infected people may become isolated, shunned, or homeless and may no longer be accepted at shelters. The stress and psychological effects on women are so great that they are at much higher risk for suicide. Sexual partners of injecting drug users are at even higher risk for suicide than are other infected people (Cohen & Alfonso, 1994; Kirschner, 1995).

Gender Issues in AIDS Research.   In addition to the vulnerability of affected women and their being

ignored in diagnosis and in medical treatment, women have also been underrepresented in clinical trials of AIDS drugs and treatment. When AIDS became highly manifest in the early and middle 1980s, biomedical, behavioral, and social research on AIDS/HIV infection in the United States and in Western countries was concentrated overwhelmingly on gay and bisexual men as research participants. Although this focus is highly understandable, given the nature of the early stages of the epidemic, the trend has continued, even with the rapid rise in the number of AIDS-infected women.

Important differences in biological factors, transmission patterns, clinical manifestations, and survival times are evident between men and women infected with the HIV virus. Men and women also differ on many psychosocial variables that may affect their immune function and hasten the progress of the disease. Questions are now being raised about whether research findings obtained primarily in men can be reliably generalized to women with AIDS/HIV infection.

In a survey of AIDS/HIV research published in scientific journals in 1984 and in 1991, Rabinowitz (1993), and Rabinowitz and colleagues (1994) found that males are still the predominant research subject. In 1991, nearly four times as many males as females were studied and in almost 25 percent of the studies the participants were not identified according to gender. Although 41 percent of the studies included both males and females, most of them featured inadequate representation of one gender, virtually always females. The authors also found that when women were included, data were not analyzed separately by gender but combined and generalized to both males and females without any justification or rationale (Rabinowitz, Sechzer, & Denmark, 1994). Thus, women, who comprise 52 percent of the adult population, are not only underinsured, underdiagnosed, and undertreated by the medical profession, but are also particularly underrepresented in clinical trials, many of which involve drug treatment for AIDS. There is a crucial need to develop a comprehensive program of education and clinical care that will deal with the special needs of women and children. It is also critical to include more women of all ages in clinical research trials so that a gender-comparative analysis of results can determine when and what type of treatment is necessary for women.

A major issue concerning a woman's risk for developing AIDS addresses the time to begin treatment. Results of a study show that infected women may be at a more advanced stage of infection with HIV than men are, even though the results of their blood tests are identical and, according to federal guidelines, treatment is not yet indicated. This suggests that infected women are treated at a more advanced stage of infection than men and are at a greater risk for developing AIDS when compared to men (Grady, 1998). Aspects of this critical finding are provided in Box 13.3.

Transmission of HIV between Women. Little attention has been given to transmission of HIV between women because the main focus has been on the "standard" transmission behaviors, such as drug use and sharing of needles and sex among men. It has been assumed that the sexual transmission of HIV from woman to woman is low. However, a recent report by Kennedy et al. (1998) has raised questions about the prevalence of HIV transmission between women. A multisite study was conducted by these authors with 871 HIV-infected women, who were then followed up for up to three and a half years. Details of this interesting and informative study are provided in Box 13.4.

Box 13.3

HIV-Infected Women at a Greater Risk for Developing AIDS

HIV-infected women may be at a greater risk for developing AIDS than men even though their blood tests are identical and, according to federal guidelines, they do not need to start treatment. A study carried out at Johns Hopkins School of Public Health measured the *virus load,* or level of virus present in the bloodstream of HIV-infected men and women. This test is important in deciding when to start treatment with antiviral drugs to prevent or delay the onset of AIDS. Guidelines issued by the U.S. Public Health Service recommend beginning treatment for both genders when the viral load rises to 10,000 copies of HIV per millimeter. This level of HIV infection is taken to indicate that the immune system is losing ground to the infection.

The results of the study showed that at a given stage of HIV infection a woman's viral load was lower than a man's even though the immune system of a woman showed as much damage as a man's. Thus, using the viral load as a marker for initiating treatment may very well delay treatment for women, with the result that when their virus load reaches the treatment point, they will be much sicker than men beginning treatment at the same virus level. Researchers who conducted the study recommended that official guidelines be changed to begin treatment earlier for women.

This finding in 650 men and women who are drug users adds fuel to the ongoing debate about just when to begin treatment. Some scientists or physicians feel that treatment with antiviral drugs should be started as soon as possible to prevent damage to the immune system; others, concerned about the side effects of antiviral drugs and drug resistance, feel that treatment should be postponed as long as possible. Still others say that, although the findings are important (and other groups have found similar differences between the sexes), it was premature to change treatment guidelines (Grady, 1998).

The results of this study may have parallels to a woman's risk for developing lung cancer described earlier in this chapter. Findings have suggested that women smokers are twice as likely to develop lung cancer. This may be due in part to women's smaller lungs receiving a more concentrated dose of smoke with its carcinogens, which may make them more vulnerable. Further studies with HIV-infected women will bring a greater understanding of this gender difference. In the meantime, establishing new procedures to detect the stage of HIV infection as an adjunct to measuring viral load may be a valuable guide in determining when to start treatment in women as well as in men.

Box 13.4

HIV Transmission between Women

The sexual behavior of women with the human immunodeficiency virus (HIV) has been largely ignored as a subject of investigation due to the belief that sexual contact between women is an unlikely transmission route for HIV. In the past, studies reported that the majority of women who became infected with HIV had engaged in high-risk behaviors, such as drug injection or sexual contact with men. However, current research indicates that female-to-female sex may be more prevalent than previously envisaged and therefore constitutes a larger risk factor for the spread of HIV than previously surmised.

Responding to this scarcity of information, the HIV Epidemiologic Research Study reported on the sexual behaviors of women infected with HIV. All 871 HIV-positive women who participated in the study met at least one of the following criteria: drug injection since 1985, sex with five or more partners in the last five years, sex with an at-risk male, or sex to obtain money or drugs. Of this group, 250 (29 percent) of HIV-infected women reported having had sex with a woman, and 67 of these women engaged in sexual behavior with one steady female partner.

The study also investigated the prevention practices employed by women to protect their partners from vaginal secretions that could spread the HIV virus. Sextoy use and receptive oral sex were examined. Thirty-four percent of women with a steady sex partner reported using sex toys and 80 percent reported receiving oral sex. Almost every participant engaged in the prevention measure of cleaning sex toys before using them again. However, using a barrier, such as a dental dam, during oral sex was not consistently practiced among these women. Thirty-one percent of this group reported using a barrier "sometimes" during oral sex, while 26 percent reported "always" using a barrier, and 43 percent never used barriers. In contrast, the consistent use of a barrier as a prevention measure is much higher among women from a cohort group who have sex with men. Fifty-three percent of these women reported always using a condom during sexual contact with men. The authors of this study (Kennedy et al., 1998) caution readers about the generalizability of the data because of the small number of women studied. Nevertheless, the sexual behavior and prevention practices among women who have sex with other women is an area that merits significant concern in this era of the AIDS epidemic.

Other Sexually Transmitted Diseases. Borgatta (1994) emphasized that many screening and treatment programs for sexually transmitted diseases are directed at women and, because of this, there may be an inadvertent perception that these diseases are wholly female problems. Except for the gay and bisexual population, screening and prevention programs for men are virtually nonexistent. Undoubtedly, many of the secondary and tertiary effects of STDs are unique to women: chronic pelvic inflammatory disease, tubal infertility, cervical cancer, preterm birth, and neonatal infection. In many other diseases, the behavior that increases the risk of the disease is considered an undesirable behavior and patients can be counseled for strategies to change and decrease risk-taking behavior. Unfortunately, there has been little "unanimity on what constitutes appropriate sexual behavior" (Borgatta, 1994, p. 102), especially to reduce the incidence of STDs. Some of the choices range from people keeping monogamous relationships, delaying initial sexual activity, decreasing the lifetime number of sexual partners, using barrier or other protection against infection, to encouraging alternative sexual practices. This issue is problematic because it is adolescents who are at the highest risk for STDs and AIDS. Although some adolescents may have information about STDs and HIV, their behavior has not seemed to change, and adolescents are still at high risk for these diseases (Borgatta, 1994). The question of whether there should be different approaches for males and females has also been raised.

Other sexually transmitted diseases have not had as much publicity and public concern as has HIV/AIDS, but are still prevalent and serious concerns. Like HIV/AIDS, these other sexually transmitted diseases (STDs) have become widespread and in certain areas uncontrollable. In 1995, the World Health Organization estimated that approximately 333 million people worldwide are infected with STDs each year (WHO, 1995). In the United States alone, it has been reported that at least 13 million people are affected, including a large proportion of adolescents with chlamydia (Burstein et al., 1998; Rathus et al., 1997). These other sexually transmitted diseases that we will discuss here include syphilis, gonorrhea, chlamydia, and the human papilloma virus.

Syphilis. The incidence of syphilis has continued to rise. By 1993, there was a total of 35,000 cases, an increase of about 6 percent from the year before (U.S. Department of Health & Human Services, 1994). The increase has parallelled the rise in cocaine use and HIV infection. Diagnosis is primarily by serologic (blood) tests, which are highly reliable but may not give positive results during the early phase of the disease. Darkfield examinations (microscopic examination of the syphilitic lesions) are specific for syphilis and provide the earliest possible testing. Such examinations require expensive microscopic equipment and may not be available at many primary-care facilities. If early diagnosis is made and treatment given, blood tests may return to negative. Serologic tests are almost always positive during the secondary stage of the disease but cannot distinguish between secondary and tertiary stages. This distinction is important because patients in secondary stage can be cured with one or several injections of penicillin. Tertiary syphilis with organ infection requires more extensive treatment.

More research is needed to develop improved diagnostic tests for the early detection of syphilis and to distinguish between the different stages of the disease. Alternative treatments to penicillin are needed but do not seem forthcoming.

Gonorrhea. Although the incidence of gonorrhea has declined in most portions of the population, there has been an increase in penicillin-resistant gonorrhea. The diagnosis of gonorrhea is usually made early because about 50 percent of males and females with early infection *are* symptomatic. This facilitates early diagnosis and treatment. Treatments for gonorrhea have improved. There are many agents that are effective after only one injection or oral dose. In comparison with the other STDs, treatment options for this disease are effective.

Chlamydia. The incidence of chlamydia is now more frequent than syphilis or gonorrhea. Prevalence may be as high as 10 percent in some populations. Chlamydia is present throughout all socioeconomic groups in the United States, in contrast to gonorrhea and syphilis, which have been associated with low socioeconomic groups. There is a high prevalence and incidence of chlamydia among adolescent females who are at the highest risk for infection (Burstein et al., 1998). Chlamydia is asymptomatic in women and frequently in men. Because of this, the organisms may reside in the subject for a prolonged period during which the disease may be transmitted. The causative organism of chlamydia lives in the cells and cannot be cultured by usual procedures. When symptomatic, chlamydia tends to cause a low-grade illness, but the disease may progress. This may lead to urethral and epididymal scarring in men and to tubal damage in women, which may lead to infertility, ectopic pregnancy, or chronic pelvic infection.

Because of the asymptomatic nature of the disease and concern for progression, effective prevention and screening are essential. Current screening for the disease is expensive, and ideal tests have not been developed. Several treatments are available, including single-dose oral treatments, but early screening is still lacking.

Human Papilloma Virus (HPV). It is estimated that the human papilloma virus (HPV) is present in 10 to 20 percent of women of reproductive age in the United States. HPV is not a reportable disease and may be asymptomatic. Various subgroups of HPV are associated with warts on the genitalia of both men and women and with flat warts that are associated with changes in the vulva, vagina, cervix, and penile skin and with cancerous lesions in these sites. Direct viral tests are difficult and very expensive, so diagnosis is based on identification of the warts and an abnormal Pap smear. There is no specific test for HPV in the offing. Although there are several treatment options for HPV, none is completely effective and recurrences are not unusual. At present there is no optimal treatment approach. Although there is much research in this area, many unanswered questions remain.

Prevention. In the area of primary prevention of STDs, there are a number of issues associated with condom use and spermicide effectiveness. Although condom use has increased and free condom distribution has even further increased their use (Cates, Stewart, & Russell, 1992), formal education apparently does not make a significant difference. In some studies, women at highest risk used condoms less frequently than women at lower risk. The new "female condom" may be a possibility for some women (Cates, Stewart et al., 1992). More efficient spermicides are also needed for primary protection. Spermicides that are basically detergents act differently against the different STD organisms. The development of specific spermicides for each of the diseases does not seem to be evident in the very near future.

Thus, primary prevention for all STDs is the same as we described above, but for secondary prevention and control of the disease, the identification and treatment of different STDs are specific for each. Tertiary prevention from the development of sequelae such as infertility and tubal disease is crucial, but, according to Borgatta (1994), programs planned to prevent or reduce tubal disease may be poorly funded, and treatment for acute pelvic infection may be inadequate and lead to chronic disease. Newer antibiotics have been proposed to treat STDs and more effectively control sequelae.

Many issues need to be addressed, such as the impact of immediate diagnosis through tests conducted in a physician's office versus delay in diagnosis by use of an outside laboratory, the question of turnaround time for such diagnostic tests, and many questions regarding the treatment of those identified with STDs and their partners. In many settings, the patient is given medication for his or her partner. Should this be done or should the partner be made to appear in person and be tested? The partner who has had no contact with the physician needs treatment. The partner may also need to be educated about STDs and their prevention, although education alone, as noted above, does not seem to make a difference.

There is little information on STDs in lesbians, about whether they can transmit vaginitis or chlamydia, although it is assumed that viral diseases like HPV, herpes, and HIV can be transmitted. Because lesbians, like heterosexual women, are no more likely to maintain a monogamous relationship for their lifetime, the majority of lesbians have had some heterosexual contact at some time during their life. Some lesbians have also had bisexual relationships. On the whole, the majority of women having sex with women will probably not seek treatment from the standard health care system, especially if they are not bisexual and not at risk for unintended pregnancy.

DISEASES PRIMARILY AFFECTING WOMEN

This section will describe two diseases that are virtually unique to women, breast cancer and osteoporosis. Although men do develop these diseases, they represent a very small proportion of the affected population. Both breast cancer and osteoporosis are considered to be primarily women's diseases.

Breast Cancer

Breast cancer is a high-mortality illness and is a major health problem in the United States as well as in other parts of the world. For women in this country, breast cancer is the second leading cause of cancer deaths, after lung cancer. Breast cancer alone now accounts for 32 percent of cancer deaths in women, with one in eight women in the United States expected to develop breast cancer (Rowland, 1998). Obviously, not all women with breast cancer will die of the disease. Just why the incidence of breast cancer continues to increase in this country is not at all clear. The causative factors have not been precisely defined, so the prevention of breast cancer still remains difficult (Kemeny, 1994; NIH-ORWH, 1992).

What Is Breast Cancer and How Does It Develop?
Cancer begins when cells in a particular site become altered and are capable of uncontrolled growth. The type of cancer cell that becomes *neoplastic* depends on the site in which it develops.

Kemeney (1994) has provided an excellent review of breast cancer and its treatment. Breast cancer usually starts inside the ducts and then enlarges locally. When confined to the ducts, it is known as *in situ carcinoma*. Once the cancer penetrates the lining of the ducts or the basement membrane, it is then able to invade the tissue around it and becomes an *invasive cancer*. Invasive cancer then has the capacity to enter the lymphatic stream, seeding cancer cells into the lymph nodes, and then seeding them into the bloodstream, by which they travel to other parts of the body (metastasis). The most common sites for *metastasis* from breast cancer are the lungs, liver, and bones (especially the vertebrae) (Kemeny, 1994).

Risk Factors.   The outstanding **risk factors** for breast cancer do not appear to be related to life-style. Breast cancer rates increase with age, from 1 in 622 women by age 35 to 1 in 9 by age 85. Family history is a strong risk factor and a gene related to at least one form of breast cancer has been identified. Women with first-degree relatives (mother, sister, daughter) with premenopausal breast cancer, compared with those without familial breast disease, have a relative risk of greater than 4.0 for developing breast cancer. For a first-degree relative with any breast cancer (not only premenopausal) the risk is 2.0 to 4.0. However, most women who develop breast cancer do not have a family history. Menstrual cycle factors, including early menarche and late menopause, increase the relative risk from 1.1 to 1.9. Age at first full-term pregnancy for women over 30 years of age also increases the risk to more than 2.0. Pregnancy factors and the menstrual cycle have been interpreted in terms of exposure to endogenous estrogen (Travis, 1988), and estrogen replacement therapy has also been associated with some

increased breast cancer risk. Alcohol consumption has been considered a risk factor. Although dietary fat has been assumed to be a risk factor, recent studies do not support this association (Colditz, 1993). On the other hand, postmenopausal obesity does increase the relative risk of breast cancer. Other proposed risk factors, such as breast injury, sexual stimulation, or breast feeding, which many women feel increase breast cancer risk, have not been supported with any empirical data (American Cancer Society, 1994a).

The psychosocial aspects of breast cancer are beginning to be addressed, albeit with a small number of studies. These are described in Box 13.5.

Treatment.   The treatment for breast cancer is based on how far the cancer has spread or the stage of the disease. Kemeny (1994) has described four stages. Stage I is a small cancer confined to the breast; stage II is a larger breast cancer that may have already involved the axillary (under the arm) lymph nodes on the same side as the breast cancer; stage III is a much more advanced cancer that has spread into the skin and chest wall and may have more extensive lymph node involvement; stage IV is a breast cancer that has metastasized or spread into organs outside the breast, like the lungs, liver, or bones.

Stages I and II are considered curable with surgery. Not all these cancers are 100 percent curable, but surgery should cure approximately 50 percent of these tumors with no further treatment. Stage III breast cancer is generally not considered curable by surgery alone, but must have additional treatment with chemotherapy or radiation therapy or both. With a Stage IV cancer, surgery is not indicated because the cancer has already spread outside the breast (Kemeny, 1994).

Early in this century, *radical mastectomy* (removal of the entire breast, chest muscle, and all the lymph nodes) was the concept of a cure for the disease, and this became the standard for tumors that had not spread beyond the breast. In the 1960s total rather than radical mastectomy was tested; the major chest muscle was not removed. Results over 20 years show no difference in survival rates. More recently, the *lumpectomy* procedure was developed and tested. The

Box 13.5_____

Psychosocial Aspects of Breast Cancer

Although written about and commented on in the popular press, it appears that the medical community has not generally studied the psychosocial and psychosexual aspects of breast cancer. From the few small studies available, women seem more comfortable with lumpectomy and tend to adjust better as far as their body image and feelings about their own sexuality are concerned than women who have had mastectomies.

In a California study of women who had undergone either lumpectomy or mastectomy, there were large differences in the sexual and body image states of the two groups. As would be expected, women with mastectomies felt much more negative about their nude appearance and more self-conscious in groups of women. These women also felt less sexually desirable and were more dissatisfied with their body image when compared with women having undergone lumpectomies. However, there was no difference in concern about the

recurrence of their cancer. Neither group showed evidence of undue depression, anxiety, or other psychological stresses.

Thus, the women with lumpectomies appeared better adjusted psychosexually and were not more concerned about recurrence of their cancer. Although other studies have reported similar results, there has as yet been no large nationwide study to examine these and other questions (Bonadonna, Valagussa, & Rossi, 1985).

The psychosexual and psychological well-being of women with breast cancer is a critical concern. These aspects have often been overlooked in rehabilitating women with the disease or in the process of a woman making an informed choice between lumpectomy and mastectomy. These concerns must be considered before any treatment for breast cancer begins (Kemeny, Wellisch, & Schain, 1988).

---

breast is not removed, but only the cancer with a rim of normal breast tissue around it. After studying results for more than 10 years with more than 2000 women, there was no significant difference in disease-free survival between all these variations of treatment (Fisher, Redmond, & Poisson, 1989). Radiation treatment after any of these surgical procedures is often carried out to help prevent the cancer from recurring. Other treatments include new antiestrogen medications like Tamoxifen. Evidence has shown that Tamoxifen has decreased the incidence of the cancer reoccurring in the other breast. Raloxifene (Evista), a new drug for osteoporosis, has also been shown to decrease the incidence of breast cancer.

Other approaches have included self-help groups that meet on a regular basis to exchange various forms of support, from information and tangible help to building self-esteem and addressing other psychological needs. It has been found that survival increased for at least two years in these women compared with women who have not been involved with such support groups.

Prevention.   At the present time there is no way to prevent breast cancer other than by trying to reduce risk factors. Unlike lung cancer, no carcinogenic agent has been identified with breast cancer. However, research with Tamoxifen (an antiestrogen medication) has yielded surprising results. Although there are contradicting reports on its efficacy in preventing cancer recurrence, all studies have shown a decrease in the incidence of a second breast cancer in the opposite breast. Recent research with Tamoxifen is investigating whether it might prevent breast cancer for women who are at high risk. This series of investigations is known as the Breast Chemoprevention Trial and is the first chemoprevention trial in the United States. In late 1998, Tamoxifen was approved by the FDA for women at high risk for breast cancer and for women who have had breast cancer. It may signal a new trend toward preventive medicine in the United States, which is long overdue for women. Another drug, raloxifene or Evista, was approved in the United States for the prevention of osteoporosis. Results of clinical trials demonstrated not only an increase in bone density in women with osteoporosis, but also a decrease in breast cancer.

Osteoporosis

Osteoporosis is a global health problem and is estimated to affect over 200 million people worldwide. This disease affects more than 25 million Americans, 80 percent of whom are women. One-third to one-half of all postmenopausal women have some degree of osteoporosis, and the rates for this disease increase dramatically with age.

What Is Osteoporosis? **Osteoporosis** is characterized by decreased skeletal mass and poor bone quality, which leads to increased fractures, typically of the hip, spine, and wrist (NIH-ORWH, 1992; Galsworthy, 1994). Each year 1.5 million fractures are attributed to osteoporosis, including 250,000 to 300,000 hip fractures. The incidence of fractures in African American and Hispanic women is one-half that of Caucasian and Asian women, but their risk is still serious. A study carried out in the state of Washington found that more than 5 percent of all hospitalizations for injuries of patients who were 65 years or older were the result of falls. More women were injured than men. One of the results of such injuries was that approximately one-half of patients with injuries due to falls were placed in a nursing facility (Brody, 1985; Kaplan et al., 1993; Riggs & Melton, 1992).

Osteoporosis is one of the few medical conditions not described by Hippocrates. This is probably because very few women lived long enough—past menopause—to develop the disease. Even in the late 1800s, women's fragile skeletons were considered a normal part of the aging process, along with changes in posture showing a dowager's hump. These changes were common in elderly Caucasian women. In the 1920s, reports and discussions about weakened bones started to appear in the German literature. The incidence of wrist fractures in women was attributed to the hazards of the long skirts that were worn by women during this time. Astley Cooper, a British surgeon, also noted fragility of bones in aged cadavers. However, in 1941, Fuller Albright concluded that "osteoporosis resulted from inadequate formation and/or excessive breakdown of bone" (Galsworthy, 1994, p. 159). Although his hypothesis was published in the *American Journal of Medicine,* little attention was given to the problem of this chronic illness primarily in women (Galsworthy, 1994).

In the 1960s, medicine began to focus not only on women, but also on elderly men and women. Although women who presented problems of osteoporosis were helped with pain relief and rehabilitation, physicians did not have sophisticated tools with which to make a diagnosis. When the technology for bone scanning was developed in the 1970s, it was possible to identify patients with osteoporosis and the disease became well known across the country and abroad.

Risk Factors. Osteoporosis is often thought of as a silent disorder because symptoms first occur in advanced stages of the disease: wrist fractures, painful and deforming vertebral fractures, and the pain and morbidity of hip fractures. Therefore, physicians will evaluate patients on a profile of risk factors that might predict the future development of the disease. Galsworthy (1994) feels that this profile is not as accurate a predictor of fracture risks as are bone density evaluations. Some of the profile risk factors used at the Osteoporosis Center of the Hospital for Special Surgery in New York City include female, Caucasian, Asian, Northern European, light hair and complexion, diet limited in calcium, sedentary life-style, postmenopausal, fracture history of spine, wrist, and hip, and family history of osteoporosis. To this list may be added past and current medications and especially the use of steroidal and other drugs that cause bone resorption.

Diagnosis. Diagnosis of osteoporosis is confirmed primarily by bone density measurements. This procedure has been shown to be a more accurate predictor of fracture risk than any other assessment. There are a variety of bone density techniques. These measurements confirm the presence of osteoporosis and determine the type of intervention that is necessary.

Because bone is a living tissue, it remodels continually during one's life-span. Remodeling is characterized by rapid resorption (when bone tissue is removed from specific areas in the body) and then a slower phase when bone tissue is re-formed at these sites. In older people, reformation may be deficient, and more and more bone tissue is lost primarily from sites in the wrist, spine, and hip in proportion to bone reformation (National Osteoporosis Foundation, 1991).

Prevention and Treatment.   For women (and men) with osteoporosis or who are at risk for developing osteoporosis, there are many treatment options. Dietary supplementation of calcium, vitamin D, and calcium-rich foods are used. Drugs are now available that protect the bones by either preventing resorptive mechanisms or building bone mass. In this way, bone loss is inhibited and the skeleton can rebuild, albeit slowly. Some of the drugs currently in use are salmon calcitonin (Miacalcin), etidronate (Didronel), alendronate (Fosomax), and the newly released raloxifine (Evista) described earlier. Estrogen replacement for postmenopausal women also helps to prevent bone loss. Other drugs awaiting FDA clearance should be available within the next few years. Exercise is also very important, especially weight-bearing exercise. Of these, walking is considered very effective, as is using a treadmill or a "stepper," which have been shown not only to prevent bone loss but also to increase bone density in the spine and hips, depending on the frequency and intensity of use (National Osteoporosis Foundation, 1991).

Prevention for younger people consists of building up their bone density levels before menopause to prevent bone loss. This includes adequate calcium and vitamin D intake and exercise with an aerobic and general strengthening component on a regular basis. These strategies should become part of one's lifestyle. The National Institutes of Health has made specific recommendations for calcium intake. Of special interest here are those recommendations for women 25 to 50 years of age (1000 mg/day) and for postmenopausal women (1000 to 1500 mg/day).

Although osteoporosis as a health problem has reached virtually epidemic proportions, there is sufficient knowledge to undertake effective therapeutic action immediately. For young women (and men), strategies to prevent bone loss should be pursued throughout their life-span.

CHANGES IN MEDICAL CARE

During the 1980s concern about women's health had gathered enough momentum to begin to effect changes in medical care and research. These changes came about as a result of responses and concerns about women's health by women in positions of authority and by pressure from scientists, both men and women, special-interest groups, the media, and the general public (LaRosa, 1994; Sechzer, Griffin, & Pfafflin, 1994). The increase in the number of women physicians has also been significant. In most medical schools, almost 40 percent or more of the students are women preparing for all specialties, including nontraditional disciplines like surgery.

Changes in Government Regulations

One of the first changes came about in 1990 with the creation of the Office of Research on Women's Health (ORWH) at the National Institutes of Health (NIH). The ORWH directs programs and initiatives concerned with a research agenda on women's health across all the institutes that comprise the NIH and encourages clinical research trials to include adequate numbers of women when the disease or disorder studied is applicable to both sexes. The ORWH also focuses on the recruitment and advancement of women in biomedical centers. With these three goals, the ORWH hopes to stimulate more research on women's health issues to prevent disease and improve the quality of life for women and to promote the identification and treatment of disease with the most advanced gender-sensitive information available (LaRosa, 1994).

A second change was the new policy of the NIH and the Alcohol, Drug, and Mental Health Administration (ADAMHA) stating that clinical research studies must include both genders so that results are applicable to the general population (NIH, 1991). The exceptions are those diseases or conditions that affect only one gender. Thus, we now have a mandate to include adequate numbers of women (as well as men) in clinical research studies of conditions or disorders that affect both males and females. Adequate justification must be given if the researchers feel that only one gender can be used.

The Food and Drug Administration (FDA) has also made changes in its policies regarding the approval of drugs for use in the general population. As of 1993, all drug testing must "include women in reasonable numbers in studies and provide the FDA with information about any significant differences found between men and women in their responses to drugs" (Fourcroy, 1994, p. 186). This new mandate will no longer exclude women of childbearing age from participation in early phases of clinical trials. The research results must also include an analysis of gender-specific differences (Fourcroy, 1994). This action by the FDA essentially reverses a policy that has been in effect since 1977. These changes with their new mandates should have an impact on research with human subjects to assure that sex and gender differences in studies, whether involving diseases or tests of new drugs, will be clarified and made available to physicians for the improved care and treatment of women. These changes will also be valuable for men's health. In the section on bias in health research, we showed that data for both men and women (when women were included) were combined and generalized to both genders. These studies did not identify results by gender, so any adverse affects for either men or women were not evident. Subsequent treatment by health-care providers has relevance for potential harm in their treatment of the patient, whether male or female. It will be important to determine the outcome of research with these regulations in force.

As indicated earlier, by 1994, the Centers for Disease Control also changed their case definition of AIDS. These new guidelines have extended the case definition to include symptoms that occur in women in the early stages of HIV infections, who usually pre-

sent with gynecological symptoms. Hopefully, this will enable women to be diagnosed earlier, to be qualified to receive medical care if they cannot afford it, and to live longer with disease than before.

Women's Medical Centers

When men see a physician, the physician usually carries out a check-up of the patient's entire body. Not so with a woman patient. Budoff, who established the first women's medical center in the United States, has stated that the "medical establishment has divided a woman's body in two parts; the medical and the reproductive" (Budoff, 1994, p. 166). Thus, the female patient needs to see a gynecologist and an internist, most often in different offices, which might involve replicating blood, urine, and other tests that are time consuming and costly. In addition, the annual or biannual mammogram necessitates visiting other offices and physicians. If the patient is at risk for osteoporosis or is at an age where bone density has to be evaluated, this means a trip to another facility. And, even though the reports of each provider are exchanged, it is time consuming though necessary for the appropriate treatment of any disorder found. There has been a growing interest in a place or center where all this care would be available and carried out by physicians and auxiliary health personnel primarily interested in women's health issues.

Over the last ten years, women's medical or health centers have been established. The first women's medical center, developed by Dr. Penny Wise Budoff, opened in Hempstead, New York, in 1985 and has served as a model for other such centers. Although beginning with only two family physicians, one endocrinologist, and one radiologist, today the Budoff Women's Medical Center has a full complement of physicians, from primary-care physicians to those with specialties across the spectrum of women's health needs.

The benefits of a women's medical center are many. It makes available a place where a woman can be seen by physicians and other health-related personnel who are truly interested in women's health. In this center a woman would have all the necessary examinations and tests without the need to see different specialists in various locations and wait for results to be exchanged between providers. A *women's medical center* is an integrated center where examination and test results are available in a shorter time and where different specialists can easily consult with each other and the patient. This can be critical, especially regarding medications and other aspects of treatment that could be reviewed directly with the patient. In such centers, there might be educational programs for preventive strategies and other relevant programs concerning women's health issues. Because there has been a marked increase in the number of women physicians, there is likely to be a majority of female personnel in such centers. The female patient might be more comfortable psychologically discussing sensitive problems with a female physician than she would with a male physician. Thus, as a patient at a women's center, a woman is made to feel special.

Another advantage of a women's center is care of the elderly. A center concerned only with women's health should not discriminate against the older patient. Therefore, for the elderly woman, a center where the physicians that she would see are free of ageism would ensure more concern about her problems and complaints and result in a higher quality of medical care. The individual woman must decide for herself whether she wants to take advantage of the integrated approach of a women's center. This decision may probably be easier for young women who are just beginning to develop a health-care program and are fully aware of their autonomy as patients and may be more critical in their choices.

SUMMARY

Physical health problems cannot be considered apart from psychological issues, particularly for women who have found so many impediments to appropriate health care. We have examined the social construction of illness, going back to Victorian times in the nineteenth century, and described how particular attitudes and practices borne of this and earlier eras have continued into the present and have affected women's health, their medical care, and the research on the diseases and disorders that they develop.

In the first part of this chapter, we recounted how the attitudes of society in general and of physicians in particular dominated the lives of women during Victorian times. We reviewed the literature on the acceptance of women's roles and inferior status, thus helping society maintain these views into present times. To our twenty-first century readers, it may be hard to understand how women accepted their socially constrained roles and how a sexuo-economic relationship with men developed.

Building on these historical associations, we went on to discuss the health problems of women and how they compare with those of men. We attempted to explain why women are sicker than men with the same health problems. The problem of stress and pain was reviewed, as well as the behaviors that develop in response to stressful situations.

The next section of this chapter reviewed issues of gender bias in women's health from a variety of approaches. We described major illnesses that affect both women and men, cardiovascular disease, lung cancer, HIV/AIDS infection, and the gender differences in these illnesses. We also described research on these diseases to determine whether treatment of data for women and men was biased and whether this pattern changed across an eight-year period. We discussed the inherent gender bias we found not only in subject selection for the studies, but also in evaluating and generalizing results of such studies to women and men without any justification. In doing so, we also evaluated the consequences of gender bias on the health of women. Breast cancer and osteoporosis, diseases primarily affecting women, were also reviewed.

In the last section of this chapter, we explored some important recent changes in medical care and speculated about the apparent attention they are bringing to gender differences in health research, as well as in diagnosis and treatment. Finally, we presented the advantages of the newly developing women's medical centers that are being established to take care of women's health problems all at one site and by physicians interested in women's health regardless of age or socioeconomic status.

In conclusion, women, with regard to their health and their psychological and physiological response to various diseases and treatments, have been understudied. Their gender, as an important component in health and research, has been undervalued. There are, however, signs of change. So as we begin the twenty-first century, we look forward to the recognition of gender as a crucial variable in the study of disease and the underlying research upon which diagnosis and treatment depend.

KEY TERMS

Acquired immunodeficiency
   syndrome (AIDS) (p. 423)
Antibody (p. 424)
Asymptomatic (p. 425)
Benign (p. 421)
Cancer (p. 421)
Cerebrovascular disease (p. 418)
Coronary artery disease (p. 418)
Fight or flight response (p. 410)
General adaptation syndrome
   (p. 411)

High-risk behavior (p. 425)
HIV (p. 423)
HIV positive (HIV+) (p. 426)
HIV-seropositive (p. 427)
Immune system (p. 425)
Maladaptive behaviors (p. 413)
Malignant (p. 421)
Opportunistic infection (p. 426)
Osteoporosis (p. 434)
Pain (p. 415)
Pain threshold (p. 415)

Pain tolerance (p. 415)
Peripheral artery disease (p. 418)
Risk factor (p. 432)
Sexually transmitted diseases
   (STDs) (p. 423)
Stress (p. 410)
   Eustress (p. 412)
   Neutral stress (p. 412)
Sympathetic nervous system (p. 412)
T cell (p. 424)
Tumor (p. 421)

DISCUSSION QUESTIONS

1. The literature on breast cancer has dealt mainly with married women, age 50 or more, yet statistics show that younger women are developing breast cancer. What are the issues facing younger women who are diagnosed with breast cancer, married or single, or in a relationship? How would they differ from those of older women?

2. As a woman, if you were faced with the diagnosis of breast cancer, what would be your choice of treatment? How would you make this decision? With whom would you consult? Would you consider having a second opinion? What would you want from your spouse or significant other? Would you tell your friends?

3. As a man, how do you think you would react if your spouse, significant other, or current girlfriend informed you that she has been diagnosed with breast cancer?

4. Do you currently see a male physician for either gynecological care and/or medical care? Have you experienced any bias or overt sexism in his treatment and attitude toward you? What do you consider the most important issues of bias and prejudice that one should look for when being treated by a male physician? If you had your choice, would you prefer to be treated by a female physician if she were on the same level of expertise as the male physician?

5. Do you think that over the next ten years female physicians will outnumber male physicians? How might medicine change?

6. Recent statistics have shown that, while smoking among males has decreased along with a decrease in lung cancer, smoking by women has increased with a concomitant increase in lung cancer. In fact, lung cancer now kills more women than breast cancer. What social and psychological factors do you think have contributed to this turn for the worse for women?

7. In many states, all newborn babies are tested anonymously for HIV infection to estimate the dimensions of the epidemic. When an infant tests positively for HIV, it is a valid indication that the mother is also infected, even though most states do not inform the mother because of individual privacy rights. Do you agree with this provision or do you feel that the mother should be notified of her HIV status? Is it possible to notify the mother without violating her privacy rights? What are the benefits of informing the mother as well as the drawbacks?

8. If you were a therapist or counselor and learned that your client was infected with HIV but refused to inform his or her partner, even though they were having sex together, how would you handle this situation?

9. Heart disease is now the number one killer of both men and women, but it seems that not only are men treated differently from women but also many tests or treatments are not very effective for women. Although some progress is being made to be more gender fair in treatment, what would you do if your mother or a close female friend or relative was diagnosed with a heart condition and worried that the treatment that you were receiving was gender biased or that it would not be effective for you as a woman?

SUGGESTED READINGS

Alexander, L. L., & LaRosa, J. H. (1994). *New dimensions on women's health.* Boston: Jones and Bartlett.

Corea, G. (1992). *The invisible epidemic: The story of women with AIDS.* New York: HarperCollins.

Love, S. M. (1990). *Dr. Susan Love's breast book.* Reading, MA: Addison-Wesley.

Shilts, R. (1987). *And the band played on.* New York: Penguin Book.

Steele, G. D., Winchester, D. P., Menck, H. R., & Murphy, G. P. *National cancer data base—Annual review of patient care.* Atlanta, GA: American Cancer Society, American College of Surgeons Commission on Cancer.

Thaul, S., & Hotra, D. (1993). *An assessment of the NIH Women's Health Initiative.* Washington, DC: Institute of Medicine.

A REFLECTION ON THE FUTURE

The times are changing. Change may be occurring too quickly for some, but change is not occurring fast enough for many boys and girls limited by their gender roles to less than full lives.
—Carol Nagy Jacklin

And how do you look backward. By looking forward. And what do they see. As they look forward. They see what they had to do before they could look backward. And there we have it all.
—Gertrude Stein

Living each day as a preparation for the next is an exciting way to live. Looking forward to something is much more fun than looking back at something—much more constructive. If we prepare ourselves so that we never have to think, "Oh, if I had only known, if I had only been ready," our lives can really be the great adventure that we so passionately want them to be.
—Hortense Odlum

The future depends entirely on what each of us does each day . . . a movement is only people moving.
—Gloria Steinem

On what basis could we form a coalition is still an open question. The idea of basing it on sexual preferences strikes me as somewhat dubious, strikes me as being less than a firm foundation. It seems to me that a coalition has to be based on the grounds of human dignity. . . . There's nothing in me that is not in everybody else, and nothing in everybody else that is not in me. . . . I'm saying I have nothing to prove. The world also belongs to me. . . . If you don't live the only life you have, you won't live some other life; you won't live any life at all.
—James Baldwin

How do we continue to forge progressive change in women's lives without being limited by the past? Can we envision a future world that involves social equality in power relations between men and women? Is it finally safe to say that psychology is being altered by the work of feminist psychologists and the new scholarship on women? In the not too distant past, the psychology of women and the psychology of gender were marginalized areas within psychology, but now research findings in these fields are being incorporated into the general domain of psychology. Indeed, these findings have altered, if not revolutionized, theory and method in psychology and other behavioral and social sciences. For example, issues that were once deemed women's issues are now seen as part of the human montage. Margaret Matlin has pointed out that in psychology texts under the letter *r,* you would find "reticular activating system" or even "rat," but not "rape." But now, rape and other issues germane to women have been incorporated in the general knowledge base of psychology and have enriched our understanding of all people.

Psychology is evolving to become a discipline that reflects and encompasses the behavior of *all* people in a social context, not just men, as it has in the past. The inequities women have endured and the equalities that they pursue command the attention of psychologists today. We are in an era of rapid social change with profound implications for changing gender roles. As we have discussed throughout this book, this is evident in many areas of life, including education, home, and family, the workplace, science, mental and physical health, and global issues affecting women.

If the future looks progressively better for both girls and women, it is a future filled with challenges and dangers. The preceding chapters identified problems that need to be addressed and resolved at the individual, social, and societal levels. The issues within these chapters indicate areas of needed reenergizing, rethinking, and reform. Regardless of whether one locates the causes of women's oppression in political, economic, sociological, or psychological factors, we must join forces to fight what some have called a backlash against feminism and feminists. Bearing this in mind, let us turn to certain issues that merit special attention in a future psychology of women and gender.

CRITICAL ISSUES FOR THE FUTURE

Images of Women

Sexism is on the defensive, but it is still openly permissible in a context in which racism or ethnocentrism would not be tolerated. Women are subjected to a daily barrage of representations in religion, education, science, and the media that are inaccurate and harmful. As we have seen vividly in Chapter 2, most religions relegate women to a secondary role in the official activities of the congregation and perpetuate women's devalued status. As we saw in Chapter 6, educators still treat children on the basis of presumed innate gender differences, rather than on the basis of individual differences. Gender-based expectations that teachers have of students may foster gender-differentiated skills and self-perceptions that limit them later on. Throughout this book, we have pointed out that although biological differences between men and women may have important implications for behavior and other outcomes, the effects of historical, cultured, and social contexts are too often ignored, minimized, or deemed trivial.

Perhaps nowhere are stereotyped images of women more ubiquitous— and damaging—than in the popular media, where women are still too often valued and defined by their physical attractiveness and where older women, disabled women, and others who do not conform to rigidly defined standards of appropriate female appearance and behavior are invisible. Psychology can do its part to change negative, inaccurate, and harmful images of women by continuing to undermine faulty beliefs that gender differences are large and due mainly to biological factors and that the needs of society are best served by traditional gender roles.

Occupational Barriers

Women today do obtain positions in occupations that are traditionally dominated by men. There is, however, a cost for many women entering fields that have been unoccupied by women or occupied by only a few women. As we have discussed in Chapters 7 and 11, sexual harassment, lack of promotion, and a hostile atmosphere may greet the most competent and ambitious woman. The expectation among contemporary young women is that barriers have been removed; the reality is quite different.

There is an increasing recognition of the need for family-oriented policies for men and women in the workplace by both the government and private industry. In 1993, President Clinton proposed and Congress passed the Family Leave Act, which allows 12 weeks of unpaid leave for reasons related to care of a family member in all companies of over 50 employees. Unfortunately, family supportive policies are still more the exception than the rule in U.S. businesses and organizations. But even where such policies exist, they are often not exploited by workers. The reasons for this are many and complex, but may include the fact that the leave is inadequate for many people's needs and may stigmatize or marginalize workers who choose to take it. Moreover, in a country where high-quality day care is scarce, many women feel that they cannot pursue high-powered careers once they begin

their families, and this may lead them to defer or forego childbearing. It appears that policies and laws do not always achieve their purposes in contemporary society.

In 1980, women earned approximately 60 percent of men's wages. By 1995, this had increased to 72 percent of men's wages. Despite these gains, pay equity remains a critical goal for women in all occupations. To increase gender diversity in the workplace, we need to continue to support affirmative-action programs and policies that break the glass ceiling and bring women into leadership roles within organizations. Psychologists can help us to achieve a better understanding of how such policies can be successfully justified and implemented.

Housework: The Revolution Left Undone

Perhaps nothing better represents the power inequity between men and women than the traditional division of household labor by sex. It is doubtful that gender roles outside the home can change very much if they do not change within the home. Some recent studies pointed to the fact that men reported an increase in their chores at home to the point of near parity with women. Other studies, however, which rely on couples writing down what they do each day, show little change in men's participation in family chores. But it should be noted that the higher a couple's income and education are, the more shared the household responsibilities are because of the greater likelihood of affording outside help. Young women need to understand that if past trends persist and budgets are limited, they may be working two shifts, one at home and one at work. Will that satisfy them? Are these the lives we envision for our daughters? What can be done to make the division of household labor more gender fair?

Redefining Masculinity

It has been a theme of this book that there continue to be significant limitations placed on the female gender role, including low pay, status, and power in the home, workplace, and larger world and disproportionately

444 EPILOGUE

heavy workloads in the home. There are significant problems found with the male gender role as well. To name a few: limited personal and social relationships and physical health problems stemming from overwork and unhealthy life-style choices. The culture of masculinity and its negative impact on men, women, and children require careful and sustained study. To date, masculinity is rarely construed as a problem and as such it needs to be brought into national discourse.

CHANGES IN THE FIELD OF PSYCHOLOGY

A number of trends in psychology merit attention. One significant trend concerns psychology as both a discipline that studies women and a discipline that attracts female students. An increasing number of psychologists are women. A number of implications flow from this, some of them troubling, but more of them positive. Some psychologists are concerned that as a profession becomes more "feminized," that is when the proportion of women increases beyond 50 percent, the status and pay of the profession declines. However, as we have seen, the perspectives and experiences of women are appropriately changing what psychologists study and how it is studied. Clearly, many benefits to psychology come from the influx of feminist women. Such women will be able to impart not only survival strategies to women through mentoring and networking, but also nurture feminist psychologists who challenge the status quo (Denmark, 1992).

Science and its associated research methods have been subjected to increasing scrutiny and critique by feminist psychologists. The experimental method, for example, was once thought to characterize the only approach for a scientific psychology. Although this method is appropriate for many basic research questions, it is limited in the study of major status characteristics such as gender, race, ethnicity, and class to which people cannot be randomly assigned. Furthermore, the experimental method presents its own problems and difficulties, which were previously buried in the mythology that all science was "objective" and "value-free." Indeed, feminist reviews of research methods demonstrate the fallibility of such thinking (Rabinowitz & Sechzer, 1993). While some psychologists may mourn any erosion of the authority of the experimental method, other psychologists have developed scientific skepticism about the overreliance on classical methods. The result is a willingness to consider what was once heretical: qualitative research methods. The use of such qualitative research methods as ethnography, discourse analysis, and clinical interviews is increasing and enriching the field. Some psychologists consider the integration of quantitative and qualitative methods to represent the best approach to many research questions.

SMALL WORLD: INTERNATIONAL REALM OF WOMEN'S ACTIVITIES

As we highlighted in Chapter 4 and mainstreamed throughout this book, gender interacts with culture, race, ethnicity, and class, and to consider it apart from these rich variables is to miss its essence. There is no "ideal" woman or man. Women and men come only in different ethnicities, cultural backgrounds, social classes, and so on. It is only at the intersections of these variables that we get a glimpse of the variations and possibilities that exist within gender categories. The psychology of the future needs to find more and better ways to conceptualize and study gender at the intersections. Indeed, the journey to gender equality may be quite different in different societies and cultures. As Burn (1996) notes, "Countries that are openly stratified and accepting of class differences may foster a greater acceptance of inequality. Women's movements in these countries may have to rely on a different rationale than those in Western countries in order to garner support" (p. 151). As we contemplate women's issues across cultures, we need to consider that Western-style feminist values may conflict with the values of cherishing cultural diversity. But just as we must not impose Western values on others, we must also continue to champion universal values like the equality of all people and challenge cultural practices that are sexist, racist, homophobic, or discriminatory in other ways. Promoting equality and well-being among all people in a multicultural world is a central challenge for psychology, particularly for feminist psychology, as we enter the twenty-first century.

GLOSSARY

Acculturation The adoption by an individual or a group of the culture patterns of another group; a process of social change caused by the interaction of significantly diverse cultures.

Achievement motivation The desire to accomplish something of importance due to one's own efforts, the desire to excel at what one does.

Adolescence The period between childhood and maturity.

African American Descendant of Africans who were brought to the United States as slaves.

Ageism Discrimination on the basis of age.

AIDS (acquired immune deficiency syndrome) A progressive deterioration of the immune system caused by HIV (human immunodeficiency virus) that suppresses the immune system's ability to fight various infections and malignancies. A diagnosis of HIV/AIDS is made on the basis of a blood test.

American Indian (Native American Indian) Overinclusive term referring to anyone whose ancestors are from one of the 587 American Indian tribes.

Androgen insensitivity A disorder in which a genetically male fetus does not respond to the masculinizing effects of his androgens.

Androgens Hormones like testosterone that develop and sustain secondary sex characteristics in males. Androgens are considered the male hormones.

Androgenital syndrome Occurs when genetically normal female fetuses are physically masculinized by a surplus of androgens.

Anorexia nervosa A serious eating disorder characterized by an intense fear of obesity, intentional starvation, and a distorted body image.

Antibody A special protein created by the body's immune system that fights specific agents causing infections in the body. With HIV infections, the infecting virus cannot be destroyed by antibodies.

Apostle Any of the 12 disciples sent out by Christ to teach the gospel (the Christian doctrine of the redemption of man through Jesus as Christ).

Asian American Overinclusive term referring to people whose ancestors are from China, Japan, Korea, India, Southeast Asia, and South Asia.

Assimilation The process by which immigrants or other newcomers become accepted by the people of the culture to which they have adapted.

Asymptomatic Without obvious symptoms. In the case of HIV, it means that a person can be infected with the virus but have no signs or symptoms. However, even though asymptomatic, an infected individual can still infect others.

Attributions for achievement Social psychologists have determined that people make judgments about the likely causes of events including their successes and failures. Attributions differ along the dimensions of internality, stability, and controllability. In achievement situations, they are generally made to ability, effort, luck, or task difficulty.

Aversive racism A phenomenon whereby covert forms of discrimination prevail even among those who loudly proclaim their egalitarianism.

Battered women Women subjected to physical and emotional abuse. A somewhat problematic term because it puts the focus on the victims and their stigmatized identities rather than the perpetrators and may keep victims silent and ashamed.

B.C.E. Before the Common Era; the same as B.C., Before Christ.

Behavior setting A basic environmental unit that entails the naturally occurring spatial and temporal features that surround behavior and the appropriate behavioral match.

Behavior therapy A system of therapies based on principles of learning theory.

Benign tumors Cells that are encapsulated and do not spread. They can be removed completely.

Bias in research methods Bias occurs in every part of the research process, from question formulation and research design to data analysis and interpretation.

Bisexual A person sexually attracted to both males and females.

Bisexuality Sexual activity with and/or the desire for people of both sexes.

Black Term used for African Americans, people from the Caribbean (e.g., West Indians), "Black" Hispanics, and recent immigrants from Africa.

Blatant sexism Occurs when women are treated in a transparently harmful and unequal way.

Brahma The supreme and eternal essence or spirit of the universe.

Brass ceiling Women's exclusion from combat, which precludes their advancement in the military.

Bronze Age Occuring between the Stone Age and the Iron Age; during this period, bronze tools and weapons were developed.

Bulimia nervosa A serious eating disorder characterized by cycles of binging and purging by episodes of self-induced vomiting and the habitual use of laxatives.

Cancer A large group of diseases characterized by uncontrolled growth and spread of abnormal cells independent of the rest of the body that metastasize to other parts of the body (see also *tumor*).

Capacitation The process that makes the sperm capable of penetrating the ovum.

C.E. Common Era; the same as A.D., from Anno Domini, the Latin for "In the year of the Lord."

Cerebrovascular disease Occurs when the blood supply of an artery to a part of the brain changes due to a blockage (clot) or a break in the vessel.

Chicanos/Chicanas Men and women of Mexican origin.

Chromosomes The genetic material in the nucleus of every cell of the body. The sperm and ova each have 23 cells; all the other cells of the body have 46.

Class The socioeconomic status of the individual or group.

Classism A society that stigmatizes poor people, working-class people, and their cultures while valuing the affluent and their cultures solely because of their relative wealth.

Climacteric The aging process between 45 and 65 years of age.

Cognitive–behavioral therapy A type of psychotherapy that uses behavior therapy and attempts to identify and restructure dysfunctional thoughts.

Cohabitation Unmarried couples living together.

Cohort A group of people born within the same year or years.

Conception The union of a sperm cell and a viable ovum; the onset of pregnancy, marked by implantation of the blastocyst (zygote) in the endometrium of the uterus.

Conceptus The fertilized ovum at any stage of development from fertilization until birth.

Contextualistic behaviorism A perspective that emphasizes that "behaviors" have no a priori categorical meanings, but must be understood and defined through a careful analysis of the context in which the behaviors occur.

Contingent worker An individual who is working part-time as a temporary employee or on a per diem basis.

Contraceptives Methods of birth control. These vary in their levels of effectiveness, cost and ease of use, sharing of responsibility between males and females, and protection from sexually transmitted diseases (STDs).

Conventional reasoning Kohlberg's second stage of moral development in which children abide by internal moral standards that are based entirely on those of their parents and/or society.

Coronary artery disease Illnesses caused by atherosclerosis, a narrowing of the coronary arteries supplying blood to the heart. Atherosclerotic plaques deposited in the vessels of the heart narrow the vessels until little or no blood can pass through.

Covert sexism A form of sexism that is intentional, hidden, and often hostile.

Cultural approach Explains the origin of gender stereotypes from a sociocultural perspective in which children are socialized to act in accordance with their cultural dictates.

Cultural deprivation model Explains the condition of African Americans within the context of racism, prejudice, and discrimination by arguing that problems of ethnic identity, self-esteem, school failure, chronic unemployment, family disturbances, and higher rates of more serious psychiatric disorders are caused by oppressive environmental circumstances.

Cultural feminism Emphasizes characteristics and qualities of women that have been devalued and ignored in our society.

Culture A group's program for survival in and adaptation to its environment; the cultural program consists of knowledge, shared beliefs, concepts, and values shared by group members through systems of communication

Cunnilingus Oral–genital sexual activity performed on women.

Date rape Rape in the context of a dating or romantic relationship.

Depression An affective disorder characterized by sadness, loss of interest in situations usually pleasant, a negative view of self, feelings of hopelessness, helplessness, and passivity, suicidal intent, loss of weight and appetite with sleep disturbances.

Division 35   The American Psychological Association's Division of the Psychology of Women, which was established in 1973.

Dominant culture   The culture that owns and controls the means of production and commerce; has the power to grant and take away livelihoods; owns and controls the channels of communication in the society; decides what, how, and who gets addressed in the media.

Dominant generation   Comprised of individuals in their middle years who are responsible for the care-giving for both the young and old.

Double standard of aging   The differential standards applied to aging men and women. Typically, aging women are devalued for their reduced physical attractiveness, while aging men remain highly valued for their continued competence and autonomy.

Ecological model   Theoretical perspective in psychology in which human behavior is understood in terms of the interaction between the person and the environment.

Effect size   A statistic that tells us how large the effect of a variable is or how large the difference between two groups is. The most commonly used measure of effect size is Cohen's *d*. Effect sizes below 0.3 are considered small; between 0.3 and 0.7, moderate; and above 0.7, large.

Egalitarian marriages   Relatively uncommon marriages in which the husbands and wives are partners in the truest sense of the term. Neither spouse is dominant or submissive, roles are flexible, and responsibilities are shared.

Electra complex   According to Freudian theory, the sexual attraction of a young girl toward her father. This is usually associated with hostility toward the mother.

Emaciation   A state of weight loss of at least 25 percent of total body weight and 15 percent below the normal weight for one's age, height, and gender.

Emic   Attributes and traits that are culturally specific.

Embryo   The fertilized ovum that will eventually become the offspring. It is called an embryo from the second week after fertilization until the end of the eighth week of pregnancy.

Empty nest syndrome   When children leave the home and parents are left to cope with their absence.

Endogamy   The custom of marrying only within one's tribe or clan.

Endogenous depression   A depression resulting from disordered biological functioning.

Engendering psychology   Cultivating a psychology in which gender considerations are mainstreamed throughout the discipline.

Epistle   Any of the letters in the New Testament written by an Apostle; a selection from the Epistles read as part of the mass or communion in church.

Estrogen   A hormone present in both females and males, but with its highest concentration in females. It is considered the female hormone. It is produced by the ovaries and adrenal glands in the female and by the testes and the adrenals in the male; in the female it stimulates breast growth at puberty, maintains the lining of the uterus, and controls the menstrual cycle.

Ethnicity   A sense of commonality transmitted over generations by the family and reinforced by the surrounding community based on perceived similarity by virtue of a common ancestry.

Ethnocultural group   A population of people that is largely self-perpetuating, shares fundamental cultural values, makes up a field of communication and interaction, and has a membership that identifies itself and is identified by others as constituting a category distinguishable from other categories of the same order.

Etic   Attributes and traits that are universal.

Eustress   Internal or external stressors that induce stress, but may also initiate responses that have some potential beneficial effects.

Exchange theory   A theory of interpersonal attraction which holds that people pursue relationships in which the value of the resources that they will obtain from their partner is greatest relative to the value of the resources that they can offer in return.

Exogamy   The custom of marrying only outside of one's tribe or clan. Outbreeding.

Exogenous depression   A depression precipitated by a life stressor. Also called *reactive depression.*

Fear of success   A construct named by Matina Horner to explain why women do not achieve as well as men. According to Horner, women feel that success involves loss of femininity and social rejection. Research has not generally supported the idea that women fear success more than men.

Fellatio   Oral–genital sexual activity performed on men.

Feminism   The belief that women and men are equal, should be equally valued, and have equal rights.

Feminization of poverty An increasing trend over time for women to be overrepresented among the poor in the United States.

Fertilization A process that begins with the fusion of the sperm and ova (egg) and ends with the formation of the zygote.

Fetal alcohol syndrome Symptoms presented by an infant exposed to heavy amounts of alcohol during gestation, which include growth deficiencies and nervous system alterations.

Fetus The unborn offspring in the postembryonic period from the ninth week after fertilization until birth.

Fight or flight response A response by which the body is swiftly aroused, usually in response to an external threatening stimulus. The response is initiated through the sympathetic nervous and endocrine systems, resulting in the individual either fleeing or fighting the object of the threat.

First-wave of feminism Feminism begun in 1903 with the founding of the women's Social and Political Union.

Follicular phase This first phase begins when ovarian follicles begin to mature.

Foreplay General name given for a variety of acts that are intended to be sexually arousing and a prelude for later intercourse.

Gender 1. A concept that refers to how differences between boys and girls and men and women are arranged in the social context of society. 2. Psychological features and social categories created by human cultures to describe the traits and behaviors that are regarded by the culture as appropriate to women and men.

Gender harassment Generalized sexist remarks and behavior that convey insulting, degrading, or sexist attitudes toward women.

Gender identity The process, occurring in early childhood, of coming to identify oneself as female or male.

Gender identity disorder Gender confusion in which children display cross-gender role behaviors and express a wish to belong to the other sex.

Gender schema theory Theory proposed by Bem, which suggests that children create knowledge structures that organize gender-related information in memory and are used to evaluate new information according to gender.

Gender stereotypes 1. Cognitive representations of males and females. 2. An organized set of beliefs about the psychological traits and characteristics and the activities appropriate to men or women.

Gendered division of labor A phenomenon in which the division of occupations into two genders is grounded in stereotypes of innate sex differences in traits and abilities.

General adaptation syndrome Hans Selye first described this syndrome as a means by which an individual responds to stress. The syndrome is characterized by (1) a nonspecific mobilization stage that initiates sympathetic nervous system activity; (2) a resistance stage, by which the individual attempts to cope with the threat; (3) a stage of exhaustion, which takes place if the individual cannot overcome the threat and thus its physiological responses are depleted.

Genital mutilation, female (FGM) A practice occurring in many parts of Africa and the Middle East in which girls and young women have the foreskin of the clitoris removed and/or the clitoris and labia removed; often the two sides of the vulva are sewn together with unsterilized equipment and without anesthesia as part of a rite of passage.

Glass ceiling The phenomenon in the workplace whereby women are unable to attain the highest levels in the corporate ladder hierarchy.

Gonad A ridge of tissue that forms around the sixth week of gestation that is sexually undifferenciated.

Grafenberg or G-spot A hypothesized place in the vagina that, when stimulated, presumably produces a distinct and powerful orgasm in women. Evidence for the existence of a G-spot is not conclusive.

Graying of America The phenomenon in the United States whereby increased medical awareness and technology cause increased longevity for individuals.

Hegemony Political domination and power, especially the leadership or domination of one state over others in a group.

Heilman's lack of fit model The idea that gender biases stem largely from an incongruity between an applicant's perceived attributes and the requirements of the position.

Heterosexism An ideological system that denies, denigrates, and stigmatizes any nonheterosexual form of behavior, identity, relationship, or community.

Heterosexual A male or female with sexual orientation toward the other sex.

High risk or unsafe behavior In the case of HIV/AIDS and other sexually transmitted diseases, specific sexual or drug-related activities that increase the chances of contracting or transmitting HIV or other viruses. High-risk behaviors are those that allow blood, semen, or vaginal fluid of one person to contact the blood or mucous membranes (in the eyes, mouth, rectum, vagina) of another person. HIV can also be transmitted through breast milk. Two of the highest-risk behaviors are having intercourse without using a condom (barrier protection) and sharing intravenous (IV) needles in drug use. Unprotected anal intercourse is a particularly high risk behavior.

Hispanic   All people of Spanish origin, which includes a variety of nationalities, ethnicities, and races.

HIV   Abbreviation for human immunodeficiency virus. HIV is a slow-acting virus that is believed to be the cause of AIDS.

HIV positive (HIV+), HIV-seropositive   Terms used to describe a person infected with HIV.

Homogamy   The notion that people tend to marry others highly similar to themselves on demographic, physical, and psychological characteristics.

Homosexual   A male or female with a sexual orientation toward partners of his or her own sex.

Horizontal hostility   Members of a subordinate group expressing self-hatred and hostility in a horizontal direction toward one's own kind (e.g., infighting among members of a subordinate group, violence and crime directed toward members of their own group).

Hormone   A chemical substance secreted by the endocrine system of females and males and carried directly to the organ or tissue upon which it acts.

Immune system   The system that protects the body from infection. Specialized cells in the immune system and proteins in the blood and in other bodily fluids work together to eliminate disease-causing agents or other toxic foreign substances from the body.

Incest   Sexual relations between people of any age who are so closely related that such relations are prohibited and punishable by law.

Inferiority model   A vast array of theories that explicitly or implicitly link African Americans' status in society to inherent genetic defects.

Insider's perspective   A research perspective based on the ideas and hypotheses of an insider social scientist who is from the culture or group being researched.

Involuntary minority   People and their descendants who were originally forced against their will by Euro-Americans through slavery, conquest, and colonization to marginally participate in U.S. society;

they tend to define themselves and their cultures in opposition to the cultural values of the majority.

Issei   First-generation Japanese Americans born and raised in Japan.

Karma   Belief that a person's actions in any one of his or her states of existence will determine his or her fate and status in the next life. One's destiny.

Late mid-life astonishment   Occurs when a woman in her 50s realizes the onset and stigma of aging.

Lateralization   The extent to which one hemisphere of the brain organizes a particular process of behavior.

Latinos/Latinas   Men and women from Latin America; some politically conscious men and women prefer these terms to Hispanic.

Liberal feminism   Focuses on equality of women and men.

Linguistic sexism   The perpetuation and reinforcement of sexist ideology through the content of a language.

Luteal phase   The third phase of the menstrual cycle, which begins after ovulation. The corpus luteum produces large amounts of progesterone and estrogen to prepare the uterus for the implantation of the fertilized egg.

Maladaptive behaviors   Behaviors inappropriate to the typical behavior of the individual. They can occur as a response to stress or stressors when the individual is unable to adapt or cope with these.

Malignant tumors   Cells that grow diffusely through normal tissue and are difficult to remove and continue to spread (*metastasize*) to other parts of the body.

Marianismo   A concept in Hispanic culture that considers women morally and spiritually superior to men.

Marital rape   Very severe kinds of rape; marital rape occurs when a husband has sexual relations with his wife against her will. Marital rape is not recognized as rape in many countries and is often not taken seriously in our own society.

Marriage gradient   The tendency for men to marry "down" in age, social, and economic class, whereas women tend to marry "up" on these dimensions.

Masturbation   Solitary sexual activity practiced by means of manual stimulation of the genitals, with or without the aid of artificial stimulation.

Matching hypothesis   The idea that people tend to develop romantic relationships with those who are similar to them, especially in physical attractiveness.

Menarche   The onset of the menstrual period in girls, which occurs during puberty and signals the start of womanhood.

Menopause   The time when a woman's menstrual cycle slows down and finally stops. This usually occurs sometime between a woman's late forties and early fifties.

Men's movement   Organized military, political, religious, and economic events undertaken to benefit men.

Menstrual cycle   This cycle occurs approximately every month and continues until about the late forties or early fifties. The menstrual cycle has four phases.

Menstrual phase   The fourth phase of the menstrual cycle. A flow of blood begins from the lining of the uterus in females after they have reached puberty.

Mesolithic Age   *Meso* means mid or middle. The Mesolithic Age refers to the period between the Paleolithic and Neolithic ages during which certain animals and plants were domesticated. The Mesolithic Age ranged from about 10,000 B.C.E. until approximately 7000 B.C.E.

Meta-analysis   A statistical technique that combines the data from different studies that test the same hypothesis in order to determine whether there was an overall effect of a variable.

Model minority   Stereotypic belief that Asian Americans have overcome discrimination and are an exemplary group.

Modern gender-role ideology   Belief that both husband and wife participate in stereotypical masculine behavior (breadwinning) and stereotypical feminine behavior (homemaking).

Modern marriage   Senior partner–junior partner relationships, which capture the notion that husbands and wives are almost equals in most respects, but in important matters the husband's will predominates.

Monotheism   The doctrine or belief that there is only one God.

Morality of constraint   Also called *heteronomous morality*. This is Piaget's first stage of moral development that lasts until 9 to 10 years old. Children base moral judgments on objective consequences, believe that rules are immutable, and believe in imminent justice or natural retribution for wrongdoing.

Morality of cooperation   Also called *autonomous morality*. This is Piaget's second stage of moral development during which children base their moral judgments on intentions rather than their consequences, regard rules as social convention, and realize the imprudence of believing in imminent justice.

Mosque   A Moslem (Muslim) temple or place of worship.

Motherhood mandate   The enormous social pressure to have children that girls and women experience; the belief that females must have children in order to be real and complete women.

Motherhood mystique   Idealized images and stereotypes that surround the notion of motherhood; for instance, the notions that only women are loving and nurturing enough to raise children, that mothering means subordinating personal goals to the children's and family's needs, and that motherhood is uniquely joyous and fulfilling for women.

Mutual marriage   Type of marriage in which the husband and wife exhibit nontraditional gender roles. Both partners provide instrumentality and expressiveness.

Myotonia   The contraction of muscles that occurs during sexual arousal.

Neolithic Age   *Neo* means new, recent, latest. The Neolithic Age refers to the latest period of the Stone Age, from approximately 7000 to about 1000 B.C.E. During this period of human culture, polished stone, tools, metal tools, pottery, weaving, rearing of stock, and agriculture were developed.

Neurasthenia   A type of neurosis, usually the result of emotional conflicts, characterized by fatigue, weakness, irritability, anxiety, and often localized pains or distress without apparent physical causes; formerly thought to result from weakness or exhaustion of the nervous system (especially of women in the nineteenth century).

Neutral stress   Stressors that invoke responses that neither threaten nor improve an organism's well-being.

Nirvana   The state of perfect blessedness achieved by the extinction of all desires and pleasures, culminating in the ultimate absorption of the soul after death into the supreme spirit (Brahma).

Nisei   Second-generation Japanese Americans who were born in the United States and experienced American backlash during World War II, resulting in the internment of many.

Nonnormative rape   Rape that is not supported or tolerated by society; this conforms to the stereotypical notion of rape: the "surprise attack on a virtuous woman."

Nonoverlapping distributions   Frequency distributions in which virtually all members of one group score higher or lower than the other group.

Normative rape   Rape that is supported or at least tolerated by society; it includes rape by intimates, such as husbands, as well as punitive rape and rape during wartime.

Occupational segregation   A phenomenon in which specific occupations are characterized as either female or male.

Opportunistic infections   Infections that develop in people whose immune systems are weakened, as in AIDS. Some of the more common opportunistic infections identified with AIDS in both men and women are *Pneumocystis carini* pneumonia (PCP), mycobacterium intracellulare (MAI), toxoplasmosis, and Kaposi's sarcoma (usually a rare form of cancer). Women presenting with gynecological problems that have been associated with HIV/AIDS are pelvic inflammatory disease (PID), human papilloma virus (HPV), cervical cancer, candida infections of the vagina and cervix, and genital herpes.

Osteoporosis   1. A disorder primarily seen in postmenopausal women. It is characterized by decreased bone mass and increased incidence of spinal and hip fracture. The loss of estrogen after menopause is associated with this problem. 2. The process of bone demineralization and thinning of the bones that results in a high risk of vertebral and/or hip fracture. It is especially seen in older women and those who have been on medications like cortisone, which depletes calcium from the bones.

Ostrich effect   A phenomenon in which women believe that sex bias operates in society, but deny having personally experienced these disadvantages.

Outsider's perspective   A research perspective based on the ideas and hypotheses of an outsider social scientist who is not from the culture or group that he or she researches.

Ovaries   Paired reproductive glands in the female located on each side of the uterus that contain and release eggs or ova and secrete hormones such as estrogen and progesterone. These are the female gonads.

Ovulation phase   The second phase of the menstrual cycle when the egg or ovum is released from the ovary.

Ovum   The female egg.

Pain   An unpleasant emotional response associated with actual or potential tissue damage.

Pain threshold   The point at which pain is first perceived.

Pain tolerance   The upper limit or the highest intensity of pain that a human or animal will accept.

Paleolithic Age   *Paleo* means ancient or *old world.* The Paleolithic Age represents an old world cultural period, the earliest part of the Stone Age, going back at least as far as 25,000 B.C.E. During this period man developed flint, stone, and bone tools and lived by hunting, fishing, and gathering plant foods. This period lasted until approximately 10,000 B.C.E. when the Mesolithic Age began.

Pantheism   The doctrine that God is not a personality but that all the laws, forces, and manifestations of the universe are God.

Parental imperative   Parental roles force female and male adults into positions consistent with their respective gender roles.

Parthenogenesis   The belief that reproduction took place by the development of an unfertilized ovum, seed, or spore.

Paul   A Jew of Tarsus (a city of South Turkey near the Mediterranean sea) who became the apostle of Christianity to the Gentiles. Paul wrote several Epistles in the New Testament. He lived sometime in the 60s C.E.

Pauline   Characteristic of the Apostle Paul; his writings or doctrines.

Penis envy   A girl's desire to be a male and have a penis.

Peripheral artery disease   Decreased blood flow to the arms or legs, resulting in a lack of oxygen to the affected part.

Polyandry   The practice of having two or more husbands at the same time.

Polygamy   The practice of having two or more wives at the same time.

Polytheism   The belief in and worship of many gods and goddesses.

Pornography   Sexually explicit material whose primary purpose is to produce sexual arousal for commercial purposes; it objectifies people by reducing them to their body parts.

Postconventional reasoning   Kohlberg's third stage of moral development in which morality is completely internalized and not based on the standards of others.

Postpartum experience   Literally *after birth,* this denotes a period of time ranging from the first days to the first year following delivery when women are adjusting to what it means to be a mother.

Preconvential reasoning   Kohlberg's first stage of moral development in which a child's moral reasoning is dictated by external rewards and punishments.

Pre-embryo stage   The interval between the completion of fertilization until the appearance of a single primitive streak.

Premenstrual syndrome (PMS)   A syndrome of psychological and physical symptoms including anxiety, depression, hyperirritability, retention of fluid, weight gain, and discomfort that some women experience a few days before menstruation.

Primitive streak   The embryonic structure that arises on about the fourteenth day of development.

Progesterone   A hormone produced in both sexes, but it is primarily known as a female hormone and during pregnancy is present in a high concentration.

Prostitution   The exchange of sex for money, gifts, and favors; prostitution is characterized by widespread gender inequality.

Pseudohermaphrodite   A person who is born with ambiguous genitalia, the gonads of one sex and the genitals of the other sex.

Puberty   The period of rapid physical growth that humans experience during adolescence.

Puritan   A member of a Protestant group in England and the U.S. colonies who, in the sixteenth and seventeenth centuries, wanted a greater reformation of the church in order to purify it of elaborate ceremonies and forms.

Quaker   A popular name for a member of the society of Friends. It is a Christian religion that was founded about 1650 in England by George Fox. The Friends have no formal creed, rites, liturgy, or priesthood and reject violence in all relationships, including war. The word *Quaker* is said to originate from George Fox's admonition to "quake" at the word of the lord.

Quid pro quo harassment   Sexual bribery or sexual coercion, referring to harassment that has rewards or punishment attached to it.

Racism   The subordination of certain groups of people based on their origins and physical characteristics.

Radical feminism   Focuses on the control of women by men. Radical feminism is based on the belief that men's oppression of women is primary and serves as a model for all other oppression.

Rape   Vaginal, oral, or anal penetration by an object or body part, against consent or through force or threat of bodily harm or when an individual is unable to consent.

Rape myths   Attitudes and beliefs that are generally false but are widely and persistently held, and serve to deny and justify male sexual aggression against women.

Rape trauma syndrome   A particular form of posttraumatic stress disorder characterized by two phases: an acute phase, usually lasting for several weeks, in which rape survivors exhibit severe disorganization; and a second, long-term reorganization, which may take several years, characterized by fears of recurrence, frightening dreams, and mistrust of personal relationships.

Reentry women   Middle-aged women who return to school or work once their children have left the home.

Refractory period   The time following orgasm during which an individual is unable to experience orgasm again.

Reincarnation   The belief that after death the soul will undergo a rebirth in another body.

Risk factor   Conditions or factors that will increase the likelihood of developing a disease or disorder.

Role overload   Occurs when a woman is required to fulfill several roles simultaneously. For example, a wife who is employed outside the home is also responsible for all household duties and child-rearing responsibilities.

Romantic love   A powerful notion in Western culture, this kind of love is marked by strong sexual or physiological arousal paired with an idealized image of the beloved.

Safe(r) sex   Sexual practices that eliminate or substantially reduce the chances that HIV or other STDs will be transmitted from an infected to an uninfected person.

Sansei   Third-generation Japanese Americans.

Scarcity hypothesis   The notion that human beings have a set amount of time and energy.

Science   A branch of knowledge or study dealing with a body of facts or truths systematically arranged and showing the operations of general laws.

Seduction theory   An early notion of Freud's; this theory proposed that women's neuroses were caused by actual childhood sexual abuse, rather than by distorted wishes and desires.

Seductive behavior   Unwanted sexual advances for which there is no penalty attached to a woman's noncompliance.

Semenarche   Also called *spermarch*. This refers to a boy's first ejaculation, which occurs during puberty and is a marker for sexual maturity.

Sex   The physical differences in the genetic composition and reproductive structures and functions of men and women.

Sex discrimination   The harmful and unequal treatment of individuals due to their sex.

Sexism   1. Differential treatment of individuals based on their sex. 2. The subordination of women and the assumption of the superiority of men solely on the basis of sex.

Sex-role spillover   A carryover into the workplace (or academy) of gender-based expectations for behavior, for example, the expectation that women will be nurturant, compliant, or sexy.

Sexual abuse of children   Any form of sexual contact that occurs before age 18, with a relative or a person at least five years older than the child or with someone who forces himself or herself on the child regardless of the age difference.

Sexual dysfunction   In women it is often defined as inability to experience orgasms under any circumstances, including high levels of stimulation (primary dysfunction), failure to achieve orgasm under many circumstances, for example, vaginal intercourse (secondary dysfunction), and inhibited sexual desire, or a general lack of interest in sex.

Sexual fantasies   Mental imagery that people find sexually arousing.

Sexual harassment   Unwelcome sexual advances, requests for sexual favors, or other verbal or physical contact of a sexual nature (1) when such behavior is made a term of employment, (2) when submission to such terms is used as the basis of employment conditions, or (3) when the verbal or physical conduct creates a hostile environment.

Sexual orientation   The focus of one's sexual and romantic desires and behaviors toward one's own sex, the other sex, or both.

Sexuality   Denotes the feelings and behaviors of males and females about sex.

Sexually transmitted diseases (STD)   Infectious diseases spread through sexual contact, such as HIV/AIDS, other viral infections, bacterial infections, and fungal and parasitic diseases.

Shakti   After the Indian goddess Shakti. To have Shakti means to have the power of creation and destruction.

Social constructionism   This view, largely credited to Foucault, holds that human behavior is determined by historical, cultural, and social conditions.

Socialist feminism   Focuses on social relations and how social institutions preserve and promote male dominance.

Sociobiology   Theory developed by E. O. Wilson, which holds that psychological traits are selected through an evolutionary process. Adaptive traits are selected because they serve to perpetuate the species.

Sperm   The male germ cell as compared with the female ovum. Sperm are produced by the testes.

Statistically significant differences   Differences between or among groups that are reliable or reproducible; that is, they are unlikely to be due to chance alone.

Stereotypes   Generalized and oversimplified beliefs about groups of people.

Stereotyping   Cognitive perspective used to describe gender differences. People learn to streamline information processing by grouping people into categories based on some similarity among members.

Stone Age   The period of human culture during which stone implements were developed and used. The Stone Age is usually divided into *paleolithic, mesolithic,* and *neolithic* periods. *Litho* means stone or rock. *Lithic* refers to a particular period or stage in the use of stone.

Stress   Stress is the effect produced by external (i.e., physical or environmental) events or by internal (i.e., physiological or psychological) factors referred to as *stressors,* which alter an organism's biological equilibrium.

Structural approach   Emphasizes the common positions that certain groups occupy within the social structure. Focus is on structural constraints that channel our experience, from the family to the societal level.

Subtle sexism   Harmful and unequal treatment of women that is less apparent and less visible to others and ourselves.

Suttee   A now outlawed but still practiced Hindu custom of self-immolation; the widow threw herself onto the funeral pyre of her husband's body and was cremated with him.

Symbiotic marriage   Type of marriage in which husband and wife conform to traditional gender roles. The husband provides instrumentality and the wife provides expressiveness.

Sympathetic nervous system   The part of the nervous system that mobilizes the body for action.

Systematic desensitization   A type of behavior therapy used in the treatment of phobias that associates a relaxed state with presentation of gradually increasing negative stimuli.

Talmud   The collection of Hebrew or Jewish writings that constitute the Jewish civil and religious law. Talmud means *learning.*

T cell   Also called *CD4 cell.* A type of lymphocyte (white blood cell) that is crucial for normal functioning of the person's immune system. T cells or CD4 cells are the primary target of HIV. The nature of this virus is such that it is able to encode itself into the genetic material of the T cell/CD4 cell and later can use the machinery of the cell to replicate new virus particles. The body's immune system becomes weakened and eventually destroyed because CD4/T cells are the main control mechanisms of the immune system. Because HIV can reduce the number of T/CD4 cells, a test to determine the number of T/CD4 cells is used as a marker of the severity of HIV and the condition of the immune system.

Testes   The pair of male reproductive glands contained in the scrotum, called the male gonads.

Testosterone   In sexual function, this hormone is considered the most important. It is present in both females and males, but has its highest concentration in males. It is referred to as the male hormone and is secreted by the testes and adrenal glands in the male and by the ovaries and adrenals in the female.

Tokenism   The hiring of women as "tokens" in the workplace to satisfy antidiscrimination laws.

Torah   The complete body of Jewish religious literature.

Traditional gender-role ideology   This belief holds that husbands are breadwinners and wives are homemakers.

Traditional marriage   Increasingly uncommon, this is a marriage in which the husband is the dominant partner and the wife submissive; the husband basically supports the family economically, and marital roles are relatively rigid.

Trimester   The three-month period used to describe the progression of a pregnancy in three periods.

Trophy wives   Young, highly attractive women who men stereotypically marry during the mid-life crisis period.

Tumor   A neoplasm or new growth. A mass of cells that grows independently of the rest of the body.

Uterus   The hollow muscular organ in the female in which menstruation occurs, as well as implantation of the fertilized ovum, nourishment and growth of the fetus, and finally the last stage of pregnancy—labor, through which the infant is delivered.

Vagina   The tubular organ in the female composed of muscle located between the urinary bladder and the rectum. It is the vestibule for sexual intercourse and serves as a vehicle for sperm to reach the ova in the Fallopian tubes. It also serves as the passage for the infant from the uterus to the outside world during labor.

Vasocongestion   Increased blood supply to the genitals that causes the penis, vaginal lips, and clitoris to swell.

Vedic   An old Indian language and precursor of Sanskrit. The early sacred literature was written in this language and is referred to as the *Vedas.* Before the development of Hinduism, the people of this time were called Vedic.

Visual–spatial ability   An umbrella category for three classes of abilities: spatial visualization, which includes finding a figure embedded in a complex background; spatial perception, which includes locating a true vertical or horizontal line in the midst of distracting information; and mental rotation, which includes correctly identifying a figure that has been rotated so that it is presented at a different angle.

Voluntary minority   People and their descendants who have voluntarily come to the United States because they believe that the move will ultimately lead to more economic opportunities and greater political freedom; they apparently do not interpret their presence and/or reception in the United States in terms of having been forced on them by Euro-Americans.

White   Subsumes many ethnocultural groups (e.g., Anglo Americans, Irish Americans, and Polish Americans).

White privilege   Unearned advantages or privileges and conferred dominance for White people based on their fair skin color, which operate basically outside their awareness, but nevertheless perpetuate oppressive conditions for people of color.

Zona pellucida   A jellylike substance surrounding the mature ovum.

Zygote   The single cell produced by the penetration of the ovum by the sperm; the union of the two gametes.

REFERENCES

AAUW Report. (1992). *How schools shortchange girls.* Washington, DC: AAUW Educational Foundation.

AAUW Report. (1998). *Separated by sex: A critical look at single-sex education for girls.* Washington, DC: AAUW Educational Foundation.

Abbey, A. (1982). Sex differences in attributions for friendly behavior. Do males misperceive females' friendliness? *Journal of Personality and Social Personality, 42,* 830–838.

Abbey, A., Andrews, F., & Halman, L. J. (1991). Gender's role in responses to infertility. *Psychology of Women Quarterly, 15,* 295–316.

Abbey, A., & Melby, C. (1986). The effect of nonverbal cues on gender differences in perceptions of sexual intent. *Sex Roles, 15,* 283–298.

Abramson, L. (1990, May 4). Uncaring women's health care. *New York Times.*

Abusharaf, R. (1998). Unmasking tradition. *The Sciences.* March/April, 22–27. Aids surveillance update. (October, 1994). New York City Department of Health.

Acker, J. (1990). Hierarchies, jobs, bodies: A theory of gendered organizations. *Gender & Society, 4,* 139–158.

Adami, H. O. (1992). Long-term consequences of estrogen and estrogen-progestin replacement. *Cancer Causes and Control, 3,* 83–90.

Adams, C. J. (Ed.). (1965). *A readers guide to the great religions.* New York: The Free Press, p. 287f (cited by J. B. Noss, and D. S. Noss, p. 496).

Adams, J. W., Kottke, J. L., & Padgitt, J. S. (1983). Sexual harassment of university students. *Journal of College Student Personnel, 24,* 484–490.

Adelmann, P. (1993). Psychological well-being and homemaker vs. retiree identity among older women. *Sex Roles, 29*(3/4), 195–212.

Ader, D. N., & Johnson, S. B. (1994). Sample description, reporting and analysis of sex in psychological research: A look at APA and APA division journals in 1990. *American Psychologist, 49,* 216–220.

Adkins-Regan, E. (1988). Sex hormones and sexual orientation in animals. *Psychobiology, 16,* 335–347.

Adler, L. L. (1999). Autonomy in a cross-cultural perspective. In M. B. Nadien & F. L. Denmark (Eds.), *Females and autonomy: A life-span perspective* (p. 14). Boston: Allyn and Bacon.

Adler, N., David, H. P., Major, B, N., Roth, S. H., Russo, N. F., & Wyatt, G. E. (1990, April 6). Psychological responses after abortion. *Science, 248,* 41–44.

Adler, P. A., Kless, S. J., & Adler, P. (1992). Socialization to gender roles: Popularity among elementary school boys and girls. *Sociology of Education, 65,* 169–187.

Agras, W. S., Rossiter, E. M., Arnow, B., Schneider, J. A., Telch, C. F., Raeburn, S. D., Bruce, B., Perl, M., & Koran, L. M. (1992). Pharmacologic and cognitive-behavioral treatment for bulimia nervosa: A controlled comparison. *American Journal of Psychiatry, 149,* 82–87.

Agrawal, R., & Kumar, A. (1992). Everyday memory in adulthood. *Psychological Studies, 37*(2–3), 161–172.

Ahlstrom, S. E. (1972). *A religious history of the American people.* New Haven, CT: Yale University Press.

Aitken, L. S., Fenaughty, A. M., West, S. G., Johnson, J. J., & Luckett, T. L. (1995). Perceived determinants of risk for breast cancer and the relations among objective risk, perceived risk, and screening behavior over time. *Women's Health: Research on Gender, Behavior, and Policy, 1*(1), 27–50.

Alan Guttmacher Institute. (1991). *Facts in brief.* New York: Author.

Alington, D. E., & Troll, L. E. (1984). Social change and equality: The roles of women and economics. In G. Baruch & J. Brooks-Gunn (Eds.), *Women in midlife* (pp. 181–202). New York: Plenum Press.

Allen, E. (1988). West Indians. In L. Comas-Diaz & E. Griffith (Eds.), *Clinical guidelines in cross-cultural mental health* (pp. 305–333). New York: Wiley.

Allen, L. S., Hines, M., Shryne, J. E., & Gorski, R. A. (1989). Two sexually dimorphic cell groups in the human brain. *Journal of Neuroscience, 9,* 497–506.

Allgeier, E. R., & McCormick, N. B. (1983). *Changing boundaries: Gender roles and sexual behavior.* Palo Alto, CA: Mayfield.

Allison, J. A., & Wrightsman, L. S. (1993). *Rape: The misunderstood crime.* Newbury Park, CA: Sage.

Almquist, E. M. (1989). The experiences of minority women in the United States: Intersections of race, gender and class. In J. Freeman (Ed.), *Women: A feminist perspective* (4th ed.) (pp. 414–445). Mountain View, CA: Mayfield.

Alton-Lee, A., Nuthall, G., & Patrick, J. (1993). Reframing classroom research: A lesson from the private world of children. *Harvard Educational Review, 63*(1), 50–84.

Alvidrez, J., & Weinstein, R. S. (1993, March). Early teacher expectations and later academic achievement. Paper presented at the biennial meeting of the Society for Research in Child Development, New Orleans, LA.

Amaro, H. (1988). Considerations for prevention of HIV infection among Hispanic women. *Psychology of Women Quarterly, 12,* 429–443.

Amaro, H. (1995). Love, sex, and power: Considering women's realities in HIV prevention. *American Psychologist, 50,* 437–447.

Amaro, H., & Russo, N. F. (1987). Hispanic women and mental health: An overview of contemporary issues in research and practice. *Psychology of Women Quarterly, 11,* 393–407.

Amatea, E. S., & Fong-Beyette, M. L. (1987). Through a different lens: Examining professional women's interrole coping by focus and mode. *Sex Roles, 17*(5/6), 237–252.

Amato, P. R., & Booth, A. (1995). Changes in gender role attitudes and perceived marital quality. *American Sociological Review, 60,* 58–66.

American Association of University Women. (1992). *The AAUW report: How schools shortchange girls.* Washington, DC: AAUW.

American Cancer Society. (1991). *Cancer facts and figures.* Atlanta, GA: American Cancer Society.

American Cancer Society. (1994a). Breast cancer: Cause and prevention. *American Cancer Society Cancer Response System.* #407068.

American Cancer Society. (1994b). Breast cancer: Methods of detection. *American Cancer Society Cancer Response System.* #407013. Author.

American Psychiatric Association. (1994). *Diagnostic and statistical manual of mental disorders* (4th ed.). Washington, DC: Author.

American Psychological Association Committee on Lesbian and Gay Concerns. (1986). Cited by B. Greene (1994).

Anatomy *is* destiny. (1997, March 17). *New York Post,* p. 17.

Anderson, B. L. (1998). Breast cancer: Biobehavioral aspects. In A. E. Blechman & K. D. Brownell (Eds.), *Behavioral medicine and women: A comprehensive handbook* (pp. 570–576). New York: Guilford Press.

Anderson, B. S. & Zinsser, J. P. (1988). *A history of their own: Women in Europe from prehistory to the present* (Vol. 1) (pp. 53–54). New York: Harper & Row.

Andrews, L. B. (1984). *New conceptions.* New York: St. Martin's.

Aneshensel, C. S., Frerichs, R. R., & Clark, V. A. (1981). Family roles and sex differences in depression. *Journal of Health and Social Behavior, 22,* 379–393.

Angier, N. (1998, September 1). Nothing becomes a man more than a woman's face. *New York Times,* p. F3.

Angier, N. (1999). *Woman: An intimate geography.* Boston: Houghton Mifflin.

Antill, J. K. (1983). Sex role complementarity versus similarity in married couples. *Journal of Personality and Social Psychology, 45,* 145–155.

Antonovsky, A. (1987). *Unraveling the mystery of health.* San Francisco: Jossey-Bass.

Anzaldúa, G. (Ed.). (1990). *Making face, making soul— Haciendo caras: Creative and critical perspectives by feminists of color.* San Francisco: Aunt Lute Foundation.

Apfelbaum, E. (1979). Relations of domination and movements for liberation: An analysis of power between groups. In W. G. Austin & S. Worchel (Eds.), *The social psychology of intergroup relations* (pp. 188–204). Monterey, CA: Brooks/Cole Publishing.

Arber, S., & Ginn, J. (1994). Women and aging. *Reviews in Clinical Gerontology, 4*(4), 349–358.

Arias, I., & Pape, K. T. (1994). Physical abuse. In L. L'Abate (Ed.), *Handbook of developmental family psychology and psychopathology* (pp. 284–308). New York: Wiley.

Aries, F. (1962). *Centuries of childhood.* New York: Knopf.

Arling, G. (1976a). The elderly widow and her family, neighbors, and friends. *Journal of Marriage and Family, 38,* 757–769.

Arling, G. (1976b). Resistance to isolation among elderly widows. *International Journal of Aging and Human Development, 7,* 67–76.

Asch, S. E. (1951). Effects of group pressure upon the modification and distortion of judgments. In H. Guetzkow (Ed.), *Groups, leadership and men* (pp. 177–190). Pittsburgh, PA: Carnegie Press.

Attie, I., & Brooks-Gunn, J. (1989). The development of eating problems in adolescent girls: A longitudinal study. *Developmental Psychology, 25,* 70–79.

Azibo, D. A. (1988). Understanding the proper and improper usage of the comparative research framework. *Journal of Black Psychology, 15,* 81–91.

Babchuk, N., & Anderson, T. (1989). Older widows and married women: Their intimates and confidantes. *International Journal of Aging and Human Development, 28*(1), 21–33.

Baber, K. M., & Allen, K. R. (1992). *Women and families: Feminist reconstructions.* New York: Guilford.

Bacquet, C. R., Horm, J. W., Gibbs, T., & Greenwald, P. (1991). Socioeconomic factors and cancer incidence among blacks and whites. *Journal of the National Cancer Institute, 83,* 551–557.

Bailey, J. M., & Pillard, R. C. (1991). A genetic study of male sexual orientation. *Archives of General Psychiatry, 48,* 1089–1096.

Bailey, J. M., Pillard, R. C., Neale, M. C., & Agyei, Y. (1993). Heritable factors influence sexual orientation in women. *Archives of General Psychiatry, 50,* 217–223.

Baltes, P. B., Smith, J., & Staudinger, U. M. (1991). Wisdom and successful aging. *Nebraska Symposium of Motivation, 39,* 123.

Bambara, T. C. (Ed.) (1970). *The Black woman: An anthology.* New York: Signet.

Barba, R., & Cardinale, L. (1991). Are females invisible students: An investigation of teacher-student questioning interactions. *School Science and Mathematics, 91,* 306–310.

Barbanel, L. (1990). Women therapists at midlife. *Psychotherapy in Private Practice, 8*(2), 79–85.

Barbee, A. P., Cunningham, M. R., Winstead, B. A., Derlega, V. J., Gulley, M. R., Yankeelov, P. A., & Druen, P. B. (1993). Effects of gender role expectations on the social support process. *Journal of Social Issues, 49,* 175–190.

Bardwell, J. R., Cochran, S. W., & Walker, S. (1986). Relationship of parental education, race, and gender to sex-role stereotyping in five-year-old kindergartners. *Sex Roles, 15,* 275–281.

Barer, B. M. (1994). Men and women aging differently. *International Journal of Aging and Human Development, 38*(1), 29–40.

Barker, K. (1993). Changing assumptions and contingent solutions: The costs and benefits of women working full- and part-time. *Sex Roles, 1/2,* 47–71.

Barker, K. (1998). Toiling for piece-rates and accumulating deficits: Contingent work in higher education. In K. Barker & K. Christensen (Eds.), *Contingent work: American employment relations in transition,* (pp. 195–220). Ithaca, NY: ILR/Cornell University Press.

Barker, K., & Christensen, K. (1998). Introduction. In K. Barker & K. Christensen (Eds.), *Contingent work: American employment relations in transition,* (pp. 1–18). Ithaca, NY: ILR/Cornell University Press.

Barker, R. (1968). *Ecological psychology.* Stanford, CA: Stanford University Press.

Barker-Benfield, G. J. (1976). The horrors of half known life: Male attitudes towards women and sexuality in nineteenth century America. New York: Harper and Row. Cited by Breiger, G. H. (1980) *History of medicine.* In *A guide to the culture of science, technology and medicine.* p. 153. New York. Free Press.

Barnes, N. S. (1987). Buddhism. In A. Sharma (Ed.), *Women in world religions* (pp. 105–133). Albany, NY: State University of New York Press.

Barnett, O. W., & La Violette, A. D. (1993). *It could happen to anyone: Why battered women stay.* Newbury Park, CA: Sage.

Barnett, R. C., & Baruch, G. K. (1987). Mothers' participation in childcare: Patterns and consequences. In F. J. Crosby (Ed.), *Spouse, parent and worker* (pp. 91–108). New Haven, CT: Yale University Press.

Barnett, R. C., Marshall, N. L., Raudenbush, S. W., & Brennan, R. T. (1983). Gender and the relationship between job experience and psychological distress: A study of dual-earner couples. *Journal of Personality and Social Psychology, 64,* 794–806.

Barnett, R. C., & Rivers, C. (1996). *She works/he works: How two-income families are happier, healthier, and better off.* San Francisco: Harper San Francisco.

Baron, L., & Straus, M. A., (1989). *Four theories of marital rape in American society: A state-level analysis.* New Haven, CT: Yale University Press.

Baron, R. A., & Bell, P. A. (1977). Sexual arousal and aggression by males: Effects of type of erotic stimuli and prior provocation. *Journal of Social and Personality Psychology, 35,* 79–87.

Barrett, C. (1996). *The Egyptian gods and goddesses: The mythology and beliefs of ancient Egypt.* London: Diamond Books.

Barringer, F. (1992, October 7). Family-leave debate: A profound ambivalence. *New York Times,* pp. A1, A22L.

Barringer, F. (1993, April 15). Sex survey of American males finds 1% are gay. *New York Times,* pp. A1, A9.

Bart, P. B., & Grossman, M. (1978). Menopause. In M. T. Notman & C. C. Nadelson (Eds.), *The woman patient: Medical and psychological interfaces* (pp. 337–354). New York: Plenum Press.

Bar-Tal, D., & Saxe, L. (1976). Perceptions of similarly and dissimilarly attractive couples and individuals. *Journal of Personality and Social Psychology, 33,* 772–781.

Barth, F. (1969). *Ethnic groups and boundaries.* Boston: Little, Brown.

Baruch, G. K., Beiner, L., & Barnett, R. C. (1987). Women and gender in research on work and family stress. *American Psychologist, 42,* 130–136.

Baskin, J. (1984). The separation of Jewish women in rabbinic Judaism. In Y. Y. Haddad & E. B. Findley (Eds.), *Women, religion and social change* (pp. 4–5). Albany, NY: State University of New York Press.

Basow, S. A. (1986). *Gender stereotypes: Traditions and alternatives.* Monterey, CA: Brooks/Cole.

Basow, S. A. (1992). *Gender: Stereotypes and roles* (3rd ed.). Pacific Grove, CA: Brooks/Cole.

Bates, G. (1981). On the nature of the hot flash. *Clinical Obstetrics and Gynecology, 24*(1), 231–241.

Baum, M. J., Erskine, M. S., Kornberg, E., & Weaver, C. E. (1990). Prenatal and neonatal testosterone exposure interact to affect differentiation of sexual behavior and partner preference in female ferrets. *Behavioral Neuroscience, 104,* 185–198.

Beal, C. (1994). *Boys and girls: The development of gender roles.* New York: McGraw-Hill.

Beckman, L. J., & Houser, B. B. (1982). The consequences of childlessness on the social-psychological well-being of older women. *Journal of Gerontology, 37*(2), 243–250.

Begley, S. (1995, February 13). Three is not enough. *Newsweek,* 67–69.

Belensky, M. F., Clinchy, B. M., Goldberg, N. R., & Tarole, J. M. (1986). *Women's ways of knowing: The development of self, voice, and mind.* New York: Basic Books.

Bell, A. P., & Weinberg, M. S. (1978). *Homosexualities: A study of diversity among men and women.* New York: Simon & Schuster.

Bell, A. P., Weinberg, M. S., & Hammersmith, S. K. (1901). *Sexual preference.* Bloomington, IN: Indiana University Press.

Bell, I. P. (1989). The double standard: Age. In J. Freeman (Ed.), *Women: A feminist perspective* (4th ed.) (pp. 236–244). Mountain View, CA: Mayfield.

Bell, J. (Ed.). (1995). *Famous Black quotations.* New York: Warner Books.

Belsky, J. (1979). Mother–father–infant interaction: A naturalistic observation study. *Developmental Psychology, 15,* 601–607.

Belsky, J. (1992). The research findings on gender issues in aging men and women. In B. R. Wainrib (Ed.), *Gender issues across the life cycle.* New York: Springer.

Bem, D. J. (1996). Exotic becomes erotic: A developmental theory of sexual orientation. *Psychological Review, 103,* 320–335.

Bem, S. L. (1974). The measurement of psychological androgyny. *Journal of Consulting and Clinical Psychology, 42*(2), 155–162.

Bem, S. L. (1981). Gender schema theory: A cognitive account of sex typing. *Psychological Review, 88,* 354–364.

Bem, S. L. (1994, August 17). In a male-centered world, female differences are transformed into female disadvantages. *Chronicle of Higher Education,* B1–B3.

Benbow, C. P., & Stanley, J. C. (1980). Sex differences in mathematical ability: Fact or artifact? *Science, 210,* 1262–1264.

Beneke, T. (1993). Men on rape. In A. Minas (Ed.), *Gender basics: Feminist perspectives on women and men* (pp. 352–357). Belmont, CA: Wadsworth.

Benin, M., & Agostinelli, J. (1988). Husbands' and wives' satisfaction with the division of labor. *Journal of Marriage and the Family, 50,* 349–361.

Bennett, A. (1989). *Death of the organization.* New York: William Morrow & Co.

Benokraitis, N. V., & Feagin, J. R. (1995). *Modern sexism: Blatant, subtle, and covert discrimination* (2nd ed.). Englewood Cliffs, NJ: Prentice-Hall.

Benson, R. C. (1983). *Handbook of obstetrics and gynecology.* Los Altos, CA: Lange Medical Publishers.

Benward, J., & Densen-Gerber, J. (1975). Incest as a causative factor in antisocial behavior: An exploratory study. *Contemporary Drug Problems, 4,* 323–340.

Berardo, D. H., Shehan, C. L., & Leslie, G. R. (1987). A residue of transition: Jobs, careers, and spouse's time in housework. *Journal of Marriage and the Family, 49,* 381–390.

Berger, C. R. (1988). Uncertainty and information exchange in developing relationships. In S. Duck & D. F. Hay (Eds.), *Handbook of personal relationships: Theory, research, and interventions* (pp. 239–255). Chichester, UK: John Wiley & Sons.

Berk, R., & Berk, S. (1979). *Labor and leisure at home: Content and organization of the household day.* Beverly Hills, CA: Sage.

Bernard, J. (1972). *The future of marriage.* New York: World.

Bernard, J. (1975). Notes on changing lifestyles, 1970–1974. *Journal of Marriage and the Family, 37,* 582–593.

Berndt, T. J. (1992). Friendships and friends' influence in adolescence. *Current Directions in Psychological Science, 1,* 156–159.

Berscheid, E. (1988). Some comments on love's autonomy—Or whatever happened to old-fashioned lust? In R. J. Sternberg & M. L. Barnes (Eds.), *The psychology of love* (pp. 359–374). New Haven, CT: Yale University Press.

Bertilson, H., Springer, K., & Fierke, K. (1982). Underrepresentation of female referents as pronouns: Examples and pictures in introductory college textbooks. *Psychological Reports, 51,* 923–931.

Betancourt, H., & Lopez, S. R. (1993). The study of culture, ethnicity, and race in American psychology. *American Psychologist, 48,* 629–637.

Beyer, S. (1990). Gender differences in the accuracy of self-evaluations of performance. *Journal of Personality and Social Psychology, 59,* 960–970.

Bhatia, M. S., Dhar, N. K., Singhal, P. K., Nigam, V. R., et al. (1990). Temper tantrums: Prevalence and etiology in a nonreferral outpatient setting. *Clinical Pediatrics, 29*(6), 311–315.

Bianchi, S. (1995). The changing demographic and socioeconomic characteristics of single-parent families. In S. Hanson, M. L. Heims, & D. J. Julian (Eds.), *Single-parent families: Diversities, myths and realities* (pp. 71–97). New York: Hayworth Press.

Bieber, I., Dair, H. J., Dince, P. R., Drellich, M. G., Grand, H. G., Grundlach, R. H., Kremer, M. W., Rifkin, A. H., Wilbur, C. B., & Bieber, T. B. (1962). *Homosexuality: A psychoanalytic study of male homosexuals.* New York: Basic Books.

Biernat, M. (1991). Gender stereotypes and the relationship between masculinity and femininity: A developmental analysis. *Journal of Personality and Social Psychology, 61*(3), 351–365.

Bigler, R. S., & Liben, L. S. (1992). Cognitive mechanisms in children's gender stereotyping: Theoretical and educational implications of a cognitive-based intervention. *Child Development, 63,* 1351–1363.

Biller, H. B. (1981). Father absence, divorce, and personality development. In M. E. Lamb (Ed.), *The role of the father in child development* (2nd ed.) (pp. 489–552). New York: Wiley.

Billy, J. O. G., Tanfer, K., Grady, W. R., & Keplinger, D. H. (1993). The sexual behavior of men in the United States. *Family Planning Perspectives, 25*(2), 52–60.

Bingham, S. G., & Scherer, L. L. (1993). Factors associated with responses to sexual harassment and satisfaction with outcome. *Sex Roles, 29,* 239–269.

Binion, V. J. (1990). Psychological androgyny: A black female perspective. *Sex Roles, 22*(7/8), 487–507.

Biological imperatives. (1973, January 8). *Time,* pp. 34–35.

Biondo, B. (1998, February 13–15). Are common chemicals scrambling your hormones? *USA Weekend,* p. 18.

Birchler, G. R., Fals-Stewart, W., & Hersen, M. (1996). Marital discord. In V. B. Van Hasselt et al. (Ed.), *Psychological treatment of older adults: An introductory text* (pp. 315–333). New York: Plenum Press.

Black, S. M., & Hill, C. E. (1984). The psychological well-being of women in their middle years. *Psychology of Women Quarterly, 8,* 282–292.

Blader, J. C., & Marshall, W. L. (1989). Is assessment of sexual arousal in rapists worthwhile? A critique of current methods and the development of a response compatibility approach. *Clinical Psychology Review, 9,* 569–587.

Blake, J. (1982). Demographic revolution and family evolution: Some implications for American women. In P. W. Berman & E. R. Rainey (Eds.), *Women: A developmental perspective.* Washington, DC: NIH Publication No. 82–2298.

Blau, F. D., & Ferber, M. A. (1987). Occupations and earnings of women workers. In S. Koziara, M. Moskow, & L. D. Tanner (Eds.), *Working women: Past, present, future* (pp. 37–68). Washington, DC: Bureau of National Affairs.

Blier, R. (1984). *Science and gender: A critique of biology and its theories on women.* New York: Pergamon Press.

Block, M. R., & Sinnot, J. D. (Eds.). (1979). *The battered elder syndrome.* College Park, MD: University of Maryland Press.

Bloom, B. L. (1988). *Health psychology: A psychosocial perspective.* Englewood Cliffs, NJ: Prentice Hall.

Blumenthal, S. J. (1996). Women's mental health: The new national focus. In J. A. Sechzer, S. M. Pfafflin, F. L. Denmark, A. Griffin, & S. J. Blumenthal (Eds.), *Women and mental health: Annals of the New York Academy of Sciences* (pp. 1–16). New York: The New York Academy of Sciences.

Blumstein, P., & Schwartz, P. (1983). *American couples: Money, work, and sex.* New York: William Morrow.

Blumstein, P., & Schwartz, P. (1990). Intimate relationships and the creation of sexuality. In D. P. McWhirter, S. A. Sanders, & J. M. Reinish (Eds.), *Homosexuality/heterosexuality: Concepts of sexual orientation* (pp. 307–320). New York: Oxford University Press.

Blumstein, P. W., & Schwartz, P. (1976). Bisexuality in women. *Archives of Sexual Behavior, 5,* 171–181.

Blyth, D. A., & Foster-Clark, F. S. (1987). Gender differences in perceived intimacy with different members of adolescents' social networks. *Sex Roles, 17,* 595–605.

Bodner, R. J. (1998). Pain. In E. A. Blechman & K. D. Brownell (Eds.), *Behavioral medicine and women* (pp. 695–699). New York: Guilford Press.

Bohan, J. (1996). *Psychology and sexual orientation.* New York: Routledge Press.

Bohannan, P. (Ed.). (1970). Divorce and after. Garden City, NY: Doubleday.

Bonadonna, G., Valagussa, P., & Rossi, A. (1985). Ten-year experience with CMF-based adjuvant chemotherapy in resectable breast cancer. *Breast Cancer Research and Treatment, 2,* 95–115.

Booth, D. A. (1989). Mood- and nutrient-conditioned appetites: Cultural and physiological bases for eating disorders. In L. H. Schneider, S. J. Cooper, & K. A. Halmi (Eds.), *The psychobiology of human eating disorders: Preclinical and clinical perspectives. Annals of the New York Academy of Sciences, 575,* 122–135.

Booth-Butterfield, M. (1986). Stifle or stimulate? The effects of communication task structure on apprehension in non-apprehensive students. *Communication Education, 35*(4), 337–348.

Borgatta, L. (1994). Sexually transmitted diseases. In J. A. Sechzer, A. Griffin, & S. M. Pfafflin (Eds.), *Forging a women's health research agenda: Policy issues for the 1990's: Annals of the New York Academy of Sciences, 736,* 102–113. New York: The New York Academy of Sciences.

Bose, U. (1985). Child-rearing attitudes of working and non-working mothers. *Psychological Research Journal, 9*(2), 54–61.

Boston Women's Health Book Collective. (1984). *The new our bodies, ourselves.* New York: Simon & Schuster.

Boston Women's Health Book Collective. (1992). *The new our bodies, ourselves.* New York: Simon & Schuster.

Boswell, J. (1988). *The kindness of strangers: The abandonment of children in Western Europe from late antiquity to the Renaissance.* New York: Pantheon.

Boyd-Franklin, N. (1987). Group therapy for black women. *American Journal of Orthopsychiatry, 57,* 394–401.

Boyd-Franklin, N. (1989). *Black families in therapy.* New York: Guilford Press.

Bradshaw, C. (1994). Asian and Asian American women: Historical and political considerations in psychotherapy. In L. Comas-Diaz & B. Greene (Eds.), *Women of color: Integrating ethnic and gender identities in psychotherapy* (pp. 72–113). New York: Guilford Press.

Brannon, L. (1996). *Gender: Psychological perspectives.* Boston: Allyn and Bacon.

Brannon, L. (1999). *Gender: Psychological perspectives.* Boston: Allyn & Bacon.

Brannon, L., & Feist, J. (1992). *Health psychology: An introduction to behavior and health.* Belmont, CA: Wadsworth.

Brannon, R. C. (1976). No "sissy stuff": The stigma of anything vaguely feminine. In D. David & R. Brannon (Eds.), *The forty-nine percent majority* (pp. 235–249). Reading, MA: Addison-Wesley. Cited in Harrison, Chen, & Ficarrotto (1995).

Breazile, J. E. (1987). Physiologic basis and consequence of distress in animals. *Journal of the American Medical Association 19*(10), 1212–1215.

Brewer, M. B., Dull, V., & Lui, L. (1981). Perceptions of the elderly: Stereotypes as prototypes. *Journal of Personality and Social Psychology, 41,* 656–670.

Brice, J. (1982). West Indians. In M. McGoldrick, J. K. Pearce, & J. Giordano (Eds.), *Ethnicity and family therapy* (pp. 123–133). New York: Guilford Press.

Brickman, P., Janoff-Bulman, R., & Rabinowitz, V. C. (1987). Meaning and value. In P. Brickman (Ed.), *Commitment, conflict, and caring.* Englewood Cliffs, NJ: Prentice-Hall.

Bridgeman, B., & Moran, R. (1996). Success in college for students with discrepancies between performance on multiple choice and essay tests. *Journal of Educational Psychology, 88,* 333–340.

Bridges, J. S., & McGrail, C. A. (1989). Attributions of responsibility for date and stranger rape. *Sex Roles, 21,* 273–286.

Brieger, G. H. (1984). History of medicine. In P. T. Durbin (Ed.), *A Guide to the Culture of Science, Technology and Medicine* (pp. 121–194). New York: The Free Press.

Brod, H. (1995). Pornography and the alienation of male sexuality. In M. Kimmel & M. Messner (Eds.), *Men's lives* (3rd ed.). Boston: Allyn and Bacon.

Brody, J. (1994, March 21). Notions of beauty transcend culture. *New York Times,* p. A14.

Brody, J. A. (1985). Prospects for an aging population. *Nature, 315,* 463–466.

Bronstein, P., Clauson, J., Stoll, M. F., & Abrams, C. L. (1993). Parenting behavior and children's social, psychological, and academic adjustment in diverse family structures. *Family Relations, 42,* 268–276.

Brooks-Gunn, J. (1987). The impact of puberty and sexual activity upon the health and education of adolescent girls and boys. *Peabody Journal of Education, 64,* 88–112.

Brooks-Gunn, J. (1988). Antecedents and consequences of variations in girls' maturational timing. *Journal of Adolescent Health Care, 9,* 365–373.

Brooks-Gunn, J., & Furstenberg, F. F. (1989). Adolescent sexual behavior. *American Psychologist, 44,* 249–257.

Brooks-Gunn, J., & Matthews, W. S. (1979). *He and she: How children develop their sex role identity.* Englewood Cliffs, NJ: Prentice Hall.

Brooks-Gunn, J., & Ruble, D. N. (1983). Dysmenorrhea in adolescence. In S. Golub (Ed.), *Menarche: The transition from girl to woman* (pp. 251–261). Lexington, MA: Lexington Books.

Brooks-Gunn, J., Samelson, M., Warren, M. P., & Fox, R. (1986). Physical similarity of and disclosure of menarcheal status to friends: Effects of age and pubertal status. *Journal of Early Adolescence, 6,* 3–14.

Brooks-Gunn, J., & Warren, M. P. (1988). The psychological significance of secondary sexual characteristics in nine- to eleven-year-old girls. *Child Development, 59,* 1061–1069.

Brooks-Gunn, J., & Zahaykevich, M. (1989). Parent–daughter relationships in early adolescence: A developmental perspective. In K. Kreppner & R. Lerner (Eds.), *Family systems and life-span development* (pp. 223–246). Hillsdale, NJ: Erlbaum.

Brophy, J. (1985). Interactions of male and female teachers. In L. C. Wilinson & C. B. Marrett (Eds.), *Gender influences in classroom interactions* (pp. 115–142). Orlando, FL: Academic Press.

Broverman, I. K., Broverman, D. M., Clarkson, F. E., Rosenkrantz, P. S., & Vogel, S. R. (1970). Sex-role stereotypes and clinical judgements of mental health. *Journal of Consulting and Clinical Psychology, 34,* 1–7.

Broverman, I. K., Vogel, S. R., Broverman, D. M., Clarkson, F. E., & Rosenkrantz, P. S. (1972). Sex-role stereotypes: A current appraisal. *Journal of Social Issues, 28,* 59–78.

Brown, D. R., & Gary, L. E. (1985). Social support network differentials among married and nonmarried black families. *Psychology of Women Quarterly, 9,* 229–241.

Brown, J. K. (1982). A cross-cultural exploration of the end of the childbearing years. In A. M. Voda, M. Dinnerstein, & S. R. O'Donnell (Eds.), *Changing perspectives on menopause* (pp. 51–59). Austin, TX: University of Texas Press.

Brown, L. S. (1990). The meaning of a multicultural perspective for theory building in feminist therapy. In L. S. Brown & M. P. P. Root (Eds.), *Diversity and Complexity in Feminist Therapy* (pp. 1–21). New York: Haworth Press.

Brown, M. S. (1981). Culture and childrearing. In A. N. Clark (Ed.), *Culture and childrearing* (pp. 3–35). Philadelphia: F. A. Davis.

Browne, A. (1987). *When battered women kill.* New York: Macmillan/Free Press.

Browne, A. (1993). Violence against women by male partners: Prevalence, outcomes, and policy implications. *American Psychologist, 48,* 1077–1087.

Browne, A., & Finkelhor, D. (1986). Impact of child sexual abuse: A review of the research. *Psychological Bulletin, 99,* 66–77.

Browning, C., Reynolds, A. L., & Dworkin, S. H. (1991). Affirmative psychotherapy for lesbian women. *Counseling Psychology, 19,* 177–196.

Bryant, J., & Brown, D. (1989). Uses of pornography. In D. Zillman & J. Bryant (Eds.), *Pornography: Research advances and policy considerations* (pp. 25–55). Hillsdale, NJ: Erlbaum.

Budoff, P. W. (1994). Women's centers: A model for future health care. In J. A. Sechzer, A. Griffin, & S. M. Pfafflin (Eds.), *Forging a women's health research agenda: Policy issues for the 1990's: Annals of the New York Academy of Sciences, 736,* 165–170. New York: The New York Academy of Sciences.

Buhrmester, D., & Furman, W. (1987). The development of companionship and intimacy. *Child Development, 58,* 1101–1113.

Bullivant, M. (1984). *Cultural maintenance and evolution.* Clevedon, England: Multilingual Matters.

Bullough, V. L. (1974). *The subordinate sex.* Baltimore, MD: Books on Demand.

Bumpass, L. L., Sweet, J. A., & Cherlin, A. (1991). The role of cohabitation in declining rates of marriage. *Journal of Marriage and the Family, 53,* 913–927.

Burack, R. C., & Liang, J. (1987). The early detection of cancer in the primary care setting: Actors associated with the acceptance and completion of recommended procedures. *Preventive Medicine, 16,* 739–751.

Burgess, A. W., & Holmstrom, L. L. (1974). Rape trauma syndrome. *American Journal of Psychiatry, 131,* 981–986.

Burn, S. M. (1996). *The social psychology of gender.* New York: McGraw-Hill.

Burnam, M. A., Stein, J. A., Golding, J. M., & Siegel, J. M. (1988). Sexual assault and mental disorders in a community population. *Journal of Consulting and Clinical Psychology, 56,* 843–850.

Burstein, G. R., Gaydos, C. A., Diener-West, M., Howell, M. R., Zenilman, J. M., & Quinn, T. C. (1998). Incident chlamydia trachomatis infections among inner-city adolescent females. *Journal of the American Medical Association, 280*(6), 521–526.

Burt, M. R. (1980). Cultural myths and supports for rape. *Journal of Personality and Social Psychology, 38,* 217–230.

Busch, C. M., Zonderman, A. B., & Costa, P. T. (1994). Menopausal transition and psychological distress in a nationally representative sample: Is menopause associated with psychological distress? *Journal of Aging and Health, 6,* 209–228.

Bush, T. L. (1990). The epidemiology of cardiovascular disease in postmenopausal women. In M. Flint, F. Kronenberg, & W. Utian (Eds.), *Multidisciplinary perspectives on menopause: Annals of the New York Academy of Sciences, 592,* 263–271. New York: The New York Academy of Sciences.

Buss, D. M. (1988). The evolution of intrasexual competition: Tactics of mate selection. *Journal of Personality and Social Psychology, 54,* 616–628.

Buss, D. M. (1989). Sex differences in human mate preferences: Evolutionary hypotheses tested in 37 cultures. *Behavioral and Brain Sciences, 12,* 1–49.

Buss. (1990). [Beall & Sternberg]

Buss, D. M. (1994). What do people desire in a mate? The evolution of human sexual strategies. *Journal of NIH Research, 6,* 37–40.

Bussey, K., & Bandura, A. (1984). Influence of gender constancy and social power on sex-linked modeling. *Journal of Personality and Social Psychology, 47,* 1292–1302.

Bussey, K., & Bandura, A. (1992). Self-regulatory mechanisms governing gender development. *Child Development, 63,* 1236–1250.

Butler, R. N. (1978). The doctor and the aged patient. In W. Reichel (Ed.), *The Geriatric Patient* (pp. 199–206). New York: Harcourt Press.

Cadden, J. (1993). *Meanings of sex differences in the Middle Ages: Medicine, science and culture.* Cambridge, England: Cambridge University Press.

Cahill, T. (1998) *The gifts of the Jews.* New York: Bantam Doubleday Dell.

Cameron, P., & Biber, H. (1973). Sexual thought throughout the life span. *Gerontologist, 13,* 144–147.

Campbell, B. (1993). To be black, gifted, and alone. In V. Cyrus (Ed.), *Experiencing race, class, and gender in the United States* (pp. 106–111). Mountain View, CA: Mayfield.

Campbell, D. T. (1967). Stereotypes and the perception of group differences. *American Psychologist, 22,* 817–829.

Campbell, J. (1962). *The masks of God: Oriental mythology.* New York: Viking.

Campbell, J. (1964). *The masks of God: Occidental mythology.* New York: Viking.

Campbell, S. M., Peplau, L., & DeBro, S. C. (1992). Women, men, and condoms: Attitudes and experiences of college students. *Psychology of Women Quarterly, 16,* 273–288.

Canetto, S. S., Kaminski, P. L., & Felicio, D. M. (1995). Typical and optimal aging in women and men: Is there a double standard? *International Journal of Aging and Human Development, 40*(3), 187–207.

Canino, G. (1982). This Hispanic woman: Sociocultural influences on diagnosis and treatment. In R. Becerra, M. Karno, & J. Escobar (Eds.), *The Hispanic: Mental health: Issues and strategies* (pp. 117–138). New York: Grune & Stratton.

Cannon, W. (1929). *Bodily changes in pain, hunger, fear and rage: An account of recent researches into the function of emotional excitement.* New York: Appelton Press.

Caplan, P. J., & Hall-McCorquodale, I. (1985). The scape-goating of mothers: A call for change. *American Journal of Orthopsychiatry, 55,* 610–613.

Carmody, D. L. (1989). *Women and world religions* (2nd ed.). Englewood Cliffs, NJ: Prentice-Hall.

Caron, S. L., Davis, C. M., Haldeman, W. A., & Stickle, M. (1993). Prediction of condom-related behaviors among first-year college students. *Journal of Sex Research, 30,* 252–259.

Carrol, J. L., Volk, K. D., & Hyde, J. S. (1985). Differences between males and females in motives for engaging in sexual intercourse. *Archives of Sexual Behavior, 14,* 131–139.

Carroll, J. L., & Wolpe, P. R. (1996). *Sexuality and gender in society.* New York: HarperCollins.

Carroll, T. F. (1983). *Women, religion, and development in the Third World.* New York: Praeger.

Carson, R. (1969). *Interaction concepts of personality.* Chicago: Aldine.

Carter, B. (1992). Stonewalling feminism. *Family Therapy Networker, 16,* 64–69.

Cascardi, M., Langhinrichsen, J., & Vivian, D. (1992). Marital aggression: Impact, injury, and health correlates for husbands and wives. *Archives of Internal Medicine, 152,* 357–363.

Cash, T. F., Gillen, B., & Burns, D. S. (1977). Sexism and 'beautyism' in personnel consultant decision making. *Journal of Applied Psychology, 62,* 301–310.

Catania, J. A., Coates, T. J., Stall, R., Turner, H., Peterson, J., Hearst, N., Dolcini, M. M., Hudes, E., Gagnon, J., Wiley, J., & Groves, R. (1992). Prevalence of AIDS-related risk factors and condom use in the United States. *Science, 258,* 1101–1106.

Catell, J. M. (1903). Cited in A. Fausto-Sterling, *Myths of gender: Biological theories about women and men* (2nd ed.). New York: HarperCollins.

Cates, W., Stewart, F. H., & Russell, J. (1992). Commentary: The quest for women's prophylactic methods—hopes vs.

science. *American Journal of Public Health, 82*(11), 1479–1482.

Cauchon, D. (1991, April 4). Women will break through glass ceiling. *USA Today,* p. 9A.

Cazenave, N. A., & Zahn, M. A. (1992). Women, murder, and male domination: Police reports of domestic violence in Chicago and Philadelphia. In E. C. Viano (Ed.), *Intimate violence: Interdisciplinary perspectives* (pp. 83–97). Washington: Hemisphere Publication Corporation.

Centers for Disease Control. (1989). Trends in lung cancer incidence—United States, 1973–1986. *Morbidity and Mortality Weekly Report 38,* 505–513.

Centers for Disease Control. (1990). Heterosexual behaviors and factors that influence condom use among patients attending a sexually transmitted disease clinic—San Francisco. *Morbidity and Mortality Weekly Report, 39,* 685–689.

Centers for Disease Control. (1992). Abortion surveillance—United States, 1989. *Mortality and Morbidity Weekly Report, 41,* 955–966.

Centers for Disease Control. (1993). HIV/AIDS surveillance—Fourth quarter edition—U.S. AIDS cases reported through December, 1992. Washington, DC: U.S. Department of Health and Human Services.

Centers for Disease Control and Prevention. (1998). *HIV/AIDS surveillance report, 10*(2), 1–43.

Chambers, D. L. (1989). Accommodation and satisfaction: Women and men lawyers and the balance of work and family. *Law and Social Inquiry, 14,* 251–287.

Chan, C. S. (1987). Asian American women: Psychological responses to sexual exploitation and cultural stereotypes. *Women & Therapy, 6,* 33–38.

Chan, C. S. (1991). *Asian Americans: An interpretive history.* Boston: Twayne.

Chan, D. W. (1990). Sex knowledge, attitudes, and experiences of Chinese medical students in Hong Kong. *Archives of Sexual Behavior, 19,* 73–93.

Chaplin, J. (1988). *Feminine counseling in action.* London: Sage.

Chapman, C. R., & Bonica, J. J. (1985). *Chronic pain.* Kalamazoo, MI: Upjohn.

Cherlin, A. J. (1981). *Marriage, divorce, remarriage.* Cambridge, MA: Harvard University Press.

Cherlin, A. J. (1998). Marriage and marital dissolution among Black Americans. *Journal of Comparative Family Studies, 29,* 147–158.

Cherlin, A. J., & Furstenberg, F. F. (1985). Styles and strategies of grandparenting. In V. L. Bengston & J. F. Robertson (Eds.), *Grandparenthood* (pp. 97–116). Beverly Hills, CA: Sage.

Cherry, F., & Deaux, K. (1978). Fear of success versus fear of gender-inappropriate behavior. *Sex Roles, 4,* 97–101.

Chideya, F. (1995). *Don't believe the hype.* New York: Penguin.

Chisholm, J. F. (1996). *Mental health issues in African-American women.* New York: New York Academy of Sciences.

Chodorow, N. (1978). *The reproduction of mothering.* Berkeley, CA: University of California Press.

Chodorow, N. (1979). Feminism and difference: Gender, relation and difference in psychoanalytic perspective. *Socialist Review, 9*(4), 51–70.

Chow, E. N.-L. (1985). The acculturation experience of Asian American women. In A. Sargeant (Ed.), *Beyond sex roles* (2nd ed.) (pp. 238–261). St. Paul, MN: West.

Christensen, K., & Murphree, M. (1988). Introduction to Conference Proceedings. In K. Christensen & M. Murphree (Eds.), *Flexible workstyles: A look at contingent labor.* Conference Summary (pp. 1–4). Washington, DC: U.S. Department of Labor, Women's Bureau.

Chu, J. (1988). Social and economic profile of Asian Pacific American women: Los Angeles county. In G. Y. Okihito, S. Hume, A. A. Hansen, & J. M. Liu (Eds.), *Reflections on shattered windows: Promises and prospects for Asian American studies* (pp. 193–205). Pullman: Washington State University Press.

Clarke-Stewart, K. A. (1978). And Daddy makes three: The father's impact on mother and young child. *Child Development, 49,* 466–478.

Cobbs, P. M. (1972). Ethnotherapy in groups. In L. Soloman & B. Berson (Eds.), *New perspectives on encounter groups* (pp. 383–403). San Francisco: Jossey-Bass.

Cohen, M. A. A., & Alfonso, C. A. (1994). Dissemination of HIV: How serious is it for women, medically and psychologically. In J. A. Sechzer, A. Griffin, & S. M. Pfafflin (Eds.), *Forging a women's health research agenda: Policy issues for the 1990's: Annals of the New York Academy of Sciences, 736,* 114–121. New York: The New York Academy of Sciences.

Cohen, O. J., & Fauci, A. S. (1998). HIV/AIDS in 1998—Gaining the upper hand? *Journal of the American Medical Association, 280*(1), 87–88.

Cohen, P. (1998, July 11). Daddy dearest: Do you really matter? *New York Times,* pp. B7, B9.

Cohen, S. (1984). The chronic intractable benign pain syndrome. *Drug Abuse & Alcoholism Newsletter, 13*(4), 240.

Colasanto, D. (1989, October 25). Gay rights support has grown since 1982, Gallup poll finds. *San Francisco Chronicle,* p. A21.

Colditz, G. A. (1993). Epidemiology of breast cancer: Findings from the Nurses' Health Study. *Cancer, 7* (Supplement), 1480–1489.

Cole, C., Hill, F., & Dayley, L. (1983). Do masculine pronouns used generically lead to thoughts of men? *Sex Roles, 9,* 737–750.

Cole, J. (Ed.) (1986). *All American women: Lives that divide, ties that bind.* New York: Macmillan.

Cole, M., Gay, J., Glick, J. A., & Sharp, D. (1971). *The cultural context of learning and thinking: An exploration in experimental anthropology.* New York: Basic Books.

Cole, S. S., & Cole, T. M. (1993). Sexuality, disability, and reproductive issues through the lifespan. *Sexuality and Disability, 11*(3), 189–205.

Coles, R., & Stokes, G. (1985). *Sex and the American teenager.* New York: Harper & Row.

Coltrane, S. (1997). Families and gender equity. *National Forum, 77,* 31–34.

Columbia Encyclopedia. (5th ed. 1993). *Mary, mother of Jesus.* New York: Columbia University Press. Retrieved July 9,1999 from the World Wide Web: http://infoplease.lycos.com/ce5/CE033140.html.

Comas-Diaz, L. (1992, Spring). The future of psychotherapy with ethnic minorities. *Psychotherapy, 29*(1), 88–94.

Comas-Diaz, L., & Greene, B. (Eds.). (1994). *Women of color: Integrating ethnic and gender identities in psychotherapy.* New York: Guilford Press.

Comas-Diaz, L., & Jacobsen, F. (1991). Ethnocultural transference and countertransference in the therapeutic dyad. *American Journal of Orthopsychiatry, 61*(3), 392–402.

Combahee River Collective. (1979). A Black feminist statement. In Z. Eisenstein (Ed.), *Capitalist patriarchy and the case for socialist feminism* (pp. 135–139). New York: Monthly Review Press.

Comfort, A. (1974). *More joy of sex.* New York: Simon & Schuster.

Committee on Lesbian and Gay Concerns. (1986). *APA policy statement on lesbian and gay issues.* Washington, DC: American Psychological Association.

Committee on Pain and Distress in Laboratory Animals, Institute of Laboratory Animal Resources (ILAR), National Research Council. *Recognition and alleviation of pain and distress in laboratory animals* (pp. 1–9). Washington, DC: National Academy Press.

Constantinople, A. (1979). Sex-role acquisition: In search of the elephant. *Sex Roles, 5,* 121–133.

Cook, E., (1990). Gender and psychological distress. *Journal of Counseling & Development, 2,* 371–375.

Coombs, R. H., & Kenkel, W. F. (1996). Sex differences in dating aspirations and satisfaction with computer-selected partners. *Journal of Marriage and the Family, 28,* 62–66.

Cordua, G. D., McGraw, K. O., & Drabman, R. S. (1979). Doctor or nurse: Children's perceptions of sex-typed occupations. *Child Development, 50,* 590–593.

Corea, G. (1992). *The invisible epidemic: The story of women and AIDS.* New York: HarperCollins.

Cosentino, C. E., & Collins, M. (1996). Sexual abuse of children: Prevalence, effects, and treatment. In J. A. Sechzer, S. M. Pfafflin, F. L. Denmark, A. Griffen, & S. J. Blumenthal (Eds.), *Women and mental health: Annals of the New York Academy of Sciences, 789,* 45–65. New York: The New York Academy of Sciences.

Cosse, W. J. (1992). Who's who and what's what? The effects of gender on development in adolescence. In B. R. Wainrib (Ed.), *Gender issues across the life cycle* (pp. 5–16). New York: Springer.

Courtney, A. E., & Whipple, T. W. (1985). Female role portrayals in advertising and communication effectiveness: A review. *Journal of Advertising, 14*(3), 4–8, 17.

Cowan, C. P., & Cowan, P. A. (1992). *When partners become parents: The big life change for couples.* New York: Basic Books.

Cozby, P. C. (1973). Self-disclosure: A literature review. *Psychological Bulletin, 79,* 73–91.

Craik, F. I. M. (1977). Age differences in human memory. In J. E. Birren & K. W. Schaie (Eds.), *Handbook of the psychology of aging* (pp. 384–420). New York: Van Nostrand Reinhold.

Crandall, V. C. (1969). Sex differences in expectancy of intellectual and academic reinforcement. In C. P. Smith (Ed.), *Achievement-related motives in children* (pp. 11–45). New York: Russell Sage Foundation.

Crandall, V. C. (1978, August). *Expecting sex differences and sex differences in expectancies: A developmental analysis.* Paper presented at a meeting of the American Psychological Association, Toronto, Canada.

Crawford, M., & Chaffin, R. (1997). The meanings of difference: Cognition in social and cultural context. In P. J. Caplan, M. Crawford, J. S. Hyde, & J. T. E. Richardson (Eds.), *Gender differences in human cognition* (pp. 81–130). London: Oxford University Press.

Crawford, M., & Marecek, J. (1989). Psychology reconstructs the female: 1968–1988. *Psychology of Women Quarterly, 13,* 147–165.

Crockett, L. J., & Petersen, A. C. (1987). Pubertal status and psychosocial development: Findings from the early adolescent study. In R. M. Lerner & T. T. Foch (Eds.), *Biological–psychosocial interactions in early adolescence* (pp. 173–188). Hillsdale, NJ: Erlbaum.

Crosby, F. (1982). *Relative deprivation and working women.* New York: Oxford University Press.

Crosby, F. (1984). Relative deprivation in organizational settings. In B. Staw & L. L. Cummings (Eds.), *Research in organizational behavior* (Vol. 6) (pp. 51–93). Greenwich, CT: JAI Press.

Crosby, F., Clayton, S., Alkinis, O., & Hemker, K. (1986). Cognitive biases in the perception of discrimination: The importance of format. *Sex Roles, 14,* 637–646.

Crosby, F. J., Pufall, A., Snyder, R. C., O'Connell, M., & Whalen, P. (1989). The denial of personal disadvantage among you, me and all the other ostriches. In M. Crawford & M. Gentry (Eds.), *Gender and thought: Psychological perspectives* (pp. 79–99). New York: Springer-Verlag.

Crouter, A. C., McHale, S. M., Bartko, W. T. (1993). Gender as an organizing feature in parent-child relationships. *Journal of Social Issues, 49,* 161–174.

Curran, B. A. (1986). American lawyers in the 1980s: A profession in transition. *Law and Society Review, 20,* 19–52.

Curtin, J. P. (1994). Gynecologic cancer: Prevention and screening strategies for the 1990's. In J. A. Sechzer, A. Griffin, & S. M. Pfafflin (Eds.), *Forging a women's health research agenda: Policy issues for the 1990's: Annals of the New York Academy of Sciences, 736,* 140–146. New York: The New York Academy of Sciences.

Cyrus, V. (Ed.). (1993). *Experiencing race, class, and gender in the United States.* Mountain View, CA: Mayfield.

D'Augelli, A. R. (1989). Homophobia in a university community: Views of prospective resident assistants. *Journal of College Student Development, 30,* 546–552.

D'Augelli, A. R. (1992). Lesbian and gay male undergraduates' experiences of harassment and fear on campus. *Journal of Interpersonal Violence, 7,* 383, 395.

D'Augelli, A. R. (1994). Lesbian and gay male development: Steps toward an analysis of lesbians' and gay men's lives. In B. Greene & G. M. Herek (Eds.), *Lesbian and gay psychology: Theory, research, and clinical applications* (pp. 118–132). Psychological Perspectives on Lesbian and Gay Issues, Vol. 1. Thousand Oaks, CA: Sage.

Dally, A. (1991). *Women under the knife* (p. xxiv) London: Hutchinson Radius.

Dan, A. J., & Bernhard, L. A. (1989). Menopause and other health issues for midlife women. In S. Hunter & M. Sundel (Eds.), *Midlife myths: Issues, findings, and practice implications* (pp. 51–66). Newbury Park, CA: Sage.

Danza, R. (1983). Menarche: Its effects on mother–daughter and father–daughter interactions. In S. Golub (Ed.), *Menarche* (pp. 99–105). Lexington, MA: Lexington Books.

Davenport, D. S., & Yurich, J. (1991). Multicultural gender issues. *Journal of Counseling and Development, 70,* 64–71.

Davidson, J. M. (1989). Sexual emotions, hormones, and behavior. *Advances, 6*(2), 56–58.

Davis, A. Y. (1981). *Women, race & class.* New York: Random House.

Davis, S. (1990). Men as success objects and women as sex objects: A study of personal advertisements. *Sex Roles, 23,* 43–50.

Dawson, D. A. (1991). Family structure and children's health and well-being: Data from the 1988 National Health Interview Survey on Child Health. *Journal of Marriage and the Family, 53,* 573–584.

De Angelis, B. (1997). *The real rules: How to find the right man for the real you.* New York: Bantam Doubleday Dell.

Dearwater, S. R., Coben, J. H., Campbell, J. C., Nah, G., Glass, N., McLoughlin, E., Bekemeier, B. (1998). Prevalence of intimate partner abuse in women treated at community hospital emergency departments. *Journal of the American Medical Association, 280,* 433–438.

Deaux, K. (1995). How basic can you be? The evolution of research on gender stereotypes. *Journal of Social Issues, 51,* 11–20.

Deaux, K., & Emswiller, T. (1974). Explanations of successful performance on sex-linked tasks: What is skill for the male is luck for the female. *Journal of Personality and Social Psychology, 29,* 80–85.

Deaux, K., & Hanna, R. (1984). Courtship in the personals column: The influence of gender and sexual orientation. *Sex Roles, 11,* 363–375.

Deaux, K., & Kite, M. (1993). Gender stereotypes. In F. L. Denmark & M. A. Paludi (Eds.), *Psychology of women: A handbook of issues and theories* (pp. 107–139). Westport, CT: Greenwood Press.

Deaux, K., White, L., & Farris, E. (1975). Skill vs. luck: Field and lab studies of male and female preferences. *Journal of Personality and Social Psychology, 32,* 629–636.

Debold, E., Wilson, M., & Malave, I. (1993). *Mother–daughter revolution: From betrayal to power.* Reading, MA: Addison-Wesley.

DeFour, D. C. (1996). The interface of racism and sexism on college campuses. In M. A. Paludi et al. (Ed.), *Sexual harassment on college campuses: Abusing the ivory tower.* Albany, NY: SUNY Press.

De Groot, S. C. (1980). Female and male returnees: Glimpses of two distinct populations. *Psychology of Women Quarterly, 5,* 358–361.

DeKeseredy, W., & Kelly, K. (1993). The incidence and prevalence of women abuse in Canadian university and college dating relationships. *Canadian Journal of Sociology, 18,* 137–159.

Delamont, S. (1990). *Sex roles and the school* (2nd ed.). London: Routledge.

Delaney, J., Lupton, M. J., & Toth, E. (1988). *The curse: A cultural history of menstruation* (rev. ed.). Urbana, IL: University of Illinois.

Delgado, J. L., & Trevino, F. (1985). The state of Hispanic health in the United States. In *The state of Hispanic America,* Vol. II. Oakland, CA: National Hispanic Center for Advanced Studies and Policy Analysis.

DeLorey, C. (1984). Health care and midlife women. In G. Baruch & J. Brooks-Gunn (Eds.), *Women in midlife* (pp. 277–301). New York: Plenum Press.

Demo, D. H. (1992). Parent–child relations: Assessing recent changes. *Journal of Marriage and the Family, 54,* 104–117.

Denmark, F. L. (1975). Growing up male. In E. Zuckerman (Ed.), *Women and men: Roles, attitudes, and power relationships.* New York: Radcliffe Club.

Denmark, F. L. (1976). The psychology of women: Its definition and the development of the field. Invited address presented at the Eastern Psychological Association, New York.

Denmark, F. L. (1992). *Changing sex ratios in psychology: For better or for worse?* Paper presented at the American Psychological Association, August 1992, Washington, DC.

Denmark, F. L. (1994). Engendering psychology. *American Psychologist, 49*(4), 329–334.

Denmark, F. L. (1999). From enhancing the development of adolescent girls. In N. G. Johnson, M. C. Roberts, & J. Worell (Eds.), *Beyond appearance: A new look at adolescent girls* (pp. 377–404). Washington, DC: APA.

Denmark, F. L., & Fernandez, L. C. (1993). Historical development of the psychology of women. In F. L. Denmark & M. A. Paludi (Eds.), *Psychology of women: A handbook of issues and theories* (pp. 3–22). Westport, CT: Greenwood Press.

Denmark, F. L., & Francois, F. (1987). Research context of studies for sex differences in mathematics performance. In J. A. Sechzer & S. M. Pfafflin (Eds.), Psychology and educational policy. *Annals of the New York Academy of Sciences, 517,* 61–68.

Denmark, F. L., Nielson, K. A., & Scholl, K. (1993). Life in the United States of America. In L. L. Adler (Ed.), *International handbook on gender roles* (pp. 452–467). Westport, CT: Greenwood Press.

Denmark, F. L., Novick, K., & Pinto, A. (1996). Women, work, and family: Mental health issues. *Annals of the New York Academy of Sciences, 789,* 101–117.

Denmark, F. L., & Paludi, M. A. (1993). *Psychology of women: A handbook of issues and theories.* Westport, CT: Greenwood Press.

Denmark, F. L., Russo, N. F., Frieze, I. H., & Sechzer, J. A. (1988). Guidelines for avoiding sexism in psychological research. *American Psychologist, 43,* 582–585.

Denmark, F. L., Sechzer, J. A., & Rabinowitz, V. C. (1994). Studies of sex and gender in lung cancer research. *American Psychological Association Conference on Psychosocial and Behavioral Factors in Women's Health.* Washington, DC: APA.

Denmark, F. L., Sechzer, J. A., & Rabinowitz, V. C. (1995). Studies of sex and gender in lung cancer research II. *Annual Convention of the American Psychological Society.* New York: Appelton Press.

Denmark, F. L., Shaw, J. S., & Ciali, S. D. (1985). The relationship among sex roles, living arrangements, and the division of household responsibilities. *Sex Roles, 12*(5/6), 617–625.

Denmark, F. L., & Waters, J. A. (1977). Male and female in children's readers: A cross-cultural analysis. In Y. H. Poortinga (Ed.), *Basic problems in cross-cultural psychology* (pp. 190–270). Amsterdam: Swets and Zeitlinger B.V.

Denny, N., Field, J., & Quadagno, D. (1984). Sex differences in sexual needs and desires. *Archives of Sexual Behavior, 13,* 233–245.

Derlega, V. J., Winstead, B. A., Wong, P. T. P., & Hunter, S. (1985). Gender effects in an initial encounter: A case where men exceed women in disclosure. *Journal of Personal and Social Relations, 2,* 25–44.

DeVellis, B. M., Wallston, B. S., & Acker, I. (1984). Childfree by choice: Attitudes and adjustment of sterilized women. *Population and Environmental, Behavioral and Social Issues, 1,* 152–162.

De Young, M. (1982). *The sexual victimization of children.* Jefferson, NC: McFarland.

Dewhurst, J. (1978). Fertility in 47,XXX and 45,X patients. *Journal of Medical Genetics, 15,* 132–135.

Diamond, M. (1982). Sexual identity, monozygotic twins, reared in discordant sex roles, and a BBC follow-up. *Archives of Sexual Behavior, 11,* 181–186.

Diamond, M. (1993). Homosexuality and bisexuality in different populations. *Archives of Sexual Behavior 22,* 291–310.

Diamond, M., & Sigmundson, K. (1997). Sex reassignment at birth. *Archives of Pediatric Adolescent Medicine, 151,* 298–304.

Diamond, N. (1973). The status of women in Taiwan: One step forward, two steps back. In M. B. Young (Ed.), *Women in China* (pp. 211–242). Ann Arbor, MI: Center for Chinese Studies, University of Michigan.

Diehl, L. A. (1988). The paradox of G. Stanley Hall: Foe of coeducation and educator of women. In L. T. Benjamin (Ed.), *A history of psychology: Original sources and contemporary research* (pp. 295–310). New York: McGraw-Hill.

Digest of educational statistics. (1976). Washington, DC: Department of Health, Education, and Welfare, Education Division, National Center for Educational Statistics.

Digest of educational statistics. (1992). Washington, DC: Department of Health, Education, and Welfare, Educational Division, National Center for Educational Statistics.

DiMaggio, P., & Mohr, J. (1985). Cultural capital, educational attainment, and marital selection. *American Journal of Sociology, 90,* 1231–1261.

Dinnerstein, D. (1976). *The mermaid and the minotaur.* New York: Harper & Row.

Dirix, M. E. (1869). *Woman's complete guide to health.* New York: W. A. Townsend and Adams. [cited by Ehrenreich & English, 1981, p. 340]

Dix, T. (1993). Attributing dispositions to children: An interactional analysis of attribution in socialization. *Personality and Social Psychology Bulletin, 19*(5), 633–643.

Dodson, B. (1987). *Sex for one: The joy of selfloving.* New York: Crown.

Donnerstein, E. (1983). Erotica and human aggression. In R. Green & E. Donnerstein (Eds.), *Aggression: Theoretical and empirical reviews.* New York: Academic Press.

Donnerstein, E., & Berkowitz, L. (1982). Victim reactions in aggressive–erotic films as a factor in violence against women. *Journal of Personality and Social Psychology, 41,* 710–724.

Donnerstein, E., & Linz, D. (1993). Sexual violence in the mass media. In M. Costanzo & S. Oskamp (Eds.), *Violence and the law* (pp. 9–36). Thousand Oaks, CA: Sage.

Donnerstein, E., & Linz, D. (1995). Mass media sexual violence and male viewers: Current theory and research. In M. S. Kimmel & M. A. Messner (Eds.), *Men's lives* (3rd ed.) (pp. 381–392). Boston: Allyn & Bacon.

Doress, P. B., Siegal, D. L., & the Midlife and Old Women Book Project. (1987). *Ourselves, growing older.* New York: Simon & Schuster.

Dornbusch, S. M., & Gray, K. D. (1988). Single-parent families. In S. M. Dornbusch & M. H. Strober (Eds.), *Feminism, children, and the new families* (pp. 274–295). New York: Guilford Press.

Dornbusch, S. M., Gross, R. T., Duncan, P. D., & Ritter, P. L. (1987). Stanford studies of adolescence using the national health examination survey. In R. M. Lerner & T. T. Foch (Eds.), *Biological–psychosocial interactions in early adolescence* (pp. 189–205). Hillsdale, NJ: Erlbaum.

Douglas, M. (1969). *Purity and danger: An analysis of the concept of pollution and taboo.* London: Ark Publications.

Douthitt, R. A. (1989). The division of labor within homes: Have gender roles changed? *Sex Roles, 20,* 693–704.

Dovidio, J. F., & Gaertner, S. L. (1986). *Prejudice, discrimination, and racism.* New York: Academic Press.

Downs, W. R. (1993). Developmental considerations for the effects of childhood sexual abuse. *Journal of Interpersonal Violence, 8,* 331–345.

Downs, W. R., Miller, B. A., Testa, M., & Panek, D. (1992). Long-term effects of parent-to-child violence for women. *Journal of Interpersonal Violence, 7,* 365–382.

Doyle, J. A. (1989). *The male experience* (2nd ed.). Dubuque, IA: William C. Brown.

Doyle, J. A., & Paludi, M. A. (1991). *Sex and gender: The human experience.* Dubuque, IA: William C. Brown.

Dr. Spurzheim's observations on insanity (1825). *Lancet,* vii, 124–125. Cited in P. Tyrer (1993). Who is failing the mentally ill? *Lancet, 341,* 1199–1201.

Dresden, M. J. (1961). Mythology of ancient Iran. In S. N. Kramer (Ed.), *Mythology of the Ancient World* (pp. 342–344). Garden City, NY: Doubleday.

Dubow, E. F., Huesmann, L. R., & Eron, L. D. (1987). Childhood correlates of adult ego development. *Child Development, 58,* 859–869.

Dunn, M. E., & Trost, J. E. (1989). Male multiple orgasms: A descriptive study. *Archives of Sexual Behavior, 18,* 377–387.

DuRivage, V. L. (1992). New policies for the part-time and contingent workforce. In V. L. duRivage (Ed.), *New policies for the part-time and contingent workforce* (pp. 89–122). Armonk, NY: M. E. Sharpe.

Durkin, K. F. (1997). Misuse of the Internet by pedophiles: Implications for law enforcement and probation practice. *Federal Probation, 61,* 14–18.

Durret, M. E., O'Bryant, S., & Pennebaker, J. W. (1975). Childrearing report of white, black, and Mexican American families. *Developmental Psychology, 2,* 871.

Dutton, D. G., & Painter, S. (1981). Traumatic bonding: The development of emotional attachments in battered women and other relationships of intermittent abuse. *Victimology: An International Journal, 1,* 139–155.

Dyson, A. H. (1994). The Ninjas, the X-men, and the ladies: Playing with power and identity in an urban primary school. *Teachers College Record, 96*(2), 219–239.

Dziech, B. W., & Weiner, L. L. (1984). *The lecherous professor: Sexual harassment on campus.* Boston: Beacon Press.

Eagly, A. (1987). *Sex differences in social behavior: A social-role interpretation.* Hillsdale, NJ: Erlbaum.

Eagly, A., & Mladinic, A. (1998). Are people prejudiced against women? Some answers from research on attitudes, gender stereotypes, and judgments of competence. In W. Stroebe & M. Hewstone (Eds.), *European review of social psychology* (pp. 1–63). New York: Wiley.

Eagly, A. H. (1995a). Reflections on the commenters' views. *American Psychologist, 50,* 169–171.

Eagly, A. H. (1995b). The science and politics of comparing women and men. *American Psychologist, 50,* 145–158.

Eccles, J. S. (1987). Gender roles and women's achievement-related decisions. *Psychology of Women Quarterly, 11,* 135–172.

Eckholm, E. (1992, October 6). What happens to infants when their mothers go to work? *New York Times,* pp. A1, A21.

Eckholm, H. (1994, November 20). Changing visions of madness in America. *New York Times,* pp. 40–41.

Ehhrenreich, B., & English, D. (1979). *For her own good: 150 years of the experts' advice to women.* London: Pluto Press.

Ehrenreich, B., & English, D. (1981). The sexual politics of illness. In P. Conrad & R. Kern (Eds.), *The sociology of health and illness: Critical perspectives* (pp. 327–350). New York: St. Martin's Press.

Ehrhardt, A. A., Grisanti, G. C., & Meyer-Bahlburg, H. F. (1977). Prenatal exposure to medroxyprogesterone acetate (MPA) in girls. *Psychoneuroendocrinology 2,* 391–398.

Ehrhardt, A. A., Meyer-Balburg, H. F. L., Rosen, L. R., Feldman, J. F., Veridiano, N. P., Zimmerman, I., & McEwen, B. S. (1985). Sexual orientation after prenatal exposure to exogenous estrogen. *Archives of Sexual Behavior, 14,* 57–77.

Elder, G. H., Caspi, A., & Downey, G. (1986). Problem behavior and family relationships: A multigenerational analysis. In A. Sorensen, F. Weinert, & L. Sherrod (Eds.), *Human development and the life course.* Hillside, NJ: Erlbaum.

Elias, M. (1984, February 7). Women pay for working hard. *USA Today,* p. 1D.

Elias, M. (1997, April 4). 2½-year study of day care isn't the last word. *USA Today,* pp. 1A, 11A.

Ellis, L., & Ames, M. A. (1987). Neurohormonal functioning and sexual orientation: A theory of homosexuality–heterosexuality. *Psychological Bulletin, 101,* 233–258.

Else, L., Wonderlick, S. A., Beatty, W. W., Christie, D. W., et al. (1993). Personality characteristics of men who physically abuse women. *Hospital and Community Psychiatry, 44,* 54–58.

Ember, C. R., & Ember, M. (1990). *Anthropology* (6th ed., Instructor's ed.). Englewood Cliffs, NJ: Prentice-Hall.

Ember, C. R., & Ember, M. (1995). Issues in cross-cultural studies of interpersonal violence. In R. B. Ruback & N. A. Weiner (Eds.), *Interpersonal violent behaviors: Social and cultural aspects* (pp. 25–42). New York: Springer.

Enarson, E. P. (1984). Woods-working women: Sexual integration in the U.S. forest service. Birmingham, AL: University of Alabama Press.

Encyclopedia Britannica. (1999, July 12). *Hebrew.* Retrieved July 14, 1999 from the World Wide Web: http://search.eb.com/bol/topic?thes_id=182911.

Encyclopedia Britannica. (1999, July 12). *Christianity.* Retrieved July 24, 1999 from the World Wide Web: http://search.eb.com/bol/topic?tmap_id=41297000 &tmap_typ=ai.

Epstein, C. F. (1986). Family and career: Why women can "have it all." In C. Tavris (Ed.), *Every woman's emotional well-being: Heart and mind, body and soul.* Englewood Cliffs, NJ: Prentice-Hall.

Erikson, E. (1950). *Childhood and society.* New York: W. W. Norton.

Escobar, J. I. (1993). Psychiatric epidemiology. In A. C. Gaw (Ed.), *Culture, ethnicity* (pp. 43–73). Washington, DC: American Psychiatric Press.

Espin, O. M. (1987). Issues of identity in the psychology of Latina lesbians. In Boston Lesbian Psychologies Collective, *Lesbian psychologies: Explorations and challenges.* Urbana, IL: University of Illinois Press.

Espin, O. M. (1994). Feminist approaches. In L. Comas Diaz & B. Greene (Eds.) *Women of color: Integrating ethnic and gender identities in psychotherapy* (pp. 265–286). New York: Guilford Press.

Estrich, S. (1987). *Real rape.* Cambridge, MA: Harvard University Press.

Etaugh, C. (1993). Women in the middle and later years. In F. L. Denmark & M. A. Paludi (Eds.), *Psychology of women: A handbook of issues and theories* (pp. 213–246). Westport, CT: Greenwood Press.

Etaugh, C., Levine, D., & Mennella, A. (1984). Development of sex biases in children: 40 years later. *Sex Roles, 10,* 911–922.

Etienne, M., & Leacock, E. (1980). *Women and colonization: Anthropological perspectives.* New York: Praeger.

Ettinger, B. (1993). Use of low-dosage 17 beta-estradiol for the prevention of osteoporosis. *Clinical Therapy, 15,* 950–962.

Evans, R. J. (1976). *The feminist movement in Germany.* London: Sage.

Evans-Pritchard, E. E. (1937). *Witchcraft, oracles, and magic among the Azande.* Oxford: Oxford University Press.

Ewing, W. (1993). The civic advocacy of violence. In A. Minas (Ed.), *Gender basics: Feminist perspectives on women and men* (pp. 200–205). Belmont, CA: Wadsworth.

Eyer, D. (1994). Mother–infant bonding: A scientific fiction. *Human Nature, 5*(1), 69–94.

Fabe, M., & Wikler, N. (1978). *Up against the clock.* New York: Random House.

Fagot, B., Hagan, R., Leinbach, M., & Kronsberg, S. (1985). Differential reactions to assertive and communicative acts of toddler boys and girls. *Child Development, 56,* 1499–1505.

Fagot, B. I. (1991, April). *Peer relations in boys and girls from two to seven.* Paper presented at the biennial meeting of the Society for Research in Child Development, Seattle, WA.

Fagot, B. I., Leinbach, M. D., & O'Boyle, C. (1992). Gender labeling, gender stereotyping, and parenting behaviors. *Developmental Psychology, 28*(2), 225–230.

Fain, T. C., & Anderton, D. L. (1987). Sexual harassment: Organizational context and defuse status. *Sex Roles, 5/6,* 291–311.

Family Leave Act, Public Law 103–3, signed into law on February 5, 1993.

Fantini, M., & Cardenas, R. (1980). *Parenting in a multicultural society.* New York: Longman.

Fausto-Sterling, A. (1985). *Myths of gender: Biological theories about women and men* (2nd Rev. ed.). New York: Basic Books.

Fausto-Sterling, A. (1992). *Myths of gender: Biological theories about women and men.* New York: Basic Books.

Fausto-Sterling, A. (1993). The five sexes: Why male and female are not enough. *The Sciences,* March/April, 20–25.

Faxon, D. P., Ghalilli, K., Jacobs, A. K., Ruocco, N. A., Christellis, E. M., Kellett, M. A., Jr., Varrichione, T. R., & Ryan, T. J. (1992). The degree of vascularization and outcome after multivessel coronary angioplasty. *American Heart Journal, 123*(4, Pt. 1), 854–859.

Feather, N. T., & Simon, J. G. (1975). Reactions to male and female success and failure in sex-linked occupations: Impressions of personality, causal attributions, and perceived likelihood of different consequences. *Journal of Personality and Social Psychology, 31,* 20–31.

Featherston, E. (Ed.). (1994). *Skin deep: Women writing on color, culture and identity.* Freedom, CA: The Crossing Press.

Federbush, M. (1974). The sex problems of school math books. In J. Stacey, S. Beraud, & J. Daniels (Eds.), *And Jill came tumbling after: Sexism in American education.* New York: Dell.

Fein, E., & Schneider, S. (1995). *The rules: Time-tested secrets for capturing the heart of Mr. Right.* New York: Warner Books.

Fein, E., & Schneider, S. (1997). *The rules II: More rules to live and love by.* New York: Warner Books.

Feingold, A. (1988). Cognitive gender differences are disappearing. *American Psychologist, 43,* 95–103.

Feingold, A. (1991). Sex differences in the effect of similarity and physical attractiveness on opposite-sex attraction. *Basic and Applied Social Psychology, 12,* 357–367.

Feldman-Summers, S., & Kiesler, S. B. (1974). Those who are number two try harder: The effects of sex on attributions of causality. *Journal of Personality and Social Psychology, 30,* 846–855.

Fennema, E., & Sherman, J. (1977). Sex-related differences in mathematics, achievement, spatial visualization, and affective factors. *American Vocational Research Journal, 14,* 51–71.

Ferree, M. M., & Hall, E. J. (1990). Visual imagery of American society: Gender and race in introductory sociology textbooks. *Gender and Society, 4,* 500–533.

Festinger, L. (1957). *A theory of cognitive dissonance.* Palo Alto, CA: Stanford University Press.

Fidell, L. S. (1980). Sex role stereotypes and the American physician. *Psychology of Women Quarterly, 4,* 313–330.

Fidell, L. S. (1984). Sex roles in medicine. In C. Widom (Ed.), *Sex roles and psychopathology* (pp. 375–389). New York: Plenum Press.

Field, T. (1978). Interaction behaviors of primary versus secondary caretaker fathers. *Developmental Psychology, 14,* 183–184.

Fine, M. (1988). Sexuality, schooling, and adolescent females: The missing discourse of desire. *Harvard Educational Review, 58,* 29–53.

Fine, M., & Asch, A. (1981). Disabled women: Sexism without the pedestal. *Journal of Sociology and Social Welfare, 8,* 233–248.

Fine, M., & Asch, A. (1988). *Women with disabilities: Essays in psychology, culture, and politics.* Philadelphia: Temple University Press.

Finkelhor, D. (1979). *Sexually victimized children.* New York: Free Press.

Finkelhor, D. (1984). *Child sexual abuse: Theory and research.* New York: Free Press.

Finkelhor, D. (1986). Sexual abuse: Beyond the family systems approach. *Journal of Psychotherapy and the Family, 2,* 53–65.

Finkelhor, D. (1987). The sexual abuse of children: Current research reviewed. *Psychiatric Annals, 17,* 233–241.

Finkelhor, D. (1990). Early and long term effects of child sexual abuse: An update. *Professional Psychology: Research and Practice, 21,* 325–330.

Finkelhor, D., & Hotaling, G. T. (1984). Sexual abuse in the national incidence study of child abuse and neglect: An appraisal. *Child Abuse and Neglect, 8,* 23–32.

Finkelhor, D., & Russell, D. (1984). Women as perpetrators: Review of the evidence. In D. Finkelhor (Ed.), *Child sexual abuse: Theory and research.* New York: The Free Press.

Finkelhor, D., & Yllo, K. (1982). Forced sex in marriage: A preliminary research report. *Crime and Delinquency, 28,* 459–478.

Finkelhor, D., & Yllo, K. (1985). *License to rape: Sexual abuse of wives.* New York: Holt, Rinehart and Winston.

Fischer, J. L., & Narus, L. R. (1981). Sex-role development in late adolescence and adulthood. *Sex Roles, 7,* 97–106.

Fischer, T. D. (1987). Family communication and the sexual behavior and attitudes of college students. *Journal of Youth and Adolescence, 16,* 481–495.

Fishbein, H. D., & Imai, S. (1993). Preschoolers select playmates on the basis of gender and race. *Journal of Applied Developmental Psychology, 14*(3), 303–316.

Fisher, B., Redmond, C., & Poisson, R. (1989). Eight-year results of a randomized clinical trial comparing total mastectomy and lumpectomy with or without irradiation in the treatment of breast cancer. *New England Journal of Medicine, 320,* 822–828.

Fisher, B., Redmond, C., & Risher, E. R. (1985). Ten year results of a randomized clinical trial comparing radical mastectomy and total mastectomy with or without radiation. *New England Journal of Medicine, 312,* 674–681.

Fisher, W. A. (1995). Understanding and promoting AIDS-preventive behavior: Insights from the theory of reasoned action. *Health Psychology, 14,* 255–264.

Fiske, S. T., Bersoff, D. N., Borgida, E., Deaux, K., & Heilman, M. E. (1991). Social science research on trial: Use of sex stereotyping research in Price Waterhouse v. Hopkins. *American Psychologist, 46,* 1049–1060.

Fiske, S. T., & Taylor, S. E. (1991). *Social cognition* (2nd ed.). New York: McGraw-Hill.

Fitting, M. D., Salisbury, S., Davies, N., & Mayclin, D. K. (1978). Self-concept and sexuality of spinal cord injured women. *Archives of Sexual Behavior, 7,* 143–156.

Fitzgerald, L. F. (1993). Sexual harassment: Violence against women in the workplace. *American Psychologist, 48,* 1070–1076.

Fitzgerald, L. F. (1996). Sexual harassment: The definition and measurement of a construct. In M. A. Paludi (Ed.), *Sexual harassment on college campuses: Abusing the ivory power* (pp. 25–47). New York: State University of New York Press.

Fitzgerald, L. F., & Ormerod, A. J. (1991). Perceptions of sexual harassment: The influence of gender and context. *Psychology of Women Quarterly, 15,* 281–294.

Fitzgerald, L. F., & Ormerod, A. J. (1993). Breaking silence: The sexual harassment of women in academia and the workplace. In F. L. Denmark & M. A. Paludi (Eds.), *Psychology of women: A handbook of issues and theories* (pp. 553–581). Westport, CN: Greenwood Press.

Fitzgerald, L. F., & Shullman, S. L. (1993). Sexual harassment: A research analysis and agenda for the 1990's. *Journal of Vocational Behavior, 42,* 5–27.

Fitzgerald, L. F., Shullman, S. L., Bailey, N., Richards, M., Swecker, J., Gold, A., Ormerod, A. J., & Weitzman, L. (1988). The incidence and dimensions of sexual harassment in academia and the workplace. *Journal of Vocational Behavior, 32,* 152–175.

Fitzgerald, L. F., & Weitzman, L. M. (1990). Men who harass: Speculation and data. In M. A. Paludi, et al. (Ed.), *Ivory power: Sexual harassment on campus* (pp. 125–140). Albany, NY: SUNY Press.

Flaks, D. K., Ficher, I., Masterpasqua, F., & Joseph, G. (1995). Lesbians choosing motherhood: A comparative study of lesbian and heterosexual parents and their children. *Developmental Psychology, 31,* 105–114.

Flower, L. (1997). *The elements of world religions.* New York: Element Books.

Follingstad, D. R., Brennan, A. F., Hause, E. S., Polek, D. S., & Rutledge, L. L. (1991). Factors moderating physical and psychological symptoms of battered women. *Journal of Family Violence, 6,* 81–95.

Forcey, L. R. (1987). *Mothers of sons: Toward an understanding of responsibility.* New York: Praeger.

Fortes, M. (1962). *The web of kinship among the Tallensi.* London: Oxford University Press.

Foster, C., Squyres, S., & Jacobs, N. (Eds.). (1996). *Women's changing role. The information series on current topics.* New York: Wylie—Information Plus.

Foucault, M. (1978). *The history of sexuality,* Vol. 1 (R. Hurley, Trans.). New York: Pantheon.

Fourcroy, J. L. (1994). Women and the development of drugs: Why can't a woman be more like a man? In J. A. Sechzer, A. Griffin, & S. M. Pfafflin (Eds.), *Forging a women's health research agenda: Policy issues for the 1990's. Annals of the New York Academy of Sciences, 736* (pp. 174–195).

Fowers, B. J. (1991). His and her marriages: A multivariate study of gender and marital satisfaction. *Sex Roles, 24,* 209–221.

Fowlkes, M. R. (1987). The myth of merit and male professional careers: The roles of wives. In N. Gerstel and H. E. Ross (Eds.), *Work and families* (pp. 347–360). Philadelphia: Temple University Press.

Fox, L. H. (1987). Sex differences among the mathematically gifted. In J. A. Sechzer & S. M. Pfafflin (Eds.), *Psychology and Educational Policy. Annals of the New York Academy of Sciences, 517* (pp. 99–112).

Fox, M., Gibbs, M., & Auerbach, D. (1985). Age and gender dimensions of friendship. *Psychology of Women Quarterly, 9,* 489–502.

Fox, R. C. (1996). Bisexuality in perspective: A review of theory and research. In B. A. Firestein (Ed.), *Bisexuality: The psychology and politics of an invisible minority.* Thousand Oaks, CA: Sage.

Fox-Keller, E. F. (1982). Feminism and science. In N. O. Keohane, et al. (Eds.), *Feminist theory: A critique of ideology* (p. 312). Chicago: University of Chicago Press.

Franz, C. E., & Stewart, A. J. (1994). *Women creating lives: Identities, resilience, & resistance.* Boulder, CO: Westview.

Frayser, S. (1985). *Varieties of sexual experience: An anthropological perspective on human sexuality.* New Haven, CT: Human Relations Area Files Press.

Freed, R. S., & Freed, S. A. (1989). Beliefs and practices resulting in female deaths and fewer females than males in India. *Population and Environment, 10,* 144–161.

Freeman, E. W., Boxer, A. S., Rickels, K., Tureck, R., & Mastroianni, L., Jr. (1985). Psychological evaluation and support in a program of in vitro fertilization and embryo transfer. *Fertility and Sterility, 43,* 48–53.

Freeman, J. (1984). Women, law, and public policy. In J. Freeman (Ed.), *Women: A feminist perspective* (pp. 365–404). Palo Alto, CA: Mayfield.

Freiberg, P. (1991). Self-esteem gender gap widens in adolescence. *APA Monitor, 22*(4), 29.

Frenkel, K. A. (1990, November). Women and computing. *Communications of the ACM, 33,* 34–46.

Freud, S. (1912). The psychology of love. In J. Strahey (Ed.), *The standard edition of the complete psychological works of Sigmund Freud,* Vol. 11, p. 189.

Freud, S. (1924). The dissolution of the Oedipus complex. In Ernest Jones (Ed.), *The standard edition of the complete psychological works of Sigmund Freud,* Vol. 19. London: Hogarth Ltd., 1961, pp. 172–179.

Freud, S. (1925/1961). Some psychical consequences of the anatomical distinction between the sexes. In J. Strahey (Ed.), *The standard edition of the complete psychological works of Sigmund Freud,* Vol. 19, 243–258. London: Hogarth Press and the Institute of Psychoanalysis.

Freud, S. (1931). Female sexuality. In J. Strahey (Ed.), *Sigmund Freud, collected papers,* Vol. V (pp. 252–272). London: Hogarth Press and the Institute of Psychoanalysis.

Freud, S. (1959). Some psychological consequences of the anatomical distinction between the sexes. In *The collected papers,* Vol. V, p. 186.

Frey, K. S., & Ruble, D. N. (1992). Gender constancy and the "cost" of sex-typed behavior: A test of the conflict hypothesis. *Developmental Psychology, 28*(4), 714–721.

Friedman, A., Tzukerman, Y., & Wienberg, H., & Todd, J. (1992). The shift in power with age: Changes in perception of the power of women and men over the life cycle. *Psychology of Women Quarterly, 16,* 513–525.

Friend, R., Rafferty, Y., & Bramel, D. (1990). A puzzling interpretation of the Asch "conformity" study. *European Journal of Social Psychology, 20,* 29–44.

Frieze, I. H. (1983). Investigating the causes and consequences of marital rape. *Signs, 8,* 532–552.

Frieze, I. H., Whitley, B. E., Jr., Hanusa, B. H., & McHugh, M. C. (1982). Assessing the theoretical models for sex differences in causal attributions for success and failure. *Sex Roles, 8,* 333–343.

Frintner, M. P., & Rubinson, L. (1993). Acquaintance rape: The influence of alcohol, fraternity membership, and sports team membership. *Journal of Sex Education and Therapy, 19,* 272–284.

Fuhrer, R., Antonucci, T. C., & Dartigues, J. F. (1992). The co-occurrence of depressive symptoms and cognitive impairment in a French community: Are there gender differences? *European Archives of Psychiatry and Clinical Neuroscience, 242*(2/3), 161–171.

Fujitomi, S., & Wong, D. (1976). The new Asian American woman. In S. Cox (Ed.), *Female psychology: The emerging self* (pp. 236–248). Chicago: Science Research Associates.

Fuller, A. H. (1961). *Buraji: Portrait of a Lebanese Moslem village*. Cambridge, MA: Harvard University Press.

Funk, R. E. (1993). *Stopping rape: A challenge for men*. Philadelphia: New Society Publishers.

Gaddis, A., & Brooks-Gunn, J. (1985). The male experience of pubertal change. *Journal of Youth and Adolescence, 14,* 61–69.

Gagnon, J. H. (1977). *Human sexualities*. Glenview, IL: Scott, Foresman.

Gagnon, J. H., & Simon, W. (1973). *Sexual conduct: The social origins of human sexuality*. Chicago: Aldine.

Galsworthy, T. D. (1994). Osteoporosis: Statistics, intervention and prevention. In J. A. Sechzer, A. Griffin, & S. M. Pfafflin (Eds.), *Forging a women's health research agenda: Policy issues for the 1990's. Annals of the New York Academy of Sciences, 736,* 158–164. New York: The New York Academy of Sciences.

Gamwell, L., & Tomas, N. (1995). *Madness in America: Cultural and medical perceptions of mental illness before 1914* (pp. 19–21). Cornell Studies in the History of Psychiatry. Ithaca, NY: Cornell University Press.

Gara, M. A., Woolfolk, R. L., Cohen, B. D., Goldstein, R. B., Allen, L. A., & Novelany, J. (1993). Perception of self and other in major depression. *Journal of Abnormal Psychology, 102*(1), 93–100.

Garb, H. (1997). Race bias, social class bias, and gender bias in clinical judgment. *Clinical psychology: Science and practice, 4*(2), 99–120.

Garber, M. (1995). *Vice versa: Bisexuality and the eroticism of everyday life*. New York: Simon & Schuster.

Garcia, L. T. (1986). Exposure to pornography and attitudes about women and rape: A correlational study. *Journal of Sex Research, 22,* 378–385.

Garfinkel, P. E., & Garner, D. M. (1982). *Anorexia nervosa: A multidimensional perspective*. New York: Bruner/Mazel.

Garland, A. W. (1988). *Women activists: Challenging the abuse of power*. New York: Feminist Press.

Garner, D. M., & Bemis, K. M. (1982). A cognitive–behavioral approach to anorexia nervosa. *Cognitive Therapy Research, 6,* 1223–1250.

Gary, L. E. (1987). Attitudes of Black adults toward community mental health centers. *Hospital and Community Psychiatry, 38,* 1100–1105.

Gazetas, P., Estabrook, A., O'Neil, J., & Sciacca, R. (1994). Importance of adequate staging and of hormone receptors in women over age 70 with breast cancer. New York: Columbia University Medical Center.

Gelles, R. J., & Straus, M. A. (1988). *Intimate violence*. New York: Simon & Shuster.

Genesis Rabbah, 18, 2. Cited by Swidler, 1976, p. 72.

Gerdes, E. P. (1995). Women preparing for traditionally male professions: Physical and psychological symptoms associated with work and home stress. *Sex Roles, 32*(11/12).

Geringer, W. M., Marks, S., Allen W. J., & Armstrong, K. A. (1993). Knowledge, attitudes, and behavior related to condom use and STDs in a high risk population. *Journal of Sex Research, 36,* 75–83.

Gerrard, M. (1987). Sex, sex guilt, and contraceptive use revisited: The 1980s. *Journal of Personality and Social Psychology, 52,* 975–980.

Gibbons, J. L., Lynn, M., Stiles, D. A., de Berducido, E. J., Richter, R., Walker, K., & Wiley, D. (1993). Guatemalan, Filipino, and U.S. adolescents' images of women as office workers and homemakers. *Psychology of Women Quarterly, 17*(4), 373–388.

Gilbert, L. A. (1993). Women at midlife: Current theoretical perspectives and research. *Women and Therapy, 14*(1/2), 105–115.

Gilbert, L. A. (1994). Reclaiming and returning gender to context: Examples from studies of heterosexual dual-earner families. *Psychology of Women Quarterly, 18,* 539–584.

Gillen, K., & Muncer, S. J. (1995). Sex differences in the perceived causal structure of date rape: A preliminary report. *Aggressive Behavior, 21,* 101–112.

Gilligan, C. (1982). *In a different voice: Psychological theory and women's development*. Cambridge, MA: Harvard University Press.

Gilligan, C., & Attanucci, J. (1988). Two moral orientations: Gender differences and similarities. *Merrill–Palmer Quarterly, 34,* 223–237.

Gilman, A. G., Rall, T. W., Neis, A. S., & Taylor, P. (Eds.). (1990). *Goodman and Gilman's pharmacological basis of therapeutics*. New York: Pergamon Press.

Gilman, C. P. (1892). *The yellow wallpaper*. The New England Magazine. Reissued 1989 as *The yellow wallpaper and other writings by Charlotte Perkins Gilman*. New York: Bantam Books.

Gilman, C. P. (1975). *The living of Charlotte Perkins Gilman: An autobiography*. New York: Harper Books.

Gilroy, F. D., & Steinbacher, R. (1991). Sex selection technology utilization: Further implications for sex-ratio imbalance. *Social Biology, 38,* 285–288.

Gimbutas, M. (1982). Prehistoric religions: Old Europe. In *The Encyclopedia of Religion,* Vol. II (pp. 506–515); *The goddesses and gods of Old Europe*. Berkeley: University of California Press. Cited by Carmody, 1989, pp. 14–21.

Ginorio, A. B., Gutierrez, L., Cauce, A. M., & Acosta, M. (1995). Psychological issues for Latinas. In H. Landrine (Ed.), *Bringing cultural diveristy to feminist psychology: Theory, research, and practice* (pp. 241–264). Washington, DC: American Psychological Association.

Glass, S. P., & Wright, T. L. (1992). Justifications for extramarital relationships: The association between attitudes, behaviors, and gender. *Journal of Sex Research, 29,* 361–387.

Glazer, N., & Moynihan, D. P. (1970). *Beyond the melting pot* (2nd ed.). Cambridge, MA: MIT Press.

Glenn, E. N. (1986). *Issei, nisei, war bride: Three generations of Japanese American women in domestic service.* Philadelphia: Temple University Press.

Glenn, N. D., & Weaver, C. N. (1988). The changing relationship of marital status to reported happiness. *Journal of Marriage and the Family, 50,* 317–324.

Glick, P. (1991). Trait-based and sex-based discrimination in occupational prestige, occupational salary, and hiring. *Sex Roles, 25*(5/6), 351–378.

Glick, P. C. (1986). The family life cycle and social change. *Family Relations, 38,* 123–129.

Glick, P. C., & Lin, S. L. (1986). Recent changes in divorce and remarriage. *Journal of Marriage and Family, 48*(4), 737–747.

Goffman, E. (1969). *The presentation of self in everyday life.* London: Allen Lane.

Goffman, E. (1979). *Gender advertisements.* Cambridge, MA: Harvard University Press.

Golan, N. (1986). *The perilous bridge.* New York: Free Press.

Gold, D., & Andres, D. (1978). Developmental comparisons between ten-year-old children with employed and non-employed mothers. *Child Development, 49,* 75–84.

Goldberg, H. (1980). *The new male: From self-destruction to self-care.* New York: Signet.

Goldenberg, N. R. (1985). *Changing of the gods: Feminism and the end of traditional religions.* Boston: Beacon Press.

Goldman, B. D. (1978). Developmental influences of hormones on neuroendocrine mechanisms of sexual behavior: Comparisons with other sexually dimorphic behaviors. In J. B. Hutchinson (Ed.), *Biological determinants of sexual behavior* (pp. 127–152). (Cited by Masters, Johnson, & Kolodny, 1995, p. 203). New York: HarperCollins.

Gondolf, E. W., & Hanneken, J. (1987). The gender warriors: Reformed batterers on abuse, treatment, and change. *Journal of Family Violence, 2,* 177–191.

Goode, E. (1996). Gender and courtship entitlement: Responses to personal ads. *Sex Roles, 34*(3/4), 141–169.

Goode, W. J. (1974). A theory of strain. *American Sociological Review, 25,* 483–496.

Goodman, H. (1982). Assertiveness breeds attempt. *Psychology Today, 16,* 75.

Goodman, J., & Croyle, R. T. (1989). Social framework testimony in employment discrimination cases. *Behavioral Science and the Law, 7,* 227–241.

Goodman, L. A., Koss, M. P., Fitzgerald, L. F., Russo, N. F., & Keita, G. P. (1993). Male violence against women: Current research and future directions. *American Psychologist, 48,* 1054–1058.

Gordon, M. J., & Riger, S. (1989). *The female fear.* New York: Free Press.

Gordon, R. R., & Gordon, K. K. (1967). Factors in postpartum emotional adjustment. *American Journal of Orthopsychiatry, 37,* 359–360.

Gore, S., & Mangione, T. W. (1983). Social roles, sex roles, and psychological distress: Additive and interactive models of sex differences. *Journal of Health and Social Behavior, 24,* 300–312.

Gormly, A. V., Gormly, J. B., & Weiss, H. (1987). Motivations for parenthood among young adult college students. *Sex Roles, 16,* 31–39.

Gorski, R. A., Gordon, J. H., Shryne, J. E., & Southam, M. A. (1978). Evidence for a morphological sex difference within the medial preoptic area of the rat brain. *Brain Research, 148,* 333–346.

Gottfredson, L. S. (1981). Circumscription and compromise: A developmental theory of occupational aspirations. *Journal of Counseling Psychology Monograph, 28,* 545–579.

Gould, S. J. (1980). *The panda's thumb: More reflections in natural history.* New York: W. W. Norton.

Gracely, R. H., McGrath, P., & Dubner, R. (1978). Ratio scales of sensory and affective verbal pain descriptors. *Pain, 5,* 5–18.

Grady, D. (1998, November 6). Study says HIV tests underestimate women's risk. *New York Times,* p. A18.

Graham, N., & Wish, E. D. (1994). Drug use among female arrestees: Onset, pattern, and relationship to prostitution. *Journal of Drug Issues, 24,* 315–329.

Graham, S. (1992). Most of the subjects were White and middle class. *American Psychologist, 47*(5), 629–639.

Grambs, J. D. (1989). *Women over forty: Visions and realities.* New York: Springer.

Gray, P. (1993, February 15). What is love? *Time,* 47–49.

Green, B. L., & Russo, N. F. (1993). Work and family roles: Selected issues. In F. L. Denmark & M. A. Paludi (Eds.), *Psychology of Women: A handbook of issues and theories.* Westport, CT: Greenwood.

Green, R. (1980). Native American women. *Signs: Journal of Women in Culture and Society, 6,* 248–267.

Green, R., & Crooks, P. D. (1988, December). Family member adjustment and family dynamics in established single-parent and two-parent families. *Social Service Review,* 600–616.

Greenblatt, R. (1979). Update on the male and female climacteric. *American Geriatrics Society, 27*(11), 481–490. Cited by Masters, Johnson, and Kolodny, 1995, p. 268.

Greene, B. (1992). Black feminist psychotherapy. In E. Wright (Ed.), *Feminism and psychoanalysis.* Oxford, England: Blackwell.

Greene, B. (1994a). African American women. In L. Comas-Diaz & B. Greene (Eds.), *Women of color: Integrating ethnic and gender identities in psychotherapy* (pp. 10–29). New York: Guilford Press.

Greene, B. (1994b). African American women: Derivatives of racism and sexism in psychotherapy. In E. Tobach & B. Rosoff (Eds.), *Genes and gender series,* Vol. 7. *Challenging racism and sexism: Alternatives to genetic explanations* (pp. 122–139). New York: Feminist Press.

Greene, B. (1994c). Lesbian and gay sexual orientations: Implications for clinical training, practice, and research. In B. Greene & G. M. Herek (Eds.), *Lesbian and gay psychology: Theory, research, and clinical applications* (pp. 1–24). Psychological Perspectives on Lesbian and Gay Issues, Vol. 1. Thousand Oaks, CA: Sage.

Greene, B. (1996). African-American women: Considering diverse identities and societal barriers in psychotherapy. In J. A. Sechzer, S. M. Pfafflin, F. L. Denmark, A. Griffin, & S. J. Blumenthal (Eds.), *Women and mental health: Annals of the New York Academy of Sciences, 789,* 191–209. New York: The New York Academy of Sciences.

Greene, B. (1997). Psychotherapy with African American women: Integrating feminist and psychodynamic models. *Smith College Studies in Social Work, 67*(3), 299–322.

Greene, J. G., & Cooke, D. J. (1980). Life stress and symptoms at the climacterium. *British Journal of Psychiatry, 136,* 486–491.

Greenfield, P. (1994). Independence and interdependence as developmental scripts: Implications of theory, research and practice. In P. Greenfield & R. Cocking (Eds.), *Cross-cultural roots of minority child development* (pp. 1–37). Hillsdale, NJ: Erlbaum.

Greenhaus, J. H., & Parasuraman, S. (1993). Job performance attributions and career advancement prospects. An examination of race and gender effects. *Organizational Behavior and Human Decision Processes, 55,* 273–297.

Grief, J. B. (1979). Fathers, children, and joint custody. *American Journal of Orthopsychiatry, 49,* 311–319.

Griffen, J. (1979). A cross-cultural investigation of behavioral changes at menopause. In J. Williams (Ed.), *Psychology of women* (pp. 488–495). New York: W.W. Norton.

Griffith, E., & Baker, F. (1993). Psychiatric care of African Americans. In A. Gaw (Ed.), *Culture, ethnicity, & mental illness* (pp. 147–174). Washington, DC: American Psychiatric Press.

Grodsky, P. B. (1995). Personal communication.

Gross, A., Smith, R., & Wallston, B. (1983). The men's movement: Personal vs. political. In J. Freeman (Ed.), *Social movements of the sixties and seventies* (pp. 71–81). New York: Longman.

Groth, A. N., & Birnbaum, H. J. (1979). *Men who rape: The psychology of the offender.* New York: Plenum.

Groth, N. A., & Burgess, A. W. (1980). Male rape: Offenders and victims. *American Journal of Psychiatry, 137,* 806–810.

Gruber, J. S., & Bjorn, L. (1982). Blue-collar blues: The sexual harassment of women auto workers. *Work and Occupations, 9,* 271–298.

Guinier, L., Fine, M., Balin, J., Bartow, A., & Stachel, D. L. (1994). Becoming gentlemen: Women's experiences at one Ivy League law school. *University of Pennsylvania Law Review, 143*(1), 1–110.

Gulik, R. M., Mellors, J. W., Havlir, D., Eron, J. J., Gonzalez, C., McMahon, D., Jonas, L., Meibohm, A., Holder, D., Schleif, W. A., Condra, J. H., Emini, E., Isaacs, R., Chodakewitz, J. A., & Richman, D. D. (1998). Simultaneous vs. sequential initiation of therapy with indavir, zidovudine and lamivudine for HIV-1 infection: 100 week follow-up. *Journal of the American Medical Association, 280*(1), 35–41.

Gutek, B. A. (1985). *Sex in the workplace.* San Francisco: Jossey-Bass.

Gutek, B. A. (1993). Responses to sexual harassment. In S. Oskamp & M. Costanzo (Eds.), *Gender issues in contemporary society* (pp. 197–216). Newbury Park, CA: Sage.

Gutek, B. A. (1996). Sexual harassment at work: When an organization fails to respond. In M. S. Stockdale (Ed.), *Sexual harassment in the workplace: Perspectives, frontiers, and response strategies* (pp. 272–290). Thousand Oaks, CA: Sage.

Gutek, B. A., & Morasch, B. (1982). Sex ratios, sex-role spillover, and sexual harassment of women at work. *Journal of Social Issues, 38,* 55–74.

Gutmann, D. (1987). *Reclaimed powers: Towards a psychology of later life.* New York: Basic Books.

Haber, L. C., & Austin, J. K. (1992). How married couples make decisions. *Western Journal of Nursing Research, 14*(3), 322–342.

Hackel, L., & Ruble, D. N. (1992). Change in the marital relationship after first baby: Predicting the impact of expectancy disconfirmation. *Journal of Personality and Social Psychology, 62,* 944–957.

Haddad, Y. Y. (1985). Islam women and revolution in twentieth-century Arab thought. In Y. Y. Haddad and E. B. Findly (Eds.), *Women, Religion and Social Change* (pp. 275–306). Albany, NY: State University of New York Press.

Hafner, R. G., & Minge, P. J. (1989). Sex-role stereotypes in women with agoraphobia and their husbands. *Sex Roles, 20,* 705–711.

Hagan, J., Zatz, M., Arnold, B., & Kay, F. (1991). Cultural, capital, gender, and structural transformation of legal practice. *Law and Society Review, 25,* 239–262.

Hagen, R. I., & Kahn, A. (1975). Discrimination against competent women. *Journal of Applied Social Psychology, 5,* 362–367.

Hall, D. T., & Gordon, F. E. (1973). Effects of career choices on married women. *Journal of Applied Psychology, 58,* 42–48.

Hall, G. C. N., & Hirschman, R. (1991). Toward a theory of sexual aggression: A quadripartite model. *Journal of Consulting and Clinical Psychology, 59,* 662–669.

Hall, G. C. N., Shondrick, D. D., & Hirschman, R. (1993). The role of sexual arousal in sexually aggressive behavior: A meta-analysis. *Journal of Consulting and Clinical Psychology, 61,* 1091–1095.

Hall, G. S. (1904). *Adolescence: Its psychology and its relations to physiology, anthropology, sociology, sex, crime, religion, and education* (Vols. 1 & 2). New York: Appleton.

Hall, G. S. (1906, June 4). Coeducation. *American Academy of Medicine,* 1–4.

Hall, G. S. (1908). Feminization in school and home. *World's Work, 16,* 10237–10244.

Hall, J. A. (1984). *Nonverbal sex differences.* Baltimore: Johns Hopkins University Press.

Hall, J. A., Epstein, A. M., DeCiantis, M. L., & McNeil, B. J. (1993). Physicians' liking for their patients: More evidence for the role affect in medical care. *Health Psychology, 12,* 140–146.

Hall, R. M., & Sandler, B. R. (1982, July 7). The classroom climate: A chilly one for women? Washington, DC: Project on the Status and Education of Women, Association of American Colleges.

Haller, J. S., & Haller, R. M. (1974). *The physician and sexuality in Victorian America.* Urbana, IL: University of Illinois Press.

Halmi, K. A. (1996). Eating disorder research in the past decade. In J. A. Sechzer, S. M. Pfafflin, F. L. Denmark, A. Griffin, and S. J. Blumenthal (Eds.), *Women and mental health. Annals of the New York Academy of Sciences, 789,* 67–77.

Halmi, K. A., Schneider, L. H., & Cooper, S. J. (1989). Preface. In L. H. Schneider, S. J. Cooper, & K. A. Halmi (Eds.), *The psychobiology of human eating disorders: Preclinical and clinical perspectives. Annals of the New York Academy of Sciences, 575,* xi. New York: The New York Academy of Sciences.

Halpern, D. F. (1997). Sex differences in intelligence: Implications for education. *American Psychologist, 52,* 1091–1102.

Halvorsen, R. (1998). The ambiguity of lesbian and gay marriages: Change and continuity in the symbolic order. *Journal of Homosexuality, 35,* 207–231.

Hamer, D. H., Hu, S., Magnuson, V. L., Hu, N., & Pattacucci, A. M. (1993). A linkage between DNA markers on the X chromosome and male sex orientation. *Science, 261,* 321–327.

Hannan, E. L., Bernard, H. R., Kilburn, H. C., & O'Donnel, J. F. (1992). Gender differences in mortality rates for coronary bypass surgery. *American Heart Journal, 123*(4, Pt. 1), 855–872.

Hanson, R. K. (1990). The psychological impact of sexual assault on women and children: A review. *Annals of Sex Research, 3,* 187–232.

Hanson, S. (1986). Father/child relationships: Beyond Kramer vs. Kramer. In R. A. Lewis & M. D. Sussman (Eds.), *Men's changing roles in the family* (pp. 135–150). New York: Haworth Press.

Hardesty, C., & Bokemeier, J. (1989). Finding time and making do: Distribution of household labor in nonmetropolitan marriages. *Journal of Marriage & the Family, 51,* 253–267.

Harding, M. E. (1971). *Women's mysteries: Ancient and modern.* New York: G. P. Putnam's Sons.

Harding, S. (1986). *The science question in feminism.* Ithaca, NY: Cornell University Press.

Hardy, J. D., Wolff, H. G., & Goodell, H. (1952). *Pain sensation and reactions.* Baltimore, MD: Williams & Wilkens.

Hare-Mustin, R., & Marecek, J. (1989). The meaning of difference: Gender theory, postmodernism, and psychology. *American Psychologist, 43*(6), 455–464.

Hariton, E. B., & Singer, J. L. (1974). Women's fantasies during sexual intercourse: Normative and theoretical implications. *Journal of Consulting and Clinical Psychology, 42,* 331–322.

Harmon, A. (1999, March 22). With the best of intentions, a game maker fails. *New York Times Business Day.*

Harold, S. (1992). Education in later life: The case of older women. *Educational Gerontology, 18*(5), 511–527.

Harper, E. B. (1969). Fear and status of the woman. *Southwestern Journal of Anthropology, 25,* 81–95.

Harré, R., & Lamb, R. (1986). *The dictionary of personality and social psychology.* Cambridge, MA: MIT Press.

Harrington, N. T., & Leitenberg, H. (1994). Relationship between alcohol consumption and victim behaviors immediately preceding sexual aggression by an acquaintance. *Violence and Victims, 9,* 315–324.

Harris, M. B., Begay, C., & Page, P. (1989). Activities, family relationships, and feelings about aging in a multicultural elderly sample. *International Journal of Aging and Human Development, 29*(2), 103–117.

Harris, M. H. (1923). A thousand years of Jewish history (10th ed.). New York: Bloch.

Harrison, A. A., & Saeed, L. (1977). Let's make a deal: An analysis of revelations and stipulations in lonely hearts advertisements. *Journal of Personality and Social Psychology, 35,* 257–264.

Harrison, J., Chin, J., & Ficarrotto, T. (1995). Warning: Masculinity may be dangerous to your health. In M. S. Kimmel & Michael A. Messner (Eds.), *Men's lives* (pp. 237–249). Boston: Allyn and Bacon.

Hartley, S. F., & Piettraczyk, L. M. (1979). Persecuting the sex of offspring: Technologies, attitudes, and implications. *Social Biology, 26,* 232–246.

Hatcher, R. A., Trussel, J., Stwart, G., Kowal, D., Guest, F., Cates, W. Jr., & Policar, M. (1994). *Contraceptive technology 1990–1992* (16th Rev. ed.). New York: Irvington.

Hatfield, E., & Sprecher, S. (1986). Measuring passionate love in intimate relationships. *Journal of Adolescence, 9,* 383–410.

Hayden-Thompson, L., Rubin, K. H., & Hymel, S. (1987). Sex preferences in sociometric choices. *Developmental Psychology, 23,* 558–562.

Haynes, S. G., Harvey, C., Montes, H., Nickens, H., & Cohen, B. (1990). Patterns of cigarette smoking among Hispanics in the United States: Results from the HANES, 1982–1984. *American Journal of Public Health, 80,* 47–53.

Hays, H. R. (1964). *The dangerous sex: The myth of feminine evil.* New York: G. P. Putnam and Sons.

Healy, B. (1991). The Yentyl syndrome. *New England Journal of Medicine, 325,* 274–276.

Hedges, L. V., & Nowell, A. (1995). Sex differences in mental test scores, variability, and number of high-scoring individuals. *Science, 269,* 41–45.

Heffernan, K. (1998). Bulimia nervosa. In A. E. Blechman & K. D. Brownell (Eds.), *Behavioral medicine and women: A comprehensive handbook* (pp. 358–363). New York: Guilford Press.

Hegeler, S., & Mortesen, M. (1977). Sexual behavior in elderly Danish males. In R. Gemme & C. Wheeler (Eds.), *Progress in sexology* (pp. 285–292). New York: Plenum Press.

Heider, F. (1958). *The psychology of interpersonal relations.* New York: Wiley.

Heilman, M. (1983). Sex bias in work settings: The lack of fit model. *Research and Organizational Behavior, 5,* 269–298.

Heinz, J. P., & Laumann, E. O. (1982). *Chicago lawyers: The social structure of the bar.* New York: Russell Sage.

Heise, L. (1994). *Violence against women: The hidden health burden.* WorldBank Discussion Papers, Washington, DC. From Landes, Foster, & Cessna, (1995). New York: Wylie—Information Plus.

Helms, J. E., & Talleyrand, R. M. (1997). Race is not ethnicity. *American Psychologist, 52,* 1246–1247.

Helson, R., Mitchell, V., & Moane, G. (1984). Personality and patterns of adherence and nonadherence to the social clock. *Journal of Personality and Social Psychology, 46,* 1079–1096.

Helstrom, A. W., & Blechman, A. E. (1998). Section editor's overview. In A. E. Blechman & K. D. Brownell (Eds.), *Behavioral medicine and women: A comprehensive handbook* (pp. 813–815). New York: Guilford Press.

Hemming, H. (1985). Women in a man's world: Sexual harassment. *Human Behavior, 38,* 67–79.

Henderson, B. E., Pagnani-Hill, A., & Ross, R. A. (1991). Decreased mortality in users of estrogen replacement therapy. *Archives of Internal Medicine, 151,* 75–78.

Hendrick, C., & Hendrick, S. (1986). A theory and method of love. *Journal of Personality and Social Psychology, 50,* 392–402.

Henry, T. (1998, October 14). Girls lagging as gender gap widens in tech education. *USA Today,* p. 4D.

Henshaw, S. K., & Silverman, J. (1988). The characteristics and prior contraceptive use of U.S. abortion patients. *Family Planning Perspectives, 20,* 158–168.

Herbert, B. (1997, October 30). China's missing girls. *New York Times,* p. A31.

Herek, G. H. (1995). Psychological heterosexism and antigay violence: The social psychology of bigotry and bashing. In M. S. Kimmel & M. A. Messner (Eds.), *Men's lives* (3rd ed.) (pp. 341–353). Boston: Allyn and Bacon.

Herrnstein, R. J., & Murray, C. (1994). *The bell curve: Intelligence and class structure in American life.* New York: Free Press.

Hersch, P. (1991, January–February). Secret lives: Lesbian and gay teens in fear of discovery. *Family Therapy Networker,* 36–39, 41–43.

Hetherington, E. M. (1967). The effects of familial variables on sex-typing, on parent–child similarity, and on imitation in children. In J. P. Hill (Ed.), *Minnesota symposia on child psychology,* Vol. 1 (pp. 82–107). Minneapolis, MN: University of Minnesota Press.

Hetherington, E. M. (1989). Coping with family transitions: Winners, losers, and survivors. *Child Development, 60,* 1–14.

Hetherington, E. M., Cox, M., & Cox, R. (1982). Effects of divorce on parents and children. In M. Lamb (Ed.), *Nontraditional families* (pp. 233–288). Hillsdale, NJ: Erlbaum.

Higginbotham, E. (1997). Introduction. In A. Stromberg, B. A. Gutek, & L. Larwood (Eds.), *Women and work: Exploring race, ethnicity and class,* Vol. 6 (pp. xv–xxxii). Beverly Hills, CA: Sage.

Highness, E. L. (1995). Difference as a knowledge issue and a scientific paradigm. Unpublished manuscript, Graduate and University Center of the City University of New York.

Hill, C. T., Peplau, L. A., & Rubin, Z. (1981). Differing perceptions in dating couples: Sex roles vs. alternative explanations. *Psychology of Women Quarterly, 5,* 418–434.

Hill, I. (1989). *The bisexual spouse.* New York: Harper & Row.

Hill, J. P. (1988). Adapting to menarche: Familial control and conflict. In M. R. Gunnar & W. A. Collins (Eds.), *Development during the transition to adolescence. Minnesota symposia on child development,* Vol. 21 (pp. 207–223). Hillsdale, NJ: Erlbaum.

Hill, J. P., & Holmbeck, G. N. (1987). Familial adaptation to biological change during adolescence. In R. M. Lerner & T. T. Foch (Eds.), Biological–psychosocial interactions in early adolescence (pp. 207–223). Hillsdale, NJ: Erlbaum.

Hill, J. P., & Lynch, M. E. (1983). The intensification of gender-related role expectations during early adolescence. In J. Brooks-Gunn & A. C. Peterson (Eds.), *Girls at puberty: Biological and psychosocial perspectives* (pp. 201–228). New York: Plenum Press.

Hill, M. E., & Augoustinos, M. (1997). Re-examining gender bias in achievement attributions. *Australian Journal of Psychology, 49,* 85–90.

Hilton, T. L. (1987). Demography, demagoguery, and test performance. In J. A. Sechzer & S. M. Pfafflin (Eds.), *Psychology and Educational Policy. Annals of the New York Academy of Sciences, 517,* 29–38.

Hite, S. (1981). *The Hite report on male sexuality.* New York: Knopf.

Hochschild, A. (1989). *The second shift: Working parents and the revolution at home.* New York: Viking.

Hochschild, A. (1997). *The time bind: When work becomes home and home becomes work.* New York: Metropolitan Books.

Hochschild, A. R. (1978). *The unexpected community: Portrait of an old-age subculture.* Berkeley, CA: University of California Press.

Hodson, S., & Pryor, B. (1984). Sex discrimination in the courtroom: Attorney's gender and credibility. *Psychological Reports, 55,* 483–486.

Hoeffer, B. (1981). Children's acquisition of sex-role behavior in lesbian-mother families. *American Journal of Orthopsychiatry, 51,* 536–544.

Hoffman, C., & Hurst, N. (1990). Gender stereotypes. *Journal of Personality and Social Psychology, 58,* 197–208.

Hoffman, L. (1972). Early childhood experiences and women's achievement motives. *Journal of Social Issues, 28,* 129–155.

Hoffman, L., Clinebell, S., & Kilpatrick, J. (1997). Office romances: The new battleground over employees' rights to privacy and the employers' right to intervene. *Employee Responsibilities and Rights Journal, 10,* 263–275.

Hoffman, L. W. (1989). Effects of maternal employment in the two-person family. *American Psychologist, 44,* 283–292.

Hofman, M. A., & Swaab, D. F. (1989). The sexually dimorphic nucleus in the preoptic area in the human brain: A comparative morphometric study. *Journal of Anatomy, 164,* 55–72.

Hogg, J., & Frank, M. (1992). Toward an interpersonal model of codependence and contradependence. *Journal of Counseling & Development, 70,* 371–375.

Holcomb, D. R., Holcomb, L. C., Sondag, K., & Williams, N. (1991). Attitudes about date rape: Gender differences among college students. *College Student Journal, 25,* 434–439.

Holden, C. (1997). Changing sex is hard to do. *Science, 275,* 1745.

Holden, C. (1997, April 25). Early puberty getting more common. *Science, 276,* 537.

Hollingworth, L. S. (1914). Functional periodicity: An experimental study of the mental and motor abilities of women during menstruation. *Teachers College Contributions to Education, 69.*

Hollingworth, L. S. (1916). Social devices for impelling women to bear and rear children. *American Journal of Sociology, 22,* 19–29.

Hollis, L. A. (1994). Women's issues in later adulthood: Psychosocial adjustment, satisfaction, and health. Poster paper presented at the American Psychological Association Women's Health Conference, Washington, DC.

Holloway, M. H. (1994, August). Trends in women's health: A global view. *Scientific American,* 76–83.

Hong, L. K., & Duff, R. W. (1994). Widows in retirement communities: The social context of subjective well-being. *Gerontologist, 34,* 347–352.

hooks, b. (1981). *Ain't I a woman?* Boston: South End Press.

hooks, b. (1984). *Feminist theory: From margin to center.* Boston: South End Press.

hooks, b. (Ed.). (1992). Eating the other. In b. hooks (Ed.), *Black looks: Race and representation* (pp. 21–39). Boston: Gloria Watkins/South End Press.

hooks, b. (1993a). *Sisters of the yam.* Boston: South End Press.

hooks, b. (1993b). Violence in intimate relationships: A feminist perspective. In A. Minas (Ed.), *Gender basics: A feminist perspective on women and men* (pp. 205–209). Belmont, CA: Wadsworth.

Hopkins v. *Price Waterhouse,* 618 F. Supp. 1109 (D. D.C. 1985).

Hopkins, J., Campbell, B., & Marcus, M. (1987). Role of infant-related stressors in post-partum depression. *Journal of Abnormal Psychology, 96,* 237–241.

Hopps, J. (1982). Oppression based on color. *Social Work, 27*(1), 3–5.

Horn, J. L., & Donaldson, G. (1980). Cognitive development II: Adulthood development of human abilities. In O. G. Brim & J. Kagan (Eds.), *Constancy and change in human development.* Cambridge, MA: Harvard University Press.

Horner, M. (1969, June). Fail bright women. *Psychology Today,* 36.

Hossain, Z., & Roopnarine, J. L. (1993). Division of household labor and child care in dual-earner African-American families and infants. *Sex Roles, 29,* 571–583.

Hotaling, C. T., & Sugarman, D. B. (1986). An analysis of risk markers in husband and wife violence: The current state of knowledge. *Violence and Victims, 1,* 101–124.

House, W. C. (1974). Actual and perceived differences in male and female expectancies and minimal goal levels as a function of competition. *Journal of Personality, 42,* 493–509.

Houseknecht, S. K. (1979). Timing of the decision to remain voluntarily childless: Evidence for continuous socialization. *Psychology of Women Quarterly, 4,* 81–96.

Howard, J. A., Blumstein, P., & Schwartz, P. (1987). Social or evolutionary theories: Some observations on preferences in human mate selection. *Journal of Personality and Social Psychology, 53,* 194–200.

Hoyenga, K. B., & Hoyenga, K. T. (1993). *Gender related differences: Origins and outcome.* Boston: Allyn and Bacon.

Hsu, L. K. G. (1990). *Eating disorders.* New York: Guilford Press.

Huang, K., & Uba, L. (1992). Premarital sexual behavior among Chinese college students in the United States. *Archives of Sexual Behavior, 21,* 227–240.

Huff, C. W., & Cooper, J. (1987, June). Sex bias in educational software: The effects of designers' stereotypes on the software they design. *Journal of Applied Social Psychology, 17,* 519–532.

Hughes, J. O., & Sandler, B. R. (1988). Peer harassment: Hassles for women on campus. *Project on the Status and Education of Women.* Washington, DC: Association of American Colleges.

Hulin, C. L., Fitzgerald, L. F., & Drasgow, I. (1996). Organizational influences on sexual harassment. In M. S. Stockdale (Ed.), *Sexual harassment in the workplace: Perspectives, frontiers, and response strategies* (pp. 127–150). Thousand Oaks, CA: Sage.

Hull, L. W. H. (1959). *History and philosophy of science.* London: William Cloves and Sons, pp. 1–33.

Hull, T. H. (1990). Recent trends in sex ratios at birth in China. *Population and Development Review, 16,* 63–83.

Humm, M. (1992). First wave feminism. *Modern feminisms: Political, literary, cultural.* New York: Columbia University Press.

Hung, J., Chaitman, B. R., Lam, J., Lesperance, J., Dupras, G., Fines, P., & Bourassa, M. G. (1984). Noninvasive diagnostic test choices for the evaluation of coronary artery disease in women: A multivariate comparison of cardiac fluoroscopy, exercise electrocardiography and exercise thallium myocardial perfusion scintigraphy. *Journal of the American College of Cardiology, 4*(1), 8–22.

Hunt, M. (1974). *Sexual behavior in the 1970's.* New York: Dell Books.

Hunter College Women's Studies Collective. (1995). *Women's realities, women's choices.* New York: Oxford University Press.

Hunter, R. H. F. (1995). *Sex determination, differentiation and intersexuality in placental mammals* (p. iv). Cambridge, England: Cambridge University Press.

Hurtado, A., Hayes-Bastista, D. E., Burciaga-Valdez, R., & Hernandez, A. (1992). *Redefining California: Latino social engagement in a multicultural society.* Los Angeles, CA: UCLA Chicano Studies Research Center.

Huston, A. C., & Alvarez, M. (1990). The socialization context of gender role development in early development. In R. Montemayer, G. R. Adams, & T. P. Gullota (Eds.), *From childhood to adolescence: A transitional period?* (pp. 156–179). Newbury Park, CA: Sage.

Hyde, J. S. (1981). How large are cognitive gender differences? A meta-analysis using w2 and d. *American Psychologist, 36,* 892–901.

Hyde, J. S. (1984). Children's understanding of sexist language. *Developmental Psychology, 20*(4), 697–706.

Hyde, J. S. (1985). *Half the human experience* (pp. 29–30). Lexington, MA: D. C. Heath.

Hyde, J. S. (1996a). *Half the human experience: The psychology of women* (5th ed.). Lexington, MA: D. C. Heath.

Hyde, J. S. (1996b). *Understanding human sexuality.* New York: McGraw-Hill.

Hyde, J. S., & Essex, M. J. (Eds.). (1991). *Parental leave and childcare: Setting a research and policy agenda.* Philadelphia: Temple University Press.

Hyde, J. S., Essex, M. J., & Horton, F. (1993). Fathers' parental leave: Attitudes and experiences. *Journal of Family Issues, 14,* 616–638.

Hyde, J. S., Fennema, E., & Lamon, S. J. (1990). Gender differences in mathematics performance: A meta-analysis. *Psychological Bulletin, 107,* 139–155.

Hyde, J. S., Klein, M. H., Essex, M. J., & Clark, R. (1995). Maternity leave and women's mental health. *Psychology of Women Quarterly, 19,* 257–285.

Hyde, J. S., Krajnik, M., & Skuldt-Niederberger, K. (1991). Androgyny across the life span: A replication and longitudinal follow-up. *Developmental Psychology, 27,* 516–519.

Hyde, J. S., & Plant, E. A. (1995). Magnitude of psychological gender differences. *American Psychologist, 50,* 159–161.

Ickovics, J. R., & Rodin, J. (1992). Women and AIDS in the United States: Epidemiology, natural history, and mediating mechanisms. *Health Psychology, 11,* 1–16.

Iglitzen, L. B., & Ross, R. (Eds.). (1986). *Women in the world 1975–1985: The women's decade.* Santa Barbara, CA: ABC/Clio.

Iijima Hall, C. (1997). Cultural malpractice: The growing obsolescence of psychology with the changing U.S. population. *American Psychologist, 52*(6), 642–651.

Imamoglu, E. O., Kuller, R., Imamoglu, V., & Kuller, M. (1993). The social psychological worlds of Swedes and Turks in and around retirement. *Journal of Cross-Cultural Psychology, 24*(1), 26–41.

Imperato-McGinley, J., & Peterson, R. (1976). Male pseudohermaphroditism: The complexities of male phenotypic development. *American Journal of Medicine, 61,* 251–272.

Imperato-McGinley, J., Peterson, R. E., Gaultieret, T., & Sturla, E. (1979). Androgens and the evolution of male gender identity among male pseudohermaphrodites with 5a-reductase deficiency. *New England Journal of Medicine, 300*(22), 1233–1237.

Indian Health Service. (1989). *Indian health service: Trends in Indian health.* Washington, DC: U.S. Department of Health and Human Services.

Ingrassia, M. (1995, April 24). The body of the beholder. *Newsweek,* 66–67.

Ingrassia, M., & Beck, M. (1994, July 4). Patterns of abuse. *Newsweek,* 26–33.

Ireland, M. S. (1993). *Reconceiving women: Separating motherhood from female identity.* New York: Guilford.

Irwin, J. L. (1979). *Womanhood in radical Protestantism 1525–1675.* Toronto, Canada: Edwin Mellon Press.

Israel, J., Poland, N., Reame, N., & Warner, D. (1980). *Surviving the change: A practical guide to menopause.* Detroit, MI: Cinnabar.

Iwao, S. (1993). *The Japanese woman: Traditional image and changing reality.* New York: Free Press.

Jaccoma, G., & Denmark, F. L. (1974). Boys or girls: The hows and whys. Unpublished master's thesis, Hunter College, New York, NY.

Jacklin, C. N. (1981). Methodological issues in the study of sex-related differences. *Developmental Review, 1,* 266–273.

Jackson, A. P. (1993). Black, single, working mothers in poverty: Preferences for employment, well-being, and perceptions of preschool-age children. *Social Work, 38*(1), 26–34.

Jackson, M. (1987). "Facts of life" or the eroticization of women's oppression? Sexology and the social construction of homosexuality. In P. Caplan (Ed.), *The cultural construction of sexuality* (pp. 52–61). London: Tavistock.

Jacobs, G., Dauphinais, P., Gross, S., & Guzman, L. (1991). *American Psychological Association site visitation report.* Washington, DC: American Psychological Association.

Jacobs, J. (1998, August). Annual meeting of the American Sociology Association, San Francisco, CA.

Jacobs, P. A. (1969). The chromosome basis of some types of intersexuality in man. *Journal of Reproduction and Fertility,* Supplement 7, 73–78. Cited by Hunter, 1995, p. 214.

Jacobs, R. H. (1994). His and her aging: Differences, difficulties, dilemmas, delights. *Journal of Geriatric Psychiatry, 27*(1), 113–128.

Jaimes, M. A. (1982). Towards a new image of American Indian women. *Journal of American Indian Education, 22*(1), 18–32.

Janelli, L. M. (1993). Are there body image differences between older men and women? *Western Journal of Nursing Research, 15*(3), 327–339.

Janowsky, J. S., Oviatt, S. K., & Orwoll, E. S. (1994). Testosterone influences in spatial cognition in older men. *Behavioral Neuroscience, 108,* 325–332.

Janus, S. S., & Janus, C. L. (1993). *The Janus report on sexual behavior.* New York: Wiley.

Jaques, E. (1965). Death and the mid-life crisis. *International Journal of Psycho-Analysis and the Bulletin of the International Psycho-Analytic Association, 46*(4), 502–512.

Jeffe, S. B. (1995, April 20). Equity the key for women. *USA Today,* p. 13A.

Jensen, A. R. (1985). The nature of the black–white difference on various psychometric tests: Spearman's hypothesis. *Behavioral and Brain Sciences, 8,* 193–263.

Johnson, C. L. (1994). Differential expectations and realities: Race, socioeconomic status, and health of the oldest old. *International Journal of Aging and Human Development, 38,* 13–27.

Johnson, K., & Ferguson, T. (1990), *Trusting ourselves: The sourcebook on the psychology of women.* New York: Atlantic Monthly Press.

Johnson, M. M. (1963). Sex role learning in the nuclear family. *Child Development, 34,* 319–333.

Johnson, M. M. (1977). Fathers, mothers, and sex typing. In E. M. Hetherington & R. D. Parke (Eds.), *Contemporary readings in child psychology.* New York: McGraw-Hill.

Johnson, P. (1976). Women and power: Toward a theory of effectiveness. *Journal of Social Issues, 32,* 99–110.

Johnson, W. D., Kayser, K. L., & Pedraza, P. M. (1984). Angina pectoris and coronary bypass surgery: Patterns of prevalence and recurrence in 3,105 consecutive patients followed up to 11 years. *American Heart Journal, 108*(4), 1190–1197.

Jones, E. F., Forrest, J. D., Goldman, N., Henshaw, S. K., Lincoln, R., Rosoff, J. I., Westoff, C. F., & Wolf, D. (1985). Teenage pregnancy in developed countries: Determinants and policy implications. *Family Planning Perspectives, 17,* 53–62.

Jones, J. (1985). Labor of love, labor of sorrow: Black women, work, and family from slavery to the present. New York: Basic Books.

Jones, J. M. (1991). Psychological models of race: What have they been and what should they be? In J. Goodchilds (Ed.), *Psychological perspectives on human diversity in America* (pp. 3–46). Washington, DC: American Psychological Association.

Jordan, J. (1997). *The relational model is a source of empowerment for women.* In M. R. Walsh (Ed.), *Women, men, and gender: Ongoing debates* (pp. 373–379). New Haven, CT: Yale University Press.

Jue, D., Meador, K. J., Zamrini, E. Y., Allen, M. E., et al. (1992). Differential effects of aging on directional and absolute errors in visuospatial memory. *Neuropsychology, 6*(4), 331–339.

Kahn, A. S., & Yoder, J. D. (1989). The psychology of women and conservatism: Rediscovering social change. *Psychology of Women Quarterly, 13,* 417–432.

Kaiser, K. (1990). Cross-cultural perspectives on menopause. In M. Flint, F. Kronenberg, & W. Utian (Eds.), Multidisciplinary perspectives on menopause. *Annals of the New York Academy of Sciences, 592,* 430–432.

Kalick, S. M., & Hamilton, T. E. (1986). The matching hypothesis reexamined. *Journal of Personality and Social Psychology, 51,* 673–682.

Kalleberg, A. L., & VanBuren, M. E. (1996). Is bigger better? Explaining the relationship between organization size and job rewards. *American Sociological Review,* 47–66.

Kallman, F. J. (1952). Comparative twin study on the genetic aspects of male homosexuality. *Journal of Nervous and Mental Disease, 115,* 283–298.

Kammeyer, K. C. W. (1990). *Marriage and family: A foundation for personal decisions* (2nd ed.). Boston: Allyn & Bacon.

Kamo, Y. (1991). A nonlinear effect of the number of children on the division of household labor. *Sociological Perspective, 34,* 205–218.

Kanamine, L. (1997, March 11). Citadel punishes 10 for harassment. *USA Today,* p. 1A.

Kanter, R. M. (1977a). *Men and women of the corporation.* New York: Basic Books.

Kanter, R. M. (1977b). Some effects of proportions on group life: Skewed sex ratios and responses to token women. *American Journal of Sociology, 82,* 965–990.

Kantrowitz, B., & Kalb, B. (1998, May 11). Boys will be boys. *Newsweek,* 54–60.

Kaplan, H. S. (1979). *Disorders of sexual desire.* New York: Simon & Shuster.

Kaplan, R. M., Sallis, Jr., J. F., & Patterson, T. L. (1993). *Health and human behavior* (pp. 162–164). New York: McGraw-Hill.

Karkau, K. (1973). *Sexism in the fourth grade.* Pittsburgh, PA: Know, Inc.

Katz, D. M. (1997). Too young to date? In A. M. Meehan & E. Astor-Stetson (Eds.), *Adolescent psychology* (pp. 162–163). Guilford, CT: Dushkin Publishing Group/Brown & Benchmark Publishers.

Katz, P. A. (1979). The development of female identity. In C. B. Kopp & M. Kirpatrick (Eds.), *Becoming female: Perspectives on development* (pp. 3–28). New York: Plenum Press.

Katz, P. A., & Ksansnak, K. R. (1994). Developmental aspects of gender role flexibility and traditionality in middle childhood and adolescence. *Developmental Psychology, 30*(2), 272–282.

Kaufert, P. (1982). Myth and the menopause. *Sociology of Health and Illness, 4,* 141–166.

Kaufman, J. (1998). Adolescent females' perception of autonomy and control. In M. B. Nadien & F. L. Denmark (Eds.), *Females and autonomy: A lifespan perspective* (pp. 43–72). Boston: Allyn & Bacon.

Kaw, E. (1993). Medicalization of racial features: Asian American women and cosmetic surgery. *Medical Anthropology Quarterly, 7,* 74–89.

Keith, J. B., McCreary, C., Collins, K., & Smith, C. P. (1991). Sexual activity and contraceptive use among low-income urban Black adolescent females. *Adolescence, 26,* 269–785.

Keller, E. F. (1982). Feminism and science. In M. Humm (Ed.), *Modern feminism: Political, literary, cultural* (pp. 312–317). New York: Columbia University Press.

Kelley, K., & Streeter, D. (1992). The roles of gender in organizations. In K. Kelley (Ed.), *Issues, theory, and research in industrial/organizational psychology* (pp. 285–337). Amsterdam: Elsevier Science Publishers.

Kelly, M. P., Strassberg, D. S., & Kircher, J. R. (1990). Attitudinal and experiential correlates of anorgasmia. *Archives of Sexual Behavior, 19,* 165–177.

Kemeny, M. M. (1994). Breast cancer in the United States. In J. A. Sechzer, A. Griffin, & S. M. Pfafflin (Eds.), *Forging a women's health research agenda: Policy issues for the 1990's. Annals of the New York Academy of Sciences, 736,* 122–130.

Kemeny, M. M., Wellisch, D. K., & Schain, W. S. (1988). Psychosocial outcome in a randomized surgical trial for treatment of primary breast cancer. *Cancer, 62,* 1231–1237.

Kendall, D. (1997). *Race, class and gender in a diverse society.* Boston: Allyn & Bacon.

Kennedy, M., Moore, J., Schuman, P., Schoenbaum, E., Zierler, S., Rompalo, A., & Chu, S. Y. (1998). Sexual behavior of HIV-infected women reporting recent sexual contact with women. *Journal of the American Medical Association, 280*(1), 29–30.

Kerig, P. K., Cowan, P. A., & Cowan, C. P. (1993). Marital quality and gender differences in parent–child interaction. *Developmental Psychology, 29*(6), 931–939.

Keshet, J. K. (1980). From seperation to stepfamily: A subsystem analysis. *Journal of Family Issues, 4,* 146–153.

Kibria, N., Barnett, R. C., Baruch, G. K., Marshall, N. L., & Pleck, J. H. (1990). Homemaking-role quality and the psychological well-being and distress of employed women. *Sex Roles, 22*(5/6), 327–347.

Kilbourne, J. (1987). *Killing us softly: Advertising images of women.* Film available from Jean Kilbourne, Cambridge Documentary Films, P.O. Box 385, Cambridge, MA 02139-0004.

Kilmartin, C. T. (1994). *The masculine self.* New York: Macmillan.

Kim, E. H., & Otani, J. (1983). Asian women in America. In E. H. Kim (Ed.), *With silk wings: Asian American women at work.* Oakland, CA: Asian Women United of California.

Kim, T. L. (1993). Life in Korea. In L. L. Adler (Ed.), *International handbook on gender roles* (pp. 187–198). Westport, CT: Greenwood Press.

Kimmel, D. C. (1988). Ageism, psychology, and public policy. *American Psychologist, 43,* 175–178.

Kimura, D. (1987). Are men's and women's brains really different? *Canadian Journal of Psychology, 28,* 133–147.

Kimura, D., & Hampson, E. (1994). Cognitive patterns in men and women is influenced by fluctuations in sex hormones. *Psychological Science, 3,* 57–61.

Kincaid-Elders, E. (1982). Bad maps for an unknown region: Menopause from a literary perspective. In A. M. Voda, M. Dinnerstein, & S. R. O'Donnell (Eds.), *Changing perspectives on menopause* (pp. 24–38). Austin, TX: University of Texas Press.

King, M. C. (1992). Occupational segregation by race and sex, 1940–1988. *Monthly Labor Review, 115*(4), 30–37.

Kinsey, A. C., Pomeroy, W. B., & Martin, C. E. (1948). *Sexual behavior in the human male.* Philadelphia: W. B. Saunders.

Kinsey, A. C., Pomeroy, W. B., Martin, C. E., & Gebhard, P. H. (1953). *Sexual behavior in the human female.* Philadelphia: W. B. Saunders.

Kirschner, J. T. (1995). AIDS and suicide. *Journal of Family Practice, 41*(5), 493–496.

Kistner, J., Metzler, A., Gatlin, D., & Risi, S. (1993). Classroom racial proportions and children's peer relations: Race and gender effects. *Journal of Educational Psychology, 85*(3), 446–452.

Kite, M. E., Deaux, K., & Miele, M. (1991). Stereotypes of young and old: Does age outweigh gender? *Psychology and Aging, 6,* 19–27.

Kitson, G. C., & Sussman, M. B. (1982). Marital complaints, demographic characteristics and symptoms of mental distress in divorce. *Journal of Marriage and the Family, 44*(1), 87–101.

Kitzinger, S. (1978). *Women as mothers: How they see themselves in different cultures.* New York: Random House.

Kitzinger, S. (1983). *Women's experience of sex.* London: Dorling Kindersley.

Klein, J. (1980). *Jewish identity and self esteem: Healing wounds through ethnotherapy.* New York: Institute on Pluralism and Group Identity.

Klein, V. (1950). The sterotype of femininity. *Journal of Social Sciences, 6,* 3–12.

Klein. (1990). Women and computing. *Communications of the Association for Computing Machinery, 33,* 34–36.

Kleinke, C. L., & Meyer, C. (1990). Evaluation of rape victims by men and women with high and low beliefs in a just world. *Psychology of Women Quarterly, 14,* 343–353.

Klonoff, E. A., & Landrine, H. (1995). The schedule of sexist events: A measure of lifetime and recent sexist discrimination in women's lives. *Psychology of Women Quarterly, 19,* 439–472.

Knafo, D., & Jaffe, Y. (1984). Sexual fantasizing in males and females. *Journal of Research in Personality, 18,* 451–467.

Knudsen, D. D. (1991). Child sexual coercion. In E. Grauerholz & M. A. Koralewski (Eds.), *Sexual coercion: A sourcebook on its nature, causes, and prevention* (pp. 17–28). Lexington, MA: Lexington Books.

Koestner, R., & Wheeler, L. (1988). Self-presentation in personal advertisements: The influence of implicit notions of attraction and role expectations. *Journal of Personal Relationships, 5,* 149–160.

Koff, E., Rierdan, J., & Silverstone, E. (1978). Changes in representation of body image as a function of menarcheal status. *Developmental Psychology, 14,* 635–642.

Kohlberg, L. (1976). Moral stages and moralization: The cognitive–developmental approach. In T. Lickona (Ed.), *Moral development and behavior* (pp. 31–53). New York: Holt, Rinehart, and Winston.

Kolata, G. (1998, September 9). Researchers report success in method to pick baby's sex. *New York Times,* p. A1.

Konrad, A. M., & Gutek, B. (1986). Impact of work experiences on attitudes toward sexual harassment. *Administration Science Quarterly, 3*(3), 422–438.

Koran 81.i-14 (cp. Rev. 6.12–14); Pelican trs., p. 17, II.3-11 (cited by Ringgren & Strom, 1967, p. 181).

Korman, S. K. (1983). Nontraditional dating behavior: Date-initiation and date expense-sharing among feminists and non-feminists. *Family Relations, 32,* 575–581.

Korman, S. K., & Leslie, G. (1982). The relationship between feminist ideology and date expense-sharing to perceptions of sexual aggression in dating. *Journal of Sex Research, 18,* 114–129.

Kortenhaus, C. M., & Demarest, J. (1993). Gender role stereotyping in children's literature: An update. *Sex Roles, 28,* 219–232.

Kosberg, J. I. (1988). Preventing elder abuse: Identification of high risk factors prior to placement decisions. *Gerontologist, 28,* 43–50.

Koss, M. P. (1990). Changed lives: The psychological impact of sexual harassment. In M. Paludi (Ed.), *Ivory power: Sex and gender harassment in the academy* (pp. 73–92). Albany, NY: State University of New York Press.

Koss, M. P. (1993). Rape: Scope, impact, intervention, and public policy responses. *American Psychologist, 48,* 1062–1069.

Koss, M. P., & Dinero, T. E. (1989). Discriminant analysis of risk factors for sexual victimization among a national sample of college women. *Journal of Consulting and Clinical Psychology, 57,* 242–250.

Koss, M. P., Dinero, T. E., Seibel, C., & Cox, S. (1988). Stranger and acquaintance rape: Are there differences in the victim's experience? *Psychology of Women Quarterly, 12,* 1–24.

Koss, M. P., Gidycz, C. A., & Wisniewski, N. (1987). The scope of rape: Incidence and prevalence of sexual aggression and victimization in a national sample of higher education students. *Journal of Consulting and Clinical Psychology, 55,* 162–170.

Koss, M. P., Heise, L., & Russo, N. F. (1994). The global health burden of rape. *Psychology of Women Quarterly, 18,* 509–537.

Koss, M. P., & Heslet, L. (1992). Somatic consequences of violence against women. *Archives of Family Medicine, 1,* 53–59.

Krantz, S. E. (1988). Divorce and children. In S. M. Dornbusch & M. H. Strober (Eds.), *Feminism, children, and the new families* (pp. 249–273). New York: Guilford Press.

Krause, N., & Markides, K. S. (1985). Employment and psychological well-being in Mexican-American women. *Journal of Health and Social Behavior, 26,* 15–26.

Kravitz, J. (1975). The relationship of attitudes to discretionary physician and dentist use by race and income. In R. Anderson, J. Kravits, & O. W. Anderson (Eds.), *Equity in health services: Empirical analyses in social policy* (pp. 73–93). Cambridge, MA: Balinger.

Krefting, L. A., Berger, P. K., & Wallace, M. J., Jr. (1978). The contribution of sex distribution, job content, and occupational classification to job sex typing: Two studies. *Journal of Vocational Behavior, 13,* 181–191.

Krishnaswamky, S. (1984). A note on female infanticide: An anthropological inquiry. *Indian Journal of Social Work, 45,* 297–302.

Kritchevsky, D. (1990). Nutrition and breast cancer. *Cancer, 66,* 1321–1325.

Kronenberg, F. (1990). Hot flashes: Epidemiology and physiology. In M. Flint, F. Kronenberg, & W. Utian (Eds.), *Multidisciplinary perspectives on menopause* (pp. 52–86). New York: Annals of the New York Academy of Sciences.

Kruger, A. (1994). The midlife transition: Crisis or chimera? *Psychological Reports, 75,* 1299–1305.

Kuhn, T. (1970). *The structure of scientific revolutions.* Chicago: University of Chicago Press.

Kumekawa, E. (1993). Sansei ethnic identity and the consequences of perceived unshared suffering for third generation Japanese Americans. In Y. Song & E. Kim (Eds.), *American mosiac: Selected readings on America's multicultural heritage* (pp. 204–214). Englewood Cliffs, NJ: Prentice Hall.

Kuo, W. H. (1984). Prevalence of depression among Asian-Americans. *Journal of Nervous and Mental Disease, 172,* 449–457.

Kurdek, L. A. (1994). The nature and correlates of relationship quality in gay, lesbian, and heterosexual cohabiting couples: A test of the individual difference, interdependence, and discrepancy models. In B. Greene & G. M. Herek (Eds.), *Lesbian and gay psychology: Theory, research, and clinical applications* (pp. 133–155). Psychological Perspectives on Lesbian and Gay Issues, Volume 1. Thousand Oaks, CA: Sage.

Kutner, N. G. (1984). Women with disabling health conditions: The signnificance of employment. *Women and Health, 9*(4), 21–31.

Lacey, J. H., & Birchnell, S. A. (1986). Abnormal eating behavior. In M. J. Christie and P. G. Mellett (Eds.), *The psychosomatic approach: Contemporary practice of wholeperson care.* New York: Wiley.

Lackey, P. N. (1989). Adults' attitudes about assignments of household chores to male and female children. *Sex Roles, 20*(5/6), 271–280.

Lacks, M. S., Williams, C. S., O'Brien, S., Pillemer, K. A., & Charlson, M. E. (1998). The mortality of elder mistreatment. *Journal of the American Medical Association, 280,* 428–432.

Lafontaine, E., & Tredeau, L. (1986). The frequency, sources, and correlates of sexual harassment among women in traditional male occupations. *Sex Roles, 15.*

LaFromboise, T., Bennett, C., James, A., & Running Wolf, P. (1995). American Indian women and psychology. In H. Landrine (Ed.), *Bringing cultural diversity to feminist psychology: Theory, research, and practice* (pp. 197–239). Washington, DC: American Psychological Association.

LaFromboise, T., Berman, J., & Sohi, B. (1994). American Indian women. In L. Comas-Diaz & B. Greene (Eds.), *Women of color: Integrating ethnic and gender identities in psychotherapy* (pp. 30–71). New York: Guilford Press.

LaFromboise, T. D., Heyle, A. M., & Ozer, E. J. (1990). Changing and diverse roles of women in American Indian cultures. *Sex Roles, 22,* 455–476.

Lagrew, D. C., & Adashek, J. A. (1998). Lowering the cesarean section rate in a private hospital: Comparison of individual physicians' rates, risk factors, and outcomes. *American Journal of Obstetrics and Gynecology, 178,* 1207–1215.

Lamb, M. (Ed.). (1987). *The father's role: Cross-cultural perspectives.* Hillsdale, NJ: Erlbaum.

Lamb, M., Pleck, J., & Levine, R. (1987). Effects of increased paternal involvement on fathers and mothers. In C. Lewis & M. O'Brien (Eds.), *Reassessing fatherhood* (pp. 108–125). London: Sage.

Lamb, M. E. (1979). Paternal influences and the father's role. *American Psychologist, 34,* 938–943.

Lamm, B. (1977). Men's movement hype. In J. Snodgrass (Ed.), *For men against sexism* (pp. 153–157). Albion, CA: Times Change Press.

Landes, A., Foster, C., & Cessna, C. (Eds.). (1994). *Women's changing role. The information series on current topics.* New York: Wylie—Information Plus.

Landes, A., Foster, C., & Cessna, C. (Eds.). (1995). *Violent relationships: Battering and abuse among adults. The information series on current topics.* New York: Wylie—Information Plus.

Landrine, H. (1985). Race X class stereotypes of women. *Sex Roles, 13,* 65–75.

Landrine, H. (Ed.). (1995). *Bringing cultural diversity to feminist psychology: Theory, research, and practice.* Washington, DC: American Psychological Association.

Langer, W. L. (Ed.). (1948). *An encyclopedia of world history.* Boston: Houghton-Mifflin.

LaRosa, J. H. (1994). Office of Research on Women's Health: National Institutes of Health and the women's health agenda. In J. A. Sechzer, A. Griffin & S. M. Pfafflin (Eds.), *Forging a women's health research agenda: Policy issues*

for the 1990's, Annals of the New York Academy of Sciences, 736,* 196–204.

LaRossa, R., & LaRossa, M. M. (1981). *How infants change families.* Beverly Hills, CA: Sage.

Larrabee, G. J., & Crook, T. H. (1993). Do men show more rapid age-associated decline in simulated everyday verbal memory than do women? *Psychology and Aging, 8*(1), 68–71.

Larson, R. J., Csikszentmihalyi, N., & Graef, R. (1982). Time alone in daily experience: Loneliness or renewal? In L. A. Peplau & D. Perlman (Eds.), *Loneliness: A sourcebook of current theory, research and therapy* (pp. 40–53). New York: Wiley.

Lauer, K. O. (1985). His husband, her wife: The dynamics of the pride system in marriage. *Journal of Evolutionary Psychology, 6,* 329–340.

Laumann, E. O., Gagnon, J. H., Michael, R. T., & Michaels, S. (1994). *The social organization of human sexuality: Sexual practices in the United States.* Chicago: University of Chicago Press.

Laws, J. L., & Schwartz, P. (1977). *Sexual scripts.* Hinsdale, IL: Dryden.

Lawson, C. (1992, August 6). Violence at home: "They don't want anyone to know." *New York Times,* pp. C1–7.

Leaper, C., Hauser, S. T., Kremen, A., Powers, S., Jacobson, A. M., Noam, G. G., Weiss-Perry, B., & Follansbee, D. (1989). Adolescent–parent interactions in relation to adolescents' gender and ego developmental pathway: A longitudinal study. *Journal of Early Adolescence, 9,* 335–361.

Leaper, C., Smith, L., Sprague, R., & Schwartz, R. (1991). *Single-parent mothers, married mothers, married fathers, and the socialization of gender in preschool children.* Paper presented at the biennial meeting of the Society for Research in Child Development, Seattle, WA.

Lederer, W. (1968). *The fear of women.* New York: Grune and Stratton.

Lee, V. E., & Marks, H. M. (1990). Sustained effects of the single-sex secondary school experience on attitudes, behaviors, and values in college. *Journal of Educational Psychology, 82,* 578–592.

Lee, V. E., Marks, H. M., & Byrd, T. (1994). Sexism in single-sex and coeducational independent secondary school classrooms. *Sociology of Education, 67,* 92–120.

Legato, M. A. (1994). Cardiovascular disease in women: What's different? What's new? What's unresolved? In J. A. Sechzer, A. Griffin, & S. M. Pfafflin (Eds.), *Forging a women's health research agenda: Policy issues for the 1990's, Annals of the New York Academy of Sciences, 736,* 147–157.

Lego, S. (1992). Masochism: Implications for psychiatric nursing. *Archives of Psychiatric Nursing, 6,* 224–229.

Leidner, R. (1991). Selling hamburgers and selling insurance: Gender, work, and identity in interactive service jobs. *Gender and Society, 5*(2), 154–177.

Leigh, W. (1994). The health status of women of color. In C. Costello & A. Stone (Eds.), *The American woman:*

1994–95 where we stand—women and health (pp. 154–196). New York: W. W. Norton.

Leitenberg, H., & Henning, K. (1995). Sexual fantasy. *Psychological Bulletin, 117,* 469–496.

Lempers, J. D., Clark-Lempers, D., & Simons, R. L. (1989). Economic hardship, parenting, and distress in adolescence. *Child Development, 60,* 25–39.

Lennon, M. C., & Rosenfield, S. (1992). The interaction of job and family conditions. *Journal of Health and Social Behavior, 33,* 316–327.

LePage-Lees, P. (1997). Struggling with a nontraditional past: Academically successful women from disadvantaged backgrounds discuss their relationship with "disadvantage." *Psychology of Women Quarterly, 21,* 365–385.

Lerner, M. J. (1980). *The belief in a just world: A fundamental delusion.* New York: Plenum.

Lerner, R. M., & Olson, C. K. (1997). "My body is so ugly!" In A. M. Meehan & E. Astor-Stetson (Eds.), *Adolescent psychology* (pp. 20–22). Guilford, CT: Dushkin Publishing Group/Brown & Benchmark Publishers.

Lester, B. M., Latasse, L., & Seifer, R. (1998). Cocaine exposure and children: The meaning of subtle effects. *Science, 282,* 633–634.

LeVay, S. (1991). A difference in hypothalmic structure between heterosexual and homosexual men. *Science, 253,* 1034–1037.

Levenson, R. W., Carstensen, L. L., & Gottman, J. M. (1994). Influence of age and gender on affect, physiology, and their interrelations: A study of long-term marriages. *Journal of Personality and Social Psychology, 67,* 56–68.

Levenson, R. W., & Gottman, J. (1985). Physiological and affective predictors of change in relationship satisfaction. *Journal of Personality and Social Psychology, 49,* 85–94.

Levine, S. A. (1985). A definition of stress. In G. Moberg (Ed.), *Animal Stress* (pp. 51–70). Bethesda, MD: American Physiological Society.

Levinson, D. J., Darrow, C. N., Klein, E. B., Levinson, M. H., & McKee, B. (1978). *The seasons of a man's life.* New York: Knopf.

Levinson, R. M., McCollum, K. T., & Kutner, N. G. (1984). Gender homophily in preferences for physicians. *Sex Roles, 10,* 315–325.

Lévi-Strauss, C. (1969). *The elementary structures of kinship.* London: Eyre and Spotiswoode.

Levy, J. (1969). Possible basis for the evolution of lateral specialization of the human brain. *Nature, 224,* 614–618.

Levy, J. (1972). Lateral specialization of the human brain. Behavioral manifestations and possible evolutionary basis. In J. A. Kiger (Ed.), *The Biology of Behavior* (pp. 169–180). Corvallis, OR: Oregon State University Press.

Lewin, K. (1935). *A dynamic theory of personality.* New York: McGraw-Hill.

Lewin, M., & Tragos, L. M. (1987). Has the feminist movement influenced adolescent sex role attitudes? A reassessment after a quarter century. *Sex Roles, 16*(3–4), 125–135.

Lewin, T. (1991, February 8). Studies on teen-age sex cloud condom debate. *New York Times,* p. A14.

Lewin, T. (1998, March 12). All-girl schools questioned as a way to attain equity. *New York Times,* p. A12.

Lewis, M. (1972). Parents and children: Sex-role development. *School Review, 80,* 229–240.

Lewis, P. H. (1995, July 3). Critics troubled by computer study on pornography. *New York Times,* p. 37, 40.

Lewittes, H. J. (1988). Just being friendly means a lot: Women, friendship, and aging. *Women & Health, 14,* 139–159.

Liang, J. (1982). Sex differences in life satisfaction among the elderly. *Journal of Gerontology, 37,* 100–108.

Libby, M. N., & Aries, E. (1989). Gender differences in preschool children's narrative fantasy. *Psychology of Women Quarterly, 13,* 293–306.

Liben, L. S., & Signorella, M. L. (1993). Gender-schematic processing in children: The role of initial interpretations of stimuli. *Developmental Psychology, 29*(1), 141–149.

Liefer, M. (1977). Psychological changes accompanying pregnancy and motherhood. *Genetic Psychology Monographs, 95,* 55–96.

Liefer, M. 1980. *Psychological effects of motherhood: A study of first pregnancy.* New York: Praeger.

Life Magazine Home Page. (1996, December). *The Mystery of Mary.* Retrieved July 9, 1999 from the World Wide Web: http://pathfinder.com@fil7w/gcA86aAOQaQ/Life/essay/Mary/Mary01.html.

Lindgren, J. R., & Taub, N. (1993). *The law of sex discrimination.* Minneapolis, MN: West Publishing.

Lindsay, R. (1993). Hormone replacement therapy for prevention and treatment of osteoporosis. *American Journal of Medicine, 95,* 37s–39s.

Lindsay, R., & Cosman, F. (1990). Estrogen in prevention and treatment of osteoporosis. In M. Flint, F. Kronenberg, & W. Utian (Eds.), *Multidisciplinary perspectives on menopause: Annals of the New York Academy of Sciences* (pp. 326–333). The New York Academy of Sciences.

Lindsey, B. (Ed.). (1980). *Comparative perspectives of Third World women: The impact of race, sex, and class.* New York: Praeger.

Linn, M. C., & Petersen, A. C. (1985). Emergence and characterization of sex differences in spatial ability: A meta-analysis. *Child Development, 56,* 1479–1498.

Linz, C. (1992). Setting the stage: Facts and figures. In J. A. Krentz (Ed.), *Dangerous men and adventurous women: Romance writers on the appeal of romance* (pp. 11–14). Philadelphia: University of Pennsylvania Press.

Linz, D. G., Donnerstein, E., & Penrod, J. (1984). The effects of multiple exposures to filmed violence against women. *Journal of Communication, 34,* 130–147.

Lipman, E. J. (1970). *The Mishnah: Oral teachings of Judaism.* New York: Viking Press.

Lips, H. M. (1997). *Sex and gender: An introduction.* Mountain View, CA: Mayfield.

Lobel, T. E., Agami-Rozenblatt, O., & Bempechat, J. (1993). Personality correlates of career choice in the kibbutz: A comparison of career and non-career women. *Sex Roles, 29*(5/6), 359–370.

Lobel, T. E., & Menashri, J. (1993). Relations of conceptions of gender-role transgressions and gender constancy to gender-typed toy preferences. *Developmental Psychology, 29*(1), 150–155.

Lobo, R. A. (1990). Estrogen and cardiovascular disease. In M. Flint, F. Kronenberg, & W. Utian (Eds.), *Mutlidisciplinary perspectives on menopause: Annals of the New York Academy of Sciences* (pp. 286–294). The New York Academy of Sciences.

Loftus, E. F. (1991). Resolving legal questions with psychological data. *American Psychologist, 46,* 1046–1048.

Loftus, E. F. (1993). The reality of repressed memories. *American Psychologist, 48,* 518–537.

Lollis, C. M., Johnson, E. H., Antoni, M. H., & Hinkle, Y. (1996). Characteristics of African Americans with multiple risk factors associated with HIV/AIDS. *Journal of Behavioral Medicine, 19,* 55–71.

Long, E. C. J., & Andrews, D. W. (1990). Perspective taking as a predictor of marital adjustment. *Journal of Personality and Social Psychology, 59,* 126–131.

Long, J., & Porter, K. L. (1984). Multiple roles of midlife women. In G. Baruch & J. Brooks-Gunn (Eds.), *Women in midlife* (pp. 109–159). New York: Plenum Press.

Lonsway, K. A. (1996). Preventing acquaintance rape through education: What do we know? *Psychology of Women Quarterly, 20,* 229–265.

Lonsway, K. A., & Fitzgerald, L. F. (1994). Rape myths: In review. *Psychology of Women Quarterly, 18,* 133–164.

Lopata, H. (1971). *Occupation housewife.* New York: Oxford University Press.

Lopata, H. Z. (1973). *Widowhood in an American city.* Cambridge, MA: Schenckman.

Lorber, J. (1994). *Paradoxes of gender.* New Haven, CT: Yale University Press.

Lord, C., Ross, L., & Lepper, M. (1979). Biased assimilation and attitude polarization: The effects of prior theories on subsequently considered evidence. *Journal of Personality and Social Psychology, 37,* 2098–2109.

Lorde, A. (1984). *Sister outsider.* Freedom, CA: Crossing Press.

Los Cocco, K. A., & Spitze, G. (1990). Working conditions, social support, and the well-being of female and male factory workers. *Journal of Health and Social Behavior, 31,* 313–327.

Lott, B. (1987). *Women's lives. Themes and variations in gender learning.* Monterey, CA: Brooks/Cole.

Lott, B. (1991). *Women's lives: Themes and variations on gender learning* (2nd ed.). Monterey, CA: Brooks/Cole.

Lott, B. (1994). *Women's lives: Themes and variations in gender learning* (3rd ed.). Pacific Grove, CA: Brooks/Cole.

Lott, B. (1995). Distancing from women: Interpersonal sexist discrimination. In B. Lott & D. Maluso (Eds.), *The social psychology of interpersonal discrimination* (pp. 12–49). New York: Guilford Press.

Lottes, I. L., & Kuriloff, P. J. (1994). Sexual socialization differences by gender, Greek membership, ethnicity and religious background. *Psychology of Women Quarterly, 18,* 203–219.

Louis Harris and Associates. (1993, July 14). Commonwealth Fund Survey of Women. New York: Commonwealth Fund.

Low, B. S. (1989). Cross-cultural patterns in the training of children: An evolutionary perspective. *Journal of Comparative Psychology, 103,* 311–319.

Lowie, R., & Hollingworth, L. S. (1916). Science and feminism. *Scientific Monthly, 3,* 277–284.

Lown, J., & Dolan, E. (1988). Financial challenges in remarriage. *Lifestyles: family and economic issues, 9,* 73–88.

Luine, V. (1985). Estradiol increase in choline acetyltranferase activity in specific basal forebrain nuclei and projection areas of female rats. *Experimental Neurology, 80,* 484–490.

Luine, V., Rentas, L., Sterback, L., & Beck, K. (1996). Estradiol effects of rat spatial memory. *Society of Neuroscience Abstracts, 22,* 1387.

Luine, V., & Rodriguez, M. (1994). Effects of estradiol in radial arm maze performance of young and aged rats. *Behavioral and Neural Biology, 62,* 230–236.

Lye, D. N., & Biblarz, T. J. (1993). The effects of attitudes toward family life and gender roles on marital satisfaction. *Journal of Family Issues, 14*(2), 157–188.

Maccoby, E., & Jacklin, C. (1974). *The psychology of sex differences.* Stanford, CA: Stanford University Press.

Macdonald, B., & Rich, C. (1983). *Look me in the eye: Old women, aging, and ageism.* San Francisco: Spinsters Ink.

MacKinnon, C. (1993). Francis Biddle's sister: Pornography, civil rights, and speech. In A. Minas (Ed.), *Gender basics: Feminist perspectives on women and men* (pp. 391–395). Belmont, CA: Wadsworth.

MacKinnon, C. A. (1979). *Sexual harassment of working women.* New Haven, CT: Yale University Press.

Magnusson, D., Strattin, H., & Allen, V. L. (1985). Biological maturation and social development: A longitudinal study of some adjustment processes from mid-adolescence to adulthood. *Journal of Youth and Adolescence, 14,* 267–283.

Malamuth, N. M. (1981). Rape fantasies as a function of exposure to violent–sexual stimuli. *Archives of Sexual Behavior, 10,* 33–47.

Malamuth, N. M., & Check, J. V. P. (1983). Sexual arousal to rape depictions: Individual differences. *Journal of Abnormal Psychology, 92,* 55–67.

Malamuth, N. M., & Donnerstein, E. (1982a). The effects of aggressive pornographic mass media stimuli. In L. Berkowitz (Ed.), *Advances in experimental social psychology,* Vol. 15. New York: Academic Press.

Malamuth, N. M., & Donnerstein, E. (1982b). As cited in E. Donnerstein & D. Linz (1993). Mass media, sexual violence and male viewers: Current theory and research. In M. S. Kimmel & M. A. Messner (Eds.), *Men's lives* (3rd ed.). Boston: Allyn & Bacon.

Malamuth, N. M., Haber, S., & Feshback, S. (1980). Testing hypotheses regarding rape: Exposure to sexual violence, sex differences, and the "normality" of rapists. *Journal of Research in Personality, 14,* 121–137.

Malamuth, N. M., Sockloskie, R. J., Koss, M. P., & Tanaka, J. S. (1991). Characteristics of aggressors against women: Testing a model using a national sample of college women. *Journal of Consulting and Clinical Psychology, 59,* 670–681.

Malgady, R., Rogler, L., & Costantino, G. (1987). Ethnocultural and linguistic bias in mental health evaluation of Hispanics. *American Psychologist, 42,* 228–234.

Maltz, W., & Holman, B. (1987). *Incest and sexuality: A guide to understanding and healing.* Lexington, MA: Lexington Books/D. C. Heath.

Mandler, G. (1980). Recognizing the judgment of previous occurrence. *Psychology Review, 87,* 252–271.

Mann, J. (1997, April 11). Falling short of equality. *Washington Post,* p. E3.

Mansfield, P. K., & Voda, A. M. (1993). From Edith Bunker to the 6:00 News: How and what midlife women learn about menopause. *Women and Therapy, 14*(1/2), 89–104.

Manson, J. E., Stampfer, M. J., Colditz, G. A., Willett, W. C., Rosner, B., Speizer, F. E., & Hennekens, C. H. (1991). A prospective study of aspirin use and primary prevention of cardiovascular disease in women. *Journal of the American Medical Association, 266,* 521–527.

Mantecon, V. H. (1993). Where are the archetypes? Searching for symbols of women's midlife passage. *Women and Therapy, 14*(1/2), 77–88.

Maracek, J., & Hare-Mustin, R. T. (1991). A short history of the future: Feminism and clinical psychology. *Psychology of Women Quarterly, 15,* 521–536. Cited by Matlin (1996), 480–481.

Maracek, J., & Kravitz, D. (1977). Women and mental health: A review of feminist change efforts. *Psychiatry, 40,* 323–329. Cited by Matlin (1996), 480–482.

Maracek, J., Kravetz, D., & Finn, S. (1979). A comparison of women who enter feminist therapy and women who enter traditional therapy. *Journal of Consulting and Clinical Psychology, 47,* 734–742.

Marano, H. E. (1993, November/December). Inside the heart of marital violence. *Psychology Today,* 48–91.

Marano, H. E. (1997, July 1). Puberty may start at 6 as hormones surge. *New York Times,* p. C1.

Marantz, S. A., & Mansfield, A. F. (1977). Maternal employment and the development of sex-role stereotyping in five-to-eleven-year-old girls. *Child Development, 48,* 668–673.

Margolin, L. (1989). Gender and the prerogatives of dating and marriage: An experimental assessment of a sample of college students. *Sex Roles, 20,* 91–102.

Markson, E. W., & Gognalons-Nicolet, M. (1990). Midlife: Crisis or nodal point? Some cross-cultural views. In B. B. Hess & E. W. Markson (Eds.), *Growing old in America* (4th ed.) (pp. 55–65). New Brunswick, NJ: Transaction.

Markson, E. W., & Taylor, C. A. (1993). Real versus reel world: Older women and the Academy awards. *Women and Therapy, 14*(1/2), 77–88.

Marshall, E. (1993). Search for a killer: Focus shifts from fat to hormones. *Science, 259,* 618–621.

Marshall, W. A., & Tanner, J. M. (1969). Variation in the pattern of pubertal changes in girls. *Archives of Disease in Childhood, 44,* 291–303.

Martin, E. (1991). The egg and the sperm: How science has constructed a romance based on stereotypical male–female roles. *Signs, 16,* 485–501.

Martin, K. A., & Freeman, M. W. (1993). Postmenopausal hormone-replacement therapy. *New England Journal of Medicine, 328,* 1115–1117.

Maspero, G. (1914). Chansons populaires. In Gaston Maspero, *Chansons Populaires Recueillies dans la Haute-Egypte: De 1900 à 1914.* Cairo: Imprimerie de l'Institute Francais d'Archeologie Orientale.

Masson, J. M. (1984, February). Freud and the seduction theory. *The Atlantic,* 12.

Masters, W. H., & Johnson, V. E. (1966). *Human sexual response.* Boston: Little, Brown.

Masters, W. H., & Johnson, V. E. (1979). *Homosexuality in perspective.* Boston: Little, Brown.

Masters, W. H., Johnson, V. E., & Kolodny, R. C. (1994). *Heterosexuality.* New York: HarperCollins.

Masters, W. H., Johnson, V. E., & Kolodny, R. C. (1995). *Human sexuality* (5th ed.). New York: HarperCollins.

Matlin, M. (1993). *The psychology of women* (2nd. ed.). Fort Worth, TX: Harcourt Brace Jovanovich.

Matlin, M. (1996). *The psychology of women* (3rd ed.). Fort Worth, TX: Harcourt Brace.

Maybach, K. L., & Gold, S. R. (1994). Hyperfemininity and attraction to macho and non-macho men. *Journal of Sex Research, 31*(2), 91–98.

Mbawa, K. (1992). Botswana children's career aspirations and views of sex roles. *Journal of Social Psychology, 133*(4), 587–588.

McAdoo, J. L. (1986). A Black perspective on the father's role in child development. In R. A. Lewis & M. D. Sussman (Eds.), *Men's changing roles in the family* (pp. 117–134). New York: Haworth Press.

McCann, U. D., & Agras, W. S. (1990). Successful treatment of nonpurging bulimia nervosa with desipramine: A double-blind, placebo controlled study. *American Journal of Psychiatry, 147,* 1509–1513.

McClelland, D. C., Atkinson, J. W., Clark, R. A., & Lowell, F. L. (1953). *The achievement motive.* New York: Appleton-Century-Croft.

McCormick, N. B. (1987). Sexual scripts: Social and therapeutic implications. *Sexual and Marital Therapy, 2,* 3–27.

McCusker, J., & Morrow, G. R. (1980). Factors relevant to the use of cancer early detection techniques. *Preventive Medicine, 9,* 388–397.

McDonald, K., & Parke, R. D. (1986). Parent–child physical play: The effects of sex and age on children and parents. *Sex Roles, 15,* 367–378.

McDonald, S. M. (1989). Sex bias in the representation of male and female characters in children's picture books. *Journal of Genetic Psychology, 150,* 389–401.

McElmurry, B. J., & Huddleston, D. (1987). *The perimenopausal woman: Perceived threats to sexuality and self-care responses.* Paper presented at the 7th Conference of the Society for Menstrual Cycle Research, Ann Arbor, MI.

McEwan, B. (1981). Neuronal gonadal steroid actions. *Science, 211*(4488), 1303–1311.

McFarlane, J. M. (1998). Premenstrual disorders. In A. E. Blechman & K. D. Brownell (Eds.), *Behavioral medicine and women: A comprehensive handbook* (pp. 457–462). New York: Guilford Press.

McFarlane, J. M., & Williams, T. M. (1994). Placing premenstrual syndrome in perspective. *Psychology of Women Quarterly, 18,* 339–373.

McGlone, J. (1980). Sex differences in human brain asymmetry: A critical survey. *Behavioral and Brain Sciences, 3,* 215–217.

McGoldrick, M., Pearce, J. K., & Giordano, J. (Eds.). (1982). *Ethnicity & family therapy* (pp. 123–133). New York: Guilford Press.

McGrath, E., Keita, G. P., Strickland, B., & Russo, N. F. (1990). *Women and depression: Risk factors and treatment issues.* Washington, DC: American Psychological Association.

McHale, S., & Huston, T. (1985). A longitudinal study of the transition to parenthood and its effects on the marriage relationship. *Journal of Family Issues, 6,* 409–433.

McHugh, P. R., Moran, T. H., & Killilea, M. (1989). The approaches to the study of human disorders in food ingestion and body weight maintenance. In L. H. Schneider, S. J. Cooper, & K. A. Halmi (Eds.), *The psychobiology of human eating disorders: Preclinical and clinical perspectives. Annals of the New York Academy of Sciences, 575,* 1–12.

McKee, L. (1982). Fathers' participation in infant care, a critique. In L. McKee & M. O'Brien (Eds.), *The father figure* (pp. 120–138). London: Tavistock.

McLaren, A. (1984). *Reproductive rituals: The perception of fertility in England from the sixteenth century to the nineteenth century.* New York: Methuen.

McLaughlin, D. K., & Lichter, D. (1997). Poverty and the marital behavior of young women. *Journal of Marriage and the Family, 59,* 582–594.

McLaughlin, M., Cormier, L. S., & Cormier, W. H. (1988). Relation between coping strategies and distress, stress, and marital adjustment of multiple role women. *Journal of Counseling Psychology, 35*(2), 187–193.

McLean, P., & Woody, S. (1998). Depression. In A. E. Blechman & K. D. Brownell (Eds.), *Behavioral medicine and women: A comprehensive handbook* (pp. 752–756). New York: Guilford Press.

McLemore, S. D. (1991). *Racial and ethnic relations in America.* Boston: Allyn & Bacon.

Mednick, M. T., & Thomas, V. G. (1993). Women and the psychology of achievement: A view from the eighties. In F. L. Denmark & M. A. Paludi (Eds.), *Psychology of women: A handbook of issues and theories.* Westport, CT: Greenwood Press.

Menning, B. E. (1977). *Infertility: A guide for the childless couple.* Englewood Cliffs, NJ: Prentice-Hall.

Mersky, H. (1976). Pain terms: A list with definitions and notes on usage. *Pain 6,* 249–250.

Meyer, B. (1980). The development of girls' sex-role attitudes. *Child Development, 51,* 508–514.

Meyer, I. H. (1995). Minority stress and mental health in gay men. *Journal of Health and Social Behavior, 36,* 38–56.

Meyer, V. F. (1991). A critique of adolescents pregnancy prevention research: The invincible white male. *Adolescence, 26,* 217–222.

Milano, G., Etienne, M. C., Cassuto-Viguier, E., Thyss, A., Santini, J., Frenay, M., Renee, N., Schneider, M., & Demard, F. (1992). Influence of sex and age on Fluorouracil clearance. *Journal of Clinical Oncology, 10*(7), 1171–1175.

Miller, B. A., Downs, W. R., & Testa, M. (1992). Long-term effects of parent-to-child violence for women. *Journal of Interpersonal Violence, 7*(3), 365–382.

Miller, J. B. (1976). *Toward a new psychology of women.* Boston: Beacon Press.

Miller, K. E. (1993, March). Same-sex and opposite-sex friendship quality and perceived social competence: Developmental overlap. Paper presented at the biennial meeting of the Society for Research in Child Development, New Orleans.

Millner, D. (1997). *The sistahs' rules: Secrets for meeting, getting, and keeping a good black man.* New York: Quill/William Morrow.

Mirowsky, J., & Ross, C. E. (1980). Minority status, ethnic culture and distress: A comparison of Blacks, Whites, Mexicans and Mexican Americans. *American Journal of Sociology, 86,* 479–495.

Missing persons: 60 million women. (1992). *Health, 14,* 16.

Mitchell, S. W. (1877). *Fat and blood and how to make them.* Philadelphia: Lippincott.

Mitchell, V., & Helson, R. (1990). Women's prime of life: Is it the 50s? *Psychology of Women Quarterly, 14,* 451–470.

Mittwoch, U. (1977). To be right is to be born male. *New Scientist, 73,* 74–76.

Moen, P. (1992). *Women's two roles: A contemporary dilemma.* New York: Auburn House.

Mogil, J. S., Sternberg, W. F., Kest, B., Marek, P., & Liebeskind, J. C. (1993). Sex differences in the antagonism of swim stress-induced analgesia: Effects of gonadectomy and estrogen replacement. *Pain, 53,* 17–25.

Mona, L. R., Gardos, M. A., & Brown, R. C. (1994). Sexual self-views of women with disabilities: The relationship among age-of-onset, nature of disability, and sexual self-esteem. *Sexuality and Disability, 12,* 261–275.

Money, J. (1975). Ablatio penis: Normal male infant sex-reassigned as a girl. *Archives of Sexual Behavior, 4,* 65–72.

Money, J. (1987). Propaedeutics of diecious G-1/R: Theoretical foundations for understanding dimorphic gender-identity/role. In J. M. Reinisch, L. A. Rosenblum, & S. A. Sanders (Eds.), *Masculinity/femininity: Basic perspectives* (pp. 13–28). New York: Oxford University Press.

Money, J. (1988). *Gay, straight and in-between.* New York: Oxford University Press.

Money, J. (1990). Agenda and credenda of the Kinsey Scale. In D. P. McWirter (Ed.), *Homosexuality/heterosexuality: Concepts of sexual orientation* (pp. 41–60). New York: Oxford University Press.

Money, J., & Ehrhardt, A. E. (1972). *Man & woman, boy & girl.* Baltimore, MD: Johns Hopkins Press.

Money, J., & Tucker, P. (1975). Sexual signatures: On being a man or woman (pp. 95–98). Boston: Little, Brown. Cited by M. Diamond, and K. Sigmundson (1997), 298–304.

Montague, H., & Hollingworth, L. S. (1914). The comparative variability of the sexes at birth. *American Journal of Sociology, 20,* 335–370.

Morahan-Martin, J. (1991). Consider the children: Is parenthood being devalued? *The Psychological Record, 41,* 303–314.

Moreau, D. (1996). Depression in the young. In J. A. Sechzer, S. M. Pfafflin, F. L. Denmark, A. Griffin, & S. Blumenthal (Eds.), *Women and mental health: Annals of the New York Academy of Sciences, 789,* 181–190. New York: The New York Academy of Sciences.

Morford, M. P. O., & Lenardon, R. J. (1995). *Classical mythology* (5th ed.) (pp. 63–65). White Plains, NY: Longman.

Morgan, D. L. (1985). Nurses' perceptions of confusion in the elderly: Influence of resident and setting characteristics. *Journal of Health and Social Behavior, 26,* 102–112.

Morgan, K. S., & Brown, L. S. (1993). Lesbian career development, work behavior, and vocational counseling. In L. D. Garrets & D. C. Kimmel (Eds.), *Psychological perspectives on lesbian and gay male experiences* (pp. 267–286). New York: Columbia University Press.

Morse, D. (1969). *The peripheral worker.* New York: Columbia University Press.

Morton, A. (1997). *Diana: Her True Story.* New York: Simon & Schuster.

Morton, T. U. (1978). Intimacy and reciprocity of exchange: A comparison of spouses and strangers. *Journal of Personality and Social Psychology, 36,* 72–81.

Mullins, L. C., & Mushel, M. (1992). The existence and emotional closeness of relationships with children, friends, and spouses: The effect of loneliness among older persons. *Research on Aging, 14*(4), 448–470.

Murray, B. (1998, October). Survey reveals concerns of today's girls. *APA Monitor, 29,* 12.

Murrell, A. J. (1996). Sexual harassment and women of color: Issues, challenges, and future directions. In M. S. Stockdale (Ed.), *Sexual harassment in the workplace: Perspectives, frontiers, and response strategies* (pp. 51–66). Thousand Oaks, CA: Sage.

Mussen, P. H., & Rutherford, E. (1963). Parent–child relations and parental personality in relation to young children's sex-role preferences. *Child Development, 34,* 489–507.

Muster, N. J. (1992). Treating the adolescent victim-turned-offender. *Adolescence, 27,* 441–450.

Myer, M. H. (1985). A new look at mothers of incest victims. *Journal of Social Work and Human Sexuality, 3,* 47–58.

Nadien, M. (1996). Aging women: Issues of mental health and maltreatment. *Annals of the New York Academy of Sciences, 789,* 129–145.

Narroll, R. (1964). Ethnic unit classification. *Current Anthrolpology, 5*(4), 283–312.

National Center for Health Statistics. (1991). *Health, United States, 1990.* Hyattsville, MD: Public Health Service.

National Institutes of Health. (1991, February 3). *Guide for grants and contracts.* NIH/ADAMHA policy concerning inclusion of women in study populations.

National Institutes of Health–Office of Research on Women's Health. (1992). *Opportunities for research on women's health.* Department of Health & Human Services, Public Health Service, National Institutes of Health. NIH Publication No. 92-3457A, September 1992.

National Osteoporosis Foundation. (1991). *Boning up on osteoporosis: A guide to prevention and treatment.* Washington, DC: Author.

National Research Council. (1992). *Recognition and alleviation of pain and distress in laboratory animals: A report of the institute of laboratory animal resources committee on pain and distress in laboratory animals.* Washington, DC: National Academy Press.

National Research Council. (1993). *Losing generations: Adolescents in high-risk settings.* Washington, DC: National Academy Press.

Neft, N., & Levine, A. D. (1997). *Where women stand: An international report on the status of women in 140 countries.* New York: Random House.

Nelson, C., & Tienda, M. (1985). The structuring of Hispanic ethnicity: Historical and contemporary perspectives. *Ethnic and Racial Studies, 8,* 49–73.

Neto, F., Williams, J. E., & Widner, S. C. (1991). Portugese children's knowledge of sex stereotypes. Effects of age, gender, and socioeconomic status. *Journal of Cross-Cultural Psychology, 22*(3), 376–388.

Neugarten, B., & Gutmann. (1964). *Personality in middle and later life.* New York: Atherton.

Neugarten, B. L., & Kraines, R. J. (1965). "Menopausal symptoms" in women of various ages. *Psychosomatic Medicine, 27,* 266.

Nevid, J. S. (1984). Sex differences in factors of romantic attraction. *Sex Roles, 11,* 401–411.

Nevid, J. S., Fichner-Rathus, L., & Rathus, S. (1995). *Human sexuality in a world of diversity* (2nd ed.). Boston: Allyn & Bacon.

Newmann, J. P. (1986). Gender, life-strains, and depression. *Journal of Health and Social Behavior, 27,* 161–178.

Niditch, S. (1991). Portrayal of women in the Hebrew Bible. In J. Baskin (Ed.), *Jewish women in historical perspective* (pp. 25–42). Detroit, MI: Wayne State University Press.

Niemela, P., & Lento, R. (1993). The significance of the 50th birthday for women's individuation. *Women and Therapy, 14*(1/2), 117–127.

Nieto-Gomez, A. (1976). A heritage of LaHembra. In S. Cox (Ed.), *Female psychology: The emerging self* (pp. 226–235). Chicago: Science Research Associates.

Nilsen, A. P., Bosmajian, H., Lee-Gershuny, H., & Stanley, J. P. (1977). *Sexism and language.* Urbana, IL: National Council of Teachers of English.

Nilson, L. (1978). The social standing of a housewife. *Journal of Marriage and the Family, 40,* 541–548.

Norton, A. J., & Moorman, J. E. (1987). Current trends in marriage and divorce among American women. *Journal of Marriage and the Family, 49*(1), 3–14.

Nosek, M. A., Howland, C. A., Young, M. E., Georgiou, D., Rintala, D. H., Foley, C. C., Bennett, L. L., & Smith, Q. (1994). Wellness models and sexuality among women with disabilities. *Journal of Applied Rehabilitation Counseling, 25,* 50–58.

Noss, J. B. (1949). *Man's Religions.* New York: Macmillan.

Noss, J. B. (1974). *Man's religions* (5th ed.). New York: Macmillan.

Noss, J. B., & Noss, D. S. (1984). *Man's Religions* (7th ed.). New York: Macmillan.

Nyberg, K. L., & Alston, J. P. (1976–1977). Analysis of public attitudes toward homosexual behavior. *Journal of Homosexuality, 2,* 99–107.

Oakley, A. (1980). *Women confined.* New York: Schocken.

O'Connell, A. N., & Rotter, G. (1979). The influence of stimulus age and sex on person perception. *Journal of Gerontology, 34,* 220–228.

O'Connor, P. (1992). *Friendships between women.* New York: Guilford Press.

Offen, (1988). Defining feminism: A comparative historical approach. *Signs: Journal of Women in Culture and Society, 14*(11), 119–157.

Offen, K. (1990). From feminism and sexual difference in historical perspective. In D. L. Rhode (Ed.), *Theoretical perspectives on sexual difference* (pp. 13–20). New Haven, CT: Yale University Press.

Offer, D., Ostrov, E., Howard, K. I., & Atkinson, R. (1988). *The teenage world. Adolescents' self-image in ten countries.* New York: Plenum.

Ogbu, J. U. (1982). Black education: A cultural–ecological perspective. In H. McAdoo (Ed.), *Black families* (pp. 139–154). Beverly Hills, CA: Sage.

Ogbu, J. U. (1994). From cultural differences to differences in cultural frame of reference. In P. Greenfield & R. Cocking (Eds.), *Cross-cultural roots of minority child development* (pp. 365–391). Hillsdale, NJ: Erlbaum.

Ohno, S. (1979) *Major sex-determining genes.* Berlin, Springer-Verlag.

O'Leary, K. D., Barling, J., Arias, I., Rosenbaum, A., Malone, J., & Tyree, A. (1989). Prevalence and stability of physical aggression between spouses: A longitudinal analysis. *Journal of Consulting and Clinical Psychology, 57,* 263–268.

Oliver, M. B., & Hyde, J. S. (1993). Gender differences in sexuality: A meta-analysis. *Psychological Bulletin, 114,* 29–51.

Oliver, S. J., & Toner, B. B. (1990). The influence of gender role typing in the expression of depressive symptoms. *Sex Roles, 22,* 775–790.

Oquendo, M., Horwath, E., & Martinez, A. (1992). Ataques de nervios: Proposed diagnostic criteria for a culture-specific syndrome. *Culture, Medicine, and Psychiatry, 16,* 367–376.

Orenstein, P. (1995, April 27). Show girls equity at work: Shattering the glass ceiling needed in the classroom as well as in the boardroom. *USA Today,* p. 13A.

Orlofsky, J. L. (1982). Psychological androgyny, sex-typing, and sex-role ideology as predictors of male–female interpersonal attraction. *Sex Roles, 8,* 1057–1073.

Ornish, D. (1982). *Stress, diet, and your heart: A lifetime program for healing your heart without surgery.* New York: Penguin.

Ornish, D., Brown, S. E., Sherwitz, L. W., Billings, J. H., Armstrong, W. T., Ports, T. A., McLanahan, S. M., Kirkeeide, R. L., Brand, R. J., & Gould, K. L. (1990). Can lifestyle changes reverse coronary heart disease? *Lancet, 336,* 129–133.

Orr, E., & Ben-Eliahu, E. (1993). Gender differences in idiosyncratic sex-typed self-images and self-esteem. *Sex Roles, 29*(3/4), 271–296.

Ortiz, V. (1994). Women of color: A demographic overview. In M. Zinn & G. Dill (Eds.), *Women of color in U.S. society* (pp. 13–40). Philadelphia: Temple University Press.

O'Sullivan, C. (1995). Fraternities and the rape culture. In M. S. Kimmel & M. A. Messner (Eds.), *Men's lives* (3rd ed.) (pp. 354–357). Boston: Allyn & Bacon.

O'Sullivan, C. S. (1991). Acquaintance gang rape on campus. In A. Parrot & L. Bechofer (Eds.), *Acquaintance rape: The hidden crime* (pp. 140–156). New York: Wiley.

Overall, C. (1992). What's wrong with prostitution? Evaluating sex work. *Signs, 17,* 705–724.

Packer, J. (1986). Sex differences in the perception of street harassment. The dynamics of feminist therapy (pp. 331–338). New York: Haworth.

Padilla, A. M., Salgado de Snyder, N. V., Cervantes, R. C., & Baezconde-Garbanati, L. (1987, Summer). Self regulation and risk-taking behavior: A Hispanic perspective. In *Research Bulletin* (pp. 1–5). Los Angeles: Spanish Speaking Mental Health Research Center.

Padilla, E. R., & O'Grady, K. E. (1987). Sexuality among Mexican-Americans: A case of sexual stereotyping. *Journal of Personality and Social Psychology, 52,* 5–10.

Pagelow, M. D. (1984). *Family violence.* New York: Praeger.

Pagelow, M. D. (1992). Adult victims of domestic violence: Battered women. *Journal of Interpersonal Violence, 7*(1), 87–120.

Palca, J. (1990). Women left out at NIH. *Science, 248,* 1601–1602.

Pallitt, K. (1997, June 27). What's right about divorce? *New York Times,* p. A29.

Palmore, E. (1971). Attitudes toward aging as shown by humor. *Gerontologist, 11,* 181–186.

Palmore, E. B., Burchett, B., Fillenbaum, G. G., George, L., & Wallman, L. M. (1985). *Retirement: Causes and consequences.* New York: Springer.

Paludi, M. A. (1984). Psychometric properties and underlying assumptions of four objective measures of fear of success. *Sex Roles, 10,* 765–781.

Paludi, M. A. (1992). *The psychology of women.* New York: Brown & Benchmark.

Paradise, L. V., & Wall, S. M. (1986). Children's perceptions of male and female principals and teachers. *Sex Roles, 14,* 1–7.

Parke, R. D. (1978). Perspectives on father–infant interaction. In J. D. Osofsky (Ed.), *Handbook of infant development* (pp. 549–590). New York: Wiley.

Parks, M. R., Stan, C. M., & Eggert, L. L. (1983). Romantic involvement and social network involvement, *Social Psychology Quarterly, 46*(2), 116–131.

Parrinder, G. (1983). *World religions: From ancient history to the present.* New York: Facts on File.

Patlak, M. (1997). The long and short of it. New medications for growth disorders. In A. M. Meehan & E. Astor-Stetson (Eds.), *Adolescent psychology* (pp. 37–39). Guilford, CT: Dushkin Publishing Group/Brown & Benchmark Publishers.

Patterson, C. (1992). Children of lesbian and gay parents. *Child Development, 63,* 1025–1042.

Patterson, C. (1994). Children of the lesbian baby-boom: Behavioral adjustment, self-concepts, and sex-role identity. In B. Greene & G. M. Herek (Eds.), *Lesbian and gay psychology: Theory, research, and clinical applications* (pp. 156–175). New York: Sage.

Patterson, C. J., & Redding, R. E. (1996). Lesbian and gay families with children: Implications of social science research for policy. *Journal of Social Issues, 52*(3), 29–50.

Patterson, C. J., & Schwartz, P. (1994). The social construction of conflict in intimate same-sex couples. In D. D. Cahn (Ed.), *Conflict in personal relationships* (pp. 3–26). Hillsdale, NJ: Erlbaum.

Payne, D. E., & Mussen, P. H. (1956). Parent–child relations and father identification among adolescent boys. *Journal of Abnormal and Social Psychology, 52,* 358–362.

Pearlman, S. F. (1992). Heterosexual mothers/lesbian daughters: Parallels and similarities. *Journal of Feminist Family Therapy, 4*(2), 1–25.

Pearlman, S. F. (1993). Late mid-life astonishment: Disruptions to identity and self-esteem. *Women and Therapy, 14*(1/2), 1–12.

Pease, J. (1993). Professor Mom: Woman's work in a man's world. *Sociological Forum, 8*(1), 133–139.

Penner, L. A., Thompson, J. K., & Coovert, D. L. (1991). Size overestimation among anorexics: Much ado about very little? *Journal of Abnormal Psychology, 100,* 90–93.

Penning, M. J., & Strain, L. A. (1994). Gender differences in disability, assistance, and subjective well-being in later life. *Journal of Gerontology, 49*(4), 202–208.

Peplau, L. A. (1991). Lesbian and gay relationships. In J. Gonsiorek & J. Weinrich (Eds.), *Homosexuality: Research implications for public policy* (pp. 177–196). Newbury Park, CA: Sage.

Peplau, L. A., & Cochran, S. D. (1990). A relational perspective on homosexuality. In D. P. McWhirter, S. A. Sanders, & J. M. Reinisch (Eds.), *Homosexuality/heterosexuality: Concepts of sexual orientation* (pp. 321–349). New York: Oxford University Press.

Peplau, L. A., Garnets, L. D., Spalding, L. H., Conley, T. D., & Veniegas, R. C. (1998). Critique of Bem's "Exotic becomes Erotic" theory of sexual orientation. *Psychological Review, 105,* 387–394.

Peplau, L. A., & Gordon, S. L. (1985). Women and men in love: Gender differences in close heterosexual relationships. In V. E. O'Leary, R. K. Unger, & B. S. Wallston (Eds.), *Women, gender, and social psychology* (pp. 257–291). Hillsdale, NJ: Erlbaum.

Peplau, L. A., Rubin, Z., & Hill, C. T. (1977). Sexual intimacy in dating relationships. *Journal of Social Issues, 33,* 86–109.

Perkins, W. (1596). *A discourse on the damned art of witchcraft.* London: n.p. Cited by Reuther (1983), pp. 222–224. *Religion and Sexism.* New York: Simon & Schuster.

Perry, J. D., & Whipple, B. (1981). Pelvic muscle strength of female ejaculation: Evidence in support of a new theory of orgasm. *Journal of Sex Research, 17,* 22–39.

Persson, I., Adami, H. O., Bergkvist, L., Lindgren, A., Petterson, B., Hoover, R., & Schairer, C. (1989). Risk of endometrial cancer after treatment with oestrogens alone or in conjunctin with progestins: Results of a prospective study. *British Medical Journal, 298,* 147–151.

Petersen, A. C. (1983). Menarche: Meaning of measures and measuring meaning. In S. Golub (Ed.), *Menarche: The transition from girl to woman* (pp. 63–76). Lexington, MA: Lexington Books.

Peterson, A. C., & Crockett, L. J. (1987). Biological correlates of spatial ability and mathematical performance. In J. A. Sechzer & S. M. Pfafflin (Eds.), *Psychology and Educational Policy. Annals of the News York Academy of Sciences, 517,* 69–86.

Petrakis, N. (1988). Chinese and breast cancer. In *Summary of Breaking the Barriers Conference by Asian American Health Forum, Inc. (AAHF).* San Francisco: AAHF.

Pharr, S. (1988). *Homophobia: A weapon of sexism.* Inverness, CA: Chardon Press.

Philliber, W., & Hiller, D. (1983). Relative occupational attainment of spouses and later changes in marriage and wife's work experience. *Journal of Marriage and the Family, 45,* 161–170.

Phinney, J. S. (1996). When we talk about American ethnic groups, what do we mean? *American Psychologist, 51,* 918–927.

Piaget, J. (1932). *The moral judgment of the child.* London: Kegan, Paul, Trench, & Trubner.

Piedmont, R. L. (1995). Another look at fear of success, fear of failure, and test anxiety: A motivational analysis using the five-factor model. *Sex Roles, 32,* 139–158.

Pinderhughes, E. (1989). *Understanding race, ethnicity, and power: The key to efficacy in clinical practice.* New York: Free Press.

Pinel, J. P. J. (1993). *Biopsychology.* Boston: Allyn & Bacon.

Pleck, J. H., Sonestein, F. L., & Ku, L. (1993). Masculinity ideology: Its impact on adolescent males' heterosexual relationships. *Journal of Social Issues, 49,* 11–19.

Polatnick, M. R. (1993). Why men don't rear children. In A. Minas (Ed.), *Gender basics: Feminist perspectives on women and men* (pp. 500–508). Belmont, CA: Wadsworth.

Polivy, J., & Thomson, L. (1988). Dieting and other eating disorders. In E. A. Blechman & K. D. Brownell (Eds.), *Handbook of behavioral medicine for women* (pp. 345–355). New York: Pergamon.

Pool, R. (1993). Evidence for homosexuality gene. *Science, 261,* 291–292.

Portes, A., & Truelove, C. (1987). Making sense of diversity: Recent research on Hispanic minorities in the United States. *Annual Review of Sociology, 13,* 359–385.

Poulin-Dubois, D., Serbin, L. A., Kenyon, B., & Derbyshire, A. (1994). Infants' intermodal knowledge about gender. *Developmental Psychology, 30*(3), 436–442.

Powderly, W. G., Landay, A., & Lederman, M. M. (1998). Recovery of the immune system with antiviral therapy: The end of opportunism? *Journal of the American Medical Association, 280*(1), 72–77.

Powell, E. (1991). *Talking back to sexual pressure.* Minneapolis: Compcare Publishers.

Powell, G. N. (1986). Effects of sex role identity and sex on definitions of sexual harassment. *Sex Roles, 14,* 9–19.

Power, T. G., McGrath, M. P., Hughes, S. O., & Manire, S. H. (1994). Compliance and self-assertion: Young children's responses to mothers versus fathers. *Developmental Psychology, 30*(6), 980–989.

Powlishta, K. K., Serbin, L. A., Doyle, A. B., & White, D. R. (1994). Gender, ethnic, and body type biases: The generality of prejudice in childhood. *Developmental Psychology, 30*(4), 526–536.

Prelevic, G. M., Balint-Peric, L., & Petrovic, J. (1990). The effects of intranasal calcitonin on bone metabolism in women with premature menopause. In M. Flint, F. Kronenberg, & W. Utian (Eds.), *Multidisciplinary perspectives on menopause: Annals of the New York Academy of Sciences, 736,* 463–465. New York: The New York Academy of Sciences.

Preston, K., & Stanley, K. (1987). "What's the worst thing. . . ?": Gender-directed insults. *Sex Roles, 17,* 209–219.

Price, D. D., & Dubner, R. (1977). Neurons that subserve the sensory-discriminative aspects of pain. *Pain, 3,* 307–338.

Price, J. H., & Miller, P. A. (1984). Sexual fantasies of Black and White college students. *Psychological Reports, 54,* 1007–1014.

Price, S. J., & McKenry, P. C. (1988). *Divorce.* Newbury Park, CA: Sage.

Prilleltensky, I. (1989). Psychology and the status quo. *American Psychologist, 44,* 795–802.

Pryor, J. B. (1987). Sexual harassment proclivities in men. *Sex Roles, 17,* 269–290.

Pryor, J. B., & Merluzzi, T. V. (1985). The role of expertise in processing social interaction scripts. *Journal of Experimental Social Psychology, 21,* 362–379.

Purcell, P., & Stewart, L. (1990). Dick and Jane in 1989. *Sex Roles, 22,* 177–185.

Pyant, C. T., & Yanico, B. J. (1991). Relationship of racial identity and gender role attitudes to black women's psychological well-being. *Journal of counseling psychology, 38,* 315–322.

Quina, K. (1996). Sexual harassment and rape: A continuum of exploitation. In M. A. Paludi (Ed.), *Sexual harassment on college campuses: Abusing the ivory power.* Albany, NY: SUNY Press.

Rabinowitz, V. C. (1993). Sex bias in human research: More questions about generalization. Symposium on "Sex Bias in Research: Are Males and Females the Same?" *Annual Meeting of the American Association for the Advancement of Science,* Boston, p. 45.

Rabinowitz, V. C. (1996). Coping with sexual harassment. In M. A. Paludi (Ed.), *Sexual harassment on college campuses: Abusing the ivory power* (pp. 199–213). New York: State University of New York Press.

Rabinowitz, V. C., & Sechzer, J. A. (1993). Feminist perspectives on research methods. In F. L. Denmark & M. A. Paludi (Eds.), *Psychology of women: A handbook of issues and theories* (pp. 23–66). Westport, CT: Greenwood Press.

Rabinowitz, V. C., Sechzer, J. A., Denmark, F. L., & Weeks, B. M. (1994). Sex and gender bias in AIDS research: A content analysis. *American Psychological Association Conference on Psychosocial and Behavioral Factors in Women's Health.* Washington, DC: APA.

Rabinowitz, V. C., & Weseen, S. (1997). Elu(ci)d(at)ing epistemological impasses: Re-viewing the qualitative/quantitative debates in psychology. *Journal of Social Issues, 53*(4), 605–630.

Radloff, L. (1975). Sex differences in depression: The effects of occupation and marital status. *Sex Roles, 1,* 249–265.

Raisman, G., & Field, P. M. (1971). Sexual dimorphism in the preoptic areas of the rat. *Science, 173,* 20–22.

Ramsey, P. G. (1991). Young children's awareness and understanding of social class differences. *Journal of Genetic Psychology, 152*(1), 71–82.

Rathus, S. (1988). *Human sexuality.* New York: Holt, Rinehart, and Winston.

Rathus, S., Nevid, J. S., & Fichner-Rathus, L. (1997). *Human sexuality in a world of diversity* (3rd ed.). Boston: Allyn and Bacon.

Rathus, S. A., Nevid, J. S., & Fichner-Rathus, L. (1998). *Essentials of human sexuality.* Boston: Allyn & Bacon.

Rawlings, E. I., & Carter, D. K. (1977). *Psychotherapy for women.* Springfield, IL: Charles C Thomas. Cited by Matlin (1996), p. 480–482.

Rawlings, E. I., & Carter, D. K. (1992). Feminist and nonsexist psychotherapy. In *Psychotherapy for women.* Springfield, IL: Charles C Thomas.

Rawlings, S., & Saluter, A. (1995). *Household and family characteristics.* Washington, DC: U.S. Bureau of the Census.

Reddy, D. M., Fleming, R., & Adesso, V. J. (1992). Gender and health. In S. Maes, H. Leventhal, & M. Johnston (Eds.), *International Review of Health Psychology* (Vol. 2) (pp. 3–32). West Sussex, England: Wiley.

Reed, R. (1988). Education and achievement of young black males. In J. T. Gibbs (Ed.), *Young, black, and male in America* (pp. 37–96). Dover, MA: Auburn.

Reedy, M. N., Birren, J. E., & Schaie, K. W. (1981). Age and sex differences in satisfying relationships across the life span. *Human Development, 24,* 52–66.

Reid, J. D. (1995). Development in later life: Older lesbians and gay lives. In A. R. D'Augelli & C. J. Patterson (Eds.), *Lesbian, gay, and bisexual identities over the life span: Psychological perspectives* (pp. 215–242). New York: Oxford University Press.

Reid, P. T. (1993). Poor women in psychological research: Shut up and shut out. *Psychology of Women Quarterly, 17,* 133–150.

Reid, P. T., & Paludi, M. A. (1993). Developmental psychology of women: Conception to adolescence. In F. L. Denmark & M. A. Paludi (Eds.) *Psychology of women: A handbook of issues and theories* (pp. 191–212). Westport, CT: Greenwood Press.

Reilly, M. E., Lott, B., & Gallogly, S. M. (1986). Sexual harassment of university students. *Sex Roles, 15,* 333–358.

Reiner, W. (1997). To be male or female—that is the question. *Archives of Pediatric & Adolescent Medicine, 151,* 224–225.

Reinisch, J. M. (1990). *The Kinsey Institute's new report on sex: What you must know to be sexually literate.* New York: St. Martin's Press.

Reis, H. T., Senchak, M., & Solomon, B. (1985). Sex differences in the intimacy of social interaction: Further examination of potential explanations. *Journal of Personality and Social Psychology, 48,* 1204–1217.

Reis, P., & Stone, A. J. (Eds.). (1992). *American Women 1992–93: A status report.* New York: W. W. Norton.

Reiss, I. L. (1986). *Journey into sexuality: An exploratory voyage.* Englewood Cliffs, NJ: Prentice Hall.

Reitz, R. (1981). *Menopause: A positive approach.* London: Unwin.

Reskin, B. F. (1993). Sex segregation in the workplace. In J. Blake & J. Hagen (Eds.), *American Sociological Review* (Vol. 19) (pp. 241–270). Palo Alto, CA: Annual Reviews.

Reskin, B. F., & Hartmann, H. I. (1986). *Women's work, men's work: Sex segregation on the job.* Washington, DC: National Academy Press.

Reskin, B. F., & Padavic, I. (1994). *Women and men at work.* Thousand Oaks, CA: Pine Forge Press.

Reskin, B. F., & Roos, P. A. (1987). Sex segregation and status hierarchies. In C. Bose & G. Spitze (Eds.), *Ingredients for women's employment policy* (pp. 3–21). Albany: State University of New York Press.

Resnick, H. S., Kilpatrick, D. G., Walsh, C., & Veronen, L. J. (1991). Marital rape. In R. T. Ammerman & M. Hersen (Eds.), *Case studies in family violence* (pp. 329–355). New York: Plenum.

Rhodes, A. L. (1983). Effects of religious denominations on sex differences in occupational expectations. *Sex Roles, 9,* 93–108.

Rice, F. P. (1990). *Intimate relationships, marriages, and families.* Mountain View, CA: Mayfield.

Rice, J. K., & Hemmings, A. (1988, Spring). Women's colleges and women achievers: An update. *Signs: Journal of Women in Culture, 13,* 3.

Rice, P. L. (1987). *Stress and health.* Pacific Grove, CA: Brooks/Cole.

Rice, P. L. (1992). *Stress and health* (2nd ed.). Pacific Grove, CA: Brooks Cole.

Rich, A. (1976). *Of women born: Motherhood as experience and institution.* New York: Norton.

Rich, A. (1977). *Of women born.* New York: Bantam.

Rich, A. (1980). Compulsory sexuality and lesbian existence. *Signs: Journal of Women in Culture, 5,* 647–650.

Rich-Edwards, J. W., Manson, J. E., Hennekins, C. H., & Buring, J. E. (1995). The primary protection of coronary heart disease in women. *New England Journal of Medicine, 332*(26), 1758–1766.

Richardson, L. W. (1988). *The dynamics of sex and gender: A sociological perspective.* Boston: Houghton-Mifflin.

Richmond-Abbott, M. (1984). Sex-roles of mothers and children in divorced, single-parent families. *Journal of Divorce, 8,* 34–46.

Richmond-Abbott, M. (1992). *Masculine and feminine: Gender roles across the life cycle* (2nd ed.). New York: McGraw-Hill.

Riege, W. H., & Inman, V. (1981). Age differences in nonverbal memory tasks. *Journal of Gerontology, 36,* 51–58.

Riger, S. (1992). Epistemological debates, feminist voices: Science, social values, and the study of women. *American Psychologist, 47,* 730–740.

Riggs, B. L., & Melton, J., III. (1992). The prevention and treatment of osteoporosis. *New England Journal of Medicine, 327,* 620–627.

Ringgren, H. & Strom, A. V. (1967). *Religions of mankind: Today and yesterday* (pp. 44–50). Philadelphia: Fortress Press.

Risman, B. J. (1987). Intimate relationships from a microstructural perspective: Men who mother. *Gender & Society, 1,* 6–32.

Rivers, R. (1995). Clinical issues and interventions with ethnic minority women. In J. Aponte, R. Rivers, & J. Wohl (Eds.), *Psychological interventions and cultural diversity* (pp. 181–198). Boston: Allyn and Bacon.

Roberts, T. (1991). Gender and the influence of evaluations on self-assessments in achievement settings. *Psychological Bulletin, 19,* 297–308.

Robinson, S. P. (1985). Hindu paradigms of women: Images and values. In Y. Y. Haddad & E. B. Findly (Eds.), *Women, religion and social change* (pp. 190–194). Albany: State University of New York Press.

Rodin, J., & Ickovics, J. R. (1990). Women's health: Review and research agenda as we approach the 21st century. *American Psychologist, 45,* 1018–1034.

Rogers, K. (1966). *The troublesome helpmate: A history of misogyny in literature.* Seattle, WA: University of Washington Press.

Rogers, R. W. (1908). *The religion of Babylonia and Assyria.* New York: Eaton & Mains.

Rohrbaugh, J. B. (1979). *Women: Psychology's puzzle.* New York: Basic Books.

Rollins, B. C. (1989). Marital quality at midlife. In S. Hunter & M. Sundel (Eds.), *Midlife myths: Issues, findings, and practice implications.* Newbury Park, CA: Sage.

Rollins, J. H. (1996). *Women's minds, women's bodies. The psychology of women in a biosocial context.* Upper Saddle River, NJ: Prentice Hall.

Root, M. (1992). Reconstructing the impact of trauma on personality. In L. S. Brown & M. Ballou (Eds.), *Personality and psychopathology: Feminist reappraisals* (pp. 229–266). New York: Guilford Press.

Root, M. (1995). The psychology of Asian American women. In H. Landrine (Ed.), *Bringing cultural diveristy to feminist psychology: Theory, research, and practice* (pp. 265–301). Washington, DC: American Psychological Association.

Rosaldo, M. Z., & Lamphere, L. (1974). *Woman, culture and society.* Stanford, CA: Stanford University Press.

Roscoe, B., Diana, M. S., & Brooks, R. H. (1987). Early, middle, and late adolescents' views on dating and factors influencing partner selection. *Adolescence, 22,* 59–68.

Rosen, B. N., & Peterson, L. (1990). Gender differences in children's outdoor play injuries: A review and an integration. *Clinical Psychology Review, 10,* 187–205.

Rosenberg, J., Perlstadt, H., & Phillips, W. R. F. (1993). Now that we are here: Discrimination, disparagement, and harassment at work and the experience of women lawyers. *Gender & Society, 7*(3), 415–433.

Rosenberg, R. (1982). *Beyond separate spheres: Intellectual roots of modern feminism.* New Haven, CT: Yale University Press.

Rosenhan, D. L., & Seligman, M. E. P. (1984). *Abnormal Psychology.* New York: W. W. Norton.

Ross, C. A., Anderson, G., Heber, S., & Norton, G. R. (1990). Dissociation and abuse among multiple personality patients, prostitutes, and exotic dancers. *Hospital and Community Psychiatry, 41,* 328–330.

Ross, C. E., & Mirowsky, J. (1988). Child care and emotional adjustment to wives' employment. *Journal of Health and Social Behavior, 29,* 127–138.

Ross, H., & Taylor, H. (1989). Do boys prefer Daddy or his physical style of play? *Sex Roles, 20*(1/2), 23–31.

Ross, S. I., & Jackson, J. M. (1991). Teachers' expectations for Black males' and Black females' academic achievement. *Personality and Social Psychology Bulletin, 17,* 78–82.

Rosser, S. V. (1992). *Biology and feminism: A dynamic interaction.* New York: Twayne.

Rossi, A. (1979). Transition to parenthood. In P. Rose (Ed.), *Socialization and the life cycle* (pp. 132–145). New York: St. Martin's Press.

Rostovsky, S. S., & Travis, C. B. (1996). Menopause research and the dominance of the biomedical model 1984–1994. *Psychology of Women Quarterly, 20,* 285–312.

Rothbaum, B. O., Foa, E. B., Riggs, D. S., Murdock, T., & Walsh, W. (1992). A prospective examination of post-traumatic stress disorder in rape victims. *Journal of Traumatic Stress, 5,* 455–475.

Rothblum, E. D. (1983). Sex-role stereotypes and depression in women. In V. Franks & E. D. Rothblum (Eds.), *The stereotyping of women: Its effects on mental health* (p. 83–111). New York: Springer.

Rothblum, E. D. (1988). Introduction: Lesbianism as a model of a positive lifestyle for women. *Women and Therapy, 8,* 1–12.

Rothblum, E. D. (1994). Lesbians and physical appearance: Which model applies? In B. Greene & G. M. Herek (Eds.),

Lesbian and gay psychology: Theory, research, and clinical applications. Psychological Perspectives on Lesbian and Gay Issues, Vol. 1. Thousand Oaks, CA: Sage.

Rowe, M. P. (1996). Dealing with harassment: A systems approach. In M. S. Stockdale (Ed.), *Sexual harassment in the workplace: Perspectives, frontiers, and response strategies* (pp. 241–271). Thousand Oaks, CA: Sage.

Rowland, J. H. (1998). Breast cancer: Psychosocial aspects. In A. E. Blechman & K. D. Brownell (Eds.), *Behavioral medicine and women: A comprehensive handbook* (pp. 577–587). New York: Guilford Press.

Rozee, P. D. (1993). Forbidden or forgiven? Rape in cross-cultural perspective. *Psychology of Women Quarterly, 17,* 499–514.

Rubin, J., Provenzano, F. J., & Luria, Z. (1974). The eye of the beholder: Parents' views on sex of newborns. *American Journal of Orthopsychiatry, 44,* 512–519.

Rubin, L. (1980). Blue-collar marriage and the sexual revolution. In A. Skolnik & J. Skolnik (Eds.), *The family in transition* (3rd ed., p. 160). Boston: Little, Brown.

Rubin, L. (1983). *Intimate stranger: Men and women together.* New York: Harper & Row.

Rubin, R., Reinisch, J., & Haskett, R. (1981). Postnatal gonadal steroid effects on human behavior. *Science, 211*(4488), 1318–1324.

Rubin, Z., Peplau, L. A., & Hill, C. T. (1981). Loving and leaving: Sex differences in romantic attachments. *Sex Roles, 7,* 821–835.

Ruether, R. R. (1993). *Sexism and god-talk: Toward a feminist theology.* Boston: Beacon Press.

Rusbult, C. E., & Martz, J. M. (1995). Remaining in an abusive relationship: An investment model analysis of nonvoluntary dependence. *Personality and Social Psychology Bulletin, 21,* 558–571.

Russell, D. (1986). *The secret trauma: Incest in the lives of girls and women.* New York: Basic Books.

Russell, D. E. H. (1982). *Rape in marriage.* New York: Macmillan.

Russell, D. E. H. (1993). *Against pornography.* Berkeley, CA: Russell Publications.

Russell, D. E. H. (1995). The prevalence, trauma, and sociocultural causes of incestuous abuse of females: A human rights issue. In R. J. Kleber & C. R. Figley (Eds.), *Beyond trauma: Cultural and societal dynamics.* New York: Plenum.

Russell, G. F. M. (1979). Bulimia nervosa: An ominous variant of anorexia nervosa. *Psychological Medicine, 9,* 392–448.

Russell, G. F. M., Szmukler, G. I., & Dare, C. (1987). An evaluation of family therapy and anorexia nervosa and bulimia nervosa. *Archives of General Psychiatry 44,* 1047–1056.

Russo, N. F. (1976). The motherhood mandate. *Journal of Social Issues, 32,* 143–154.

Russo, N., & Denmark, F. (1984). Women, psychology, & public policy. *American Psychologist, 39*(10), 161–165.

Russo, N. F., & Denmark, F. L. (1987). Contributions of women to psychology. *Annual Review of Psychology, 38,* 279–298.

Russo, N., & Green, B. (1993). Women and mental health. In F. Denmark & M. Paludi (Eds.), *Psychology of women: A handbook of issues and theories* (pp. 379–436). Westport, CT: Greenwood.

Russo, N. F., & Green, B. L. (1993). Women and mental health. In F. L. Denmark & M. A. Paludi (Eds.), *Psychology of women: A handbook of issues and theories* (pp. 379–436). Westport, CT: Greenwood Press.

Ryan, E. B., & Carranza, M. A. (1975). Valuative reactions of adolescents toward speakers of standard English and Mexican-American accented English. *Journal of Personality and Social Psychology, 31,* 855–863.

Ryan, E. B., Carranza, M. A., & Moffie, R. W. (1977). Reactions towards varying degrees of accentedness in the speech of Spanish–English bilinguals. *Language and Speech, 20,* 24–26.

Ryan, W. (1971). *Blaming the victim.* New York: Random House.

Rybarczyk, B. (1994). Diversity among American men: The impact of aging, ethnicity, and race. In C. T. Kilmartin (Ed.), *The masculine self* (pp. 113–131). New York: Macmillan.

Saal, F. E., Johnson, C. B., & Weber, N. (1989). Friendly or sexy? It may depend on whom you ask. *Psychology of Women Quarterly, 13,* 263–276.

Sadker, M., & Sadker, D. (1994) *Failing at fairness: How America's schools cheat girls.* New York: Charles Scribner's Sons.

Sadker, M., Sadker, D., & Klein, S. (1991). The issue of gender in elementary and secondary education. In G. Grant (Ed.), *Review of research in education,* Vol. 17 (pp. 269–334). Washington, DC: American Educational Research Association.

Safilios-Rothschild, C. (1979). *Sex-role socialization and discrimination: A synthesis and critique of the literature.* Washington, DC: National Institute of Education.

Saluter, A. F. (1992). Marital status and living arrangements: March 1992. *Current Population Reports, Series P,* 420–468.

Sanday, P. R. (1981). The socio-cultural context of rape: A cross-cultural study. *Journal of Social Issues, 37,* 5–27.

Sanders, S. A., & Reinisch, J. M. (1999). Would you say you "had sex" if. . . . *Journal of the American Medical Association, 281,* 275–277.

Sarafino, E. R. (1994). *Health psychology: Biopsychosocial interactions.* New York: Wiley.

Sargent, C., & Harris, M. (1992). Gender ideology, childrearing, and child health in Jamaica. *American Ethnologist, 19*(3), 523–537.

Satyaswaroop, P. G., Zaino, R. J., & Mortel, R. (1983). Human endometrial adenocarcinoma transplanted into nude mice: Growth regulation by estradiol. *Science, 219,* 58–60.

Savin-Williams, R. C. (1979). Dominance hierarchies in groups of early adolescents. *Child Development, 50,* 923–935.

Sayers, J. (1992). Feminism, psychoanalysis and psychotherapy. In J. M. Ussher & P. Nicolson (Eds.), *Gender issues in clinical psychology* (pp. 194–211). London: Routledge.

Scanzoni, L., & Scanzoni, J. J. (1976). *Men, women, and change: A sociology of marriage and the family.* New York: McGraw-Hill.

Scanzoni, J., & Szinovacz, M. (1980). *Family decision-making: A developmental sex role model.* Beverly Hills, CA: Sage.

Scarf, M. (1979). The more sorrowful sex. *Psychology Today, 12*(11), 44–52, 89.

Scarr, S. (1988). Race and gender as psychological variables. *American Psychologist, 43,* 56–59.

Schaie, K. W. (1994). *The course of adult intellectual development.* Unpublished manuscript. University Park: Pennsylvania State University.

Schatten, G., & Schatten, H. (1983). The energetic egg. *The Sciences, 23*(5), 28–34.

Schatz, M. S., & Bane, W. (1991). Empowering the parents of children in substitute care: A training model. *Child Welfare, 70,* 665–678.

Schlegal, A. (1973). The adolescent socialization of the Hopi girl. *Ethnology, 12,* 449–462.

Schlegal, A., & Barry, H., III. (1991). *Adolescence: An anthropological inquiry.* New York: Plenum Press.

Schlesinger, B. (1982). Lasting marriages in the 1980s. *Conciliation Courts Review, 20,* 43–49.

Schlossberg, N. K. (1984). The midlife woman as student. In G. Baruch & J. Brooks-Gunn (Eds.), *Women in midlife* (pp. 315–339). New York: Plenum Press.

Schmelkin, L. P., Wachtel, A. B., Schneiderman, B. E., & Hecht, D. (1988). The dimensional structure of medical students' perceptions of diseases. *Journal of Behavioral Medicine, 11,* 171–184.

Schneider, B. F. (1987). Graduate women, sexual harassment, and university policy. *General Hospital Psychiatry, 58,* 46–65.

Schneir, M. (Ed.). (1972). *Feminism: The essential historical writings.* New York: Vintage.

Schrire, C., & Steiger, W. I. (1974). A matter of life and death: An investigation into the practice of female infanticide in the Arctic. *Man, 9,* 161–184.

Schur, E. M. (1984). *Labeling women deviant: Gender, stigma and control.* Philadelphia: Temple University Press.

Schwartz, R. A. (1986). Abortion on request: The psychiatric implications. In J. D. Butler & D. F. Walbert (Eds.), *Abortion and the law* (3rd ed.) (pp. 323–337). Dublin, Ireland: Round Hall Sweet & Maxwell.

Scrimshaw, S. (1984). Infanticide in human populations: Social and individual concerns. In G. Hausfater & S. Hrdy (Eds.), *Infanticide: Comparative and evolutionary perspectives* (pp. 463–486). New York: Aldine.

Searles, P., & Berger, R. J. (1987). The current status of rape reform legislation: An examination of state statutes. *Women's Rights Law Reporter, 10,* 25–43.

Seavey, C. A., Katz, P. A., & Zalk, S. R. (1975). Baby X: The effects of gender labels on adult responses to infants. *Sex Roles, 1,* 103–109.

Sechzer, J. A. (1993). Sex bias in animal research: A question of generalization. Symposium on "Sex Bias in Research: Are Males and Females the Same?" *Annual Meeting of the American Association for the Advancement of Science.* Boston: AAAS.

Sechzer, J. A., Denmark, F. L., & Rabinowitz, V. C. (1993). Gender bias in women's health research. Proceedings of the NIH–Office of Research on Women's Health, *Recruitment and Retention of Women in Clinical Trials.* Huntsville, MD.

Sechzer, J. A., Griffin, A., & Pfafflin, S. M. (1994). Women's health and paradigm change. In J. A. Sechzer, A. Griffin, & S. M. Pfafflin (Eds.), *Forging a women's health research agenda: Policy issues for the 1990's. Annals of the New York Academy of Sciences, 736,* 2–20.

Sechzer, J. A., Pfafflin, S. M., Denmark, F. L., Griffin, A., & Blumenthal, S. J. (1994). Women and mental health: An introduction. In J. A. Sechzer, S. M. Pfafflin, F. L. Denmark, A. Griffin, & S. J. Blumenthal (Eds.), *Women and Mental Health. Annals of the New York Academy of Sciences, 789,* vii–x.

Sechzer, J. A., Rabinowitz, V. C., Denmark, F. L., McGinn, M. F., Weeks, B. M., & Wilkins, C. L. (1994). Sex and gender bias in animal research and in clinical studies of cancer, cardiovascular disease, and depression. In J. A. Sechzer, A. Griffin, & S. M. Pfafflin (Eds.), *Forging a women's health research agenda: Policy issues for the 1990's: Annals of the New York Academy of Sciences, 736,* 21–48. New York: The New York Academy of Sciences.

Sechzer, J. A., Zmitrovich, A., & Denmark, F. L. (1985, October). Sex bias in research. Symposium on "Sex and Gender Bias in Psychological Research." *Program of the Section of Psychology of the New York Academy of Sciences,* New York, NY.

Seed, M. (1994). Postmenopausal hormone replacement therapy, coronary heart disease and plasma lipoproteins. *Drugs, 47*(Suppl. 2), 25–34.

Seegmiller, B. (1993). Pregnancy. In F. Denmark & M. Paludi (Eds.), *Psychology of women: A handbook of issues and theories* (pp. 437–474). Westport, CT: Greenwood.

Seller, M. (1981). G. Stanley Hall & Edward Thorndike on the education of women: Theory and policy in the progressive era. *Educational Studies, 11,* 365–374.

Selye, H. (1956) *The stress of life.* New York: McGraw-Hill.

Serafino, E. P. (1994). *Health psychology: Biopsychosocial interactions.* New York: Wiley.

Serbin, L. A., Connor, J. M., Buchardt, C. J., & Citron, C. C. (1979). Effects of peer presence on sex-typing of children's play behavior. *Journal of Experimental Child Psychology, 27,* 303–309.

Serbin, L. A., Moller, L., Powlishta, K., & Gulko, J. (1991, April). *The emergence of gender segregation and behav-*

ioral compatibility in toddlers' peer preferences. Paper presented at the biennial meeting of the Society for Research in Child Development, Seattle, WA.

Serbin, L. A., O'Leary, K. D., Kent, R., & Tonick, I. (1973). A comparison of teacher response to preacademic and problem behavior of boys and girls. *Child Development, 44,* 796–804.

Serril, M. S. (1993, June 21). Defiling the children. *Newsweek,* 52–55.

Shaffer, D. R., & Wegley, C. (1974). Success orientation and sex role congruence as determinants of the attractiveness of competent women. *Journal of Personality, 42,* 586–600.

Shafter, R. (1992). Women and masochism: An introduction to trends in psychoanalytic thinking. *Issues in Ego Psychology, 15,* 56–62.

Shapiro, H. I. (1988). *The new birth-control book: A complete guide for women and men.* Englewood Cliffs, NJ: Prentice Hall.

Shaywitz, B. A., Shaywitz, S. E., Pugh, K. R., Constable, R. T., Skudlarski, P., Fulbright, R. K., Bronen, R. A., Fletcher, J. M., Shankweller, D. P., Katz, L., & Gore, G. C. (1995). Sex differences in the functional organization of the brain for language. *Nature, 373,* 607–609.

Sheehy, G. (1974). *Passages.* New York: Bantam Books.

Shelton, B. A. (1992). *Women, men and time: Gender differences in paid work, housework, and leisure.* New York: Greenwood Press.

Shenk, D., & Fullmer, E. (1996). Significant relationships among older women: Cultural and personal constructions of lesbianism. In K. A. Roberto (Ed.), *Relationships between women in later life* (pp. 75–89). New York: Harrington Park Press/Haworth Press.

Shepard, G. B. (1991). A glimpse of kindergarten—Chinese style. *Young Children, 47,* 11–15.

Sherwin, B. B. (1998). Estrogen and cognitive functioning in women. *Estrogen and Cognition, 217,* 17–22.

Sherwin, L. N. (1987). *Psychosocial dimensions of the pregnant family.* New York: Springer.

Shields, S. (1975). Functionalism, Darwinism, and the psychology of women. *American Psychologists, 30,* 739–754.

Shlapentokh, V. (1984, February 4). In Soviet Union, women emerge superior. *New York Times,* p. 23.

Shochley, W. (1971). Negro I.Q. Deficit: Failure of a malicious coincidence model warrants new research proposals. *Review of Educational Research, 41,* 227–248.

Short, R. V. (1982). Sex determination and differentiation. In C. R. Austin & R. V. Short (Eds.), *Reproduction in mammals* (2nd ed.) (Vol. 2) (pp. 70–113).

Shorter, E. (1975). *The making of the modern family.* New York: Basic Books.

Showalter, E. (1985). *The female malady: Women, madness, and culture, 1830–1980.* New York: Penguin.

Shulman, A. K. (1980). Theories of mate selection. In W. Henslin (Ed.), *Marriage and family in a changing society.* New York: Free Press.

Shum, L. M. (1996). Asian-American women: Cultural and mental health issues. In J. A. Sechzer, S. M. Pfafflin, F. L. Denmark, A. Griffin, & S. Blumenthal (Eds.), *Women and mental health. Annals of the New York Academy of Sciences, 789* (181–190). New York: The New York Academy of Sciences.

Sidel, R. (1993). Who are the poor? In V. Cyrus (Ed.), *Experiencing race, class, and gender in the United States* (pp. 123–128). Mountain View, CA: Mayfield.

Sidorowicz, L. S., & Lunney, G. S. (1980). Baby X revisited. *Sex Roles, 6,* 67–73.

Signorelli, N. (1989). Television and conceptions about sex roles: Maintaining conventionality and the status quo. *Sex Roles, 21*(5/6), 341–352.

Silverman, I., & Eals, M. (1992). Sex differences in spatial abilities: Evolutionary theory and data. In J. Barkow, L. Cosmides, & J. Tooby (Eds.), *The adapted mind: Evolutionary psychology and the generation of culture* (pp. 533–549). New York: Oxford University Press.

Silverstein, L. B. (1996). Fathering is a feminist issue. *Psychology of Women Quarterly, 20,* 3–37.

Silverstein, L. B., & Phares, V. (1996). Expanding the mother-child paradigm: An examination of dissertation research 1986–1994. *Psychology of Women Quarterly, 20*(1), 39–53.

Simmons, R. G., & Blyth, D. A. (1987). *Moving into adolescence: The impact of pubertal change and school context.* New York: Aldine De Gruyter.

Simmons, R. G., Blyth, D. A., Van Cleave, E. F., & Bush, D. M. (1979). Entry into early adolescence: The impact of school structure, puberty, and early dating on self-esteem. *American Sociological Review, 44,* 948–967.

Simon, R. W. (1992). Parental role strain, salience of parental identity and gender differences in psychological distress. *Journal of Health and Social Behavior, 33,* 25–35.

Singer, J., & Singer, I. (1972). Types of female orgasm. *Journal of Sex Research, 8,* 255–267.

Singh, D. (1993). Adaptive significance of waist-to-hip ratio and female physical attractiveness. *Journal of Personality and Social Psychology, 65,* 293–307.

Singh, S. (1994). Gender differences in work values and personality characteristics among Indian executives. *Journal of Social Psychology, 134*(5), 699–700.

Slonim-Nevo, V. (1992). First premarital intercourse among Mexican-American and Anglo-American adolescent women: Interpreting ethnic differences. *Journal of Adolescent Research, 7,* 332–351.

Small, H. (1996). *Love's madness: Medicine, the novel, and female insanity.* Oxford, England: Oxford University Press.

Small, M. F. (1999). A woman's curse. *The Sciences, 39*(1), 24–29.

Smetana, J. G. (1988). Concepts of self and social convention: Adolescents' and parents' reasoning about hypothetical and actual family conflicts. In M. Gunnar & W. A. Collins (Eds.), *Development during the transition to adolescence: Minnesota symposia on child psychology* (Vol. 21) (pp. 79–119). Hillsdale, NJ: Erlbaum.

Smith, A. D. (1977). Adult age differences in cued recall. *Developmental Psychology, 13,* 326–331.

Smith, G. J. (1985). Facial and full-length ratings of attractiveness related to the social interactions of young children. *Sex Roles, 12,* 287–293.

Smith, H. (1994). *Worlds religions: A guide to our wisdom traditions.* New York: HarperCollins.

Smith, H. S., Handy, R. T., & Loetscher, L. A. (1960). *American Christianity, Volume I. 1607–1620.* New York: Charles Scribner.

Smith, J. I. (1985). Women, religion and social change in early Islam. In Y. Y. Haddad & E. B. Findly (Eds.), *Women, religion and social change* (pp. 19–36). Albany, NY: State University of New York Press.

Smith, W. D., Burlew, A. K., Mosley, M. H., & Whitney, W. M. (1978). *Minority issues in mental health.* Reading, MA: Addison-Wesley.

Smuts, B. (1995). The evolutionary origins of patriarchy. *Human Nature, 6,* 1–32.

Snipp, C. M., & Aytac, I. A. (1990). The labor force participation of American Indian women. *Research in human capital and development, 6,* 189–211.

Sommers, C. H. (1994). *Who stole feminism? How women have betrayed women.* New York: Simon & Schuster.

Song, Y. (1993). Asian American women's experience in the crossfire of cultural conflict. In Y. Song & E. Kim (Eds.), *American mosaic: Selected readings on America's multicultural heritage* (pp. 186–203). Englewood, Cliffs, NJ: Prentice Hall.

Sonnert, G., & Holton, G. (1995). *Who succeeds in science? The gender dimension.* New Brunswick, NJ: Rutgers University Press.

Sonnert, G., & Holton, G. (1996). Career patterns of women and men in the sciences. *American Scientist, 84,* 63–71.

Spalter-Roth, R., Kalleberg, A. L., Rasell, E., Cassirer, N., Reskin, B. F., Hudson, K., Appelbaum, E., & Dooley, B. L. (1997). *Managing work and family: Nonstandard work arrangements among managers and professionals.* Washington, DC: Economic Policy Institute.

Specter, M. (1998, July 10). Population implosion worries graying Europe. *New York Times,* pp. A1, A6.

Spelman, E. V. (1988). *The inessential woman: Problems of exclusion in feminist thought.* Boston: Beacon Press.

Spence, J. T., Helmreich, R. L., & Stapp, J. (1974). The personal attributes questionnaire: A measure of sex-role stereotypes and masculinity/femininity. *JSAS Catalog of Selected Documents in Psychology, 4,* 43.

Spickard, P. R. (1992). The illogic of American racial categories. In M. P. P. Root (Ed.), *Racially mixed people in America* (pp. 12–23). Newbury Park, CA: Sage.

Sprecher, S. (1985). Sex differences in bases of power in dating relationships. *Sex Roles, 12*(3/4), 449–462.

Spurlock, J. (1984). Black women in the middle years. In G. Baruch & J. Brooks-Gunn (Eds.), *Women in midlife* (pp. 245–260). New York: Plenum Press.

Squyres, S., Jacobs, N., & Quiram, J. (Eds.). (1996). Minorities: A changing role in American society. *The information series on current topics.* New York: Wylie—Information Plus.

Stack, C. (1974). *All our kin.* New York: Harper & Row.

Stacy, R. D., Prisbell, M., & Tollefsrud, K. (1992). A comparison of attitudes among college students toward sexual violence committed by strangers and by acquaintances: A research report. *Journal of Sex Education and Therapy, 18,* 257–263.

Stahly, G. B. (1996). Battered women: Why don't they just leave? In J. C. Chrisler, C. Golden, & P. D. Rozee (Eds.), *Lectures on the psychology of women.* New York: McGraw-Hill.

Stampfer, M. J., Colditz, G. A., Willett, W. C., Manson, J. E., Rosner, B., Speiser, F. E., & Hennekens, C. H. (1991). Postmenopausal, estrogen therapy and cardiovascular disease: Ten-year follow-up from the nurses' health study. *New England Journal of Medicine, 325,* 756–762.

Stanley, J. (1977). Paradigmatic woman: The prostitute. In D. Shores (Ed.), *Papers in language variation* (pp. 303–321). Birmingham: University of Alabama Press.

Staples, R. (1993). Black men/Black women: Changes in roles and relationships. In A. Minas (Ed.), *Gender basics: Feminist perspectives on women and men* (pp. 252–262). Belmont, CA: Wadsworth.

Staples, R., & Johnson, L. B. (1993). *Black families at the crossroads: Challenges and prospects.* San Francisco: Jossey-Bass.

Stark, E., & Flitcraft, A. (1988). Violence among intimates: An epidemiological review. In V. B. Van Hasselt & R. L. Morrison (Eds.), *Handbook of family violence* (pp. 293–317). New York: Plenum.

States, M. S., & Bane, W. (1991). Empowering the parents of children in substitute care: A training model. *Child Welfare, 70,* 665–678.

Stead, D. (1996, January 7). Breaking the glass ceiling with the power of words. *New York Times,* p. 6F.

Steckel, A. (1987). Psychosocial development of children of lesbian mothers. In F. N. Bozett (Ed.), *Gay and lesbian parents* (pp. 75–85). New York: Praeger.

Steele, C. M. (1997). A threat in the air: How stereotypes shape intellectual identity and performance. *American Psychologist, 52,* 613–629.

Steele, C. M., & Aronson, J. (1995). Stereotype threat and the intellectual test performance of African Americans. *Journal of Personality and Social Psychology, 69,* 797–811.

Steering Committee of the Physician's Health Study Research Group (1989). Final report from the aspirin component of the ongoing physician's health study. *New England Journal of Medicine, 321,* 129–135.

Steig, R. L., & Williams, R. C. (1983). Chronic pain as a biosociocultural phenomenon: Implications for treatment. *Seminars in Neurology, 3,* 370–376.

Steil, J. M. I. (1997). *Marital equality: Its relationship to the well-being of husbands and wives.* Thousand Oaks, CA: Sage.

Steil, J. M., & Turetsky, B. (1987). Marital influence levels and symptomatology among wives. In F. Crosby (Ed.), *Relative deprivation and working women* (pp. 74–90). New York: Oxford University Press.

Stein, J. H., & Reiser, L. W. (1994). A study of white middle-class adolescent boys' responses to "semenarche" (the first ejaculation). *Journal of Youth and Adolescence, 23,* 373–384.

Steinbacher, R., & Gilroy, F. D. (1996). Technology for sex selection: Current status and utilization. *Psychological Reports, 79,* 728–730.

Steinberg, L. (1981). Transformations in family relations at puberty. *Developmental Psychology, 17,* 833–840.

Steinberg, L. (1993). *Adolescence* (3rd ed.). New York: McGraw-Hill.

Steinhart, E. (1992). The effects of perceived status and degree of accentedness on listeners' social judgments. Unpublished doctoral project, Pace University, New York.

Steinmetz, S. K., & Lucca, J. S. (1988). Husband battering. In V. B. Van Hasselt, R. L. Morrison, A. S. Bellack, & M. Hersen (Eds.), *Handbook of family violence* (pp. 233–246). New York: Plenum.

Sternbach, R. A., & Tursky, B. (1965). Ethnic differences among housewives in psychophysical and skin potential responses to electric shock. *Psychophysiology, 1,* 241–246.

Sternberg, R. J. (1988). Triangulating love. In R. J. Sternberg & M. L. Barnes (Eds.), *The psychology of love* (pp. 119–138). New Haven, CT: Yale University Press.

Sternberg, R. J., & McGrane, P. A. (1993). *Intellectual development across the life span.* Unpublished manuscript, Yale University, New Haven, CT.

Stevens, E. (1973). Machismo and marianismo. *Transaction Society, 10*(6), 57–63.

Stevens, E. P. (1993). Marianismo: The other face of machismo in Latin America. In A. Minas (Ed.), *Gender basics: Feminist perspectives on women and men.* Belmont, CA: Wadsworth.

Stevenson, M. R., & Black, K. N. (1988). Paternal absence and sex-role development: A meta-analysis. *Child Development, 59*(3), 793–814.

Stewart, A. J. (1998). Doing personality research: How can feminist theories help? In B. M. Clinchy & J. K. Norem (Eds.), *The gender and psychology reader* (pp. 54–68). New York: New York University Press.

Stieg, R. L., & Williams, R. C. (1983). Chronic pain as a biosociocultural phenomenon: Implications for treatment. *Seminars in Neurology, 3,* 370–376. Cited by Bloom, 1988, p. 240.

Stockard, J., & Johnson, M. M. (1992). *Sex and gender in society.* Englewood Cliffs, NJ: Prentice Hall.

Stolberg, S. (1998, April 3). Rise in smoking by young blacks erodes a success story. *New York Times,* p. A24.

Stoller, E. P., & Cutler, S. J. (1992). The impact of gender on configurations of care among married elderly couples. *Research on Aging, 14*(3), 313–330.

Stoltenberg, J. (1993). Gays and the pornography movement. In A. Minas (Ed.), *Gender basics: Feminist perspectives on women and men.* Belmont, CA: Wadsworth.

Stoltzman, S. M. (1986). Menstrual attitudes, beliefs, and symptom experiences of adolescent females, their peers, and their mothers. *Health Care for Women International, 7,* 97–114.

Stone, G. C. (1979). Health and the health system: A historical overview and conceptual framework. In G. C. Stone, F. Cohen, & N. E. Adler (Eds.), *Health psychology—A handbook* (pp. 1–17). San Francisco: Jossey-Bass.

Storer, J. H. (1992). Gender and kin role transposition as an accommodation to father-daughter incest. In T. L. Whitehead & B. V. Reid (Eds.), *Gender constructs and social issues* (pp. 70–102). Urbana, IL: University of Illinois Press.

Storms, M. D. (1981). A theory of erotic orientation development. *Psychological Review, 88,* 340–353.

Straus, M., Gelles, R., & Steinmetz, S. (1980). *Behind closed doors: Violence in America.* Garden City, NY: Doubleday.

Straus, M. A., & Gelles, R. J. (1986). Societal change and change in family violence from 1975 to 1985 as revealed by two national surveys. *Journal of Marriage and the Family, 48,* 465–479.

Strawbridge, W. J., Kaplan, G. A., Camacho, T., & Cohen, R. D. (1992). The dynamics of disability and functional change in an elderly cohort: Results from the Alameda County Study. *Journal of the American Geriatrics Society, 40*(8), 799–806.

Stricken, L. J., Rock, D. A., & Burton, N. W. (1993). Sex differences in predictions of college grades from scholastic aptitude scores. *Journal of Educational Psychology, 85,* 710–718.

Strickland, B. R. (1988). Sex related differences in health and illness. *Psychology of Women Quarterly, 12,* 381–399.

Struckman-Johnson, C. (1991). Male victims of acquaintance rape. In A. Parrot & L. Bechofer (Eds.), *Acquaintance rape: The hidden crime* (pp. 192–213). New York: Wiley.

Stuenkel, C. A. (1989). Menopause and estrogen replacement therapy. *Psychiatric Clinics of North America, 12*(1), 133–152.

Stueve, A., & O'Donnell, L. (1984). The daughter of aging parents. In G. Baruch & J. Brooks-Gunn (Eds.), *Women in midlife* (pp. 203–225). New York: Plenum Press.

Sudarkasa, N. (1988). Interpreting the African heritage in Afro-American family organization. In H. P. McAdoo (Ed.), *Black families* (2nd ed.) (pp. 27–43). Newbury Park, CA: Sage.

Sue, S. (1988). Psychotherapeutic services for ethnic minorities, *American Psychologist, 43,* 301–308.

Sugarman, D. B., & Hotaling, G. T. (1989). Violent men in intimate relationships. An analysis of risk markers. *Journal of Applied Social Psychology, 19,* 1034–1048.

Sukemune, S., Shiraishi, T., Shirakawa, Y., & Matsumi, J. T. (1993). Life in Japan. In L. L. Adler (Ed.), *International handbook of gender roles* (pp. 174–186). Westport, CT: Greenwood Press.

Sullivan, J. P., & Mosher, D. L. (1990). Acceptance of guided imagery of marital rape as a function of macho personality. *Violence and Victims, 5,* 275–286.

Swaab, D. F., & Fliers, E. (1985). A sexually dimorphic nucleus in the human brain. *Science, 188,* 1112–1115.

Swerdlow, M. (1989). Men's accommodations to women entering a nontraditional occupation: A case of rapid transit operatives. *Gender & Society 3,* 373–387.

Swidler, A. (1983). Love and adulthood in American culture. In A. Skolmad & J. Skolnick (Eds.), *Family in transition* (pp. 223–228) (4th ed.). Boston: Little, Brown.

Swidler, L. (1976). *Women in Judaism: The status of woman in formative Judaism.* Metuchen, NJ: Scarecrow Press.

Swim, J. K., & Sanna, L. J. (1996). He's skilled; she's lucky: A meta-analysis of observers' attributions for women's and men's successes and failures. *Personality and Social Psychology Bulletin, 22,* 507–519.

Symons, D. (1979). *The evolution of human sexuality.* Garden City, NY: Doubleday.

Szmukler, G. I., Eisler, I., Russell, G. F. M., & Dare, C. (1985). Anorexia nervosa, "parental expressed emotion" and dropping out of treatment. *British Journal of Psychiatry, 147,* 265–271.

Taeuber, C. (Ed.). (1991). *Statistical handbook on women in America.* Phoenix, AZ: Oryx Press.

Tafoya, T. (1989). Circles and cedar: Native Americans and family therapy. In G. W. Saba, B. M. Karrer, & K. V. Hardy (Eds.), *Minorities and family therapy* (pp. 71–96). Binghamton, NY: Haworth Press.

Tallichet, S. E. (1995). Gendered relations in the mines and the division of labor underground. *Gender & Society, 9*(6), 697–711.

Tamir, L. M. (1982). *Men in their forties: The transition to middle age.* New York: Springer.

Tangri, S., Burt, M. R., & Johnson, L. B. (1982). Sexual harassment at work: Three explanatory models. *Journal of Social Issues, 38,* 33–54.

Tannahill, R. (1982). *Sex in history.* New York: Stein and Day.

Tannen, D. (1990). *You just don't understand: Men and women in conversation.* New York: Morrow.

Tavard, G. (1973). *Woman in Christian tradition.* Notre Dame, IN: University of Notre Dame Press. Cited by Swidler, 1976, pp. 27–28.

Tavris, C., & Sadd, S. (1977). *The Redbook report on female sexuality.* New York: Delacorte.

Taylor, S. E. (1995). *Health psychology* (3rd ed.). New York: McGraw-Hill.

Terpstra, D. E. (1986). Organizational costs of sexual harassment. *Journal of Employment Counseling, 23,* 112–119.

Terpstra, D. E., & Baker, D. D. (1986). A framework for the study of sexual harassment. *Basic and Applied Social Psychology, 7,* 17–34.

Thoits, P. A. (1987a). Gender and marital status differences in control and distress: Common stress versus unique stress explanations. *Journal of Health and Social Behavior, 28,* 7–22.

Thoits, P. A. (1987b). Position paper. In A. Eichler & D. L. Parron (Eds.), *Women's mental health: Research agenda for the future* (DHHS publication number ADM87–1542). Washington, DC: U.S. Government Printing Office.

Thomas, A., & Sillen, S. (1979). *Racism & psychiatry.* Secaucus, NJ: Citadel Press.

Thompson, L. (1991). Family work: Women's sense of fairness. *Journal of Family Issues, 12,* 181–196.

Thornhill, N. W., & Thornhill, R. (1991). Coercive sexuality of men: Is there psychological adaptation to rape? In E. Grauerholz & M. A. Koralewski (Eds.), *Sexual coercion: A sourcebook in its nature, causes, and prevention* (pp. 91–107). Lexington, MA: Lexington Books/D. C. Heath.

Thornton, A. (1989). Changing attitudes toward family issues in the United States. *Journal of Marriage and the Family, 51,* 873–894.

Thorpe, T. C. (1989). Caregiving: What do midlife lesbians view as important? *Journal of Gay and Lesbian Psychotherapy, 1*(1), 87–103.

Thurston, B. (1998). *Women in the new testament: Questions and commentary.* New York: Crossroad-Herder.

Tidball, M. E. (1973). Perspective on academic women and affirmative action. *Educational Record, 54,* 130–135.

Till, F. J. (1980). *Sexual harassment: A report on the sexual harassment of students.* Report of the National Advisory Council on Women's Educational Programs, U.S. Department of Education.

Time, 1973, January 8. Cited by Diamond and Sigmundson, 1997, p. 299.

Todd, J., Friedman, A., & Kariuki, P. W. (1990). Women growing stronger with age: The effect of status in the United States and Kenya. *Psychology of Women Quarterly, 14,* 567–577.

Tolman, D. L. (1992). Voicing the body: A psychological study of adolescent girls' sexual desire. Unpublished dissertation, Harvard University.

Tomkiewicz, J., & Hughes, R. E. (1993). Women who choose business administration versus women who choose administrative services: How they differ. *Journal of Applied Social Psychology, 23*(11), 867–874.

Tong, R. (1982). Feminism, pornography and censorship. *Social Theory and Practice, 8,* 1–17.

Tong, R. (1989). *Feminist thought: A comprehensive introduction.* Boulder, CO: Westview Press.

Torack, R. M. (1982). Historical aspects of normal and abnormal brain fluids. *Archives of Neurology, 39,* 197–201.

Toubia, N. (1993). *Female genital mutilation: Call for global action.* New York: Women, Ink.

Touchette, N. (1993). Estrogen signals a novel route to pain relief. *Journal of NIH Research, 5,* 53–58.

Travis, C. B. (1988). *Women and health psychology: Biomedical issues.* Hillsdale, NJ: Erlbaum.

Travis, C. B. (1998). *Woman and health psychology: Mental health issues.* Hillsdale NJ: Erlbaum. Cited by Matlin, 1996, pp. 480–482.

Triandes, H. (1994). *Culture and social behavior.* New York: McGraw Hill.

Troll, L. E. (1989). Myths of midlife intergenerational relationships. In S. Hunter & M. Sundel (Eds.), *Midlife myths* (pp. 210–231). Newbury Park, CA: Sage.

Turner, B. & Turner, C. (1992). Who treats minorities? Paper presented at the meeting of the Eastern American Psychological Association, April, 1992, Boston.

Tursky, B., & Sternbach, R. A. (1967). Further physiological correlates of ethnic differences in responses to shock. *Psychophysiology, 4,* 67–74.

Uchitelle, L. (1974, November 28). Women in their 50s follow many paths into workplace. *New York Times,* pp. A1, B8.

Uchitelle, L. (1996, August 23). Despite drop, rate of layoff remains high. *New York Times,* p. A1.

Udall, L. (1977). *Me and mine: The life story of Helen Sekequaptewa.* Tucson, AZ: University of Arizona Press.

Udry, J. R., & Billy, J. O. G. (1987). Initiation of coitus in early adolescence. *American Sociological Review, 52,* 841–855.

Udry, J. R., Billy, J. O. G., Morris, N. M., Groff, T. R., Raj, M. H. (1985). Serum androgenic hormones motivate sexual behavior in adolescent boys. *Fertility and Sexuality, 43,* 90–94.

Udvardy, M. (1992). The fertility of the post-fertile: Concepts of gender, aging, and reproductive health among the Giriama of Kenya. *Journal of Cross-Cultural Gerontology, 7*(4), 289–306.

Unger, R. K. (1979). *Female and male psychological perspectives.* New York: Harper & Row.

Unger, R. K. (1981). Sex as a social reality: Field and laboratory research. *Psychology of Women Quarterly, 5,* 645–653.

Unger, R. K. (1995). Conclusion: Cultural diversity and the future of feminist psychology. In H. Landrine (Ed.), *Bringing cultural diveristy to feminist psychology: Theory,*

research, and practice (pp. 413–431). Washington, DC: American Psychological Association.

Unger, R. K., & Crawford, M. (1992). *Women and gender: A feminist psychology.* New York: McGraw-Hill.

Unger, R. K., & Crawford, M. (1996). *Women and gender: A feminist psychology* (2nd ed.). New York: McGraw-Hill.

United Nations. (1991). *The world's women 1970–1990: Trends and statistics.* New York: Author.

United Nations. (1993). Rape and the abuse of women in the territory of former Yugoslavia (*UN Document E/CN.4/1993/L.21*). Geneva, Switzerland: Author.

United Nations Conference on Female Genital Mutilation. (1998). A paper presented by the Honorable Jane F. Kuka, New York.

Urbancic, J. C. (1987). Incest trauma. *Journal of Psychosocial Nursing, 25,* 33–35.

U.S. Bureau of the Census. (1988a). *Current population reports: Population profile of the United States, 1987.* Special Studies, Series P-23, No. 150. Washington, DC: U.S. Government Printing Office.

U.S. Bureau of the Census. (1988b). *Statistical abstract of the United States: 1987.* Washington, DC: U.S. Government Printing Office.

U.S. Bureau of the Census. (1991). Marital status and living arrangements: March, 1990. *Current Population Reports,* Series P-20, No. 450. Washington, DC: U.S. Government Printing Office.

U.S. Bureau of the Census. (1992). Current population reports, series p. 20, no. 459. *The Asian and Pacific Islander population in the United States: March 1991 and 1990.* Washington, DC: U.S. Government Printing Office.

U.S. Bureau of the Census. (1993). Educational attainment in the U.S. In *Current Population Report Series* (pp. 20–476). Washington, DC: U.S. Government Printing Office.

U.S. Bureau of the Census. (1994, February). New racial and ethnic information debunks stereotypes. *Monthly News from the U. S. Bureau of the Census: Census and You,* 29(2), 4–5. Washington, DC: U.S. Government Printing Office.

U.S. Bureau of the Census. (1998c, February 18). Press-Release ch98–126. Washington, DC: U.S. Government Printing Office.

U.S. Bureau of the Census. (1998d, July 27). *Current population survey.* Washington, DC: U.S. Government Printing Office.

U.S. Department of Commerce, Bureau of the Census. (1990). *Statistical abstract of the United States.* Washington, DC: U.S. Government Printing Office.

U.S. Department of Commerce. (1998). *U.S. Census Bureau: The official statistics.* Washington, DC: U.S. Government Printing Office.

U.S. Department of Health & Human Services. (1992). *Sexually transmitted diseases.* Washington, DC: U.S. Government Printing Office.

U.S. Department of Health and Human Services. (1996). Vol. 46, No. 11. Washington, DC: U.S. Government Printing Office.

U.S. Department of Health and Human Services, Centers for Disease Control, Operational Research Section, Behavioral and Prevention Research Branch, Division of STD/HIV Prevention, Center for Prevention Services. (1992b). *What we have learned from the AIDS Community Demonstration Projects.* Atlanta: Centers for Disease Control.

U.S. Department of Labor. (1993). *20 facts on women workers.* Washington, DC: U.S. Government Printing Office.

U.S. Merit Systems Protection Board. (1981). *Sexual harassment of federal workers: Is it a problem?* Washington, DC: U.S. Government Printing Office.

Ussher, J. (1989). *The psychology of the female body.* London: Routledge.

Valian, V. (1998). *Why so slow? The advancement of women.* Cambridge, MA: MIT Press.

Van Goozen, S. H. M., Cohen-Kettenis, P. T., Gooren, L. J. G., Frijda, N. H., & Van de Poll, N. E. (1995). Gender differences in behavior: Activating effects of cross-sex hormones. *Psychoneuroendocrinology, 20,* 343–363.

Van Keep, P. A. (1976). Psychosocial aspects of the climacteric. In P. A. Van Keep, R. B. Greenblatt, & M. Albeaux-Fernet (Eds.), *Consensus on menopause research.* Baltimore, MD: University Park Press.

Vannoy, D. (1991). Social differentiation, contemporary marriage, and human development. *Journal of Family Issues, 12*(3), 251–267.

Vasta, R., Knott, J. A., & Gaze, C. E. (1996). Can spatial training erase the gender differences on the water-level task? *Psychology of Women Quarterly, 20,* 549–568.

Vaughn, B. E., Block, J. H., & Block, J. (1988). Parental agreement on child rearing during early childhood and the psychological characteristics of adolescents. *Child Development, 59,* 1020–1033.

Vazquez-Nuttall, E., Romero-Garcia, I., & DeLeon, B. (1987). Sex roles and perceptions of feminity and masculinity of Hispanic women: A review of the literature. *Psychology of Women Quarterly, 11,* 409–426.

Vega, W. A., Warheit, G. J., & Meinhardt, K. (1984). Marital disruption and the prevalence of depressive symptomatology among Anglos and Mexican Americans. *Journal of Marriage and Family, 46,* 817–824.

Veniegas, R. C., & Peplau, L. A. (1997). Power and the quality of same-sex friendships. *Psychology of Women Quarterly, 21,* 279–297.

Verbrugge, L. M. (1979). Female illness rates and illness behavior. *Women and Health, 4*(1), 61–75.

Verbrugge, L. M. (1980). Sex differences in complaints and diagnoses. *Journal of Behavioral Medicine, 3*(4), 327–355.

Vierck, C. J., Jr. (1976). Extrapolations from the pain research literature to problems of adequate veterinary care. *Journal of the American Veterinary Association, 168*(6), 510–513.

Villarosa, L. (Ed.). (1994). *Body & soul: The Black women's guide to physical health and emotional well-being.* New York: Harper & Row.

Vredenberg, K., Krames, L., & Flett, G. L. (1986). Sex differences in the clinical expression of depression. *Sex Roles, 14,* 37–49.

Wade, C., & Tavris, C. (1994). The longest war: Gender and culture. In W. J. Lonner & R. S. Malpass (Eds.), *Psychology and culture* (pp. 121–126). Boston: Allyn & Bacon.

Waits, T. M., Johnson, D. H., Hainsworth, J. D., Hande, K. R., Thomas, M., & Grieco, F. A. (1992). Prolonged administration of oral etoposide in non-small cell lung cancer: A phase II trial. *Journal of Clinical Oncology, 10*(2), 292–296.

Wakefield, H., & Underwager, R. (1991). Female child sexual abusers: A critical review of the literature. *American Journal of Forensic Psychology, 9,* 43–69.

Waldman, C. (1992, May 4). Deadbeat dads. *Newsweek,* 46–52.

Waldron, I. (1976). Why do women live longer than men? *Social Science and Medicine, 10,* 349–362.

Walker, A. J., Pratt, C. C., & Wood, B. (1993). Perceived frequency of role conflict and relationship quality for caregiving daughters. *Psychology of Women Quarterly, 17,* 207–221.

Walker, L. E. (1990). A feminist therapist views the case. In D. W. Cantor (Ed.), *Women as therapists: A multitheoretical casebook* (pp. 78–95). New York: Springer. Cited by Matlin (1996), pp. 480–482.

Walker, L. E. A. (1979). *The battered woman.* New York: Harper & Row.

Wallach, H. R., Matlin, M. W., & Young, D. (1992). *College women's expectations about pregnancy, childbirth, and infant care: A prospective study.* Paper presented at Eastern Psychological Association, Boston.

Wallerstein, J. S. (1997, June 27). *New York Times.*

Wallerstein, J. S., & Blakeslee, S. (1989). *Second chances: Men, women and children a decade after divorce.* New York: Ticknor and Fields.

Wallerstein, J. S., & Kelly, J. B. (1980). *Surviving the breakup: How children and parents cope with divorce.* New York: Basic Books.

Wallston, B. S., DeVellis, B. M., & Wallston, K. (1983). Licensed practical nurses' sex role stereotypes. *Psychology of Women Quarterly, 7,* 199–208.

Walsh, P., & Connor, C. L. (1979). Old men and young women: How objectively are their skills assessed? *Journal of Gerontology, 34,* 561–568.

Ward, M. C. (1999). *A world full of women* (2nd ed.). Boston: Allyn & Bacon.

Waterman, J. (1986). Family dynamics of incest with young children. In K. MacFarlane & J. Waterman (Eds.), *Sexual abuse of young children: Evaluation and treatment* (pp. 197–203). New York: Guilford.

Waterman, J., & Lusk, R. (1986). Scope of the problem. In K. MacFarlane & J. Waterman (Eds.), *Sexual abuse of children: Evaluation and treatment* (pp. 3–14). New York: Guilford.

Watson, G., & Williams, J. (1992). Feminist practice in therapy. In J. M. Ussher & P. Nicholson (Eds.), *Gender issues in clinical psychology* (pp. 212–236). London: Routledge.

Webb, T. E., & VanDevere, C. A. (1985). Sex differences in the development of depression. *Sex Roles, 12,* 91–95.

Wechsler, D. (1972). "Hold" and "Don't Hold" test. In S. M. Chown (Ed.), *Human ageing* (pp. 25–34). New York: Penguin.

Weidiger, P. (1975). *Menstruation and menopause.* New York: Knopf.

Weigel, D., & Weigel, R. (1990). Congruency of preferences for family-based gender roles and family satisfaction in two-generation farm families. *Sex Roles, 22,* 649–659.

Weinberg, M. S., Williams, C. J., & Pryor, D. W. (1994). *Dual attraction: Understanding bisexuality.* New York: Oxford University Press.

Weiner, B. (1974). *Achievement motivation and attribution theory.* Morristown, NJ: General Learning Press.

Weiner, B. (1986). *An attributional theory of motivation and emotion.* New York: Springer-Verlag.

Weinraub, M., & Frankel, J. (1977). Sex differences in parent–infant interaction during free play, departure, and separation. *Child Development, 48,* 1240–1249.

Weisman, C. S., & Teitelbaum, M. A. (1985). Physician gender and the physician–patient relationship: Recent evidence and relevant questions. *Social Science and Medicine, 20,* 1119–1127.

Weiss, L. (1971). Additional evidence of a gradual loss of germ cells in the pathogenesis of streak ovaries in Turner's syndrome. *Journal of Medical Genetics, 6,* 540–544.

Weissberg, M. P. (1983). *Dangerous secrets: Maladaptive responses to stress.* New York: W. W. Norton.

Weissman, M. M., & Klerman, G. L. (1979). Sex differences and the epidemiology of depression. *Archives of General Psychiatry, 34,* 98–111.

Welch, D. (1987). American Indian women: Reaching beyond the myth. In C. Calloway (Ed.), *New directions in American Indian history* (pp. 31–48). Norman, OK: University of Oklahoma Press.

Welsh, D. P., & Powers, S. I. (1991). Gender differences in family interaction. In R. M. Lerner, A. C. Petersen, & J. Brooks-Gunn (Eds.), *Encyclopedia of adolescence* (pp. 334–339). New York: Garland Press.

Wendell, S. (1993). Toward a feminist theory of disability. In A. Minas (Ed.), *Gender basics: Feminist perspectives on women and men* (pp. 50–58). Belmont, CA: Wadsworth.

Wenger, N. K., Speroff, L., & Packard, B. P. (1993). Cardiovascular health and disease in women. *New England Journal of Medicine, 329*(4), 247–256.

Werry, J. S. (1986). Physical illness, symptoms, and allied disorders. In H. C. Quay & J. S. Werry (Eds.), *Psychopathologi-* cal disorders of childhood (3rd ed.) (pp. 232–293). New York: Wiley.

Weseen, S. (1999). *The myths of motherhood.* Unpublished manuscript. New York: The City University of New York.

West, C. (1994). *Race matters.* New York: Random House.

West, C., & Zimmerman, D. H. (1987). Going gender. *Gender and Society, 1,* 125–151.

Westkott, M. C. (1997). On the new psychology of women: A cautionary view. In M. R. Walsh (Ed.), *Women, men, and gender: Ongoing debates* (pp. 362–372). New Haven, CT: Yale University Press.

Westkott, M. (1998). Culture and women's health. In A. E. Blechman & K. D. Brownell (Eds.), *Behavioral medicine and women: A comprehensive handbook* (pp. 816–820). New York: Guilford Press.

Wheeler, L., Reis, H. T., & Bond, M. H. (1989). Collectivism–individualism in everyday social life: The middle kingdom and the melting pot. *Journal of Personality and Social Psychology, 45,* 945–953.

Wheeler, L., Reis, H., & Nezlek, J. (1994). Loneliness, social interaction, and sex roles. *Journal of Personality and Social Psychology, 45,* 943–953.

Wheeler, M. (1974). *No-fault divorce.* Boston: Beacon Press.

White, E. (Ed.). (1994). *The Black women's health book: Speaking for ourselves* (2nd ed.). Seattle, WA: Seal Press.

White, K. M., Speisman, J. C., Jackson, D., Bartis, S., & Costos, D. (1986). Intimacy maturity and its correlates in young married couples. *Journal of Personality and Social Psychology, 50,* 152–162.

White, S. W., & Kowalski, R. M. (1994). Deconstructing the myth of the nonaggressive woman: A feminist analysis. *Psychology of Women Quarterly, 18*(4), 487–508.

Wickelgren, I. (1997). Estrogen stakes claim to cognition. *Science, 276,* 675–678.

Wilbur, J., Dan, A., Hedricks, C., & Holm, K. (1990). The relationship among menopausal status, menopausal symptoms, and physical activity in midlife women. *Family and Community Health, 13*(3), 67–78.

Wilcox, V. L. (1992). Effects of patient's age, gender, and depression on medical students beliefs, attitudes, intentions, and behavior. *Journal of Applied Social Psychology, 22,* 1093–1110.

Will, J., Self, P., & Datan, N. (1976). Maternal behavior and perceived sex of infant. *American Journal of Orthopsychiatry, 46,* 135–139.

Willett, W. C., Hunter, D. J., Stampfer, M. J., Colditz, G., Manson, J. E., Speigelman, D., Rosner, B. M., Hennekens, C. H., & Speiser, F. E. (1992). Dietary fat and fiber in relation to risk of breast cancer. *Journal of the American Medical Assocation, 268,* 2037–2044.

Williams, C. L. (1989). *Gender differences at work: Women and men in nontraditional occupations.* Berkeley, CA: University of California Press.

Williams, E., Radin, N., & Allegro, T. (1992). Sex role attitudes of adolescents raised primarily by their fathers: An 11-year follow-up. *Merrill–Palmer Quarterly, 38*(4), 457–476.

Williams, G. H. (Ed.). (1962). *The radical reformation.* Philadelphia: Westminster Press.

Williams, J. E., & Best, D. L. (1982). *Measuring sex stereotypes: A thirty nation study.* Beverly Hills, CA: Sage.

Williams, J. E., & Best, D. L. (1990). *Measuring sex stereotypes: A thirty-nation study* (rev. ed.). Beverly Hills, CA: Sage.

Williams, J. E., & Best, D. L. (1990). *Measuring sex stereotypes: A multination study* (rev. ed.). Newbury Park, CA: Sage.

Williams, J. H. (1987). *Psychology of women.* New York: W. W. Norton.

Williams, J. H. (1987). *Psychology of women: Behavior in a biosocial context* (3rd ed.). New York: W. W. Norton.

Wilmoth, G., & Adelstein, D. (1988). *Psychological sequelae of abortion and public policy.* Paper presented at the 96th American Psychological Association Convention, Atlanta, GA.

Wilson, E. O. (1975). *Sociobiology: The new synthesis.* Cambridge, MA: Harvard University Press.

Wilson, E. O. (1978). *On human nature.* Cambridge, MA: Harvard University Press.

Wilson, J. (1978). *Religion in American society.* Englewood Cliffs, NJ: Prentice Hall.

Wilson, J. D. (1990). Androgens. In A. G. Gilman, T. W. Rall, A. S. Nies, & P. Taylor (Eds.), *Goodman and Gilman's pharmacological basis of therapeutics* (8th ed.) (pp. 1414–1418). New York: Pergamon Press.

Wilson, M. (1992, August). The effect of diverse family structures in the African-American community. Paper presented at the 100th Annual Convention of the American Psychological Association, Washington, DC.

Wincze, J. P., Hoon, P., & Hoon, E. F. (1977). Sexual arousal in women: A comparison of cognitive and physiological responses by continuous measurement. *Archives of Sexual Behavior, 6,* 121–133.

Wines, M. (1992, May 21). Views on single motherhood are multiple at White House. *New York Times,* p. 1, B16.

Winkler, K. J. (1990, October 10). Evidence of "cultural vitality." *Chronicle of Higher Education,* pp. A5, A8.

Wise, L. L., Steel, L., & MacDonald, C. (1979). *Origins and career consequences of sex differences in high school mathematics achievement.* Palo Alto, CA: American Institutes for Research.

Witherington, B., III. (1984). *Women in the ministry of Jesus.* Cambridge, MA: Cambridge University Press. [cited by Carmody, 1989]

Witt, S. H. (1976). Native women today: Sexism and the Indian woman. In S. Cox (Ed.), *Female psychology: The emerging self* (pp. 249–259). Chicago: Science Research Associates.

Wolf, N. (1991). *The beauty myth: How images of beauty are used against women.* New York: Morrow.

Wolff, B. B. (1978). Behavioral measurement of human pain. In R. A. Sternbach (Ed.), *The psychology of pain* (pp. 129–168). New York: Raven Press.

Wolff, C. (1971). *Love between women.* New York: Harper & Row.

Women's Health Advocate (1997, December). Body image: The last frontier of women's rights. *Women's Health Advocate, 4,* 10.

Wong, D. Y. (1983). Asian/Pacific American women: Legal issues. In *Civil rights issues of Asian and Pacific Americans: Myths and realities* (pp. 153–164). Washington, DC: U.S. Government Printing Office.

Wong, D. Y., & Hayashi, D. (1989). Behind unmarked doors: Developments in the garment industry. In Asian American Women United of California (Ed.), *Making waves: An anthology of writings by and about Asian American women* (pp. 159–171). Boston: Beacon Press.

Wood, A. D. (1973, Summer). The fashionable diseases: Women's complaints and their treatment in nineteenth century America. *Journal of Interdisciplinary History, 4,* 25–42.

Woodhouse, A. (1982). Sexuality, femininity, and fertility control. *Women's Studies International Forum, 5,* 1–15.

World Bank. (1993). *World Development Report 1993: Investing in Health.* New York: Oxford University Press.

World Health Organization. (1948). *Constitution of the World Health Organization.* Geneva, Switzerland: WHO Basic Documents.

Worobey, J. L., & Angel, R. J. (1990). Functional capacity and living arrangements of unmarried elderly persons. *Journals of Gerontology, 45*(3), 95–101.

Worrell, J., & Remer, P. (1992). *Feminist perspectives in therapy: An empowerment model for women.* New York: Wiley. Cited by Matlin, 1996, p. 480–482.

Wu, X., & DeMaris, A. (1996). Gender and marital status differences in depression: The effects of chronic strains. *Sex Roles, 34*(5/6), 299–319.

Wyatt, G. E. (1989). Reexamining factors predicting Afro-American and white American women's age at first coitus. *Archives of Sexual Behavior, 18,* 271–298.

Wyatt, G. E. (1994). The sociocultural relevance of sex research: Challenges for the 1990s and beyond. *American Psychologist, 49,* 748–754.

Wyche, K. F. (1993). Psychology and African American women: Findings from applied research. *Applied & Preventative Psychology, 2,* 115–121.

Yalom, I. D. (1980). *Existential psychotherapy.* New York: Basic Books.

Yamada, M. (1983). Asian Pacific American women and feminism. In C. Moraga & G. Anzaldira (Eds.), *This bridge called my back: Writings by radical women of color.* New York: Kitchen Table–Women of Color Press.

Yankelovich, D. (1981). *New rules.* New York: Random House.

Yarkin, K. L., Town, J. P., & Wallston, B. S. (1982). Blacks and women must try harder: Stimulus persons' race and sex and attributions of causality. *Personality and Social Psychology Bulletin, 8,* 21–24.

Yates, G. L., MacKenzie, R. G., Pennbridge, J., & Swofford, A. (1991). A risk profile comparison of homeless youth involved in prostitution and homeless youth not involved [Special Issue: Homeless Youth]. *Journal of Adolescent Health, 12,* 545–548.

Yee, B. W. (1990). Gender and family issues in minority groups. *Generations, 14*(3), 39–42.

Ying, Y. (1988). Depressive symptomatology among Chinese-Americans as measured by CES-D. *Journal of Clinical Psychology, 44*(5), 739–746.

Yoder, J. D. (1999). *Women and gender: Transforming psychology.* Upper Saddle River, NJ: Prentice-Hall.

Yoder, J. D., & Schleicher, T. L. (1996). Undergraduates regard deviation from occupational gender stereotypes as costly for women. *Sex Roles, 34*(3/4), 171–188.

Young, C. (1989). Psychodynamics of coping and survival of the African American female in a changing world. *Journal of Black Studies, 20,* 208–223.

Young, K. K. (1987). Introduction to women in world religions. In A. Sharma (Ed.), *Women in World Religions* (pp. 1–36). Albany, NY: State University of New York Press.

Yu, A. Y. (1993). Life in Hong Kong. In L. L. Adler (Ed.), *International handbook on gender roles* (pp. 108–121). Westport, CT: Greenwood Press.

Yu, L. C., & Carpenter, L. (1991). Women in China. In L. L. Adler (Ed.), *Women in cross-cultural perspective* (pp. 189–203). Westport, CT: Praeger.

Zaehner, R. C. (1958). *The comparison of religions* (pp. 30–68). Boston: Beacon Press.

Zahaykevich, Sirey, & Brooks-Gunn, unpublished [Unger & Crawford]

Zalk, S. R. (1996). Men in the academy: A psychological profile of harassers. In M. A. Paludi (Ed.), *Sexual harassment on college campuses: Abusing the ivory power* (pp. 81–113). New York: State University of New York Press.

Zborowski, M. (1969). *People in pain.* San Francisco: Jossey-Bass.

Zelinski, E. M., Gilewski, M. J., & Schaie, K. W. (1993). Individual differences in cross-sectional and 3-year longitudinal memory performance across the adult life span. *Psychology and Aging, 8*(2), 176–186.

Zeman, N. (1990, Summer/Fall). The new rules of courtship (Special Edition). *Newsweek,* 24–27.

Zillman, D., & Bryant, J. (1982). Pornography, sexual callousness, and the trivialization of rape. *Journal of Communication, 32,* 10–21.

Zillman, D., & Bryant, J. (1984). Effects of massive exposure to pornography. In N. H. Malamuth & E. Donnerstein (Eds.), *Pornography and sexual aggression* (pp. 115–138). New York: Academic Press.

Zimiles, H., & Lee, V. E. (1991). Adolescent family structure and educational progress. *Developmental Psychology, 27,* 314–320.

Zola, I. K. (1966). Culture and symptoms: An analysis of patient's presenting complaints. *American Sociological Review, 31,* 615–630.

Zucker, K. J., Bradley, S. J., Lowry-Sullivan, C. B., Kuksis, M., Birkenfeld-Adams, A., & Mitchell, J. N. (1993). A gender identity interview for children. *Journal of Personality Assessment, 61*(3), 443–456.

Women of Color and, perspectives on, 112–113
women's suffrage in U.S. and, 65
Feminist critique in psychology, issues of, 13–19
approaches to research, 15–16
mapping solutions for gender fair research, 16–19
problems and biases in research, 14–15
Feminist therapy, 396–398
Feminization of poverty, 123, 390
Fertility, moon as symbol of, 31
Fertilization, 80
timing of, 144
Fetal alcohol syndrome, 91
Fetus, 81, 294
Fidelity, 233–234
Fight or flight response, 410–411
Filipinos, 167 (*see also* Asian Americans)
Financial abuse of elders, 377
Fisher, Mary, 65
Five Pillars of Islam, 68
Five Sexes, The (Fausto-Sterling), 90–91
Five Worldly Vows, 38, 39
Flexibility of gender roles, 148
in old age, 333–334
Flex time, 221–223
Fluid intelligence, 334–335
Fluid reasoning, 183
Fluorouracil (5FU), sex and age differences in, 422
Flush (hot flashes), 101–102, 323–324, 325
Folklore about pregnancy, 293
Follicular phase, 99
Food and Drug Administration (FDA), 102, 436
"Force only" rape, 353
Foreplay, 231, 249
Fosomax (drug), 102
Fox, George, 65
Frequency distributions, 177
Friendships, 304–306
in adolescence, 165
male, 354
in mid-life, 326
widowhood and, 331
Functionalism, 11
Future, critical issues for the, 442–444

Galen, 421
Gametes, 78–80
Gandhi, Indira, 43
Gandhi, Mahatma, 43
Gang rape, 353–354
Gautama, Siddhartha, 39
Gay marriage, 280–281
Gay men, 92–95 (*see also* Homosexuality)
anti-gay violence and, 374–375
cohabiting, 285–287
family dynamics of, 244–246
in later life, 330
as parents, 321
personal ads of, 313
prevalence of, 243–244

sexual behavior and techniques among, 250, 287
Gender:
as analytic tool, 18
beliefs about, 5–6
distinction between sex and, 3–7
as socially constructed concept, 4
Gender bias (*see* Bias, gender)
Gender-earnings ratio, 116
Gender-fair research, 15–19
issues in conducting, 15–16
mapping solutions for, 16–19
Gender harassment, 342, 343
Gender identity, 145 (*see also* Gender role development)
acquisition of language and, 157
nature versus nurture and development of, 75–77
sex reassignment and, 74–75
territorialism about occupation and, 210–211
Gender identity disorder (GID), 148
Gender inequality, partner abuse and, 362
Gender role(s):
flexibility of, 148, 333–334
modern ideology, 315
traditional ideology, 315
Gender role development, 141–170
children's attitudes toward females and males, 149–151
expectations and, 142–144
guide to major phases of, 143
images of femininity and masculinity, 148–149
moral development, 142, 145–148
parenting and, 151–156
in puberty and adolescence, 162–166
race, ethnicity, culture and class effects on, 149, 166–168
scientific theories on growing up, 144–145
socializing forces in, 156–162
Gender-role inequality, 115–118
Gender schemas, 26–27 (*see also* Gender stereotypes)
Gender schema theory, 149–150
Gender socialized behaviors, 114–115
Gender stereotypes, 6–7
in children's literature, 159
double standard of labeling and diagnosis of mental disorders and, 385
education and, 133
factors involved in formation of, 26
fathers and, 154–155, 156
origins in mythology, 27–34
overview of, 26–27
physical health and, 408–409
religion and (*see* Religion, gender stereotypes originating in)
about Women of Color, 119–120
General adaptation syndrome, 411
Generativity versus stagnation, 311
Genes, 78–80

sex-determining, 82
Genesis, story of, 28–29
Genetics:
cardiovascular disease and, 419
genetic conditions affecting sex and gender, 89–91
homosexuality and, 93–94
Genital mutilation, female (FGM), 116–118, 233, 355, 376–377
Genitals, external, 83–84, 85
Genital stimulation, mutual, 250
Giriama of Kenya, postmenopausal women of, 325
Glass ceiling, 135, 206, 213–215
Glass Ceiling Commission, 213
Glucose metabolism, 419
Goddesses, 29–33
Gonadotropin release, control of, 94
Gonads, 82, 84
streak, 88
Gonorrhea, 430
Good boy-good girl orientation, 147
Good Friday, 54
Gospels, 57, 58
Government regulations, changes in, 435–436
Graaf, Reguier de, 87
Grades in school, 185–186
Grafenberg, E., 253
Grafenberg spot (G-spot), 253
Graham, Katharine, 213, 224
Grandparent role, 333
grandmothers, 304, 329
Graying of America, 321
Greek mythology, 27, 32
Groupthink, 354
Growth spurt, 97
Guilt, initiative versus, 311

Hanukkah, 46
Happiness:
marriage and, 279–280, 315–316
of single versus married people, 312
Harasser, status of, 343
Harvey, William, 87
Hazing at law school, 212–213
Health, defined, 407–408 (*see also* Mental health; Physical health)
Health care, 301
Healy, Bernadine, 421
Heart attack, 418
Heart disease (*see* Cardiovascular disease (CVD))
He as generic pronoun, use of, 156
Hebrew Bible, 49
Hebrew religion, early development of, 47–50 (*see also* Judaism, gender stereotypes in)
Heckler, Margaret M., 126
Hegemony, 110
Heilman's lack of fit model, 209
Hellenism, 50
Hemispheric differentiation, 174
Henry VIII, King, 63

Mullerian duct-inhibiting substance, 82, 89
Mullerian ducts, 82
Multiple orgasms, 254–255
Multiple roles, 219–221
Murder, partner abuse and, 360, 363, 364
Muslim, meaning of word, 66 (see also Islam, gender stereotypes in)
Mutual genital stimulation, 250
Mutual marriage, 314
Myocardial infarction (heart attack, MI), 418
Myotonia, 251
Mysogyny, 157
Mythology, gender stereotypes originating in, 27–34 (see also Religion, gender stereotypes originating in)
in China before Confucius, 33–34
women as source of evil, 27–33
Myths:
creation, 28–29, 33
of motherhood, 290–291
rape, 357, 372
of workplace, 200–201

National Academy of Sciences, 189
National Cancer Institute, 94
SEER (Surveillance, Epidemiology, and End Results) Program of, 128
National Family Violence Survey (1985), 364
National Institutes of Health, 434
National Institutes of Health-Office of Research on Women's Health (NIH-ORWH), 409–410, 411, 435
National Opinion Research Center (NORC), 241
Native American Indians, 109
gender development among, 167
Native American Indian women (see also Women of Color):
employment of, 134
historical overview of experiences of, 124
in later life, 329
mental health among, 127
physical health among, 411
stereotypes of, 119–120
Natural biological model of sexual harassment, 217–218, 345
Nature versus nurture, gender identity development and, 75–77
Nazi Holocaust, 46
Nebuchadnezzar, 48
Neolithic Age, 29
Neoplastic cells, 421
Nesting behaviors, 294
Neurasthenia, 382, 406
Neurological aspects of homosexuality, 94
Neurology, rise of, 384
Neutral stress, 412
New Male, The (Goldberg), 20
New Our Bodies, Ourselves, The (Boston Women's Health Book Collective), 359
New Testament, 54
Nigeria, violence against women in, 355

Night sweat, 101–102, 323–324, 325
Nirvana, 38, 39
Nisei, 118
Nobel Prize, 189
No-fault divorce, 316
Nonaggressive pornography, 372
Noninsulin-dependent diabetes mellitus (NIDDM), 411
Nonnormative rape, 350
Nonoverlapping distributions, 177
Nonsexist therapy, 396
Normative rape, 349–350
Norms, achievement motivation and, 188
Nuns, 40, 66
Nursing schools, gender composition of, 210
Nurture versus nature, gender identity development and, 75–77

Obesity, 411
among Women of Color, 128–132
Objectification of women, 214
Obscenity (see Pornography)
Observational learning, 145, 395
Obsessive rape, 353
Obstetricians, 295
Occupational barriers, 443
Occupational segregation, 202–207
glass ceiling and, 135, 206, 213–215
sex discrimination in hiring and, 207–209
sexual harassment and, 217, 218
Oedipus complex, 76, 144, 145–146, 244, 395
Operationalizations in gender-fair research, 16
Opportunistic infections, 426
Oral sex, 249–250
Oral stage, 76, 144
Organizational climate, sexual harassment and, 218–219
Organizational model of sexual harassment, 217–218, 345
Orgasm(s):
disability and, 258
factors related to, 253
masturbation and, 249
multiple, 254–255
sexual dysfunction and, 255
Orgasmic phase of sexual arousal, 251, 252
Orthodox Judaism, 46
Osteoporosis, 100, 325, 434–435
Ostrich effect, 215
Outgroup homogeneity effect, 354
Outsider's perspective, 111
Ovaries, 78, 84
Ovariotomy, 406
Overload, role, 222, 314, 316, 320
Ovist theory of reproduction, 87
Ovulation phase, 99
Ovum, 78–79

Packwood, Robert, 341
Pain:
definition and measurement of, 415

distress induced by, 413
distress not induced by, 413–414
as major stressor, 415–417
sexual pain disorders, 255
sociocultural expressions of, 416
treatment of, 417
types of, 415
Pain perception, 415, 416–417
Pain sensitivity range, 415
Pain threshold, 415
Pain tolerance, 415
Paleolithic Age, 29
Palestine:
Jesus and women in pre-Christian, 58–59
in time of Christ, 56
Pandora, story of, 27
Pangenesis, 86
Pankhurst, Emmeline, 12
Pantheism, 34
Papal Infallibility, doctrine of, 60, 62
Paradise Lost (Milton), 45
Parental imperative, 333–334
Parental leave, 223
Parenthood
experience of, 319–321
transition to, 298
in young adulthood, 319–321
Parenting, effective, 136
Parenting, gendered, 287–306
enforcing motherhood, 291–293
experience of mothering, 293–302
fatherhood, 302–304
gender role development and, 151–156
motherhood mandate, 289–290
motherhood mystique, 290–291
reasons for becoming parents, 287–289
Parents:
caring for elderly, 327
choosing not to be, 291–292
effect on children, 154–156
single, 135–137, 153–154, 292–293, 318–319, 320
Parthenogenesis, 30
Partner abuse, 359–366
consequences for abused women, 364–365
definitions and prevalence of, 360–361
personal and societal responses to, 365–366
predictors of, 363
research on, 363–364
theories of, 361–363
Partners, sex with, 249–250
Part-time work, 221–223
Passages (Sheehy), 311–312
Passive smoking, 421
Passover, 46
Paternal leave, 222–223
Patriarchal cultures, 30
Patriarchal system:
of Aryans, 34–36
in Christianity, 59–60, 61
Islamic, 68
partner abuse and, 362–363
of Rabbinic Judaism, 51

Patriarch of Constantinople, 61
Paul, Apostle, 59
Pauline Christianity, 59
Pedophiles, 367
Peer group:
  gang rape and, 356
  influence in adolescence, 162, 165
  polarization into male and female
    cliques, 148
  as socializing force, 161–162
  support for sexual aggression by male,
    352
Pelvic inflammatory disease, 425
Penile erection, 251
Penis envy, 77, 144, 244, 395
Penn, William, 65
Pennsylvania Hospital, 383
Pentecost, 46, 54
People of color (see Race and ethnicity)
People's Republic of China (see China)
Perception(s):
  adolescent, of working women, 202
  of behaviors constituting sexual
    harassment, 345
  pain, 415, 416–417
  of personal control, 329
  of sexual harassment, variables
    influencing, 343
  spatial, 182, 183
Performance, expectations for academic,
  191
Peripheral artery disease, 418
Personal advertisements, gender
  stereotypes reflected in, 313
Personal relationships (see Intimate
  relationships)
Personal responses:
  to partner abuse, 365–366
  to rape and sexual assault, 359
  to sexual harassment, 348
Pesticides, 185
Phallic stage, 76, 144
Phalloplasty, 75
Pharisees, 49, 51, 55, 57
Phimosis, 74
Phobias, 395
Phrenology, 384
Physical health, 403–439
  bias in women's health research, issues
    of, 417–431
  breast cancer, 128, 411, 421, 431–433
  cardiovascular disease, 102, 128–129,
    409, 418–421
  diseases unique to women, 431–435
  gender stereotypes and consequences
    for, 408–409
  health status of women, 407
  lung cancer, 411, 421–423
  medical care for women, 406–407,
    435–437
  morbidity and mortality, gender
    comparisons in, 409–410
  osteoporosis, 100, 325, 433–435
  partner abuse and, 364

politics of illness, 405–407
rape and, 358
sexual harassment and, 348
sexually transmitted diseases, 238, 259,
  358, 423–431
stress and, 410–417
in Victorian times, 405–406
well-being and, 407–408
of Women of Color, 128–133, 411
Physical maltreatment of elders, 377
Physical violence (see Violence and
  exploitation, gendered)
Physiologic stressors, 412
Pill, birth control, 259
Pius XII, Pope, 60
Plateau phase of sexual arousal, 251, 252
Plato, 66
Play:
  parent-child, 152, 155
  as socializing force, 157–158
Playboy survey, 240, 241
PMDD, 393
PMS, 392–393
Pneumocystis carini pneumonia, 425, 426
Politics of illness, 405–407
  health status of women, 407
  medical treatments for women, 406–407
  in Victorian times, 405–406
Polyandry, 52
Polygamy, 52, 68
Polymorphously perverse condition, 244
Polytheism, 34
Polytheistic cultures, 29
Pornography, 257, 370–373
Portuguese children, gender attitudes in, 151
Positive reinforcement, 395
Possessing the Secret of Joy (Walker), 376
Postconventional reasoning, 147
Postpartum experience, 298–300
Posttraumatic stress disorder (PTSD), 394
  partner abuse and, 364–365
  rape victims and, 358
  violence in schools and, 194
Poverty:
  academic high achievers and
    disadvantage, 194
  cultural vitality and, 111
  feminization of, 123, 390
  mental health and, 398–399
  mothering in, 301
Power:
  breadwinning, 291
  consensual sexual relationship in context
    of unequal, 343–344
  gendered violence and exploitation and,
    340
  in marriage, 314–315
  rape culture and maintenance of male,
    356
  in religious hierarchy, 66
  sexual harassment and position of, 218,
    347
Power rapes, 356
Power relations, 18

Practical needs, marriage to meet, 275
Preconventional reasoning, 146–147
Preformist theory of reproduction, 87
Pregnancy:
  adolescent, 234, 261, 411
  ectopic, 411
  experience of, 293–295
  hormonal levels in, homosexuality and,
    95
  partner abuse during, 364
  perceived as disease, 406, 407
  trimesters, 81, 84–86, 294
Prejudice, 5 (see also Discrimination;
  Sexism)
  ageism, 103, 322
  AIDSism, 427
Premarital cohabitation, 283
Premarital sex, 235, 240–241, 276
Premenstrual dysphoric disorder (PMDD),
  393
Premenstrual syndrome (PMS), 392–393
Prenatal drug exposure, 91–92, 95
Prenatal stress, 95
Presbyterians, 63
Prescriptions about pregnancy, 293
Prestige:
  job, 208–209
  in religious hierarchy, 66
Primary cardiac arrest, 418
Primary orgasmic dysfunction, 255
Primitive cultures, women as source of evil
  in, 29–31
Problem-focused coping methods, 219
Problem solving, gender comparisons in,
  181
Pro-choice movement, 296
Professional-level employment, 135, 292
Progesterone, 84
Project Access, 189
Pro-life movement, 296
Promiscuity, 235
Property, women as, 45
Prostate cancer, 103
Prostate gland, 103
Prostitution, 232, 373–374
  Madonna-whore dichotomy and,
    232–233, 235
Protestant Episcopal Church, 63
Protestantism, 59, 62–66
Protestant Reformation, 62
Prozac, 391
Pseudohermaphroditism, 76, 89–90
Psychoanalysis and Women (Miller), 395
Psychoanalytic theories:
  gender identity and, 75–76
  on gender role development, 144
  of parenting, 288–289
  of sexual orientation, 244–246
Psychoanalytic therapy, 395
Psychological heterosexism, 375
Psychological maltreatment of elders, 377
Psychological theories of sexual
  orientation, 244
Psychologic stressors, 412

522

Psychologists, female, 444
Psychology:
    changes in field of, 444
    of men, 9–10, 20
    of women, 2, 19–20
Psychosexual development, 76–77, 144
Psychosocial development, 310–311
Psychotherapeutic intervention for
    depression, 391
Psychotic affective disorder, 127
PTSD (*see* Posttraumatic stress disorder
    (PTSD))
Puberty, 96–98
    defined, 163
    gender role development in, 162–166
    parent-child relations during, 164–165
    timing of, social development and,
        163–164
Pubic hair, 97
Puerto Rican women, 125
Punitive rape, 350
Purging, binge eating and, 386, 387
Puritanism, 64–65
Pythagoras, 86

Quakerism, 65–66
Qualitative research methods, 444
Quality of life among Women of Color,
    126–137
    education, 133–134, 194, 276
    employment, 134–135
    family type, 135–137
    mental health, 127–128
    physical health, 128–133, 411
Quality time, 136
Question formulation in gender-fair
    research, 15, 17
Quickening, 294
Quid pro quo (contingency) harassment,
    342, 343
Qur'an (Koran), 66, 67–68

Rabbis, 51–52, 66
Race and ethnicity (*see also* Class, social;
    Culture(s); Women of Color):
    AIDS and, 424
    in America, 121–123
    causes of death by, 130–131
    cognitive ability and academic
        achievement and, 194
    confusion surrounding ethnic-racial
        categorization, 108–110
    depression and, 390
    ethnicity, 120–121
    feminist perspectives and, 112–113
    gender typing across, 166–167
    intermarriage and, 277
    later life and, 329
    marriage rates and, 276
    masturbation and, 248
    mental health and, 398–399
    occupational and labor force
        participation of women by, 199
    occupational segregation and, 204

physical health of women and, 128–129,
    411
psychology of women and, 19–20
reaction to retirement and, 333
sexual harassment and, 347
sexuality and, 237–239
stereotypes of women by, 7
teacher attention in school and, 161
terminology for, 109–110
theoretical and empirical research on
    people of color, 110–112
treatment in mental asylums and, 383
voluntary versus involuntary minorities,
    121–122
widowhood and, 331
Racism, 111, 124, 167
Radiation treatment for breast cancer, 432
Radical feminism, 13
Radical mastectomy, 432
Raloxifene (Evista), 102, 433
Ramphela, Mamphela, 224
Rape, 349–359
    aggressive pornography and attitudes
        toward, 372
    categories of, 352–354
    cultural significance of, 354–358
    definitions and prevalence of, 349–351
    effects of, on women, 358
    personal and societal responses to,
        358–359, 360
    rapists, characteristics of, 351–352
    reasons for, 354–356
    relationship of rapist and rape victim, 351
    victims of, 351
Rape deterrence strategies, 359
Rape fantasy, 256–257
Rape myths, 357, 372
Rape-prone versus rape-free societies, 350
Rape trauma syndrome, 358
Reconstructionism, 46
Redbook survey, 241
Redlining, 124
Red Sea, parting of, 48
Reentry women, 194, 310, 328
Reformed Tradition (Calvinist tradition), 63
Reform Judaism, 46
Refractory period, 251, 254
Regulations, government, 435–436
Reincarnation (Samsara), 37
Reinforcement, 145
    of maladaptive behaviors, 414
    positive, 395
Relational-development, 398
Relational therapy, 397–398
Religion (*see also specific religions*):
    abortion and, 296
    contraceptive use and, 238
    divorce and, 317
    gay marriage and, 281
    sexuality and, 237–239
Religion, gender stereotypes originating in,
    27–69
    in China before Confucius, 33–34
    in India, 34–44

monotheistic religions, 44–69 (*see also*
    Christianity, gender stereotypes in;
    Islam, gender stereotypes in; Judaism,
    gender stereotypes in)
    women as source of evil, 27–33
Remarriage, 316, 317, 319
Remodeling of bone, 434
Reproduction, sexual selection in, 86–88
Reproductive system:
    female, 99
    internal, development of, 82–83
    male, 100
Republic (Plato), 66
Research, 2
    AIDS, gender issues in, 427–428
    changes in government regulations and,
        435–436
    feminist reviews of, 444
    gender-fair, 15–19
    on intimate relationships, 269
    on partner abuse, 363–364
    on sexual harassment, 346–347
    social change and, 21
    traditional, nonsexist, and feminist
        approaches to, 15–16
Research, gender bias in, 404–405, 409
    on depression, 392
    research methods, 14–15
    in women's health research, 417–431
Research design in gender-fair research, 16
Research methods, 14–15, 176–177
Resistance against rape, 359
Resolution phase of sexual arousal, 251, 252
Resurrection of Jesus, 57
Retirement, 310, 332–334
Rhythm method, 260–261
Right-to-life (pro-life) movement, 296
Risk factors:
    for breast cancer, 432
    for cardiovascular disease, 419
    divorce and, 316–317
    for osteoporosis, 434
Roe v. *Wade*, 296
Role conflict, part-time work and, 222
Role confusion, identity versus, 311
Role models, 145
Role overload, 314, 316
    part-time work and, 222
    of single parent, 320
Roles, multiple, 219–221 (*see also* Gender
    role development; Gender role(s))
Roman Catholicism, 59
Romance novels, sexual scripts in, 236
Romantic love, 270–271, 273, 275
Rosh Hashanah, 46
*Rules: Time-Tested Secrets for Capturing
    the Heart of Mr. Right, The* (Fein and
    Schneider), 272

Sacramental Agent, Church as, 60
Sacraments, 54
Sadducees, 51, 55
Sadism, 362
Sadistic rapes, 356

experience of parenthood in, 320
gender role socialization in, 153–154
Singles, in early adulthood, 312–314
Single-sex education, 160, 186, 192–194
Slavery, 124
Smith, William Kennedy, 352
Smoking, cigarette, 132–133, 421, 423
Social change, psychological research and, 21
Social class (see Class, social)
Social constructionism, 21
on sexuality, 230–231
Social Darwinism, 10
Social effects of divorce, 317
Socialist feminism, 12–13
Socialization:
achievement patterns in science and, 189–190
contraceptive use and, 261–262
in double standard, 234–237
gender socialized behaviors, 114–115
of lesbians and gay men, 286
male, 354
origin of sexual harassment in, 345
parenting and childhood gender, 151–156
for sexual communication, 352
Socializing forces, 156–162
advertising, 159–160
children's literature, 159, 186
language, 156–157
media, 158
peers, 161–162
play and competition, 157–158
school, 160–161
Social learning theory, 144–145
Social-order-maintaining orientation, 147
Social role analysis, 26
Social Security benefits, part-time work and, 223
Social support:
friendships and, 304–306
gender differences in seeking and receiving, 304
networks among single parents, 320
during pregnancy, 294
in widowhood, 331
Social World of Ancient Israel, The (Matthews and Benjamin), 50
Societal responses:
to child sexual abuse, 369
to partner abuse, 366
to problem of rape, 359
Society, sex discrimination in, 9–12
Society of Friends (Quakers), 65–66
Sociobiological theory of rape, 354–355
Sociobiology, 21
Sociocultural approach:
model of sexual harassment, 217–218, 345–346
to partner abuse, 362–363
Socioeconomic status (see Class, social)
Sociological theories of sexual orientation, 246
Socratic method in law schools, 212

Software, sexist educational, 192
Spatial perception, 182, 183
Spatial reasoning, 185
Spatial visualization, 182, 183
Spermarche (semenarche), 164
Sperm cell, 78, 79–80
Spermicides, 431
Spinal cord injuries, sexuality and, 257–258
Sports, competitive, 157–158
Spousal bereavement, 310, 330–332
Spouse abuse (see Partner abuse)
Stagnation, generativity versus, 311
Standardized tests, 185–186
Stanton, Elizabeth Cady, 12
Statistical issues, 177–178
Statistically significant differences, 178
Status rape, 350
Statutory rape, 350
STDs (see Sexually transmitted diseases (STDs))
Stepmothers, 292
Stereotypes and stereotyping, 185 (see also Gender stereotypes)
ageist, 322
beliefs about gender based on, 5–6
defined, 26
about gay and lesbian couples, 285–286
about menopause, 324
occupational segregation and, 211–212
of patients, by physicians, 391
of researchers, 2
Sterilization, 259
Stigma, social:
of aging, 310, 321–327
AIDSism, 427
menopause and, 324–325
occupational segregation and, 211–212
Stomach cancer, 411
Stone Center at Wellesley College, 397
Stranger rape, 353
Streak gonads, 88
Street harassment, 344–345
Stress, 410–417
coping with, 414–415
defined, 410
early contributions on, 410–415
internal versus external, 216–217
of migration, 398–399
neutral, 412
prenatal, 95
of professional Women of Color, 135
at work, 216–221
Stress management, cognitive-behavioral, 426
Stressor(s), 410
examples of potential, 412
pain as, 415–417
Stroke (cerebrovascular disease), 128–129, 411, 418
Structural approach, 5
Subculture, 118
Subincision, practice of, 32
Subjects in AIDS research, 427
Submission fantasies, 257

Subordinates, horizontal hostility between, 121
Subordination and equivalence, conflict in Catholicism between, 59–60
Substitute marriage, 283
Subtle sexism, 8–9
Success:
attributions for, 188–191
fear of, 188
Sudras, 36
Sumerian literature, women in, 30
Superego, 146
Super Mom, myth of, 219–220
Surgery:
breast cancer, 432–433
to control intractable chronic pain, 417
coronary bypass, 419–420
Surveillance, Epidemiology, and End Results (SEER) Program, 128
Surveys:
on rape, 351
of sex in U.S., 239–242
Suttee (sati), custom of, 42, 355
Symbiotic marriage, 314
Sympathetic nervous system, 412
Synagogues, 49, 52
Syphilis, 430
Systematic desensitization, 395
Systemic lupus erythematosus, 411

Taboos:
menstruation as, 33
about pregnancy, 293
among primitive tribes, 33
Taiwan, evolving marital customs in, 315
Talmud, 49–50, 52
Tamoxifen, 433
T cell lymphocytes, CD4 helper-inducer, 424
Teacher expectations, 186–187
Teachers as socializing force, 160–161
Teaching authority, Church as, 60
Teenagers (see Adolescence)
Television:
double standards of aging on, 322
as socializing force, 158
Temperament, sexual orientation and, 246
Temper tantrum prevalence, social class and, 168
Ten Commandments, 48
Teratogenic malformations, 91–92
Testes, 78, 79–80
development of, 84
transformation of undifferentiated gonads into, 82
Testicular feminization syndrome, 89–90
Testosterone, 82
brain organization and, 174–175
male climacteric and decreased, 102–103
Tests, 176
sex differences on cognitive, 180–181
standardized, 185–186
Textbooks, sexism in, 186